Current Trends and Advances in Computer-Aided Intelligent Environmental Data Engineering

Intelligent Data-Centric Systems

Current Trends and Advances in Computer-Aided Intelligent Environmental Data Engineering

Edited by

Gonçalo Marques
*Polytechnic of Coimbra, ESTGOH, Rua General Santos Costa,
Oliveira do Hospital, Portugal*

Joshua O. Ighalo
*Department of Chemical Engineering, Nnamdi Azikiwe University, Awka, Nigeria;
Department of Chemical Engineering, Faculty of Engineering and Technology,
University of Ilorin, Ilorin, Nigeria*

Series Editor

Fatos Xhafa
Universitat Politècnica de Catalunya, Spain

ACADEMIC PRESS
An imprint of Elsevier

Academic Press is an imprint of Elsevier
125 London Wall, London EC2Y 5AS, United Kingdom
525 B Street, Suite 1650, San Diego, CA 92101, United States
50 Hampshire Street, 5th Floor, Cambridge, MA 02139, United States
The Boulevard, Langford Lane, Kidlington, Oxford OX5 1GB, United Kingdom

ISBN: 978-0-323-85597-6

For Information on all Academic Press publications
visit our website at https://www.elsevier.com/books-and-journals

Publisher: Mara Conner
Editorial Project Manager: Joshua Mearns
Production Project Manager: Sreejith Viswanathan
Cover Designer: Victoria Pearson Esser

Typeset by MPS Limited, Chennai, India

Working together
to grow libraries in
developing countries

www.elsevier.com • www.bookaid.org

Contents

List of contributors xvii

CHAPTER 1 An introduction to *Current Trends and Advances in Computer-Aided Intelligent Environmental Data Engineering* 1

Joshua O. Ighalo and Gonçalo Marques

Introduction 1

Book structure and relevant audience 2

Intelligent systems in environmental engineering research 3

Looking to the future 4

References 4

SECTION 1 Data-centric and intelligent systems in air quality monitoring, assessment and mitigation

CHAPTER 2 Application of deep learning and machine learning in air quality modeling 11

Ditsuhi Iskandaryan, Francisco Ramos and Sergio Trilles

Introduction 11

Data profiling 12

    Datasets 12

    Air quality data and indices 13

Learning from data 14

    Data integration and data preprocessing 15

    Machine learning and deep learning algorithms 17

    Validation metrics 18

Conclusions and further thoughts 19

Acknowledgments 20

References 20

CHAPTER 3 Advances in data-centric intelligent systems for air quality monitoring, assessment, and control 25

Samuel Eshorame Sanni, Emmanuel Emeka Okoro, Emmanuel Rotimi Sadiku and Babalola Aisosa Oni

Introduction 25

Overview of AI-based technologies and data-centric systems for pollution control 26

Artificial intelligence...26
Data-centric system design principles..28
Data-centric/decision support systems...28
Data interpretation and mining methods..30
Fundamental principles of data mining with AI...31
Machine learning and AI models..32
AI methods for air quality monitoring...38
Review of a few previous and more recent studies on air
quality modeling..42
Future opportunities: the next data wave...47
Conclusions...48
References...49

CHAPTER 4   **Intelligent systems in air pollution research: a review**...................**59**

Ali Sohani, Mohammad Hossein Moradi, Krzysztof Rajski,
Yousef Golizadeh Akhlaghi, Mitra Zabihigivi, Uwe Wagner and
Thomas Koch

Introduction...59
The definition of atmosphere..60
The structure of atmosphere..60
Different contaminants in the air...62
Tropospheric ozone (O_3)..62
Nitrogen dioxide (NO_2)...62
Particulate matter...64
Carbon monoxide and carbon dioxide..65
Sulfur dioxide..66
Reviewing the literature..66
A new studied case..69
Research methodology...70
    The employed machine learning method...70
The investigated city..70
Input and output parameters..71
Error-related criteria..71
Results and discussion...72
    The specifications and validation of the developed models........................72
Uncertainty of different models...73
Analyzing error for smaller ranges of the input parameters............................74
Conclusions..79
References...79

CHAPTER 5   ESTABLISH—a decision support system for monitoring the quality of air for human health **83**

Mihaela Balanescu, Andrei Birdici, Iacob Crucianu, Alexandru Drosu, George Iordache, Adrian Sandu Pasat, Carmen Poenaru and George Suciu

Introduction 83
Related work 84
ESTABLISH pilot study: user requirements 85
ESTABLISH decision support system 90
   ESTABLISH architecture 90
Deployment, data acquisition, and integration 91
Preliminary testing of sensors 91
   Scenario A—different type of equipment 93
   Scenario B—same type of equipment 94
Data acquisition and integration from wearable devices 94
Data acquisition and integration from environmental monitoring devices 97
Visualization of the air quality index 97
ESTABLISH platform presentation 98
User guide for patients 99
User guide for therapists 100
Conclusions 101
Acknowledgment 102
References 102

CHAPTER 6   Indoor air pollution: a comprehensive review on public health challenges and prevention policies **105**

Jagriti Saini, Maitreyee Dutta and Gonçalo Marques

Introduction 105
Indoor air quality and public health 107
   Respiratory illness 107
   Cardiovascular dysfunctions 107
   Neuropsychiatric complications 108
   Chronic pulmonary disease 108
   Cancer 108
   Low birth weight and infant mortality 108
   Cataract 109
   Sick building syndrome 109
Enhanced indoor air quality and prevention strategies 109
Technologies and control policies for enhanced indoor air quality 112
   Indoor air quality management technologies 112

Control policies for indoor air quality 113

Discussion 114

Conclusion 117

References 119

SECTION 2 Data-centric and intelligent systems in water quality monitoring, assessment and mitigation

CHAPTER 7   **Data-centric intelligent systems for water quality monitoring, assessment and control** **129**

Samuel Eshorame Sanni, Emmanuel Emeka Okoro, Emmanuel Rotimi Sadiku and Bablola Aisosa Oni

Introduction 129

Problems associated with numerical modeling in hydraulic transport and water quality prediction 131

Why artificial intelligence? 131

AI methods and machine learning methods for water quality modeling and contaminant hydrology 132

Recent advances in water quality modeling 146

Conclusion 149

References 150

Further reading 159

CHAPTER 8   **ANN prognostication and GA optimization of municipal solid waste leachate treatment using aluminum electrodes via electrocoagulation-flocculation method** **161**

Chinenye Adaobi Igwegbe, Okechukwu Dominic Onukwuli, Joshua O. Ighalo, Chukwuemeka Daniel Ezeliora and Pius Chukwukelue Onyechi

Introduction 161

Methodology 164

Batch electrocoagulation experiments 164

Artificial neural network modeling 166

Genetic algorithm optimization of the ECF process 169

Statistical analysis on the data 169

Calculation of electrode and electrical consumption 170

Results and discussion 170

ANN modeling results 170

Genetic algorithm optimization results 173

Statistical analysis results 175

Electrode and electrical power consumption during the ECF process................ 177
Conclusion 177
Acknowledgment 177
References... 178

CHAPTER 9   Application of deep learning and machine learning methods in water quality modeling and prediction: a review **185**
Ugochukwu Ewuzie, Oladotun Paul Bolade and Abisola Opeyemi Egbedina

Introduction.. 185
Deep learning and machine learning in WQ modeling and prediction 188
Overview of learning methods 189
Supervised learning 189
Unsupervised learning 190
Reinforcement learning 190
Semisupervised learning.. 190
Machine learning architectures used in water quality modeling
and prediction 191
Artificial neural network 191
Neural networks models 192
    Multilayer perceptron neural network (MLP-ANN or MLP)....................... 192
    Radial basis function (RBF-ANN) 192
    Self-organizing maps 193
Support vector machines 193
Decision trees 193
Deep learning architectures used in water quality modeling
and prediction 194
Convolutional neural network 195
Recurrent neural network 196
Generative unsupervised models... 197
Application of ML and DL models in WQ prediction of different
water systems.. 198
Modeling and prediction of different water systems... 198
Data collection.. 199
Input data selection... 204
Data splitting... 204
Data preprocessing 205
Model structure determination 207
Model training 208
Performance evaluation measures.. 209
Challenges facing DL and ML predictions... 210

Conclusion and future prospect..210
References...211

CHAPTER 10 Intelligent systems in water pollution research: a review **219**
Ali Sohani, Kiana Berenjkar, Mohammad Hassan Shahverdian,
Hoseyn Sayyaadi and Erfan Goodarzi
Introduction..219
Water standards 220
    The basis of water standards 220
    Harmful effects of salt..221
Water desalination technologies...222
    Phase-changing desalination...222
    Without phase-changing desalination 230
Reviewing the literature 233
Selected case study from the literature 236
    The investigated system 236
    The selected city...236
    The utilized machine learning approaches...237
    The obtained results..237
Conclusions...240
References...240

CHAPTER 11 A long short-term memory deep learning approach for
river water temperature prediction **243**
Salim Heddam, Sungwon Kim, Ali Danandeh Mehr,
Mohammad Zounemat-Kermani, Ahmed Elbeltagi, Anurag Malik
and Ozgur Kisi
Introduction..243
Materials and methods..245
    Study area and data 245
    Performance assessment of the models..246
Methodology 246
    Gaussian process regression 246
    Gene expression programming..248
    Online sequential extreme learning machine......................................248
    Support vector regression 251
    Long short-term memory 251
    Multiple linear regression 253
Results and discussion..253
    USGS 01104430 station 253
    USGS 14207200 station 256

USGS 422302071083801 station 258
USGS 422622122004000 station 259
    Discussion 264
Conclusions and future recommendations 265
References 266

SECTION 3 Data-centric and intelligent systems in land pollution research

**CHAPTER 12 Data-centric and intelligent systems in land
pollution research** **273**
*Mohammad Hossein Moradi, Ali Sohani, Mitra Zabihigivi, Uwe Wagner,
Thomas Koch and Hoseyn Sayyaadi*
Introduction 273
Application of deep learning and machine learning methods in flow
modeling of landfill leachate 274
    Main concepts 274
    Selected recent studies 275
Application of deep learning and machine learning methods in soil quality
assessment and remediation 277
    Main concepts 277
    Selected recent studies 281
Establishing a nexus between nonbiodegradable waste and
data-centric systems 283
    Main concepts 283
    Selected recent studies 286
Case studies of evaluations and analysis of solid waste management
techniques by deep learning and machine learning methods 290
    The complexity of solid waste management techniques 290
    The analyzed case study 292
Conclusions 294
References 294

**CHAPTER 13 Application of artificial intelligence in the mapping and
measurement of soil pollution** **297**
*Chukwunonso O. Aniagor, Marcel I. Ejimofor, Stephen N. Oba
and Matthew C. Menkiti*
Introduction 297
Methodology 298
    Systematic review protocol 298

Search and selection criteria 299
Quality check and data extraction.. 299
Theoretical background of the different AI models 300
    Artificial intelligence models applied in the field 300
Artificial neural network 300
    The multilayer perceptron neural network............................... 302
    The backpropagation neural network....................................... 302
    The radial basis function neural network................................. 302
Support vector machines 304
Adaptive neurofuzzy inference system 304
Random forest... 305
Gradient boosted machine 306
Bayesian machine learning... 306
Hybrid models 307
Application domain of the different AI models 307
    AI models in soil pollution mapping 307
AI models in soil pollutant measurement 309
Conclusions.. 312
References.. 313
Further reading 318

**CHAPTER 14 Artificial intelligence in the reduction and management
of land pollution**.. 319
*Marcel I. Ejimofor, Chukwunonso O. Aniagor, Stephen N. Oba,
Matthew C. Menkiti and Victor I. Ugonabo*
Introduction.. 319
The use of artificial intelligence and robotics in system modification for
effective on-spot minimization of wastes in process industries........... 320
    Artificial intelligence in the disposal and smart recycling of wastes 321
Convolutional neural network model system of waste classification 322
Support vector machine.. 323
Artificial intelligence-robotics pickup system 323
Artificial intelligence and robotics in waste recycling...................... 324
Robotic recycle sorting system 325
    Working principle of the robotic sorting system........................ 325
    Advantages and disadvantages of recycling robotic sorting system 325
Artificial intelligence-robotic quality assessment system 325
Reforestation for land pollution management: impact of drones and
neural network 326
Land pollution management via sustainable green agriculture: use of machine
learning and robotics 328

Conclusion 329
References... 330
Further reading 333

SECTION 4 Data-centric and intelligent systems in noise pollution research and other environmental engineering issues

CHAPTER 15 Advanced soft computing techniques in modeling noise pollution health impacts... **337**
Manoj Yadav, Bhaven Tandel and M. Mansoor Ahammed
Introduction... 337
Effect of noise pollution on human health 338
    Hearing impairment.. 338
    Interference with speech communication 339
    Sleep disturbances 339
    Cardiovascular and physiological 339
    Disturbances in mental health 339
    The effects of noise on performance 339
    Negative social behavior and annoyance reactions 340
Noise pollution health-impact modeling... 340
    Exploratory factor analysis.. 340
    Structural equation modeling 341
Stage 1: Defining individual constructs.. 342
Stage 2: Developing and specifying the measurement model 342
Stage 3: Designing a study to produce empirical results 343
Stage 4: Assessing measurement model validity.............................. 344
Stage 5: Specifying the structural model.. 344
Stage 6: Assessing the structural model validity.............................. 345
    Adaptive neuro-fuzzy inference system...................................... 345
SEM and ANFIS case studies 347
Conclusion 349
References... 349

CHAPTER 16 Intelligent and knowledge-based waste management: smart decision-support system.. **353**
Emmanuel Emeka Okoro and Samuel Eshorame Sanni
Introduction... 353
Trends in exploration and production wastes in the oil and gas industry 354
    Exploration waste in the oil and gas industry 355
    Production and refining waste in the oil and gas industry.......... 357

Oil and gas waste management.. 359
Conventional waste management approach in oil and gas industry 361
   Waste handling hierarchy... 361
   Waste treatment techniques in oil and gas industry 363
Environmental impact of oil and gas generated wastes 364
Challenges of conventional waste management systems 366
Expert system for oil and gas waste management system 367
   Sensor application in waste management expert system.............. 368
   Algorithm of the proposed sensor approach......................... 370
Gaps in waste management expert system 371
Effective utilization of expert systems in oil and gas industry waste
management.. 373
Conclusion 374
References... 375

CHAPTER 17 Computer-aided modeling of solid waste conversion: case study of maize (*Zea mays*) residues air gasification............. 381

Adewale George Adeniyi, Joshua O. Ighalo
and Chinenye Adaobi Igwegbe

Introduction.. 381
Methodology 382
   Component specifications... 382
   Model specifications.. 382
   Model description 383
Results and discussion... 384
   Effect on temperature on product selectivity............................. 385
   Effect of pressure on product selectivity 385
   Effect of air − fuel ratio on product selectivity.......................... 387
Conclusion 388
References... 389

CHAPTER 18 Neural network model for biological waste management systems... 393

Ravi Rajamanickam and Divya Baskaran

Introduction.. 393
Materials and methods... 394
Data-driven modeling approaches.. 394
Artificial neural network-based predictive modeling 394
Choosing the activation function 395

Choosing the appropriate training algorithm 396
Data preprocessing and randomization 397
Data division.. 397
Internal parameters of the network and performance evaluation........................ 397
Sensitivity analysis 398
Statistical analysis... 398
Results and discussions 398
    Process modeling of biological reactors for DCM removal........................... 398
Artificial neural modeling of the different biological reactors 399
    Effect of internal network parameters on the network
    architecture-modified RBC 400
Predictive capability of the model for modified RBC 401
Sensitivity analysis of inputs... 404
Removal of DCM in biotrickling filter.. 406
    Effect of internal network parameters on the network architecture................ 406
Predictive capability and sensitivity of the ANN model..................................... 407
Conclusion 412
References.. 412

**CHAPTER 19 The role of artificial neural network in bioproducts
development: a case of modeling and optimization studies** **417**
*Abiola Ezekiel Taiwo, Anthony Ikechukwu Okoji,
Andrew C. Eloka-Eboka and Paul Musonge*
Introduction.. 417
Bioproduct development.. 418
Product formulation 419
Product deformulation 420
Selected optimization tools used in bioprocess development as
computational intelligence.. 420
    Artificial intelligence.. 420
Genetic algorithm 423
Fuzzy logic 424
Application of optimization tools in bioprocessing operations............................ 424
Bioremediation.. 425
Biofuel production 426
Biopharmacy.. 426
Future development or trend 427
Conclusion 427
References.. 427

CHAPTER 20 Modeling of grains sun drying: from theoretical methods to intelligent systems... **433**

Joshua O. Ighalo, Adewale George Adeniyi and Chinenye Adaobi Igwegbe

Introduction.. 433

An account of early theoretical modeling efforts................................. 435

Intelligent systems in the modeling of grains sun drying 437

Conclusion 438

References... 439

Index 443

List of contributors

Adewale George Adeniyi
Department of Chemical Engineering, Faculty of Engineering and Technology, University of Ilorin, Ilorin, Nigeria

M. Mansoor Ahammed
Civil Engineering Department, S.V. National Institute of Technology, India

Chukwunonso O. Aniagor
Department of Chemical Engineering, Nnamdi Azikiwe University, Awka, Nigeria

Mihaela Balanescu
R&D Department, Beia Consult International, Bucharest, Romania

Divya Baskaran
Department of Chemical Engineering, Sri Venkateswara College of Engineering, Sriperumbudur, Tamil Nadu, India

Kiana Berenjkar
Lab of Optimization of Thermal Systems' Installations, Faculty of Mechanical Engineering-Energy Division, K. N. Toosi University of Technology, Tehran, Iran

Andrei Birdici
R&D Department, Beia Consult International, Bucharest, Romania

Oladotun Paul Bolade
Department of Petroleum Chemistry, American University of Nigeria, Yola, Nigeria

Iacob Crucianu
SIVECO Romania SA, Bucharest, Romania

Ali Danandeh Mehr
Department of Civil Engineering, Antalya Bilim University, Antalya, Turkey

Alexandru Drosu
R&D Department, Beia Consult International, Bucharest, Romania

Maitreyee Dutta
National Institute of Technical Teacher's Training & Research, Chandigarh, India

Abisola Opeyemi Egbedina
Department of Chemistry, University of Ibadan, Ibadan, Nigeria

Marcel I. Ejimofor
Department of Chemical Engineering, Nnamdi Azikiwe University, Awka, Nigeria

Ahmed Elbeltagi
College of Environmental and Resource Sciences, Zhejiang University, Hangzhou, China; Agricultural Engineering Department, Faculty of Agriculture, Mansoura University, Mansoura, Egypt

Andrew C. Eloka-Eboka
Centre of Excellence in Carbon-based Fuels, School of Chemical and Minerals Engineering, North-West University, Potchefstroom, South Africa

Ugochukwu Ewuzie
Department of Pure and Industrial Chemistry, Abia State University, Uturu, Nigeria

Chukwuemeka Daniel Ezeliora
Department of Industrial/Production Engineering, Nnamdi Azikiwe University, Awka, Nigeria

Yousef Golizadeh Akhlaghi
EPSRC National Centre for Energy Systems Integration School of Engineering, Urban Sciences Building, Newcastle University, Newcastle, United Kingdom

Erfan Goodarzi
Lab of Optimization of Thermal Systems' Installations, Faculty of Mechanical Engineering-Energy Division, K. N. Toosi University of Technology, Tehran, Iran

Salim Heddam
Faculty of Science, Agronomy Department, Hydraulics Division, Laboratory of Research in Biodiversity Interaction Ecosystem and Biotechnology, University 20 Août 1955, Skikda, Algeria

Joshua O. Ighalo
Department of Chemical Engineering, Faculty of Engineering and Technology, University of Ilorin, Ilorin, Nigeria; Department of Chemical Engineering, Nnamdi Azikiwe University, Awka, Nigeria

Chinenye Adaobi Igwegbe
Department of Chemical Engineering, Nnamdi Azikiwe University, Awka, Nigeria

George Iordache
R&D Department, Beia Consult International, Bucharest, Romania

Ditsuhi Iskandaryan
Institute of New Imaging Technologies (INIT), Jaume I University, Castelló, Spain

Sungwon Kim
Department of Railroad Construction and Safety Engineering, Dongyang University, Yeongju, Republic of Korea

Ozgur Kisi
Department of Civil Engineering, School of Technology, Ilia State University, Tbilisi, Georgia; Institute of Research and Development, Duy Tan University, Da Nang, Vietnam

Thomas Koch
Institute of Internal Combustion Engines, Karlsruhe Institute of Technology, Karlsruhe, Germany

Anurag Malik
Punjab Agricultural University, Regional Research Station, Bathinda, India

Gonçalo Marques
Polytechnic of Coimbra, ESTGOH, Rua General Santos Costa, Oliveira do Hospital, Portugal

Matthew C. Menkiti
Department of Chemical Engineering, Nnamdi Azikiwe University, Awka, Nigeria

Mohammad Hossein Moradi
Institute of Internal Combustion Engines, Karlsruhe Institute of Technology, Karlsruhe, Germany

Paul Musonge
Faculty of Engineering, Mangosuthu University of Technology, Durban, South Africa

Stephen N. Oba
Department of Chemical Engineering, Nnamdi Azikiwe University, Awka, Nigeria

Anthony Ikechukwu Okoji
Department of Chemical Engineering, Landmark University, Omu-Aran, Nigeria

Emmanuel Emeka Okoro
Department of Petroleum Engineering, Covenant University, Ota, Nigeria

Babalola Aisosa Oni
Department of Chemical Engineering, Covenant University, Ota, Nigeria

Okechukwu Dominic Onukwuli
Department of Chemical Engineering, Nnamdi Azikiwe University, Awka, Nigeria

Pius Chukwukelue Onyechi
Department of Industrial/Production Engineering, Nnamdi Azikiwe University, Awka, Nigeria

Carmen Poenaru
R&D Department, Beia Consult International, Bucharest, Romania

Ravi Rajamanickam
Department of Chemical Engineering, Annamalai University, Chidambaram, India

Krzysztof Rajski
Wroclaw University of Science and Technology, Faculty of Environmental Engineering, Wroclaw, Poland

Francisco Ramos
Institute of New Imaging Technologies (INIT), Jaume I University, Castelló, Spain

Emmanuel Rotimi Sadiku
Department of Metallurgy, Polymer and Chemical Engineering, Tshwane University of Technology, Pretoria, South Africa

Jagriti Saini
National Institute of Technical Teacher's Training & Research, Chandigarh, India

Adrian Sandu Pasat
R&D Department, Beia Consult International, Bucharest, Romania

Samuel Eshorame Sanni
Department of Chemical Engineering, Covenant University, Ota, Nigeria

Hoseyn Sayyaadi
Lab of Optimization of Thermal Systems' Installations, Faculty of Mechanical Engineering-Energy Division, K.N. Toosi University of Technology, Tehran, Iran

Mohammad Hassan Shahverdian
Lab of Optimization of Thermal Systems' Installations, Faculty of Mechanical Engineering-Energy Division, K.N. Toosi University of Technology, Tehran, Iran

Ali Sohani
Lab of Optimization of Thermal Systems' Installations, Faculty of Mechanical Engineering-Energy Division, K.N. Toosi University of Technology, Tehran, Iran

George Suciu
R&D Department, Beia Consult International, Bucharest, Romania

Abiola Ezekiel Taiwo
Department of Chemical Engineering, Landmark University, Omu-Aran, Nigeria

Bhaven Tandel
Civil Engineering Department, S.V. National Institute of Technology, India

Sergio Trilles
Institute of New Imaging Technologies (INIT), Jaume I University, Castelló, Spain

Victor I. Ugonabo
Department of Chemical Engineering, Nnamdi Azikiwe University, Awka, Nigeria

Uwe Wagner
Institute of Internal Combustion Engines, Karlsruhe Institute of Technology, Karlsruhe, Germany

Manoj Yadav
Civil Engineering Department, S.V. National Institute of Technology, India

Mitra Zabihigivi
Institute of Internal Combustion Engines, Karlsruhe Institute of Technology, Karlsruhe, Germany

Mohammad Zounemat-Kermani
Department of Water Engineering, Shahid Bahonar University of Kerman, Kerman, Iran

An introduction to *Current Trends and Advances in Computer-Aided Intelligent Environmental Data Engineering*

Joshua O. Ighalo[1,2] and Gonçalo Marques[3]

[1]*Department of Chemical Engineering, Faculty of Engineering and Technology, University of Ilorin, Ilorin, Nigeria*
[2]*Department of Chemical Engineering, Nnamdi Azikiwe University, Awka, Nigeria* [3]*Polytechnic of Coimbra, ESTGOH, Rua General Santos Costa, Oliveira do Hospital, Portugal*

Introduction

In 10 years, several new application areas for intelligent data-centric systems, artificial intelligence, and other computing-based technologies have emerged (Philip Chen & Zhang, 2014). This is the first book aiming to synthesize recent developments, present case studies, and discuss new methods in the area of knowledge. Numerous methods for enhanced data analysis are available in the literature. Furthermore, the application of these methods in the environmental science field is of utmost importance for enhanced public health (Saini et al., 2020b). In particular, cyberphysical systems can provide a continuous flow of data retrieved from cost-effective sensors that can be used in multiple applications (Karagulian et al., 2019). However, to transform these data into knowledge, it is necessary to apply computer-aided methods (Marques, Aleixo et al., 2019, Marques, Ferreira et al., 2019, Marques, Pitarma et al., 2019). The application of these methods will significantly promote people's daily routines. Therefore it is imperative to merge multiple technological fields such as cyber-physical systems and artificial intelligence (AI) to build novel solutions to solve complex public challenges and contribute to overall public health and well-being.

This book, *Current Trends and Advances in Computer-Aided Intelligent Environmental Data Engineering*, presents the latest findings on how AI-based tools are being applied in environmental engineering research. These systems can transform the data collected by intelligent sensors in to relevant and reliable information to support decision-making. These tools include knowledge-based systems, genetic algorithms, artificial neural networks, support vector machine and long—short-term memory (LSTM).

The book explores the various intelligent systems used in the modeling of environmental engineering data in 5 times. This introductory chapter has been prepared by the editors of the book to discuss how intelligent systems have been applied across the various research areas in

Current Trends and Advances in Computer-Aided Intelligent Environmental Data Engineering.
DOI: https://doi.org/10.1016/B978-0-323-85597-6.00012-4

environmental engineering. The book aims to provide an in-depth review of the latest research findings and technological developments in the field of sensors data, addressing enhanced computer-aided methods and applications which transform these data into knowledge.

Book structure and relevant audience

Current Trends and Advances in Computer-Aided Intelligent Environmental Data Engineering is structured into four key sections based on the critical areas of the application of computer-based technologies in environmental engineering. Each section has at least a review chapter. The sections are made up primarily of the latest research, case studies, and methods synthesis. The book merges two engineering disciplines: computer engineering and environmental engineering. The key novelty herein is to present the leading computer-aided technologies, applications, algorithms, systems, and future scope considering this multidisciplinary domain that incorporates the data collected from smart sensors, smart sensor networks that will be processed using enhanced data analytics, and machine intelligence techniques.

The book is a fundamental information source for multiple groups ranging from academics to industrial professionals. Moreover, this book involves individuals from two main areas, computer science engineering and environmental science. Graduate and undergraduate students from those areas will find this book a relevant source to support their cross-domain research activities that deal with environmental data. The book provides a useful data source for software developers and data scientists to support their industrial activities. Furthermore, this book provides a fundamental basis to support decision-making for the chemical plant manager and environmental policymakers. The primary audience is the international academic community, with a particular focus on computer and environmental engineers. Academicians and researchers in environmental science and engineering will be interested in the book because it directly presents the latest research in this new field. This will help to broaden their scope of knowledge and give them new perspectives on previous problems. Environmental engineering professionals and policymakers will find this book of interest because it looks at new ways to solve their environmental problems and develop other industrial policies tailored toward data science and artificial intelligence. Computer engineering professionals will also be captivated by this book because it presents a different area of application for the methods they have been developing. Moreover, the book also offers methods for research students to imitate and learn from while trying to get to grip with the rigors of data science and artificial intelligence.

The expertise of the book editors is well balanced within the two major areas described. The first editor, Gonçalo Marques, has worked extensively in data-centric systems for air pollution (Saini et al., 2020a), noise monitoring (Marques & Pitarma, 2019a, 2019b, 2019c, 2019d, 2020a, 2020b), water quality (Marques & Pitarma, 2019a, 2019b, 2019c, 2019d, 2020a, 2020b), and medical (Marques & Pitarma, 2019a, 2019b, 2019c, 2019d, 2020a) applications. The second editor, Joshua O. Ighalo, has worked extensively on a variety of environmental engineering problems such as water pollution remediation (Hevira et al., 2020; Ighalo et al., 2020a, 2020b; Ighalo & Eletta, 2020) and solid waste management (Adeniyi, Ighalo, & Marques, 2020; Adeniyi, Ighalo, & Abdulkareem,

2020; Hussain, 2020; Ighalo & Adeniyi, 2020a, 2020b, 2020c). Both editors have also worked together in applying intelligent systems to process engineering problems (Hevira et al., 2020; Ighalo et al., 2020c; Ighalo & Eletta, 2020). This cross-domain approach enables the design and development of novel computer-aided methods that lead to emergent applications in environmental data engineering.

Intelligent systems in environmental engineering research

Over the years, intelligence systems based on research data have been employed in numerous areas of environmental engineering. One of the first key domains was in air pollution modeling (Cabaneros et al., 2019). The application of intelligent systems in air pollution has risen steadily over the past two decades, as explained in a recent review (Cabaneros et al., 2019). These applications have become more pertinent as poor air quality has resulted in respiratory illnesses and other health challenges in various parts of the globe (Carracedo-Martíne et al., 2010). The first section of this book discusses data-centric and intelligent systems in air quality monitoring, assessment, and mitigation.

Due to changes in lifestyle and urbanization, a greater variety of pollutants is now being observed in water bodies (Adeniyi & Ighalo, 2019; Ighalo & Adeniyi, 2020a, 2020b, 2020c). More sophistication is now required for the monitoring and assessment of water quality (Adeniyi & Ighalo, 2019; Ighalo & Adeniyi, 2020a, 2020b, 2020c). Relatively recently, the authors of this book conducted a comprehensive evaluation of the monitoring of water quality based on Internet-based techniques (Ighalo et al., 2021). This is among the recent improvements in the research area based on the influence of computer science and engineering. Another area includes the use of deep learning, machine learning, neural networks, fuzzy inference systems, and other intelligent computer-based systems. The second section of this book discusses data-centric and intelligent systems in water quality monitoring, assessment, and mitigation.

There are other relevant areas of environmental engineering that data-centric and intelligent systems have now also become more popular. In land and soil pollution, explored in the third section, intelligent systems have been employed to predict soil pollution levels (Bonelli et al., 2017; Sakizadeh et al., 2017; Tarasov et al., 2018), soil pollutant transport (Buszewski & Kowalkowski, 2006), and to assist in analytical procedures (Sirven et al., 2006). Noise pollution issues have also been investigated by researchers with the aid of data-centric and intelligent systems (Kranti et al., 2012; Nedic et al., 2014). Researchers have modeled roadway traffic noise (Cammarata et al., 1995; Hamad et al., 2017), noise barrier optimization (Zannin et al., 2018), noise source classification (Stoeckle et al., 2001), and the prediction of annoyance evaluation (Steinbach & Altinsoy, 2019). The fourth section presents an in-depth discussion of noise pollution applications using computer-aided methods and other interesting areas of environmental research applications of data-centric and intelligent systems such as solid and hazardous waste management (Adamović et al., 2018; Bayar et al., 2009; Bunsan et al., 2013) and life-cycle analysis (Song et al., 2017; Xin et al., 2020).

Looking to the future

Based on the experience of the authors in examining the research area, several conclusions can be drawn both for the current scenario and as statements of future perspectives. There has been a steady increase in the application of data-centric and intelligent systems on environmental engineering data in virtually all environmental engineering research areas. Furthermore, more intricate and sophisticated architectures will be developed that would greatly improve prediction accuracy. Data-centric and intelligent systems are not very common in developing countries where research involving modeling and prediction remains largely by conventional mathematical techniques. This will change as the younger generation of researchers in these areas becomes more willing to explore these opportunities and resources. This book presents the latest finding on how data-centric and intelligent systems are being applied in environmental engineering research. These tools can transform the data collected by intelligent sensors to relevant and reliable information to support decision-making. The editors of the book expect that this initiative will support future cross-domain applications for the design of computer-aided intelligent environmental data engineering.

References

Adamović, V. M., Antanasijević, D. Z., Ristić, M., Perić-Grujić, A. A., & Pocajt, V. V. (2018). An optimized artificial neural network model for the prediction of rate of hazardous chemical and healthcare waste generation at the national level. *Journal of Material Cycles and Waste Management*, *20*(3), 1736−1750. Available from https://doi.org/10.1007/s10163-018-0741-6.

Adeniyi, A. G., & Ighalo, J. O. (2019). Biosorption of pollutants by plant leaves: An empirical review. *Journal of Environmental Chemical Engineering*, *7*(3), 103100. Available from https://doi.org/10.1016/j.jece.2019.103100.

Adeniyi, A. G., Ighalo, J. O., & Marques, G. (2020). Utilisation of machine learning algorithms for the prediction of syngas composition from biomass bio-oil steam reforming. *International Journal of Sustainable Energy*, *40*(4), 310−325. Available from https://doi.org/10.1080/14786451.2020.1803862.

Adeniyi, A. G., Ighalo, J. O., & Abdulkareem, S. A. (2020). Al, Fe and Cu waste metallic particles in conductive polystyrene composites. *International Journal of Sustainable Engineering*, 1−7.

Bayar, S., Demir, I., & Engin, G. O. (2009). Modeling leaching behavior of solidified wastes using back-propagation neural networks. *Ecotoxicology and Environmental Safety*, *72*(3), 843−850. Available from https://doi.org/10.1016/j.ecoenv.2007.10.019.

Bonelli, M. G., Ferrini, M., & Manni, A. (2017). Artificial neural networks to evaluate organic and inorganic contamination in agricultural soils. *Chemosphere*, *186*, 124−131. Available from https://doi.org/10.1016/j.chemosphere.2017.07.116.

Bunsan, S., Chen, W. Y., Chen, H. W., Chuang, Y. H., & Grisdanurak, N. (2013). Modeling the dioxin emission of a municipal solid waste incinerator using neural networks. *Chemosphere*, *92*(3), 258−264. Available from https://doi.org/10.1016/j.chemosphere.2013.01.083.

Buszewski, B., & Kowalkowski, T. (2006). A new model of heavy metal transport in the soil using nonlinear artificial neural networks. *Environmental Engineering Science*, *23*(4), 589−595. Available from https://doi.org/10.1089/ees.2006.23.589.

Cabaneros, S. M., Calautit, J. K., & Hughes, B. R. (2019). A review of artificial neural network models for ambient air pollution prediction. *Environmental Modelling and Software*, *119*, 285−304. Available from https://doi.org/10.1016/j.envsoft.2019.06.014.

Cammarata, G., Cavalieri, S., & Fichera, A. (1995). A neural network architecture for noise prediction. *Neural Networks*, *8*(6), 963−973. Available from https://doi.org/10.1016/0893-6080(95)00016-S.

Carracedo-Martíne, E., Taracido, M., Tobias, A., Saez, M., & Figueiras, A. (2010). Case-crossover analysis of air pollution health effects: A systematic review of methodology and application. *Environmental Health Perspectives*, *118*(8), 1173−1182. Available from https://doi.org/10.1289/ehp.0901485.

Hamad, K., Ali Khalil, M., & Shanableh, A. (2017). Modeling roadway traffic noise in a hot climate using artificial neural networks. *Transportation Research Part D: Transport and Environment*, *53*, 161−177. Available from https://doi.org/10.1016/j.trd.2017.04.014.

Hevira, L., Zilfa, R., Ighalo, J. O., & Zein, R. (2020). Biosorption of indigo carmine from aqueous solution by *Terminalia catappa* shell. *Journal of Environmental Chemical Engineering*, *8*(5), 104290. Available from https://doi.org/10.1016/j.jece.2020.104290.

Hussain, C. M. (2020). Utilization of recycled polystyrene and aluminum wastes in the development of conductive plastic composites: Evaluation of electrical properties. In J. O. Ighalo, & A. G. Adeniyi (Eds.), *Handbook of environmental materials management* (pp. 1−9). Springer Nature.

Ighalo, J. O., & Adeniyi, A. G. (2020a). A comprehensive review of water quality monitoring and assessment in Nigeria. *Chemosphere*, *260*, 127569.

Ighalo, J. O., & Adeniyi, A. G. (2020b). Adsorption of pollutants by plant bark derived adsorbents: An empirical review. *Journal of Water Process Engineering*, *35*, 101228. Available from https://doi.org/10.1016/j.jwpe.2020.101228.

Ighalo, J. O., & Adeniyi, A. G. (2020c). A perspective on environmental sustainability in the cement industry. *Waste Disposal & Sustainable Energy*, *2*(3), 161−164. Available from https://doi.org/10.1007/s42768-020-00043-y.

Ighalo, J. O., & Eletta, O. A. A. (2020). Response surface modelling of the biosorption of Zn(II) and Pb(II) onto *Micropogonias undulatus* scales: Box−Behnken experimental approach. *Applied Water Science*, *10*(8), 197−209. Available from https://doi.org/10.1007/s13201-020-01283-3.

Ighalo, J. O., Adeniyi, A. G., & Marques, G. (2020a). Application of artificial neural networks in predicting biomass higher heating value: An early appraisal. *Energy Sources, Part A: Recovery, Utilization and Environmental Effects*. Available from https://doi.org/10.1080/15567036.2020.1809567.

Ighalo, J. O., Adeniyi, A. G., & Marques, G. (2020b). Application of linear regression algorithm and stochastic gradient descent in a machine-learning environment for predicting biomass higher heating value. *Biofuels, Bioproducts and Biorefining*. Available from https://doi.org/10.1002/bbb.2140.

Ighalo, J. O., Adeniyi, A. G., & Marques, G. (2021). *Internet of things for water quality monitoring and assessment: A comprehensive review. Studies in computational intelligence* (Vol. 912, pp. 245−259). Springer. Available from https://doi.org/10.1007/978-3-030-51920-9_13.

Ighalo, J. O., Ajala, O. J., Umenweke, G., Ogunniyi, S., Adeyanju, C. A., Igwegbe, C. A., & Adeniyi, A. G. (2020c). Mitigation of clofibric acid pollution by adsorption: A review of recent developments. *Journal of Environmental Chemical Engineering*, *8*(5), 10426. Available from https://doi.org/10.1016/j.jece.2020.104264.

Karagulian, F., Barbiere, M., Kotsev, A., Spinelle, L., Gerboles, M., Lagler, F., Redon, N., Crunaire, S., & Borowiak, A. (2019). Review of the performance of low-cost sensors for air quality monitoring. *Atmosphere*, *10*(9), 506. Available from https://doi.org/10.3390/atmos10090506.

Kranti, K., Manoranjan, P., & Kumar, K. V. (2012). Road traffic noise prediction with neural networks—a review. *An International Journal of Optimization and Control: Theories & Applications (IJOCTA)*, *2*(1), 29−37. Available from https://doi.org/10.11121/ijocta.01.2012.0059.

Marques, G., & Pitarma, R. (2019a). *A cost-effective real-time monitoring system for water quality management based on Internet of Things. Science and technologies for smart cities* (pp. 312−323). Springer.

Marques, G., & Pitarma, R. (2019b). *Noise mapping through mobile crowdsourcing for enhanced living environments*. Lecture notes in computer science (including subseries Lecture notes in artificial intelligence and lecture notes in bioinformatics) (Vol. 11538, pp. 670–679). Springer Verlag. Available from https://doi.org/10.1007/978-3-030-22744-9_52.

Marques, G., & Pitarma, R. (2019c). *Smartwatch-based application for enhanced healthy lifestyle in indoor environments. Advances in intelligent systems and computing* (Vol. 888, pp. 168–177). Springer Verlag. Available from https://doi.org/10.1007/978-3-030-03302-6_15.

Marques, G., & Pitarma, R. (2019d). *Using IOT and social networks for enhanced healthy practices in buildings. Smart innovation, systems and technologies* (Vol. 111, pp. 424–432). Springer Science and Business Media Deutschland GmbH. Available from https://doi.org/10.1007/978-3-030-03577-8_47.

Marques, G., & Pitarma, R. (2020a). A real-time noise monitoring system based on Internet of Things for enhanced acoustic comfort and occupational health. *IEEE Access, 8*, 139741–139755. Available from https://doi.org/10.1109/ACCESS.2020.3012919.

Marques, G., & Pitarma, R. (2020b). *Promoting health and well-being using wearable and smartphone technologies for ambient assisted living through Internet of Things, . Lecture notes in networks and systems* (Vol. 81, pp. 12–22). Springer. Available from https://doi.org/10.1007/978-3-030-23672-4_2.

Marques, G., Aleixo, D., & Pitarma, R. (2019). *Enhanced hydroponic agriculture environmental monitoring: An Internet of Things approach, . Lecture notes in computer science (including subseries Lecture notes in artificial intelligence and lecture notes in bioinformatics)* (Vol. 11538, pp. 658–669). Springer Verlag. Available from https://doi.org/10.1007/978-3-030-22744-9_51.

Marques, G., Ferreira, C. R., & Pitarma, R. (2019). Indoor air quality assessment using a CO_2 monitoring system based on Internet of Things. *Journal of Medical Systems, 43*(3), 67. Available from https://doi.org/10.1007/s10916-019-1184-x.

Marques, G., Pitarma, R., Garcia, N. M., & Pombo, N. (2019). Internet of things architectures, technologies, applications, challenges, and future directions for enhanced living environments and healthcare systems: A review. *Electronics (Switzerland), 8*(10), 1081. Available from https://doi.org/10.3390/electronics8101081.

Nedic, V., Despotovic, D., Cvetanovic, S., Despotovic, M., & Babic, S. (2014). Comparison of classical statistical methods and artificial neural network in traffic noise prediction. *Environmental Impact Assessment Review, 49*, 24–30. Available from https://doi.org/10.1016/j.eiar.2014.06.004.

Philip Chen, C. L., & Zhang, C. Y. (2014). Data-intensive applications, challenges, techniques and technologies: A survey on big data. *Information Sciences, 275*, 314–347. Available from https://doi.org/10.1016/j.ins.2014.01.015.

Saini, J., Dutta, M., & Marques, G. (2020a). A comprehensive review on indoor air quality monitoring systems for enhanced public health. *Sustainable Environment Research, 30*, 6.

Saini, J., Dutta, M., & Marques, G. (2020b). Indoor air quality prediction systems for smart environments: A systematic review. *Journal of Ambient Intelligence and Smart Environments, 12*(5), 433–453.

Sakizadeh, M., Mirzaei, R., & Ghorbani, H. (2017). Support vector machine and artificial neural network to model soil pollution: A case study in Semnan Province, Iran. *Neural Computing and Applications, 28*(11), 3229–3238. Available from https://doi.org/10.1007/s00521-016-2231-x.

Sirven, J. B., Bousquet, B., Canioni, L., Sarger, L., Tellier, S., Potin-Gautier, M., & Le Hecho, I. (2006). Qualitative and quantitative investigation of chromium-polluted soils by laser-induced breakdown spectroscopy combined with neural networks analysis. *Analytical and Bioanalytical Chemistry, 385*(2), 256–262. Available from https://doi.org/10.1007/s00216-006-0322-8.

Song, R., Keller, A. A., & Suh, S. (2017). Rapid life-cycle impact screening using artificial neural networks. *Environmental Science and Technology, 51*(18), 10777–10785. Available from https://doi.org/10.1021/acs.est.7b02862.

Steinbach, L., & Altinsoy, M. E. (2019). Prediction of annoyance evaluations of electric vehicle noise by using artificial neural networks. *Applied Acoustics, 145*, 149–158. Available from https://doi.org/10.1016/j.apacoust.2018.09.024.

Stoeckle, S., Pah, N., Kumar, D. K., & McLachlan, N. (2001). *Environmental sound sources classification using neural networks. ANZIIS 2001—Proceedings of the 7th Australian and New Zealand intelligent information systems conference* (pp. 399−403). Institute of Electrical and Electronics Engineers Inc. Available from https://doi.org/10.1109/ANZIIS.2001.974112.

Tarasov, D. A., Buevich, A. G., Sergeev, A. P., & Shichkin, A. V. (2018). High variation topsoil pollution forecasting in the Russian Subarctic: Using artificial neural networks combined with residual kriging. *Applied Geochemistry*, *88*(Part B), 188−197. Available from https://doi.org/10.1016/j.apgeochem.2017.07.007.

Xin, J., Akiyama, M., Frangopol, D. M., Zhang, M., Pei, J., & Zhang, J. (2020). Reliability-based life-cycle cost design of asphalt pavement using artificial neural networks. *Structure and Infrastructure Engineering*, *17*(6), 872−886. Available from https://doi.org/10.1080/15732479.2020.1815807.

Zannin, P. H. T., Do Nascimento, E. O., da Paz, E. C., & Do Valle, F. (2018). Application of artificial neural networks for noise barrier optimization. *Environments—MDPI*, *5*(12), 1−20. Available from https://doi.org/10.3390/environments5120135.

Data-centric and intelligent systems in air quality monitoring, assessment, and mitigation

Application of deep learning and machine learning in air quality modeling

Ditsuhi Iskandaryan, Francisco Ramos and Sergio Trilles

Institute of New Imaging Technologies (INIT), Jaume I University, Castelló, Spain

Introduction

Polluted air causes various diseases in humans and also negatively affects the environment (Brook et al., 2003; Mills et al., 2009; Yang et al., 2004). According to the World Health Organization (WHO), every year nine people out of every 10 breathe highly polluted air, and 7 million people die because of air pollution.[1] Therefore this problem has become one of the most alarming situations for governments and society. However, it remains challenging to reduce the causes of air pollution. Predicting air quality with higher accuracy is one of the most pressing challenges for data analysts and can be considered to be one of the central topics in data science. When exploring the reasons behind air pollution, first should be mentioned urbanization, with the movement of people from rural to urban areas. This process is integrated with industrialization, which in turn involves the construction of new factories, the creation of heating systems, heavy use of vehicles, etc. This transformation, as a result, causes a deterioration in air quality, with this process being especially pronounced in developing countries, where urbanization is taking place at a rapid pace (Qiu et al., 2019).

A possible solution to help to reduce this problem is to harness the power and capacity of technology to predict air quality. The main aim is to generate useful information to help organize and plan daily life and avoid exposure to air pollution. Two of the powerful predictive tools currently in use are machine learning (ML) and deep learning (DL). These techniques are used to find patterns based on external factors, and can predict air quality with higher accuracy (Iskandaryan et al., 2020a, 2020b). As external factors, mention should be made of meteorological data, weather forecast data, spatial data, etc., which are as crucial as ML and DL models to obtain higher accuracy, and their general description is provided in the following sections.

The main goal of this chapter is to provide the reader with a generic workflow of learning from air quality stations data to forecast air quality predictions. This workflow is based on three sections, including data profiling, data learning, and conclusions. It should be emphasized that this work targets the concept of air quality prediction from the perspective of data science researchers, and it can be useful for works devoted to air quality prediction. Section 2 provides detailed information

---

[1] https://www.who.int/health-topics/air-pollution#tab = tab_1

Current Trends and Advances in Computer-Aided Intelligent Environmental Data Engineering.
DOI: https://doi.org/10.1016/B978-0-323-85597-6.00018-5

about air quality data and indices, external datasets used along with air quality data to increase the accuracy of the methods. Section 3 introduces the integration and preprocessing steps of those data, the ML and DL algorithms used for the purpose of learning data, and validation metrics used to evaluate the methods. Finally, Section 4 summarizes the work and suggests further avenues for research.

Data profiling

This section cover the following aspects: (1) datasets that are used with air quality prediction to increase performance accuracy and (2) pollutants and a general description of indices and the standards.

Datasets

Air quality is highly dependent on many external factors. To control and accurately predict air quality, it is essential to consider these factors. It is therefore advantageous to include, along with air quality data, other datasets that affect air quality. Those datasets can be classified into the following categories (Iskandaryan et al., 2020a) (Fig. 2.1).

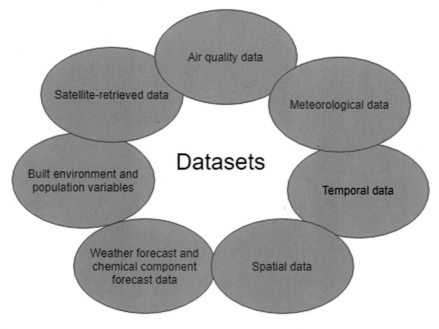

FIGURE 2.1

Datasets used for air quality prediction. These datasets are grouped into the following categories: meteorological data, temporal data, spatial data, built environment and population variables, satellite-retrieved data, weather forecast data, and chemical component forecast data.

Meteorological data—the most used dataset along with air quality data. For example, Liu et al. included precipitation, humidity, temperature, wind force, and wind direction with air quality data [carbon monoxide (CO), nitrogen dioxide (NO_2), ground-level ozone (O_3), particulate matter with a diameter equal to 2.5 μm ($PM_{2.5}$), particulate matter with a diameter equal to 10 μm (PM_{10})] (Liu et al., 2019). The aim of the work was to predict $PM_{2.5}$ by combining the aforementioned variables and applying ML techniques. Another example is the work done by Deters et al., where they used 6 years' records of meteorological data together with air quality data to predict $PM_{2.5}$ (Deters et al., 2017).

Temporal data—includes the day of the month, day of the week, and hour of the day. Ma et al. used $PM_{2.5}$, PM_{10}, CO, NO_2, sulfur dioxide (SO_2), O_3, temperature, pressure, relative humidity, wind speed, wind direction, and the recorded month, day, and hour of these observations to predict $PM_{2.5}$ in Wayne County in Michigan (Ma et al., 2020).

Spatial data—proximity to transportation, topographical characteristics, neighborhood characteristics, the locations of the stations, planetary boundary layer height, altitude, and elevation. In addition to air quality and meteorological data, Abu Awad et al. used proximity to transportation, topographical characteristics, and neighborhood characteristics to forecast black carbon (Abu Awad et al., 2017).

Built environment and population variables—land use data, traffic intensity features, sound pressure, pollution point source, transportation source, point of interest (POI) distribution, factory air pollution emission, road network distribution, anthropogenic emission inventory, emissions, population density, human movements (floating population and estimated traffic volume), and social media data. Contreras and Ferri utilized traffic intensity features (traffic level in the surrounding stations and traffic level 3 hours before) and weather conditions to predict NO, NO_2, SO_2, and O_3 levels (Contreras & Ferri, 2016).

Satellite-retrieved data—aerosol optical depth, satellite-retrieved SO_2 from ozone monitoring instrument-SO_2, Ultraviolet (UV) Index, Normalized Difference Vegetation Index (NDVI). Li et al. used meteorological data, temporal data, land use data, satellite-retrieved SO_2 from ozone monitoring instrument-SO_2, pollution point source, and transportation source to predict SO_2 levels in China (Li et al., 2019).

Weather forecast and chemical component forecast data—organic carbon, black carbon, etc. Ling et al. used air quality, meteorological data, weather forecast data, traffic flow data, factory air pollutant emission data, POI distribution data, and road network distribution data to forecast Air Quality Index (AQI) (Ling et al., 2019).

Air quality data and indices

Air pollution is created from chemical elements that are derived from natural and anthropogenic sources. There are several pollutants that have the most severe effects on human health and the environment, including $PM_{2.5}$, PM_{10}, nitrogen oxide (NO_x), O_3, and SO_2. Depending on the area, some pollutants can be dominant and have a greater impact, therefore the prediction target, the dominant pollutant, differs from region to region.

There are different approaches to available observe and investigate certain pollutants. AQI is used to monitor and report air quality, which helps to convert air pollution into a number which in turn is helpful from the points of public understanding of view and easy comparison (Thom & Ott,

1967). However, the interpretation of air quality indices varies depending on the area. There are a number of reasons for these differences, such as historical impacts, local air quality problems, quality of life, etc. In addition, the methodology of calculation behind AQI is different, and interestingly there is no one internationally accepted approach. It is challenging to define one approach that could be efficient and cover all the aforementioned differences (Kanchan & Goyal, 2015; Plaia & Ruggieri, 2011). Below, several popular indices are introduced (Ramos et al., 2018). Some focus on one pollutant, some while others have a multipollutant approach by applying different methods for aggregation.

The US Environmental Protection Agency (EPA) AQI—refers to the highest individual pollutant (O_3, $PM_{2.5}$, PM_{10}, CO, NO_2, and SO_2) of the given area. Therefore it is not able to aggregate more than one pollutant. This index varies from 0 to 500 with the following categories: Good (0−50), Moderate (51−100), Unhealthy for Sensitive Groups (101−150), Unhealthy (151−200), Very Unhealthy (201−300), and Hazardous (301−500).

The Canada Air Quality Health Index (AQHI)—the main goal of the AQHI is to monitor air quality impact on health and avoid harmful effects. This index provides a number from 1 to 10 + and, based on these, air quality is categorized in the following classes: Low (1−3); Moderate (4−6); High (7−10); and Very High above 10. To calculate the AQHI, the concentrations of NO_2, $PM_{2.5}$, and O_3 are taken into consideration.

Common Air Quality Index (CAQI) (Van Den Elshout et al., 2014)—can differentiate traffic conditions from city background conditions. It varies from 0 (very low) to above 100 (very high). CAQI is formed by selecting the highest value from the list of subindices calculated for each pollutant (O_3, PM_{10}, CO, NO_2, SO_2, and $PM_{2.5}$).

Daily Air Quality Index (DAQI) (Ayres et al., 2011)—uses a scale with four levels of Low (1−3), Moderate (4−6), High (7−9), and Very High (10). To calculate DAQI the following pollutants are considered: O_3, NO_2, SO_2, $PM_{2.5}$, and PM_{10}.

France Air Quality Index, ATMO Index[2]—is defined on a scale of 1−10. The ATMO Index calculates considering the concentrations of SO_2, NO_2, O_3, $PM_{2.5}$, and PM_{10}.

As can be seen, the categories and scales of these categories vary depending on the indices.

Learning from data

Nowadays, thanks to technology, it is possible to observe, collect, and save big data. Learning from these data is an essential procedure, the aim of which is to discover useful patterns and priceless information. However, analyzing the data remains challenging and time consuming. Different techniques and methods are used to overcome the aforementioned problems. Fig. 2.2 shows the steps for extracting knowledge and information from raw data, including data integration, data preprocessing, machine learning, and validation, which in turn lead to making a decision and solving different problems (Alasadi & Bhaya, 2017; García et al., 2016). The figure also indicates the components of data preprocessing and machine learning. Data preprocessing includes outlier detection, missing value treatment, normalization, discretization, feature selection, and imbalanced

---

[2]https://atmo-france.org/

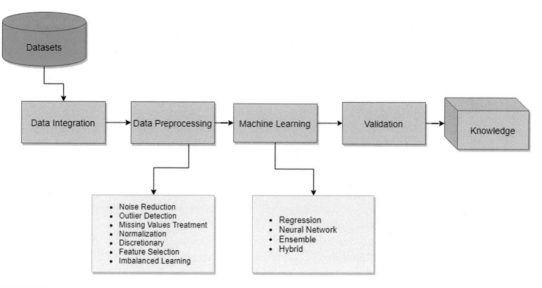

FIGURE 2.2

Steps involved in data learning process. The diagram shows the steps of extracting knowledge and information from raw data, including datasets, data integration, data preprocessing, machine learning, validation, and knowledge.

learning. Machine learning and deep learning include regression, neural network, ensemble, and hybrid models. Each step is detailed in the following sections.

Data integration and data preprocessing

To effectively and efficiently analyze huge datasets, it is important to enhance the quality of the raw data. Referring to Fig. 2.2, it can be seen that the first step is to combine and integrate datasets from multiple and various sources into one platform. The next step is data preprocessing and includes noise reduction, outlier detection, missing value treatment, normalization, discretization, feature selection, and imbalanced learning.

Noise reduction and outlier detection: having noise can significantly worsen the performance accuracy, particularly in the case of applying instance-based learners. There are some techniques which observe data, find noise, and remove or filter it, in other words, they generate noise-free data from row data. Several authors (Gupta & Gupta, 2019; Xingquan & Xindong, 2004) have presented the different types of noise with corresponding identification and handling methods: attribute noise—filtering, polishing; class noise—ensemble techniques, distance-based algorithm, single learning-based technique, removing, filtering, and polishing.

Because of several errors, such as human error or instrument error, it is possible that the data could contain an outlier, and it is very important to detect and remove these values. Depending on the application and data structure, the approaches to detect outliers can differ. Hodge and Austin described three approaches: a clustering approach, a classification approach, and a novelty approach

(Hodge & Austin, 2004). Those approaches include distance-based, set-based, density-based, depth-based, model-based, and graph-based algorithms.

Missing value treatment: another issue related to data is the existence of missing values. There are three types of missing data: Missing Completely At Random (MCAR), Missing Not At Random (MNAR), and Missing At Random (MAR) (Donders et al., 2006). Depending on the number of missing values, missing data can be handled differently: by removal or imputation. In the case of a small number of missing data they can be removed; otherwise, it is recommended to carry out imputation. The latter is performed with different methods which are merged into three categories: data-driven (mean, hot-deck, cold-deck, etc.), model-based (regression-based, likelihood-based, etc.), and ML-based methods [decision trees, neural network (NN), etc.] (Farhangfar et al., 2007; Lakshminarayan et al., 1999). Junninen et al. introduced methods using for missing air quality data imputation (Junninen et al., 2004). The methods are linear, spline, and univariate nearest neighbor interpolations, regression-based imputation, multivariate nearest neighbor, self-organizing maps, and multilayer back-propagation nets.

Normalization and discretization: sometimes, in datasets, features can vary over a wide range, creating difficulties for some algorithms. Therefore feature scaling and normalization are applied to solve this problem. This can be done using one of the following methods: min−max normalization or feature scaling, z-score normalization or standardization, and unit length scaling.

Regarding discretization, it can help in easier comprehension of data than continuous values, and it is closer to knowledge-level representation; moreover, several ML algorithms can only work with discrete values. Discretization aims to remove maximum intervals with minimal loss of information. Liu et al. introduced the steps of the discretization process: sorting, choosing a cut-point, splitting/merging, and stopping (Liu et al., 2002). Examples of discretization methods are ID3, Minimum Description Length Principle (MDLP), ChiMerge, and so on.

Feature selection: this concept refers to dimensionality reduction. To analyze and interpret a huge dataset is a challenging task. Feature selection helps to remove redundant and irrelevant data, select a subset of features that better describe the data, can effectively understand and interpret the data, significantly improve performance accuracy, reduce computational time, and decrease curse of dimensionality effects. The following are commonly used methods for future selection: filter, wrapper, and embedded methods (Chandrashekar & Sahin, 2014; Kumar & Minz, 2014). Filter methods by ranking features select the most highly ranked features (correlation criteria, mutual information), wrapper methods by combining different subsets search and choose the combination which has higher performance (genetic algorithm, particle swarm optimization), and embedded methods perform feature selection during the training process (minimum redundancy maximum relevance).

Imbalanced learning: sometimes data can contain more items from one class than another. To handle this issue, imbalanced learning is applied with oversampling and undersampling approaches. The most common method of imbalanced learning is Synthetic Minority Oversampling TEchnique (SMOTE) (Chawla et al., 2002).

One example of data integration and data preprocessing is in the study by Zhang et al. (Zhang et al., 2019). In this research the authors obtained better results by first integrating different datasets, including air quality, meteorological, spatial, and weather forecast data. Then, exploring datasets and different features, they detected existing outliers, in particular, with the temperature data samples outside the range of −30°C to +40°C, pressure data samples greater than 2000 kPa, humidity samples greater than 100%, and wind direction outside of the range of 0−360 degrees being considered as outliers. These outliers were filled with new data obtained after applying the linear interpolation method. Regarding missing values, the combination of the linear interpolation and the random forest means was applied. Moreover, to remove redundant and unnecessary information, principal component analysis was used.

Another study, which included detailed information about data preprocessing, was carried out by D. Zhu et al. (2018). This work was focused on applying parameter-reducing formulations and consecutive-hour-related regularizations to forecast SO_2, $PM_{2.5}$, and O_3. After integrating air quality and meteorological data, the next step was to preprocess the combined dataset. For the main part of the dataset, the data rate was hourly, however, some variables had several records in 1 hour, and so, for these variables, the hourly mean was calculated and used. Missing values were imputed by using the closest-neighbor values for four continuous variables and one categorical variable: wind gust, pressure, altimeter reading, precipitation, and weather conditions. Finally, normalization was applied for all the features and pollutant targets.

Machine learning and deep learning algorithms

Having preprocessed data, the next step is to use them as an input for certain models. ML and DL methods have been used in many fields, and are also very powerful for air quality prediction. The ML and DL algorithms applied in this field are grouped into the following categories: NN, regression, ensemble, and hybrid models.

Regression analysis aims to predict continuous value, to depict the relationship between dependent and independent variables. Depending on this relation, the following types of regression analysis are formed: linear, multiple linear, and nonlinear. The difference between linear and multiple linear regression is the number of dependent variables for one independent variable. Nonlinear regression is used for solving more complex problems, in which case the dependence of dependent and independent variables is not linear.

Eldakhly et al. applied chance Weighted Support Vector Regression (chWSVR) to forecast PM_{10} for the next hour (Eldakhly et al., 2017). The output showed that the proposed method demonstrated better results. Oprea et al. used M5P and REPTree to forecast PM_{10} (Oprea et al., 2016). The results showed that M5P improves the accuracy of the prediction.

Neural network has recently become the most used ML technique, and works similar to the human brain. The latter fact creates difficulties in explaining how it works. NN consists of several layers, which are made of nodes, where all computations derived from processing. The input layers with corresponding weights are summed and then pass through the activation function giving the output layer. Then, by calculating the error, the process is continued until the obtained error is suitable for a certain application.

Tao et al. applied the Convolutional-based Bidirectional Gated Recurrent Unit (CBGRU) combined with 1D convnets and Bidirectional Gated Recurrent Unit (BGRU) NN to forecast $PM_{2.5}$ (Tao et al., 2019). Compared to SVR, Gradient Boosting Regression (GBR), Decision Tree Regression (DTR), Recurrent Neural Network (RNN), Long Short-Term Memory (LSTM), Gated Recurrent Unit (GRU), and BGRU, the prediction results showed that CBGRU performed better.

Liu et al. developed an Attention-based Air Quality Predictor (AAQP) with n-step recurrent prediction (Liu et al., 2019). Compare to artificial neural network (ANN), SVM, GRU, LSTM, seq2seq, seq2seq-mean, seq2seq-attention, and n-step AAQP, attention-based models demonstrated better results and also recurrent prediction gave better results compared to direct prediction. Regarding steps analysis, the results showed that 12-step AAQP was the best. The authors also compared training and prediction times for each model. Moreover, the training time (s) of 12-step AAQP (GRU) and the prediction time of 12-step AAQP (LSTM) had better performances.

Ensemble and hybrid models recently have become very popular in practice. The opportunity to integrate different models with certain strategies, by considering that each model has limitations, and controlling the strengths and weaknesses of each individual method, significantly improved performance accuracy and enabled more complex problems to be solved. At first glance, these two models seem similar, but there is a slight difference related to the integration mechanism. The ensemble method applies a homogeneous approach to combine weak methods. The following problems: statistical, computational, and representation problems, which usually appear in the case of single method implementation, can be solved with ensemble learning. It should be noted also, that the in case of having an issue related to the amount of data, small or big data, for both situations ensemble learning is a good option to apply. The most popular approaches are bagging or bootstrap aggregation and boosting. Bagging by bootstrap sampling creates subsets for base learners and then combines the outputs by voting for classification and by averaging for regression. In the case of boosting, base learners are trained sequentially on a weighted version of the data, and the final results are obtained through a weighted majority vote for classification and a weighted sum for regression. The hybrid model heterogeneously combines different ML and DL methods. Sometimes, it uses one model for prediction and another for optimization, which can increase the accuracy.

Due to the potential that these methods can provide, their use is increasing in various fields, including also air quality prediction. Zhang et al. implemented the Light Gradient Boosting Machine (LightGBM) ensemble model to predict the $PM_{2.5}$ concentration for the next day (Zhang et al., 2019). The analysis was performed on predictive and historical data. Compared to Adaboost, Gradient Boosting Decision Tree (GBDT), eXtreme Gradient Boosting (XGboost), Deep Neural Network (DNN), and also with LightGBM excluded predictive data, the results showed that the proposed method was best-performing method.

Zheng et al. applied a multiple kernel learning model with support vector classifier (MKSVC) ensemble methods for $PM_{2.5}$ prediction (Zheng et al., 2018). The following methods were used for comparison purposes: AutoRegressive Integrated Moving Average (ARIMA), Random Forest (RF) and Support Vector Machine (SVM), Multilayer Perceptron (MLP), and LSTM. As a result, MKSVC showed the best performance.

Regarding hybrid models, Li and Ngan developed a model integrating ARIMA, SVM, and ANN (Li and Ngan, 2019). The proposed method had a better performance compared to all single classifiers in the ensemble and with RF.

D. Zhu et al. (2018) and S. Zhu et al. (2018) developed a hybrid model, CEEMD-PSOGSA-SVR-GRNN, based on Complementary Ensemble Empirical Mode Decomposition (CEEMD), Particle Swarm Optimization and Gravitational Search Algorithm (PSOGSA), SVR, Generalized Regression Neural Network (GRNN), and Grey Correlation Analysis (GCA) to predict $PM_{2.5}$.

Validation metrics

Validation or evaluation metrics are the tools or mechanisms for measuring the quality of the models. They are an essential part of obtaining an effective ML or DL model. Depending on the task, application, and model, the metrics differ. In the domain of air quality prediction, more than 60 metrics are being used, from which the following metrics are the most used (Iskandaryan et al., 2020b): root mean square error (RMSE), mean absolute error (MAE), Pearson correlation coefficient (R), and mean absolute percentage error (MAPE). RMSE is used to measure the error of the model [Eq. (2.1)]. The lower the value of RMSE, the better the performance of the model, and, depending on the application, certain values can be acceptable or not. MAE measures the average value of the errors [Eq. (2.2)]. The Pearson correlation coefficient is the statistical relationship between two continuous variables [Eq. (2.3)]. MAPE measures the accuracy of the forecast system expressed as a percentage [Eq. (2.4)].

$$RMSE = \left(\frac{1}{n} \sum_{i=1}^{n} (E_i - A_i)^2 \right)^{1/2} \tag{2.1}$$

$$MAE = \frac{1}{n} \sum_{i=1}^{n} |E_i - A_i| \tag{2.2}$$

$$R = \frac{\sum_{i=1}^{n} E_i A_i - \sum_{i=1}^{n} E_i \sum_{i=1}^{n} A_i / n}{\left(\left(\sum_{i=1}^{n} E_i^2 - \left(\sum_{i=1}^{n} E_i \right)^2 / n \right) \left(\sum_{i=1}^{n} E_i^2 - \left(\sum_{i=1}^{n} A_i \right)^2 / n \right) \right)^{1/2}} \tag{2.3}$$

$$MAPE = \frac{1}{n} \sum_{i=1}^{n} \left| \frac{E_i - A_i}{A_i} \right| 100\% \tag{2.4}$$

where n is the number of instances, and E_i and A_i are the estimated and actual values at the time i, respectively. Sometimes, researchers use several metrics to be able to evaluate methods from different points of view and carry out a comparison.

Xu and Ren used RMSE, MAE, and R with other two metrics (normalized root mean square error and symmetric mean absolute percentage error) to evaluate Supplementary Leaky Integrator Echo State Network (SLI-ESN) for $PM_{2.5}$ prediction (Xu & Ren, 2019). The results showed that the proposed method outperformed other methods with the following outputs: RMSE: 9.3953, MAE: 5.8447, and R: 0.9945 for the next 1-hour prediction; RMSE: 37.6874, MAE: 25.5871, and R: 0.9108 for the next 5-hour prediction; and RMSE: 65.7108, MAE: 46.3633, and R: 0.7314 for the next 10-hour prediction.

Ma et al. applied RMSE, MAE, and MAPE to evaluate Bidirectional Long Short-Term Memory (BLSTM) network integrated with the Inverse Distance Weighting (IDW) technique for $PM_{2.5}$ prediction (Ma et al., 2019). Compared to AutoRegressive Integrated Moving Average (ARIMA), ElasticNet, SVR, GBDT, ANN, RNN, LSTM, BLSTM, and Convolutional Neural Network-LSTM (CNN-LSTM), the proposed method had the highest performance with RMSE: 8.24, MAE: 4.80, and MAPE (%): 9.01.

Conclusions and further thoughts

Considering the negative consequences of air pollution on human health and the environment, this area is of growing concern. To reduce this negative impact and improve air quality, it is important to study its progress, to discover the external factors that affect it, and to explore the pattern with further expansion. ML and DL are packages of algorithms with powerful tools that can model and perform predictions. They are also very popular for air pollution prediction.

This chapter presents the workflow of air quality prediction with a detailed description of the covered steps. First, it should be mentioned that to include only air quality data in the analysis is not sufficient. To enhance the accuracy of model performance, it is preferable to integrate all the relevant data. However, knowing in advance which variables are relevant is not an easy task. Therefore the datasets that have a certain relation with air quality data and can affect the structure of air quality should be incorporated in the analysis, which in further steps will be preprocessed. The datasets used by researchers are categorized into the following groups: meteorological data, temporal data, spatial data, built environment and population variables, satellite-retrieved data, weather forecast data, and chemical component forecast data. The combination of available datasets can contain noisy, redundant, and unstructured data. Preprocessing with its powerful techniques is being applied to solve the aforementioned issues and extract the subsets with the most relevant data. Particularly, the following components of preprocessing are described in this chapter: outlier detection, missing value treatment, normalization, discretization, feature selection, and imbalanced learning. Afterward, the selected variables go through ML and DL algorithms to obtain the final goal, that of predicting air quality. Regarding the final prediction, this can be for an individual air pollutant or certain AQI, depending on the case study and its characteristics. After selecting and choosing the item to be predicted, ML and DL models are applied and validated using evaluation metrics.

The existence of various ML and DL methods creates difficulties in choosing the best methods. Depending on the data structure, data types, and research area, these methods can perform differently. Therefore future research directions may be designed to discover the best methods for given dataset combinations.

Acknowledgments

Ditsuhi Iskandaryan has been funded by the predoctoral program PINV2018—Universitat Jaume I (PREDOC/ 2018/61). Sergio Trilles has been funded by the Juan de la Cierva—Incorporación postdoctoral program of the Ministry of Science and Innovation—Spanish Government (IJC2018-035017-I). This work has been funded by the Generalitat Valenciana through the Subvenciones para la realización de proyectos de I + D + i desarrollados por grupos de investigación emergentes program (GV/2020/035).

References

Abu Awad, Y., Koutrakis, P., Coull, B. A., & Schwartz, J. (2017). A spatio-temporal prediction model based on support vector machine regression: Ambient Black Carbon in three New England States. *Environmental Research*, *159*, 427−434. Available from https://doi.org/10.1016/j.envres.2017.08.039.

Alasadi, S. A., & Bhaya, W. S. (2017). Review of data preprocessing techniques in data mining. *Journal of Engineering and Applied Sciences*, *12*(16), 4102−4107. Available from https://doi.org/10.3923/jeasci. 2017.4102.4107.

Ayres, J. G., Smallbone, K., Holgate, S., & Fuller, G. (2011). *Review of the UK Air Quality Index*. Health Protection Agency for the Committee on the Medical Effects of Air Pollutants.

Brook, R. D., Brook, J. R., & Rajagopalan, S. (2003). Air pollution: the \heart\ of the problem. *Current Hypertension Reports*, *5*(1), 32−39. Available from https://doi.org/10.1007/s11906-003-0008-y.

Chandrashekar, G., & Sahin, F. (2014). A survey on feature selection methods. *Computers and Electrical Engineering*, *40*(1), 16−28. Available from https://doi.org/10.1016/j.compeleceng.2013.11.024.

Chawla, N. V., Bowyer, K. W., Hall, L. O., & Kegelmeyer, W. P. (2002). SMOTE: synthetic minority over-sampling technique. *Journal of Artificial Intelligence Research*, *16*, 321−357. Available from https://doi.org/10.1613/jair.953.

Contreras, L., & Ferri, C. (2016). Wind-sensitive interpolation of urban air pollution forecasts. *Procedia Computer Science*, *80*, 313−323. Available from https://doi.org/10.1016/j.procs.2016.05.343.

Deters, Z. R., Gonzalez, M., & Rybarczyk, Y. (2017). Modeling pm2. 5 urban pollution using machine learning and selected meteorological parameters. *Journal of Electrical and Computer Engineering*, *2017*(5), 1−14.

Donders, A. R. T., van der Heijden, G. J. M. G., Stijnen, T., & Moons, K. G. M. (2006). Review: a gentle introduction to imputation of missing values. *Journal of Clinical Epidemiology*, *59*(10), 1087−1091. Available from https://doi.org/10.1016/j.jclinepi.2006.01.014.

Eldakhly, N. M., Aboul-Ela, M., & Abdalla, A. (2017). Air pollution forecasting model based on chance theory and intelligent techniques. *International Journal on Artificial Intelligence Tools*, *26*(6), 1750024. Available from https://doi.org/10.1142/S0218213017500245.

Farhangfar, A., Kurgan, L. A., & Pedrycz, W. (2007). A novel framework for imputation of missing values in databases. *IEEE Transactions on Systems, Man, and Cybernetics Part A: Systems and Humans*, *37*(5), 692−709. Available from https://doi.org/10.1109/TSMCA.2007.902631.

García, S., Ramírez-Gallego, S., Luengo, J., Benítez, J. M., & Herrera, F. (2016). Big data preprocessing: methods and prospects. *Big Data Analytics*, *1*, 9.

Gupta, S., & Gupta, A. (2019). Dealing with noise problem in machine learning data-sets: a systematic review. *Procedia Computer Science*, *161*, 466−474. Available from https://doi.org/10.1016/j.procs.2019.11.146.

Hodge, V. J., & Austin, J. (2004). A survey of outlier detection methodologies. *Artificial Intelligence Review*, *22*(2), 85−126. Available from https://doi.org/10.1023/B:AIRE.0000045502.10941.a9.

Iskandaryan, D., Ramos, F., & Trilles, S. (2020a). Air quality prediction in smart cities using machine learning technologies based on sensor data: a review. *Applied Sciences (Switzerland)*, *10*(7), 2401. Available from https://doi.org/10.3390/app10072401.

Iskandaryan, D., Ramos, F., & Trilles, S. (2020b). The role of datasets in air quality prediction. *Atmosphere*.

Junninen, H., Niska, H., Tuppurainen, K., Ruuskanen, J., & Kolehmainen, M. (2004). Methods for imputation of missing values in air quality data sets. *Atmospheric Environment*, *38*(18), 2895−2907. Available from https://doi.org/10.1016/j.atmosenv.2004.02.026.

Kanchan, G. A. K., & Goyal, P. (2015). A review on air quality indexing system. *Asian Journal of Atmospheric Environment*, *9*(2), 101−113. Available from https://doi.org/10.5572/ajae.2015.9.2.101.

Kumar, V., & Minz, S. (2014). Feature selection: a literature review. *SmartCR*, *4*(3), 211−229.

Lakshminarayan, K., Harp, S. A., & Samad, T. (1999). Imputation of missing data in industrial databases. *Applied Intelligence*, *11*(3), 259−275. Available from https://doi.org/10.1023/A:1008334909089.

Li, R., Cui, L., Meng, Y., Zhao, Y., & Fu, H. (2019). Satellite-based prediction of daily SO_2 exposure across China using a high-quality random forest-spatiotemporal Kriging (RF-STK) model for health risk assessment. *Atmospheric Environment*, *208*, 10−19. Available from https://doi.org/10.1016/j.atmosenv.2019.03.029.

Li, L., & Ngan, C. K. (2019). *A weight-adjusting approach on an ensemble of classifiers for time series forecasting*. ACM international conference proceeding series (pp. 65−69). Association for Computing Machinery. Available from https://doi.org/10.1145/3325917.3325920.

Ling, C., Yifang, D., Dandan, L., Xiaoze, L., & Hanyu, L. (2019). Deep multi-task learning based urban Air Quality Index modelling. *Proceedings of the ACM on Interactive, Mobile, Wearable and Ubiquitous Technologies, 3*(1), 1−17. Available from https://doi.org/10.1145/3314389.

Liu, H., Hussain, F., Tan, C. L., & Dash, M. (2002). Discretization: an enabling technique. *Data Mining and Knowledge Discovery, 6*(4), 393−423. Available from https://doi.org/10.1023/A:1016304305535.

Liu, B., Yan, S., Li, J., Qu, G., Li, Y., Lang, J., & Gu, R. (2019). A sequence-to-sequence air quality predictor based on the n-step recurrent prediction. *IEEE Access, 7,* 43331−43345. Available from https://doi.org/10.1109/ACCESS.2019.2908081.

Ma, J., Ding, Y., Cheng, J. C., Jiang, F., Gan, V. J., & Xu, Z. (2020). A Lag-FLSTM deep learning network based on Bayesian optimization for multi-sequential-variant PM2.5 prediction. *Sustainable Cities and Society, 60,* 102237.

Ma, J., Ding, Y., Gan, V. J. L., Lin, C., & Wan, Z. (2019). Spatiotemporal prediction of PM2.5 concentrations at different time granularities using IDW-BLSTM. *IEEE Access, 7,* 107897−107907. Available from https://doi.org/10.1109/ACCESS.2019.2932445.

Mills, N. L., Donaldson, K., Hadoke, P. W., Boon, N. A., MacNee, W., Cassee, F. R., Sandström, T., Blomberg, A., & Newby, D. E. (2009). Adverse cardiovascular effects of air pollution. *Nature Clinical Practice Cardiovascular Medicine, 6*(1), 36−44. Available from https://doi.org/10.1038/ncpcardio1399.

Oprea, M., Dragomir, E. G., Popescu, M., & Mihalache, S. F. (2016). Particulate matter air pollutants forecasting using inductive learning approach. *Revista de Chimie, 67*(10), 2075−2081. Available from http://www.revistadechimie.ro/archive.asp.

Plaia, A., & Ruggieri, M. (2011). Air quality indices: a review. *Reviews in Environmental Science and Biotechnology, 10*(2), 165−179. Available from https://doi.org/10.1007/s11157-010-9227-2.

Qiu, G., Song, R., & He, S. (2019). The aggravation of urban air quality deterioration due to urbanization, transportation and economic development—Panel models with marginal effect analyses across China. *Science of the Total Environment, 651,* 1114−1125. Available from https://doi.org/10.1016/j.scitotenv.2018.09.219.

Ramos, F., Trilles, S., Muñoz, A., & Huerta, J. (2018). Promoting pollution-free routes in smart cities using air quality sensor networks. *Sensors (Switzerland), 18*(8), 2507. Available from https://doi.org/10.3390/s18082507.

Tao, Q., Liu, F., Li, Y., & Sidorov, D. (2019). Air pollution forecasting using a deep learning model based on 1D convnets and bidirectional GRU. *IEEE Access, 7,* 76690−76698. Available from https://doi.org/10.1109/ACCESS.2019.2921578.

Thom, G. C., & Ott, W. R. (1967). A proposed uniform air pollution index. *Atmospheric Environment, 10*(3), 261−264.

Van Den Elshout, S., Léger, K., & Heich, H. (2014). CAQI common air quality index—update with PM2.5 and sensitivity analysis. *Science of the Total Environment, 488−489*(1), 461−468. Available from https://doi.org/10.1016/j.scitotenv.2013.10.060.

Xingquan, Z., & Xindong, W. (2004). Class noise vs. attribute noise: a quantitative study. *Artificial Intelligence Review, 22,* 177−210. Available from https://doi.org/10.1007/s10462-004-0751-8.

Xu, X., & Ren, W. (2019). Prediction of air pollution concentration based on mRMR and echo state network. *Applied Sciences (Switzerland), 9*(9), 1811. Available from https://doi.org/10.3390/app9091811.

Yang, C. Y., Chang, C. C., Chuang, H. Y., Tsai, S. S., Wu, T. N., & Ho, C. K. (2004). Relationship between air pollution and daily mortality in a subtropical city: Taipei, Taiwan. *Environment International, 30*(4), 519−523. Available from https://doi.org/10.1016/j.envint.2003.10.006.

Zhang, Y., Wang, Y., Gao, M., Ma, Q., Zhao, J., Zhang, R., Wang, Q., & Huang, L. (2019). A predictive data feature exploration-based air quality prediction approach. *IEEE Access, 7,* 30732−30743. Available from https://doi.org/10.1109/ACCESS.2019.2897754.

Zheng, H., Li, H., Lu, X., & Ruan, T. (2018). A multiple kernel learning approach for air quality prediction. *Advances in Meteorology*, *2018*, 3506394.

Zhu, D., Cai, C., Yang, T., & Zhou, X. (2018). A machine learning approach for air quality prediction: Model regularization and optimization. *Big Data and Cognitive Computing*, *2*(1), 5.

Zhu, S., Lian, X., Wei, Lin, Che, J., Shen, X., Yang, Li., ... Li, J. (2018). PM2.5 forecasting using SVR with PSOGSA algorithm based on CEEMD, GRNN and GCA considering meteorological factors, Atmospheric Environment. *Atmospheric Environment*, *183*, 20−32. Available from https://doi.org/10.1016/j.atmosenv.2018.04.004.

Advances in data-centric intelligent systems for air quality monitoring, assessment, and control

Samuel Eshorame Sanni[1], Emmanuel Emeka Okoro[2], Emmanuel Rotimi Sadiku[3], and Babalola Aisosa Oni[1]

[1]Department of Chemical Engineering, Covenant University, Ota, Nigeria [2]Department of Petroleum and Gas Engineering, University of Port Harcourt, Port Harcourt, Nigeria [3]Department of Metallurgy, Polymer and Chemical Engineering, Tshwane University of Technology, Pretoria, South Africa

Introduction

The impact of environmental and air quality assessment on levels of contamination and pollution largely depends on the information/data quality available for decision-making. Often, it is expected that the data collected are harmonized during the assessment to enhance the decision-making process. However, problems may arise as a result of the nonuniformity of the data as received or compiled from the data source, hence poor decisions may be made. In modern times, computers play a crucial/central role in contemporary issues that are related to environmental protection, including aspects of monitoring, assessment/processing, data generation, communication, data storage, and information retrieval. Since data gathering is a continuous operation, it then suffices to say that it has ushered in the era of big data. However, full exploitation of the potential of supercomputers/data-centric systems (DCS) makes for an easy integration and enhancement of machines which help to treat these data via trained algorithms that have similar features to the human mind; this art of deploying knowledge-oriented systems to resolve data-centered issues is termed "artificial intelligence" (AI). The systems employed are known as DCS/environmental decision support systems (EDSS) (Cortes et al., 2000). Progressive advancements in human progression are evidenced by human dependence on nature's resources/environment, which may become adversely impacted if sufficient measures are not taken to avoid changes that are destructive to the environment and its inhabitants. The destructive influence of human activities on the environment can be correlated with the recent trends in population growth, rapid urbanization, and industrialization; these have led to the projections that human-focused concerns such as the need to meet basic needs including production of useful chemicals, cooking, burning etc. are the major determinants of these societal forces/influences that have altered nature's outlook/environment (Thomson, 1997) and the air we breathe. Environmental science is an interdisciplinary subject that focuses on man's influence on environmental processes (Eblen & Eblen, 1994); however, this chapter's discourse will focus explicitly on air pollution. In recent years, the unprecedented and unusual trends in industrial and anthropogenic activities, such as petroleum refining, combustion, purification, gas scrubbing, and bush burning, have become some of the major causes of air pollution, which in turn alter air quality owing to the myriad of contaminants/pollutants, particulate matter, or gases released from those sources (Jørgensen & Johnsen, 1989). The Earth's environment is dynamic and complex and as such, several aspects or activities may have a similar impact; one of which is global warming, which is caused by the release of greenhouse gases. Other effects/impacts may result from the synergistic combination of several activities, which may give a higher impact than those of the individual activities as adjudged from the reductionist theorem; an example is the reaction of NO_2 and hydrocarbons to produce tropospheric ozone (O_3). Hence, to isolate the individual effects of the combined gases as well as the final product, it becomes pertinent to consider exploiting DCS that can give the data history for the existence of the separate species (NO_2 and hydrocarbons) as well as the threshold for the formation of the product species (ozone). This then makes for easy computation/evaluation of the gathered data using trained algorithms integrated into model software, for quality air assessment, monitoring, and control, which in turn give an idea of the contribution of each species (reactant/product) to the overall effect (Hart et al., 1998). Climate change is universal and complex, due to the nature of interactions occurring at different spatiotemporal scales, hence addressing these issues requires the consideration of interactions that exist between humans and the environment within the ecosystem (Sydow et al., 1998), alongside adequate planning, supervision, prediction, and environmental process control at different scales and times. Organizations such as the International Standard Organization (ISO14001), Eco-Management and Audit Scheme (EMAS) of Europe, and National Environmental Policy Act (NEPA) of the United States are being more environmentally conscious by instigating suitable legislation to cater to the aspect of prioritizing for the consideration of the effect of environmental impact on planning and decision-making, especially for large projects, such as the Kyoto Summit—Agenda 21 (Ostrom, 1991). In the past four decades, the leap-frog advances in information technology have led to the development of new and superhardware systems which have enhanced stronger links between the outputs of multidisciplinary research in the fields of environmental and computer sciences that have created a new discipline termed "environmental informatics" (Radermacher et al., 1994), which constitutes the application of AI, geographical information systems, modeling, and simulation, as well as other graphical user interface software systems. These systems serve as catalysts for easy integration of data/information sourced from different knowledge systems within the environmental sector (Stephanopoulos & Han, 1996; Avouris & Page, 1995).

Overview of AI-based technologies and data-centric systems for pollution control

Artificial intelligence

This is the art and science of programming and capacitating systems with human abilities toward analyzing environmental incidents to make informed decisions for attaining specific goals. AI systems may be software-based/virtual, which take the form of voice assistants, image analysis software, search engines, as well as speech/face recognition systems that employ symbolic rules or learning algorithms for their adaptation to different environmental conditions based on their data history. They can also be embedded in hardware components, including robots, autonomous cars, and drones/Internet of Things (IoT) devices. Artificially intelligent systems are manmade software and hardware systems, which process information in the physical/digital dimension by examining their environment via data acquisition, reasoning, interpretation, and processing to decide on the best possible actions to take toward achieving a set goal. The main components of AI are data and algorithms, which can be integrated with hardware devices. In machine learning, a subset of AI algorithms is trained to allow for the drawing of apt inferences of certain patterns that are informed by decision analyses and tested on a set of data to decide on the actions required to attain some specific objectives. Algorithms can learn on data while they are being processed. While AI tools can act independently in terms of being able to critically examine a situation without following some sets of predetermined rules/instructions, their performances are largely dependent on and constrained by their developers since humans optimize and determine the program goals to be achieved.

AI expert system (ES) application to pollution control and management is an area currently being given significant attention. AI systems for environmental process control are a series of automated/managed subprocess routines that process information gathered via monitoring, sensing, and manipulation of process variables, such that the system mimics the human reasoning and decision-making process (Walker, 1993). The instruments employed in the data-gathering process are linked to a control structure that issues the control command. A supervisory data acquisition system is connected via network communications to control the hardware, while the data acquisition system helps to maintain the applications that are one step above the primary control function/database (Rynk, 1992). The functionality of the computer must entail applications such as computer-aided instructions, training, maintenance, configuration, plant planning, optimization, scheduling, alarm management, and operator decision support (Stock, 1989). Industrial operations involving the use of AI technologies usually span across the use of ESs, neural networks, and fuzzy logic (FL).

ESs mimic human problem-solving initiatives by duplicating the human professionalism/expertise in its knowledge bank. ESs are comprised of three major components, namely, a knowledge-base containing heuristics and facts associated with the application domain, an inference engine that scrutinizes the knowledge bank for the most suitable rules to be applied in solving a particular problem, and a working memory which acts as a storehouse for storing the newly generated information as the inference engine explores and selects the appropriate rules to be applied. Other components within the ES include a graphical user interface and explanation facility.

FL has been adopted as an alternative to classical/binary-valued logic in industrial process control as well as consumer products, aerospace, and air pollution control situations (Langari & Yen, 1995). FL plays a crucial role in diverse applications, thus helping to close the gap between symbolic processes and numerical computation, all aimed at providing a suitable rule-based linguistic-control strategy. FL is a flexible domain application for control engineering and nonbinary-valued logic application. Hence FL forms the basis for implementing control strategies toward an efficient decision-making/supervisory control process. One fundamental variance between FL and ES is the use of linguistics rather than numeric variables, alongside fuzzy conditional statements in place of exact expressions in FL relative to ES. This then makes room for the manipulation of rules that integrate linguistics and inexact data as efficient tools for reasoning through management tasks that are somewhat difficult to manage and control (Walker, 1993).

Another predominantly used AI technology is neural network technology, which entails a computational paradigm, modeled to mimic the human brain, in terms of filtering essential data from a huge chunk of irrelevant datasets with the capacity to learn from previous and present experiences, as well as predict new outcomes based on the ability to generalize on the previous experiences (Walker, 1993). Artificial neural network (ANN) models are a network of parallel machines comprised of input and output connections that mimic the mental reasoning capacity of the human brain.

Data-centric system design principles

As the size of data grows, the cost of moving the data around becomes prohibitive. Thus it becomes necessary to employ distributed intelligence to bring computation to the data. DCS consolidate modeling, simulation, analytics, big data, as well as machine learning and cognitive computing as "systems of insight." They possess other capabilities which include being fast and flexible at low energy costs, thus ushering in a new category of computers.

DCS uses a POWER architecture to share expertise and validate procedures on IP-compliant servers toward serving the evolving needs of users. A good DCS is made up of the following: a storage/hard disk, storage-class memory, main memory, and a cache. According to Agerwala and Perone (2014), the five basic principles guiding the design and functionality of DCS include:

1. *Principle 1*: Minimization of data transfer—Data mobility is quite expensive. It requires hardware and software to provide easy computation, which enables workloads to run as well as required.
2. *Principle 2*: Enables good computation across all levels of system hierarchy with special features, including active system elements, network, memory, storage, etc. Here, hardware and software components require innovations to enable advanced data computation.
3. *Principle 3*: This principle requires that the system is modular, balanced, has a composable architecture for big data analytics, and is highly efficient for modeling and simulation practice; this also suggests that the modular system's design is upgradeable and scalable from subrack to hundreds of racks.
4. *Design principle 4*: The system must have an application-driven design that uses real workloads or workflows to drive design points. In addition, its co/secondary design must have customer value.
5. *Principle 5*: The system must leverage on open POWER to expedite innovation within a broad diversity for clients.

Data-centric/decision support systems

DCSS are intelligent information-gathering systems that reduce the time spent in making quality decisions as well as ensuring consistency. They complement the efforts of decision-makers by presenting them with several criteria within compared alternatives and actual selections that result in justifiable decisions. The operations within the evaluation process must be interactive, friendly, spontaneous, and highly efficient. Fig. 3.1 is an illustration of the components of a DCS.

In engineering, some novel findings and research innovations have been made possible via the use of AI where decisions have to be made based on environmental assessments and investigations resulting from environmental processes/systems. A number of these systems are characterized by incomplete mathematical tools/models developed from limited experimental data. Thus accurate

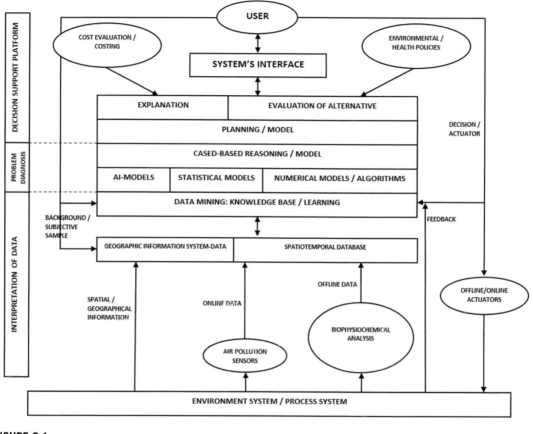

FIGURE 3.1

Schematic of data-centric systems.

Adapted from Cortes, U., Sanchez-Marrè, M., Ceccaroni, L., R-Roda, R., & Poch, M. (2000). Artificial intelligence and environmental decision support systems, Applied Intelligence, 13(1), 77–91.

and precise predictive behaviors of these systems are dependent on the ability to further exploit multiple and several incomplete knowledge banks. However, the imposition of multiple complementary problem-solving techniques (MCPTs) such as case-based reasoning (CBR) and constraint satisfaction measures often help to minimize these uncertainties (Krovvidy & Wee, 1993; Hastings et al., 1996), whereas, in AI, this phenomenon is characterized by an ill-structured domain (Robertson et al., 1991). In this domain, relationships between concepts or their attributes are not clearly defined since they are almost mutually exclusive with less contrasting agreements among professionals. In addition, the multivariant nature of environmental issues influences the final decision or selection from a list of plausible solutions. The complexity of the system and the multiplexed views/interests requires that there is sufficient homogenization/harmonization of the mechanisms that engender conflicting goals with contradicting information. The following subsections discuss the use of AI and information technology in planning, prediction, design, decision-making, as well as modeling and simulation of data-centric/decision support systems for environmental management (monitoring, protection, assessment, and control). In place of the dynamic and complex nature of the environment, it is clear that the current spate of environmental problems, including air pollution, destruction of the biosphere, water contamination, and climate change cannot be well understood through pragmatic/empirical approaches, hence the need for the adoption of mathematical models and simulation tools which are more flexible to these changes (Cortes et al., 2000).

Data interpretation and mining methods

Data mining entails the screening of data to detect patterns, identify potential opportunities/problems, and determine the similarities between previous and current events which help to provide insights into key factors and their relationships with unidentifiable data characteristics (Cortes et al., 2000). Through these, it becomes possible to gain insights into new situations.

Problem diagnosis. This simply implies the technique of troubleshooting to identify the root cause of a problem, that is, looking out for characteristic symptoms to generate and confirm idealistic hypotheses on the possible cause of a problem (Cortes et al., 2000). This, in turn, provides opportunities for passing recommendations as regards strategies to be adopted for recovery/repair based on available knowledge or partial information on previous experiences.

Decision support techniques. These involve the evaluation of alternative methods/systems to be able to explore and quantify their possible effects, compare their relative costs/benefits, and hence suggest apt action plans. Based on the studies conducted by Cortes et al. (2000), decision-support/DCS include:

1. *Environmental decision support systems (EDSSs).*
2. *Multiple objective decision support system* (Haagsma & Johanns, 1994; Bender & Simonovic, 1994).
3. *Frames*: Frames were first proposed by Marvin Minsky in 1974 as a means of separating knowledge into substructures of stereotyped situations; they are extensive forms of representing knowledge and reasoning schemes using AI. This is a knowledge-oriented tool/model that provides support for the selected air pollution model (Calori et al., 1994). It comprises relational databases that support all the required system information and relies on a rule-based ES that explains to and helps users. The relational database and ESs are usually in sync, which makes for effective knowledge management. There is also an in-built mechanism that the system uses to determine users' expertise from which it also gives selective access to information. All information (general and metainformation) about the models, is secured in a structural framework. Model selection within this framework depends on aspects tied to the physics of the problem to be simulated as well as resource availability.
4. *Mediterranean Expert (MEDEX)*: This is a forecasting tool designed for forecasting of the weather within the Mediterranean region; it provides a novice forecaster with the encoded knowledge/experience of a 20-year Mediterranean expert-meteorologist. The system's configuration is typical of FL that helps in predicting the threshold and cessation of gale-force 7 winds (Hadjimichael et al., 1996). The implementation procedure entails the system's measure

of compatibility with specified variables that are loosely defined and its ability to augment for the uncertainty and inexperience/low skills of users.

5. *The Distributed Chemical Emergencies Manager (DCHEM)*: As the name implies, this is an example of EDSS which finds application in areas involving chemical accidents such as toxic/harmful chemicals and gases (Sazonova & Osipov, 1998). Its decision-making portfolio supports the management of a special category of environmental emergencies and accidents caused by contact with electrical equipment containing/conveying toxic substances. It is one of several systems that adopt the distributed agents' technologies alongside their negotiation protocols in addressing problems.

6. *Combining Human Assessment and Reasoning Aids for Decision-making in Environmental Emergencies (CHARADE)*: This system is composed of a general system's architecture for DSS and top-notch/powerful situation assessment and intervention facilities for environmental emergency management (Avesani et al., 1993, 1995). Often, the selected application is a center for monitoring wildfire-fighting operations. In addition, the system's kernel is based on a hybrid constraint-based structure.

7. *The Intelligent Environmental Quality (INTELLEnvQ) System*: The INTELLEnvQ system architecture system comprises a knowledge base (a subsection of the rule-based) and an inference engine that make up the expert rule-based system and a forecasting module whose operation is centered on the feedforward artificial neural network (FFANN). The knowledge-based rules provide the result from environmental quality analysis (EQA) via a forecast-based approach from the data generated by ANN and other meteorological factors that may compromise environmental air quality. The INTELLEnvQ system can be used as a daily air monitoring tool.

Fundamental principles of data mining with AI

Data mining is a process that entails the use of pattern recognition, database technology, machine learning, and statistical mathematics in identifying/benchmarking new/useful correlations, patterns, and trends in the course of sorting huge chunks of data kept in repositories (Hand, 1998; Thuraisingham, 1999). Machine learning is a set of algorithms that help to automate and improve the performance of a data-mining process via borrowed experiences from history files of previously handled situations. Machine learning is one of the tools used in AI to solve problems; it simply considers the use of computational models to gain insight into human thought and behavioral patterns, all aimed at proffering expedient solutions to problems that would have taken a long time to solve if they were to be handled manually (Tanimoto, 1987). AI tools are used for data association, estimation, classification, data segmentation, and prediction; however, these tools have their strengths and weaknesses in specific fields. Based on the work of Moustakis et al. (1996), AI is associated with three major tasks (Fig. 3.2), otherwise known as factors, that include:

1. *Knowledge engineering*: This has to do with the task—acquisition of expert knowledge and refinement of the acquired knowledge to gain extra knowledge (i.e., mining the deductive database/knowledge base through inductive logical programming).
2. *Problem solving*: This has to do with scheduling, grouping, optimizing, etc.
3. *Classification and prediction*: The combination of these techniques in terms of applicability.

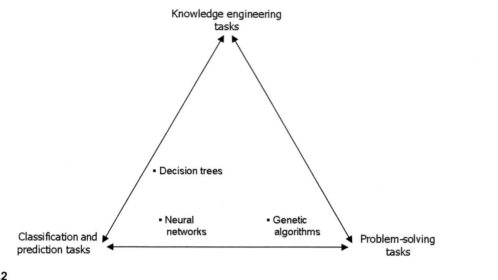

FIGURE 3.2

A simplex of three data-mining tasks using artificial intelligence.

From Adriaans, P. W., & Zantinge, D. (1996). Data mining. Harlow: Addison Wesley Longman (Adriaans and Zantinge, 1996).

Machine learning and AI models

Artificial neural network

This AI technique mimics the problem-solving capability of the human brain (Baxter et al., 2001). ANN models have similar features to the human brain; they possess the capacity to learn from repeated input data by adjusting weights assigned to the neurons in the ANN architecture (Fig. 3.3). ANN is a self-organized learning system from which patterns and conceptualized ideas can be retrieved from historical data (Baxter et al., 1999). ANNs have recently attracted serious attention as a result of their wide applicability and the ease with which complicated problems are treated. Hence, they are very potent tools for integration in models, where data relationships are not already known or are otherwise, nonlinear, complex, imprecise, and noisy (Lek & Guegan, 1999). Generally, ANN offers several advantages over conventional modeling techniques; it finds application in the following problem areas: pattern grouping/classification, clustering and categorization, approximation of functions, predictive forecasting, optimization, associative memory, and process controls (Jain et al., 1996).

Basically, in terms of its processed data, the relationship between the input and output data rests solely on the available information, without any presumptions from the neural network (Harvey, 1998). In addition, because ANN is tolerant of errors/faults during the model development and application stages, issues such as data discontinuities, variations in noise levels, data precision, and data dispersion are easily absorbed/accommodated (Foody & Arora, 1997). Its extreme speed/flexible nature, as well as recent advances in computing, have helped to reduce the time required to develop new models as well as that required to retrain these models for the incorporation of new data that reflect changes made to processes (Baxter et al., 1999). However, one of the major

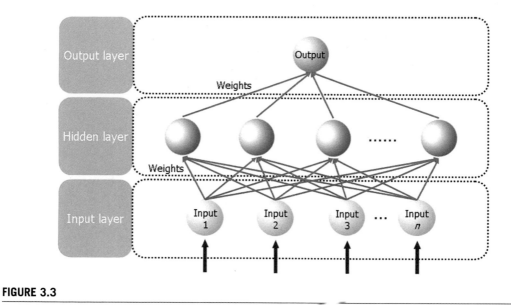

FIGURE 3.3

General structure of the artificial neural network.

Adapted from Kim, K., & Park, J. (2009). A survey of applications of artificial intelligence algorithms in eco-environmental modelling. Environmental Engineering Research, 14(2), 102–110.

disadvantages of the ANN modeling technique is that the derived models are seen to represent a black box since ANN does not yield explicit and well-defined or detailed rules. In addition, information is scarce as regards the model's applicability to data outside the domain within which the model is trained. In addition, it is note worthy that there is no ideal protocol for developing an ANN model, rather, each modeler may tend to adopt a hybrid of modeling techniques. Based on reports from the literature, ANN is data intensive and highly recommended for situations involving large datasets and prediction tasks (Zhang & Stanley, 1997), especially in situations where the model results are more significant than knowing how the model works (Berry & Linoff, 1997). Examples of ANN algorithms include the multilayer feedforward neural network that is trained by the backpropagation algorithm, that is, the backpropagation network and the Kohonen self-organized mapping (SOM), which is also known as the Kohonen network SOM. The choice of the ANN algorithm adopted in solving a particular problem depends on the nature of the problem.

The decision tree

Decision tree (DT) is a very useful method. It is very powerful and popularly known for its ability to classify data and make a meaningful prediction for the data under investigation. It is a non-parametric modeling tool that is comprised of recursively partitioned multidimensional spacing into homogeneous response groups defined by predictors (Vayssieres, 2000; Breiman et al., 1984). Thereafter, based on the results obtained from analyses, a hierarchal binary-looking tree-like structure with branches and leaves appears, as illustrated in Fig. 3.4; it depicts the rules for

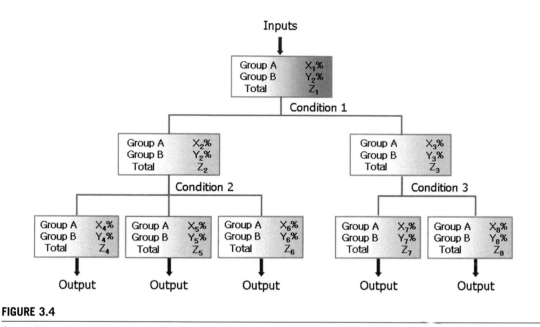

Inputs

Group A $X_1\%$
Group B $Y_2\%$
Total Z_1

Condition 1

Group A $X_2\%$
Group B $Y_2\%$
Total Z_2

Group A $X_3\%$
Group B $Y_3\%$
Total Z_3

Condition 2

Condition 3

Group A $X_4\%$
Group B $Y_4\%$
Total Z_4

Group A $X_5\%$
Group B $Y_5\%$
Total Z_5

Group A $X_6\%$
Group B $Y_6\%$
Total Z_6

Group A $X_7\%$
Group B $Y_7\%$
Total Z_7

Group A $X_8\%$
Group B $Y_8\%$
Total Z_8

Output   Output   Output   Output   Output

FIGURE 3.4

General structure of a decision tree.

Adapted from Kim, K., & Park, J. (2009). A survey of applications of artificial intelligence algorithms in eco-environmental modelling. Environmental Engineering Research, 14*(2), 102–110.*

predicting/treating new cases (Dunham, 2002; Breiman et al., 1984). The advantages of DT over other AI models include:

- There are no strict assumptions for distributing the target variable.
- It can handle nonlinear models without allowing for any form of variable transformation/change.
- Compared to other AI models such as ANN and support vector machines (SVM), it entails a shorter training time while attaining similar levels of accuracy.
- It clearly defines the relative importance of a set of input variables.
- It allows for easy data interpretation owing to its comprehensive rules.

Unlike neural networks, DT is not a "black box"; however, its disadvantages include:

- A relatively large chunk of training data is required for its successful implementation.
- DT cannot express linear relationships in simple and concise forms.
- As a result of its binary nature, it produces batch-wise or discrete/discontinuous outputs.
- It gives a nonunique solution per operation, hence it is difficult to hold a claim of its best result/solution (Iverson & Prasad, 1998; Scheffer, 2002).

Despite the shortlisted demerits of DT, researchers and software experts have proposed several algorithms, including CHAID (Kass, 1980), CART (Breiman et al., 1984), and C4.5 (Quinlan, 1993) for integration in DT as a way of taking advantage of the synergistic effect of the merits of each algorithm for improved performance and commercialization.

The least square support vector machine or support vector machine (LSSVM/LSVM)

This is a computer-based algorithm whose origin is traceable to statistical learning theory (SLT) for carrying out pattern-recognition tasks (Vapnik, 1998). This AI tool can provide reliable empirical predictions for different pragmatic applications ranging from hand written digit recognition to text grouping or classification (Tan et al., 2005). SVM is very apt for high-dimensional data and can avert problems associated with dimensionality when treating data; this is made possible by its ability to present its decision boundaries via a subset of the trained samples/support vectors. An illustration of the LSSVM is shown in Fig. 3.5.

Genetic algorithm

This is a stochastic optimization method that uses a four-stage (initialization, selection, crossover, and mutation) search algorithm to observe a set of data while making selections based on survival rates among stringed structures (Holland, 1975; Goldberg, 1989; Wong & Tan, 1994). This tool can be used in maintaining the population of species in an artificial ecosystem by screening the chromosomes of several species within the system (Fig. 3.6). A genetic algorithm (GA) is suitable for situations requiring multiparameter optimization, in which the objective function is subject to several hard and soft constraints.

Case-based reasoning (CBR)

CBR is a problem-solving tool that references and applies case histories retrieved from libraries/directories of similar situations to proffer solutions to new problems (Kolodner, 1993). It mirrors problem-solving techniques adopted by humans in solving past problems and uses such experiences

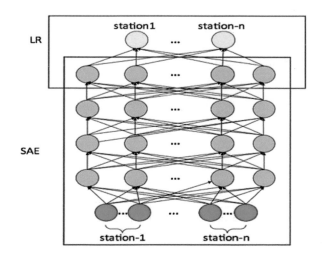

FIGURE 3.5

LSSVM model structure with stacked autoencoder (SAE) and linear regression (LR) system for air quality prediction.

Adapted from Li, X., Peng, L., Hu, Y., Shao, J., & Chi, T. (2016). Deep learning architecture for air quality predictions. Environmental Science and Pollution Research, 23*(22), 22408–22417.*

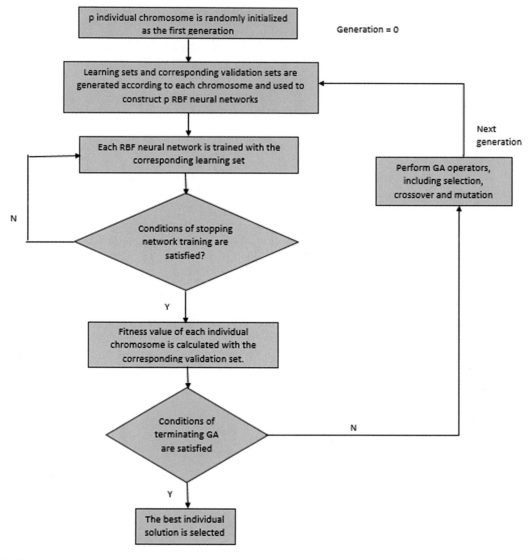

FIGURE 3.6

Configuration of the flow scheme of a sample artificial neural network genetic algorithm.

Adapted from Zhao, H., Zhang, J., Wang, K., et al. (2011). A GA-ANN model for air quality predicting. In 2010 International computer symposium (ICS2010). IEEE.

in handling fresh problems. CBR applies the specific knowledge/experience gained from a previous situation, whereas most AI techniques rely on the general knowledge obtained from a problem domain, hence, there is no possibility of overfitting (Watson, 1997; Shin & Han, 1999; Humphreys et al., 2003).

Random forest model

This model adopts a technique in which a collection of DTs is built based on data subsets where aggregation of the predictions is used to estimate the final prediction, as shown in Fig. 3.7. Yu et al. (2016) used a random forest model (RFM) in predicting the air quality from meteorology data comprised of road information, real-time traffic status, and point of interest (POI) distribution obtained from urban sensors. The RFM algorithm is useful in training and predicting data. Air quality indices (AQIs) for six components, including SO_2, NO_2, suspended particulate matter with <10 μm (i.e., PM_{10}) aerodynamic diameter, $PM_{2.5}$, CO, and O_3, were measured at the monitoring stations of some cities in China. Calculated AQIs were presented on an hourly basis using the formula published by China's Ministry of Environmental Protection. A total of 2701 pieces of data were used to test the ANN algorithm by segmenting the area (Shenyang) being investigated into 1258 grids distributed into 34 rows and 37 columns. Based on the simulation results, an accuracy of about 81% was obtained for the predicted AQIs and it was confirmed that the tool adopted, outperformed the naïve Bayes, logistic regression, single DT, and other ANN tools.

Deep belief network (DBN)

Li et al. (2016) adopted a novel spatiotemporal deep learning (STDL) air quality prediction tool, which considers spatial and temporal correlations. It also comprises a stacked autoencoder (SAE) for extracting air quality features; the data generated are trained in a layer-wise manner. In contrast to traditional time-based series prediction models, DBN can predict the air quality of several stations simultaneously, while indicating areas of temporal stability in different seasons. Compared with three other models, including the spatiotemporal artificial neural network (STANN), the autoregression moving

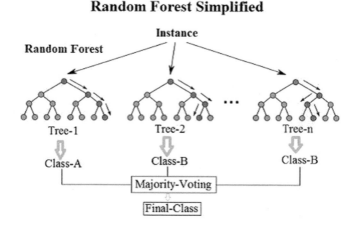

FIGURE 3.7

Configuration of the simplified random forest model.

Adapted from Jagannath, V. (2020). Random forest template for TIBCO Spotfire—TIBCO Community. *Available from https://community.tibco.com/wiki/random-forest-template-tibco-spotfirer-wiki-page (accessed 29.08.20); Kang, G. K., Gao, J. Z., Chiao, S., Lu, S., & Xie, G. (2018). Air quality prediction: Big data and machine learning approaches,* International Journal of Environmental Science and Development, *9(1), 8–16.*

average (ARMA), and the support vector regression (SVR) models, DBN demonstrated superior performance.

Radial basis function neural network (RBFNN)

The RBFNN system features include a basis function that may be Gaussian or wavelet, a wide horizon for universal approximation, fast data training, high robustness, and tolerance against noise, small data requirement when used in continuous mode, as well as good capability for problem generalization. However, it requires a large amount of trained data, neurons, and large memory and CPU time when trained in batch mode.

Adaptive network-based inference fuzzy system

This type uses the integrated gradient descent and least square methods to train parameters. Despite its advantage of requiring a short learning time, its major shortcoming is that it gives optimum results by a trial-and-error approach.

Multilayer perceptron neural network

This type engenders supervised learning. Its backpropagation algorithm is widely adopted as its algorithm for data training. It is easy to implement without any trade-offs between its consistency and accuracy, despite the changes or offsets occurring in a process. However, the multilayer perceptron neural network has a slow level of convergence with its required number of hidden neurons determined by trial and error. There are also issues of data overfitting alongside the existence of a local minimum.

The coactive neurofuzzy inference system

According to the Transportation Research Board of National Academies (2007), the coactive neurofuzzy inference system (CANFIS) is in a class of adaptive neurofuzzy inference systems that can be adopted as a universal approximator of nonlinear functions. Its topology is a dual system of neural networks and fuzzy inference systems. The exceptional ability of CANFIS is inherent in its pattern-dependent weights located between the consequent and fuzzy association layers. The CANFIS consists of a fuzzy neuron that applies two membership functions (i.e., the general bell and Gaussian functions) to its input variables. The network consists of a normalization axon that expands the generated output in values of $0-1$. Its modular networks, whose numbers correspond to the number of network outputs and processing elements, implement functional rules to a set of specified inputs. The combiner axon of CANFIS applies the outputs from the membership functions to those of the modular network. These outputs are then sent via an output layer from which the error therein is back-propagated to the membership function and the modular network.

Hint: For detailed application of some of these techniques, interested readers are advised to consult the texts cited, Hassan and Li (2010), and other articles listed in the later section on "Review of a few previous and more recent studies on air quality modeling."

AI methods for air quality monitoring

Some AI methods adopted in developing DCS are recommended for consultation in the following contexts:

1. Rule-based reasoning (Hushon, 1987; Lapointe et al., 1989; Serra et al., 1994; Chapman & Patry, 1989).
2. Planning (Kangari & Rouhani, 1989; Krovviddy et al., 1994; Charlebois et al., 1995; Avesani et al., 2000),
3. CBR (Krovvidy & Wee, 1993; Jones & Roydhouse, 1995; Branting et al., 1997; Sanchez-Marrè et al., 1997).
4. Qualitative reasoning (Kompare, 1994; Heller et al., 1995; Lundell, 1996; Mora-López & Conejo, 1998).
5. Constraint satisfaction (CHARADE, 1995; Paggio et al., 1998; Avesani et al., 2000).
6. Model-based reasoning (Chong & Walley, 1996; Englehart, 1997; Varis, 1997; Sangüesa & Burrell, 2000).
7. Connexionist reasoning (Zhu et al., 1998; Wen & Vassiliadis, 1998; Raman & Chandramouli, 1996; Tan & Smeins, 1996).
8. Evolutionary computing (Zhang et al., 1995; Halhal et al., 1997; Savic & Walters, 1997; Mulligan & Brown, 1998).
9. FL techniques (Manesis et al., 1998; Sasikumar & Mujumdar, 1998; Genovesi et al., 1999; Chang et al., 1997).

Air quality models
1. The Urban Airshed Model developed by Chang et al. (1997).
2. The Weather Research and Forecasting Model with Chemistry Features was discussed by Chuang et al. (2011).
3. The Community Multiscale Air Quality model was established by Mueller and Mallard (2011).

Air quality monitoring, assessment, and control
DCS for air quality monitoring assessment and control are expected to be able to deal with useful knowledge within the four-stage environmental management process cycle:

1. *Hazard identification (Haz-in)*: This is a process that involves the adoption of several filtering/screening criteria and reasoning as regards the activity (air pollution) being investigated. This is a continuous operation or a troubleshooting measure adopted in search of possible outcomes (potential hazards). In this process, the required data for the enhancement of the risk assessment step is generated. A good hazard identification step is often linked to efficient data mining, curation, gathering, and interpretation.
2. *Risk assessment*: This is the problem diagnosis step. In risk assessment, using the appropriate tools, quantitative/qualitative measurements of the hazards of interest are taken. The data-centric decision support system may be integrated with numerical and/or qualitative tools/mathematical model algorithms for the quantification/estimation of the hazard potential of air pollutants. The model-based system assumes form of a model-based reasoning/knowledge-based system that employs a rule-based reasoning approach or a CBR system in overcoming data heterogeneity sourced from various sources within different limits of accuracy.
3. *Risk evaluation*: As soon as the potential risks from an event have been identified and assessed, it becomes somewhat expedient to pass valued judgments concerning the degree

of certainty/uncertainties associated with a certain hypothesis. This is only made possible if the system has accumulated/trained experience (i.e., CBR) in handling similar events such that previous experiences of risk evaluations are adopted as aids for ensuring reliable future judgments.

4. *Intervention decision-making*: This is the implementation of apt methods of risk—reduction and control. Here, knowledge of the context within which the phenomenon applies must be available because it engenders and guarantees smooth balancing and interpretation of the results obtained from the risk evaluation and benefit procedures.

Air quality standards: assessment tools/mechanisms for quality assessment (Air Quality Index)

Air quality standards: The Office of Air Quality Planning and Standards (OAQPS) controls/monitors the programs of the Environmental Protection Agency (EPA) to improve the quality of air in areas whose air quality have been compromised by pollutants. The OAQPS has an extension/suboffice of the National Ambient Air Quality Standard (NAAQS), which has the task of ensuring good air quality via stipulated criteria for different pollutants. The two types of air quality standards are primary and secondary standards.

1. *Primary standards*: These are standards established to prevent severe health risks caused by air/environmental pollution.
2. *Secondary standards*: These types are enacted to provide welfare effects, such as damage to farm crops, vegetation, and buildings, because pollutants are of varying origins and have different effects.

The NAAQS also has different guidelines for time-averaged long- and short-term pollutants. Short-term standards were established to guide against acute/short-term health effects, whereas the long-term standards were developed to guide against chronic health situations; Table 3.1 shows some air quality standards and guidelines for different air pollutants.

Table 3.1 Guidelines for air quality standards.

Pollutant	Primary/ secondary	Average time	Concentration	Guideline
CO	Primary	8 h 1 h	9 ppm 35 ppm	Should not be exceeded more than once in a year
Pb	Primary and secondary	3-Month average	$0.15 \, \mu g/m^3$	Not to be exceeded
NO_2	Primary	1 h 1 year	100 ppb 53 ppb	1-h dailyMaximum concentration in the 98th percentile as averaged over 3 yearsMust not exceed the annual mean concentration
O_3	Primary and secondary	8 h	0.07 ppm	Annual fourth-highest daily maximum8-h concentration, averaged over 3 years

EPA. (2015). NAAQS table. Available from https://www.epa.gov/criteria-air-pollutants/naaqs-table (accessed 28.08.20).

Air quality control

Air quality control strategies include traffic control in terms of providing public vehicles for commuters to reduce air pollution, that is, the introduction of gas traps for industrial vessels where these gases are released, gas monitoring using sensors, the use of ice to contain global warming by induced precipitation, policy implementation for pollution control, government sanctions for violators, etc.

Data acquisition and air quality sensors

Adequate presentation of knowledge is governed by the quality of information gathered from the investigated situation. The stages involved include data cleaning, data repair, and transformation of the huge chunk of available data; hence the significance of metainformation and good background knowledge for process pruning and guidance cannot be overemphasized. This then brings to mind the idea of data mining, which entails the adoption of ESs, data storage technologies, statistical data, data visualization, as well as unmonitored machine learning schemes in which a myriad of incompatible disproportionate pieces of information from dissimilar sources are often treated together. The data obtained from various sources fall within the following categories:

1. *Diverse data*: These types range from those obtained from biophysical sources such as climate, biotic and biological interactions within the ecosystem, to those obtained from resource use, process economics, and zoning and environmental/health regulations concerning some stipulated social preferences and objectives.
2. *Variable, analytical, and volume-based data*: For this type, the magnitude of the decision problem, the number of alternatives, and quality of analytical details, determine the sizes of the data and knowledge bases.
3. *Unanticipated data*: Owing to the advancements in technology and the tasks involved in comprehending the problem at hand, some additional data and irrelevant data may become evident in the process, which then informs the need to integrate additional features in the system so that it incorporates new ways to interpret the data for accurate decision-making; usually, such changes may be somewhat expensive and time demanding.
4. *Redundant data*: To make up for the ills associated with the performance of certain data types, in terms of data interpretation and drawn inferences, redundant data may be considered suitable for inclusion as regards the situation investigated; however several inconsistencies may ensue, leading to cases of increased data heterogeneity.

Air quality monitoring systems: remote sensors

Fig. 3.8 is an illustration of a carefully positioned remote sensor.

The Urban Clouds spatial mapping air quality sensor

The Urban Clouds spatial mapping air quality sensor is a system that measures the concentrations of several pollutants and, with the help of a GSM/GPRS-modem, sends data to a storage platform provided in the "Urban Clouds." The platform renders API services that provide data to customer systems for further analysis or ingestion into machine learning-based applications. Urban Clouds comprises a customer dashboard for visualizing or downloading data in CSV format.

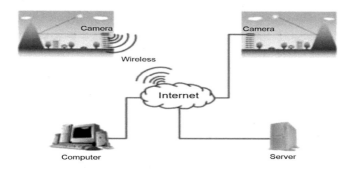

FIGURE 3.8

The schematic remote sensor with IP camera for air quality monitoring.

Adapted from Wong, C. J., MatJafri, M. Z., Abdullah, K., Lim, H. S., & Low, K. L. (2007). Temporal air quality monitoring using surveillance camera. In IEEE international geoscience and remote sensing symposium. IEEE.

The Libelium air quality IoT kit

This comprises a gateway unit connected locally to one or more remote sensors. The gateway unit relays data via a 3G/4G network connected to a cloud service/database (i.e., the MySQL database). Other sensors for air quality monitoring include the DICOM 4000/DICOM 400 for CO_2, NO_2, CO, and hydrocarbon monitoring, MQ 135 gas sensor, the indoor and outdoor particulate matter (PM_{10}, $PM_{2.5}$) monitor, Grimm 1.109 OPC (Grimm Technologies Inc., Douglasville, GA, United States), the 602-3, ELT (Sensor Corp., Bucheon, Gyeonggi-do, Korea), relative humidity monitor (Humi-01, manufactured by Digikey Electronics, MN, United States), particulate matter monitor (DP-100, LABCO, Korea), CO_2 sensor (M-530, ELT Sensor Corp., Korea), CO (COD-100, ELT Sensor Corp., Korea), TVOC (AQM-100, ELT Sensor Corp., Korea), etc.

Review of a few previous and more recent studies on air quality modeling

This section reviews some recent studies on air quality modeling. The works of Abderrahim et al. (2016), Kukkonen et al. (2003), Pawul and Śliwka (2016), and Rybarczyk and Zalakeviciute (2018) were dedicated to prediction of the concentration and pollution levels of particulate matter and gas in relation to air pollution. However, based on their findings, PM_{10} and $PM_{2.5}$ are the most dominant pollutants in most pollution predictions involving machine learning methods. Several studies also have been dedicated to forecasting nitric oxides and ozone, with a few of them dedicated to sulfur dioxide or carbon monoxide. Considering the frequency of application of some forecasting methods, ANNs have been found to trail behind the ensemble-learning packages. Gas-induced air pollution forecasts in terms of SO_2, NO_2, and NO emissions were carried out at the Polish State Environmental Monitoring System (PSEMS) stations in Zakopane and Nowy Sącz, from January 1 to December 31, 2017, using an air-circulation weather type model. Neural network architectures were built and tested for each gas type to make the best model selection for application. Each network was comprised of one layer of hidden neurons. The data adopted for the investigation were segmented into training data (70%), validation data (15%), and testing data (15%) subsets, respectively. Data for sunshine, fog, and wind duration were also provided. Prior to selection of the data,

Table 3.2 Sample data of some estimated parameters of artificial intelligence predictions of gaseous emissions.

Station	Pollutant	Correlation coefficients	Difference between the average values of the expected and predicted values (μg)	Average difference in standard deviation of the expected and predicted values	Upper and lower limits of the different air pollutants (μg)
Z	SO_2	0.98	1.87	2.39	1.6−71.9
Z	NO	0.84	5.40	7.9	0−109
Z	NO_2	0.90	4.75	4.55	4−90
Z	O_3	0.92	7.83	5.62	3−114
N	SO_2	0.92	1.7	2.19	1.3−58.7
N	NO	0.82	6.76	7.71	0−90
N	NO_2	0.82	4.88	3.92	6−78

Note: N, *Nowy Sącz;* Z, *Zakopane.*
Adapted from Pawul, M. (2019). Application of neural networks to the prediction of gas pollution of air, New Trends in Production Engineering, *2(1), 515−523.*

a correlation analysis was conducted. The concentrations of the air-polluting gases and the meteorological data were introduced in the trained data set. From the results, the average daily pollution rate, maximum and minimum temperatures, as well as snow cover thickness were determined. The best correlation indicators for all trained data set were estimated to be 0.98 for SO_2 pollution in Zakopane (see Table 3.2), while the lowest average error (distance between the expected/real value and the predicted value for SO_2-induced air pollution in Nowy Sącz) was 1.7 μg. For Zakopane and Nowy Sącz, the estimated average error rates of SO_2-induced air pollution were 1.87 and 1.7 μg, with 75% of the errors not exceeding 2.15 and 2.01 μg, respectively (Pawul, 2019). The highest average error rate was obtained for ozone (7.63 μg), which was measured only in Zakopane. Table 3.2 gives some estimated parameters of the results obtained for the best neural network.

Liu et al. (2020) carried out a time-series comparison of three air pollution algorithms. The test was completed using Linux. The algorithms include an AI-based remote sensing/monitoring algorithm, a geostationary ocean color imager (GOCI) satellite sensor-based algorithm and the moderate resolution imaging spectroradiometer (MODIS) data-based algorithm. Based on the results, the AI-remote sensing algorithm gave the shortest prediction time (i.e., 0.28 seconds) with appreciable levels of accuracy, whereas the geostationary satellite sensor and the MODIS-based algorithms gave longer prediction times of 0.72 and 1.18 seconds, respectively. Some other methods for characterizing and forecasting the dispersion of air pollutants include the simple box model that was adopted by Middleton (1998), the persistence and regression models by Shi and Harrison (1997), as well as other complex dynamic air models such as the CHIMERE as adopted by Monteiroa et al. (2005) and the community multiscale air quality model as discussed by Luecken et al. (2006) and Arasa et al. (2010). Although simple models provide a fast overview of the problem being investigated, they usually depend on very significant simple assumptions that cannot provide sufficient information for the complex interactions and processes that influence the transport and chemical behaviors of the target pollutants (Luecken et al., 2006). Mishra and Goyal (2015) carried out air pollution prediction of hourly mean concentrations of NO_2 at Taj Mahal, Agra, India, using statistical regression and an AI-based model (i.e., a public health-oriented air quality forecasting model) and 10-year air sampling data. Based on the investigation, NO_2 concentrations were found to be higher in November. As a result, data for November were used as a standard in the development of a multiple linear regression (MLR) model that was advanced into an air quality forecasting model for the prediction of NO_2 concentrations at Agra. Furthermore, a principal component analysis (PCA) of the regression models was carried out to establish the correlations between the predictor variables between meteorology-based information and NO_2. The significant variables were then considered the input parameters for the resulting ANN-multilayer perceptron model. The combined PCR and MLR models were then evaluated statistically, which gave estimated correlation coefficients (R) of 0.89 and 0.91, and 0.69 and 0.89, respectively, for the entire training and validation periods. The normalized MSE, index of agreement, and fractional bias (FB) were seen to conform to the observed values. However, the PCA-ANN model was preferred to the MLR model. According to the authors, the PCA in the hybrid PCA-ANN model helped to minimize the dimensions of the input variable in the ANN architecture, thus reducing the data training time and subsequently improving the model's accuracy; this model is suitable for visualizing ambient air quality as well as meteorological data. Multilayer perceptrons comprising of highly supervised trained algorithms have been used in handling some difficult and diverse air pollution problems. In the study conducted by Elangasinghe, Singhal, Dirks, and Salmond (2014), a method for extraction of key information from meteorological data and traffic emission patterns was used to build a reliable and efficient ANN forecasting tool for NO_2 concentrations at a location near a major highway in Auckland, New Zealand. Data such as wind speed and direction, temperature, relative humidity, solar radiation, as well as timed emissions in hours, days, months, and years were presented according to the time scales of three input optimization methods [i.e., GA, forward selection (FS), and backward elimination (BE) methods]. Based on their findings, it was observed that the GA gave predictions whose values corresponded to the smallest mean absolute error. Hence, the nature of the nonlinear function of the trained genetically optimized neural network was then determined from the model's response to perturbations induced by individual predictor variables during the sensitivity analyses. The work of Singh et al. (2013) used basic meteorological parameters to model the concentrations of PM_{10} particulates and SO_2 in determining NO_2 concentrations as a predictor variable; hence this imposes a kind of limitation to the model's application. Time-lagged models which have the capacities to give reliable air pollution forecasts from 1 to 24 hours ahead of the timed investigation have been reported (Karatzas & Kaltsatos, 2007); however, these models become unreliable, especially when there are large gaps/downtimes in the generated data which may have been caused by faulty equipment or poor calibration. Arhami et al. (2013) carried out hourly predictions of air pollution levels via ANN coupled with uncertainty analysis from Monte Carlo simulations. Chelani et al. (2002) made significant contributions to the prediction of SO_2 concentration in air using ANN, and their results were seen to be in good agreement with the observations from similar studies. Chen et al. (2014) developed a neural network ensemble technique for modeling and improving the measurement accuracy/prediction of air quality data obtained from meteorological fields adopted for air quality studies. Other machine learning methods that have been applied to air quality modeling include MLR models (Chen et al., 2014; Mishra, Goyal & Upadhyay, 2015), the hidden Markov model (Sun et al., 2013), geographic weighted regression model (Madrigano et al., 2013), support vector machine (Sun & Sun, 2016), and the neural network model (Chen et al., 2014; Feng et al., 2015; Ordieres et al., 2005). The work of Ong et al. (2015) involves the use of a deep recursive neural network for the application of an automatic encoder pre-training method for tasks involving time-series predictions; the resulting predictions were more accurate than those obtained from a compared VENUS system adopted by the Japanese government. Ozone forecasts in highly polluted urban settings were carried out using photochemical models in transport and dispersion scenarios (Jorquera et al., 1998). Also, linear regression and PCA have been adopted in air pollution studies; the classic time-series models [autoregression moving average (ARMA) models] were adopted by Kumar and Jain (2010), while for the support vector machines, a machine learning method was used in analyzing data gathered from air pollution studies (Ortiz et al., 2010). Also, Flores-Vergara et al. (2019), investigated the performance of recurring neural nets as well as long short-term memory in predicting daily-maximum tropospheric ozone concentrations in Santiago (Chile) in South America at a certain location using endogenous and exogenous time-series data (chemical and meteorological data). Based on the multitask learning criterion used in testing the trained model, the expected values predicted improved over the previous version of the model that could only make predictions 1 day ahead of the pollution incident in one-time step, by also accounting for multiple quantiles of the response distribution. Qin et al. (2017) also adopted the same recurring model for air quality prediction. From their work, the experimental measurements of real-life data gave improved prediction accuracies for high values of time series. Pak et al. (2018) used a hybrid-convolutional neural network to make reliable predictions of ozone concentrations in air. Pardo and Malpica (2017) carried out air quality forecasts in Spain (Madrid) using long short-term memory networks. Rodrigues and Pereira (2018) proved the outstanding competence and ability of the deep joint mean and quantile regression model in solving spatiotemporal/air pollution problems, whereas Salazar et al. (2019) predicted ozone hourly concentrations in air using the wavelets and ARIMA models. The work of Seguel et al. (2012) was on the determination of ozone weekend effects in Santiago, Chile, while Sousa et al. (2007) predicted ozone concentrations in a polluted environment using MLR models and ANN. Luna et al. (2014) made accurate predictions of tropospheric concentrations of O_3 using ANN and SVC in Rio de Janeiro, Brazil. A comparative study of ground-level ozone prediction was carried out by Gorai and Mitra (2017) using feedforward backpropagation (FB) and layer-recurrent neural network (LNN) models. Real-time hourly predictions of O_3 were made using a deep convolutional neural network (Eslami et al., 2020). The minimum redundancy maximum relevance (MRMR) and echo state network (ESN) models were used in making air pollution forecasts of $PM_{2.5}$ by adopting a supplementary leaky integrator echo state network (SLI-ESN) which memorizes historical data. The dataset comprised air pollution data for $PM_{2.5}$, PM_{10}, NO_2, CO, O_3, SO_2, temperature, pressure, humidity, wind speed, and wind direction. The indicators for evaluating the models include the root mean square error (RMSE), symmetric mean absolute percentage error (SMAPE), mean absolute error (MAE), normalized root mean square error (NRMSE), and the Pearson correlation coefficient (R). The approach adopted involves a prior use of the MRMR feature to handle data redundancy, which increased the computational speed. To extract evolutionary details of relevant variables, a phase space reconstruction of the gathered information was first done while the SLI-ESN was used in making the final forecast. The results obtained were compared with those obtained for other models [i.e., the ESN, leaky integrator echo state network (LI-ESN), extreme learning machine (ELM) as well as the hierarchical ELM and SAE], and it was observed that the SLI-ESN model gave the best results amongst all the models.

Exposures to PM can result in respiratory and cardiovascular diseases. Inhaled particles released in enclosed spaces/underground parking garages (UPGs) are potential threats to the human respiratory system. Oh and Kim (2020) carried out a modeling study on particulate matter (PM), total volatile carbon (TVoC), and CO in UPGs under different operating conditions, including heating, ventilation, and air-conditioning (HVAC) by means of real-time monitors and integrated sensors. Model predictions of the PM concentrations from vehicular traffic volumes and ANN were made considering several environmental factors. Measured PM_{10} concentrations from the UPGs were higher than those obtained from the model as a result of short-term sources of the particulates as induced by vehicles within the park. The average inhaled and respirable PM dosages for adults were estimated using ANN which gave R^2 values of 0.69–0.87 for the predicted values as compared with experimental measurements, respectively, thus demonstrating the feasibility of using air quality monitoring to determine the risks of human exposure to vehicle-induced pollutants in UPGs and the use of ANN in evaluating indoor air quality. Indoor air quality is affected by a constantly changing interaction of indoor and outdoor factors.

Other studies have also reported the release of particulate materials (PM_{10}, $PM_{2.5}$) in buildings to be mostly derived from outdoor particles sucked in via HVAC systems (Liu et al., 2019; Adam et al., 1994; Andrew & Chio, 2004; Carrilho da Graça, 2018; Wang et al., 2006; Sundell et al., 2010; Geens et al., 2006). Some of these ventilation systems are somewhat ineffective in completely dispersing vehicle-induced pollutants coming from enclosed underground spaces, thus they may accumulate in these indoor environments and cause serious health concerns in humans (Papakonstantinou et al., 2003; Dhawan et al., 2018; Buonanno et al., 2013; Lehnert et al., 2012; Yang et al., 2019). Although air quality sensors are adopted in monitoring air quality, these systems need to be supported by AI techniques that are quite efficient in predicting air quality so as to take proactive measures when life-threatening situations arise. This then goes further to say that much still needs to be done in the area of ventilation and heating systems using modeling techniques. No doubt, the IoT helps to secure precision in weather observations such as temperature, humidity, and wind velocity measurements. Rather than taking indoor air quality measurements and analysis, predictive mathematical models/tools can be employed for making accurate estimates of air pollutants. As contributed by indoor and outdoor sources, changes in weather, atmospheric conditions, particle dispersion/deposition, and other factors, compromise indoor air quality (Russo et al., 2015). In addition, there are only few studies as regards the use of ANN in estimating air quality in relation to health effects (Kassomenos et al., 2011; Polezer et al., 2018; Wang et al., 2008; Kachba et al., 2020). Studies on complex system prediction have proven the superiority of ANN to traditional statistical methods and deterministic models, due to their limited computational efficiencies, generalization ability, and prior knowledge of the modeled process structure (Elangasinghe, Dirks, Singhal et al., 2014; Lal & Tripathy, 2012; Nejadkoorki & Baroutian, 2011).

Liu et al. (2019) carried out a study that involved the onsite monitoring and modeling of the varying concentrations of $PM_{2.5}$, PM_{10}, CO_2, and TVoC in naturally ventilated underground car parks with high traffic volumes. Papakonstantinou et al. (2003) conducted a computational and experimental evaluation of the impact of ventilation effectiveness in an underground garage. According to them, there were close matches between the estimated and empirical values. Oh et al. (2020) modeled the human health exposure effect of respirable particles and TVoC in underground car parks aerated with different types of ventilators; the study gave reasonable predictions of the concentration levels of dominant particulate matter and their short- and long-term consequences on the human respiratory system. The effects of harmful nanoparticulates have also been modeled by Nazarenko et al. (2012), in which inhalation of and exposure to cosmetic powder were quantitatively assessed via a modeling technique that centers on a smart systems modeling procedure. The study of Yu et al. (2020) is a check on the influence of air compactness of a building envelope/space on indoor particulate concentration. The studies of Mosley et al. (2001) and Zhu et al. (2005) accounted for the penetration of ambient fine particles and freeway ultrafine particles into an indoor space, respectively. The modeling techniques adopted gave reliable estimates of the indoor particles' influx. The effects of the rate of ventilation on aerosol deposition on materials have been modeled (Adam et al., 1994); in the same vein, a simplified modeling technique for the turbulent mixing of wind-driven single-sided ventilators was studied by Carrillho da Graça (2018). Also, according to Sundell et al. (2010), Wang et al. (2008), and Buonanno et al. (2013), there is ample evidence of the effect of air ventilation rates on human health. Geens et al. (2006) carried out a review of different studies on ventilation performance for spaces in a particular location where smoking is permitted. The study of Lehnert et al. (2012) was on modeling of the exposure of humans to inhalable, respirable, and ultrafine particles of welding fumes resulting from a hot-work site. Chung and Kim (2020) established an automobile environment detection system using a modeling procedure rooted on a deep neural network; its implementation was successfully carried out using IoT-enabled in-vehicle air quality sensors. Using ANN, Lal and Tripathy (2012) made model predictions of dust particle concentrations in an open-cast coal mine. Gerharz et al. (2009) conduced a pilot study in which indoor and outdoor estimations of individual exposures to $PM_{2.5}$ from GPS profiles and diaries were modeled. Chao (2003) carried out an estimation of the penetration coefficients and deposition rates of PM as a function of particle size in naturally ventilated areas/homes that were not exposed to smoke/smokers, while Elbayoumi et al. (2015) conducted a study on the development and adoption of regression and feedforward backpropagation neural network (FFBP-NN) in predicting seasonal indoor concentrations of $PM_{2.5}$ and PM_{10} in naturally ventilated school environments. A similar study was conducted by Ul-Saufie et al. (2013), in which reasonable estimates of daily concentrations of PM_{10} were accurately predicted by adopting two combined models (regression and feedforward backpropagation models) alongside PCA.

Despite all the aforementioned efforts, it remains very important to state that the existing machine learning and AI methods are faced with the issue of ignoring the inherent features of air pollution sources, especially in terms of proximity (i.e., proximity to pollution data) of nearby sites, thus they rarely consider the distance of separation between pollution sources as well as the monitored sites. Furthermore, in machine learning, the absence/lack of consideration for independent variables has an adverse effect on the predicted outcome, hence the reason for often achieving <90% accuracies (Cheng et al., 2012; Hssina et al., 2014; Hang-Suk & Joon-Hong, 2009; Li et al., 2016; Malgorzata, 2019; Mitchell, 1991; Oeder et al., 2012; Oh & Kim, 2020; Quinlan, 1993; Rykiel, 1989, Salazar et al., 2019, Xu & Ren, 2019; Ye et al., 1998.

Future opportunities: the next data wave

According to reports, Europe and many other nations are presently weaker in terms of maximizing the potentials that are inherent in consumer applications, thus leading to a low level of competence in data access due to value shifts and data reuse. The growing pace of data around the world has been estimated to rise from 33 to 175 zettabytes from 2018 to 2025 (European Commission, 2020).

Every fresh wave of data is expected to open up opportunities for IT experts to take up strategic positions as knowledge experts in this voluminous-data economy. Consequently this has influenced the way data are being stored and processed in recent times. In today's world, about 80% of data processing and analysis takes place in the cloud, and is usually made possible by the existence of data centers and centralized computing facilities also known as DCS, while about 20% is stored in smart objects, including cars, home appliances, robots, and computer ware. Low-power electronics are a special set of devices that need be exploited as specialized future processors for AI. This is predicted to usher in the development of low-power-consuming systems with high performance.

Advances in quantum computing increase the processing speed/capacity of quantum simulators as well as their program architectures for efficient quantum computing. Sometimes, the data gathered from sensors/faulty devices are not very accurate, which in turn impacts on the quality of evaluation, assessment, and network communication problems. This then brings to mind the need to carry out big data quality assurance checks on the data modeling procedure and the model validation technique, all aimed at adopting the appropriate tools for air quality evaluation. As advances in smart sensing and the IoT come to bear, environmental sensors, such as air sensors, which lack the capacity for good precision when tested with integrated real-time big data quality evaluation and monitoring within smart cities will be complemented in terms of supporting/enhancing air quality management. The aerated environment of a city is a multilevel system whose composition is affected by several factors including pollutant concentrations, emission levels, time, location, wind speed, etc. Considering the fact that most of the established models apply machine learning to data generated from a specific location and time, it then suffices to say that the model will only be compatible for air monitoring and assessment situations for future smart cities that support real-time air quality monitoring, evaluation, and prediction. This can also be addressed using integrated and dynamic air quality models/hybrid machine learning tools that can sufficiently cater to the influence of factors such as the nature of wind flow, time series, and their impacts on different atmospheric conditions. Based on existing studies, ANN can be used successfully, in forecasting air pollution, especially in areas where data on personal exposure to poisonous particles that penetrate these buildings are lacking. This can be done by developing an indoor exposure model which uses similar data sources to make valuable predictions and evaluation of pollutant concentrations and their effects on human health. Also, to support the implementation of a good air quality management strategy, it is advisable to equip buildings where HVAC systems are installed with web-based real-time monitors for monitoring and documenting data on indoor air pollutants to ascertain the indoor air quality per time as this will help improve human health and quality of life, thus ensuring a safe and environmentally friendly atmosphere.

Conclusions

Air pollution can have severe consequences in humans, thus resulting in cases such as lung cancer, brain/liver/kidney damage, cardiac disease, and respiratory dysfunctions. It also contributes to the depletion of the ozone layer, which protects the Earth from the sun's ultraviolet rays. Thus, with modern technologies, these problems can be seen ahead of time, which in turn helps in taking proactive measures as a way of avoiding any pending harm. AI techniques/models rely on knowledge-based systems that help to accelerate the problem identification process. The integration/combination of several AI models with other models (i.e., numerical and/or statistical models) as one system enhances the level of accuracy, reliability, and usefulness of the final model relative to the individual capacities of the separate models. In today's world, there is no doubt that the aforementioned tools provide a strong basis for good decision-based actions in many real-life applications. The application of DCS is fast increasing beyond hardware devices, however, it is necessary to emphasize this, because models are system specific. Despite this positive impression, AI models that find application in environmental issues are somewhat inferior/not applicable to AI systems in other fields such as medicine or manufacturing. The emergence of information technology has led to the connection of machines and remote sensors as means of solving environmentally related problems such as air pollution and contamination toward ensuring easy computation and the development of novel cost-effective approaches for solving these problems. These have also helped to reduce the time spent in making decisions, owing to the fast computation times of these facilities, which have similar features to supercomputers. As familiarity with the modalities of DCS increases, the time spent on understanding/learning their features and functionalities reduces, which in turn allows for more participation with very good turnaround/fast decision-making processes, that is, local and global decisions are arrived at and shared in the shortest possible time frame, which guarantees effective actions based on precise/accurate decisions. One very useful computer-based decision support system concept is "integration." This concept suggests that for any software system developed for real-world application, the bridging of several information sources helps to ensure that more than one problem is presented and modeled using different problem-solving tools and a highly effective/multifaceted problem-oriented interface, which is dynamic in nature. Furthermore, air pollution modeling helps in the casual description of the relationship between emissions, meteorology, and atmospheric concentrations of pollutants, as well as how effective remediation strategies may be, in terms of providing avenues for future simulations of expected trends. Despite the aforementioned advancements with AI as an air forecasting tool, a few caveats such as the construction and the right selection of input parameters still remain a challenge that needs to be properly addressed, because, despite the fact that any set of data can be inputted into an ANN architecture for training and validation, it is not realistically possible to have several combinations tested/tried at the same time.

References

Adam, N., Kohal, J., & Riffat, S. (1994). Effect of ventilation rate on deposition of aerosol particles on materials. *Building Services Energineering Research and Technology*, *15*(3), 185–188.

Adriaans, P. W., & Zantinge, D. (1996). *Data mining*. Harlow: Addison Wesley Longman.

Agerwala, T., & Perone, M. (2014). Data centric systems: The next paradigm in computing. In *Keynote at the international conference on parallel processing*, Minneapolis, MN, September 2014.

Andrew, J., & Chio, M. D. (2004). Biological effects of Utah Valley ambient air particles in humans: A review. *Journal of Aerosol Medicine*, *17*(2), 157–164.

Arasa, R., Soler, M. R., Ortega, S., Olid, M., & Merino, M. (2010). A performance evaluation of MM5/MNEQA/CMAQ air quality modelling system to forecast ozone concentrations in Catalonia. *Tethys*, *7*, 11–23.

Arhami, M., Kamali, N., & Rajabi, M. M. (2013). Predicting hourly air pollutant levels using artificial neural networks coupled with uncertainty analysis by Monte Carlo simulations. *Environmental Science and Pollution Research, 20*(7), 4777−4789.

Avesani, P., Perini, A., & Ricci, F. (1993). Combining CBR and constraint reasoning in planning forest fire fighting. In *Proceedings of the first European workshop on case-based reasoning* (pp. 235−239).

Avesani, P., Perini, A., & Ricci, F. (1995). *The intervention planning subsystem*, Technical Report, IRST. CHARADE. Istituto per la Ricerca Scientifica e Tecnologica, Torento, Italy.

Avesani, P., Perini, A., & Ricci, F. (2000). Interactive case-based planning for forest fire management. *Applied Intelligence, 13*, 7−17.

Avouris, N. M., & Page, B. (1995). *Environmental informatics: Methodology and applications of environmental information processing*. Norwell, MA: Kluwer.

Baxter, C. W., Stanley, S. J., & Zhang, Q. (1999). Development of a full-scale artificial neural network model for the removal of natural organic matter by enhanced coagulation. *Aqua, 48*(4), 129−136.

Baxter, C. W., Zhang, Q., Stanley, S. J., Shariff, R., Tupas, R. R., & Stark, H. L. (2001). Drinking water quality and treatment: The use of artificial neural networks. *Canadian Journal of Civil Engineering, 28*(1), 26−35.

Bender, M., & Simonovic, S. P. (1994). Decision support system for long-range stream-flow forecasting. *Journal of Computing in Civil Engineering, 8*(1), 20−34.

Berry, M. J. A., & Linoff, G. (1997). *Data mining techniques for marketing, sales, and customer support*. New York: John Wiley & Sons.

Branting, K., Hastings, J. D., & Lockwood, J. A. (1997). Integrating cases and models for prediction in biological systems. *AI Applications, 11*(1), 29−48.

Breiman, L., Friedman, J. H., Olshen, R. A., & Stone, J. C. (1984). *Classification and regression trees. The Wasworth statistics/probability series*. New York: Chapman and Hall.

Buonanno, G., Marks, G. B., & Morawska, L. (2013). Health effects of daily airborne particle dose in children: Direct association between personal dose and respiratory health effects. *Environmental Pollution, 2013* (180), 246−250.

Calori, G., Colombo, F., & Finzi, G. (1994). Frame: A knowledgebase tool to support the choice of the right air pollution model. In G. Guariso, & B. Page (Eds.), *Computer support for environmental impact assessment* (pp. 211−222).

Carrilho da Graça, G. (2018). A technical note on simplified modeling of turbulent mixing in wind-driven single sided ventilation. *Building and Environment, 131*, 12−15.

Chang, N. B., Chen, Y. L., & Chen, H. W. (1997). A fuzzy regression analysis for the construction cost estimation of wastewater treatment plants. *Journal of Environmental Science and Health Part A: Environmental Science and Engineering and Toxic and Hazardous Substance Control, 32*(4), 885−899.

Chao, C. (2003). Penetration coefficient and deposition rate as a function of particle size in non-smoking naturally ventilated residences. *Atmospheric Environment, 37*(30), 4233−4241.

Chapman, D., & Patry, G. G. (1989). *Dynamic modeling and expert systems in wastewater engineering*. Chelsea: Lewis Publishers.

Charlebois, D., Matwin, S., & Goodenough, D. G. (1995). Planning with agents in intelligent data management for forestry. In IJCAI-95 *Workshop on artificial intelligence and the environment* (pp. 69−70).

Chelani, A. B., Rao, C. V. C., Phadke, K. M., & Hasan, M. Z. (2002). Prediction of sulphur dioxide concentration using artificial neural networks. *Environmental Modelling and Software, 17*(2), 161−168.

Cheng, S. Y., Li, L., Chen, D. S., & Li, J. B. (2012). A neural network-based ensemble approach for improving the accuracy of meteorological fields used for regional air quality modeling. *Journal of Environmental Management, 112*, 404−414.

Chen, Y., Qin, H., & Zhou, Z. G. (2014). A comparative study on multi-regression analysis and BP neural network of PM2.5 index. In *International conference on natural computation* (pp. 155−159). IEEE: Xiamen, China.

Chong, H. G., & Walley, W. J. (1996). Rule-base vs probabilistic approaches to the diagnosis of faults in wastewater treatment processes. *Artificial Intelligence in Engineering, 10*(3), 265–273.

Chuang, M. -T., Zhang, Y., & Kang, D. -W. (2011). Application of WRF/Chem-MADRID for real-time air quality forecasting over the Southeastern United States. *Atmospheric Environment, 45*(34), 6241–6250. Available from https://doi.org/10.1016/j.atmosenv.2011.06.071.

Chung, J.-J., & Kim, H.-J. (2020). An automobile environment detection system based on deep neural network and its implementation using IoT-enabled in-vehicle air quality sensors. *Sustainability, 12*(6), 2475.

Cortes, U., Sanchez-Marrè, M., Ceccaroni, L., R-Roda, R., & Poch, M. (2000). Artificial intelligence and environmental decision support systems. *Applied Intelligence, 13*(1), 77–91.

Dhawan, S., Sebastian, A., & Siby, J. (2018). Health risk assessment of workers in underground parking due to exposure to CO and VOC. *International Journal of Engineering Science and Technology., 2018*(5), 1388–1391.

Dunham, M. H. (2002). *Data mining: introduction and advanced topics.* Pearson Education Inc.

Eblen, R., & Eblen, W. (1994). *The encyclopaedia of the environment.* Houghton Mifflin Co, ISBN 0-395-55041-6.

Elangasinghe, A. M., Singhal, N., Dirks, K. N., & Salmond, J. A. (2014). Development of an ANN-based air pollution forecasting system with explicit knowledge through sensitivity analysis. *Atmospheric Pollution Research, 5*(4), 696–708.

Elangasinghe, M., Dirks, K., Singhal, N., Costello, S., Longley, I., & Salmond, J. (2014). A simple semi-empirical technique for apportioning the impact of roadways on air quality in an urban neighbourhood. *Atmospheric Environment, 83*, 99–108.

Elbayoumi, M., Ramli, N. A., & Yusof, N. F. (2015). Development and comparison of regression models and feedforward backpropagation neural network models to predict seasonal indoor PM2.5–10 and PM2.5 concentrations in naturally ventilated schools. *Atmospheric Pollution Research, 6*(6), 1013–1023.

Englehart, J. D. (1997). Bayesian-risk analysis for sustainable process design. *Journal of Environmental Engineering, 123*(1), 71–79.

Eslami, E., Choi, Y., Lops, Y., & Sayeed, A. (2020). A real-time hourly ozone prediction system using deep convolutional neural network. *Neural Computing and Applications, 32*, 8783–8797. Available from https://doi.org/10.1007/s00521-019-04282-x.

European Commission. (2020). *White paper on artificial intelligence: A European approach to excellence and trust,* 19.2.2020 COM (2020) 65 final. Brussels.

Feng, X., Li, Q., Zhu, Y., Hou, J., Jin, L., & Wang, J. (2015). Artificial neural networks forecasting of PM 2.5, pollution using air mass trajectory based geographic model and wavelet transformation. *Atmospheric Environment, 107*, 118–128.

Flores-Vergara, D., Ñanculef, R., Valle, C., Osses, M., Jacques, A., Domínguez, M., 2019. Forecasting ozone pollution using recurrent neural nets and multiple quantile regression. In *2019 IEEE CHILEAN conference on electrical, electronics engineering, information and communication technologies (CHILECON)* (pp. 1–6). IEEE.

Foody, G. M., & Arora, M. K. (1997). An evaluation of some factors affecting the accuracy of classification by an artificial neural network. *International Journal of Remote Sensing, 18*(4), 799–810.

Geens, A., Snelson, D., Littlewood, J., & Ryan, J. (2006). Ventilation performance for spaces where smoking is permitted: A review of previous work and field study results. *Building Services Engineering Research and Technology, 27*(3), 235–248.

Genovesi, A., Harmand, J., & Steyer, J.-P. (1999). Integrated fault detection and isolation: Application to a Winery's wastewater treatment plant. *Applied Intelligence, 13*(1), 207–224.

Gerharz, L. E., Kruger, A., & Klemm, O. (2009). Applying indoor and outdoor modeling techniques to estimate individual exposure to PM2.5 from personal GPS profiles and diaries: A pilot study. *Science of the Total Environment, 407*(18), 5184–5193.

Goldberg, D. E. (1989). *Genetic algorithms in search, optimization and machine learning* (p. 412) Addison-Wesley Publishing Co. Inc.

Gorai, A., & Mitra, G. (2017). A comparative study of the feed-forward back-propagation and layer-recurrent neural network model for forecasting ground level ozone concentration. *Air Quality, Atmosphere and Health, 10*(2), 213−223.

Haagsma, I. G., & Johanns, R. D. (1994). Decision support systems: An integrated approach. In P. Zannetti (Ed.), *Environmental systems* (vol. 2, pp. 205−212). .

Hadjimichael, M., Arunas, P., Kuciauskas, L., & R. Brody. (1996). MEDEX: A fuzzy system for forecasting mediterranean gale force winds. In *Proceedings FUZZ-IEEE96. IEEE international conference on fuzzy systems* (pp. 529−534). New Orleans, LA.

Halhal, D., Walters, G. A., Ouazar, D., & Savic, D. A. (1997). Water network rehabilitation with structured messy genetic algorithm. *Journal of Water Resources Planning and Management, 123*(3), 137−146.

Hand, D. J. (1998). Data mining: Statistics and more? *The American Statistician, 52*(2), 112−118.

Hart, J., Hunt, I., & Shankararaman, V. (1998). Environmental management systems—A role for AI? In Environmental *sciences* and *artificial intelligence* (BESAI'98) workshop (pp. 1−10).

Harvey, S. (1998). An introduction to artificial intelligence. *Appita Journal, 51*(1), 20−24.

Hassan, R., & Li, M. (2010). Urban air pollution rorecasting using artificial intelligence-based tools. In V. Villanyi (Ed.), *Air pollution*. InTech Open, ISBN: 978-953-307-143-5, InTech.

Hastings, J., Branting, K., & Lockwood, J. (1996). A multi-paradigm reasoning system for rangeland management. *Computers and Electronics in Agriculture, 16*(1), 47−67.

Heller, U., Struss, P., Guerrin, F., & Roque, W. (1995). A qualitative modelling approach to algal bloom prediction. In *Artificial intelligence and the environment workshop (IJCAI-95)* (pp. 21−26).

Holland, J. H. (1975). *Adaptation in natural and artificial systems*. University of Michigan Press.

Hssina, B., Merbouha, A., Ezzikouri, H., & Erritali, M. (2014). A comparative study of decision tree ID3 and C4.5. International Journal of Advanced Computer Science and Applications, Special Issue on Advances in Vehicular Ad Hoc Networking and Applications. Special Issue on Advances in Vehicular Ad Hoc Networking and Applications. Available from https://doi.org/10.14569/SpecialIssue.2014.040203.

Humphreys, P., McIvor, R., & Chan, F. (2003). Using case-based reasoning to evaluate supplier environmental management performance. *Expert Systems with Applications, 25*(2), 141−153.

Hushon, J. M. (1987). Expert systems for environmental problems. *Environmental Science and Technology, 21* (9), 838−841.

Iverson, L. R., & Prasad, A. M. (1998). Predicting abundance of 80 tree species following climate change in the eastern United States. *Ecological Monographs, 68*(4), 465−485.

Jagannath, V. (2020). *Random forest template for TIBCO Spotfire—TIBCO Community*. Available from https://community.tibco.com/wiki/random-forest-template-tibco-spotfirer-wiki-page (accessed 29.08.20).

Jain, A. K., Mao, J., & Mohiuddin, K. M. (1996). Artificial neural networks: A tutorial. *Computer, 29*(3), 31.

Jones, E. K., & Roydhouse, A. (1995). Retrieving structured spatial information from large databases: A progress report. In *IJCAI-95 workshop on artificial intelligence and the environment* (pp. 49−57).

Jørgensen, S. E., & Johnsen, I. (1989). *Principles of environmental science and technology, . Studies in environmental science* (vol. 33). Elsevier, ISBN 0-444-43024-5.

Jorquera, H., et al. (1998). Forecasting ozone daily maximum levels at Santiago, Chile. *Atmos. Environ, 32* (20), 3415−3424.

Kachba, Y., Chiroli, D. M. G., Belotti, J. T., Alves, T. A., Tadano, Y. S., & Siqueira, H. (2020). Artificial neural networks to estimate the influence of vehicular emission variables on morbidity and mortality in the largest metropolis in South America. *Sustainability, 12*(7), 2621. Available from https://doi.org/10.3390/su12072621.

Kang, G. K., Gao, J. Z., Chiao, S., Lu, S., & Xie, G. (2018). Air quality prediction: Big data and machine learning approaches. *International Journal of Environmental Science and Development, 9*(1), 8−16. Available from https://doi.org/10.18178/ijesd.2018.9.1.1066.

Kang-Suk, K., & Joon-Hong, P. (2009). A survey of applications of artificial intelligence algorithms in eco-environmental modelling. *Environmental Engineering Research*, *14*(2), 102−110. Available from https://doi.org/10.4491/eer.2009.14.2.102.

Kangari, R., & Rouhani, S. (1989). Reservoir management and planning expert system. In S. J. Nix, A. G. Collind, & T.-K. Tsay (Eds.), *Knowledge-based expert systems in water utility operations and management*. American Water Works Association (AWWA) Research Foundation.

Karatzas, K. D., & Kaltsatos, S. (2007). Air pollution modelling with the aid of computational intelligence methods in Thessaloniki, Greece. *Simulation Modelling Practice and Theory*, *15*(10), 1310−1319.

Kass, G. V. (1980). An exploratory technique for investigating large quantities of categorical data. *Journal of the Royal Statistical Society. Series C (Applied Statistics)*, *29*(2), 119−127.

Kassomenos, P., Petrakis, M., Sarigiannis, D., Gotti, A., & Karakitsios, S. (2011). Identifying the contribution of physical and chemical stressors to the daily number of hospital admissions implementing an artificial neural network model. *Air Quality, Atmosphere & Health*, *4*, 263−272.

Kim, K., & Park, J. (2009). A survey of applications of artificial intelligence algorithms in eco-environmental modelling. *Environmental Engineering Research*, *14*(2), 102−110. Available from https://doi.org/10.4491/eer.2009.14.2.102.

Kolodner, J. L. (1993). *Case-based reasoning*. San Francisco: Morgan Kaufmann Publisher, ISBN: 9781483294490.

Kompare, B. (1994). Qualitative modelling of environmental processes. In P. Zannetti (Ed.), *Environmental systems, vol. II: Computer techniques in environmental studies V*. Computational Mechanics Publications.

Krovvidy, S., & Wee, W. G. (1993). Wastewater treatment system from case-based reasoning. *Machine Learning*, *10*(3), 341−363.

Krovviddy, S., Wee, W. G., Suidan, M., Summers, R. S., Coleman, J. J., & Rossman, L. (1994). Intelligent sequence planning for wastewater treatment systems. *IEEE Expert*, *9*(6), 15−20.

Kukkonen, J., Partanen, L., Karppinen, A., Ruuskanen, J., Junninen, H., Kolehmainen, M., Niska, H., Dorling, S., Chatterton, T., Foxall, R., & Cawley, G. (2003). Extensive evaluation of neural network models for the prediction of NO_2 and PM10 concentrations, compared with a deterministic modelling system and measurements in central Helsinki. *Atmospheric Environment*, *37*(32), 4539−4550.

Kumar, U., & Jain, V. (2010). ARIMA forecasting of ambient air pollutants. *Stochastic Environmental Research and Risk Assessment*, *24*(5), 751−760.

Lal, B., & Tripathy, S. S. (2012). Prediction of dust concentration in open cast coat mine using artificial neural network. *Atmospheric Pollution Research*, *3*(2), 211−218.

Langari, R., & Yen, J. (1995). Introduction to fuzzy logic control. In J. Yen, R. Langari, & L. A. Zadeh (Eds.), *Industrial applications of fuzzy logic and intelligent systems*. New York: IEEE Press.

Lapointe, J., Marcos, B., Veillette, M., Laflamme, G., & Dumontier, M. (1989). Bioexpert-an expert system for wastewater treatment process diagnosis. *Computers & Chemical Engineering*, *13*(6), 619−630.

Lehnert, M., et al. (2012). Exposure to inhalable, respirable, and ultrafine particles in welding fume. *Annals of Occupational Hygiene*, *56*(5), 557−567.

Lek, S., & Guegan, J. F. (1999). Artificial neural networks as a tool in ecological modelling, an introduction. *Ecological Modelling*, *120*(2−3), 65−73.

Li, X., Peng, L., Hu, Y., Shao, J., & Chi, T. (2016). Deep learning architecture for air quality predictions. *Environmental Science and Pollution Research*, *23*(22), 22408−22417. Available from https://doi.org/10.1007/s11356-016-7812-9.

Liu, Y., Jing, Y., & Lu, Y. (2020). Research on quantitative remote sensing monitoring algorithm of air pollution based on artificial intelligence. *Journal of Chemistry*, *2020*, 7390545. Available from https://doi.org/10.1155/2020/7390545.

Liu, Z., Yin, H., Ma, S., Jin, G., Gao, J., & Ding, W. (2019). On-site assessments on variations of PM2.5, PM10, CO_2 and TVOC concentrations in naturally ventilated underground parking garages with traffic volume. *Environmental Pollution*, *247*, 626−637.

Luecken, D. J., Hutzell, W. T., & Gipson, G. L. (2006). Development and analysis of air quality modelling simulations for hazardous air pollutants. *Atmospheric Environment*, *40*(26), 5087−5096.

Luna, A. S., Paredes, M. L. L., de Oliveira, G. C. G., & Corrêa, S. M. (2014). Prediction of ozone concentration in tropospheric levels using artificial neural networks and support vector machine at Rio de Janeiro, Brazil. *Atmospheric Environment*, *98*, 98−104.

Lundell, M. (1996). *Qualitative modelling and simulation of spatially distributed parameter systems*, Ph.D. thesis. École Polytecnique fédérale de Lausanne.

Madrigano, J., Kloog, I., Goldberg, R., Coull, B. A., Mittleman, M. A., & Schwartz, J. (2013). Long-term exposure to PM2.5 and incidence of acute myocardial infarction. *Environmental Health Perspectives*, *121*(2), 192−196.

Manesis, S. A., Sapidis, D. J., & King, R. E. (1998). Intelligent control of wastewater treatment plants. *Artificial Intelligence in Engineering*, *12*(3), 275−281.

Malgorzata, P. (2019). Application of neural networks to the prediction of gas pollution of air. *New Trends in Production Engineering*, *2*(1), 515−523. Available from https://doi.org/10.2478/ntpe-2019-0055.

Mitchell, M. (1991). In L. D. Davis (Ed.), *Handbook of genetic algorithms: Book review*. New York: Van Nostrand Reinhold Publishers.

Middleton, D. R. (1998). A new box mode to forecast urban air quality: BOXURB. *Environmental Monitoring and Assessment*, *52*, 315−335.

Mishra, D., & Goyal, P. (2015). Development of artificial intelligence based NO_2 forecasting models at Taj Mahal, Agra. *Atmospheric Pollution Research*, *6*(1), 99−106.

Mishra, D., Goyal, P., & Upadhyay, A. (2015). Artificial intelligence-based approach to forecast PM 2.5, during haze episodes: A case study of Delhi, India. *Atmospheric Environment*, *102*, 239−248.

Monteiroa, A., Vautard, R., Borregoa, C., & Miranda, A. I. (2005). Long-term simulations of photo oxidant pollution over Portugal using the CHIMERE model. *Atmospheric Environment*, *39*(17), 3089−3101. Available from https://doi.org/10.1016/j.atmosenv.2005.01.045.

Mora-López, L., & Conejo, R. (1998). Qualitative reasoning model for the prediction of climatic data. In *Binding environmental sciences and artificial intelligence workshop (BESAI 98)* (pp. 55−67).

Mosley, R. B., Greenwell, D. J., Sparks, L. E., Guo, Z., Tucker, W. G., Fortmann, R., & Whitfield, C. (2001). Penetration of ambient fine particles into the indoor environment. *Aerosol Science and Technology*, *34*(1), 127−136.

Moustakis, V. S., Lehto, M., & Salevendy, G. (1996). Survey of expert opinion: Which machine learning method may be useful for which task? *International Journal of Human-Computer Interaction*, *8*(3), 221−236.

Mueller, S. F., & Mallard, J. W. (2011). Contributions of natural emissions to ozone and $PM_{2.5}$ as simulated by the community multiscale air quality (CMAQ) model. *Environmental Science and Technology*, *45*(11), 4817−4823. Available from https://doi.org/10.1021/es103645m.

Mulligan, A. E., & Brown, L. C. (1998). Genetic algorithms for calibrating water quality models. *Journal of Environmental Engineering*, *124*(3), 202−211.

EPA. (2015). *NAAQS table*. Available from https://www.epa.gov/criteria-air-pollutants/naaqs-table (accessed 28.08.20).

Nazarenko, Y., Zhen, H., Han, T., Lioy, P. J., & Mainelis, G. (2012). Nanomaterial inhalation exposure from nanotechnology-based cosmetic powders: A quantitative assessment. *Journal of Nanoparticle Research*, *14*(11), 1229.

Nejadkoorki, F., & Baroutian, S. (2011). Forcasting extreme PM10 concentrations using artificial neural networks. *International Journal of Environmental Research*, *6*(1), 277−284.

Oeder, S., et al. (2012). Toxicity and elemental composition of particulate matter from outdoor and indoor air of elementary schools in Munich, Germany. *Indoor Air*, *22*, 148−158.

Oh, H.-J., & Kim, J. (2020). Monitoring air quality and estimation of personal exposure to particulate matter using an indoor model and artificial neural network. *Sustainability, 12*(3794), 1−20. Available from https://doi.org/10.3390/su12093794.

Oh, H.-J., Sohn, J.-R., Roh, J.-S., & Kim, J. (2020). Exposure to respirable particles and TVOC in underground parking garages under different types of ventilation and their associated health effects. *Air Quality Atmosphere & Health, 13*(10), 297−308.

Ong, B. T., Sugiura, K., & Zettsu, K. (2015). Dynamic pretraining of Deep Recurrent Neural Networks for predicting environmental monitoring data. In *IEEE International* conference on big data (pp. 760−765). IEEE.

Ordieres, J. B., Vergara, E. P., Capuz, R. S., & Salazar, R. E. (2005). Neural network prediction model for fine particulate matter (PM2.5) on the United States−Mexico border in El Paso (Texas) and Ciudad Juárez (Chihuahua). *Environmental Modelling & Software, 20*(5), 547−559.

Ortiz, E., et al. (2010). Prediction of hourly O_3 concentrations using support vector regression algorithms. *Atmospheric Environment, 44*(35), 4481−4488.

Ostrom, E. (1991). *Governing the commons: The evolution of institutions for collective action.* Cambridge University Press, ISBN 0-521-37101-5.

Paggio, R., Agre, G., Dichev, C., Dochev, D., Umann, G., & Rozman, T. (1998). TRACE—a development platform for environmental decision support systems. In Binding *environmental sciences* and *artificial intelligence* (BESAI 98) *workshop* (pp. 145−160).

Pak, U., et al. (2018). A hybrid model based on convolutional neural networks and long short-term memory for ozone concentration prediction. *Air Quality, Atmosphere & Health, 11*(8), 883−895.

Papakonstantinou, K., Chaloulakou, A., Duci, A., Vlachakis, N., & Markatos, N. (2003). Air quality in an underground garage: Computational and experimental investigation of ventilation effectiveness. *Energy and Buildings, 35*(9), 933−940.

Pardo, E., & Malpica, N. (2017). Air quality forecasting in Madrid using long short-term memory networks. In *Proceedings of the IWINAC 2017* (pp. 232−239).

Pawul, M. (2019). Application of neural networks to the prediction of gas pollution of air. *New Trends in Production Engineering, 2*(1), 515−523. Available from https://doi.org/10.2478/ntpe-2019-0055.

Pawul, M., & Śliwka, M. (2016). Application of artificial neural networks for prediction of air pollution levels in environmental monitoring. *Journal of Ecological Engineering, 17*(4), 190−196.

Polezer, G., Tadano, Y. S., Siqueira, H. V., Godoi, A. F. L., Yamamoto, C. I., André, P. A., Pauliquevis, T., Andrade, M. F., Oliveira, A., Saldiva, P. H. N., et al. (2018). Assessing the impact of PM2.5 on respiratory disease using artificial neural networks. *Environmental Pollution, 235*, 394−403.

Qin, Y., et al. (2017). A dual-stage attention-based recurrent neural network for time series prediction. In *Proceedings of the 26th international joint conference on artificial intelligence* (pp. 2627−2633).

Quinlan, J. R. (1993). *C4.5: Programs for machine learning.* San Mateo: Morgan Kaufmann Publishers.

Radermacher, F. J., Riekert, W. F., Page, B., & Hilty, L. M. (1994). Trends in environmental information processing. In K. Brunnstein, & E. Raubold (Eds.), *Thirteenth world computer congress 94* (vol. 2, pp. 597−604). North Holland: Elsevier Science Publishers B.V.

Raman, H., & Chandramouli, V. (1996). Deriving a general operating policy for reservoirs using neural network. *Journal of Water Resources Planning and Management, 122*(5), 341−347.

Robertson, D., Bundy, A., Muetzelfeldt, R., Haggith, M., & Uschold, M. (1991). *Eco-logic: Logic-based approaches to ecological models.* MIT Press, ISBN 0-262-18143-6.

Rodrigues, F., & Pereira, F. C. (2020). Beyond expectation: Deep joint mean and quantile regression for spatiotemporal problems. *IEEE Transactions on Neural Networks and Learning Systems, 31*(12), 5377−5389.

Russo, A., Lind, P. G., Raischel, F., Trigo, R., & Mendes, M. (2015). Neural network forecast of daily pollution concentration using optimal meteorological data at synoptic and local scales. *Atmospheric Pollution Research*, *6*(3), 540−549.

Rybarczyk, Y., & Zalakeviciute, R. (2018). Machine learning approaches for outdoor air quality modelling: A systematic review. *Applied Sciences*, *8*(12), 2570.

Rykiel, E. J. (1989). Artificial intelligence and expert systems in ecology and natural resource management. *Ecological Modelling*, *46*(1−2), 3−8.

Rynk, R. F. (1992). *Computer-integrated monitoring and control of a composting process using an expert system*, Ph.D. dissertation. University of Massachusetts, Amhurst, MA.

Salazar, L., Nicolis, R., Ruggeri, F., Kisel'ák, J., & Stehlik, M. (2019). Predicting hourly ozone concentrations using wavelets and ARIMA models. *Neural Computing and Applications*, *31*(4), 4331−4340. Available from https://doi.org/10.1007/s00521-018-3345-0.

Sanchez-Marrè, M., Cortes, U., R-Roda, I., Poch, M., & Lafuente, J. (1997). This issue: Machine learning and adaptation in WWTP through case-based reasoning. *Microcomputers in Civil Engineering*, *12*(4), 251−266.

Sangüesa, R., & Burrell, P. (2000). Application of Bayesian network learning methods to wastewater treatment plants. *Applied Intelligence*, *13*(1), 19−40.

Sasikumar, K., & Mujumdar, P. P. (1998). Fuzzy optimization model for water quality management of river system. *Journal of Water Resources Planning and Management*, *124*(2), 79−84.

Savic, D. A., & Walters, G. A. (1997). Genetic algorithms for least cost design of water distribution networks. *Journal of Water Resources Planning and Management*, *123*(2), 67−77.

Sazonova, L., & Osipov, G. (1998). Intelligent system for fish stock prediction and allowable catch evaluation. In U. Cortés, & M. Sànchez-Marrè (Eds.), *Binding Environmental Sciences and Artificial Intelligence (BESAI 98) Workshop* (pp. 161−176).

Scheffer, J. (2002). Data mining in the survey setting: Why do children go off the rails? *Research Letters in the Information and Mathematical Sciences*, *3*, 161−189.

Seguel, R. J., et al. (2012). Ozone weekend effect in Santiago, Chile. *Environmental Pollution*, *162*, 72−79.

Serra, P., Sànchez-Marrè, M., Lafuente, J., Cortés, U., & Sànchez-Marrè, M. (1994). Artificial Intelligence and Environmental Decision Support Systems 89 Poch, DEPUR: A knowledge-based tool for wastewater treatment plants. *Engineering Applications of Artificial Intelligence*, *7*(1), 23−30.

Shi, J. P., & Harrison, R. M. (1997). Regression modelling of hourly NOx and NO_2 concentrations in urban air in London. *Atmospheric Environment*, *31*(24), 4081−4094.

Shin, K. S., & Han, I. (1999). Case-based reasoning supported by genetic algorithms for corporate bond rating. *Expert Systems with Applications*, *16*(2), 85−95.

Singh, K. P., Gupta, S., & Rai, P. (2013). Identifying pollution sources and predicting urban air quality using ensemble learning methods. *Atmospheric Environment*, *80*, 426−437.

Sousa, S., et al. (2007). Multiple linear regression and artificial neural networks based on principal components to predict ozone concentrations. *Environmental Modelling and Software*, *22*(1), 97−103.

Stephanopoulos, G., & Han, C. (1996). Intelligent systems in process engineering: A review. *Computers & Chemical Engngineering*, *20*(6/7), 743−791.

Stock, M. (1989). *AI in process control*. New York: McGraw-Hill Book Company.

Sun, W., & Sun, J. (2016). Daily PM2.5 concentration predictionbased on principal component analysis and LSSVM optimized by cuckoo search algorithm [J]. *Journal of Environmental Management*, *188*, 144−152.

Sun, W., Zhang, H., Palazoglu, A., Singh, A., Zhang, W., & Liu, S. (2013). Prediction of 24-hour-average PM (2.5) concentrations using a hidden Markov model with different emission distributions in Northern California. *Science of the Total Environment*, *443*(3), 93−103.

Sundell, J., Levin, H., Nazaroff, W. W., & Cain, W. S. (2010). Ventilation rates and health: Multidisciplinary review of the scientific literature. *Indoor Air*, *21*(3), 191−204.

Sydow, A., Rose, H., & Rufeger, O. (1998). Sustainable development and integrated assessment. *Ercim News*, *34*(32).

Tan, S. S., & Smeins, F. E. (1996). Predicting grassland community changes with an artificial neural-network model. *Ecological Modelling*, *84*(1−3), 91−97.

Tan, P.-N., Steinbach, M., & Kumar, V. (2005). *Introduction to data mining*. Boston: Addison-Wesley.

Tanimoto, S. L. (1987). *The elements of artificial intelligence*. Rockvile: Computer Science Press.

Thomson, A. J. (1997). Artificial intelligence and environmental ethics. *AI Applications*, *11*(1), 69−73.

Thuraisingham, B. (1999). *Data mining: Technologies, techniques, tools, and trends*. New York: CRC Press.

Transportation Research Board of National Academies. (2007). *Transportation research circular: Artificial intelligence*. Transportation Research circular E-C113. http://www.TRB.org.

Ul-Saufie, A., Yahaya, A., Ramli, N., Awang, N., & Hamid, H. (2013). Future daily PM10 concentrations prediction by combining regression models and feedforward backpropagation models with principle component analysis (PCA). *Atmospheric Environment*, *77*, 621−630.

Vapnik, V. (1998). *Statistical learning theory*. New York: John Wiley & Sons.

Varis, O. (1997). Bayesian decision analysis for environmental and resource management. *Environmental Modelling and Software*, *12*(2−3), 177−185.

Vayssieres, M. (2000). Classification trees: An alternative nonparametric approach for predicting species distributions. *Journal of Vegetation Science*, *11*(5), 679−694.

Walker, R. (1993). Artificial intelligence. *Paper Maker*, *56*(3), 24−26.

Wang, Q., Liu, Y., & Pan, X. (2008). Atmospheric pollutants and mortality rate of respiratory diseases in Beijing. *Science of the Total Environment*, *391*(1), 143−148.

Wang, X., Bi, X., Sheng, G., & Fu, J. (2006). Chemical composition and sources of PM10 and PM2.5 aerosols in Guangzhou, China. *Environmental Monitoring and Assessment*, *119*(1−3), 425−439.

Watson, I. (1997). *Applying case-based reasoning: Techniques for enterprise systems (The Morgan Kaufmann Series in Artificial Intelligence)* (1st ed.). San Francisco: Morgan Kaufmann Publishers.

Wen, C.-H., & Vassiliadis, C. A. (1998). Applying hybrid artificial intelligence in wastewater treatment. *Engineering Applications of Artificial Intelligence*, *11*(6), 685−705.

Wong, C. J., MatJafri, M. Z., Abdullah, K., Lim, H. S., & Low, K. L. (2007). Temporal air quality monitoring using surveillance camera. In *IEEE* international geoscience *and* remote sensing symposium, IEEE.

Wong, F., & Tan, C. (1994). Hybrid neural, genetic, and fuzzy systems. In G. J. Deboeck (Ed.), *Trading on the edge*. New York: John Wiley.

Xu, X., & Ren, W. (2019). Prediction of air pollution concentration based on mRMR and echo state network. *Applied Sciences*, *9*(9), 1811.

Yang, X., Zhao, Z., Hua, R., Su, X., Ma, L., & Chen, Z. (2019). Simulation study on the influence of urban underground parking development on underlying surface and urban local thermal environment. *Tunneling and Underground Space Technology*, *89*, 133−150.

Ye, H., Nicolai, R., & Reh, L. (1998). A Bayesian−Gaussian neural network and its applications in process engineering. *Chemical Engineering and Processing*, *37*(5), 439−449.

Yu, L., Kang, N., Wang, W., Guo, H., & Ji, J. (2020). Study on the influence of air tightness of the building envelope on indoor particle concentration. *Sustainability*, *12*(5), 1708.

Yu, R., Yang, Y., Yang, L., Han, G., & Move, O. A. (2016). RAQ—a random forest approach for predicting air quality in urban sensing systems. *Sensors*, *16*(1), 86.

Zhang, B.-T., Ohm, P., & Mhlenbein, H. (1995). Water pollution with evolutionary neural trees. In *Artificial intelligence* and the *environment* (IJCAI-95) *workshop* (pp. 32−40).

Zhang, Q., & Stanley, S. J. (1997). Forecasting raw-water quality parameters for the North Saskatchewan River by neural network modeling. *Water Research*, *31*(9), 2340−2350.

Zhao, H., Zhang, J., Wang, K., et al. (2011). A GA-ANN model for air quality predicting. In *2010 International computer symposium (ICS2010)*. IEEE.

Zhu, J., Zurcher, J., Rao, M., & Meng, M. Q.-H. (1998). An on-line wastewater quality predication system based on a time-delay neural network. *Engineering Applications of Artificial Intelligence*, *11*(6), 747−758.

Zhu, Y., Hinds, W. C., Krudysz, M., Kuhn, T., Froines, J., & Sioutas, C. (2005). Penetration of freeway ultra-fine particles into indoor environments. *Journal of Aerosol Science*, *36*(3), 303−322.

Intelligent systems in air pollution research: a review

**Ali Sohani[1], Mohammad Hossein Moradi[2], Krzysztof Rajski[3], Yousef Golizadeh Akhlaghi[4],
Mitra Zabihigivi[2], Uwe Wagner[2], and Thomas Koch[2]**

*[1]Lab of Optimization of Thermal Systems' Installations, Faculty of Mechanical Engineering-Energy Division, K.N.
Toosi University of Technology, Tehran, Iran [2]Institute of Internal Combustion Engines, Karlsruhe Institute of
Technology, Karlsruhe, Germany [3]Wroclaw University of Science and Technology, Faculty of Environmental
Engineering, Wroclaw, Poland [4]EPSRC National Centre for Energy Systems Integration School of Engineering,
Urban Sciences Building, Newcastle University, Newcastle, United Kingdom*

Introduction

Our life is heavily dependent on the air. Air is not only necessary for human to stay alive, it is also required for a large number of processes, including photosynthesis, combustion, and transportation by aircraft. According to statistics released by the World Health Organization (WHO, 2020), around 4 million people lose their lives annually due to exposure to polluted air. Therefore controlling air quality and finding ways to make it clean are serious tasks facing engineering scientists.

The quality of air is dependent on different factors, including the number of substances in it. These include water vapor (H_2O), carbon dioxide (CO_2), methane (CH_4), carbon monoxide (CO), ozone (O_3), sulfur dioxide (SO_2), nitrogen dioxide (NO_2), and particulate matter (PM). Among all these, there are three that have the greatest contributions. They are NO_2, O_3, and PM.

The growing concerns about air pollution have motivated researchers to conduct several studies for providing better ways to monitor air quality, assessment, and its mitigation (Siciliano et al., 2020). Among the research work, developing artificial intelligence and data-centric methods for prediction and clustering in the different fields related to air pollution has been a hot topic, which is reviewed here.

This research work is organized in a way that, initially, a short description of the atmosphere is presented in the section "The structure of the atmosphere," and then, the most important air contaminants are introduced in the section "Different contaminants in the air." Next, a literature review is carried out in the section "Tropospheric ozone (O_3)." Then, research work is described to illustrate the application of an artificial neural network (ANN) for forecasting NO_2 and PM_{10} for the city of Cologne, Germany, in the section "Nitrogen dioxide (NO_2)."

Current Trends and Advances in Computer-Aided Intelligent Environmental Data Engineering.
DOI: https://doi.org/10.1016/B978-0-323-85597-6.00002-1

The definition of atmosphere

Historically, the word "atmosphere" is composed of two Greek words: "atmo" meaning vapor and "sphere" which refers to a spherical region, and is used to describe the gaseous volume around us, and which is one of the five elements that the Earth is made of. The Earth's system is made of the following five items, as shown in Fig. 4.1 (Wyche & Smallbone, 2020a):

Lithosphere: The solid part that covers the Earth core is called the lithosphere. The outer portions of the mantle and the crust belong to this (Cooper et al., 2017).

Biosphere: The biosphere consists of humans, animals, insects, plants, and all living microorganisms and macroorganisms, and abiotic substances by which they obtain their required energy and other materials they require (Mencuccini et al., 2019).

Hydrosphere and cryosphere: These refer to the liquid and solid phases of water in the Earth, respectively (Levy et al., 2018).

Atmosphere: This is the air volume in our surroundings (Kosyakov et al., 2020).

The Earth—space interface: This is between the atmosphere and the region with the vacuum in space.

The structure of the atmosphere

Based on the temperature level, the atmosphere is itself divided into layers, as depicted in Fig. 4.2. They are described here, starting from the lowest part.

Troposphere: This is the closest part of the atmosphere to the ground. We are living in that region, and the most of the emissions coming from human activity is confined to that layer. A huge portion of the air mass is related to the troposphere, and the temperature falls gradually with an increase in altitude (Brune et al., 2020).

Stratosphere: This is the second layer after the troposphere. In contrast to the first layer, here the temperature starts to increase with altitude, which comes from the ozone there, at around 15—30 km

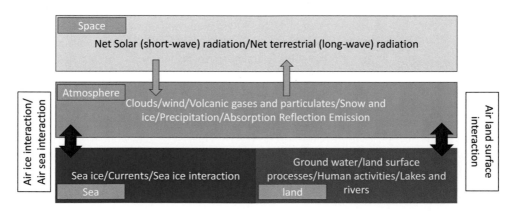

FIGURE 4.1

A graphical representation of the five elements which the Earth is made of.

Thermosphere (85–600 km thickness)

Mesosphere (35 km thickness)

Stratosphere (35 km thickness)

Troposphere (8–14 km thickness)

FIGURE 4.2

Different layers of the atmosphere.

from ground level. The ozone in the stratosphere blocks the harmful ultraviolet radiation from reaching the Earth, while it helps to emit the heating energy. The ozone in the stratosphere, which is beneficial for all living organisms on Earth, should not be confused with that in the troposphere. The latter is one of the main contributors to air pollution, as will be further discussed in detail (Domeisen et al., 2019). The mass above the middle of this layer is only 1% of the atmosphere's mass, which means the main part, that is, 99%, of the mass of the atmosphere is in troposphere and the lower part of the stratosphere (Wyche & Smallbone, 2020a).

The mesosphere is the third layer of the atmosphere from the Earth. In that region, temperature declines again while there are also high-speed winds (Becker & Vadas, 2018).

The mosphere is located immediately after the mesosphere. This is the region where ions are made through photoionization of the ultraviolet part of the received radiation from the sun.

Different contaminants in the air

When the concentration of some materials in the air increases, the air becomes "polluted." There are different contaminants in the air and herein a short description is given about the formation methods of the most important ones, and the most significant harmful effects they have. It should be noted that, in the literature, the contaminants can be categorized into primary and secondary emissions. The primary emissions refer to materials that have direct harmful effects on humans, plants, and animals. On the other hand, the secondary emissions are those that react with other materials, and the reactants of their reaction leads to damage to human health, resources, and ecosystems.

Tropospheric ozone (O_3)

An ozone molecule is composed of three oxygen atoms, as illustrated in Figs. 4.3 and 4.4. In the stratosphere, there are O_3 molecules that absorb the ultraviolet part of solar radiation which is harmful for humans. The concentration of O_3 in the troposphere is naturally low. However, due to burning fossil fuels and some other activities, NO_2 and volatile organic compounds (VOCs) are released. In the presence of the solar radiation, they react, and O_3 is formed in the troposphere. In contrast to stratospheric ozone, the tropospheric O_3 can damage the human body and cause several serious issues, including respiratory problems. The important point about the tropospheric O_3 is that more ozone molecules is produced when higher solar radiation is received. Therefore, the amount of this contaminant is higher during spring and summer, when people are more active and breathe more rapidly.

Nitrogen dioxide (NO_2)

There are different types of nitrogen oxide (NO_x), among which NO_2 is one of the most important contaminants. In organic fuels, including oil, and especially coal, NO_2 is found, and during the combustion process, it is released into the atmosphere. In addition, NO_2 is one of the gases produced during a number of industrial processes, such as welding, food manufacturing, and construction.

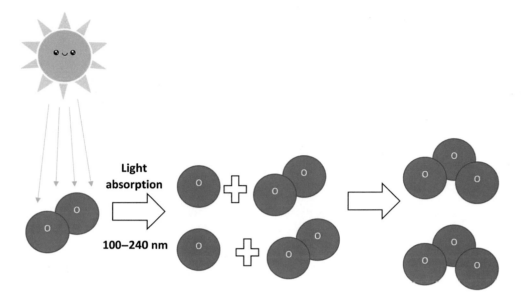

(A)

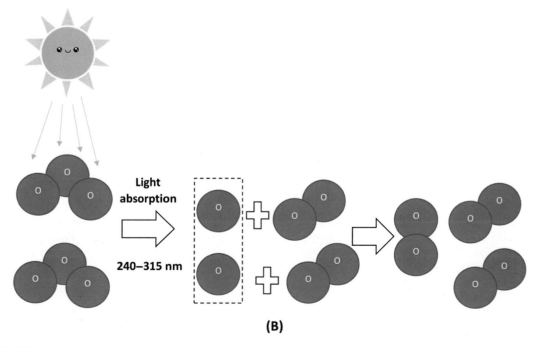

(B)

FIGURE 4.3

Stratospheric O$_3$ (A) formation and (B) destruction.

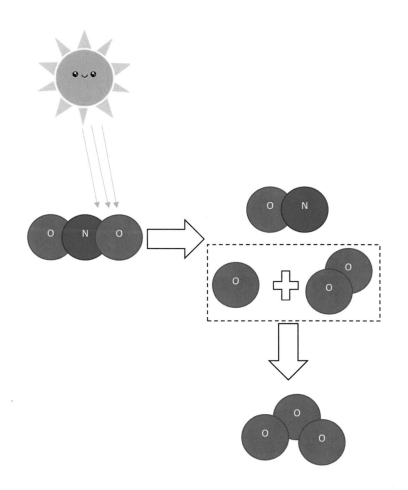

FIGURE 4.4

Formation of atmospheric O_3.

The high concentration of NO_2 in the atmosphere has a harmful impact on vegetation, and reduces the productivity level of plants. In addition, it leads to fading of the colors of fabrics and surfaces. NO_2 also poses problems to the capability of blood to carry oxygen, which leads to issues such as headache, tiredness, vertigo, blue color of skin, difficult breathing, and even death. Moreover, as indicated in Fig. 4.5, NO_2 contributes to the formation of other contaminants, such as tropospheric ozone.

Particulate matter

In addition to the gases such as NO_2 and tropospheric O_3, there are also some tiny solid particles and liquid droplets that are carried by the air. These are known as particulate matter (PM). In the literature on air pollution, there are two major groups of particulate matter: PM_{10} and $PM_{2.5}$. PM_{10}

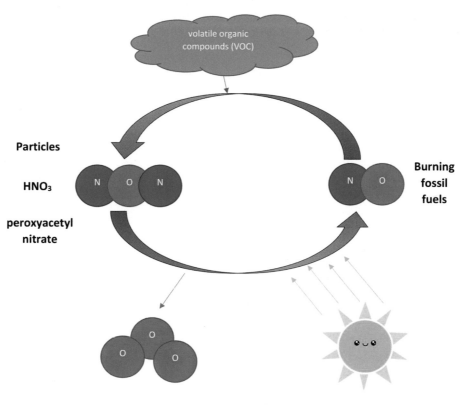

FIGURE 4.5

A schematic of the formation of NO_2 and its relation to other contaminants.

is particulate matter whose diameter is equal to or less than 10 μm, while $PM_{2.5}$ covers that with a diameter below or equal to 2.5 μm. PM_{10} comes from sources such as crushing operations, road and natural dusts, agricultural processes, and winds blowing across sands. Incomplete combustion in technologies such as engines, power plants, and biomass systems has the greatest contribution to forming $PM_{2.5}$. To obtain a better insight, in Fig. 4.6 the dimensions of $PM_{2.5}$ and PM_{10} are compared with human hair and sand.

PM enters the body by inhalation. Between PM_{10} and $PM_{2.5}$, the latter is more dangerous as it is able to travel deeper, reaching the lungs and causing serious problems in breathing, arrhythmia, and heart attacks. The results of some recent studies have also proven that exposure to PM over a long time can contribute also to low birth weight.

Carbon monoxide and carbon dioxide

Fossil fuels contain carbon atoms. When they take part in the combustion process, carbon atoms react with the air in the atmosphere. If combustion is carried out completely, that is, in the presence

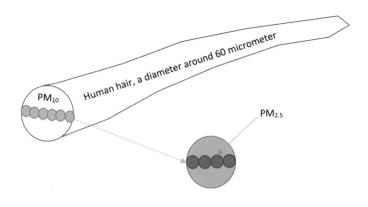

FIGURE 4.6

Comparing dimensions of PM_{10} and $PM_{2.5}$ with human hair.

of enough O_2, CO_2 is released. Otherwise, CO is formed. In addition, CO_2 is taken into account as a byproduct in the manufacturing processes of some materials like cement.

CO_2 causes a greenhouse effect. It traps the received radiation from the sun, which leads to warming of the troposphere air and the production of tropospheric O_3.

Despite the low levels of CO_2 not having a considerable impact on the human body, higher levels lead to a decreased oxygen level in the blood. When the oxygen level in the blood is reduced, problems such as fast and irregular heartbeat, headache, vomiting, and vertigo can result. In the worst cases, death can occur. It is also worth mentioning that CO_2 is transformed to O_2 during photosynthesis, and is improving vegetation (in addition to lowering the burning of fossil fuels by switching to other possibilities such as renewable energy sources) could be taken into account as a practical way to decrease the concentration of CO_2.

Sulfur dioxide

Besides nitrogen and carbon, fossil fuels also contain sulfur. In the combustion process, sulfur reacts with oxygen, which results in the formation of SO_2. Like NO_2, SO_2 can contribute to forming air contaminants, such as tropospheric O_3, sulfate aerosols, and PM. Furthermore, during rainfall, SO_2 is dissolved in water, leading to the formation of H_2SO_4 and hence acid rain.

Review of the literature

Because of their straightforward and high prediction accuracy, data-centric and artificial intelligence tools have been widely utilized to estimate the concentration of different contaminants in the air. This section provides a short description of some recently conducted studies.

Cabaneros et al. (2017) took advantage of ANN to find the concentration of NO_2 in London, United Kingdom. Their prediction approach was able to estimate the amount of contaminant in the air over a 24-hour period in the future. They compared the accuracy of ANN with other possible methods, including the stepwise regression method (SRM) and regression trees.

Mohebbi et al. (2019) provided a tool to predict the NO emission level using ANN. Shiraz City, which is located in Iran, was chosen as the case study, and a special type of dynamic neural network, called the nonlinear autoregressive exogenous type (NARX), was selected to give greater accuracy. The training process was done by employing data gathered from 2005 to 2008 while short-time prediction was followed as the goal of modeling. The prediction accuracy of NARX was compared with the conventional feedforward network, which demonstrated the superiority of NARX.

The concentration of NO_2 in the air of Algeciras Bay, Spain, was predicted using ANN in the study conducted by Van Roode et al. (2019). That study utilized the information recorded in 14 stations to generate a map of pollution. Creating these maps was done using two methods. One was the inverse distance weight approach, while the other was the least absolute shrinkage and selection operator method. The evaluation showed that the latter offered better performance than the former.

A machine learning method, which is called long short-term memory (LSTM), was employed by Awan et al. (2020) for estimation of the traffic flow. Their model gave the atmospheric conditions, in addition to CO, NO, NO_2, NO_x, and O_3 as the inputs. Having developed the model for Madrid, Spain, some ways to improve the traffic were suggested, and the impact of using them was evaluated by employing the LSTM model.

LSTM was also used in the investigation of Xayasouk et al. (2020) for prediction of $PM_{2.5}$ and PM_{10} for the capital of South Korea (Seoul). There, LSTM and deep autoencoder approaches were employed, while the input data for training the network were extracted from 25 stations in the city over a 3-year period. The provided prediction method was used for 10-day forecasting.

Kristiyanti et al. (2020) performed a research work to obtain the air quality status in Jakarta, Indonesia, which has one of the highest amounts of contaminants in the air throughout the year in the world. Their ANN model had five inputs and one output. The inputs were the concentration of NO_2, CO_2, O_3, PM_{10}, and SO_2 in the air. The output was the air quality status, which would be either good, moderate, harmful, or very harmful.

Bi et al. (2020) provided ANN models to simulate the combustion process and determine the amount of produced emissions for the combination of a fuel that was obtained by a combination of biomass and waste from a coal-mining process. The data gathered through the infrared spectroscopy process were utilized as the input for developing models. Among 21 developed topologies, a feedforward ANN, consisting of two hidden and one output layer, was obtained as the modeling tool.

Machine learning approaches have been also utilized to predict the impact of air pollution on mortality and morbidity rates. One example of such studies was the investigation carried out by Kachba et al., where ANN was employed to determine both mentioned criteria for the region of Sao Paolo, Brazil, in South America. In the developed model of the authors of that study, the impact of CO, NO_2, O_3, PM, and SO_2 concentrations on the rate of the respiratory problems was studied, while the amount of purchased fuel, roads characteristics, and life of vehicles were taken into account also. The findings of that study showed that the extreme learning machine approach and Echo state ANN were the best data-centric tools for prediction of morbidity and mortality rates, respectively (Kachba et al., 2020).

Some other research works are reported and described in Table 4.1. In this table, some key information about each study is indicated.

Table 4.1 Review of some studies that have been carried out to predict the amount of contaminants in polluted air.

Study	Prediction resolution	Input parameters			Separate error analysis for different subregions of the input parameters?	The reported range for the coefficient of determination (R^2)	
		Time	Meteorological characteristics	Maximum values of emissions on the day before prediction		NO_2	PM_{10}
Nidzgorska-Lencewicz (2018)	Hourly	✗	✓	✗	No	N.A.	0.805−0.825
Park et al. (2018)	Hourly	✓	✓	✗	No	N.A.	0.63−0.79
Yeganeh et al. (2018)	Hourly	✗	✓	✗	No	0.82	N.A.
Cujia et al. (2019)	Daily	✓	✗	✗	No	N.A.	0.362−0.689
Tzanis et al. (2019)	Hourly	✓	✓	✗	No	N.A.	0.64−0.71
Sethi and Mittal (2019)	Hourly	✓	✓	✗	No	N.A.	0.481−0.734
Valput et al. (2019)	Hourly	✗	✓	✗	No	0.20−0.57	N.A.
Gu et al. (2021)	Hourly	✓	✓	✗	No	Less than 0.8	N.A.
Shishegaran et al. (2020)	Hourly	✓	✓	✗	No	N.A.	N.A.
Fung et al. (2020)	Hourly	✓	✓	✗	No	N.A.	0.44−0.64
Cabaneros et al. (2020)	Hourly	✓	✓	✗	No	0.556−0.783	N.A.
Liu et al. (2019)	Hourly	✗	✓	✗	No	N.A.	N.A.
Turabieh et al. (2020)	Hourly	✓	✓	✗	No	0.10−0.85	0.67−0.83
Şahin et al. (2020)	Daily	✗	✓	✗	No	N.A.	N.A.
Fong et al. (2020)	Hourly	✗	✓	✗	No	N.A.	N.A.

In addition to the mentioned research works, there have been some excellent review studies that have classified and investigated the conducted studies. The papers published by Sanober and Usha Rani (2020), Araujo et al. (2020), Usmani et al. (2020), and Cabaneros et al. (2017) are good examples.

A new studied case

Based on the brief literature review conducted in the previous section, as well as the points found in the review investigations, two significant gaps could be identified, which are discussed in the following.

Ambient characteristics, including the temperature, relative humidity, air pressure, and wind velocity have been considered as the input parameters in the modeling. Sometimes, the day of the week and the time of day have been also added. However, the models have been developed in a way that one effective factor has not been considered as an input. This is a parameter that describes the level of emissions at the beginning of the prediction period. This means that the developed models work in a way that they assumed the amount of pollution in the future as being the same as the time period of the employed training data. This is a big shortcoming. The emission levels do not remain constant over this time as the level of emission varies by defining more strict emission targets and the corresponding developing novel technologies (Koch et al., 2019; Koch & Tocdter, 2018; Maniatis et al., 2019a; Maniatis et al., 2019b; Moradi et al., 2017; Wagner, 2018). Some other sources, such as changes in the road traffic, can also make a contribution to the variation of emissions.

As an example of the recently defined exhaust emission standards, Euro 6 Standard for cars could be given. Comparing the values of the produced NO_2 in the years 2006 (when Euro 4 was effective) and 2019 (when the standard Euro 6 was being imposed) at urban measuring stations in Germany demonstrates a more than 50% decrease in the annual average for some locations (The Federal Environment Agency. The Environmental Data for Germany, 2020).

In other words, if a model in the literature has been trained based on the data in 2006, it had accurate prediction until the emission level in the air was in the same range for that year. Therefore it does not provide a precise estimation in 2019. Moreover, the fact that several models in the literature have not been able to provide an accurate prediction for the values around the peak in the hourly profiles, as indicated in the review paper of Cabaneros et al. (2019), they could be originated from neglecting the input parameters that are considered here, and have not been taken into account in the previous studies.

Furthermore, as the literature review demonstrates, only one value for each of the error-related criteria, such as the coefficient of determination (R^2) and mean absolute error (MAE) have been given. This means that such a value represents the prediction accuracy for the "whole" range of input parameters. Although it has provided a good insight into the prediction of the whole data, it does not provide information about the prediction accuracy of the model in different ranges of the input parameters. Despite having a good "average" for the whole range, a model could have a relatively high error rate for a range of input parameters. Additionally, as reviewing the literature has shown, in the research works that have presented a model for hourly estimation, the accuracy has been usually moderate.

Therefore the present research work is done in this part as the next move in the investigations in the field, in which ANN models for hourly prediction of NO_2 and PM_{10}, as two main emissions in the air, are developed. The recorded data using high-tech measurement devices at a station in Cologne, Germany, were used in addition to the ambient characteristics and day of the week, and the maximum amount of pollution in the day before modeling was also considered as an input parameter. In that way, the model would be able to perform accurately when the produced emission level changed for the aforementioned reasons. Therefore it would have enough flexibility for future predictions. This is the primary novelty of this work.

In addition to presenting the error values when all the data are considered, the errors for different ranges of input parameters are also presented. This provides the ability to answer the question "Whether the model provides precise estimation in different subregions or not?" and if it is not, the places in which the accuracy should be enhanced will be found. Moreover, the possibility of a better evaluation of the model is provided in that way. This item also achieves a high accuracy which can be considered as the second novelty of this study.

Research methodology

The employed machine learning method

There are a variety of structures for an ANN. Among them, the cascade forward backpropagation type is chosen. In a cascade forward ANN, as the name suggests, the neurons in each layer do not only have a connection with the neurons in the preceding layer but also obtain one signal from the layers before the preceding layer. The developed models with this type of neural networks in previous studies showed excellent results. For modeling, the MATLAB software program is used as one of the most powerful means for this purpose. For more details about the working principle of an ANN, the published literature, including the previous studies of the research team in which ANN has been employed for modeling HVAC systems, like Sohani et al. (2017), Moradi et al. (2017), Sohani et al. (2016b), and Sohani et al. (2020) should be referred to.

The investigated city

With a population of 1,087,000 inhabitants, Cologne is the largest city in the Rhine Region and the fourth largest in Germany. Having more than 20 big companies, the city also is one of the main industrial centers in Europe. Therefore air pollution is a serious issue for this highly populated industrial city.

The data recording during 1 year, from January 1, 2019 to December 31, 2019, at station Clevischer Ring (DENW211), Cologne, Germany, and published in The Federal Environment Agency. The Environmental Data for Germany (2020) was employed as the source of data for model development [as mentioned in literature, such as Cabaneros et al. (2019), data from air pollution in 1 year is enough to provide highly accurate models for annual predictions]. As indicated in

The Federal Environment Agency (2020), the data have been gathered using high-accuracy measuring devices.

Input and output parameters

Developing models are carried out for each day separately. Modeling is done by taking seven effective parameters as the inputs:

1. *Time*,
2−5. *The meteorological variables*, and
6 and 7. *The maximum values of the emission concentration on the day before starting prediction*: The highest values of concentration for NO$_2$ and PM$_{10}$ on the previous day of prediction are selected as the input parameters for modeling.

The input and output parameters are also introduced in Table 4.2.

Error-related criteria

As an important stage in the evaluation of a model, error-related criteria should be considered; only if a model enjoys an acceptable range of error-related criteria, can it be introduced as suitable for prediction.

Therefore, and for the sake of providing a comprehensive error analysis, five key error-related criteria are chosen for investigation. The first is the coefficient of determination (R^2) that is determined from Eq. (4.1) (Sohani et al., 2021):

$$R^2 = 1 - \frac{\sum_{i=1}^{num_{data}} (Y_i - \hat{Y}_i)^2}{\sum_{i=1}^{num_{data}} (Y_i - \overline{Y})^2} \tag{4.1}$$

Table 4.2 A summary of the input and output parameters in modeling by artificial neural network.

Input or output	Type of variable	Variable
Input	Time of year	Time
	Meteorological characteristics	Air temperature
		Air relative humidity
		Wind speed
		Air pressure
	Air pollutant concentration before forecasting	The maximum values of the PM$_{10}$ concentration on the day before starting the prediction
		The maximum values of the NO$_2$ concentration on the day before starting the prediction
Output	Air pollutant concentration at the investigated time	PM$_{10}$ concentration at the investigated time
		NO$_2$ concentration at the investigated time

The second and third error parameters employed for error analysis are MAE and root mean square error (RMSE). Eqs. (4.2) and (4.3) present their methods of calculation, respectively (Sohani et al., 2016a):

$$MAE = \frac{\sum_{i=1}^{num_{data}} |Y_i - \hat{Y}_i|}{num_{data}} \tag{4.2}$$

$$RMSE = \sqrt{\frac{\sum_{i=1}^{num_{data}} (Y_i - \hat{Y}_i)^2}{num_{data}}} \tag{4.3}$$

In Eqs. (4.1–4.3), Y and $\hat{Y}$ are the actual and estimated values and num_{data} also represents number of employed data for model development. Moreover, the subscript i shows the data series number. By dividing by the mean, the normalized parameters can be obtained from Eqs. (4.4) and (4.5), which are considered as the fourth and fifth parameters (Sayyaadi & Modeling, n.d.).

$$NMAE = \frac{MAE}{\overline{Y}} \tag{4.4}$$

$$NRMSE = \frac{RMSE}{\overline{Y}} \tag{4.5}$$

Results and discussion

The specifications and validation of the developed models

The models were developed using the MATLAB software program for working days, that is, from Monday to Friday. The specifications of the developed models for different working days are indicated in Table 4.3. For valuation of the models, the comparisons between the measured and predicted data for 1 sample week (120 hours) are shown in Figs. 4.7 and 4.8. The data are for 1 week in January (from Monday to Friday). It must be mentioned that the employed data for validation in Figs. 4.7 and 4.8 had not been used for model development. (It should be noted that validation here means the validation of a simulation method, like the one done for numerical approaches, and is different than the validation process during the development of an ANN.)

From Figs. 4.7 and 4.8, it can be seen that the developed models are capable of predicting highly dynamic changes in emissions at different times and different conditions. In addition to the trend, even small fluctuations can be predicted by the developed models. Moreover, the problem of not providing an accurate prediction around the peak values in the previous investigations, which was discussed in the introduction, has been solved by employing the developed models, as observed in Figs. 4.7 and 4.8. Figs. 4.7 and 4.8 also imply that there are several peaks at different times, which comes from various issues, like traffic (e.g., around 8 a.m. each day). It highlights the fact

Table 4.3 Characteristics of the developed ANN models (*ANN*, Artificial neural network).

Number of hidden layers	Number of neurons in hidden layers	Activation function in hidden layers	Activation function in output layer
2	15–9	Tangent sigmoid-tangent sigmoid	Linear transfer

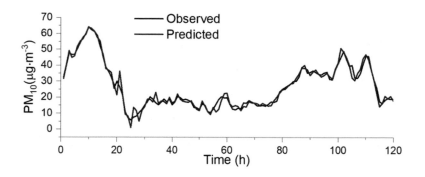

FIGURE 4.7

Comparing the prediction ability of the developed ANN models and the data used for their validation for PM_{10} (*ANN*, artificial neural network).

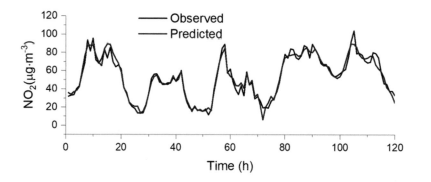

FIGURE 4.8

Comparing the prediction ability of the developed ANN models and the data used for their validation for NO_2 (*ANN*, artificial neural network).

that releasing emissions should be investigated on an hourly basis, and in the hourly investigation, the hour of the day should be considered as an input.

Uncertainty of different models

The values of the error-related criteria for the developed models also are shown in Table 4.4. The results show the high accuracy of the developed models. The average MAE for the different days (the average for the MAE values from Monday to Friday) is 4.2 $\mu g/m^3$ for NO_2 and 2.4 $\mu g/m^3$ for PM_{10}. Furthermore, the average R^2 for prediction of NO_2 and PM_{10} are 0.904 and 0.911, respectively, which are up to 10% higher than for the developed models from other studies (their values are around 0.8).

Table 4.4 Uncertainty of different models.

Day	Model	R^2 (-)	NRMSE (-)	RMSE ($\mu g/m^3$)	NMAE (-)	MAE ($\mu g/m^3$)
Monday	NO_2	0.911	0.135	6.154	0.096	4.404
	PM_{10}	0.931	0.164	3.619	0.101	2.224
Tuesday	NO_2	0.908	0.124	5.997	0.087	4.221
	PM_{10}	0.921	0.155	3.66	0.105	2.487
Wednesday	NO_2	0.908	0.13	6.158	0.091	4.303
	PM_{10}	0.916	0.18	4.266	0.099	2.339
Thursday	NO_2	0.917	0.124	5.767	0.079	3.7
	PM_{10}	0.936	0.156	3.451	0.091	1.997
Friday	NO_2	0.911	0.125	5.993	0.091	4.365
	PM_{10}	0.813	0.27	6.06	0.14	3.137
Average	NO_2	0.911	0.127	6.014	0.089	4.199
	PM_{10}	0.904	0.185	4.211	0.107	2.437

NMAE, *normalized mean absolute error;* NRMSE, *normalized root mean square error;* MAE, *mean absolute error;* RMSE, *root mean square error.*

Analyzing error for smaller ranges of the input parameters

To better assess how accurately the ANN models are in different ranges of the input parameters, the prediction errors were analyzed more precisely in smaller ranges of the input parameters. For this purpose, the range for each input parameter is divided into four parts, which have the same length, and the errors in the prediction of PM_{10} and NO_2 are presented for them individually. In addition to the normalized MAE for each range, the probability is also presented.

Furthermore, some other graphs, like Fig. 4.9B, are also plotted. In such figures, the x axis is the absolute error of NO_2 (in $\mu g/m^3$), the y axis is the absolute error of PM_{10} (in $\mu g/m^3$), and the color maps show the value for each input parameter. In those figures, x and y axes are restricted to an absolute error level of 5 $\mu g/m^3$ to specify the range in which the developed models are very accurate. In other words, they show in which spectrum of the input data the models can deliver precise results.

Time: As Fig. 4.9A demonstrates, time is a parameter that has almost the same probability in different ranges. This means that for each range, there are enough data to be trained in the model development. Moreover, based on Fig. 4.9B, in the whole spectrum of time, the developed model works well.

Temperature: According to Fig. 4.10A, more than 70% of that is distributed between 5.3°C and 24.2°C. In addition, less than 10% of the data has a temperature above 24.2°C. As a result, some data in the temperature range of 24.2°C–33.7°C are used to build the ANN model, which could be a reason for decreasing the precision in that limit. The same observation can be seen in Fig. 4.10B, where the blue and green colors that represent the range between 5.3°C and 24.2°C are dominant. It should be also noted that despite having low probability in the temperature range below 5.3°C, the prediction error for that range is in an acceptable range. This shows that only in some ranges with a low probability, does the error have an upward trend, not all.

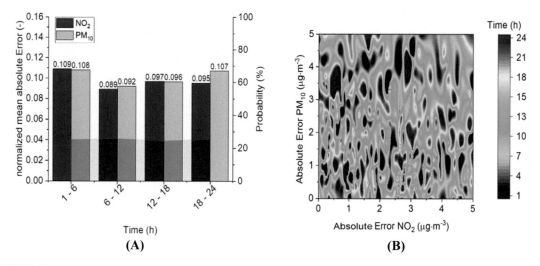

FIGURE 4.9

Investigating the accuracy of the developed ANN models for prediction of data in different subregions of time (time of the day): (A) NMAE and probability; (B) the color maps (*ANN*, artificial neural network; *NMAE*, normalized mean absolute error).

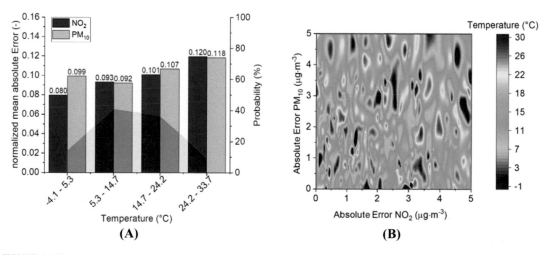

FIGURE 4.10

Investigating the accuracy of the developed ANN models for prediction of data in different subregions of the ambient temperature: (A) NMAE and probability; (B) the color maps (*ANN*, artificial neural network; *NMAE*, normalized mean absolute error).

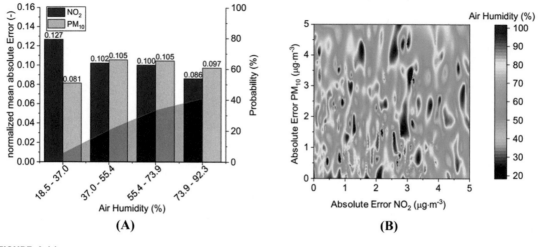

FIGURE 4.11

Investigating the accuracy of the developed ANN models for prediction of data in different subregions of the ambient relative humidity: (A) NMAE and probability; (B) the color maps (*ANN*, artificial neural network; *NMAE*, normalized mean absolute error).

Relative humidity: Following a similar method as for the temperature, the range that has a lower probability, that is, the range from 18.5% to 37.0%, has a relatively higher error level compared to the other ranges, as per Fig. 4.11A. The point also is confirmed using Fig. 4.11B, in which the corresponding colors to this range rarely appear. It is worth mentioning that despite having a higher error level, the normalized mean absolute error (NMAE) for this range is still in a very acceptable range, which is 0.127 and 0.081 for NO_2 and PM_{10}, respectively.

Wind speed: The results shown in Fig. 4.12A reveal that, like previously investigated input parameters, in the areas where the number of training data is low, that is, from the wind speed of 3.3 to 4.4 m/s, the accuracy of the models is also low. For that reason, there are only a few red points in Fig. 4.12B. In addition to having only a small amount of data for high values of wind speed, further error sources can occur, such as whirl up, which could cause extraordinary values of PM_{10} and increase the prediction errors up to 60%.

Air pressure: Most parts of Fig. 4.13B are covered by colors close to green, which shows that a large part of the accurate predictions belongs to the range around 996−1022 mbar, where the data probability is also high, as Fig. 4.13A shows. However, there should not be any concerns about increasing the error in the range outside the mentioned limit, that is, the values of 983−996 mbar, since the probability is very low.

The maximum concentration of PM_{10} from the day before starting prediction: As Fig. 4.14B shows, the density of blue is very high there. This color represents the limit between 21.6 and 51.7 µg/m³. As can be seen by evaluating Fig. 4.14A, this range has the highest probability also for this range. Despite having an almost reverse relationship with probability, the prediction accuracy remains in an acceptable range even in the range of 112.0−142.2 µg/m³, which has the lowest amount of data. For that range, the NMAEs in the prediction of NO_2 and PM_{10} are 0.142 and

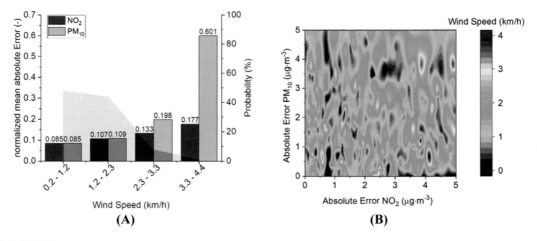

FIGURE 4.12

Investigating the accuracy of the developed ANN models for prediction of data in different subregions of the wind speed: (A) NMAE and probability; (B) the color maps (*ANN*, artificial neural network; *NMAE*, normalized mean absolute error).

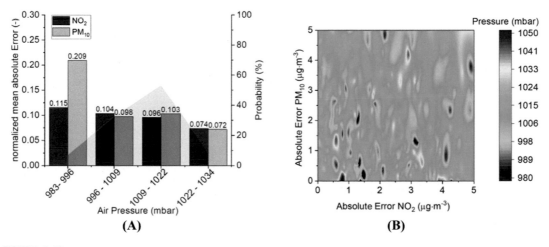

FIGURE 4.13

Investigating the accuracy of the developed ANN models for prediction of data in different subregions of the air pressure: (A) NMAE and probability; (B) the color maps (*ANN*, artificial neural network; *NMAE*, normalized mean absolute error).

0.154, respectively. This reveals that the provided models will perform very well when the emission level for polluting activities changes.

The maximum concentration of NO_2 from the day before starting prediction: The results of evaluating the error for the four divided subregions are shown in Figs. 4.15A and B. Based on

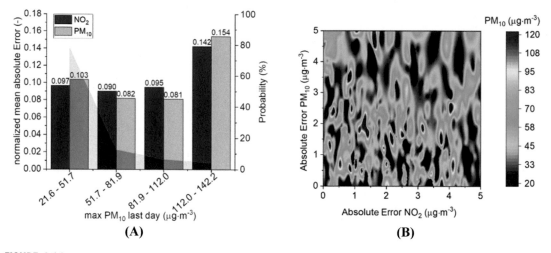

FIGURE 4.14

Investigating the accuracy of the developed ANN models for prediction of data in different subregions of the maximum concentration of PM_{10} from the day before starting prediction: (A) NMAE and probability; (B) the color maps (*ANN*, artificial neural network; *NMAE*, normalized mean absolute error).

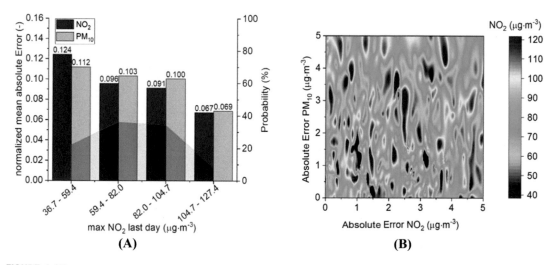

FIGURE 4.15

Investigating the accuracy of the developed ANN models for prediction of data in different subregions of the maximum concentration of NO_2 from the day before starting prediction: (A) NMAE and probability; (B) the color maps (*ANN*, artificial neural network; *NMAE*, normalized mean absolute error).

Fig. 4.15A, except for the range between 104.7 and 127.4 $\mu g/m^3$, that is, the highest range for this parameter, the other have high probability values. For that range, as Fig. 4.15A demonstrates, NMAE values are 0.067 and 0.069 for the concentration of NO_2 and PM_{10}. In addition, the NMAE for the prediction of the aforementioned emissions does not exceed 0.124 and 0.112. This point, in addition to other results discussed here, highlights the fact that the presented models have very accurate prediction in almost the whole range of the subregions for the input parameter. Especially for the concentration of NO_2 and PM_{10}, which represents the amount of the released emissions at the time of modeling, the developed models work very well, which shows that the developed models offer high flexibility to changes in emission production. This means that they could be employed for long-term precise estimation of emission levels.

Conclusions

The conducted research in this chapter has led to finding two important outcomes:

In some subregions, although the prediction error remained in an acceptable range, it was relatively greater than for other. This was a result of different issues, as discussed. The most important was the much smaller probability of data in a range than others, such as air pressure in the range of 983−996 mbar. This highlighted the necessity for error analysis for different subregions. In other words, as has been usually done, the error analysis should not be limited to giving the values of the error-related criteria for the whole range, and to be completely sure, the values for subregions should also be provided.

When the amount of contaminants in the air on the day before prediction was added to the input, the values of error-related criteria, including the coefficient of determination (R^2), were enhanced significantly compared to those reported in the literature. The developed models for the prediction of NO_2 and PM_{10} offered R^2 values of 0.911 and 0.904, respectively, which are higher than the corresponding values in previous studies. It has been shown that to achieve more accurate hourly prediction, having inputs from the amount of emission on the day before the prediction is necessary. Furthermore, by adding the parameters describing contaminant levels before starting the prediction as inputs, the models will be able to provide precise prediction in the following years, when the levels of the released emissions change.

References

Araujo, L. N., Belotti, J. T., Alves, T. A., Tadano, Y. D. S., & Siqueira, H. (2020). Ensemble method based on artificial neural networks to estimate air pollution health risks. *Environmental Modelling and Software*, *123*, 104567. Available from https://doi.org/10.1016/j.envsoft.2019.104567.

Awan, F. M., Minerva, R., & Crespi, N. (2020). Improving road traffic forecasting using air pollution and atmospheric data: experiments based on LSTM recurrent neural networks. *Sensors (Switzerland)*, *20*(13), 1−21. Available from https://doi.org/10.3390/s20133749.

Becker, E., & Vadas, S. L. (2018). Secondary gravity waves in the winter mesosphere: Results from a high-resolution global circulation model. *Journal of Geophysical Research: Atmospheres*, *123*(5), 2605−2627. Available from https://doi.org/10.1002/2017JD027460.

Bi, H., Wang, C., Lin, Q., Jiang, X., Jiang, C., & Bao, L. (2020). Combustion behavior, kinetics, gas emission characteristics and artificial neural network modeling of coal gangue and biomass via TG-FTIR. *Energy*, *213*, 118790. Available from https://doi.org/10.1016/j.energy.2020.118790.

Brune, W. H., Miller, D. O., Thames, A. B., Allen, H. M., Apel, E. C., Blake, D. R., Bui, T. P., Commane, R., Crounse, J. D., Daube, B. C., Diskin, G. S., DiGangi, J. P., Elkins, J. W., Hall, S. R., Hanisco, T. F., Hannun, R. A., Hintsa, E. J., Hornbrook, R. S., Kim, M. J., & Wolfe, G. M. (2020). Exploring oxidation in the remote free troposphere: Insights from atmospheric tomography (ATom). *Journal of Geophysical Research: Atmospheres*, *125*(1). Available from https://doi.org/10.1029/2019JD031685, e2019JD031685.

Cabaneros, S. M. L. S., Calautit, J. K. S., & Hughes, B. R. (2017). Hybrid artificial neural network models for effective prediction and mitigation of urban roadside NO_2 pollution. *Energy Procedia*, *142*, 3524−3530. Available from https://doi.org/10.1016/j.egypro.2017.12.240.

Cabaneros, S. M., Calautit, J. K., & Hughes, B. R. (2019). A review of artificial neural network models for ambient air pollution prediction. *Environmental Modelling and Software*, *119*, 285−304. Available from https://doi.org/10.1016/j.envsoft.2019.06.014.

Cabaneros, S. M., Calautit, J. K., & Hughes, B. (2020). Spatial estimation of outdoor NO2 levels in Central London using deep neural networks and a wavelet decomposition technique. *Ecological Modelling*, *424*, 109017.

Cooper, C. M., Miller, M. S., & Moresi, L. (2017). The structural evolution of the deep continental lithosphere. *Tectonophysics*, *695*, 100−121. Available from https://doi.org/10.1016/j.tecto.2016.12.004.

Cujia, A., Agudelo-Castañeda, D., Pacheco-Bustos, C., & Teixeira, E. C. (2019). Forecast of PM10 time-series data: a study case in Caribbean cities. *Atmospheric Pollution Research*, *10*(6), 2053−2062. Available from https://doi.org/10.1016/j.apr.2019.09.013.

Domeisen, D. I. V., Garfinkel, C. I., & Butler, A. H. (2019). The teleconnection of El Niño Southern oscillation to the stratosphere. *Reviews of Geophysics*, *57*(1), 5−47. Available from https://doi.org/10.1029/2018RG000596.

Fong, I. H., Li, T., Fong, S., Wong, R. K., & Tallón-Ballesteros, A. J. (2020). Predicting concentration levels of air pollutants by transfer learning and recurrent neural network. *Knowledge-Based Systems*, *192*, 105622.

Fung, P. L., Zaidan, M. A., Timonen, H., Niemi, J. V., Kousa, A., Kuula, J., et al. (2020). Evaluation of white-box versus black-box machine learning models in estimating ambient black carbon concentration. *Journal of Aerosol Science*, 105694.

Gu, J., Yang, B., Brauer, M., & Zhang, K. M. (2021). Enhancing the evaluation and interpretability of data-driven air quality models. *Atmospheric Environment*, *246*, 118125.

Kachba, Y., de Genaro Chiroli, D. M., Belotti, J. T., Alves, T. A., de Souza Tadano, Y., & Siqueira, H. (2020). Artificial neural networks to estimate the influence of vehicular emission variables on morbidity and mortality in the largest metropolis in South America. *Sustainability (Switzerland)*, *12*(7), 2621. Available from https://doi.org/10.3390/su12072621.

Koch, T., & Toedter, O. (2018). Eine bewertuung des dieselmotorischen umwelteinflusses. In *10 Internationales AVL forum abgas- und partikelemissionen*, Ludwigsburg, Germany, February 20, 2018.

Koch, P.J., Bertsch, M., Disch, C., Heinz, A., & Notheis, D. (2019). Soot formation in combustion. In *SAE international 2019* (pp. 63−82).

Kosyakov, D., Latkin, N. V., Pokryshkin, S., Berzhonskis, V., Polyakova, O., et al. (2020). Peat burning—an important source of pyridines in the earth atmosphere. *Environmental Pollution*, *266*, 115109.

Kristiyanti, A., Purwaningsih, E., Nurelasari, E., Al Kaafi, A., & Umam, A. H. (2020). Implementation of neural network method for air quality forecasting in Jakarta region. *Journal of Physics: Conference Series*, *1641*, 012037.

Levy, J. S., Fountain, A. G., Obryk, M. K., Telling, J., Glennie, C., Pettersson, R., Gooseff, M., & Van Horn, D. J. (2018). Decadal topographic change in the McMurdo Dry Valleys of Antarctica: thermokarst subsidence, glacier thinning, and transfer of water storage from the cryosphere to the hydrosphere. *Geomorphology*, *323*, 80−97. Available from https://doi.org/10.1016/j.geomorph.2018.09.012.

Liu, H., Wu, H., Lv, X., Ren, Z., Liu, M., Li, Y., et al. (2019). An intelligent hybrid model for air pollutant concentrations forecasting: Case of Beijing in China. *Sustainable Cities and Society*, *47*, 101471.

Maniatis, P., Erforth, D., Wagner, U., & Koch, T. (2019a). *Development of valve train configurations optimized for cold start and their effect on diesel soot emission. SAE technical papers (Vols. 2019, Issue September)*. Society of Automotive Engineers. Available from https://doi.org/10.4271/2019-24-0161.

Maniatis, P., Wagner, U., & Koch, T. (2019b). A model-based and experimental approach for the determination of suitable variable valve timings for cold start in partial load operation of a passenger car single-cylinder diesel engine. *International Journal of Engine Research*, *20*(1), 141−154. Available from https://doi.org/10.1177/1468087418817119.

Mencuccini, M., Manzoni, S., & Christoffersen, B. (2019). Modelling water fluxes in plants: From tissues to biosphere. *New Phytologist*, *222*(3), 1207−1222. Available from https://doi.org/10.1111/nph.15681.

Mohebbi, M. R., Karimi Jashni, A., Dehghani, M., & Hadad, K. (2019). Short-term prediction of carbon monoxide concentration using artificial neural network (NARX) without traffic data: Case study: Shiraz City. *Iranian Journal of Science and Technology—Transactions of Civil Engineering*, *43*(3), 533−540. Available from https://doi.org/10.1007/s40996-018-0210-4.

Moradi, M. H., Sohani, A., Zabihigivi, M., & Wirbser, H. (2017). A comprehensive approach to find the performance map of a heat pump using experiment and soft computing methods. *Energy Conversion and Management*, *153*, 224−242. Available from https://doi.org/10.1016/j.enconman.2017.09.070.

Nidzgorska-Lencewicz, J. (2018). Application of artificial neural networks in the prediction of PM10 levels in the winter months: A case study in the Tricity agglomeration. *Poland. Atmosphere*, *9*(6), 203.

Park, S., Kim, M., Kim, M., Namgung, H.-G., Kim, K.-T., Cho, K. H., et al. (2018). Predicting PM10 concentration in Seoul metropolitan subway stations using artificial neural network (ANN). *Journal of Hazardous Materials*, *341*, 75−82.

Şahin, F., Işik, G., Şahin, G., & Kara, M. K. (2020). Estimation of PM10 levels using feed forward neural networks in Igdir. *Turkey. Urban Climate*, *34*, 100721.

Sanober, S., & Usha Rani, K. (2020). *Review on neural network algorithms for air pollution analysis*, . *Advances in intelligent systems and computing* (1054, pp. 353−365). Springer. Available from https://doi.org/10.1007/978-981-15-0135-7_34.

Sayyaadi, H., & Modeling. (n.d.). Assessment, and Optimization of Energy Systems.

Sethi, J. K., & Mittal, M. (2019). A new feature selection method based on machine learning technique for air quality dataset. *Journal of Statistics and Management Systems*, *22*(4), 697−705. Available from https://doi.org/10.1080/09720510.2019.1609726.

Shishegaran, A., Saeedi, M., Kumar, A., & Ghiasinejad, H. (2020). Prediction of air quality in Tehran by developing the nonlinear ensemble model. *Journal of Cleaner Production*, *259*, 120825.

Siciliano, B., Dantas, G., da Silva, C. M., & Arbilla, G. (2020). The updated Brazilian national air quality standards: A critical review. *Journal of the Brazilian Chemical Society*, *31*(3), 523−535. Available from https://doi.org/10.21577/0103-5053.20190212.

Sohani, A., Hoseinzadeh, S., Samiezadeh, S., & Verhaert, I. (2021). Machine learning prediction approach for dynamic performance modeling of an enhanced solar still desalination system. *Journal of Thermal Analysis and Calorimetry*. Available from https://doi.org/10.1007/s10973-021-10744-z.

Sohani, A., Sayyaadi, H., & Hoseinpoori, S. (2016a). Modélisation et optimisation à objectifs multiples d'un refroidisseur évaporatif indirect à écoulements croisés à cycle M en utilisant le réseau neuronal de type GMDH. *International Journal of Refrigeration*, *69*, 186−204. Available from https://doi.org/10.1016/j.ijrefrig.2016.05.011.

Sohani, A., Sayyaadi, H., Hasani Balyani, H., & Hoseinpoori, S. (2016b). A novel approach using predictive models for performance analysis of desiccant enhanced evaporative cooling systems. *Applied Thermal Engineering*, *107*, 227−252. Available from https://doi.org/10.1016/j.applthermaleng.2016.06.121.

Sohani, A., Shahverdian, M. H., Sayyaadi, H., & Garcia, D. A. (2020). Impact of absolute and relative humidity on the performance of mono and poly crystalline silicon photovoltaics; applying artificial neural network. *Journal of Cleaner Production*, *276*, 123016. Available from https://doi.org/10.1016/j.jclepro.2020.123016.

Sohani, A., Zabihigivi, M., Moradi, M. H., Sayyaadi, H., & Hasani Balyani, H. (2017). A comprehensive performance investigation of cellulose evaporative cooling pad systems using predictive approaches. *Applied Thermal Engineering*, *110*, 1589−1608. Available from https://doi.org/10.1016/j.applthermaleng.2016.08.216.

The Federal Environment Agency. The environmental data for Germany, 2020. https://www.umweltbundesamt.de.

The World Health Organization (WHO). The statistics about the air pollution < https://www.who.int/health-topics/air-pollution#tab=tab_1 > ; Accessed on December 8, 2020. (2020).

Turabieh, H., Sheta, A., Braik, M., & Kovač-Andrić E. (2020). A layered recurrent neural network for imputing air pollutants missing data and prediction of NO 2, O 3, PM 10, and PM 2.5. Forecasting in Mathematics-Recent Advances, New Perspectives and Applications: IntechOpen

Tzanis, C. G., Alimissis, A., Philippopoulos, K., & Deligiorgi, D. (2019). Applying linear and nonlinear models for the estimation of particulate matter variability. *Environmental Pollution*, *246*, 89−98.

Usmani, R. S. A., Saeed, A., Abdullahi, A. M., Pillai, T. R., Jhanjhi, N. Z., & Hashem, I. A. T. (2020). Air pollution and its health impacts in Malaysia: A review. *Air Quality, Atmosphere and Health*, *13*(9), 1093−1118. Available from https://doi.org/10.1007/s11869-020-00867-x.

Valput, D., Navares, R., & Aznarte, J. L. (2019). Forecasting hourly $${\hbox {NO} _ {2}}$$ NO 2 concentrations by ensembling neural networks and mesoscale models. *Neural Computing and Applications*, 1−12.

Van Roode, S., Ruiz-Aguilar, J. J., González-Enrique, J., & Turias, I. J. (2019). An artificial neural network ensemble approach to generate air pollution maps. *Environmental Monitoring and Assessment*, *191*(12), 727. Available from https://doi.org/10.1007/s10661-019-7901-6.

Wagner, U. (2018). Combustion engines—today and in the future. 9th VERT Forum.

Wyche, K., & Smallbone, K. (2020a). Introducing the key concepts of air quality management. University of Brighton. https://www.youtube.com/watch?v = BERM_1ktwpc.

Xayasouk, T., Lee, H. M., & Lee, G. (2020). Air pollution prediction using long short-term memory (LSTM) and deep autoencoder (DAE) models. *Sustainability (Switzerland)*, *12*(6), 2570. Available from https://doi.org/10.3390/su12062570.

Yeganeh, B., Hewson, M. G., Clifford, S., Tavassoli, A., Knibbs, L. D., & Morawska, L. (2018). Estimating the spatiotemporal variation of NO2 concentration using an adaptive neuro-fuzzy inference system. *Environmental Modelling & Software*, *100*, 222−235.

ESTABLISH—a decision support system for monitoring the quality of air for human health

Mihaela Balanescu[1], Andrei Birdici[1], Iacob Crucianu[2], Alexandru Drosu[1], George Iordache[1], Adrian Sandu Pasat[1], Carmen Poenaru[1], and George Suciu[1]

[1]R&D Department, Beia Consult International, Bucharest, Romania [2]SIVECO Romania SA, Bucharest, Romania

Introduction

Outdoor air pollution is a major public health issue, leading to 4.2 million premature deaths worldwide (WHO, 2016) and half a million in the European Union (EU) in 2018 (EEA, 2019). The EU identifies seven main air pollutants (Koolen & Rothenberg, 2019): ammonia (NH_3), nitrogen oxides (NO_x), carbon monoxide (CO), and particulate matter (PM) with an aerodynamic diameter lower than 2.5 and 10 μm ($PM_{2.5}$ and PM_{10}), sulfuric oxides (SO_x), tropospheric ozone (O_3), and non-methane volatile organic compounds (NMVOCs). Ambient $PM_{2.5}$ air pollution has been of increasing public concern and was estimated to cause 2.9 million deaths and 69.7 million disability-adjusted life years in 2013 worldwide, in particular in China, Middle East, Europe, and the United States. Many studies have confirmed the associations between exposure to ambient $PM_{2.5}$ and acute and chronic adverse health effects (e.g., Feng et al., 2016; Chen et al., 2017; Santo Signorelli et al., 2019), including hospital admissions and mortality for cardiovascular (e.g., stroke, heart infarction, hypertension, and thrombosis) and respiratory diseases (asthma, chronic obstructive pulmonary disease), but also neonatal conditions (neonatal thrombosis, low birth weight).

At the EU level, the pollutants with the most critical effect on human health are PMs (mainly PM_{10} and $PM_{2.5}$) and NO_x who are specific to large urban agglomerations. Besides the already known health effects, $PM_{2.5}$ act as a carrier for various viruses (including COVID-19) and have an important impact on human health. A study performed by Harvard University shows that an increase of only 1 μg/m^3 in the $PM_{2.5}$ concentration is associated with a 15% increase in the COVID-19 death rate. Also, it has been shown that particulate air pollution contributed $\sim 15\%$ to COVID-19 mortality worldwide, 27% in East Asia, 19% in Europe, and 17% in North America (Pozzer et al., 2020). Moreover, a relationship between long-term exposure to NO_2 and coronavirus fatality was identified (Hahad et al., 2020).

Personal exposure is determined by the time spent in specific microenvironments and the concentrations in those microenvironments. People spend more than 85% of their time indoors (Klepeis et al., 2001). Thus the indoor environment is the main location in which exposures to ambient $PM_{2.5}$ occur. Overall indoor $PM_{2.5}$ concentrations are shaped by infiltration of outdoor $PM_{2.5}$ and additions from indoor sources (Adgate et al., 2007).

Current Trends and Advances in Computer-Aided Intelligent Environmental Data Engineering.
DOI: https://doi.org/10.1016/B978-0-323-85597-6.00005-7

Individual services, products, and solutions using environmental data and combining them with health data from other sources (such as wearable devices) need to be considered to improve the quality of life, reducing health costs, and supporting vulnerable groups such as the elderly or patients. In the ESTABLISH project a decision support system was developed that allows data acquisition from very heterogeneous sensor types. The ESTABLISH platform developed reliable alignment and implementation methods for self-awareness and self-adaptability, specific to the field of sensor data collection. They are based on the low-bandwidth networks of distributed, low-power devices.

Section "Scenario B—same type of equipment" presents several other platforms that try to combine physiological and environmental data. Section "ESTABLISH decision support system" is focused on presenting the ESTABLISH pilot study and user requirements. The architecture, data acquisition, integration, and visualization are addressed in the section "Deployment, data acquisition, and integration," while in the next section is presented the final form of the ESTABLISH platform. Conclusions and further works are presented in the final section.

Related work

According to the State of Health in the EU report (OCDE, 2019), life expectancy in Romania is among the lowest in the European Union, and the problems faced by the health system (high level of preventable deaths, low average doctor/person consultations, etc.) indicate significant possibilities for improving the situation at the national level. Primary care services are also underused, while emergency care is overused, even for minor health problems.

According to a recent study (Kim & Zuckerman, 2019), there are increasing numbers of indicators suggesting that the implementation of telemedicine on a large scale can significantly increase access to health care for vulnerable members of society, improve public health systems, and standardize the global health network. In Romania, most digital solutions developed for health are dedicated to fitness, weight loss, nutrition, general medical advice, or medical calls and scheduling medical sessions.

Of interest for this work are the existing wearable systems used in healthcare applications. For example, in this study (Andreu-Perez et al., 2015) are presented various implementation of sensors for monitoring the human physiology and behaviour. To conduct regular clinical tests, to monitor the progress of diseases, to make decisions about medical treatment, and to access past medical records, technical support is needed in functional medical environments. In these environments, the adoption of wearable systems and the creation of a medical experience that is more seamless is welcomed. Long-term disease management can be achieved by creating a distributed healthcare system that presents shared costs as described by Lanata et al. (2014). The performance of the flexibility (both longitudinal and temporal) of the medical examination is increased, and the work effort to continuously supervise the patients is reduced. The clinical tests can be integrated with the wearable systems to improve the management of a long-term wider medical system as discussed in Doty et al., (2015) and Saleem et al., (2017).

In this context, a platform for tailored rehabilitation programs is very much needed, and combining physiological and environmental data is an innovation in this domain. MediCall (MediCall,

2021) is an online platform supported by a private clinic, through which patients without a medical subscription can schedule online discussion sessions with doctors. The patient must create an account, after which they can choose the particular of interest and view the profiles and the program of doctors. The appointment is confirmed immediately after the online payment. MediHome (MediHome, 2021) is the option for patients with an existing medical subscription, and access is based on the subscriber code. Both services have a web version and a mobile application. Doxtar (Doxtar, 2021) is a telemedicine platform through which specialists and family doctors can offer online consultations to patients and operates based on a commission from doctors' receipts. The platform can be accessed both on the web and as a mobile application.

Doctor31 (Doctor31 2021) is a free mobile application that offers users the possibility to interpret media tests and obtain a medical preopinion based on completing an online questionnaire.

Status (Status, 2021) is an online application that supports the digitization of medical business. The application is available for doctors, patients (for interactions with doctors, updating medical data, etc.), healthcare providers (promoting services), and health insurance companies (facilitating interaction with the public). The application is accessible for a fee.

At the international level, the telemedicine solutions implemented vary depending on various factors, such as the level of financing of health systems, the regulations in force in each country, and possible restrictions on the international transfer of medical data. As a result, the digitization of health services is not homogeneous, and the success of technological solutions depends on the characteristics of the market to which they are addressed.

Doxy.me (Doxy.me, 2021) is a telemedicine platform for digitizing clinical trials and remotely establishing the patient's diagnosis. Clinical/physician staff can schedule video conferences with patients, and the login link is provided via email and text messages. The service is available for a fee. AMC Health (2021) provides telemedicine services to optimize the management of health services. The remote monitoring system ensures fast treatment and an effective communication experience for both patients and doctors or providers. The ChARM Health (2021) telemedicine streamlines the process of booking online consultations and eliminates long waiting times by providing an online medical reservation management system. Doctors can use the automatic calendar function to book time intervals and easily manage appointments.

VSee (VSee, 2021) is a telemedicine system used for the NASA space station, and is dedicated to reducing healthcare costs, increasing patients' access to health services, and increasing the efficiency of medical personnel. VSee offers simple, scalable telecare, with fast and secure communications, customized workflows for digital physician—patient interactions, integrations of medical devices and tools, and personalized patient experiences.

ESTABLISH pilot study: user requirements

The ESTABLISH pilot study developed in Bucharest, Romania, uses data from ambient sensors (air quality, atmospheric pressure, temperature, and humidity) and physiological and behavioral sensors (heart rate and respiratory rate, number of steps) to provide patients in clinical rehabilitation/keep fit programs with decision support tools related to behavior and treatment options. Therefore, for the pilot implementation, a 10 subjects' segment was selected by different gender and ages, different affections, and with different recovery plans. In the pilot study group different health affections were identified, such as for overweight, obesity, kyphosis, scoliosis, lumbar spine affections, rheumatoid arthritis, and lymphedema. The main objectives and recovery plan in addressing the previously mentioned affections are composed by weight loss, amelioration of spinal posture, an increase in spine flexibility, increasing muscle strength, improving breathing, and increasing lung ventilation, improving physical and mental health, and treating pain and inflammation. All of these are achieved through physical exercise and a good opportunity for multiple parameter monitoring is offered.

The ESTABLISH pilot's goals are to (1) monitor health parameters to constantly improve the health of the population through rehabilitation and spa care, specifically targeting the patient's functional aspects of integration in everyday life, environment, and work; (2) development of a decision support system and services based on the outdoor environment parameters and indoor location; and (3) to reduce operational costs and improve the quality of the services provided.

The pilot is held in collaboration with "Centrul Steluțelor", a support, counseling, and recovery center established by the MAME (Asociația, 2021), a nongovernmental organization (NGO) in which, annually, approximately 150 children with serious illnesses and children from low-income families receive free services such as medical information and guidance, individual and group psychological counseling, physiokinetic therapy, art therapy, and speech therapy. Within the center, both children and their families receive the support and attention they need to overcome more easily the crisis they are going through. The patients enrolled in the recovery programs coordinated by the Center expressed their agreement to participate in the ESTABLISH pilot (in person or through a tutor, as appropriate). Their participation in the ESTABLISH pilot involves wearing smart bracelets both during the recovery program and for the rest of the time to create a relevant history of their evolution through the recovery process.

The first step in the definition of the platform architecture was to establish the functionalities of the platform and to identify the potential improvements the services developed within it. Therefore, a workshop was organized with 25 participants including both patients and staff members from the center, and other medical therapists from different institutions. The workshop participants completed questionnaires concerning the perception of the air quality in their living area, risk population categories, perceived factors as main pollution sources and the major pollutants, information sources and channels and quality of the information available. Considering the data visualization components, the participants were asked to identify the visual elements that they would prefer for environmental data presentation (including for air quality). Data usability, platform access, and (if appropriate) the type of payment.

The statistics of the participants' age and gender distribution, the field of work, and their feedback considering the perception of the air quality in their living area are presented in Fig. 5.1.

About 45% of the participants considered that the air quality in their living area was moderate, while good or poor quality were described by around 22% of the participants. The pollution episodes are perceived as having a homogeneous distribution, with a higher perception during the evening (32%).

The study group (Fig. 5.2) identified the children, persons with respiratory diseases, and elderly as the categories with the highest risk from exposure to air pollutants. The perception of the main source of pollution was linked to transportation. The most significant indoor pollutant was the main dust, while outdoor pollutant identified was CO_2 emissions.

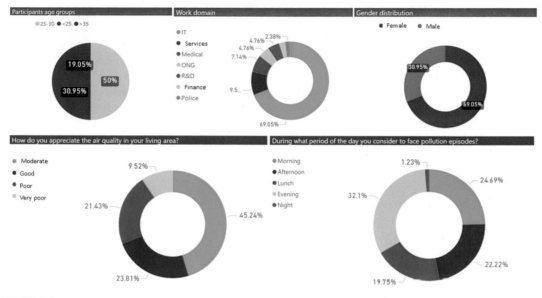

FIGURE 5.1

Presentation of the workshop results—group statistics and perception of the air quality.

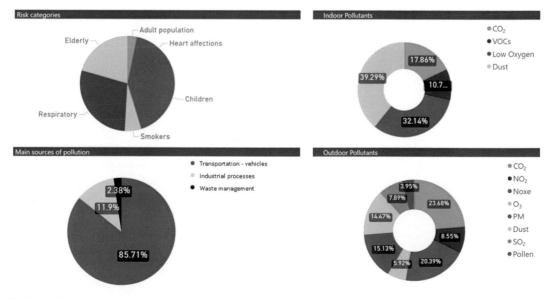

FIGURE 5.2

Presentation of the workshop results—risk categories, pollutants, and main sources.

The Internet was identified as the most important channel of communication for air quality information (64%), followed by mobile applications and social media (Fig. 5.3). The answers reveal that although the participants were concerned about the air quality and eager to be informed about it, they we not interested in the quality of the information that they received and would prefer to be informed mainly when pollution episodes occur or on a weekly basis.

Considering the development of the decision support component based on the outdoor environmental data, the participants identified the visual elements that they would prefer for air quality data presentation (Fig. 5.4).

In addition, we received positive feedback regarding the presentation of the ESTABLISH services, available within the ESTABLISH platform mockups. The data usability, platform access, and preferred type of payment were identified (Fig. 5.5).

The workshop was successful in having the opportunity to assess the end-users perspectives regarding air pollution phenomena and managed to identify the relevant methods to present air quality data in a meaningful and easy to assess way.

The main aspects retained after the workshop, further translated in the platform design, regarding the patient management service, having noted the usability concerns for managing patients' appointments and important notes and evaluations during the recovery session. To ease the data interpretation for both user categories (therapists and patients), the implementation of the visual representation of the decision support component according to initial designs was realized.

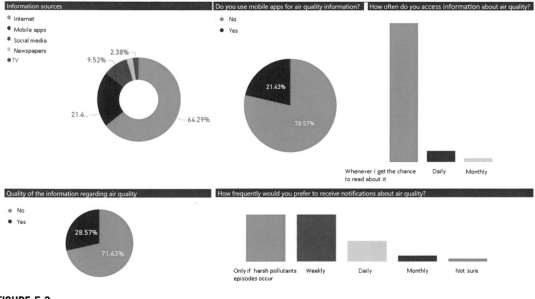

FIGURE 5.3

Presentation of the workshop results—communication channels.

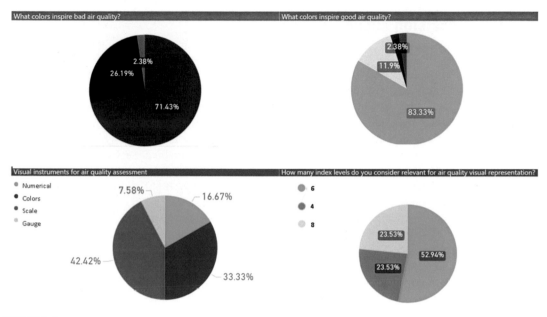

FIGURE 5.4

Presentation of the workshop results—design of visual instruments.

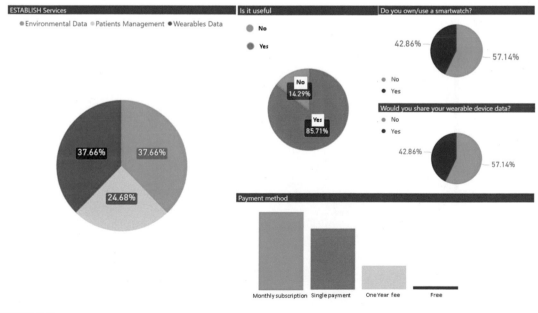

FIGURE 5.5

Presentation of the workshop results—ESTABLISH services.

ESTABLISH decision support system
ESTABLISH architecture

The conceptual architecture of the ESTABLISH platform was presented in Suciu et al. (2018) and is based on several development frameworks. It advanced a cloud architecture that allows data integration from various sources. This architecture generates several pieces of software (data collectors), thus overcoming the challenge of data heterogeneity. During the implementation phase, the ESTABLISH smart health platform was developed based on an informatic system that uses the Internet of Things and addresses a market segment in intelligent medical services, more precisely, therapists and patients that can benefit from the services available in the platform.

The applied architecture of the platform is presented in Fig. 5.6, highlighting the following software and hardware components.

A module for data acquisition from the environmental sensing devices that use several sensors (1.1), (1.2), (1.3), (1.4), (1.5), (1.6), (1.7), and (1.8) that allow the monitoring of the following parameters: relative humidity, air temperature, atmospheric pressure, suspended dust concentrations, and gaseous pollutant concentrations (SO_2, NO_2, CO, CO_2, and VOC).

A multiprotocol Gateway module (2.1): this allows the acquisition of data collected from sensors and ensures their transmission to the platform through Ethernet/4G/3G/GPRS communication protocols.

A middleware data transmission component (3.1), which enables the communication between the Gateway and the data persistence level within the ESTABLISH platform (4.1). The "Connectors" ensure the wearables data ingestion from the OEMs cloud through a REST API.

The decision support component: this is a module for processing the data collected from the sensors (5.1). The data collected from the sensors are stored in a database, they are analyzed through the decision support component to be further transmitted to the data presentation/visualization layer.

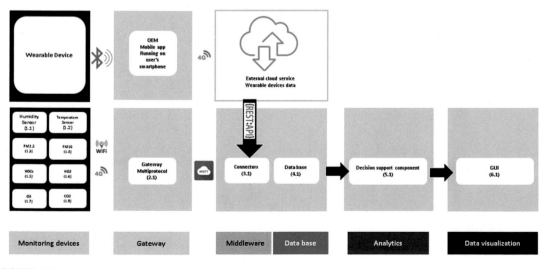

FIGURE 5.6

The architecture of the ESTABLISH platform.

The decision support component performs data processes based on the calculated values of a single composite air quality index that considers the concentration values of all air pollutants.

This index consists of two components: (1) the main component, supplied by the pollutant with the highest concentration compared to the limit values (color index—I_{color}) and (2) a secondary component determined by the values of the concentrations of the other pollutants (color intensity index—$I_{intensity}$). The way that this index is built is presented in the section "Visualization of the air quality index".

Deployment, data acquisition, and integration

Within the ESTABLISH pilot study the following monitoring devices were deployed to gather both environmental and physiological data:

OAQ#1 environmental sensing device, a Libelium Plug&Sense—Smart Cities Pro (SCP) station, is an outdoor air quality monitoring station that has the following sensors: temperature, relative humidity, pressure, PM_1, $PM_{2.5}$, PM_{10}, NO_2, CO, and O_3. The OAQ 1 device features a robust waterproof IP65 enclosure and uses a 4G communication module to send the data to cloud storage or a Gateway.

OAQ#2 is the second type of outdoor air quality monitoring station (an uRADMonitor City station). This OAQ device is equipped with the following sensors O_3, SO_2, NO_2, CO, PM_1, $PM_{2.5}$, PM_{10}, and comes in a rugged aluminum enclosure with a wall mounting support and communicates with the manufacturer cloud platform through a Wi-Fi module. The manufacturer offers a REST API to integrate the data with third-party applications.

An IAQ monitoring device is an indoor air quality monitoring station, which includes the following sensors: temperature, relative humidity, CO, NO_2, VOCs, and O_2. The IAQ device communicates with the Gateway through a Wi-Fi module.

The wearable device (a Garmin activity tracker) is a smartwatch designed for monitoring physical activities and collects physiological data such as heart rate, and other behavioral parameters like burned calories, steps, sleeping hours, etc.

Table 5.1 presents the specifications of the OAQ#1, OAQ#2, and IAQ monitoring devices with their parameters concerning air quality and the weather. In Fig. 5.7 the sensing equipment is deployed at the pilot's location, "Centrul Steluțelor."

Preliminary testing of sensors

Before being deployed, all the sensors were tested. As the PMs are sensitive to ambient conditions, a special study of the variability of the values of the measured parameter between the same type of equipment and between different equipment was performed. The measurement technique for the PM concentration enclosed in both types of equipment is an optical particle counter (OPC). The main characteristics and recommendation for the OPC technology include the following.

Advantages: real-time values with very high frequency; low investment and maintenance cost; and high flexibility considering deployment location.

Table 5.1 Device parameters for the monitoring devices (OAQ#1, OAQ#2, and IAQ).

Device/parameter	OAQ#1	OAQ#2	IAQ
Temperature	X	–	X
Relative humidity	X	–	X
Atmospheric pressure		–	X
CO		X	X
NO_2		X	X
CO_2	–	–	X
O_2	X	–	X
VOC	–	–	X
O_3	–	X	–
SO_2	–	X	–
PM_1	X	X	–
$PM_{2.5}$	X	X	–
PM_{10}	X	X	–

VOC, *Volatile organic compound.*

FIGURE 5.7

The sensing equipment deployed at the pilot's location.

Disadvantages: good or very good measurement precision; no existing standard for measurements.

Recommendations: management of air pollutant sources to reduce emissions; new insights concerning the connection between exposure and the effects of air pollutants on human health; used as a complementary network in support of the air quality reference network and to raise awareness.

The IoT equipment tested for measuring the PM_{10} and $PM_{2.5}$ concentrations were Libelium Plug and Sense SCP (Waspmote Plug&Sense, 2021) (SCP#1, SCP#2, SCP#3) and uRADMonitor (Technical, 2017) (uRAD). The testing was performed for 11 days, outdoors and in an urban environment. The testing scenarios and specification of the equipment are presented in Table 5.2 (Alphasense, 2021; Laser dust, 2016).

Scenario A—different type of equipment

The comparative analysis of PM concentrations was realized based on measurement performed for 11 days in October 2018. The results (Fig. 5.8) show that the $PM_{2.5}$ and PM_{10} concentrations follow almost the same variation curve. In addition, it can be seen that the values of the concentrations measured with uRAD equipment are lower than those measured with Libelium equipment (represented in the figure as average values).

The data obtained were statistically analyzed. The values of the main statistical parameters (Table 5.3) for the uRAD data series and the mean value of the Libelium equipment are homogeneous (with the lower mean value for uRAD). The values of Pearson correlation coefficients are significant, with the smallest value being registered between Libelium and uRAD equipment (Table 5.4).

Table 5.2 Scenario and IoT equipment (*IoT*, Internet of Things).				
IoT equipment	**Frequency of measurement**	**Sensor name**	**Scenario A—different type of equipment**	**Scenario B—same type of equipment**
Libelium Plug and Sense SCP	User selected/ 15 min	OPC-N2	Yes	Yes
uRADMonitor	1 min	Winsen ZH03A	Yes	No

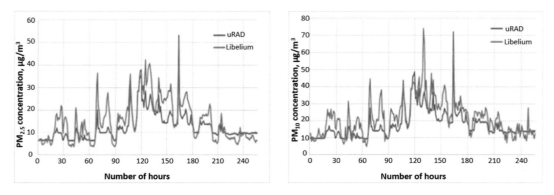

FIGURE 5.8

PMs concentration values registered in the monitoring period (*PM* Particulate matter).

Table 5.3 The values of the main statistical parameters for PM$_{2.5}$ and PM$_{10}$ measured concentrations.

Statistical parameter	PM$_{2.5}$ concentrations		PM$_{10}$ concentrations	
	uRAD	Libelium	uRAD	Libelium
Mean value	12.43	15.28	17.68	21.93
Median value	9.91	13.18	14.33	20.99
Standard deviation	6.24	9.35	8.29	10.89
Variation	38.93	87.49	68.86	118.79
Minimum value	6.20	3.43	9.39	4.95
Maximum value	53.36	49.30	72.11	74.23

Table 5.4 Prarson's correlation coefficient values for PM$_{2.5}$ and PM$_{10}$ concentrations.

	PM$_{2.5}$ concentration					PM$_{10}$ concentration			
	SCP#1	SCP#2	SCP#3	uRAD		SCP#1	SCP#2	SCP#3	uRAD
SCP#1	1				SCP#1	1			
SCP#2	0.989	1			SCP#2	0.905	1		
SCP#3	0.985	0.984	1		SCP#3	0.848	0.850	1	
uRAD	0.879	0.857	0.864	1	uRAD	0.804	0.791	0.803	1

The ANOVA method was used to evaluate the differences between the four datasets. The result of the F-test indicates that there are statistically significant differences between the measurements performed with the uRAD and with the Libelium equipment.

Scenario B—same type of equipment

In this scenario measured PM$_{2.5}$ and PM$_{10}$ concentrations were compared with the same type of equipment (Libelium Plug and Sense SCP). The data obtained showed little variation between PM$_{2.5}$ and PM$_{10}$ concentrations (Fig. 5.9).

The values of Pearson correlation coefficients are significant (the lower value is 0.803—Table 5.4). The ANOVA method was used to evaluate the differences between the three datasets. The result of the F-test indicates a high degree of homogeneity and reproducibility of the measurements made (differences between datasets are not statistically significant).

Data acquisition and integration from wearable devices

To access the data of the wearable device, a data acquisition module was built, based on Garmin Health API. Through this module the patients, who use Garmin smartwatches, can share their data (with third-party services) generated by Garmin activity trackers. The Garmin Health API allows

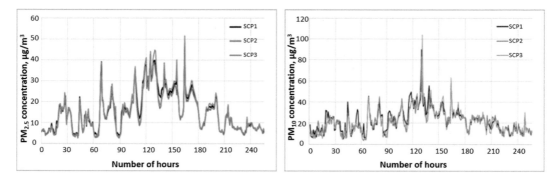

FIGURE 5.9

PM_{10} and $PM_{2.5}$ concentration values registered in the monitoring period.

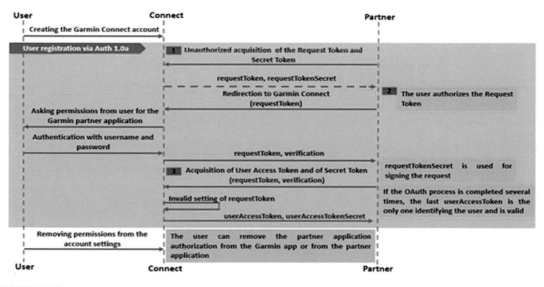

FIGURE 5.10

The authentication thread for Garmin ESTABLISH data acquisition component.

data retrieval through specific endpoints, and third-party services can access these endpoints when they need to obtain the users' data. The ESTABLISH third-party service is identified by a "client ID" (consumer key), while the request of the respective service to access the data is validated through the "client secret" (a token). The wearable data acquisition module is an application written in Python programming language and uses the Flask framework to implement the Garmin endpoints and REST architecture. In Fig. 5.10 are presented the threads for authenticating the ESTABLISH Garmin data acquisition module.

The ESTABLISH users (patients' category), who have Garmin smartwatches, can authorize data sharing with the ESTABLISH Garmin application through the ESTABLISH mobile

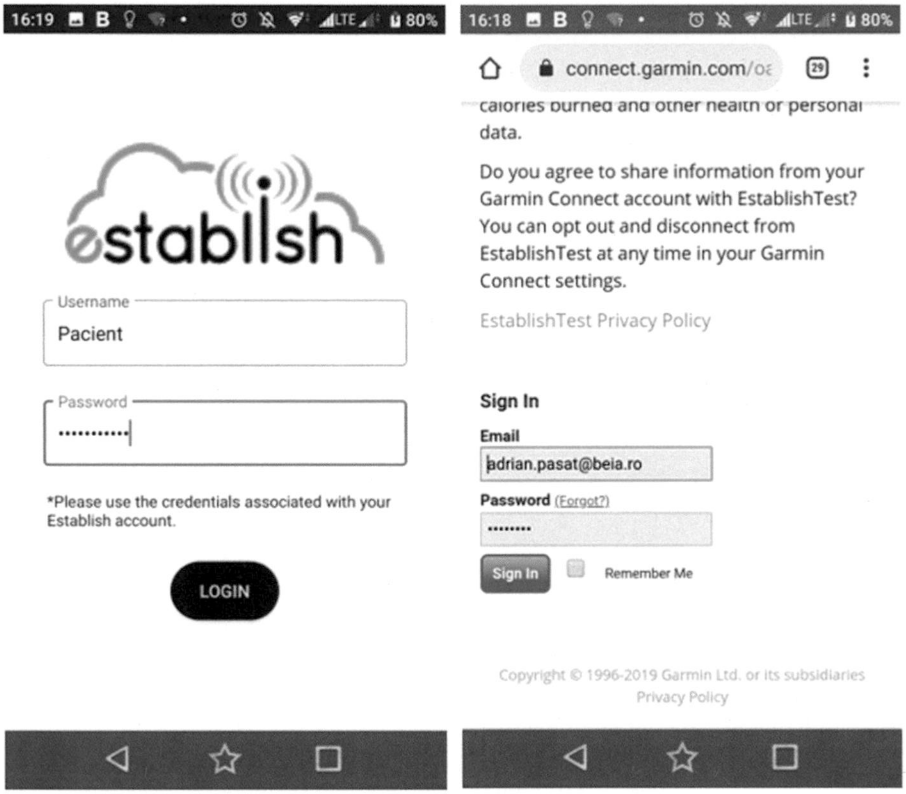

FIGURE 5.11

The ESTABLISH mobile application—presentation of the patients' authorization menu to allow Garmin data sharing.

application, see Fig. 5.11. From the mobile application, the patient accesses the "Agree" button to authorize the ESTABLISH Garmin application. After accessing the "Agree" button, the user is redirected to the ESTABLISH Garmin application page, which displays the generated tokens and the "Remove" button should the patient want to disable data sharing. After the authorization process is finalized, when the user synchronizes the Garmin smart device with the Garmin Connect mobile application, the data are passed on to the Garmin cloud. The ESTABLISH Garmin application sends a ping notification to the configured endpoints, and the message received on the callback URL receives the authentication data of Garmin users for whom the REST endpoints can be called, thus collecting new synchronized data. The response received by the HTTP GET requests is in the form of a JSON message, which is then parsed, and the new data are transmitted via the MQTT protocol to the ESTABLISH back-end platform using several topics.

The data presentation of the measurements acquired from Garmin devices is presented in the ESTABLISH platform presentation section.

Data acquisition and integration from environmental monitoring devices

The environmental data management flow process specific to the ESTABLISH pilot implementation consists of the following stages:

The OAQ#1 and IAQ monitoring devices transmit the measurements through 4G, respectively, from the Wi-Fi interface to the Meshlium Gateway (2.1). Once received in the Meshlium Multiprotocol Gateway, the data are stored in a MySQL database that ensures local persistence. Afterward, the data are parsed to the ESTABLISH back end, namely, the MQTT broker, using one of the Meshlium GW connectors.

The OAQ#2 device connects (via Wi-Fi) to a cloud platform that allows data access through a REST interface. The HTTP method used to acquire the data from the uRADMonitor Cloud is GET. Therefore, to ensure the integration of the OAQ#2 in the ESTABLISH back end, a NODE RED application was created that performs data acquisition by implementing at predefined intervals HTTP requests according to the REST API specifications. The received messages are then published to the MQTT broker, the main component of to ESTABLISH back end.

Visualization of the air quality index

The air quality index (AQI) is used to quantify air quality and the changes in pollution happening in the atmosphere. AQI is generally calculated for major air pollutants like ozone, carbon monoxide, nitrogen dioxide, and sulfur dioxide. By constantly monitoring the AQI, information about air quality is gathered and used to protect and improve personal health. AQI can be measured in different ways:

- Using a portable PM monitor (PM_{10}/$PM_{2.5}$) (IOTAP, Malmö University, 2016);
- Using an advanced sensory device that measures multiple parameters—PMs, VOCs (volatile organic compounds), temperature, humidity, and CO (e.g., Huma-i HI-150); and
- Using an "air-quality-meter" smartphone application that uses the device's camera to measure PM_{10}.

AQI can be estimated through algorithms. One example of such an algorithm is PM Nowcast. This was designed by the United States Environmental Protection Agency (USEPA) and is used for real-time reporting of the AQI for PM (PM10 or PM2.5) (AirNow, n.d.; Samir, 2018; Ricardo Energy & Environment, 2016; USEPA, 2020). Generally, PM Nowcast is calculated as:

$$Nowcast = \frac{\sum_{i=1}^{12} w^{i-1} c_i}{\sum_{i=1}^{12} w^{i-1}} \tag{5.1}$$

where c_i is PM concentrations registered over the previous 12 hours (c_1 being the most recent value) and w is calculated as:

$$w = \begin{cases} w* & \text{if } 1 - w* > \dfrac{1}{2}, \\ \dfrac{1}{2} & \text{if } 1 - w* \leq \dfrac{1}{2}. \end{cases} \tag{5.2}$$

Table 5.5 Categories of air quality based on concentration and indexes breakpoints.

C_{low}	C_{high}	I_{low}	I_{high}	Category
0	12	0	50	Good
12.1	35.4	51	100	Moderate
35.5	55.4	101	150	Unhealthy for sensitive groups
55.5	150.4	151	200	Unhealthy
150.5	250.4	201	300	Very unhealthy
250.5	350.4	301	400	Hazardous
350.5	500.4	401	500	Hazardous

$$w* = \frac{c_{max} - c_{min}}{c_{max}}, \tag{5.3}$$

where c_{max} and c_{min} are the maximum and the minimum values of the PM concentrations over the last 12 hours, respectively.

It is possible to determine AQI through the calculated PM Nowcast:

$$AQI = \frac{Nowcast - Clow}{C_{high} - C_{low}} \left(I_{high} - I_{low}\right) - I_{low}, \tag{5.4}$$

where: C_{low} is the concentration breakpoint that is $\leq$ Nowcast; C_{high} is the concentration breakpoint $>$ Nowcast; and I_{low} and I_{high} are the indexes breakpoints corresponding to C_{low} and C_{high}.

Considering the values of these parameters, a color code is defined in Table 5.5. The color code is a simple and easy-to-understand indicator that helps to evaluate the air quality in a certain location. This way users can assess if the air quality may be dangerous to them.

For correct interpretation of the colors (especially by typical users) it needs to be divided into two distinct groups: the sensitive population and the nonsensitive population. As air pollution can affect people differently, a wide range of parameters (e.g., age, lung diseases, and lung capacity) needs to be considered. In the mentioned "sensitive" category, people with heart and/or lung diseases, asthma, circulatory disorders, elderly people, and children may be included.

Transforming the measured AQI into a common and easy to use scale is a multistep process. First, the composed AQI is evaluated along with all the measured pollutants from the atmosphere. After that, it is translated into a color scheme so that any person in the area can understand the concentrations and act accordingly after they evaluate the risks. The algorithm implemented in the ESTABLISH platform is presented in detail in Svertoka et al. (2020).

ESTABLISH platform presentation

The ESTABLISH platform shows high potential to support the connection between patients and therapists, offering important benefits, as described below.

Therapists can monitor the recovery of patients through the tools of visualization of physiological data, having a new perspective on the evolution of the patient during the recovery program.

At the same time, through continuous monitoring of the recovery programs, therapists can ensure good observance of the medical protocol and can detect possible deviations from its correct use.

Patients have the prospect of a faster recovery, having a constant exchange of information and feedback from therapists regarding the development of the recovery program.

The platform allows its users to adapt faster and easier to the environment, through the decision support component, while considering the health and physical needs of each patient. This is done by timely awareness of the limitations that the physical and medical condition of each, based on the personalized profile which considers the psychological state, preferences, and behaviour (self-awareness and self-adaptations). The environmental and physiological sections are key components for the continuous monitoring of a patient's health.

The environmental section displays the environmental parameters collected by the monitoring stations and displays both messages of interest and a graph representing the AQI values of the previous 24 hours (Fig. 5.12).

The physiological section displays physiological data (Fig. 5.13) such as heart rate, number of steps taken, and calories, which are monitored using Garmin bracelets.

User guide for patients

The user account with the role of PATIENT is created to gain access to the private environment of the platform. The user authenticated as a PATIENT will be able to perform the following actions:

- View recommended activities;
- View available data in the platform; and
- Viewing activities is enabled by accessing the "My activities" button from the main menu. In this section, the patient can filter the results by date, if they wants to see the activities for a certain period of time.

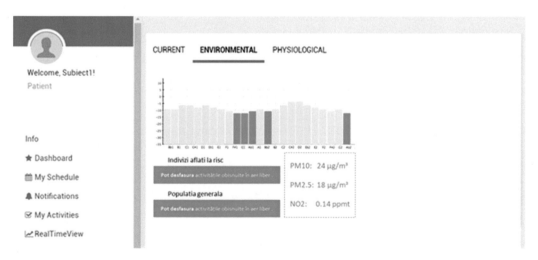

FIGURE 5.12

Environmental section of the ESTABLISH platform.

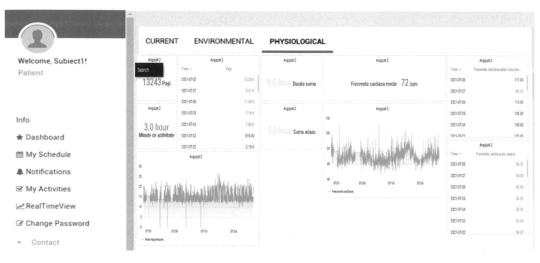

FIGURE 5.13

Physiological section of the ESTABLISH platform.

The user can also access each activity for more information, which includes the following lines:

- Title of the activity;
- Description of the activity;
- Contraindications, if applicable;
- Level of difficulty;
- Duration of the activity;
- The date on which the activity is scheduled; and
- The location where the activity will take place.

In this section, the user can add comments to the activity, with these being visible only to the user.

User guide for therapists

The user account with the role of THERAPIST is created to allow access to the private environment of the platform. The user logged in as a THERAPIST will be able to perform the following actions:

- View and add patients;
- Create and view activities for each patient;
- ESTABLISH the program for activities; and
- View available data in the platform.

Patients are viewed by accessing the "My Patients" page on the main menu. The THERAPIST user can add a new patient, view the entire list of patients, and edit the information of each patient. The "My Patients" section displays the complete list of patients along with an "Add new patient" button to add a new patient. Adding a new patient opens a new page where the patient data will be filled in, considering the necessary fields. The patient data that the physiotherapist user can enter into the platform are:

- Patient's name and surname;
- Phone number and email address;
- Home address;
- Age, height, weight, and sex;
- Diagnosis, followed by details;
- The connection data in the platform that will be sent to the patient; and
- The patient's Garmin account identification data.

The THERAPIST user can view and modify at any time the data saved in the profiles of their patients. This will be done by accessing a patient's name, which will open the user information page.

In this section, you can click the "Edit" button to edit the information, which will open a page similar to adding a new patient. In the "Patient Activities" section, the user can view the entire list of activities and filter it either by the patient's name or over a period of time.

By accessing the "Add new activity" button, the therapist can create a new activity in the section that opens, selecting the patient, the type of activity from a predefined list, where the fields "description" and "contraindications" will be filled in automatically.

If the required activity is not in the default list, it must be created separately by accessing "Settings Activities" in the main menu. In this section are presented all the predefined types of activities, which can be edited or further accessed through the "Add new activity" button to add a new activity. An activity includes a series of specific information, such as:

- Name of the activity;
- Recovery program;
- Description of the activity;
- Recommendations;
- Contraindications;
- Level of difficulty;
- Duration for carrying out the activity; and
- Pattern of repetition of the activity by the patient (per week, with the possibility of choosing a certain day for the activity).

In addition, in the "Add new activity" section, the date for carrying out the activity can be scheduled, which will later appear in the calendar in the "My Schedule" section for both the therapist and the patient.

Conclusions

The ESTABLISH platform is a system that combines different types of sensors with the purpose of improving the quality of life for different subjects. Various components, such as user requirements, data acquisition and integration in the platform, and architectural and user guides for platform usage are presented. Through the offered benefits (monitoring of the recovering process and program, permanent exchange of information and feedback), the ESTABLISH platform shows high potential to support the connection between patients and therapists with the achievement of a faster recovery of the patients. Future work will include extensive testing in relevant environments (i.e., health recovery and clinical rehabilitation centers) paving the road to reach the market.

Acknowledgments

This work has been supported by UEFISCDI Romania and MCI through projects ESTABLISH (contract no. 88/2016, project cod PN-III-P3-3.5-EUK-2016-0011), Wins@Hi (contract no. 96/2017, project cod PN-III-P3-3.5-EUK-2017-02-0038). In addition, part of the work was done under Mad@Work project (contract 18033/2020, EUREKA, ITEA Cluster).

References

Adgate, J. L., Mongin, S. J., Pratt, G. C., Zhang, J., Field, M. P., Ramachandran, G., & Sexton, K. (2007). Relationships between personal, indoor, and outdoor exposures to trace elements in PM2.5. *Science of the Total Environment*, *386*(1−3), 21−32.

AirNow. How is the NowCast algorithm used to report current air quality? (n.d.). Retrieved February 5, 2021, from <https://usepa.servicenowservices.com/airnow?id = kb_article_view&sys_kb_id = fed0037b1b62545040a1a7dbe54bcbd4>.

Alphasense. Optical particle counter. (n.d.). Retrieved from <http://www.alphasense.com/index.php/products/optical-particle-counter/>, on February 5, (2021).

AMC Health. (n.d.). Retrieved from <https://www.amchealth.com/>, on February 4, (2021).

Andreu-Perez, J., Leff, D. R., Ip, H. M., & Yang, G.-Z. (2015). From wearable sensors to smart implants—Toward pervasive and personalized healthcare. *IEEE Transactions on Biomedical Engineering*, *62*(12), 2750−2762.

Asociaţia M.A.M.E. (n.d.). Retrieved from <https://asociatiamame.com/>, on February 5, (2021).

ChARM Health. (n.d.). Retrieved from <https://www.charmhealth.com/>, on February 4, (2021).

Chen, R., Yin, P., Meng, X., Liu, C., Wang, L., Xu, X., Ross, J. A., Tse, L. A., Zhao, Z., Kan, H., & Zhou, M. (2017). Fine particulate air pollution and daily mortality. A nationwide analysis in 272 Chinese cities. *American Journal of Respiratory and Critical Care Medicine*, *196*(1), 73−81.

Doctor31 (n.d.). Retrieved from <https://www.doctor31.com/>, on February 4, (2021).

Doty, T. J., Kellihan, B., Jung, T.-P., Zao, J. K., & Litvan, I. (2015). *The wearable multimodal monitoring system: A platform to study falls and near-falls in the real-world. International conference on human aspects of IT for the aged population* (pp. 412−422)). Springer.

Doxtar. (n.d.). Retrieved from <https://www.doxtar.ro>, on February 4, (2021).

Doxy.me. (n.d.). Retrieved from <https://doxy.me/>, February 4, (2021).

EEA. (2019). *Air quality in Europe—2020 Report* (10th ed.). European Environment Agency.

Feng, S., Gao, D., Liao, F., Zhou, F., & Wang, X. (2016). The health effects of ambient PM2.5 and potential mechanisms. *Ecotoxicology and Environmental Safety*, *128*, 67−74.

Hahad, O., Lelieveld, J., Birklein, F., Lieb, K., Daiber, A., & Münzel, T. (2020). Ambient air pollution increases the risk of cerebrovascular and neuropsychiatric disorders through induction of inflammation and oxidative stress. *International Journal of Molecular Sciences*, *21*(12), 4306.

IOTAP, Malmö University. (2016). Smart health and IoT. <https://medium.com/@iotap/smart-health-and-iot-68125f95c405>.

Kim, T., & Zuckerman, J. E. (2019). Realizing the potential of telemedicine in global health. *Journal of Global Health*, *9*(2), 020307.

Klepeis, N. E., Nelson, W. C., Ott, W. R., Robinson, J. P., Tsang, A. M., Switzer, P., Behar, J. V., Hern, S. C., & Engelmann, W. H. (2001). The National Human Activity Pattern Survey (NHAPS): A resource for assessing exposure to environmental pollutants. *Journal of Exposure Science & Environmental Epidemiology*, *11*(3), 231−252.

Koolen, C. D., & Rothenberg, G. (2019). Air pollution in Europe. *ChemSusChem*, *12*(1), 164.

Lanata, A., Valenza, G., Nardelli, M., Gentili, C., & Scilingo, E. P. (2014). Complexity index from a personalized wearable monitoring system for assessing remission in mental health. *IEEE Journal of Biomedical and Health Informatics*, *19*(1), 132−139.

Libelium. Waspmote Plug&Sense: Technical guide. (n.d.). Retrieved from <http://www.libelium.com/products/plug-sense/>, on February 5, (2021).

MediHome. (n.d.). Retrieved from <https://mymedicover.atlashelp.net/ro>, on February 4, (2021).

MediCall. (n.d.). Retrieved from <https://medicover.atlashelp.net/ro>, on February 4, (2021).

Pozzer, A., Dominici, F., Haines, A., Witt, C., Munzel, T., & Lelieveld, J. (2020). Regional and global contributions of air pollution to risk of death from COVID-19. *Cardiovascular Research*, *116*(14), 2247−2253.

Ricardo Energy & Environment. Services to develop an EU air quality index. (2016). Retrieved February 5, 2021, from <https://ec.europa.eu/environment/air/pdf/Air%20quality%20index_final%20report.pdf>.

Saleem, K., Shahzad, B., Orgun, M. A., Al-Muhtadi, J., Rodrigues, J. J., & Zakariah, M. (2017). Design and deployment challenges in immersive and wearable technologies. *Behaviour & Information Technology*, *36*(7), 687−698.

Samir, L. (2018). Air quality index (AQI)—Comparative study and assessment of an appropriate model for B&H. In *Proceedings of the 12th scientific/research symposium with international participation "metallic and nonmetallic materials" B&H*, Vlašić, Bosnia and Herzegovina, April 19th−20th, 2018.

Santo Signorelli, S., Conti, G. O., Zanobetti, A., Baccarelli, A., Fiore, M., & Ferrante, M. (2019). Effect of particulate matter-bound metals exposure on prothrombotic biomarkers: A systematic review. *Environmental Research*, *177*, 108573.

State of Health in the EU. (2019). *România: Profilul de țară din 2019 în ceea ce privește sănătatea*. OECD Publishing. Available from https://ec.europa.eu/health/sites/health/files/state/docs/2019_chp_romania_romanian.pdf.

Status. (n.d.). Retrieved from <https://www.status-online.com/ro/>, on February 4, (2021).

Suciu, G., Pasat, A., Nadrag, C., & Balanescu, M. (2018). *Multi-source cloud platform for enhancing the quality of life. 18th International multidisciplinary scientific GeoConference SGEM 2018* (pp. 523−529)). SGEM.

Svertoka, E., Bălănescu, M., George, S., Pasat, A., & Drosu, A. (2020). Decision support algorithm based on the concentrations of air pollutants visualization. *Sensors*, *20*(20), 5931.

uRADMonitor. Technical documents. (2017). Retrieved February 5, 2021, from https://www.uradmonitor.com/uradmonitor-industrial/

USEPA. (n.d.). NowCast calculator. Retrieved from <https://www3.epa.gov/airnow/aqicalctest/nowcast.htm>, on February 18, (2020).

VSee. (n.d.). Retrieved February from <https://vsee.com/>, on 4, (2021).

WHO. (2016). *Ambient air pollution: A global assessment of exposure and burden of disease*. World Health Organization.

Winsen. Laser dust module manual. (2016). Retrieved from <https://www.winsen-sensor.com/d/files/PDF/Gas%20Sensor%20Module/PM2.5%20Detection%20Module/ZH03A%20Laser%20Dust%20Module%20V1.8.pdf>, on February 5, (2021).

Indoor air pollution: a comprehensive review of public health challenges and prevention policies

6

Jagriti Saini[1], Maitreyee Dutta[1], and Gonçalo Marques[2]

[1]*National Institute of Technical Teacher's Training & Research, Chandigarh, India* [2]*Polytechnic of Coimbra, ESTGOH, Rua General Santos Costa, Oliveira do Hospital, Portugal*

Introduction

Reports reveal that, typically, people spend 80−90% of their time indoors. Consequently, the indoor air environment has a substantial impact on public health (Boor et al., 2017). The inherent causes of indoor air pollution (IAP) in most developing countries are combustion sources (tobacco products, wood, coal, kerosene, gas, and oil), building materials, volatile organic compounds (VOCs), carpets, central cooling and heating systems, house cleaning products, humidification devices, personal care products, gaseous pollutants (carbon monoxide), defective ventilation, and noxious agents. Potential chemical and biological hazards causing harmful impacts on the indoor environment and human health include ozone, sulfur oxides, nitrogen, pesticides, infectious agents, formaldehyde, and biological agents (dust mites, mold, and microbial organism) (Žuškin et al., 2009). The increasing incidence of IAP causes a social burden in terms of diseases, human suffering, and discomfort. Furthermore, it is directly related to avoidable economic cost, and loss of well-being and community productivity. Reported deterioration of indoor air quality (IAQ) shows an immediate impact on occupants of hospitals, houses, offices, schools, and other community buildings (Śmiełowska et al., 2017).

Statistics collected from India in 2017 (Balakrishnan et al., 2019) revealed that 55.5% of the population was using solid fuels for cooking and heating needs. The number of deaths due to IAP in the same year was reported to be 0.48 million, and the ratio was higher in rural areas. Researchers revealed that if solid fuel usage can be lowered below the minimum permissible level, it could increase the average life expectancy by 1.7 years (Balakrishnan et al., 2019). The usage of solid fuels and the routine habits are contributing to a deterioration in IAQ levels. In the past few years, the capital city of Delhi has reported a higher level of ambient air pollution. Still, as per current news updates, the residents need to install air purifiers in their living spaces as well. *The Economic Times*, on September 24, 2019 reported a study on real-time IAQ monitoring of more than 400 homes in Delhi-NCR. The level of carbon dioxide in most of the houses was somewhere around 3900 parts per million (ppm). However, the reported safe limit is 750 ppm. Similarly, the tVOC (total VOCs) concentration was higher

Current Trends and Advances in Computer-Aided Intelligent Environmental Data Engineering.
DOI: https://doi.org/10.1016/B978-0-323-85597-6.00006-9

than 1000 micrograms per cubic meter air (μg/m^3), which is much higher when compared to the safe limit of 200 μg/m^3 (The Economic Times, 2019). BBC News reported that air pollution in India has become worse than in China. Usually, the common factors contributing to indoor and outdoor air pollution in most countries are heavy industries, fossil fuel-burning power plants, and vehicular traffic. However, in India, the predominant cause of air pollution is the burning of agricultural stubble by farmers (BBC News, 2019). The state of pollution worsens when people use fire crackers to celebrate the Diwali festival. India Today, on October 28, 2019, reported that the air quality index in multiple areas of Delhi was recorded to be 999 (extreme limit of the recording instrument) on Diwali night. The prescribed limit is usually 60 (India Today, 2019). These stats are critical for a country where more than 100,000 children below the age group of 5 years die every year due to air pollution (World Economic Forum, 2019).

According to a survey (Amegah & Jaakkola, 2016), around 2.8 billion people or 41% of households at the global level rely on solid fuels for their cooking needs. They often make use of coal, crop waste, charcoal, animal dung, and wood for heating and cooking purposes. On May 8, 2018, the World Health Organization (WHO) stated that household air pollution caused the premature deaths of more than 4 million people due to a lack of preventive measures for cooking practices (WHO, 2018). Reports reveal that out of 4.3 million people who lose their lives every year due to improper IAQ, 8% die due to lung cancer, 27% due to pneumonia, 20% because of chronic obstructive pulmonary disease (COPD), 27% as a result of ischemic heart disease, and 18% due to stroke (WHO, 2018). Women and young children who spend more time in the household are highly vulnerable to health issues caused by poor IAQ (Ritchie & Roser, 2019; Rumchev et al., 2017). These problems are not limited to rural areas. The air quality in cities is contaminated by excessive use of chemical-rich products, heating and cooling systems, and improper ventilation arrangements. The list of symptoms for building-related illness includes dizziness; irritation of the eyes, throat, and nose; nausea; and dryness in mucous membranes, wheezing, erythema, hoarseness, mental fatigue, coughing, airway infections, unspecified hypersensitivity, and headaches (Ezzati & Kammen, 2002).

The objective of this chapter is to present a comprehensive review of critical public health hazards and challenges caused by IAP. Timely recognition and identification of symptoms caused by polluting agents can help to evaluate the risks of significant impairments. An in-depth study of the health issues related to poor IAQ is essential to take preventive steps to ensure better health and well-being of occupants with varying individual sensitivity levels. Furthermore, the main contribution of this chapter is to summarize the body of knowledge in this field. The strategies and policies to avoid the dangers associated with IAQ are discussed. The creation of an effective framework for rural and urban areas for IAQ monitoring will contribute to minimizing the impact of this public challenge. It is not possible to implement a standard action plan to handle all the health issues caused by IAP. However, strategic approaches can be helpful on different levels.

The remainder of the chapter is structured as follows: the section "Indoor air quality and public health" presents an in-depth review of public health hazards caused by poor IAQ and associated challenges, "Enhanced indoor air quality and prevention strategies" is concerned with the methods to control IAQ along with preventive guidelines. Furthermore, "Technologies and control policies for enhanced indoor air quality" presents technology-inspired solutions, including possible advice on control policies for IAQ; the "Discussion" section outlines discussions on this extensive review, and the conclusion is presented in the final section.

Indoor air quality and public health

The health effects of IAQ cannot be determined by considering only pollution levels. The time that people spend indoors while breathing in polluted air must also be considered for its correct evaluation (Rumchev et al., 2017). Succinctly, exposure can be defined as contact between the human body surface and airborne contaminants. It can be external (e.g., through the skin) or internal (via the respiratory tract) (Watson et al., 1988). Medical health professionals and researchers have reported the occurrence of several harmful diseases due to IAP (WHO, 2018). Hence, future researchers are advised to work on ultrafine indoor particles (Kagan et al., 2005). In this chapter, we have focused on primary health hazards caused by IAP. This comprehensive review includes respiratory illness, chronic obstructive pulmonary disease, cancer, pulmonary tuberculosis, mortality, and cataracts.

Respiratory illness

Recent investigations demonstrate a strong association between the cases of acute respiratory infection and air pollution worldwide (Horne et al., 2018; Mason et al., 2019). Repeated exposure to biomass fuel (BMF) smoke is the most common cause of acute respiratory illness in children (Laumbach & Kipen, 2012). This source affects the upper respiratory tract. However, a middle ear infection is another uncommon fatal symptom of this disease. It can also lead to morbidity and deafness and, if not treated in time, may even cause mastoiditis (Fullerton et al., 2008). A recent study proposed by Wolkoff (2018) describes IAP as a common cause of reduced work performance and absenteeism in offices. This questionnaire-based study reported symptoms of sensory irritation in upper airways and eyes among office employees due to long-term exposure to poor IAQ.

Pollutants can penetrate the human body through the air during the inhaling and exhaling process (Yue et al., 2019). Irritation of the upper respiratory tract, especially in the trachea, is considered to be the first most identifiable symptom of IAP. Furthermore, IAP not only leads to disturbances of the voice but also plays an essential role in producing symptoms of lung cancer and asthma (Weisel, 2002). Pollutants such as particulate matters (PMs) and other respirable chemicals such as O_3 and benzene can cause severe injuries to the respiratory system (Valavanidis et al., 2013).

Cardiovascular dysfunctions

Several epidemiologic and experimental studies have revealed that IAQ has a direct connection with cardiac-related illness (Andersen et al., 2012; Nogueira, 2009). As per medical health studies, harmful air pollutants also cause some alterations to the total number of white blood cells (Steenhof et al., 2014). Animal models suggest a close relationship between air pollution exposure and hypertension (Sun et al., 2008). The high risk of potential diseases due to the burning of kerosene/diesel on human health has been compared to the risk associated with clean cooking solutions (Mitter et al., 2016). The estimated increase in cardiovascular mortality within 10 years due to the frequent burning of diesel and kerosene was 10%. However, it was reduced to 6% in the case of gas (Samet et al., 2016).

Neuropsychiatric complications

There is a critical relationship between air-suspended toxic materials with the performance of the nervous system as these harmful substances cause long-term damage to nerves (Ghorani-Azam et al., 2016). The effects of toxic indoor air include psychiatric disorders and neurological complications (Genc et al., 2012). Psychiatric disorders include antisocial behaviors, aggression, and stress, whereas neurological impairment has devastating consequences. Moreover, it has a critical impact on children. IAP also causes neurological hyperactivity, risk of neuroinflammation (Calderón-Garcidueñas et al., 2008b), and Parkinson and Alzheimer diseases (Calderón-Garcidueñas et al., 2008a).

Chronic pulmonary disease

COPD is well known as a progressive inflammatory condition of the lung parenchyma, pulmonary vessels, and airways. It is the third most common cause of death and the fifth most reported cause of disability worldwide (Andersen et al., 2012). Breathing in smoke developed by burning coal or wood for cooking food in developing countries causes severe damage to the lungs. Women and children that spend more time indoors are at higher risk of COPD due to the routine burning of fuels in the kitchen (Fullerton et al., 2008).

Cancer

Tobacco smoke is a significant risk factor for lung cancer. However, nonsmokers, especially women, in developing countries form the larger proportion of lung cancer patients (Smolle & Pichler, 2019; Vermeulen et al., 2019). An epidemiologic study conducted in China described a strong association between IAP constituents and risks of lung cancer among never-smoking women in Fyyuan and Xuanwei (Vermeulen et al., 2019). The main reason for a woman suffering from lung cancer in China is excessive exposure to coal smoke at home. The WHO reports that solid fuels used in Chinese households caused 420,000 premature deaths per year. This is 40% higher than the 300,000 premature deaths that occurred due to outdoor pollution (Zhang Junfeng Jim & Smith Kirk, 2007). Three hours of cooking using biomass smoke expose a woman to an equal amount of benzo[a]pyene as compared to smoking two packets of cigarettes per day (Fullerton et al., 2008). Long-term exposure to formaldehyde and PMs is the most common cause of cancer. Radon is considered to be the second-leading cause behind of lung cancer after cigarette smoke (Laquatra & Abdul Mujeebu, 2019). The EPA has stated that radon is the inherent cause of 21,000 lung cancer deaths per year in the United States. Moreover, almost one in seven cases of lung cancer in the United States has been reported to be due to excessive exposure to radon (Foster & Everett Jones, 2016).

Low birth weight and infant mortality

IAP is associated with reduced adverse birth outcomes (Arroyo et al., 2016; Haider et al., 2016). A study conducted by Ritz and Yu (1999) presented a direct relationship between birth weight and excessive exposure to carbon monoxide. Hence while determining the potential health hazards and challenges associated with IAP, it is crucial to analyze the birth weight-related issues. In developing countries, this factor has a significant impact on the lifestyle of poor women who spend more time indoors breathing polluted air. Statistics reveal almost 4.3 million deaths, along with 7.7% of global mortality, due to IAP (Ghergu et al., 2016).

Cataract

The cases of cataracts are high in developing countries (Lewallen & Courtright, 2002). Several epidemiological studies from India and Nepal reveal poor indoor cooking standards as the main cause of blindness and BMF as the main cause of cataracts (Pokhrel et al., 2005). The primary reason behind increasing cases of cataracts due to IAQ in developing countries is a lack of awareness. Moreover, nutritional state, smoking, and diarrhea episodes have a direct impact on cataracts.

As seen in numerous animal studies, the condensates of wood smoke, and cigarette smoke, cause significant damage to the lenses of rats, leading to opacities, discoloration, and particles of debris (Moturi, 2010; Shalini et al., 1994). The process of disease development involves excessive accumulation and absorption of toxins that cause oxidation (Mishra et al., 1999). Smoke also actuates oxidative stress while depilating plasma ascorbate, glutathione, and carotenoids that otherwise provide some antioxidant protection against the development of cataracts. During a study of 89,000 households in India, an estimated odds ratio of 1:3 was observed for blindness in females who use BMF in the home (Fullerton et al., 2008).

Sick building syndrome

IAQ is directly connected with sick building syndrome (SBS). The leading cause of this is insufficient ventilation (Jafari et al., 2015; Joshi, 2008). The typical chemical contaminants in buildings are found in upholstered furniture, cleaning agents, carpeting, adhesives, and paints, which emit VOCs. These VOCs are the primary cause of SBS. The symptoms include mental fatigue, skin irritation, nausea, dizziness, headache, and eye irritation (Lu et al., 2015). In addition, factors that contribute to SBS are dust, harmful organisms, mold, bacteria, toxic gases, chemical vapors, and harmful compounds (Norhidayah et al., 2013).

Rural women suffer more due to IAP as compared to urban female occupants due to the poorer living standards (Singh & Aligarh, 2013). The lack of knowledge and the nonavailability of resources make it difficult for rural women to improve their health conditions. Differential health impacts on urban and rural women due to IAP are described in Fig. 6.1. This shows a higher number of disease cases from rural areas and the inherent cause behind this is poor living conditions. Women in rural areas suffer excessive exposure to solid fuels as they spend more time in kitchens with inadequate ventilation arrangements (IARC Working Group on the Evaluation of Carcinogenic Risks to Humans, 2010).

Enhanced indoor air quality and prevention strategies

Air pollution and human health are closely linked to each other. It is essential to adopt potential measures to control the pollutant concentration levels in households, offices, schools, hospitals, and

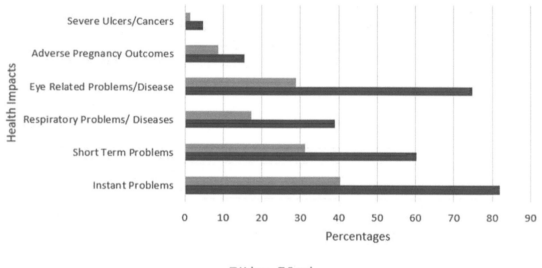

FIGURE 6.1

Differential health impacts on urban and rural women due to IAP (Singh & Aligarh, 2013) (*IAP*, indoor air pollution).

other commercial complexes to ensure comfortable and healthy IAQ levels. On the one hand, it is necessary to implement significant government policies. On the other hand, occupants need to implement strategies to improve IAQ. Before describing essential control policies, it is crucial to throw light on what can be done at an individual level.

The indoor environment needs to meet the standard guidelines for thermal comfort and IAQ (Calautit et al., 2017; Giamalaki & Kolokotsa, 2019). Thermal comfort in buildings is affected by several factors. These factors include air velocity, air humidity, air temperature, human clothing, ventilation, mean radiant temperature, biological pollutants, particle pollutants, gaseous pollutants, and activity levels. To minimize the health issues associated with various factors affecting IAQ, experts have advised several prevention methods (Laumbach & Kipen, 2012). The common sources that produce such pollutants are tobacco smoke, unvented kerosene heaters, leaking chimneys, gas appliances or gas heaters, fireplaces, and automobile exhaust in houses with attached garages need to be monitored. These sources can lead to lung cancer or impaired lung function, irritation to the throat, eyes, and nose, and respiratory diseases that are frequent in children such as flu-like symptoms and bronchitis (Lewtas, 2007). Therefore people the use of kerosene or gas heaters indoors must be avoided. This is particularly the case in areas with inadequate ventilation arrangements. It is essential to ensure scheduled repair and maintenance of furnaces and appliances.

Furthermore, the filters in heating and cooling systems must be changed before they start contaminating the living space. Reducing the combustion of solid fuels, and advanced cooking and heating systems must be made available to rural areas in developing countries (Fan et al., 2018). It is crucial to increase the circulation of fresh air. Moreover, the installation of exhaust fans is an effective approach to reduce air pollution in the kitchen. In the case of attached garages, proper ventilation arrangements must be ensured to disperse vehicle exhaust.

The tobacco smoke produced by cigarettes, smoking pipes, or tobacco pipes increases the risk of lung cancer; respiratory disease; heart diseases; irritation to the throat, eyes, and nose; pneumonia; headaches; and the chances of ear infections in children (Rosen et al., 2015). Therefore smoking should be avoided to reduce the derived adverse health issues. Addicted smokers can also obtain treatments from rehabilitation centers to adopt healthy life behaviors (Bartlett et al., 2013; Sarkar et al., 2019).

Formaldehyde emission is caused by floor finishes, varnishes, adhesives, paints, and cosmetic products such as hair care solutions and nail polish, smoke from fireplaces, urea-formaldehyde foam insulation, vehicle exhaust, tobacco smoke, and pressure wood products such as plywood wall paneling, fiberboard, hardwood, glue, and stoves (Liu et al., 2018; Salthammer et al., 2010). The primary health effects caused by formaldehyde include allergic reactions, coughing, nausea, rashes, watery eyes, fatigue, irritation to the throat, nose, and eyes, and wheezing (Delikhoon et al., 2018). Several symptoms of cancer in animals cause significant damage to the central nervous system, liver, and kidney, and are a potential reason for the increasing morbidity rate due to IAP (Kaden et al., 2010). To deal with these consequences, individuals must replace products causing substantial formaldehyde emissions with those having lower discharge ranges. Fireplaces, wood stoves, and chimneys must be cleaned efficiently and safely to clear obstructions that can otherwise cause IAP. It is preferable to use zero-VOC or low-VOC products, provide proper ventilation, and avoid using scented products such as candles and aerosol deodorizers. Dehumidifiers should be used to maintain relative humidity in the appropriate range as suggested by experts. The setup configuration should be below 30% in the winter season and 50% in summer (Fang et al., 1998).

The primary sources of radon are soil, water, and local geology. The Environment Protection Agency (EPA) and WHO state that radon is the second most common cause of the increasing cases of lung cancer, and it is also related to stomach cancer (Bruno, 1983; Al Jassim & Isaifan, 2018). Therefore it is necessary to seal foundation cracks, basement leaks, and utility junctions. Building managers must install an appropriate ventilation system for basements. Homeowners can either opt for mechanical ventilation arrangements or active soil depressurization. Studies show synergistic reactions between radon and smoking, leading to a higher number of deaths (Lantz et al., 2013; Staff, 1999).

Indoor pesticides originate from several sources such as wood-protecting agents, termiticides, insecticides, treated wood, impregnated carpets and textiles, pest-control chemicals, house dust, and lawn and garden chemicals (Ayoko et al., 2004). The common health issues caused by pesticides are acute toxicity due to short-term exposure to pesticides, headache, loss of consciousness, diarrhea, vomiting, nausea, skin and eye irritation, allergic sensations, a sore throat or a cough, respiratory tract irritation, extreme weakness, and seizures. Long-term toxicity can lead to cancer, hyperactivity disorder, attention deficit, non-Hodgkin lymphoma, anxiety and depression, asthma, Parkinson disease, or death (Sarwar & Lee, 2016). Therefore it is necessary to improve ventilation arrangement in home, office, schools, hospitals, and other commercial buildings. Moreover, it is crucial to avoid the storage of pesticides indoors and organic solutions are preferred to chemical-rich products. In addition, it is necessary to follow manufacturer instructions for all pesticide products (Hoppin et al., 2006; Wu et al., 2011).

Asbestos is found in a wide range of manufacturing products and building materials such as cement products, paper products, ceiling, floor tiles, roofing shingles, friction products, coatings, gaskets, packaging, and insulations and heat-resistant fabrics (IARC Working Group on the Evaluation of Carcinogenic Risks to Humans, 2012). Asbestos can cause pleural plaques, lung cancer, asbestosis, and mesothelioma; and smokers are always at higher risk of these chronic diseases (Schneider & Woitowitz, 1995). Consequently, it is crucial to use appropriate building materials for new constructions so that asbestos exposure can be reduced to the occupants. It is also crucial to apply strict precautions for the disposal and removal of asbestos-containing materials. Furthermore, it is important to wear gloves, a hat, and disposable clothing. Providing proper ventilation and using hand tools for breaking asbestos products instead of power tools is also essential. After removal of asbestos-containing materials, the area must be vacuum cleaned using appliances dedicated to asbestos cleaning. Moreover, it is necessary to use standard high-efficiency particulate air (HEPA) filters (Oren et al., 2001; Sublett et al., 2010).

Common sources of ozone in indoor environments are ozone generators. These sources include air cleaners that produce ozone as a by-product, and office equipment such as photocopiers and printers (Huang et al., 2019). Several health issues associated with this are lung and throat irritation, wheezing, and coughing. People that are already suffering from emphysema, bronchitis, asthma, and older adults are at high risk (Nicolas et al., 2003). Therefore it is crucial to use ozone monitors in schools, hospitals, home, and offices. Ozone-monitoring systems can provide alarms for maintaining proper ozone levels with additional ventilation arrangements.

Technologies and control policies for enhanced indoor air quality

Indoor air quality management technologies

With the proliferation of advanced technologies, professionals have designed a variety of automatic devices for enhanced IAQ. The systems and technologies available in the market can be divided into two groups: ventilation devices and filtration devices.

The heat recovery ventilator (HRV) device is designed to remove contaminated air from kitchens, baths, and other parts of the home to the outdoors. It delivers oxygen-rich, fresh air to living space through a reliable heat exchanger unit. Furthermore, in the summer, it can reduce energy bills by removing heat from incoming air. Most HRV products can be easily attached to exhaust ducts in the kitchen and bathroom by replacing ordinary noisy fans (Liu et al., 2017).

HEPA filters are also recommended for air filtration. This technology is essential for operating rooms and hospitals. The efficiency of a HEPA filter is 99.97% for 0.30 µm particle size (Sangeetha et al., 2016). The majority of particles contributing to IAP are smaller than five microns. However, traditional filter systems were not able to filter microscopic particles (Yoon et al., 2016). The HEPA filter technology must be made available to economically weak sectors of developing countries (Kabrein et al., 2016; Sublett, 2011).

Minimum efficiency reposting value (MERV) 11 filters are available in the thickness range of 2−4 inches. MERV is an industry standard recommended to filter particles in the size range of 0.3−10.0 µm (Cecala et al., 2016). A higher MERV rating ensures higher efficiency features. However, MERV 4 or lower is not recommended to improve IAQ as it cannot eliminate microscopic particles (Cecala et al., 2016). Consequently, the MERV 11 range is effective for both large and small particles, including pet dander, fungal spores, dust, mold spores, and pollens. These filters must be replaced according to the manufacturer instructions (Kabrein et al., 2016; Sublett, 2011).

Electrostatic air purifiers reduce the levels of molds, pollens, and dust from indoor environments by approximately 90% (Zhao et al., 2016). Electrostatic filters are often confused with HEPA filters. However, they are two different technologies. Electrostatic air purifiers include a polypropylene filtration system that produces static charges when contaminated air passes through it. These charges attract particles and hold them tight while circulating clean air in the premises. In short, unlike HEPA, electrostatic air purifiers do not use filters. These systems are popular due to their minimal maintenance requirements and low operational cost (Kabrein et al., 2016).

Electronic air cleaners use a nonionizing polarized system that captures airborne particles of 0.30 microns (Xu, 2014). Several systems include special arrangements for removing VOCs and unwanted odors while ensuring the flow of clean air indoors (Sublett, 2011).

Control policies for indoor air quality

Government authorities, health professionals, and individuals need to work together for the development and implementation of appropriate control policies for IAQ management. The preventive and technology solutions are already available in the market. Consequently it is necessary to ensure proper utilization of resources. Developed countries have already established several policies, strategies, and schemes to improve built environments for healthy living (Sagar et al., 2016; Gould et al., 2018; Jorquera et al., 2019; Tsai, 2017).

The control policies are effective only if people are aware of problems associated with IAQ. First, it is crucial to educate people to increase their awareness about environment protection and health effects related to IAQ (Andamon et al., 2019). Occupant health issues are the leading cause of morbidity and mortality. Moreover, awareness campaigns must be organized at all levels to implement control policies effectively. IAQ must be included in school curriculums (Singleton et al., 2018). Technical education and training programs must be conducted in organizations to achieve goals specified by WHO air quality guidelines (Agarwal et al., 2018; Argunhan & Avci, 2018; Mathew et al., 2019).

In the United States, the EPA has established the Clean Air Act that sets limits for air pollutants in industrial units such as steel mills and chemical plants (Bento et al., 2015; Hendryx & Holland, 2016). Similar regulations and legislation must be formed in developing countries also well. Furthermore, it is not just about designing policies, government authorities need to take strict action on their implementation on all levels. Regular inspection programs must be executed in schools, hospitals, organizations, and residential areas as well. Failure to achieve the desired goal must be a matter of vigorous action. However, improvements must be appreciated with recognition and financial incentives. Instead of spending all the time on planning, a ground-level performance analysis of all IAQ control policies is essential to achieving the desired results. Moreover, government authorities are also responsible for providing an appropriate arrangement for the implementation of IAQ control policies for rural and financially weak sectors (Liu et al., 2017). IAQ monitoring systems are essential to control biological, physical, chemical, and other IAPs in residential as well as public buildings.

Implementation of the above-mentioned strategies for existing and new buildings is a complicated task. The government needs to set appropriate regulations for materials to be used in new constructions, ventilation arrangements, furnishings, and fittings (Jomehzadeh et al., 2017; Persily, 2015; Stabile et al., 2016). It is essential to use certified items only from licensed manufacturers to achieve the desired IAQ levels. The existing buildings, such as schools and hospitals, must be modified to meet efficient ventilation conditions that can reduce exposure to IAP.

Around 60−70% of the population in developing countries such as Bangladesh, India, Peru, Nepal, and Kenya use solid fuels such as kerosene, firewood, cow dung, and coal for cooking and heating purposes (Agarwal et al., 2018; Ghimire et al., 2019; Jung & Huxham, 2018; Kelp et al., 2018; Mdege et al., 2019; Rupakheti et al., 2019; Sharma & Jain, 2019). This contributes to the increase in the number of deaths of women and children in economically weak sections of the community. The government needs to develop new policies for the improvement of their quality of life. Researchers and engineers also need to work side by side for the development of some budget-friendly solutions to address these challenges. It is possible to use natural gas as the best source of fuel, but at the same time, ventilation must be improved along with some behavior interventions (Zhao et al., 2016, 2019).

Discussion

The extensive review conducted in this chapter discusses IAQ in public utility buildings and residential premises. In general, they can be divided into three major groups:

1. Factors influenced by human activities in the indoor environment;
2. Factors related to specific building characteristics;
3. Factors associated with the quantity and type of chemical compounds present in the indoor air.

To address the medical health consequences caused by IAP, it is not only necessary to focus on all these factors but also to find potential methods to eliminate risks. Therefore government agencies have developed specific guidelines to improve IAQ in different countries. The main reason behind increasing cases of related medical health cases is a lack of awareness. Despite the efforts carried out in the direction of IAP management and building maintenance to reduce the effect of pollutants, people are still generally more concerned about outdoor pollution, and they often neglect the factors affecting indoor areas. However, as people typically spend most of their time indoors, it is essential to develop reliable preventive measures for enhanced IAQ.

A summary of preventive strategies useful for IAQ management is provided in Table 6.1. These preventive measures focus on four main points:

1. Improving ventilation arrangements in buildings;
2. Using appropriate building materials;
3. Making use of organic products;
4. Improving cooking practices.

It is essential to use filters to remove harmful pollutants from indoor air environments. Nowadays, it is possible to find a variety of air filters, cleaners, and ventilation systems to improve IAQ in residential and commercial buildings. Nevertheless, as indoor air is highly affected by qualitative and quantitative compositions within the building environment, it is difficult to find a reliable solution for IAQ improvement (Cincinelli & Martellini, 2017; Śmiełowska et al., 2017).

Table 6.2 summarizes the effectiveness of IAQ management technologies along with their advantages and disadvantages. The possible recommendations are also listed to facilitate the

Table 6.1 Comparison summary of IAQ management technologies.

Pollutants	Sources	Health effects	Prevention strategies	Commonly affects
By-products of combustion (NO_x, CO_2, CO)	Tobacco smoke; unvented kerosene heaters; leaking chimneys; gas appliances; automobile exhaust	Lung problems; respiratory diseases, flu-like symptoms	Timely maintenance of appliances and furnaces; avoid combustion of solid fuels; proper ventilation arrangements in buildings	Households in village areas
Tobacco smoke	Cigarettes; smoking pipes; or tobacco pipes	Lung cancer; respiratory disease; heart diseases; pneumonia; chances of ear infections in children	Reducing or avoiding tobacco smoke; isolate smoking zones from work premises	Rural areas in developing countries where people are still unaware of the harmful impacts of using tobacco pipes
Formaldehyde and VOCs	Building materials, chemical-rich cosmetic products, fireplaces, tobacco smoke, vehicle exhaust	Respiratory issues; cancer; major damage to the central nervous system, liver, and kidney	Timely cleaning of fireplaces; adequate ventilation arrangements; avoid using scented products; dehumidifier installation	Buildings near high-traffic areas; modern homes that are loaded with emission-releasing products
Radon	Soil, water, and local geology	Lung cancer; stomach cancer	Improve building health; install reliable ventilation systems; avoid smoking inside	School buildings; basements
Pesticides	Impregnated carpets and textiles; pest-control chemicals; house dust; lawn and garden chemicals	Respiratory issues; extreme weakness; seizures; cancer; dizziness asthma; Parkinson disease; death	Improve ventilation arrangements; start using organic products	Modern homes that use chemical-rich products; commercial buildings; hospital areas
Asbestos	Building materials; paper products; packaging; insulations; heat-resistant fabrics	Pleural plaques; lung cancer; asbestosis; mesothelioma	Use appropriate building products; use HEPA filters	Stores selling building materials; inadequately designed buildings
Ozone	Ozone generators; some poor-quality air cleaners; printers and photocopiers	Respiratory issues, lung diseases	Schedule routine outdoor activities to breath fresh air; use ozone monitors with alert systems	Office areas

IAQ, *indoor air quality;* VOCs, *volatile organic compounds.*

Table 6.2 Summary of the primary pollution sources for IAQ.

Type of filter	Target pollutants	Maximum recorded efficiency (approx.)	Suggested for	Advantages	Disadvantages	Remarks
Heat recovery ventilator	Mildew; mold; radon	70–90%	Areas with higher radon content or inadequate ventilation arrangements	Recovers 90% of the wasted heat; balanced heat distribution	May cause overheating; provides desired results only with efficient air-conditioning systems	Energy-saving solution for modern and traditional homes
HEPA filters	Animal dander, abundant dust pollen, mold spores, pet hair	99.97%	Asthma sensitivity, moderate to high allergen levels	Higher efficiency HEPA filters do not produce ozone	Do not capture gases; need HVAC system modifications; expensive choice; higher noise levels	Can target 0.3 μm particles with ease
MERV 11 disposable filters	Bacteria and viruses; autoemissions and *Legionella*; humidifier dust	>95%	Best choice for residential and commercial buildings	Reliable lifetime	Quite expensive	Can trap tiny 0.3 μm particles
Electrostatic air purifiers	Mold and mildew	>95%	Safe for households	Augment HEPA filtration, low-pressure drop; hence use less energy, high capture efficiencies	Do not capture gases, produce ozone causing adverse health effects, need frequent cleaning, expensive choice	Low-power requirements can save more on monthly bills
Electronic air cleaners	Viruses and bacteria; large particles and contaminants; mold; pollen; VOCs	90%	Recommended for hospital laboratories; residential and commercial buildings with proper ozone reduction strategies	Can be used for several years without replacement	Must be cleaned at least four times a year (with prime seasonal variations); increase ozone levels indoor	Can capture particles as small as 0.1 μm

IAQ, *indoor air quality*; MERV, *minimum efficiency reposting value*; VOCs, *volatile organic compounds*.

appropriate purchase decision of buyers. Therefore the selection of filter must be made based on the living conditions and factors affecting IAQ.

It is not possible to recommend one standard solution to deal with IAP in all commercial buildings, residential premises, hospitals, schools, and other living spaces. At the same time, it is crucial to focus on the cost of installation and power requirements of individual systems because it is relevant for middle- and low-income groups in the developing countries (Irfan et al., 2018). Researchers need to find potential solutions to enhance IAQ while balancing all associated factors of interest (Laumbach et al., 2015).

Fig. 6.2 represents the research areas, open questions, and essential variables associated with IAP. It presents the interconnection of various factors described in this extensive review along with the critical determinants. This taxonomy also provides an overview of the research problems, risks, and management issues. Literature that includes information related to a specific area is also highlighted for each section. In addition, Fig. 6.1 provides insights into potential health problems, and the essential elements responsible for IAQ management and control. This study is useful for government agencies to develop new policies and control mechanisms in the field of IAQ. Furthermore, this document provides relevant insights to support future research studies.

No technology or policy can improve IAQ until and unless people become aware of the matter. Hence the prime focus must be on public education. First, people need to take appropriate steps to improve their health conditions while using preventive procedures against IAP. Second, the government needs to implement regular examination of IAQ in public utility buildings such as hospitals and schools.

The most challenging part of IAQ management is to address the economically weaker sectors of society. These sectors have inadequate knowledge along with a lack of potential resources to deal with the consequences of IAP. Furthermore, it is necessary to create reliable, budget-friendly, and practically implementable solutions. The correct implementation of preventive and control policies will increase productivity at workplaces and reduce public health hazards.

Several review papers on this topic are available (Saini et al., 2020; Tran et al., 2020). However, this comprehensive review analyzes the complete body of the material representing the current state of the art, finds commonalities, and characterizes alternative approaches to similar problems. The overall objective of this chapter is to extract lessons and common threads in numerous research studies that are of general interest and applicability rather than simply enumerating the reviewed papers and outlining the work presented in each. This review chapter presents several primary pollution sources for IAQ in Table 6.1 along with a comparison of IAQ management technologies in Table 6.2.

Moreover, Fig. 6.2 presents a taxonomy on the research areas and open questions that demand focus from upcoming researchers and policymakers. The main contribution of this comprehensive review is to synthesize the existing body of knowledge in a unique way, which is not accessible to the readers by reading the included studies alone.

Conclusion

Poor IAQ leads to several risks to public health and demands the attention of authorities and individuals, particularly in developing countries. An efficient action plan must be designed to meet the

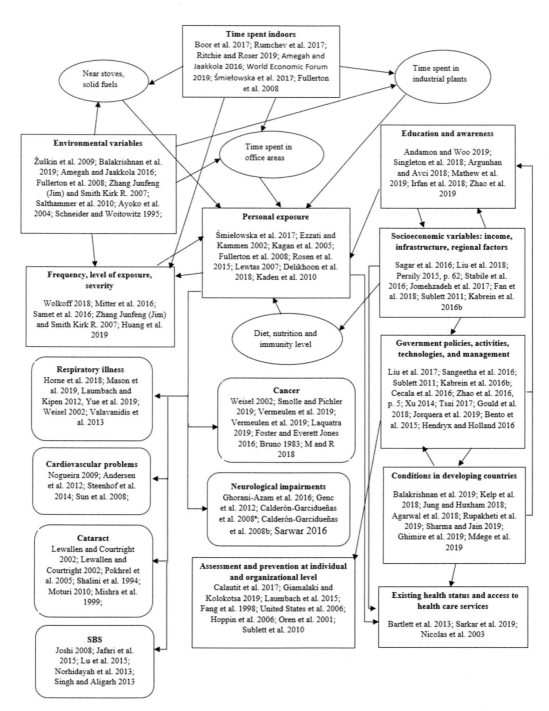

FIGURE 6.2

Research areas and open questions that demand focus from upcoming researchers and policymakers.

standard IAQ guidelines at the local and global level. Moreover, it is essential to ensure affordable and sustainable solutions. It is also essential to develop a systematic approach to monitoring trends and levels of exposure in rural and urban areas to create healthier environments. Several methods are recommended, such as improving ventilation and cooking practices in buildings, using appropriate building materials, and avoiding the use of nonorganic products to promote IAQ.

Preventive strategies for IAQ management are available, such as (1) improving ventilation arrangements in the buildings, (2) using appropriate building materials, (3) making use of organic products, and (4) improving cooking practices. However, without applying real-time supervision systems, it is not possible to detect and plan interventions to improve IAQ for enhanced occupational health. Furthermore, the development of cost-effective IAQ supervision systems for enhanced living environments is critical.

This chapter has reviewed several aspects of IAQ focusing on public health concerns, symptoms, and policies, and presented a discussion on the primary pollution sources and management technologies. The discussion on policies and technologies for IAQ management should offer an essential background for additional investigation. Therefore this chapter aims to support policymakers in developing countries working in the area of building health management for enhanced occupational health.

References

Agarwal, A., Kirwa, K., Eliot, M. N., Alenezi, F., Mcnya, D., Mitter, S. S., Velazquez, E. J., Vedanthan, R., Wellenius, G. A., & Bloomfield, G. S. (2018). Household air pollution is associated with altered cardiac function among women in Kenya. *American Journal of Respiratory and Critical Care Medicine*, *197*(7), 958−961. Available from https://doi.org/10.1164/rccm.201704-0832LE.

Al Jassim, M., & Isaifan, R. (2018). A review on the sources and impacts of radon indoor air pollution. *Journal of Environmental and Toxicological Studies*, *2*(1). Available from https://doi.org/10.16966/2576-6430.112.

Amegah, A. K., & Jaakkola, J. J. (2016). Household air pollution and the sustainable development goals. *Bulletin of the World Health Organization*, *94*(3), 215−221. Available from https://doi.org/10.2471/BLT.15.155812.

Andamon, M. M., Woo, J., Rajagopalan, P., Andamon, M. M., & Moore, T. (2019). *Indoor environmental quality of preparatory to year 12 (P-12) educational facilities in Australia: Challenges and prospects. Energy performance in the Australian built environment* (pp. 111−130). Springer. Available from http://link.springer.com/10.1007/978-981-10-7880-4_8.

Andersen, Z. J., Kristiansen, L. C., Andersen, K. K., Olsen, T. S., Hvidberg, M., Jensen, S. S., Ketzel, M., Loft, S., Sørensen, M., Tjønneland, A., Overvad, K., & Raaschou-Nielsen, O. (2012). Stroke and long-term exposure to outdoor air pollution from nitrogen dioxide: A cohort study. *Stroke*, *43*(2), 320−325. Available from https://doi.org/10.1161/STROKEAHA.111.629246.

Argunhan, Z., & Avci, A. S. (2018). Statistical evaluation of indoor air quality parameters in classrooms of a university. *Advances in Meteorology*, *2018*(1), 1−10. Available from https://doi.org/10.1155/2018/4391579.

Arroyo, V., Díaz, J., Carmona, R., Ortiz, C., & Linares, C. (2016). Impact of air pollution and temperature on adverse birth outcomes: Madrid, 2001−2009. *Environmental Pollution*, *218*, 1154−1161. Available from https://doi.org/10.1016/j.envpol.2016.08.069.

Ayoko, G. A., Pluschke, P., & Hutzinger, O. (2004). *Indoor air pollution. The handbook of environmental chemistry* (4). Springer.

Balakrishnan, K., Dey, S., Gupta, T., Dhaliwal, R. S., Brauer, M., Cohen, A. J., Stanaway, J. D., Beig, G., Joshi, T. K., Aggarwal, A. N., Sabde, Y., Sadhu, H., Frostad, J., Causey, K., Godwin, W., Shukla, D. K., Kumar, G. A., Varghese, C. M., Muraleedharan, P., & Dandona, L. (2019). The impact of air pollution on deaths, disease burden, and life expectancy across the states of India: The Global Burden of Disease Study 2017. *The Lancet Planetary Health, 3*(1), e26−e39. Available from https://doi.org/10.1016/S2542-5196(18)30261-4.

Bartlett, R., Brown, L., Shattell, M., Wright, T., & Lewallen, L. (2013). Harm reduction: Compassionate care of persons with addictions. *Medsurg Nursing: Official Journal of the Academy of Medical-Surgical Nurses, 22*(6), 349−353.

BBC News. (2019). Why is India's pollution much worse than China's? https://www.bbc.com/news/world-asia-50298972.

Bento, A., Freedman, M., & Lang, C. (2015). Who benefits from environmental regulation? Evidence from the Clean Air Act amendments. *Review of Economics and Statistics, 97*(3), 610−622. Available from https://doi.org/10.1162/REST_a_00493.

Boor, B. E., Spilak, M. P., Laverge, J., Novoselac, A., & Xu, Y. (2017). Human exposure to indoor air pollutants in sleep microenvironments: A literature review. *Building and Environment, 125,* 528−555. Available from https://doi.org/10.1016/j.buildenv.2017.08.050.

Bruno, R. C. (1983). Sources of indoor radon in houses: A review. *Journal of the Air Pollution Control Association, 33*(2), 105−109. Available from https://doi.org/10.1080/00022470.1983.10465550.

Calautit, J. K., Aquino, A. I., Shahzad, S., Nasir, D. S. N. M., & Hughes, B. R. (2017). Thermal comfort and indoor air quality analysis of a low-energy cooling windcatcher. *Energy Procedia, 105,* 2865−2870. Available from https://doi.org/10.1016/j.egypro.2017.03.634.

Calderón-Garcidueñas, L., Mora-Tiscareño, A., Ontiveros, E., Gómez-Garza, G., Barragán-Mejía, G., Broadway, J., Chapman, S., Valencia-Salazar, G., Jewells, V., Maronpot, R. R., Henríquez-Roldán, C., Pérez-Guillé, B., Torres-Jardón, R., Herrit, L., Brooks, D., Osnaya-Brizuela, N., Monroy, M. E., González-Maciel, A., Reynoso-Robles, R., & Engle, R. W. (2008a). Air pollution, cognitive deficits and brain abnormalities: A pilot study with children and dogs. *Brain and Cognition, 68*(2), 117−127. Available from https://doi.org/10.1016/j.bandc.2008.04.008.

Calderón-Garcidueñas, L., Solt, A. C., Henríquez-Roldán, C., Torres-Jardón, R., Nuse, B., Herritt, L., Villarreal-Calderón, R., Osnaya, N., Stone, I., García, R., Brooks, D. M., González-Maciel, A., Reynoso-Robles, R., Delgado-Chávez, R., & Reed, W. (2008b). Long-term air pollution exposure is associated with neuroinflammation, an altered innate immune response, disruption of the blood-brain barrier, ultrafine particulate deposition, and accumulation of amyloid beta-42 and alpha-synuclein in children and young adults. *Toxicologic Pathology, 36*(2), 289−310. Available from https://doi.org/10.1177/0192623307313011.

Cecala, A. B., Organiscak, J. A., Noll, J. D., & Zimmer, J. A. (2016). Comparison of MERV 16 and HEPA filters for cab filtration of underground mining equipment. *Mining Engineering, 68*(8), 50−58. Available from https://doi.org/10.19150/me.6712.

Cincinelli, A., & Martellini, T. (2017). Indoor air quality and health. *International Journal of Environmental Research and Public Health, 14*(11), 1286. Available from https://doi.org/10.3390/ijerph14111286.

Delikhoon, M., Fazlzadeh, M., Sorooshian, A., Baghani, A. N., Golaki, M., Ashournejad, Q., & Barkhordari, A. (2018). Characteristics and health effects of formaldehyde and acetaldehyde in an urban area in Iran. *Environmental Pollution (Barking, Essex: 1987), 242*(Pt A), 938−951. Available from https://doi.org/10.1016/j.envpol.2018.07.037.

Ezzati, M., & Kammen, D. M. (2002). The health impacts of exposure to indoor air pollution from solid fuels in developing countries: Knowledge, gaps, and data needs. *Environmental Health Perspectives, 110*(11), 1057−1068. Available from https://doi.org/10.1289/ehp.021101057.

Fan, G., Xie, J., Yoshino, H., Yanagi, U., Hasegawa, K., Kagi, N., Goto, T., Zhang, Q., Wang, C., & Liu, J. (2018). Indoor environmental conditions in urban and rural homes with older people during heating season:

A case in cold region, China. *Energy and Buildings*, *167*, 334−346. Available from https://doi.org/10.1016/j.enbuild.2018.01.064.

Fang, L., Clausen, G., & Fanger, P. O. (1998). Impact of temperature and humidity on the perception of indoor air quality. *Indoor Air*, *8*(2), 80−90. Available from https://doi.org/10.1111/j.1600-0668.1998.t01-2-00003.x.

Foster, S., & Everett Jones, S. (2016). Association of school district policies for radon testing and radon-resistant new construction practices with indoor radon zones. *International Journal of Environmental Research and Public Health*, *13*(12), 1234. Available from https://doi.org/10.3390/ijerph13121234.

Fullerton, D. G., Bruce, N., & Gordon, S. B. (2008). Indoor air pollution from biomass fuel smoke is a major health concern in the developing world. *Transactions of the Royal Society of Tropical Medicine and Hygiene*, *102*(9), 843−851. Available from https://doi.org/10.1016/j.trstmh.2008.05.028.

Genc, S., Zadeoglulari, Z., Fuss, S. H., & Genc, K. (2012). The adverse effects of air pollution on the nervous system. *Journal of Toxicology*, *2012*, 1−23. Available from https://doi.org/10.1155/2012/782462.

Ghergu, C., Sushama, P., Vermeulen, J., Krumeich, A., Blankvoort, N., van Schayck, O. C., & de Witte, L. P. (2016). Dealing with indoor air pollution: An ethnographic tale from urban slums in Bangalore. *International Journal of Health Sciences*, *6*(1), 348−361.

Ghimire, S., Mishra, S. R., Sharma, A., Siweya, A., Shrestha, N., & Adhikari, B. (2019). Geographic and socio-economic variation in markers of indoor air pollution in Nepal: Evidence from nationally-representative data. *BMC Public Health*, *19*(1), 195. Available from https://doi.org/10.1186/s12889-019-6512-z.

Ghorani-Azam, A., Riahi-Zanjani, B., & Balali-Mood, M. (2016). Effects of air pollution on human health and practical measures for prevention in Iran. *Journal of Research in Medical Sciences*, *21*, 65. Available from https://doi.org/10.4103/1735-1995.189646.

Giamalaki, M., & Kolokotsa, D. (2019). Understanding the thermal experience of elderly people in their residences: Study on thermal comfort and adaptive behaviors of senior citizens in Crete, Greece. *Energy and Buildings*, *185*, 76−87. Available from https://doi.org/10.1016/j.enbuild.2018.12.025.

Gould, C. F., Schlesinger, S., Toasa, A. O., Thurber, M., Waters, W. F., Graham, J. P., & Jack, D. W. (2018). Government policy, clean fuel access, and persistent fuel stacking in Ecuador. *Energy for Sustainable Development*, *46*, 111−122. Available from https://doi.org/10.1016/j.esd.2018.05.009.

Haider, M. R., Rahman, M. M., Islam, F., & Khan, M. M. (2016). Association of low birthweight and indoor air pollution: Biomass fuel use in Bangladesh. *Journal of Health & Pollution*, *6*(11), 18−25. Available from https://doi.org/10.5696/2156-9614-6-11.18.

Hendryx, M., & Holland, B. (2016). Unintended consequences of the Clean Air Act: Mortality rates in Appalachian coal mining communities. *Environmental Science & Policy*, *63*, 1−6. Available from https://doi.org/10.1016/j.envsci.2016.04.021.

Hoppin, J. A., Adgate, J. L., Eberhart, M., Nishioka, M., & Ryan, P. B. (2006). Environmental exposure assessment of pesticides in farmworker homes. *Environmental Health Perspectives*, *114*(6), 929−935. Available from https://doi.org/10.1289/ehp.8530.

Horne, B. D., Joy, E. A., Hofmann, M. G., Gesteland, P. H., Cannon, J. B., Lefler, J. S., Blagev, D. P., Korgenski, E. K., Torosyan, N., Hansen, G. I., Kartchner, D., & Pope, C. A. (2018). Short-term elevation of fine particulate matter air pollution and acute lower respiratory infection. *American Journal of Respiratory and Critical Care Medicine*, *198*(6), 759−766. Available from https://doi.org/10.1164/rccm.201709-1883OC.

Huang, Y., Yang, Z., & Gao, Z. (2019). Contributions of indoor and outdoor sources to ozone in residential buildings in Nanjing. *International Journal of Environmental Research and Public Health*, *16*(14), 2587. Available from https://doi.org/10.3390/ijerph16142587.

IARC Working Group on the Evaluation of Carcinogenic Risks to Humans. (2010). *Household use of solid fuels and high-temperature frying. IARC monographs on the evaluation of carcinogenic risks to humans* (Vol. 95, pp. 1−430). Lyon: International Agency for Research on Cancer.

IARC Working Group on the Evaluation of Carcinogenic Risks to Humans. (2012). *Asbestos (chrysotile, amosite, crocidolite, tremolite)*. (1st ed.). *IARC monographs on the evaluation of carcinogenic risks to humans, No. 100C*, (Vol. 1). Lyon: International Agency for Research on Cancer.

India Today. (2019). Air pollution in Delhi was 16 times worse than prescribed limit on Diwali night. https://www.indiatoday.in/diu/story/delhi-air-pollution-16-times-worse-prescribed-limit-diwali-night-1613477-2019-10-28.

Irfan, M., Cameron, M. P., & Hassan, G. (2018). *Interventions to mitigate indoor air pollution: A cost-benefit analysis. Working papers in economics 18/14*. Hamilton: University of Waikato. Available from https://ideas.repec.org/cgi-bin/refs.cgi.

Jafari, M. J., Khajevandi, A. A., Mousavi Najarkola, S. A., Yekaninejad, M. S., Pourhoseingholi, M. A., Omidi, L., & Kalantary, S. (2015). Association of sick building syndrome with indoor air parameters. *Tanaffos*, *14*(1), 55−62.

Jomehzadeh, F., Nejat, P., Calautit, J. K., Yusof, M. B. M., Zaki, S. A., Hughes, B. R., & Yazid, M. N. A. W. M. (2017). A review on windcatcher for passive cooling and natural ventilation in buildings, Part 1: Indoor air quality and thermal comfort assessment. *Renewable and Sustainable Energy Reviews*, *70*, 736−756. Available from https://doi.org/10.1016/j.rser.2016.11.254.

Jorquera, H., Montoya, L. D., Rojas, N. Y., Henríquez, C., & Romero, H. (2019). *Urban air pollution. Urban Climates in Latin America* (pp. 137−165). Springer. Available from http://link.springer.com/10.1007/978-3-319-97013-4_7.

Joshi, S. M. (2008). The sick building syndrome. *Indian Journal of Occupational and Environmental Medicine*, *12*(2), 61−64. Available from https://doi.org/10.4103/0019-5278.43262.

Jung, J., & Huxham, M. (2018). Firewood usage and indoor air pollution from traditional cooking fires in Gazi Bay, Kenya. *Bioscience Horizons: The International Journal of Student Research*, *11*, hzy014. Available from https://doi.org/10.1093/biohorizons/hzy014.

Kabrein, H., Yusof, M. Z. M., & Leman, A. M. (2016). Progresses of filtration for removing particles and gases pollutants of indoor; limitations and future direction; review article. *ARPN Journal of Engineering and Applied Sciences*, *11*(6), 3633−3639.

Kaden, D., Mandin, C., Nielsen, G., & Wolkoff, P. (2010). *WHO guidelines for indoor air quality: Selected pollutants*. Geneva: World Health Organization. Available from https://www.ncbi.nlm.nih.gov/books/NBK138711/.

Kagan, V. E., Bayir, H., & Shvedova, A. A. (2005). Nanomedicine and nanotoxicology: Two sides of the same coin. *Nanomedicine: Nanotechnology, Biology, and Medicine*, *1*(4), 313−316. Available from https://doi.org/10.1016/j.nano.2005.10.003.

Kelp, M. M., Grieshop, A. P., Reynolds, C. C. O., Baumgartner, J., Jain, G., Sethuraman, K., & Marshall, J. D. (2018). Real-time indoor measurement of health and climate-relevant air pollution concentrations during a carbon-finance-approved cookstove intervention in rural India. *Development Engineering*, *3*, 125−132. Available from https://doi.org/10.1016/j.deveng.2018.05.001.

Lantz, P. M., Mendez, D., & Philbert, M. A. (2013). Radon, smoking, and lung cancer: The need to refocus radon control policy. *American Journal of Public Health*, *103*(3), 443−447. Available from https://doi.org/10.2105/AJPH.2012.300926.

Laquatra, J., & Abdul Mujeebu, M. (2019). *Indoor air quality. Indoor environmental quality*. IntechOpen. Available from https://www.intechopen.com/books/indoor-environmental-quality/indoor-air-quality.

Laumbach, R., Meng, Q., & Kipen, H. (2015). What can individuals do to reduce personal health risks from air pollution? *Journal of Thoracic Disease*, *7*(1), 96−107. Available from https://doi.org/10.3978/j.issn.2072-1439.2014.12.21.

Laumbach, R. J., & Kipen, H. M. (2012). Respiratory health effects of air pollution: Update on biomass smoke and traffic pollution. *The Journal of Allergy and Clinical Immunology*, *129*(1), 3−11. Available from https://doi.org/10.1016/j.jaci.2011.11.021.

Lewallen, S., & Courtright, P. (2002). Gender and use of cataract surgical services in developing countries. *Bulletin of the World Health Organization, 80*(4), 300−303.

Lewtas, J. (2007). Air pollution combustion emissions: Characterization of causative agents and mechanisms associated with cancer, reproductive, and cardiovascular effects. *Mutation Research/Reviews in Mutation Research, 636*(1−3), 95−133. Available from https://doi.org/10.1016/j.mrrev.2007.08.003.

Liu, W., Shen, G., Chen, Y., Shen, H., Huang, Y., Li, T., Wang, Y., Fu, X., Tao, S., Liu, W., Huang-Fu, Y., Zhang, W., Xue, C., Liu, G., Wu, F., & Wong, M. (2018). Air pollution and inhalation exposure to particulate matter of different sizes in rural households using improved stoves in central China. *Journal of Environmental Sciences, 63*, 87−95. Available from https://doi.org/10.1016/j.jes.2017.06.019.

Liu, G., Xiao, M., Zhang, X., Gal, C., Chen, X., Liu, L., Pan, S., Wu, J., Tang, L., & Clements-Croome, D. (2017). A review of air filtration technologies for sustainable and healthy building ventilation. *Sustainable Cities and Society, 32*, 375−396. Available from https://doi.org/10.1016/j.scs.2017.04.011.

Lu, C.-Y., Lin, J.-M., Chen, Y.-Y., & Chen, Y.-C. (2015). Building-related symptoms among office employees associated with indoor carbon dioxide and total volatile organic compounds. *International Journal of Environmental Research and Public Health, 12*(6), 5833−5845. Available from https://doi.org/10.3390/ijerph120605833.

Mason, T. G., Schooling, C. M., Chan, K. P., & Tian, L. (2019). An evaluation of the air quality health index program on respiratory diseases in Hong Kong: An interrupted time series analysis. *Atmospheric Environment, 211*, 151−158. Available from https://doi.org/10.1016/j.atmosenv.2019.05.013.

Mathew, M., McLeod, R., Salman, D., & Thomas, P. (2019). Should current indoor environment and air quality standards be doing more to protect young people in educational buildings? <https://repository.lboro.ac.uk/articles/Should_current_indoor_environment_and_air_quality_standards_be_doing_more_to_protect_young_people_in_educational_buildings_/9458243>.

Mdege, N., Fairhurst, C., Ferdous, T., Hewitt, C., Huque, R., Jackson, C., Kellar, I., Parrott, S., Semple, S., Sheikh, A., Swami, S., & Siddiqi, K. (2019). Muslim communities learning about second-hand smoke in Bangladesh (MCLASS II): Study protocol for a cluster randomised controlled trial of a community-based smoke-free homes intervention, with or without indoor air quality feedback. *Trials, 20*(1), 11. Available from https://doi.org/10.1186/s13063-018-3100-y.

Mishra, V. K., Retherford, R. D., & Smith, K. R. (1999). Biomass cooking fuels and prevalence of blindness in India. *Journal of Environmental Medicine, 1*(4), 189−199. Available from https://doi.org/10.1002/jem.30.

Mitter, S. S., Vedanthan, R., Islami, F., Pourshams, A., Khademi, H., Kamangar, F., Abnet, C. C., Dawsey, S. M., Pharoah, P. D., Brennan, P., Fuster, V., Boffetta, P., & Malekzadeh, R. (2016). Household fuel use and cardiovascular disease mortality: Golestan cohort study. *Circulation, 133*(24), 2360−2369. Available from https://doi.org/10.1161/CIRCULATIONAHA.115.020288.

Moturi, N. W. (2010). Risk factors for indoor air pollution in rural households in Mauche division, Molo district. *Kenya. African Health Sciences, 10*(3), 230−234.

Nicolas, M., Ramalho, O., & Maupetit, F. (2003). Impact of ozone on indoor air quality: A Preliminary Field Study. Healthy. *Buildings, 1*, 247−252.

Nogueira, J. B. (2009). Air pollution and cardiovascular disease. Revista Portuguesa de Cardiologia : Orgao Oficial Da Sociedade Portuguesa de Cardiologia = Portuguese. *Journal of Cardiology, 28*(6), 715−733.

Norhidayah, A., Chia-Kuang, L., Azhar, M. K., & Nurulwahida, S. (2013). Indoor air quality and sick building syndrome in three selected buildings. *Procedia Engineering, 53*, 93−98. Available from https://doi.org/10.1016/j.proeng.2013.02.014.

Oren, I., Haddad, N., Finkelstein, R., & Rowe, J. M. (2001). Invasive pulmonary aspergillosis in neutropenic patients during hospital construction: Before and after chemoprophylaxis and institution of HEPA filters. *American Journal of Hematology, 66*(4), 257−262. Available from https://doi.org/10.1002/ajh.1054.

Persily, A. (2015). Challenges in developing ventilation and indoor air quality standards: The story of ASHRAE Standard 62. *Building and Environment*, *91*, 61−69. Available from https://doi.org/10.1016/j.buildenv.2015.02.026.

Pokhrel, A. K., Smith, K. R., Khalakdina, A., Deuja, A., & Bates, M. N. (2005). Case-control study of indoor cooking smoke exposure and cataract in Nepal and India. *International Journal of Epidemiology*, *34*(3), 702−708. Available from https://doi.org/10.1093/ije/dyi015.

Ritchie, H., & Roser, M. (2019). Indoor air pollution. <https://ourworldindata.org/indoor-air-pollution>.

Ritz, B., & Yu, F. (1999). The effect of ambient carbon monoxide on low birth weight among children born in southern California between 1989 and 1993. *Environmental Health Perspectives*, *107*(1), 17−25.

Rosen, L. J., Myers, V., Winickoff, J. P., & Kott, J. (2015). Effectiveness of interventions to reduce tobacco smoke pollution in homes: A systematic review and meta-analysis. *International Journal of Environmental Research and Public Health*, *12*(12), 16043−16059. Available from https://doi.org/10.3390/ijerph121215038.

Rumchev, K., Zhao, Y., & Spickett, J. (2017). Health risk assessment of indoor air quality, socioeconomic and house characteristics on respiratory health among women and children of Tirupur, South India. *International Journal of Environmental Research and Public Health*, *14*(4), 429. Available from https://doi.org/10.3390/ijerph14040429.

Rupakheti, D., Kim Oanh, N. T., Rupakheti, M., Sharma, R. K., Panday, A. K., Puppala, S. P., & Lawrence, M. G. (2019). Indoor levels of black carbon and particulate matters in relation to cooking activities using different cook stove-fuels in rural Nepal. *Energy for Sustainable Development*, *48*, 25−33. Available from https://doi.org/10.1016/j.esd.2018.10.007.

Sagar, A., Balakrishnan, K., Guttikunda, S., Roychowdhury, A., & Smith, K. R. (2016). India leads the way: a health-centered strategy for air pollution. *Environmental Health Perspectives*, *124*(7), 116−117. Available from https://doi.org/10.1289/EHP90.

Saini, J., Dutta, M., & Marques, G. (2020). A comprehensive review on indoor air quality monitoring systems for enhanced public health. *Sustainable Environment Research*, *30*(1), 6. Available from https://doi.org/10.1186/s42834-020-0047-y.

Salthammer, T., Mentese, S., & Marutzky, R. (2010). Formaldehyde in the indoor environment. *Chemical Reviews*, *110*(4), 2536−2572. Available from https://doi.org/10.1021/cr800399g.

Samet, J. M., Bahrami, H., & Berhane, K. (2016). Indoor air pollution and cardiovascular disease: New evidence from Iran. *Circulation*, *133*(24), 2342−2344. Available from https://doi.org/10.1161/CIRCULATIONAHA.116.023477.

Sangeetha, D.N., Subramanian, V., Jose, M.T., & Venkatraman, B. (2016). A preliminary study on shelf life of high efficiency particulate air (HEPA) filter used in nuclear facilities. In Proceedings of the international conference on radiological safety in workplace, nuclear facilities and environment (Vol. 47), Kalpakkam, India, February 22−25, 2016. http://inis.iaea.org/search/search.aspx?orig_q = RN:47088568.

Sarkar, A., Roy, D., Chauhan, M., Makwana, N. R., Parmar, D. V., & Yadav, S. (2019). A study on the pattern of self-reported tobacco addiction in hypertensive patients in Gujarat, India. *Addiction & Health*, *11*(1), 35−42. Available from https://doi.org/10.22122/ahj.v11i1.223.

Sarwar, M., & Lee, A. (2016). Indoor risks of pesticide uses are significantly linked to hazards of the family members. *Cogent Medicine*, *3*(1), 1155373. Available from https://doi.org/10.1080/2331205X.2016.1155373.

Schneider, J., & Woitowitz, H. J. (1995). Asbestos-related mesotheliomas in housewives from indoor air pollution. *International Journal of Hygiene and Environmental Medicine*, *196*(6), 495−503.

Shalini, V. K., Luthra, M., Srinivas, L., Rao, S. H., Basti, S., Reddy, M., & Balasubramanian, D. (1994). Oxidative damage to the eye lens caused by cigarette smoke and fuel smoke condensates. *Indian Journal of Biochemistry & Biophysics*, *31*(4), 261−266.

Sharma, D., & Jain, S. (2019). Impact of intervention of biomass cookstove technologies and kitchen characteristics on indoor air quality and human exposure in rural settings of India. *Environment International*, *123*, 240−255. Available from https://doi.org/10.1016/j.envint.2018.11.059.

Singh, A. L., & Aligarh, S. J. (2013). A comparative analysis of indoor air pollution due to domestic fuel used in rural and urban households: A case study. *Transactions, 35*(2), 287−298.

Singleton, R., Salkoski, A. J., Bulkow, L., Fish, C., Dobson, J., Albertson, L., Skarada, J., Ritter, T., Kovesi, T., & Hennessy, T. W. (2018). Impact of home remediation and household education on indoor air quality, respiratory visits and symptoms in Alaska Native children. *International Journal of Circumpolar Health, 77*(1), 1422669. Available from https://doi.org/10.1080/22423982.2017.1422669.

Śmiełowska, M., Marć, M., & Zabiegała, B. (2017). Indoor air quality in public utility environments—A review. *Environmental Science and Pollution Research, 24*(12), 11166−11176. Available from https://doi.org/10.1007/s11356-017-8567-7.

Smolle, E., & Pichler, M. (2019). Non-smoking-associated lung cancer: A distinct entity in terms of tumor biology, patient characteristics and impact of hereditary cancer predisposition. *Cancers, 11*(2), 204. Available from https://doi.org/10.3390/cancers11020204.

Stabile, L., Dell'Isola, M., Frattolillo, A., Massimo, A., & Russi, A. (2016). Effect of natural ventilation and manual airing on indoor air quality in naturally ventilated Italian classrooms. *Building and Environment, 98*, 180−189. Available from https://doi.org/10.1016/j.buildenv.2016.01.009.

National Research Council Staff. (1999). *Health effects of exposure to radon: BEIR VI.* Washington, DC: The National Academies Press. Available from https://public.ebookcentral.proquest.com/choice/publicfullrecord.aspx?p = 3375739.

Steenhof, M., Janssen, N. A. H., Strak, M., Hoek, G., Gosens, I., Mudway, I. S., Kelly, F. J., Harrison, R. M., Pieters, R. H. H., Cassee, F. R., & Brunekreef, B. (2014). Air pollution exposure affects circulating white blood cell counts in healthy subjects: The role of particle composition, oxidative potential and gaseous pollutants—The RAPTES project. *Inhalation Toxicology, 26*(3), 141−165. Available from https://doi.org/10.3109/08958378.2013.861884.

Sublett, J. L. (2011). Effectiveness of air filters and air cleaners in allergic respiratory diseases: A review of the recent literature. *Current Allergy and Asthma Reports, 11*(5), 395−402. Available from https://doi.org/10.1007/s11882-011-0208-5.

Sublett, J. L., Seltzer, J., Burkhead, R., Williams, P. B., Wedner, H. J., & Phipatanakul, W.American Academy of Allergy Asthma & Immunology. (2010). Air filters and air cleaners: Rostrum by the American Academy of Allergy, Asthma & Immunology Indoor Allergen Committee. *The Journal of Allergy and Clinical Immunology, 125*(1), 32−38. Available from https://doi.org/10.1016/j.jaci.2009.08.036.

Sun, Q., Yue, P., Ying, Z., Cardounel, A. J., Brook, R. D., Devlin, R., Hwang, J.-S., Zweier, J. L., Chen, L. C., & Rajagopalan, S. (2008). Air pollution exposure potentiates hypertension through reactive oxygen species-mediated activation of Rho/ROCK. *Arteriosclerosis, Thrombosis, and Vascular Biology, 28*(10), 1760−1766. Available from https://doi.org/10.1161/ATVBAHA.108.166967.

The Economic Times. (2019). Not just outdoor, indoor air in Delhi polluted too: Study. <https://economictimes.indiatimes.com/news/politics-and-nation/not-just-outdoor-indoor-air-in-delhi-polluted-too-study/articleshow/71279705.cms>.

Tran, V. V., Park, D., & Lee, Y.-C. (2020). Indoor air pollution, related human diseases, and recent trends in the control and improvement of indoor air quality. *International Journal of Environmental Research and Public Health, 17*(8), 2927. Available from https://doi.org/10.3390/ijerph17082927.

Tsai, W.-T. (2017). Overview of green building material (GBM) policies and guidelines with relevance to indoor air quality management in Taiwan. *Environments, 5*(1), 4. Available from https://doi.org/10.3390/environments5010004.

Valavanidis, A., Vlachogianni, T., Fiotakis, K., & Loridas, S. (2013). Pulmonary oxidative stress, inflammation and cancer: Respirable particulate matter, fibrous dusts and ozone as major causes of lung carcinogenesis through reactive oxygen species mechanisms. *International Journal of Environmental Research and Public Health, 10*(9), 3886−3907. Available from https://doi.org/10.3390/ijerph10093886.

Vermeulen, R., Downward, G. S., Zhang, J., Hu, W., Portengen, L., Bassig, B. A., Hammond, S. K., Wong, J. Y. Y., Li, J., Reiss, B., He, J., Tian, L., Yang, K., Seow, W. J., Xu, J., Anderson, K., Ji, B.-T., Silverman, D., Chanock, S., & Lan, Q. (2019). Constituents of household air pollution and risk of lung cancer among never-smoking women in Xuanwei and Fuyuan, China. *Environmental Health Perspectives*, *127*(9), 97001. Available from https://doi.org/10.1289/EHP4913.

Watson, A. Y., Bates, R. R., & Kennedy, D. (1988). *Air pollution, the automobile, and public health*. Washington, DC: The National Academies Press. Available from http://www.ncbi.nlm.nih.gov/books/NBK218150/.

Weisel, C. P. (2002). Assessing exposure to air toxics relative to asthma. *Environmental Health Perspectives*, *110*(Suppl 4), 527–537.

WHO. (2018). Household air pollution and health. <https://www.who.int/news-room/fact-sheets/detail/household-air-pollution-and-health>.

Wolkoff, P. (2018). Indoor air humidity, air quality, and health—An overview. *International Journal of Hygiene and Environmental Health*, *221*(3), 376–390. Available from https://doi.org/10.1016/j.ijheh.2018.01.015.

World Economic Forum. (2019). The dark side of Diwali, festival of lights. https://www.weforum.org/agenda/2019/11/diwali-air-pollution-delhi-health/.

Wu, Y., Miao, H., & Fan, S. (2011). *Separation of chiral pyrethroid pesticides and application in pharmacokinetics research and human exposure assessment. Pesticides in the modern world—Effects of pesticides exposure*. IntechOpen. Available from https://doi.org/10.5772/16617.

Xu, Z. (2014). *Fundamentals of air cleaning technology and its application in cleanrooms*. Springer. Available from http://link.springer.com/10.1007/978-3-642-39374-7.

Yoon, Y., Kim, S., Lee, J., Choi, J., Kim, R.-K., Lee, S.-J., Sul, O., & Lee, S.-B. (2016). Clogging-free microfluidics for continuous size-based separation of microparticles. *Scientific Reports*, *6*, 26531. Available from https://doi.org/10.1038/srep26531.

Yue, K., Sun, X., Tang, J., Wei, Y., & Zhang, X. (2019). A simulation study on the interaction between pollutant nanoparticles and the pulmonary surfactant monolayer. *International Journal of Molecular Sciences*, *20*(13), 3281. Available from https://doi.org/10.3390/ijms20133281.

Zhang Junfeng (Jim)., & Smith Kirk, R. (2007). Household air pollution from coal and biomass fuels in China: Measurements, health impacts, and interventions. *Environmental Health Perspectives*, *115*(6), 848–855. Available from https://doi.org/10.1289/ehp.9479.

Zhao, X., Wang, S., Yin, X., Yu, J., & Ding, B. (2016). Slip-effect functional air filter for efficient purification of PM2.5. *Scientific Reports*, *6*(1), 35472. Available from https://doi.org/10.1038/srep35472.

Zhao, N., Zhang, Y., Li, B., Hao, J., Chen, D., Zhou, Y., & Dong, R. (2019). Natural gas and electricity: Two perspective technologies of substituting coal-burning stoves for rural heating and cooking in Hebei Province of China. *Energy Science & Engineering*, *7*(1), 120–131. Available from https://doi.org/10.1002/ese3.263.

Žuškin, E., Schachter, E. N., Mustajbegović, J., Pucarin-Cvetković, J., Doko-Jelinić, J., & Mučić-Pucić, B. (2009). Indoor air pollution and effects on human health. *Periodicum Biologorum*, *111*(1), 37–40.

Data-centric and intelligent systems in water quality monitoring, assessment, and mitigation

Data-centric intelligent systems for water quality monitoring, assessment, and control

Samuel Eshorame Sanni[1], Emmanuel Emeka Okoro[2], Emmanuel Rotimi Sadiku[3] and Babalola Aisosa Oni[1]

[1]Department of Chemical Engineering, Covenant University, Ota, Nigeria [2]Department of Petroleum and Gas Engineering, University of Port Harcourt, Port Harcourt, Nigeria [3]Department of Metallurgy, Polymer and Chemical Engineering, Tshwane University of Technology, Pretoria, South Africa

Introduction

The flow of pollutants (industrial wastes and accidental spillages) into aquatic systems has become a serious menace to the ecosystem, the Earth's environment, as well as human lives (Azizullah et al., 2011; Fang et al., 2018; Wu et al., 2016). The recent increase in the frequency of water pollution incidents is somewhat alarming, and calls for drastic measures to gain full control of the situation (Shao et al., 2006; Wang et al., 2019a, 2019b; Wu et al., 2017). To guide against the risks associated with water pollution, it is pertinent to understand the nature and sources of these pollutants, their toxicodynamics/kinetics alongside water dynamics, all aimed at developing adequate water protection schemes/systems toward ensuring a high reduction in the number of pollution incidents and indiscriminate wastewater discharges via quick and effective wastewater disposal systems. This then suggests the need to develop accurate and efficient pollutant tracers and source trackers, which will help keep track of the locations, types/quantities of pollutants, and periods when these pollutants are released into aquatic systems (Shao et al., 2006; Wang et al., 2019a, 2019b; Wu et al., 2017). To achieve this, adequate water quality assessment and pollutant-source-tracking strategies can be ensured via monitoring stations where the movement of these pollutants can be tracked along a path from source to destination. Owing to the diverse nature of hydrological/water transformation processes, river dynamics, and water sources from which these pollutants are released; every pollutant source has distinct water quality characteristics (Kai et al., 2019; Wang et al., 2014). In recent times, population growth in some regions of the world has greatly impacted climate change, which in turn, has a recursive effect on water usage patterns, water quality, and the availability of groundwater (Carlson et al., 2011; Chen, 2019; Taylor et al., 2013; Mining et al., 2018; Wakode et al., 2018). The impact of urbanization on climate in arid and semiarid regions has been reported to have a direct impact on surface land cover, rate of evaporation, rainfall levels, surface runoffs, and the Earth's temperature, which also have negative consequences on the groundwater refill rate and accessibility (Kalhor & Emaminejad, 2019; Shahid & Hazarika, 2010; Trichakis et al., 2011). Thus, to improve on the efficiencies of water quality assessment and monitoring processes, there is a high demand placed on the use of artificial intelligence as a means of ensuring swift responses to the world's water pollution concerns.

Modern advances in computing technology have led to the increased use of AI rather than numerical models in simulating flow and water quality in coastal environments. However, more importantly, emphasis is on the application of algorithmic procedures that are able to address problems related to water quality/pollution. Prior to this, numerical models were employed which despite lacking user-friendliness, are also void of knowledge transfer at the model-interpretation phase. Hence there is a need to address these constraints on model application as well as to close the undesirable gaps between model developers and users. Model selection is usually not an easy task, especially when adequate information on the scenarios under investigation is not available (Chau, 2006). This then informs the need to incorporate some existing heuristic knowledge about the model manipulation steps, which in turn furnish the user with adequate information toward ensuring suitable intelligent manipulation of the inherent calibration parameters. Some numerical models applied in water quality simulation include the finite element, finite difference (FD) (Chau, 2006), boundary element, and Eulerian–Lagrangian methods, whose time-stepping algorithms are either implicit, explicit, or characteristic-based with respect to their shape functions/orders (i.e., first, second, or higher orders). The mathematical modeling step is usually simplified into a spatial one-, two-, or three-dimensional depth-average model (Chau et al., 1996; Chau & Jiang, 2001, 2002; Cheng et al., 1984; Tucciarelli & Termini, 2000). The subject, "hydraulics and water quality modeling," generally involves some heuristics and empirical experience, which are implemented via simplification and modeling approaches that lean on the experiences/skills of professionals (Yu & Righetto, 2001). However, the levels of accuracy attained during the model-prediction step largely depend on nonzero tolerance for errors in the establishment of boundary conditions, model variables, as well as the numerical scheme used (Martin et al., 1999). As previously mentioned, the selection of a suitable numerical model as the solution to a practical water quality problem is somewhat herculean (Ragas et al., 1997), hence detailed knowledge of the applications and limitations of prospective models is required. To appropriately model the water quality of rivers, oceans, streams, ponds, etc., information, such as water depth, velocity, grid spacing, etc., ought to be known. In addition, there is also ample evidence that, for nonexpert users, the length of time expended on model manipulation procedures is highly dependent on the experience of the user. Therefore it has become pertinent to include some established training features that will aid easy selection, design, and application of these models. In addition, the complex nature of the numerical simulation of water hydraulics and quality has necessitated the integration of AI in some existing mathematical models for easy selection and application. Recently, there has been increased interest in the application of AI (Chau & Ng, 1996; Chau & Yang, 1993; Chau & Zhang, 1995) owing to the possibility of simulating human expertise within a well-defined/descriptive domain at the problem-solving phase; this entails incorporating descriptive, procedural, and reasoning knowledge/abilities in the problem analysis stage, which also permits the successful development of intelligent management/data-centric systems with the use of shells in application software, such as MATLAB, Visual Basic, and C++ to ensure adequate/efficient water quality modeling. Over the past few decades, the continuous advancements in AI have made it possible to integrate existing technologies and experiences into numerical modeling systems as a way of abating this challenge. Some AI technologies adopted for water quality modeling include genetic algorithm (GA), knowledge-based system (KBS), artificial neural network (ANN), the fuzzy inference system (FIS), etc.

Problems associated with numerical modeling in hydraulic transport and water quality prediction

Numerical modeling is the digitalization of knowledge transformation as regards a physical phenomenon with the aim of simulating behaviors, to translate the numerical output into a comprehensible format (Abbott, 1993). One major problem often encountered in process modeling is model manipulation, especially at the model development stage, because a slight variation in the phenomenological parameters may result in several outputs/deviations from the expected outcome. This makes knowledge of model manipulation essential; the steps involved include identification of the process type (chemical/physical process), physical observations/monitoring, mathematical description of hydraulics or water quality, discretization procedure of the governing equations for the process, suitable/accurate algorithm(s) for solving the discretized equations, as well as an analysis and interpretation of the output. Nonetheless, skill is a basic requirement in identifying the failure of a model, especially when comparing simulated output with real-life data as well as passing heuristic judgments in line with some observed environmental changes. Many model users lack the requisite knowledge for using a set of input data in a generated algorithm for the successful evaluation of the outcomes of precise investigations. Hence they may encounter problems such as design inferiority, which in turn leads to model underutilization or failure (Chau, 2006).

Why artificial intelligence?

The ultimate aim in water quality engineering is to achieve a satisfactory simulation. With the advent of computers, the underscored limitations of numerical models have only known some limited controls owing to the fact that computers are limited in memory and speed. This then led to the idea of striking a balance between model accuracy and speed during the model manipulation step as a way of limiting the constraints imposed by assuming that certain basic parameters are usually constant. For instance, in 2D coastal modeling, some authors assumed a constant bottom friction coefficient (Chau & Jin, 1995) to simplify their problem, while the work of Baird and Whitelaw (1992) reported water quality modeling by predicting algal behavior in relation to its respiration rate and water temperature. In simulating an eutrophication process, consideration for the variation of sunlight intensity within the water column is also a necessity (Chau & Jin, 1998). All of the highlighted examples are clear indications that human intelligence adopts existing knowledge as a means of trimming down the number of available choices/alternatives that help to improve the accuracy of the model manipulation step through the alteration of one or a few variables. This is because the modification of many variables at the same time may result in losses or marginal errors along the direction/path of manipulation. To augment for these lapses, AI technologies have been employed because of their capacity to mimic several behavioral trends while complementing the inherent deficiencies of numerical models. Therefore it then suffices to point out that although first-generation models are systems of linear equations applied in proffering solutions to environmental problems, due to the complex dynamics of the situations arising from hydraulic transport and water quality problems, nonlinear solutions have been established to help alleviate some of these challenges. As a further improvement to the existing models, came the third-generation models which are applied to specific domain problems (Cunge, 1989; Falconer et al., 1992). They possess features that facilitate their application in solving related problems, with examples including the 2D/3D FD numerical models for making reasonable parametric predictions of the hydraulic changes/water quality alteration that arise during tidal flows (Chau et al., 1996; Chau & Jin, 1998, 1995). The fourth-generation models have a wider range of application, parameter specification, grid formation, preprocessing/postprocessing features, and capacity to manage real-life data. Hence they are referred to as intelligent front ends that facilitate other simulation tools that help to combat some specific hydrological/water quality concerns (Knight & Petridis, 1992; Recknagel et al., 1998). In lieu of this, their shortcomings include their inability to fully address knowledge elicitation and transfer (Abbott, 1991). These lapses have also ushered in the need to develop and apply expert systems that are fitted with human capacities to reason and solve the uncertainties associated with water pollution problems with special considerations for their sources, nature, interactions, and forces that cause particulate/gaseous migrations into water bodies (Ragas et al., 1997). Hence the fifth-generation models are fitted with AI technologies/algorithms and machine learning features that are often employed in computational hydrodynamics as separate entities, which help to furnish nonexperienced users with the requisite steps for handling water pollution and other related problems (Chau & Chen, 2001).

AI methods and machine learning methods for water quality modeling and contaminant hydrology

Knowledge-based systems

These are highly interactive computerized tools that help in mimicking and automating human-expert decision-making and reasoning processes to proffer solutions to particular domain problems by providing answers to questions, rendering advice, drawing inferences, and justifying conclusions. Fig. 7.1 is an illustration of the KBS process (Chau, 2006). The knowledge base houses information/general facts about the situation of interest, the associated rule of thumb, and a set of causal models that are applicable to a particular problem domain. The KBS-inference section uses the knowledge base as a guide to control the decision-making process by contextualizing the problem in the problem domain.

The contextualized problem domain consists of facts about the current state of the problem, hence it is dynamically oriented by the inferential mechanism, which extracts pieces of information from the knowledge base and operator. The KBS is comprised of a knowledge acquisition module, which provides the link/interface between experts and the KBS; its role is to provide a way of keying in specific knowledge in the knowledge base. The link/interface between experts and the KBS helps to translate the user-specified input to a usable or machine-readable format. In the KBS, there is also an explanation module which explains how inferences are drawn and applied, that is, explanations on why certain information is demanded and the manner in which a conclusion is drawn. KBS is deemed suitable for addressing situations that require skilled expertise, professional judgment, and the

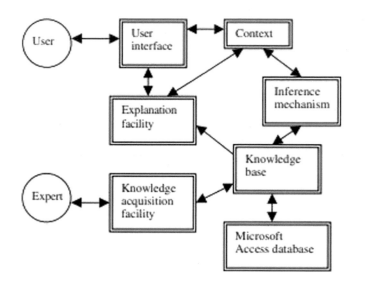

FIGURE 7.1

The KBS work flow. *KBS*, Knowledge-based system.

From Chau, K.W. (2006). A review on integration of artificial intelligence into water quality modelling. Marine Pollution Bulletin, 52
(7), 726–733. https://doi.org/10.1016/j.marpolbul.2006.04.003. Reprinted with permission from Elsevier.

application of rule of thumb. KBS finds application in several areas, including engineering (Chau & Albermani, 2002), medicine, social sciences, biotechnology, etc. Some studies have considered the integration of KBS in numerical modeling of coastal flows (Blanpain & Chocat, 1994; Uzel et al., 1988). These models are confined to 1D flow situations of river network/planning owing to their non-complex nature and selection procedure/rules of engagement. The study of Chau and Yang was on the use of an integrated expert system in handling issues related to fluvial hydrodynamics (Chau & Yang, 1993). A decision support system (DSS) for effective river basin planning and management has been developed (Jamieson & Fedra, 1996). The application of integrated intelligent systems in environmental models was adopted by Bobba et al. (2000) in tackling several hydrological issues. The work of Booty et al. (2001) involves the design and implementation of a DSS for toxic/poisonous chemicals in some of the Great Lakes by making use of technologies such as 1D model-spatial algorithms, statistics, KBS, and other information technology tools. The established knowledge bases are endowed with heuristic rules that do not allow for model manipulation, but are suitable for the model selection subroutine. Therefore, however simple a case is, adequate programming of the knowledge representation and selection processes are necessary despite being somewhat herculean. Hence, for 2D/3D modeling, the integration of KBS and its solution algorithm as one entity/system, makes the solution complex. In essence, the administered solution should be able to provide expert advice on the model selection process alongside the parameters needed to model particular situations. Based on the fact that many concerted efforts and long-term sacrifices have been committed to the development of most established system software programs (Fortran, Pascal, C++, Visual Basic, etc.), which are in machine-readable format, this then implies that it would amount to high costs/redundancy if they were to be rewritten and replaced.

The architectural prototype of an integrated KBS is illustrated in Fig. 7.2 (Chau, 2006). The expert system shell/visual rule studio (VRS) runs as an ActiveX Designer in the Microsoft Visual Basic 6.0 environment. The VRS (hybrid expert system) takes advantage of the production rules and the objective-programmed examples for some expert-tackled problems.

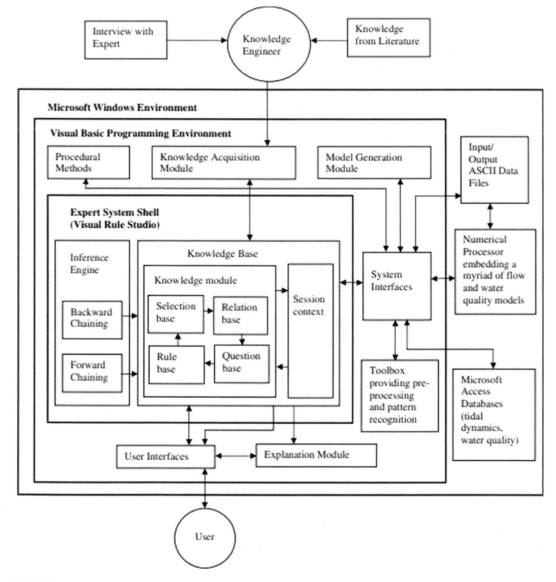

FIGURE 7.2

A prototype KBS with the ability to manipulate flow and water quality. *KBS*, Knowledge-based system.

From Chau, K.W. (2006). A review on integration of artificial intelligence into water quality modelling. Marine Pollution Bulletin, 52 (7), 726–733. https://doi.org/10.1016/j.marpolbul.2006.04.003. *Reprinted with permission from Elsevier.*

Genetic algorithm

GA is a stochastic search procedure that employs computational models of natural evolutionary origin in the development of computer-based solution systems (Goldberg, 1989). The search procedures of GA are based on mechanisms describing natural genetics and biologically inspired activities, which can be adopted as optimization tools that help minimize/maximize the target-objective function. Their modus operandi works on the concept of survival of the fittest merged with an information-exchange program via random genetic operations that simulate nature to generate an effectively managed mechanism. GA is iteratively fashioned to produce sample population strings that simulate a natural collection of biological organisms, where old generations of such organisms are conceived, born, and nurtured until their due time for reproduction. GA is not constrained by assumptions/search space, especially in terms of its continuity equations/existing derivatives. Some genetic operators (i.e., selection, dominance, deletion, migration, inversion, intrachromosomal duplication, mutation, segregation, crossover, sharing, translocation, etc.) have been integrated into GA. According to some reports, GA has the capacity to proffer suitable solutions to problems ranging from simple to highly complex, multivariable problems (Chau et al., 1996; Chau & Jiang, 2001, 2002; Cheng et al., 1984; Tucciarelli & Termini, 2000). In simulating and predicting the flow scenario and water quality management using numerical models, incorrect use of the model parameters acquired via experimentation often introduces unintended errors, thus ensuring numerical instability. However, it is interesting to note that GA provides the platform for determining appropriate parameter combinations for the case under investigation. Some statistical parameters such as percentage error of peak value, peak time, total water volume flow rate, and composition are very pertinent parameters for water quality modeling. The parametric calibrations that are usually carried out to determine some established constants are usually based on tidal measures, as well as the accumulation of water constituents over several years. Furthermore, tests such as sensitivity analysis on crossover/mutation probability, sample-size, and maximum evaluations can be performed as a way of determining the most suitable algorithm or solution pathway for the situation under investigation. In essence, GAs are applicable in situations where models with more transparent knowledge representations can be used to describe the problem of interest; this in turn facilitates a good understanding of the behavioral and predictive patterns, regularities, and interrelationships that exist within certain phenomena using specific model algorithms (Chau, 2006). The use of GA in the calibration of a water quality model has been carried out (Ng & Perera, 2003) while the GA optimization of municipal wastewater treatment to determine river water quality was investigated by Heon et al. (2004). Chau (2002) also employed GA in calibrating and modeling flow and water quality where the model was found to accurately mimic the basic characteristics of the flow and quality of water investigated.

Artificial neural network

ANN is a system whose architecture is like that of the brain entrenched by neurons. The ANN structure is comprised of noncomplex models comprising of a black box of processing elements linked by variable weights (Garrett, 1994). Fig. 7.3 shows the structural view of an ANN architecture whose three layers are interconnected by nodes or neurons (Chau, 2006). It comprises of input and output layers where data are made available to the neural network and given as responses within the network to the input signals. There are also one or more intermediate layers (hidden layers), which lie between the input and output layers; these help in determining the levels of complex associations that exist between patterns. The neurons within the intermediate and output layers

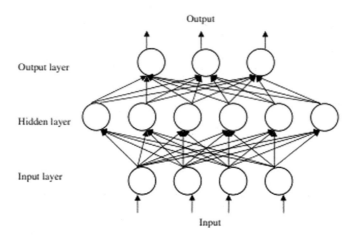

FIGURE 7.3

Structural view of ANN architecture. *ANN,* Artificial neural network (Chau & Albermani, 2003).

From Chau, K.W., & Albermani, F. (2003). Knowledge-based system on optimum design of liquid retaining structures with genetic algorithms. Journal of Structural Engineering, 129(10), 1312–1321. https://doi.org/10.1061/(ASCE)0733-9445(2003)129:10 (1312). Reprinted with permission from Elsevier.

help in processing the input data by multiplying each input by its corresponding weight. The sum of these products is then computed and processed using a nonlinear transfer function such as the S-shaped sigmoid curve (Rumelhart et al., 1994).

ANN models are flexible tools that apply complex functions in training some sets of input and output data when dealing with a great deal of information. ANN models are very useful tools for tackling complex, nonlinear processes without having to assume any preexisting relationship between the input and output variables. Learning in ANN involves adjusting the weighted interconnections during pattern matching, combinatorial optimization, data compression, and function optimization. The ability of ANN adaptation in situations of uncertainty and complex scenarios has been reported over a wide range of applications (Chau & Cheng, 2002; Sérodes & Rodriguez, 1996). ANNs have also found significant application in water quality modeling (Lek & Guégan, 1999; Zou et al., 2002). The work of Kralisch et al. (2003) involves the use of ANN in the optimization of watershed management as a means of maintaining an equilibrium between water quality and other associated challenges in the agricultural sector. Maier et al. (2004) employed ANN in estimating some water quality parameters alongside the optimum alum doses in a water source. In environmental water quality management, water dynamics is often linked to environmental parameters that are not accurately determined as input parameters without consideration for optimal choices. However, there is limited knowledge about the learning process in several application domains that have led to the discovery of other ANN techniques.

Fuzzy inference systems

The pioneers of the fuzzy inference system (FIS) were Zadeh and Kacprzyk (1992). This is an important tool that finds relevance in the modeling of complex imprecise systems. Within the system's set theory, the component elements are mapped to some set of values using a function whose interval lies between 0 and 1. In FIS, the assessment of the membership functions of a variable is always done parallel to its probabilistic estimation using stochastic models. In modeling practices, involving FIS, membership functions and selection of suitable models for the decision maker are decided from statistical surveys. FIS modeling operates on the basis of "if–then" logic; the "if" component is the fuzzy explanatory variable-vector-set bearing membership functions, while "then" denotes the consequence or complementary action. The optimization of a problem involves the development and determination of the maximum or minimum value of an objective function within some sets of constraints. However, when the objective or constraints are hazy/vague, the problem is described as a fuzzy optimization problem. Generally, fuzzy logic (FL) is launched as a refinement to conventional methods of optimization, where the crisp objective function and its constraints are improvised with fuzzy constraints (Chau, 2006; Cheng & Chau, 2001; Cheng et al., 2002). The theoretical concepts of FL are useful in the modeling of water quality, by providing alternative methods, especially in situations where information about the objective function and constraints are not clearly/precisely defined. A few other works involving the use of FIS include the FL synthetic evaluation of river quality modeling by Chang et al. (2014) and the adoption of heuristic knowledge and data mining techniques in modeling the eutrophication process of Lake Taihu and Lake Chad (Carlson et al., 2011; Chen, 2019; Taylor et al., 2013; Mining et al., 2018; Wakode et al., 2018). In addition, the study of Liou et al. involved the use of a stage fuzzy set theory in determining river quality in Taiwan (Liou et al., 2003). A bloom-predictor design for the prediction of daily fluctuations of dissolved oxygen (DO), pH, temperature, and oxy-reduction potential in water was carried out by Marsili-Libelli (2004). Although most of the existing studies are focused on freshwater riverine systems, literature on the application of FIS to coastal systems is relatively scarce.

Integrated long-short-term memory network

Point sources are essential paths through which pollutants gain entry into rivers. Hence it becomes very necessary to identify the basic features/properties and monitor the origins of these pollutants. Integrated long-short-term memory (LSTM) uses cross-correlation and association rules such as a priori, in identifying the features of some water pollutants/contaminants as well as to track the industrial point sources of these foreign bodies in water. Furthermore, cross-correlation helps to identify dependencies/interrelationships between complex substances and then uses their degrees of association/correlation to quantify the existing relationships of such substances (Podobnik et al., 2009). Usually, the interdependence between substances is premised by endogenous mechanisms; hence it is not necessary to identify correlations in large datasets via the cross-correlation method, especially when the interrelationships between the substances/pollutants are complicated and causal. Based on reports, the cross-correlation technique is very effective in identifying possible interactions between water quality monitors/indicators within a basin while reliably tracking the behavioral influence of pollutants from the point sources. In a study conducted by Wang et al. (2019a, 2019b), water quality was monitored in the Shandong province of China. The data generated were verified/tested using a hybrid AI system that adopts a cross-correlation method in generating a cross-correlation map describing water quality in the province. From the map, pollutants with high correlation tendencies to influence water quality in the area were identified. After this some sets of association rules (a priori) were used to track/match the pollutants with industries generating such substances within the study area. These data were then inputted to the LSTM to establish the mechanism by which the LSTM traced the water pollutants that were identified. According to the investigation, the variation in water quality was affected by the presence of industry, as well as the different distributions and production frequencies of the pollutants from the point sources. Also, the water quality correlation maps helped to identify regular and random fluctuations in point source pollutant emissions owing to the variation in water quality/characteristics as adjudged by water quality indices which gave clear indications of the industries whose production processes have a strong impact on water quality. Based on their study, the LSTM model is very useful for accurately tracing the point sources that may be responsible for future alterations to the water quality of aquatic systems. Table 7.1 contains some ANN models and machine learning algorithms applied to water pollution situations (Garrett, 1994).

Table 7.1 Input parameters and output data for some ANN and machine learning tools applied to water pollution

Input	Output	AI method	Dataset			R^2	RMSE	Ref.
			Tr	Val	Tes			
Initial Cd^{2+} conc., pH, adsorbent dosage, and contact time	Cd^{2+} expulsion efficiency	GA-ANN	65	19	9	0.94	0.989	Nag et al. (2018)
Initial BR46 and Cu^{2+} conc., pH, contact time, and adsorbent dosage	Cu^{2+} and BR46 removal efficiencies	MLPNN ANFIS	38	6	6	0.9871 (Cu^{2+}, MLPNN) 0.999 Cu^{2+}, ANFIS	1.248 (Cu^{2+}, MLPNN) 0.353 (Cu^{2+}, ANFIS)	Dolatabadi et al. (2018)
Initial Pb^{2+}, contact time, pH, and adsorbent dosage	Pb^{2+} removal efficiency	GA-ANN	19	3	3	0.999	0.374	Yasin et al. (2014)
Concentration of complex and eluent, pH, quantity of tea waste, volume and flow rate of eluent	Removal efficiencies of Mn^{2+} and Co^{2+}	PSO-ANN	76%	12%	12%	0.9807 Mn^{2+}	0.1 Co^{2+}	Khajeh et al. (2017)
Initial pH, adsorbent dosage, temperature, and contact time	Cu^{2+} expulsion efficiencies	RBFNN	50	-	50	0.999	0.0125	Turan et al. (2011)
Initial conc. of Cd^{2+} and MB, adsorbent-mass, pH, and contact time	Cd^{2+} and MB expulsion efficiencies	MLPNN	36	8	8	0.9896 (MLPNN) 0.9912 (BRT)	0.0048 (MLPNN) 0.0036 (BRT)	Mazaheri et al. (2017)

Table 7.1 Input parameters and output data for some ANN and machine learning tools applied to water pollution *Continued*

Input	Output	AI method	Dataset			R^2	RMSE	Ref.
			Tr	Val	Tes			
Initial As^{3+} conc., pH, contact time, temperature, material dosage, and agitation speed	As^{3+} removal efficiency	MLPNN	63	-	42	0.975	0.541	Mandal et al. (2015)
Initial conc. of ions, adsorbent dosage, and removal time	Adsorption of Pb^{2+} and Cu^{2+}	MLPNN	15	-	5	0.9905 (Pb^{2+}) 0.9632 (Cu^{2+})	0.95 (Pb^{2+}) 1.87 (Cu^{2+})	Khandanlou et al. (2016)
Collector conc., frother conc., pH, impeller speed, and flotation time	Expulsion efficiencies of (Ni^{2+}) and H_2O	GA-ANN	54	-	13	0.974 (Ni^{2+})	0.208 (Ni^{2+})	Hoseinian et al. (2017)
Initial Pb^{2+} and MG, materials dosage, pH, and ultrasonication time	Pb^{2+} and MG expulsion efficiencies	MLPNN	20	6	6	0.9997 (Pb^{2+}) 0.9999 (MG)	0.0316 (Pb^{2+}) 0.0632 (MG)	(MG) Dil et al. (2017)
Initial conc. of CV, adsorbent dosage, pH, and period of sonication	Adsorption of CV	MLPNN	75	-	25	0.9998	0.031	Dil et al. (2016)
Adsorbent mass, pH, time of sonication, initial MB, and MG conc.	MB and MG expulsion efficiencies	MLPNN RBFNN	46	10	10	0.9785 (MB, MLPNN) 0.9984 (MB, RBFNN)	MLPNN) 0.0022 (MB, RBFNN)	Asfaram et al. (2017)
Initial methylene blue conc., adsorbent mass, pH, and sonication time	Methylene blue removal efficiency	LS-SVM	75	-	25	0.9995	0.000162	Asfaram et al. (2016a)

(Continued)

Table 7.1 Input parameters and output data for some ANN and machine learning tools applied to water pollution *Continued*

Input	Output	AI method	Dataset			R^2	RMSE	Ref.
			Tr	Val	Tes			
Initial methylene blue and MG conc., pH, adsorbent mass, and ultrasonication time	Efficiency of MB and MG removal	MLPNN	70	15	15	0.9997 (MB) 0.9990 (MG	0.0245 (MB) 0.0346 (MG	Asfaram et al. (2016b)
Initial methyl orange conc., adsorbent dosage, and contact time	Removal efficiency of methyl orange	PSO-ANN	270	-	90	0.97	0.03	Agarwal et al. (2016)
Initial IC and SO conc., adsorbent mass, and time of sonication	IC and SO removal efficiencies	MLPNN	70	15	15	0.9991 (IC) 0.9997 (SO	0.00792 (IC) 0.00746 (SO)	Dastkhoon et al. (2017)
Initial BGD conc., amount of ZnS-NP-AC, and contact time	BGD expulsion efficiency	PSO-ANN	252	-	108	0.9558	0.0458	Ghaedi et al. (2015)
Initial conc. of MG, DB and MB, adsorbent mass, and sonication time	Removal efficiencies of MG, DB, and MB	MLPNN	70%	15%	15%	0.9989 (MG) 0.9992 (DB) 0.9993 (MB)	0.0077 (MG) 0.0010 (DB) 0.0047 (MB)	Bagheri et al. (2016)
Adsorbent dosage, initial conc. of EY, and contact time	Removal efficiency of EY	GA-ANN	252	54	54	0.9991	0.0122	Assefi et al. (2014)
Initial MG conc., contact time, pH, and adsorbent dosage	Adsorption of MG	GA-SVR	176	-	75	0.9195	0.0583	Ghaedi et al. (2016a)
Initial conc. of BGD and EB, adsorbent dosage, and contact time	Removal efficiencies of BGD and EB	MLPNN	41	-	13	0.9589 (BGD) 0.9455 (EB)	0.0458 (BGD) 0.0469 (EB)	Jamshidi et al. (2016)
Initial conc. of methyl orange and contact time	Adsorption of methyl orange	MLPNN	60%	20%	20%	0.998	10.08	Tanhaei et al. (2016)

Table 7.1 Input parameters and output data for some ANN and machine learning tools applied to water pollution *Continued*

Input	Output	AI method	Dataset			R^2	RMSE	Ref.
			Tr	Val	Tes			
Adsorbate conc., pH, temperature, and contact	2-Chlorophenol removal efficiency	RBFNN	320	160	160	0.96	2.46	Singh et al. (2013)
MLSS, HRT, and contact time	Carbon oxygen demand efficiency	MLPNN	70%	15%	15%	0.9999	0.1486	Hazrati et al. (2017)
Initial pH, WTR dose, dye conc., and final pH	Color removal efficiency	RSM-ANN	60%	20%	20%	0.972	0.4	Gadekar and Ahammed (2019)
Initial naphthalene conc., salinity, fluence rate, temperature, and contact time	Naphthalene retention efficiency	MLPNN	116	38	38	0.943	0.042	Jing et al. (2014)
Initial pH, $[H_2O_2]/[Fe^{2+}]$ mole ratio, and Fe^{2+} dosage	Mass ratio and COD removal efficiency	MLPNN	11	3	4	0.984 (MCR) 0.968 (MRE)	1.54 (MCR) 1.86 (MRE)	Sabour and Amiri (2017)
Dosage conc. of precipitate, pH, and solution conductivity	SO_3^{2+}, SO_4^{2+}, removal efficiency	MLPNN	70%	15%	15%	0.9955	—	Kartic et al. (2018)

Data-centric systems: Application of AI and machine learning tools for water quality assessment

Data-centric monitoring tools are used for assessing, monitoring, and gathering information on the quality of water. They help to gather information that serves as input parameters for onward processing by machine learning and AI technologies; some studies that used these systems are described under the following subheadings.

Gradient boosting regression

Sharafati et al. (2020) developed a new strategy for predicting the monthly groundwater short- and long-term lead contamination of the Rafsanjan aquifer in Iran via a machine learning method also known as gradient boosting regression. Satellite-based systems such as the Tropical Rainfall

Measuring Mission and Gravity Recovery and Climate Experiment (GRACE) were employed in gathering data that served as inputs/variables to be predicted at different time lags. As a way of establishing the optimal input parameter combinations, a nonlinear feature picking tool, also known as the gamma test (GT), was employed. Performance prediction of the spatial analysis of the aquifer was done using the R^2 and normalized root mean square error metrics. The results obtained from the study showed that gradient boosting regression (GBR) was more accurate in measuring the groundwater level of the aquifer, whereas the performance of the GRACE tool was more effective in predicting the influence of variables such as pumping rate and water depth. The correlation between the observed and predicted groundwater levels shows that the coefficient of determination was in the range of 0.66−0.94 for lead (Pb) concentrations measured at different times. The spatiotemporal patterns of the predicted results confirmed that regions with high water depths and water flow rates were seen to have more accurate measurements from the north to south and west to east of the Rafsanjan aquifer and vice versa. In essence, they encouraged the application of machine learning by water resource planners when making decisions toward ensuring the accurate modeling of hydrological systems.

Support vector machine, the decision tree, and the artificial neuron fuzzy inference system

Costache (2019) conducted an investigation into the flash-flood susceptibility/potential and basin mapping of the Prahoa river in Romania. The area of the river basin considered in this study is about $260 \, km^2$, of which 70% of the area was adopted as training data, while the other 30% was considered as revalidation data. Parameters (i.e., hydrological, lithological, and morphological parameters) such as slope angle, aspect ratio, topographic wetness index, hydrological soil group, and land use were chosen for statistical tests and incorporated into four models, namely, support vector machine (SVM) frequency ratio, logistic regression frequency ratio, support vector machine weights of evidence, and logistic regression weights of evidence. Based on the findings, a total of about 33% of the area investigated was identified as low and high flood-flash points. The estimated flood-prone areas spanned through the 0.724−0.904 range with accuracies lying within 0.708−0.801 for the training and validation area data. Some studies have shown the capability of AI and machine learning tools in ensuring the risk assessment mapping of flood-susceptible areas using AI-data-based techniques (Bui et al., 2019; Hong, Panahi, et al., 2018; Hong, Tsangaratos, et al., 2018; Khosravi et al., 2018; Zhao et al., 2019). Identifying flood-prone areas alongside their frequencies and magnitudes of occurrence are very important steps in ensuring timely mitigation practices for combatting flood hazards. Although continuous fluctuations in the Earth's climatic conditions/human factors make it somewhat herculean to accurately map and forecast flash-flood hotspots, with the help of SVM, decision tree, artificial neuron fuzzy inference system (ANFIS), and other AI models, the task becomes more easily achievable. Model efficiencies can be evaluated by determining the area under the receiver's operating characteristic curve (Bui et al., 2019; Chen, Liu, et al., 2017; Chen, Xie, et al., 2017). This curve determines the ability of a statistical tool to accurately predict the likelihood of occurrence of flooding at a specific location (Costache, 2019; Hong, Panahi, et al., 2018). Recently, there have also been proposals in the light of adopting hybrid models owing to the lapses of some of these models as well as the search for improved levels of accuracy. Studies of some hybrid models have been carried out which have helped in flagging early flood warning signals in Vietnam (Bui et al., 2019), Iran (Khosravi et al., 2018) and China

(Hong, Panahi, et al., 2018; Hong, Tsangaratos, et al., 2018; Zhao et al., 2019). A study was conducted on the surface measurements (363 measurements) of chlorophyll-a (Chl-a) and DO content of a lake, for which Fijani et al. (2019) developed an integrated two-layer framework hybrid decomposition technique using the extreme learning machine tool for estimating the desired water quality parameters of the Chl-a and DO contents of the lake. Shi et al. (2018) proposed the use of the wavelet neural network alongside some high-frequency measurements for the rapid detection of water quality. Based on these findings, the proposed hybrid technique can successfully determine the tendency of occurrence of two anomalies/events of total pollutant variation in the lake within a time scale of 15 minutes by employing high-frequency online ANN sensors.

Gama test and artificial neuron fuzzy inference system for suspended sediment load modeling of water quality

Suspended sediment load (SSL) is an indicator that helps to determine the influence of research conducted on water quality, changes in land use, and the impact of engineering practices on flowing streams (Agarwal et al., 2016; Asfaram, Ghaedi, Azqhandi, et al., 2016; Asfaram, Ghaedi, Hajati, et al., 2016; Asfaram et al., 2017; Assefi et al., 2014; Bagheri et al., 2016; Dastkhoon et al., 2017; Dil et al., 2017; Dolatabadi et al., 2018; Gadekar & Ahammed, 2019; Ghaedi et al., 2016; Ghaedi et al., 2015; Mazaheri et al., 2017; Hazrati et al., 2017; Hoseinian et al., 2017; Jamshidi et al., 2016; Jing et al., 2014; Khajeh et al., 2017; Khandanlou et al., 2016; Mandal et al., 2015; Nag et al., 2018; Navamani Kartic et al., 2018; Sabour & Amiri, 2017; Singh et al., 2013; Tanhaei et al., 2016; Turan et al., 2011; Yasin et al., 2014; Ye et al., 2020). The prior estimation of the quantity of suspended solids in water is the most reliable approach, but the cost implications have limited the commercial application of gage stations. Some authors have employed the SSL model in determining the amount of suspended solids in rivers (Buyukyildiz & Kumcu, 2017; Choubin et al., 2018; Nourani et al., 2019; Sharghi et al., 2019; Yilmaz et al., 2018). However, in the work of Buyukyildiz and Kumcu (2017), it was mentioned that the use of three input variables (current and previous day's flow rate as well as previous SSL data) was the best input combination for such a modeling assignment. The results of Yilmaz et al. (2018) also attest to the reliability of the current day's water flow rate as very useful information for effectively forecasting the SSL in a river. The results from their works also affirm the reliability and superiority of AI models over conventional approaches (correlation coefficient analysis and classical regression analyses). For uncontaminated streams/water bodies, some studies have tested the applicability of AI in the assessment and early signaling of the tendency for contamination of rivers (Chang et al., 2014; Liu & Lu, 2014), groundwater (Agarwal et al., 2016; Asfaram, Ghaedi, Azqhandi, et al., 2016; Asfaram, Ghaedi, Hajati, et al., 2016; Asfaram et al., 2017; Assefi et al., 2014; Bagheri et al., 2016; Dastkhoon et al., 2017; Dil et al., 2017; Dolatabadi et al., 2018; Gadekar & Ahammed, 2019; Ghaedi et al., 2016; Ghaedi et al., 2015; Mazaheri et al., 2017; Hazrati et al., 2017; Hoseinian et al., 2017; Jamshidi et al., 2016; Jing et al., 2014; Khajeh et al., 2017; Khandanlou et al., 2016; Mandal et al., 2015; Nag et al., 2018; Navamani Kartic et al., 2018; Sabour & Amiri, 2017; Singh et al., 2013; Tanhaei et al., 2016; Turan et al., 2011; Yasin et al., 2014; Ye et al., 2020), lakes (Li et al., 2017; García Nieto et al., 2019), and oceans (Thoe et al., 2012; Wei et al., 2015). Water quality alteration and pollution are usually influenced by natural and human factors. Thus early warning signals and assessment information are affected by some input conditions which ought to be carefully examined to ascertain the key factors that adversely alter water purity. Chang et al. (2014) carried out monthly data monitoring of the arsenic (As) content of a northern Taiwan river; the results were also validated by AI prediction models. About 37 datasets of 1-month antecedent rainfall were recorded at a rainfall gage-station, while 13 water quality parameters were also measured all through the months over a 3-year span at a water quality monitoring station. A nonlinear analytical factor (i.e., the gama test, GT) was selected for the analysis. Three variables [i.e., rainfall (R), nitrite-nitrogen (NO_2-N), and temperature (T)], were extracted from a total of 14 effective parameters and fitted into the ANFIS models (ANFIS-GT, ANFIS-CC, and ANFIS-all) for further analysis owing to the fact that the variables were found to have a strong correlation with arsenic concentration. Based on the investigation, the ANFIS-GT model performed better than the ANFIS-CC and ANFIS-all models, with percentage margins of 50% and 52% improvements, respectively, in terms of the calculated root mean square error (RMSE). In addition, it was discovered that low temperature, high nitrite-nitrogen, and 1 month of high amount of antecedent rainfall/precipitation would increase the surface water arsenic concentration over the 3-year period. Fig. 7.4 is an illustration of the structural overview of a typical ANFIS configuration.

The decision tree, ruled induction, fuzzy logic, multilayer perceptron neural network, and radial basis function neural network

The study of Yoo et al. (2016) involved the assessment of groundwater quality using a hybrid model comprised of decision tree (DT) and ruled induction in predicting groundwater pollution

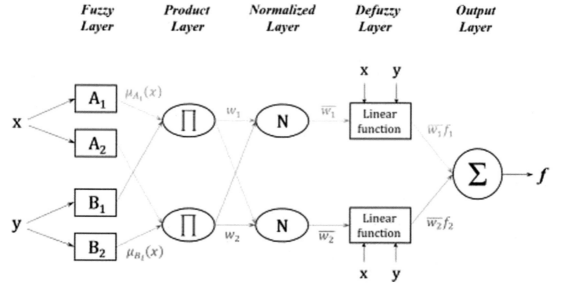

FIGURE 7.4

An overview of the structural form of ANFIS. *ANFIS*, Artificial neuron fuzzy inference system.

From Ye, Z., Yang, J., Zhong, N., Tu, X., Jia, J., & Wang, J. (2020). Tackling environmental challenges in pollution controls using artificial intelligence: A review. Science of the Total Environment, 699, *134279. https://doi.org/10.1016/j.scitotenv.2019.134279.*
Reprinted with permission from Elsevier.

sensitivity patterns with data obtained from a CCl_3-contaminated site within the Woosan Industrial Park of South Korea. The hydrological parameters adopted as input parameters include net recharge, aquifer geospatial data, and soil media, because they were found to have an influence on the groundwater sensitivity to CCl_3. The infiltration of landfill leachate was modeled and simulated using FL, radial basis function neural network (RBFNN), and multilayer perceptron neural network (MLPNN) to evaluate the environmental effect of leachate penetration at a specific location (Bagheri et al., 2017). Based on the results, molybdenum, sodium, and chemical oxygen demand (COD) were seen to have a high influence on leachate intake by groundwater. Fig. 7.5 shows the structural view of a typical RFBNN with one output. The work of Thoe et al. (2012) is a comprehensive study which involved the prediction of the next-day's bacterial concentration/counts in some selected beaches in Hong Kong. They used multiple linear regression and ANN in tracking as well as estimating water quality limits, and the results were found to outperform some current beach strategies adopted for tracking water quality within some permissible limits. Overall, the ANN estimator was found to be very reliable in providing high-end concentration estimates, although it recorded more false alarms/false-positive predictions, which were speculated to be caused by a deficiency in the availability of routine monitors/control systems at extreme conditions including strong winds and typhoons/rainstorms. Fig. 7.6A and B show how data are processed within a neuron and the MLPNN architecture, while Table 7.2 shows some AI models and machine learning algorithms applied to control systems (Huang et al., 2014; Jaramillo et al., 2018; Jing et al., 2015; Lin et al., 2012; Sun et al., 2017; Ye et al., 2020).

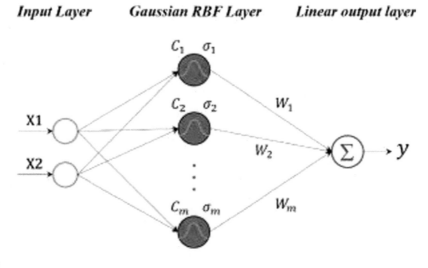

FIGURE 7.5

The structural view of the RBFNN with single output. *RBFNN*, Radial basis function neural network.

From Ye, Z., Yang, J., Zhong, N., Tu, X., Jia, J., & Wang, J. (2020). Tackling environmental challenges in pollution controls using artificial intelligence: A review. Science of the Total Environment, 699, *134279. https://doi.org/10.1016/j.scitotenv.2019.134279.*

Reprinted with permission from Elsevier.

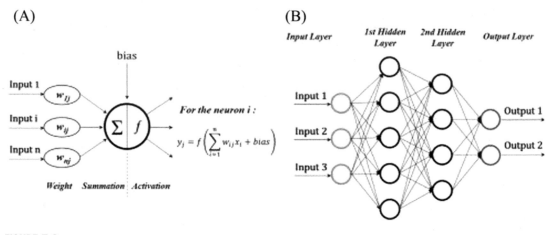

FIGURE 7.6

Data processing in: (A) a neuron and (B) the MLPNN architecture. *MLPNN*, Multilayer perceptron neural network.

From Ye, Z., Yang, J., Zhong, N., Tu, X., Jia, J., & Wang, J. (2020). Tackling environmental challenges in pollution controls using artificial intelligence: A review. Science of the Total Environment, 699, *134279. https://doi.org/10.1016/j.scitotenv.2019.134279.*

Reprinted with permission from Elsevier.

Recent advances in water quality modeling

Over the last few decades, AI technology has been shown to be an excellent tool for modeling and optimizing processes involving pollutant removal (dyes/heavy metals, etc.) from wastewaters owing to its self-learning adaptive features. Among the factors influencing the pollutant removal process are initial pollutant concentration, pH of the medium, contact time, and adsorbent dosages; these serve as input parameters to the network of neurons (i.e., the neural network), while the performance of the model is determined in terms of its ability to accurately predict the pollutant removal efficiency as an output variable (Dil et al., 2017; Dolatabadi et al., 2018; Nag et al., 2018). Generally, the MLPNN is used in predicting output values for such systems based on some specified input conditions, while the backpropagation algorithm is often adopted as the training function (Antwi et al., 2018; Khandanlou et al., 2016). Based on some findings, when compared to MLPNN, the RBFNN is a more flexible and efficient tool for simulating and optimizing adsorption processes involving the removal of heavy metal ions and dyes from contaminated streams (Asfaram et al., 2017; Messikh et al., 2015; Singh et al., 2013; Turan et al., 2011). The reliability of RBFNN for operations of this kind is due to its modular network structure and unsupervised learning characteristics. Yu and Righetto (2001) carried out a study on the use of batch MLPNN models (i.e., BP-ANN); pH, DO, oxidation-reduction potential, initial chromium (VI) concentrations, dosage, and contact time were supplied as the input variables to determine the Cr(VI) removal efficiency of the process. A nanovalent (nZVI) batch reactor was adopted at the experimental phase of the study. Therein three probes were installed to monitor the DO, the oxidation-reduction potential, and pH, while the desired data were acquired online. The resulting datasets generated from the Cr(VI) removal experiments were randomly selected for training and testing. Hence it was observed that

Table 7.2 Some AI models and machine learning algorithms applied in intelligent control systems.

S. no.	Influential factors	Control parameters	AI method	Control type	Process	Scale	Effects with respect to conventional techniques	Ref.
1	DO and pH	Aerobic phase length (APL)	SVM	Online	SBR	Lab	Reduced APL by 9.54 days	Jaramillo et al. (2018)
2	Influent NH^{4+}-N, COD/N, effluent TN, and water temperature	N_2O emission	MLPNN	Offline	A/O	Full and pilot	Reduced N_2O emission down to 0.21% of N-load	Sun et al. (2017)
3	UV fluence rate, salinity, temperature, initial naphthalene conc., and reaction time	Naphthalene removal efficiency	GA-ANN	Offline	AOPs	Lab	Reduction in cost of treatment by 20.4%	Jing et al. (2015)
4	Influent COD, TN, rate of inflow, pH, ORP, return mixed liquid ratio, and nitrate conc. of the last anoxic zone	Effluent COD, TN, and operating cost	FNN	Online	A/O	Lab	Reduction in effluent COD, TN, and operating costs by 14%, 10.5%, and 17%, respectively	Huang et al. (2014)
5	Influent coliform counts, turbidity, color, ORP, pH, and temperature	Effluent coliform counts	MLPNN	Online	AOPs	Lab	Result in energy saving and capacity reduction of 13.2%−15.7%	Lin et al. (2012)

AI, *Artificial intelligence;* COD, *chemical oxygen demand;* DO, *dissolved oxygen;* GA-ANN, *genetic algorithm-artificial neural network;* MLPNN, *multilayer perceptron neural network;* ORP, *oxidation-reduction potential;* SBR, *sequencing batch reactor;* SVM, *support vector machine;* TN, *total nitrogen;* A/O, *anoxic/oxic;* AOPs, *advanced oxidation processes;* FNN, *fuzzy neural network.*

the trained MLPNN models gave precise results, thus exhibiting good potential for optimizing the nZVI batch-Cr(VI) removal process. Dolatabadi et al. (2018) used a 5-7-2 MLPNN model and ANFIS in predicting the adsorptive capacity of sawdust during the simultaneous adsorption of Cu (II) and Basic Red46 (BR46) from a contaminated solution. Fifty samples, separated into 38, 6, and 6 training, validation, and testing samples, respectively, were used in testing the performance of the models in terms of their predictive accuracies for Cu(II) and Basic Red46 (BR46) removal from the solution. From the results, the MLPNN and ANFIS models gave excellent results, with regression values ranging from 0.98 to 0.99 for both contaminants. In the study conducted by Khandanlou et al. (2016) for Cu(II) adsorption, 20 experimental datasets were split into 15 training datasets and 5 testing datasets, which were further used in training the MLPNN model. However, despite using a small portion of the available data for the ANN training, the estimated adsorption efficiency of Cu (II) was 74.04%, which was judged to be very close to the actual/measured value (75.54%) at optimum conditions; this further suggests that the model can give accurate results within the confines of nonabundant experimental data. Furthermore, although arguable, they asserted that there are no strict regulations for selecting the data needed to train a model toward ensuring high levels of accuracy. From a study involving 270 experimental datasets, out of which 90 were selected for testing as presented by Agarwal et al. (2016), a particle swarm optimization-based ANN model was used to investigate the adsorption of methyl orange as a contaminant from a solution. Ghaedi et al. (2016) combined two models [the support vector machine (SVM) and GA] as tools for forecasting the adsorption of malachite green (MG) using multiwalled carbon nanotubes. The data used in carrying out the research were grouped into training data (176 samples) and testing subsets comprising of 75 samples. Both models gave accurate predictions of dye expulsion without use of the validation subsets. The response surface method, MLPNN, and RBFNN were adopted in making predictions of methylene blue dye and MG adsorption onto a novel adsorbent (Asfaram et al., 2017). According to the investigation, the RBFNN model gave the highest R^2 and the lowest RMSE values. The work of Singh et al. (2013) involves the use of MLPNN, RBFNN, and three nonlinear AI models in estimating the removal efficiency of 2-chlorophenol from a solution using nonlinear data. Based on their findings, the RBFNN model exhibited the best predictive and generalization abilities relative to the other models; their findings were also supported by the work of Turan et al. (2011), in which an investigation into the adsorption of copper from pumice-leached industrial waste was carried out. Due to its ability to map principles with input noises of high tolerances, RBFNN has been confirmed as a very efficient tool for the prediction of heavy metal ionic concentrations and dye expulsion from wastewaters, although this tool requires more training data (Buyukyildiz & Kumcu, 2017). The use of AI in the estimation of the presence of nutrients, persistent organic pollutants, chemical oxygen, etc. has also been carried out (Agarwal et al., 2016; Asfaram, Ghaedi, Azqhandi, et al., 2016; Asfaram, Ghaedi, Hajati, et al., 2016; Asfaram et al., 2017; Assefi et al., 2014; Bagheri et al., 2016; Dastkhoon et al., 2017; Dil et al., 2017; Dolatabadi et al., 2018; Gadekar & Ahammed, 2019; Ghaedi et al., 2016; Ghaedi et al., 2015; Mazaheri et al., 2017; Hazrati et al., 2017; Hoseinian et al., 2017; Jamshidi et al., 2016; Jing et al., 2014; Khajeh et al., 2017; Khandanlou et al., 2016; Mandal et al., 2015; Nag et al., 2018; Navamani Kartic et al., 2018; Sabour & Amiri, 2017; Singh et al., 2013; Tanhaei et al., 2016; Turan et al., 2011; Yasin et al., 2014; Ye et al., 2020). The three-layer BP-ANN model by Antwi et al. (2018) was used in estimating the chemical oxygen expulsion from industrial waste water treatment in an up-flow anaerobic sludge blanket reactor for processing starch. The six input parameters for the model included organic loading rate, pH, NH_4^+-N, biogas yield, COD, and effluent volatile fatty acid. The nonlinear interrelationship between the dependent and independent variables associated with the digestion process was determined using the BP-ANN model.

AI models connected to automatic control systems for wastewater treatment processes have been used to construct intelligent control strategies for aerobic content monitoring of some wastewater treatment processes to reduce the total aeration time and ensure cost-effectiveness toward ensuring adequate compliance with effluent standards (Asadi et al., 2017; Foscoliano et al., 2016;

Ruan et al., 2017; Sun et al., 2017; Wen et al., 2017). Online DO monitoring is an essential and integral part of intelligence control. FL-based intelligent control systems (i.e., FNN and ANFIS controllers) have been adopted in water pollution situations where high accuracies were achieved in terms of the estimated effluent quality; the process was also described as being cost-effective for the biological treatment of wastewater (Huang et al., 2014; Jaramillo et al., 2018; Jing et al., 2015; Lin et al., 2012; Sun et al., 2017; Ye et al., 2020). A real-time intelligent control system was designed by Wen et al. (2017). The DO system consists of a feedforward controller whose origin is traceable to a RBF network and a proportional integral differential controller (feedback controller) situated on a BP network. The former helped to optimize input parameters for the feedback control system, while the latter helped to ensure the stability of effluent quality via precise real-time monitoring of DO concentrations within wastewater treatment plants (WWTPs). The tool developed by Ding et al. (2011) is a novel intelligent control system for optimization of the aeration process in a conventional sequencing batch biofilm reactor (SBBR) while taking into consideration the resulting effects of microbial activity as it relates to three key controlling parameters, namely, DO, temperature, and intermittent aeration in relation to the SBBR-IC system. In addition, the new system dropped the aeration time and HRT by 50% and 56%, respectively, when the results obtained were compared with those of traditional SBBRs; higher CODs were also recorded from the new system. Generally, for wastewater treatment processes, aeration is highly energy intensive and may occupy about 50%–75% of the total energy expenditure in a WWTP (Gude, 2015; Longo et al., 2016). There are also issues of large time variations/disturbances in the random quality of the wastewater inlet stream. Despite the huge costs associated with WWTPs, AI-based aeration intelligent control systems are a promising solution to the high operational cost of WWTPs. Foscoliano et al. (2016) presented a recurrent neural network for capturing the input–output behavior of nitrogen compounds in a bioreactor. The dynamic matrix control was selected as the control system. Based on these findings, the tool was able to give accurate data on ammonia, nitrate, and cost of energy reduction during the activated sludge treatment process. Ruan et al. (2017) developed a strategy for reducing the cost of processes such as anaerobic/anoxic/oxic (A/A/O) processes during the treatment stages of wastewater from paper making; the GA-fuzzy wavelet neural network software sensor was adopted in monitoring DO concentrations and it was observed that the operating cost was reduced by 20% while maintaining effluent quality standards. Jaramillo et al. proposed an online system for estimation of the time taken for aerobic removal of nitrate compounds with the use of closed-loop monitoring of the medium's pH and DO using the features of the SVM (Jaramillo et al., 2018). In the bid to ascertain the end-point of the aerobic process, a decision rule/relationship between stagewise ammonium degradation and complete ammonium degradation was generated using an SVM classifier. Based on the predictions, the proposed strategy gave a significant decrease of 7.52% in the aerobic degradation time, which corresponds to a period of 9.54 days. For further reading on machine learning systems application to waste water treatment, the study by Ye et al. (2020) alongside other referenced texts can be consulted.

Conclusion

Water pollution is a complex phenomenon that requires a hybrid of technical and smart approaches all aimed at proffering water quality control measures for the efficient management and conservation of water resources. It is no longer debatable that AI and machine learning tools have gained significant attention in the efficient prediction and forecasting of contaminant influx and early warning signs of their intricacies, especially with the assistance of data-gathering tools/systems (data-centric systems), which keep a close watch on the environment, thus providing data for the efficient modeling and description of water hydrology, water quality, and water pollution indices. The use of several tools including FL, SVM, MLPNN, RBFNN, and DT have shown tremendous levels of accuracies over conventional linear/nonlinear models, hence the need to consider integrating two or more of these AI tools for improved levels of accuracies. These expert systems are very efficient because they are trained to reason like humans and perform tasks based on routine exercises as informed by some specific input data, toward generating very reliable results, thus ensuring accurate decision-making. Therefore, beyond what is found in the current literature, more of these smart tools and data-centric systems should be tried for the accurate determination, assessment, and prediction of several hazardous contaminants that find their way into groundwaters, lakes, streams, rivers, and aquifers. Furthermore, the era of computing with AI has made it possible to obtain quick and reliable information/solutions to water contamination problems owing to the flexible and adaptable interfaces/network architectures of these tools. This then suggests that the uses of AI, machine learning, and data-centric systems are the future solutions for the myriad of challenges associated with the world's water pollution/contamination phenomena.

References

Abbott, M. B. (1991). *Hydroinformatics: Information technology and the aquatic environment.* Aldershot: Avebury Technical.

Abbott, M. B. (1993). The electronic encapsulation of knowledge in hydraulics, hydrology and water resources. *Advances in Water Resources*, *16*(1), 21−39. Available from https://doi.org/10.1016/0309-1708 (93)90027-D.

Agarwal, S., Tyagi, I., Gupta, V. K., Ghaedi, M., Masoomzade, M., Ghaedi, A. M., & Mirtamizdoust, B. (2016). Kinetics and thermodynamics of methyl orange adsorption from aqueous solutions—Artificial neural network-particle swarm optimization modeling. *Journal of Molecular Liquids*, *218*, 354−362. Available from https://doi.org/10.1016/j.molliq.2016.02.048.

Antwi, P., Li, J., Meng, J., Deng, K., Koblah Quashie, F., Li, J., & Opoku Boadi, P. (2018). Feedforward neural network model estimating pollutant removal process within mesophilic upflow anaerobic sludge blanket bioreactor treating industrial starch processing wastewater. *Bioresource Technology*, *257*, 102−112. Available from https://doi.org/10.1016/j.biortech.2018.02.071.

Asadi, A., Verma, A., Yang, K., & Mejabi, B. (2017). Wastewater treatment aeration process optimization: A data mining approach. *Journal of Environmental Management*, *203*, 630−639. Available from https://doi.org/10.1016/j.jenvman.2016.07.047.

Asfaram, A., Ghaedi, M., Ahmadi Azghandi, M. H., Goudarzi, A., & Hajati, S. (2017). Ultrasound-assisted binary adsorption of dyes onto Mn@ CuS/ZnS-NC-AC as a novel adsorbent: Application of chemometrics for optimization and modeling. *Journal of Industrial and Engineering Chemistry*, *54*, 377−388. Available from https://doi.org/10.1016/j.jiec.2017.06.018.

Asfaram, A., Ghaedi, M., Azghandi, M. H. A., Goudarzi, A., & Dastkhoon, M. (2016a). Statistical experimental design, least squares-support vector machine (LS-SVM) and artificial neural network (ANN) methods for modeling the facilitated adsorption of methylene blue dye. *RSC Advances*, *6*(46), 40502−40516. Available from https://doi.org/10.1039/c6ra01874b.

Asfaram, A., Ghaedi, M., Hajati, S., & Goudarzi, A. (2016b). Synthesis of magnetic γ-Fe_2O_3-based nanomaterial for ultrasonic assisted dyes adsorption: Modeling and optimization. *Ultrasonics Sonochemistry*, *32*, 418−431. Available from https://doi.org/10.1016/j.ultsonch.2016.04.011.

Assefi, P., Ghaedi, M., Ansari, A., Habibi, M. H., & Momeni, M. S. (2014). Artificial neural network optimization for removal of hazardous dye Eosin Y from aqueous solution using Co2O3-NP-AC: Isotherm and kinetics study. *Journal of Industrial and Engineering Chemistry*, *20*(5), 2905−2913. Available from https://doi.org/10.1016/j.jiec.2013.11.027.

Azizullah, A., Khattak, M. N. K., Richter, P., & Häder, D. P. (2011). Water pollution in Pakistan and its impact on public health—A review. *Environment International*, *37*(2), 479−497. Available from https://doi.org/10.1016/j.envint.2010.10.007.

Bagheri, A. R., Ghaedi, M., Asfaram, A., Hajati, S., Ghaedi, A. M., Bazrafshan, A., & Rahimi, M. R. (2016). Modeling and optimization of simultaneous removal of ternary dyes onto copper sulfide nanoparticles loaded on activated carbon using second-derivative spectrophotometry. *Journal of the Taiwan Institute of Chemical Engineers*, *65*, 212−224. Available from https://doi.org/10.1016/j.jtice.2016.05.004.

Bagheri, M., Bazvand, A., & Ehteshami, M. (2017). Application of artificial intelligence for the management of landfill leachate penetration into groundwater, and assessment of its environmental impacts. *Journal of Cleaner Production*, *149*, 784−796. Available from https://doi.org/10.1016/j.jclepro.2017.02.157.

Baird, J. I., & Whitelaw, K. (1992). Water quality aspects of estuary modeling. In R. A. Falconer (Ed.), *Water quality modeling* (pp. 119−126). London: Routledge.

Blanpain, O., & Chocat, B. (1994). *Introduction of expertise in a hydroinformatics system: Choice of hydraulic and hydrologic models. Hydroinformatics '94*. Rotterdam: Balkema.

Bobba, A. G., Singh, V. P., & Bengtsson, L. (2000). Application of environmental models to different hydrological systems. *Ecological Modelling*, *125*(1), 15−49. Available from https://doi.org/10.1016/S0304-3800(99)00175-1.

Booty, W. G., Lam, D. C. L., Wong, I. W. S., & Siconolfi, P. (2001). Design and implementation of an environmental decision support system. *Environmental Modelling and Software*, *16*(5), 453−458. Available from https://doi.org/10.1016/S1364-8152(01)00016-0.

Bui, D. T., Tsangaratos, P., Ngo, P. T. T., Pham, T. D., & Pham, B. T. (2019). Flash flood susceptibility modeling using an optimized fuzzy rule based feature selection technique and tree based ensemble methods. *Science of the Total Environment*, *668*, 1038−1054. Available from https://doi.org/10.1016/j.scitotenv.2019.02.422.

Buyukyildiz, M., & Kumcu, S. Y. (2017). An estimation of the suspended sediment load using adaptive network based fuzzy inference system, support vector machine and artificial neural network models. *Water Resources Management*, *31*(4), 1343−1359. Available from https://doi.org/10.1007/s11269-017-1581-1.

Carlson, M. A., Lohse, K. A., McIntosh, J. C., & McLain, J. E. T. (2011). Impacts of urbanization on groundwater quality and recharge in a semi-arid alluvial basin. *Journal of Hydrology*, *409*(1−2), 196−211. Available from https://doi.org/10.1016/j.jhydrol.2011.08.020.

Chang, F. J., Chung, C. H., Chen, P. A., Liu, C. W., Coynel, A., & Vachaud, G. (2014). Assessment of arsenic concentration in stream water using neuro fuzzy networks with factor analysis. *Science of the Total Environment*, *494−495*, 202−210. Available from https://doi.org/10.1016/j.scitotenv.2014.06.133.

Chau, K. (2002). *Calibration of flow and water quality modeling using genetic algorithm. Lecture notes in computer science (including subseries lecture notes in artificial intelligence and lecture notes in bioinformatics)* (Vol. 2557, p. 720). Springer Verlag. Available from https://doi.org/10.1007/3-540-36187-1_69.

Chau, K. W. (2006). A review on integration of artificial intelligence into water quality modelling. *Marine Pollution Bulletin*, *52*(7), 726−733. Available from https://doi.org/10.1016/j.marpolbul.2006.04.003.

Chau, K. W., & Albermani, F. (2002). Expert system application on preliminary design of water retaining structures. *Expert Systems with Applications*, *22*(2), 169−178. Available from https://doi.org/10.1016/S0957-4174(01)00053-7.

Chau, K. W., & Albermani, F. (2003). Knowledge-based system on optimum design of liquid retaining structures with genetic algorithms. *Journal of Structural Engineering*, *129*(10), 1312−1321. Available from https://doi.org/10.1061/(ASCE)0733-9445(2003)129:10(1312).

Chau, K. W., & Chen, W. (2001). An example of expert system on numerical modelling system in coastal processes. *Advances in Engineering Software*, *32*(9), 695−703. Available from https://doi.org/10.1016/S0965-9978(01)00023-0.

Chau, K. W., & Cheng, C. T. (2002).). *Real-time prediction of water stage with artificial neural network approach. Lecture notes in computer science (including subseries lecture notes in artificial intelligence and lecture notes in bioinformatics)* (Vol. 2557, p. 715). Springer Verlag. Available from https://doi.org/10.1007/3-540-36187-1_64.

Chau, K. W., & Jiang, Y. W. (2001). 3D numerical model for Pearl River Estuary. *Journal of Hydraulic Engineering*, *127*(1), 72−82. Available from https://doi.org/10.1061/(ASCE)0733-9429(2001)127:1(72).

Chau, K. W., & Jiang, Y. W. (2002). Three-dimensional pollutant transport model for the Pearl River Estuary. *Water Research*, *36*(8), 2029−2039. Available from https://doi.org/10.1016/S0043-1354(01)00400-6.

Chau, K. W., & Jin, H. (1998). Eutrophication model for a coastal bay in Hong Kong. *Journal of Environmental Engineering*, *124*(7), 628−638. Available from https://doi.org/10.1061/(ASCE)0733-9372(1998)124:7(628).

Chau, K. W., & Jin, H. S. (1995). Numerical solution of two-layer, two-dimensional tidal flow in a boundary-fitted orthogonal curvilinear co-ordinate system. *International Journal for Numerical Methods in Fluids*, *21*(11), 1087−1107. Available from https://doi.org/10.1002/fld.1650211106.

Chau, K. W., & Ng, V. (1996). Un système expert basé sur l'état actuel des connaissances dans la conception de butees pour les canalisations d'eau à Hong Kong. *Journal of Water Supply: Research and Technology—AQUA*, *45*(2), 96−99.

Chau, K. W., & Yang, W. W. (1993). Development of an integrated expert system for fluvial hydrodynamics. *Advances in Engineering Software*, *17*(3), 165−172. Available from https://doi.org/10.1016/0965-9978(93)90076-6.

Chau, K. W., & Zhang, X. N. (1995). An expert system for flow routing in a river network. *Advances in Engineering Software*, *22*(3), 139−146. Available from https://doi.org/10.1016/0965-9978(95)00026-S.

Chau, K. W., Jin, H. S., & Sin, Y. S. (1996). A finite difference model of two-dimensional tidal flow in Tolo Harbor, Hong Kong. *Applied Mathematical Modelling*, *20*(4), 321−328. Available from https://doi.org/10.1016/0307-904X(95)00127-6.

Chen, J. (2019). Satellite gravimetry and mass transport in the earth system. *Geodesy and Geodynamics*, *10*(5), 402−415. Available from https://doi.org/10.1016/j.geog.2018.07.001.

Chen, J., Liu, J., He, Y., Huang, L., Sun, S., Sun, J., Chang, K. L., Kuo, J., Huang, S., & Ning, X. (2017). Investigation of co-combustion characteristics of sewage sludge and coffee grounds mixtures using thermogravimetric analysis coupled to artificial neural networks modeling. *Bioresource Technology*, *225*, 234−245. Available from https://doi.org/10.1016/j.biortech.2016.11.069.

Chen, W., Xie, X., Wang, J., Pradhan, B., Hong, H., Bui, D. T., Duan, Z., & Ma, J. (2017). A comparative study of logistic model tree, random forest, and classification and regression tree models for spatial prediction of landslide susceptibility. *Catena*, *151*, 147−160. Available from https://doi.org/10.1016/j.catena.2016.11.032.

Cheng, C., & Chau, K. W. (2001). Fuzzy iteration methodology for reservoir flood control operation. *Journal of the American Water Resources Association*, *37*(5), 1381−1388. Available from https://doi.org/10.1111/j.1752-1688.2001.tb03646.x.

Cheng, R. T., Casulli, V., & Milford, S. N. (1984). Eulerian-Lagrangian solution of the convection-dispersion equation in natural coordinates. *Water Resources Research*, *20*(7), 944−952. Available from https://doi.org/10.1029/WR020i007p00944.

Cheng, C. T., Ou, C. P., & Chau, K. W. (2002). Combining a fuzzy optimal model with a genetic algorithm to solve multi-objective rainfall-runoff model calibration. *Journal of Hydrology*, *268*(1−4), 72−86. Available from https://doi.org/10.1016/S0022-1694(02)00122-1.

Choubin, B., Darabi, H., Rahmati, O., Sajedi-Hosseini, F., & Kløve, B. (2018). River suspended sediment modelling using the CART model: A comparative study of machine learning techniques. *Science of the Total Environment*, *615*, 272−281. Available from https://doi.org/10.1016/j.scitotenv.2017.09.293.

Costache, R. (2019). Flash-Flood Potential assessment in the upper and middle sector of Prahova river catchment (Romania). A comparative approach between four hybrid models. *Science of the Total Environment*, *659*, 1115−1134. Available from https://doi.org/10.1016/j.scitotenv.2018.12.397.

Cunge, J. (1989). Review of recent developments in river modelling. In R. A. Falconer, P. Goodwin, & R. G. S. Matthew (Eds.), *Hydraulic and environmental modelling of coastal, estuarine and river waters* (pp. 393−404). Aldershot: Avebury Technical.

Dastkhoon, M., Ghaedi, M., Asfaram, A., Ahmadi Azqhandi, M. H., & Purkait, M. K. (2017). Simultaneous removal of dyes onto nanowires adsorbent use of ultrasound assisted adsorption to clean waste water: Chemometrics for modeling and optimization, multicomponent adsorption and kinetic study. *Chemical Engineering Research and Design*, *124*, 222−237. Available from https://doi.org/10.1016/j.cherd.2017.06.011.

Dil, E. A., Ghaedi, M., Asfaram, A., Hajati, S., Mehrabi, F., & Goudarzi, A. (2017). Preparation of nanomaterials for the ultrasound-enhanced removal of Pb^{2+} ions and malachite green dye: Chemometric optimization and modeling. *Ultrasonics Sonochemistry*, *34*, 677−691. Available from https://doi.org/10.1016/j.ultsonch.2016.07.001.

Dil, E. A., Ghaedi, M., Ghaedi, A., Asfaram, A., Jamshidi, M., & Purkait, M. K. (2016). Application of artificial neural network and response surface methodology for the removal of crystal violet by zinc oxide nanorods loaded on activate carbon: kinetics and equilibrium study. *Journal of Taiwan Institute of Chemical Engineering*, *59*, 210−220. Available from https://doi.org/10.1016/j.jtice.2015.07.023.2.

Ding, D., Feng, C., Jin, Y., Hao, C., Zhao, Y., & Suemura, T. (2011). Domestic sewage treatment in a sequencing batch biofilm reactor (SBBR) with an intelligent controlling system. *Desalination*, *276*(1−3), 260−265. Available from https://doi.org/10.1016/j.desal.2011.03.059.

Dolatabadi, M., Mehrabpour, M., Esfandyari, M., Alidadi, H., & Davoudi, M. (2018). Modeling of simultaneous adsorption of dye and metal ion by sawdust from aqueous solution using of ANN and ANFIS. *Chemometrics and Intelligent Laboratory Systems*, *181*, 72−78. Available from https://doi.org/10.1016/j.chemolab.2018.07.012.

Falconer, R. A., Chandler-Wilde, S. N., & Liu, S. Q. (1992).), . *Hydraulic and environmental modelling: Proceedings of the second international conference on hydraulic and environmental modelling of coastal, estuarine and river waters* (Vol. I, pp. 3−39). Routledge.

Fang, Q., Wang, G., Xue, B., Liu, T., & Kiem, A. (2018). How and to what extent does precipitation on multitemporal scales and soil moisture at different depths determine carbon flux responses in a water-limited grassland ecosystem? *Science of the Total Environment*, *635*, 1255−1266. Available from https://doi.org/10.1016/j.scitotenv.2018.04.225.

Fijani, E., Barzegar, R., Deo, R., Tziritis, E., & Konstantinos, S. (2019). Design and implementation of a hybrid model based on two-layer decomposition method coupled with extreme learning machines to support real-time environmental monitoring of water quality parameters. *Science of the Total Environment*, *648*, 839−853. Available from https://doi.org/10.1016/j.scitotenv.2018.08.221.

Foscoliano, C., Del Vigo, S., Mulas, M., & Tronci, S. (2016). Predictive control of an activated sludge process for long term operation. *Chemical Engineering Journal, 304*, 1031−1044. Available from https://doi.org/10.1016/j.cej.2016.07.018.

Gadekar, M. R., & Ahammed, M. M. (2019). Modelling dye removal by adsorption onto water treatment residuals using combined response surface methodology-artificial neural network approach. *Journal of Environmental Management, 231*, 241−248. Available from https://doi.org/10.1016/j.jenvman.2018.10.017.

García Nieto, P. J., García-Gonzalo, E., Alonso Fernández, J. R., & Díaz Muñiz, C. (2019). Water eutrophication assessment relied on various machine learning techniques: A case study in the Englishmen Lake (Northern Spain). *Ecological Modelling, 404*, 91−102. Available from https://doi.org/10.1016/j.ecolmodel.2019.03.009.

Garrett, J. H. (1994). Where and why artificial neural networks are applicable in Civil Engineering. *Journal of Computing in Civil Engineering, 8*, 129−130. Available from https://doi.org/10.1061/(ASCE)0887-3801 (1994)8:2(129).

Ghaedi, M., Ansari, A., Bahari, F., Ghaedi, A. M., & Vafaei, A. (2015). A hybrid artificial neural network and particle swarm optimization for prediction of removal of hazardous dye brilliant green from aqueous solution using zinc sulfide nanoparticle loaded on activated carbon. *Spectrochimica Acta—Part A: Molecular and Biomolecular Spectroscopy, 137*, 1004−1015. Available from https://doi.org/10.1016/j.saa.2014.08.011.

Ghaedi, M., Dashtian, K., Ghaedi, A. M., & Dehghanian, N. (2016). A hybrid model of support vector regression with genetic algorithm for forecasting adsorption of malachite green onto multi-walled carbon nanotubes: Central composite design optimization. *Physical Chemistry Chemical Physics, 18*(19), 13310−13321. Available from https://doi.org/10.1039/c6cp01531j.

Goldberg, D. E. (1989). *Genetic algorithms in search, optimization and machine learning*. Boston, MA: Addison-Wesley Longman Publishing Co., Inc.

Gude, V. G. (2015). Energy and water autarky of wastewater treatment and power generation systems. *Renewable and Sustainable Energy Reviews, 45*, 52−68. Available from https://doi.org/10.1016/j.rser.2015.01.055.

Hazrati, H., Moghaddam, A. H., & Rostamizadeh, M. (2017). The influence of hydraulic retention time on cake layer specifications in the membrane bioreactor: Experimental and artificial neural network modeling. *Journal of Environmental Chemical Engineering, 5*(3), 3005−3013. Available from https://doi.org/10.1016/j.jece.2017.05.050.

Heon, C. J., Ki, S. S., & Sung, R. H. (2004). A river water quality management model for optimising regional wastewater treatment using a genetic algorithm. *Journal of Environmental Management, 73*(3), 229−242. Available from https://doi.org/10.1016/j.jenvman.2004.07.004.

Hong, H., Panahi, M., Shirzadi, A., Ma, T., Liu, J., Zhu, A. X., Chen, W., Kougias, I., & Kazakis, N. (2018). Flood susceptibility assessment in Hengfeng area coupling adaptive neuro-fuzzy inference system with genetic algorithm and differential evolution. *Science of the Total Environment, 621*, 1124−1141. Available from https://doi.org/10.1016/j.scitotenv.2017.10.114.

Hong, H., Tsangaratos, P., Ilia, I., Liu, J., Zhu, A. X., & Chen, W. (2018). Application of fuzzy weight of evidence and data mining techniques in construction of flood susceptibility map of Poyang County, China. *Science of the Total Environment, 625*, 575−588. Available from https://doi.org/10.1016/j.scitotenv.2017.12.256.

Hoseinian, F. S., Rezai, B., & Kowsari, E. (2017). The nickel ion removal prediction model from aqueous solutions using a hybrid neural genetic algorithm. *Journal of Environmental Management, 204*, 311−317. Available from https://doi.org/10.1016/j.jenvman.2017.09.011.

Huang, M., Ma, Y., Wan, J., Wang, Y., Chen, Y., & Yoo, C. (2014). Improving nitrogen removal using a fuzzy neural network-based control system in the anoxic/oxic process. *Environmental Science and Pollution Research, 21*(20), 12074−12084. Available from https://doi.org/10.1007/s11356-014-3092-4.

Jamieson, D. G., & Fedra, K. (1996). The "WaterWare" decision-support system for river-basin planning. 1. Conceptual design. *Journal of Hydrology*, *177*(3−4), 163−175. Available from https://doi.org/10.1016/0022-1694(95)02957-5.

Jamshidi, M., Ghaedi, M., Dashtian, K., Ghaedi, A. M., Hajati, S., Goudarzi, A., & Alipanahpour, E. (2016). Highly efficient simultaneous ultrasonic assisted adsorption of brilliant green and eosin B onto ZnS nanoparticles loaded activated carbon: artificial neural network modeling and central composite design optimization. *Spectrochimica Acta, Part A: Molecular and Biomolecular Spectroscopy*, *153*, 257−267. Available from https://doi.org/10.1016/j.saa.2015.08.024.Z.

Jaramillo, F., Orchard, M., Muñoz, C., Antileo, C., Sáez, D., & Espinoza, P. (2018). On-line estimation of the aerobic phase length for partial nitrification processes in SBR based on features extraction and SVM classification. *Chemical Engineering Journal*, *331*, 114−123. Available from https://doi.org/10.1016/j.cej.2017.07.185.

Jing, L., Chen, B., & Zhang, B. (2014). Modeling of UV-induced photodegradation of naphthalene in marine oily wastewater by artificial neural networks. *Water, Air, and Soil Pollution*, *225*(4), 1−14. Available from https://doi.org/10.1007/s11270-014-1906-0.

Jing, L., Chen, B., Zhang, B., & Li, P. (2015). Process simulation and dynamic control for marine oily wastewater treatment using UV irradiation. *Water Research*, *81*, 101−112. Available from https://doi.org/10.1016/j.watres.2015.03.023.

Kai, X., Hailong, L., Meghan, S., Xiaoying, Z., Xuejing, W., Yan, Z., Xiaolang, Z., & Haiyan, L. (2019). Coastal water quality assessment and groundwater transport in a subtropical mangrove swamp in Daya Bay, China. *Science of the Total Environment*, *646*, 1419−1432. Available from https://doi.org/10.1016/j.scitotenv.2018.07.394.

Kalhor, K., & Emaminejad, N. (2019). Sustainable development in cities: Studying the relationship between groundwater level and urbanization using remote sensing data. *Groundwater for Sustainable Development*, *9*, 100243. Available from https://doi.org/10.1016/j.gsd.2019.100243.

Kartic, D. N., Narayana, B. C. A., & Arivazhagan, M. (2018). Removal of high concentration of sulfate from pigment industry effluent by chemical precipitation using barium chloride: RSM and ANN modeling approach. *Journal of Environmental Management*, *206*, 69−76. Available from https://doi.org/10.1016/j.jenvman.2017.10.017.

Khajeh, M., Sarafraz-Yazdi, A., & Moghadam, A. F. (2017). Modeling of solid-phase tea waste extraction for the removal of manganese and cobalt from water samples by using PSO-artificial neural network and response surface methodology. *Arabian Journal of Chemistry*, *10*, S1663−S1673. Available from https://doi.org/10.1016/j.arabjc.2013.06.011.

Khandanlou, R., Fard Masoumi, H. R., Ahmad, M. B., Shameli, K., Basri, M., & Kalantari, K. (2016). Enhancement of heavy metals sorption via nanocomposites of rice straw and Fe_3O_4 nanoparticles using artificial neural network (ANN). *Ecological Engineering*, *91*, 249−256. Available from https://doi.org/10.1016/j.ecoleng.2016.03.012.

Khosravi, K., Pham, B. T., Chapi, K., Shirzadi, A., Shahabi, H., Revhaug, I., Prakash, I., & Tien Bui, D. (2018). A comparative assessment of decision trees algorithms for flash flood susceptibility modeling at Haraz watershed, northern Iran. *Science of the Total Environment*, *627*, 744−755. Available from https://doi.org/10.1016/j.scitotenv.2018.01.266.

Knight, B., & Petridis, M. (1992). Flowes: An intelligent computational fluid dynamics system. *Engineering Applications of Artificial Intelligence*, *5*(1), 51−58. Available from https://doi.org/10.1016/0952-1976(92)90097-4.

Kralisch, S., Fink, M., Flügel, W. A., & Beckstein, C. (2003). A neural network approach for the optimisation of watershed management. *Environmental Modelling and Software*, *18*(8−9), 815−823. Available from https://doi.org/10.1016/S1364-8152(03)00081-1.

Lek, S., & Guégan, J. F. (1999). Artificial neural networks as a tool in ecological modelling, an introduction. *Ecological Modelling, 120*(2−3), 65−73. Available from https://doi.org/10.1016/S0304-3800(99)00092-7.

Li, B., Yang, G., Wan, R., Hörmann, G., Huang, J., Fohrer, N., & Zhang, L. (2017). Combining multivariate statistical techniques and random forests model to assess and diagnose the trophic status of Poyang Lake in China. *Ecological Indicators, 83*, 74−83. Available from https://doi.org/10.1016/j.ecolind.2017.07.033.

Lin, C. H., Yu, R. F., Cheng, W. P., & Liu, C. R. (2012). Monitoring and control of UV and UV-TiO$_2$ disinfections for municipal wastewater reclamation using artificial neural networks. *Journal of Hazardous Materials, 209−210*, 348−354. Available from https://doi.org/10.1016/j.jhazmat.2012.01.029.

Liou, S. M., Lo, S. L., & Hu, C. Y. (2003). Application of two-stage fuzzy set theory to river quality evaluation in Taiwan. *Water Research, 37*(6), 1406−1416. Available from https://doi.org/10.1016/S0043-1354(02)00479-7.

Liu, M., & Lu, J. (2014). Support vector machine—An alternative to artificial neuron network for water quality forecasting in an agricultural nonpoint source polluted river? *Environmental Science and Pollution Research, 21*(18), 11036−11053. Available from https://doi.org/10.1007/s11356-014-3046-x.

Longo, S., d'Antoni, B. M., Bongards, M., Chaparro, A., Cronrath, A., Fatone, F., Lema, J. M., Mauricio-Iglesias, M., Soares, A., & Hospido, A. (2016). Monitoring and diagnosis of energy consumption in wastewater treatment plants. A state of the art and proposals for improvement. *Applied Energy, 179*, 1251−1268. Available from https://doi.org/10.1016/j.apenergy.2016.07.043.

Maier, H. R., Morgan, N., & Chow, C. W. K. (2004). Use of artificial neural networks for predicting optimal alum doses and treated water quality parameters. *Environmental Modelling and Software, 19*(5), 485−494. Available from https://doi.org/10.1016/S1364-8152(03)00163-4.

Mandal, S., Mahapatra, S. S., Sahu, M. K., & Patel, R. K. (2015). Artificial neural network modelling of As (III) removal from water by novel hybrid material. *Process Safety and Environmental Protection, 93*, 249−264. Available from https://doi.org/10.1016/j.psep.2014.02.016.

Marsili-Libelli, S. (2004). Fuzzy prediction of the algal blooms in the Orbetello lagoon. *Environmental Modelling and Software, 19*(9), 799−808. Available from https://doi.org/10.1016/j.envsoft.2003.03.008.

Martin, J. L., McCutcheon, S. C., & Schottman, R. W. (1999). *Hydrodynamics and transport for water quality modeling*. Boca Raton: CRC Press.

Mazaheri, H., Ghaedi, M., Ahmadi Azghandi, M. H., & Asfaram, A. (2017). Application of machine/statistical learning, artificial intelligence and statistical experimental design for the modeling and optimization of methylene blue and Cd(ii) removal from a binary aqueous solution by natural walnut carbon. *Physical Chemistry Chemical Physics, 19*(18), 11299−11317. Available from https://doi.org/10.1039/c6cp08437k.

Messikh, N., Chiha, M., Ahmedchekkat, F., & Al Bsoul, A. (2015). Application of radial basis function neural network for removal of copper using an emulsion liquid membrane process assisted by ultrasound. *Desalination and Water Treatment, 56*(2), 399−408. Available from https://doi.org/10.1080/19443994.2014.936513.

Mining, M., Moeck, C., Radny, D., & Shirmer, M. (2018). Impact of urbanization on groundwater recharge rates in Dübendorf, Switzerland. *Journal of Hydrology, 563*, 1135−1146.

Nag, S., Mondal, A., Roy, D. N., Bar, N., & Das, S. K. (2018). Sustainable bioremediation of Cd(II) from aqueous solution using natural waste materials: Kinetics, equilibrium, thermodynamics, toxicity studies and GA-ANN hybrid modelling. *Environmental Technology and Innovation, 11*, 83−104. Available from https://doi.org/10.1016/j.eti.2018.04.009.

Navamani Kartic, D., Aditya Narayana, B. C. H., & Arivazhagan, M. (2018). Removal of high concentration of sulfate from pigment industry effluent by chemical precipitation using barium chloride: RSM and ANN modeling approach. *Journal of Environmental Management, 206*, 69−76. Available from https://doi.org/10.1016/j.jenvman.2017.10.017.

Ng, A. W. M., & Perera, B. J. C. (2003). Selection of genetic algorithm operators for river water quality model calibration. *Engineering Applications of Artificial Intelligence, 16*(5−6), 529−541. Available from https://doi.org/10.1016/j.engappai.2003.09.001.

Nourani, V., Molajou, A., Tajbakhsh, A. D., & Najafi, H. (2019). A wavelet based data mining technique for suspended sediment load modeling. *Water Resources Management*, *33*(5), 1769−1784. Available from https://doi.org/10.1007/s11269-019-02216-9.

Podobnik, B., Grosse, I., Horvatić, D., Ilic, S., Ivanov, P. C., & Stanley, H. E. (2009). Quantifying cross-correlations using local and global detrending approaches. *European Physical Journal B*, *71*(2), 243−250. Available from https://doi.org/10.1140/epjb/e2009-00310-5.

Ragas, A. M. J., Haans, J. L. M., & Leuven, R. S. E. W. (1997). Selecting water quality models for discharge permitting. *European Water Pollution Control*, *7*(5), 59−67.

Recknagel, F., Fukushima, T., Hanazato, T., Takamura, N., & Wilson, H. (1998). Modelling and prediction of phyto- and zooplankton dynamics in Lake Kasumigaura by artificial neural networks. *Lakes and Reservoirs: Research and Management*, *3*(2), 123−133. Available from https://doi.org/10.1111/j.1440-1770.1998.tb00039.x.

Ruan, J., Zhang, C., Li, Y., Li, P., Yang, Z., Chen, X., Huang, M., & Zhang, T. (2017). Improving the efficiency of dissolved oxygen control using an on-line control system based on a genetic algorithm evolving FWNN software sensor. *Journal of Environmental Management*, *187*, 550−559. Available from https://doi.org/10.1016/j.jenvman.2016.10.056.

Rumelhart, D. E., Widrow, B., & Lehr, M. A. (1994). The basic ideas in neural networks. *Communications of the ACM*, *37*(3), 87−92. Available from https://doi.org/10.1145/175247.175256.

Sabour, M. R., & Amiri, A. (2017). Comparative study of ANN and RSM for simultaneous optimization of multiple targets in Fenton treatment of landfill leachate. *Waste Management*, *65*, 54−62. Available from https://doi.org/10.1016/j.wasman.2017.03.048.

Sérodes, J. B., & Rodriguez, M. J. (1996). Prédiction de l'évolution du chlore résiduel dans les réservoirs des réseaux de distribution: Application des réseaux neuroneaux. *Journal of Water Supply: Research and Technology—AQUA*, *45*(2), 57−66.

Shahid, S., & Hazarika, M. K. (2010). Groundwater drought in the northwestern districts of Bangladesh. *Water Resources Management*, *24*(10), 1989−2006. Available from https://doi.org/10.1007/s11269-009-9534-y.

Shao, M., Tang, X., Zhang, Y., & Li, W. (2006). City clusters in China: Air and surface water pollution. *Frontiers in Ecology and the Environment*, *4*(7), 353−361. Available from https://doi.org/10.1890/1540-9295(2006)004[0353:CCICAA]2.0.CO;2.

Sharafati, A., Asadollah, S. B. H. S., & Neshat, A. (2020). A new artificial intelligence strategy for predicting the groundwater level over the Rafsanjan aquifer in Iran. *Journal of Hydrology*, *591*, 125468. Available from https://doi.org/10.1016/j.jhydrol.2020.125468.

Sharghi, E., Nourani, V., Najafi, H., & Gokcekus, H. (2019). Conjunction of a newly proposed emotional ANN (EANN) and wavelet transform for suspended sediment load modeling. *Water Science and Technology: Water Supply*, *19*(6), 1726−1734. Available from https://doi.org/10.2166/ws.2019.044.

Shi, B., Wang, P., Jiang, J., & Liu, R. (2018). Applying high-frequency surrogate measurements and a wavelet-ANN model to provide early warnings of rapid surface water quality anomalies. *Science of the Total Environment*, *610−611*, 1390−1399. Available from https://doi.org/10.1016/j.scitotenv.2017.08.232.

Singh, K. P., Gupta, S., Ojha, P., & Rai, P. (2013). Predicting adsorptive removal of chlorophenol from aqueous solution using artificial intelligence based modeling approaches. *Environmental Science and Pollution Research*, *20*(4), 2271−2287. Available from https://doi.org/10.1007/s11356-012-1102-y.

Sun, S., Bao, Z., Li, R., Sun, D., Geng, H., Huang, X., Lin, J., Zhang, P., Ma, R., Fang, L., Zhang, X., & Zhao, X. (2017). Reduction and prediction of N$_2$O emission from an anoxic/oxic wastewater treatment plant upon DO control and model simulation. *Bioresource Technology*, *244*, 800−809. Available from https://doi.org/10.1016/j.biortech.2017.08.054.

Tanhaei, B., Ayati, A., Lahtinen, M., Mahmoodzadeh Vaziri, B., & Sillanpää, M. (2016). A magnetic mesoporous chitosan based core-shells biopolymer for anionic dye adsorption: Kinetic and isothermal study and application of ANN. *Journal of Applied Polymer Science*, *133*(22), 43466. Available from https://doi.org/10.1002/app.43466.

Taylor, R. G., Scanlon, B., Döll, P., Rodell, M., van Beek, R., Wada, Y., Longuevergne, L., Leblanc, M., Famiglietti, J. S., Edmunds, M., Konikow, L., Green, T. R., Chen, J., Taniguchi, M., Bierkens, M. F. P., MacDonald, A., Fan, Y., Maxwell, R. M., Yechieli, Y., & Treidel, H. (2013). Ground water and climate change. *Nature Climate Change*, *3*, 322−329. Available from https://doi.org/10.1038/nclimate1744.

Thoe, W., Wong, S. H. C., Choi, K. W., & Lee, J. H. W. (2012). Daily prediction of marine beach water quality in Hong Kong. *Journal of Hydro-Environment Research*, *6*(3), 164−180. Available from https://doi.org/10.1016/j.jher.2012.05.003.

Trichakis, I. C., Nikolos, I. K., & Karatzas, G. P. (2011). Artificial neural network (ANN) based modeling for karstic groundwater level simulation. *Water Resources Management*, *25*(4), 1143−1152. Available from https://doi.org/10.1007/s11269-010-9628-6.

Tucciarelli, T., & Termini, D. (2000). Finite-element modeling of floodplain flow. *Journal of Hydraulic Engineering*, *126*(6), 416−424. Available from https://doi.org/10.1061/(ASCE)0733-9429(2000)126:6(416).

Turan, N. G., Mesci, B., & Ozgonenel, O. (2011). The use of artificial neural networks (ANN) for modeling of adsorption of Cu(II) from industrial leachate by pumice. *Chemical Engineering Journal*, *171*(3), 1091−1097. Available from https://doi.org/10.1016/j.cej.2011.05.005.

Uzel, A. R., Edwards, R. J., & Button, B. L. (1988). A study into the feasibility of an intelligent knowledge based system (IKBS) in computational fluid mechanics (CFM). *Engineering Applications of Artificial Intelligence*, *1*(3), 187−193. Available from https://doi.org/10.1016/0952-1976(88)90005-X.

Wakode, H. B., Baier, K., Jha, R., & Azzam, R. (2018). Impact of urbanization on groundwater recharge and urban water balance for the city of Hyderabad, India. *International Soil and Water Conservation Research*, *6*(1), 51−62. Available from https://doi.org/10.1016/j.iswcr.2017.10.003.

Wang, G., Li, J., Sun, W., Xue, B., Yinglan, A., & Liu, T. (2019a). Non-point source pollution risks in a drinking water protection zone based on remote sensing data embedded within a nutrient budget model. *Water Research*, *157*, 238−246. Available from https://doi.org/10.1016/j.watres.2019.03.070.

Wang, G., Yinglan, A., Xu, Z., & Zhang, S. (2014). The influence of land use patterns on water quality at multiple spatial scales in a river system. *Hydrological Processes*, *28*(20), 5259−5272. Available from https://doi.org/10.1002/hyp.10017.

Wang, P., Yao, J., Wang, G., Hao, F., Shrestha, S., Xue, B., Xie, G., & Peng, Y. (2019b). Exploring the application of artificial intelligence technology for identification of water pollution characteristics and tracing the source of water quality pollutants. *Science of the Total Environment*, *693*, 133440. Available from https://doi.org/10.1016/j.scitotenv.2019.07.246.

Wei, L., Hu, Z., Dong, L., & Zhao, W. (2015). A damage assessment model of oil spill accident combining historical data and satellite remote sensing information: A case study in Penglai 19−3 oil spill accident of China. *Marine Pollution Bulletin*, *91*(1), 258−271. Available from https://doi.org/10.1016/j.marpolbul.2014.11.036.

Wen, X., Gong, B., Zhou, J., He, Q., & Qing, X. (2017). Efficient simultaneous partial nitrification, anammox and denitrification (SNAD) system equipped with a real-time dissolved oxygen (DO) intelligent control system and microbial community shifts of different substrate concentrations. *Water Research*, *119*, 201−211. Available from https://doi.org/10.1016/j.watres.2017.04.052.

Wu, B., Wang, G., Jiang, H., Wang, J., & Liu, C. (2016). Impact of revised thermal stability on pollutant transport time in a deep reservoir. *Journal of Hydrology*, *535*, 671−687. Available from https://doi.org/10.1016/j.jhydrol.2016.02.031.

Wu, B., Wang, G., Wang, Z., Liu, C., & Ma, J. (2017). Integrated hydrologic and hydrodynamic modeling to assess water exchange in a data-scarce reservoir. *Journal of Hydrology*, *555*, 15−30. Available from https://doi.org/10.1016/j.jhydrol.2017.09.057.

Yasin, Y., Ahmad, F. B. H., Ghaffari-Moghaddam, M., & Khajeh, M. (2014). Application of a hybrid artificial neural network-genetic algorithm approach to optimize the lead ions removal from aqueous solutions using intercalated tartrate-Mg-Al layered double hydroxides. *Environmental Nanotechnology, Monitoring and Management, 1–2*, 2–7. Available from https://doi.org/10.1016/j.enmm.2014.03.001.

Ye, Z., Yang, J., Zhong, N., Tu, X., Jia, J., & Wang, J. (2020). Tackling environmental challenges in pollution controls using artificial intelligence: A review. *Science of the Total Environment, 699*, 1342679.

Yilmaz, B., Aras, E., Nacar, S., & Kankal, M. (2018). Estimating suspended sediment load with multivariate adaptive regression spline, teaching-learning based optimization, and artificial bee colony models. *Science of the Total Environment, 639*, 826–840. Available from https://doi.org/10.1016/j.scitotenv.2018.05.153.

Yoo, K., Shukla, S. K., Ahn, J. J., Oh, K., & Park, J. (2016). Decision tree-based data mining and rule induction for identifying hydrogeological parameters that influence groundwater pollution sensitivity. *Journal of Cleaner Production, 122*, 277–286. Available from https://doi.org/10.1016/j.jclepro.2016.01.075.

Yu, L., & Righetto, A. M. (2001). Depth-averaged turbulence $\tilde{k}$-$\tilde{w}$ model and applications. *Advances in Engineering Software, 32*(5), 375–394. Available from https://doi.org/10.1016/S0965-9978(00)00100-9.

Zadeh, L., & Kacprzyk, J. (1992). *Fuzzy logic for the management of uncertainty.* New York: John Wiley & Sons, Inc.

Zhao, G., Pang, B., Xu, Z., Peng, D., & Xu, L. (2019). Assessment of urban flood susceptibility using semi-supervised machine learning model. *Science of the Total Environment, 659*, 940–949. Available from https://doi.org/10.1016/j.scitotenv.2018.12.217.

Zou, R., Lung, W. S., & Guo, H. (2002). Neural network embedded Monte Carlo approach for water quality modeling under input information uncertainty. *Journal of Computing in Civil Engineering, 16*(2), 135–142. Available from https://doi.org/10.1061/(ASCE)0887-3801(2002)16:2(135).

Further reading

Bindal, S., & Singh, C. K. (2019). Predicting groundwater arsenic contamination: Regions at risk in highest populated state of India. *Water Research, 159*, 65–76. Available from https://doi.org/10.1016/j.watres.2019.04.054.

Chen, Q., & Mynett, A. E. (2003). Integration of data mining techniques and heuristic knowledge in fuzzy logic modelling of eutrophication in Taihu Lake. *Ecological Modelling, 162*(1–2), 55–67. Available from https://doi.org/10.1016/S0304-3800(02)00389-7.

Ghaedi, A. M., Ghaedi, M., Pouranfard, A. R., Ansari, A., Avazzadeh, Z., Vafaei, A., Tyagi, I., Agarwal, S., & Gupta, V. K. (2016). Adsorption of Triamterene on multi-walled and single-walled carbon nanotubes: Artificial neural network modeling and genetic algorithm optimization. *Journal of Molecular Liquids, 216*, 654–665. Available from https://doi.org/10.1016/j.molliq.2016.01.068.

Huang, M., Wan, J., Ma, Y., Wang, Y., Li, W., & Sun, X. (2009). Control rules of aeration in a submerged biofilm wastewater treatment process using fuzzy neural networks. *Expert Systems with Applications, 36*(7), 10428–10437. Available from https://doi.org/10.1016/j.eswa.2009.01.035.

Qiao, J. F., Hou, Y., Zhang, L., & Han, H. G. (2018). Adaptive fuzzy neural network control of wastewater treatment process with multiobjective operation. *Neurocomputing, 275*, 383–393. Available from https://doi.org/10.1016/j.neucom.2017.08.059.

Shamiri, A., Wong, S. W., Zanil, M. F., Hussain, M. A., & Mostoufi, N. (2015). Modified two-phase model with hybrid control for gas phase propylene copolymerization in fluidized bed reactors. *Chemical Engineering Journal, 264*, 706–719. Available from https://doi.org/10.1016/j.cej.2014.11.104.

Wang, J., Zhao, J., Lei, X., & Wang, H. (2018). New approach for point pollution source identification in rivers based on the backward probability method. *Environmental Pollution*, *241*, 759–774. Available from https://doi.org/10.1016/j.envpol.2018.05.093.

Yu, R. F., Chi, F. H., Cheng, W. P., & Chang, J. C. (2014). Application of pH, ORP, and DO monitoring to evaluate chromium(VI) removal from wastewater by the nanoscale zero-valent iron (nZVI) process. *Chemical Engineering Journal*, *255*, 568–576. Available from https://doi.org/10.1016/j.cej.2014.06.002.

Zhang, B., Yang, C., Zhu, H., Li, Y., & Gui, W. (2016). Evaluation strategy for the control of the copper removal process based on oxidation-reduction potential. *Chemical Engineering Journal*, *284*, 294–304. Available from https://doi.org/10.1016/j.cej.2015.07.094.

Zhang, Y., & Pan, B. (2014). Modeling batch and column phosphate removal by hydrated ferric oxide-based nanocomposite using response surface methodology and artificial neural network. *Chemical Engineering Journal*, *249*, 111–120. Available from https://doi.org/10.1016/j.cej.2014.03.073.

ANN prognostication and GA optimization of municipal solid waste leachate treatment using aluminum electrodes via electrocoagulation-flocculation method

Chinenye Adaobi Igwegbe[1], Okechukwu Dominic Onukwuli[1], Joshua O. Ighalo[1,2], Chukwuemeka Daniel Ezeliora[3], and Pius Chukwukelue Onyechi[3]

[1]*Department of Chemical Engineering, Nnamdi Azikiwe University, Awka, Nigeria* [2]*Department of Chemical Engineering, Faculty of Engineering and Technology, University of Ilorin, Ilorin, Nigeria* [3]*Department of Industrial/Production Engineering, Nnamdi Azikiwe University, Awka, Nigeria*

Introduction

Leachate generation is a major problem for municipal solid waste landfills and causes a significant threat to the safety of surface water and groundwater (Raghab et al., 2013). Leachate can be defined as a liquid that passes through a landfill and has extracted dissolved and suspended matter from it (Raghab et al., 2013). Leachate results from precipitation entering the landfill from moisture that exists in the waste when it is composed. The discharge of landfill leachate can lead to serious environmental problems (Aziz et al., 2011; Gandhimathi et al., 2013). If not treated for safe discharge before percolation into the soil and subsoil, contaminating the groundwater, surface water, and soil, it could be a major source of water contamination, with the probability of the outbreak of dangerous diseases (acute and chronic toxicities) (Aziz et al., 2011; Gotvajn et al., 2009; Sanphoti et al., 2006; Ziyang et al., 2009). This negative aspect is associated with municipal sanitary landfill disposal methods (Bashir et al., 2012; Kashitarash et al., 2012). Generally, leachate is characterized by high values of ammonical nitrogen (NH_3-N), heavy metals (e.g., copper, iron, zinc, lead, manganese, etc.), chlorinated organic and inorganic salts (e.g., chloride, sulfate, sodium, etc.), halogenated hydrocarbons, suspended solids, inorganic salts, humic acid, kaolin, dyes, phosphate, and magnesium, which contribute to biochemical oxygen demand (BOD), chemical oxygen demand (COD), pH, color, fatty acids, turbidity, and suspended solids (Kamaruddin et al., 2017; Raghab et al., 2013; Renou et al., 2008; Uygur & Kargi, 2004) as well as strong color and bad odor (Raghab et al., 2013). Leachate production is rapid in tropical countries since the rainfall normally exceeds the quantity that can be evaporated during the rainy season (Aziz et al., 2014). Therefore there is the need for treatment to avoid seepage into water bodies. The age, waste composition, and climatic conditions of the landfill are among the most important factors that affect leachate characteristics

Current Trends and Advances in Computer-Aided Intelligent Environmental Data Engineering.
DOI: https://doi.org/10.1016/B978-0-323-85597-6.00013-6

(Aziz et al., 2011; Gandhimathi et al., 2013). In addition, leachate quality and quantity are influenced by the landfill age, landfill hydrology, precipitation, weather variation, waste type, and composition, depending on the standard of living of the surrounding population (Abbas et al., 2009; Baig et al., 1999; Kamaruddin et al., 2017; Lim et al., 2016; Renou et al., 2008).

Several techniques have been applied for the treatment of solid waste landfill leachate, including coagulation-flocculation (Cheng & Chi, 2002; Ghafari et al., 2009; Kumar & Bishnoi, 2017; Zouboulis et al., 2004), advanced oxidation process (Shabiimam & Anil, 2012; Sun et al., 2009), electro-Fenton method (Amuda, 2006), Fenton reaction (Trujillo et al., 2006), coagulation-adsorption (Bazrafshan & Ahmadi, 2017; Chaouki et al., 2017; Gandhimathi et al., 2013), nanofiltration and reverse osmosis (Košutića et al., 2014; Theepharaksapan et al., 2011), bipolar membrane electrodialysis (Ilhan et al., 2014), electrocoagulation (EC) (Ilhan, Kurt, Apaydin, & Gonullu, 2008; Sekman, Top, Varank, & Bilgili, 2011; Turro et al., 2011), biodegradation (Lim et al., 2016; Tamrat et al., 2012; Xu et al., 2010; Yang & Zhou, 2008), adsorption (Ching et al., 2011; Kalderis et al., 2008; Sivakumar, 2013), chemical precipitation (Chen et al., 2013; Di Iaconi et al., 2010; Zhang et al., 2009), nanofiltration (Linde & Jönsson, 1995), reverse osmosis (Theepharaksapan et al., 2011), and dissolved air flotation (Ahmadi & Mostafapour, 2017).

However, EC is a simple, neat, and very efficient method, that is easy to operate and produces a decreased quantity of sludge. EC combines electrochemistry, coagulation, and flotation processes in water purification. This technology is a treatment process that uses electrical current to treat and flocculate contaminants without the addition of any form of coagulant (Igwegbe et al., 2019). In the EC technique, these cations (active precursor coagulant) are generated in situ through the electrolytic dissolution or corrosion of sacrificial anodes; usually, iron or aluminum plates are used (Fig. 8.1) (Moussa et al., 2016). EC has been used to eliminate a wide range of water pollutants (Naje et al., 2016), including turbidity (Kobya et al., 2003; Kobya & Delipinar, 2008), which is the amount of cloudiness in water. Water turbidity is caused by the presence of suspended particles (Mucha & Kułakowski, 2016). Different studies have also been reported on electrochemical

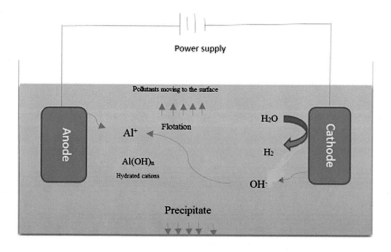

FIGURE 8.1

A schematic representation of a basic EC cell. *EC,* Electrocoagulation.

treatment of water by exhausting aluminum (Ilhan et al., 2008; Kobya et al., 2003), iron (Igwegbe, 2019; Kobya et al., 2003; Kobya & Delipinar, 2008), stainless steel (Arslan-Alaton et al., 2009; Murthy & Parmar, 2011; Nizam et al., 2016; SenthilKumar et al., 2010), magnesium (Devlin et al., 2019; Vasudevan et al., 2010), copper electrodes (Danial et al., 2017; Prajapati et al., 2016; Safwat et al., 2019; Zarei et al., 2018), etc. The electrochemical reactions that occur at the anode and cathode during the EC when aluminum (Al) electrodes are used are displayed as Eqs. (8.1)−(8.3) (Ghalwa et al., 2017; Mouedhen et al., 2008):

Anode:

$$Al_{(s)} \rightarrow Al^{3+}_{(aq)} + 3e^-$$ (8.1)

Cathode:

$$3H_2O_{(l)} + 3e^- \rightarrow \frac{3}{2}H_{2(g)} + 3OH^-$$ (8.2)

When the anode potential is sufficiently high, secondary reactions may occur, especially oxygen evolution:

$$2H_2O_{(l)} \rightarrow O_{2(g)} + 4H^+ + 4e^-$$ (8.3)

Aluminum ions (Al^{3+}) produced by electrolytic dissolution of the anode [Eq. (8.1)] immediately undergo spontaneous hydrolysis reactions which generate various monomeric species such as $Al(OH)^{2+}_{(aq)}$ and $Al(OH)_3$ and are finally polymerized to $Al_n(OH)_{3n}$.

A number of researchers (Bhatti et al., 2011; Bui et al., 2016; Maleki et al., 2014; Vinitha et al., 2018; Zangooei et al., 2016) have focused on modeling the electrocoagulation-flocculation (ECF) process using ANNs (artificial neural networks). However, there is not much published information on the application of ANN modeling on electrochemical purification for solid waste landfill leachate. The objective of this study is to ascertain the prognostic ability of ANNs in modeling leachate treatment using EC via aluminum electrodes. This study also aims to examine the efficiency of ECF processes for the reduction of turbidity from solid waste leachate using aluminum rods.

ANNs are used for predicting the outcome and behavior of systems, designing different processes, and analyzing already existing processes (Ghosh et al., 2015). ANN is centered on the biological neural system structure (Kareem & Pathak, 2016). Currently, ANN is implemented by various disciplines to predict the outputs due to its ability to engage learning algorithms and characterize the interactions between output and input for nonlinear systems (Behin & Farhadian, 2016; Pilkington et al., 2014). This relationship can be recognized using error functions such as MSE (mean square error) and R^2 (regression analysis coefficient). Generally, the ANN requires a very large number of data points to perform better in the training of networks (Igwegbe, Onukwuli, et al., 2019). The multilayer perceptrons (MLPs) are usually trained with a backpropagation (BP) algorithm. Herein, error minimization was achieved using the Levenberge−Marquardt (LM) method other than the conjugate gradient and gradient descent methods since the LM requires more memory but less time (Billah et al., 2016). It has been also reported that the LM gives higher R^2 and lower MSE than the other methods. A two-layer feed-forward network with sigmoid hidden neurons and linear output neurons (fitnet) can fit multidimensional mapping problems well arbitrarily, given consistent data and enough neurons in its hidden layer.

To prognosticate the optimum responses and optimum values of the experimental elements, the GA (genetic algorithm) can be used. GA is a computing technique used to discover the exact solution to maximizing a system. GA imitates genetics, natural selection, and evolution, and is centered on optimizing, evaluating, and improving a problem until a discontinuing measure is attained (Tumuluru & Heikkila, 2019). Many authors have used GA to maximize their results (Azari et al., 2019; Betiku & Ajala, 2014; Dawood & Li, 2013; Tumuluru & Heikkila, 2019).

The aim of this work is to study and employ ANN for modeling turbidity reduction in municipal waste leachate through aluminum electrodes. The optimum turbidity removal and optimum parameters that influence the treatment process (initial pH, current density, electrolysis time, settling time, and temperature) were also obtained using the GA tool. The data were also statistically analyzed using Minitab software.

Methodology
Batch electrocoagulation experiments

The municipal waste leachate was obtained on June 14, 2018, from a dumping site at Agu-Awka, Nigeria (latitude: 6°12′45.68″ N, longitude: 7°04′19.16″ E) at a single point. It has been in operation since 2013. The leachate was kept in containers at 4°C prior to use to avoid changes in its characteristics. The characteristics of the leachate are listed in Table 8.1.

The ECF experiments were carried out in the Chemical Engineering laboratory, Nnamdi Azikiwe University, Awka, Nigeria. ECF studies were carried out using regulated DC power supply (HUPE Model LLLN003C) of 220 V and 0−3 A capacity. The voltage and current were maintained using the rheostat. The effects of various operating parameters such as initial pH, current density (A), electrolysis time (min), settling time (min), and temperature (K) on the EC process using Al (99.5%) plates as the sacrificial electrodes were investigated.

Before each experiment, the pH of the wastewater was adjusted using an HCl or NaOH solution within the range of pH 2−10. The electrodes were placed vertically in the reactor at a depth of 8 cm and connected at the monopolar parallel mode at an electrode distance of 5 cm. The current density could be regulated at a given level at a constant voltage of 220 V. Different currents were

Table 8.1 Leachate characteristics.

Parameter	Unit	Value
pH	−	7.8
Temperature	°C	30.1
Turbidity	NTU	613
Total suspended solids	mg/L	414
Total dissolved solids	mg/L	230
Total solids	mg/L	644
Electrical conductivity	μS/cm	123
Biochemical oxygen demand	mg/L	1413
Chemical oxygen demand	mg/L	3972

passed into the 500 mL of leachate. All runs were performed at different temperatures, with each beaker placed on a stirrer to agitate the electrolyte with a constant charge time of 15 min, flocculation time of 15 minutes (30 rpm), with a magnetic stirrer immersed in 20 mL of the samples being withdrawn from each of the beakers and their respective coagulation-adsorption efficiency (%R) was calculated for different turbidities at different settling times using Eq. (8.4):

$$\%R = \frac{TUR_i - TUR_f}{TUR_i} \times 100 \qquad (8.4)$$

where TUR_i is the initial turbidity and TUR_f is the final turbidity.

The turbidity values were determined using the EPA Method 180.1 (O'Dell, 1993). After each run, the electrodes were cleaned thoroughly to remove any surface grease or solid residues. A schematic illustration of the ECF process is presented in Fig. 8.2.

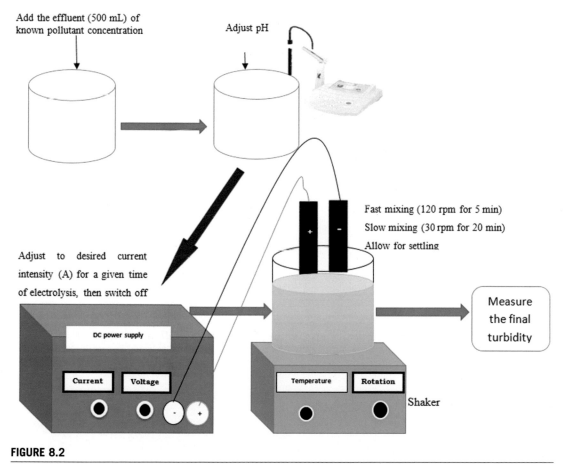

FIGURE 8.2

A schematic illustration of the electrocoagulation-flocculation process used in this study.

Artificial neural network modeling

An MLP-based feedforward ANN, which makes use of the backpropagation learning algorithm, was applied for the modeling. The network consists of an input layer, a hidden layer, and an output layer (Fig. 8.3).

   The MLP technique used in this work was developed in MATLAB® (The Math Works Inc., 2018). The following five input neurons (or variables) (Table 8.2) were considered for the ECF experiments: pH, current intensity, electrolysis time, settling time, and temperature. A hidden layer of determined neurons (determined by trial-and-error technique) and an output layer of one neuron representing the removal efficiency (turbidity reduction) were used for the modeling. The model dataset utilized in the design of the ANN was built using a central composite design-response surface methodology experimental plan of five-level factors, coded as −1 (low), 0 (central point), 1 (high), −α, and +α (Table 8.1) was generated by Design expert software (v. 11.0.0), which led to 50 experiments (Table 8.2). The experiments were carried out according to the runs seen in Table 8.2 using the procedure described in the previous section to obtain the experimental or actual response (output) at each run.

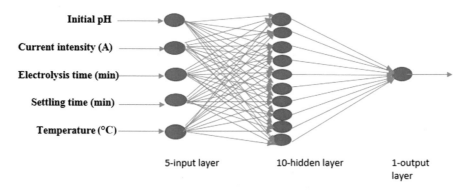

FIGURE 8.3

The MLP neural network used in this study. *MLP*, multilayer perceptron.

Table 8.2 Process variables and their levels for ECF experiment (full factorial). *ECF,* **electrocoagulation-flocculation.**

	Range of actual and coded variables				
Variables	**−α**	**−1**	**0**	**+1**	**+α**
X_1: initial pH	2	4	6	8	10
X_2: current intensity (A)	1	1.5	2	2.5	3
X_3: electrolysis time (min)	2	4	6	8	10
X_4: settling time (min)	0	10	20	30	40
X_5: Temperature (°C)	30	40	50	60	70

Then, the data presented in Table 8.3 were divided into three sets [the training, validating, and testing sets giving 85% (42 samples), 10% (five samples), and 5% (three samples), respectively] for the input layer. Experimental turbidity reduction efficiencies or values were used for the output layer. The Neural Fitting app (nftool) was used to select data, create, and train the network. To obtain a better prediction of the output responses, the best number of neurons in the hidden layer, training samples, validating samples, and testing samples were chosen by the trial-and-error method. The network MLP was trained with the Levenberg−Marquardt backpropagation algorithm (trainlm). A transigmoid transfer function (transig) at the hidden layer and a linear transfer function (purelin) at the output layer were applied.

Table 8.3 Dataset used for the ANN modeling, the actual and predicted efficiencies using ANN at the Nbest. *ANN*, artificial neural network.

Run	Input					Output	
	pH	Current dosage (A)	Electrolysis time (min)	Settling time (min)	Temperature (°C)	Experimental values (%)	ANN predicted values (%)
1	4	1.5	4	10	40	86.39	86.72
2	4	2.5	8	10	60	94.08	94.06
3	4	1.5	4	10	60	87.55	87.69
4	6	2	6	20	50	94.34	93.95
5	4	1.5	8	30	60	97.63	97.57
6	4	2.5	4	30	40	96.44	96.45
7	8	2.5	4	30	40	93.16	93.80
8	4	1.5	8	30	40	96.46	96.42
9	4	2.5	4	10	40	88.55	88.58
10	8	1.5	4	30	60	90.66	90.62
11	10	2	6	20	50	91.79	91.83
12	8	1.5	4	10	60	83.89	84.44
13	8	1.5	8	10	40	91.94	91.91
14	6	2	6	20	50	93.12	93.95
15	6	1	6	20	50	92.00	92.02
16	4	1.5	4	30	40	91.85	91.96
17	6	2	2	20	50	94.17	94.17
18	4	1.5	4	30	60	92.39	92.40
19	4	2.5	8	30	40	96.38	96.37
20	4	2.5	4	10	60	93.12	93.11
21	6	2	10	20	50	99.77	99.77
22	6	2	6	0	50	73.65	73.65
23	4	2.5	8	30	60	97.82	97.80
24	6	2	6	40	50	85.19	85.22
25	6	2	6	20	50	93.30	93.95
26	8	2.5	8	10	60	95.30	95.17
27	6	2	6	20	50	94.38	93.95

(Continued)

Table 8.3 Dataset used for the ANN modeling, the actual and predicted efficiencies using ANN at the Nbest. *ANN*, artificial neural network. *Continued*

Run	Input					Output	
	pH	Current dosage (A)	Electrolysis time (min)	Settling time (min)	Temperature (°C)	Experimental values (%)	ANN predicted values (%)
28	6	2	6	20	50	93.48	93.95
29	8	2.5	4	10	60	90.94	90.93
30	8	2.5	8	30	60	94.93	94.92
31	6	2	6	20	70	95.80	95.82
32	2	2	6	20	50	98.52	97.32
33	4	1.5	8	10	60	94.72	94.63
34	8	1.5	8	30	40	92.21	92.24
35	8	1.5	4	30	40	89.67	89.63
36	6	2	6	20	30	94.72	94.70
37	4	2.5	4	30	60	94.38	94.38
38	4	1.5	8	10	40	93.12	93.15
39	6	2	6	20	50	94.75	93.95
40	8	2.5	8	10	40	92.75	94.87
41	6	2	6	20	50	93.54	93.95
42	8	2.5	4	30	60	92.98	92.98
43	8	2.5	8	30	40	95.20	95.12
44	8	1.5	8	30	60	94.04	94.06
45	8	2.5	4	10	40	85.05	85.04
46	4	2.5	8	10	40	91.86	91.85
47	6	2	6	20	50	94.34	93.95
48	6	3	6	20	50	99.96	101.72
49	8	1.5	8	10	60	88.39	88.35
50	8	1.5	4	10	40	82.81	82.82

The network was trained for different numbers of iterations to obtain the best number of neurons for the hidden layer. The number of nodes (N) varied from 3 to 12. Its performance was evaluated using the MSE and R^2 existing in the MATLAB software. The regression coefficient measures the correlation between the predicted responses (outputs) and the experimental responses (targets). An R^2 close to 1 implies a better relationship. A low MSE also implies a better relationship. The training stops automatically when there is an increase in the MSE of the validation samples.

The best N was chosen based on the values of R^2, root mean square error (RMSE), SSE, and AAD and the plots of the training, validation, and testing made. The RMSE, AAD, and SSE equations are given in Eqs. (8.5)–(8.7) (Ahmadi & Igwegbe, 2020; Igwegbe, Mohmmadi, et al., 2019)

$$\text{RMSE} = \left(\frac{1}{n} \sum_{i=1}^{n} (\%R_{i,pred} - \%R_{i,exp})^2 \right)^{1/2} \tag{8.5}$$

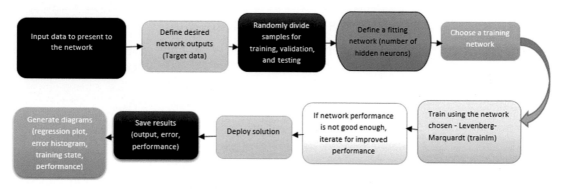

FIGURE 8.4

The steps used in the ANN modeling of this study using the nftool in MATLAB. *ANN*, artificial neural network.

$$\mathrm{SSE} = \sum_{i=1}^{n=1} (\%R_{i,pred} - \%R_{i,exp})^2 \tag{8.6}$$

$$\mathrm{AAD} = \left[\frac{1}{n} \sum_{i=1}^{n} \left(\frac{\%R_{i,pred} - \%R_{i,exp}}{\%R_{i,exp}}\right)\right] \times 100 \tag{8.7}$$

where $\%R_{i,pred}$ is the predicted efficiency, $\%R_{i,exp}$ is the experimental efficiency, and n is the number of data points.

Fig. 8.4 shows the steps involved in ANN modeling using the nftool in MATLAB.

Genetic algorithm optimization of the ECF process

The ECF process was maximized using the GA optimization technique via the GA tool in ANSYS software (version 16.0.1). The global optimum solution was also obtained.

Statistical analysis of the data

The data were analyzed statistically using the main effect analysis plots to examine whether the parameters considered (initial pH, current density, electrolysis time, settling time, and temperature) have an influence on the percentage turbidity removal. The normal probability plot was made also made to demonstrate the significant rate of the individual parameters. The Pearson correlations were used to correlate the relationship between the parameters and the response values to reveal the level of their relationships. The significant level adopted in this research is 0.05. The statistical analysis was done using the Minitab software.

Calculation of electrode and electrical consumption

The theoretical electrical energy consumption (EEC) per m³ of the effluent and electrode consumption (ELC) were also determined using Eqs. (8.8) and (8.9), respectively (Elkacmi et al., 2017; Irki, 2018)

$$\text{EEC}\left(\frac{\text{kWh}}{\text{m}^3}\right) = \frac{U \times i \times t_{EC}}{V} \times 10^{-3} \tag{8.8}$$

$$\text{ELC}\left(\frac{\text{kg}}{\text{m}^3}\right) = \frac{i \times t_{EC} \times M_w}{z \times F \times V} \times 10^{-3} \tag{8.9}$$

where U = cell voltage (V), i = current (A), t_{EC} = operating time (h), M_w = molecular mass of aluminum (26.98 g/mol), z = number of electrons transferred (3), F = Faraday's constant = 96485.34 A s/mol, V = volume of solution (m³).

Results and discussion
ANN modeling results

The experimental and ANN-predicted turbidity reduction efficiencies at best N (Nbest) are presented in Table 8.3. The R^2, RMSE, SSE, and AAD values for the different numbers of nodes are presented in Table 8.4. The best number of neurons (Nbest) was observed as 10, having the lowest RMSE, SSE, and AAD, and highest R^2 value. The MSEs of 0.04374, 1.16665, and 1.63636 were observed for the training (with $R^2 = 0.99893$), validation (with $R^2 = 0.94262$), and testing sets (with $R^2 = 0.99774$), respectively. The R^2 values are close to 1 and the RMSE, SSE, and AAD values are low, indicating that the ANN can be used to model the turbidity removal from leachate using Al electrodes (Table 8.4). These error values (RMSE, SSE, and AAD) also impede the predicted and experimental responses from being close and accurate.

Table 8.4 The R^2 and MSE values at the different numbers of neurons, N.

N	R^2	RMSE	SSE	AAD
3	0.9323	0.0131	0.0172	0.0007
4	0.9202	0.0147	0.0216	0.00180
5	0.9625	0.0097	0.0094	0.00001
6	0.9313	0.0130	0.01692	0.00015
7	0.9589	0.0105	0.01097	0.00246
8	0.9464	0.0115	0.01333	0.00091
9	0.9842	0.0065	0.00417	0.00018
10 (Nbest)	**0.9886**	**0.0053**	**0.00279**	**0.00106**
11	0.9736	0.0082	0.00677	0.00087
12	0.9733	0.00823	0.00678	0.00119

The linear fit model obtained by the plot of the ANN validation outputs, Y versus the targets, T (the experimental value), is shown in Fig. 8.5 and Eq. (8.7). These model equations were used to predict the ANN model output response values.

R^2 of 0.99893, 0.94262, 0.99774, and 0.99427 were obtained for the training, validation, testing, and all plots, respectively (Fig. 8.5). These values indicate that the ANN as a modeling tool is adequate for the data. Also, it is obvious that the ANN was capable of predicting the reduction of turbidity from leachate using Al electrodes since the ANN predicted and experimental values are close (Table 8.2 and Fig. 8.5). Fig. 8.6 shows the performance plots of the best trained network and the regression plots, respectively, using the LMb algorithm. The training of the data was stopped with an MSE error of 1.1667 at epoch 10; this is close to the acceptable range. Fig. 8.7 also shows

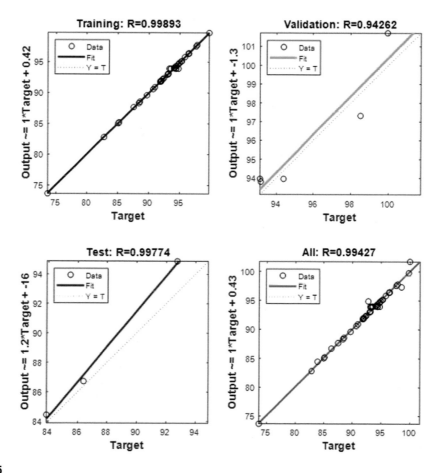

FIGURE 8.5

Regression plots for the ANN model for turbidity reduction on the leachate using Al electrodes at the Nbest. *ANN*, artificial neural network.

$$Y = (0.82)T + (14)(7)$$

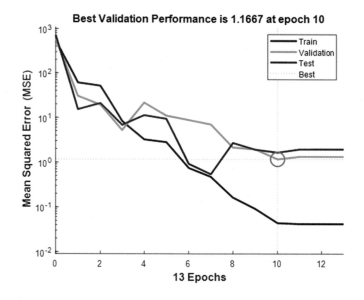

FIGURE 8.6

Performance plots for the ANN model for turbidity reduction on the leachate using Al electrodes at the Nbest. *ANN*, artificial neural network.

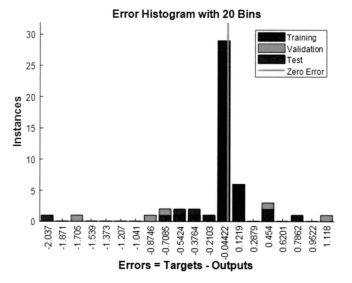

FIGURE 8.7

Error histogram plots for the ANN predicted turbidity reduction on the leachate at the Nbest. *ANN*, artificial neural network.

that the predicted and actual values are close, as more than 25 of the trained data points have zero error.

Genetic algorithm optimization results

The application of GA shows the optimal solutions for the experimental results (Fig. 8.8). Fig. 8.8 shows the table of schematic that deals with the optimization analysis and the optimal solutions for the experimental results. This shows that the experimental trials developed 1476 design local points or solutions before achieving the optimal solutions. The optimal solutions for the input process parameters for pH, current dosage, electrolysis time, settling time, and temperature were 3.6004, 1.3502 A, 3.6004 minutes, 9.001 minutes, and 36.004°C, respectively; while the optimal solution of the response parameters shows that the optimal solution for the response is 99.98%. The sensitivity analysis shows the input process parameters analysis to the response variable (Fig. 8.9). This figure shows that pH is the most influential input process parameter among the other factors used for the experimental trials. Experiments were carried out in triplicates using the optimum conditions

Table of Schematic A2: Optimization		▾ ⊟ X
	A	**B**
1	⊟ Optimization Study	
2	Maximize P6; P6 >= 73.65	Goal, Maximize P6 (Default importance); Strict Constraint, P6 values greater than or equals to 73.65 (Default importance)
3	⊟ Optimization Method	
4	MOGA	The MOGA method (Multi-Objective Genetic Algorithm) is a variant of the popular NSGA-II (Non-dominated Sorted Genetic Algorithm-II) based on controlled elitism concepts. It supports multiple objectives and constraints and aims at finding the global optimum.
5	Configuration	Generate 1000 samples initially, 500 samples per iteration and find 1 candidates in a maximum of 200 iterations.
6	Status	Converged after 1476 evaluations.
7	⊟ Candidate Points	
8		Candidate Point 1
9	P1 - pH	3.6004
10	P2 - Current dosage (A)	1.3502
11	P3 - Electrolysis time (min)	3.6004
12	P4 - Settling time (min)	9.001
13	P5 - Temperature (0C)	36.004
14	P6 - Experimental values (%)	⋆⋆⋆ 99.98

FIGURE 8.8

Optimization analysis and the optimal solutions for the results.

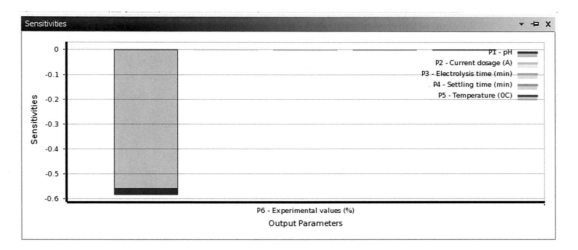

FIGURE 8.9

The sensitivity analysis on the GA optimization. *GA*, genetic algorithm.

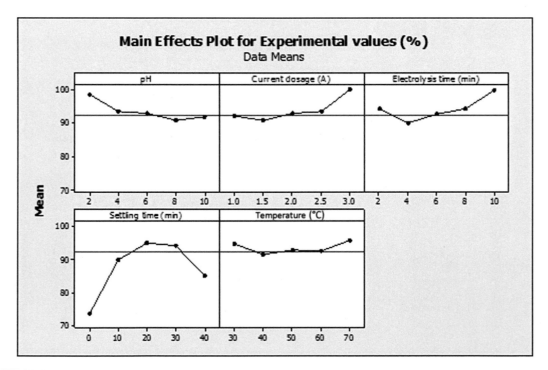

FIGURE 8.10

Main effects plot for the experimental values (%)

to validate the result, and 99.84% was obtained; this is close to 99.98%, which proves that the GA optimization tool is efficient.

Statistical analysis results

The main effect analysis showed that the independent variables vary along the mean of the response variable. This shows that the parameters have an influence on the response variable (Fig. 8.10). The results (Fig. 8.11) revealed that the factors (parameters) and the response (turbidity reduction) are all significance, with a significance level that is less than 0.005. This shows that the experimental data trials experimented for the processes are all significant to effectively and efficiently reveal the results of the experiments. The correlation results (Table 8.5) revealed that pH, current dosage, electrolysis time and settling time (the independent variables), are strongly significant to the response variable (the dependent variable). Meanwhile, temperature is the only independent variable that is not significant for the response variable.

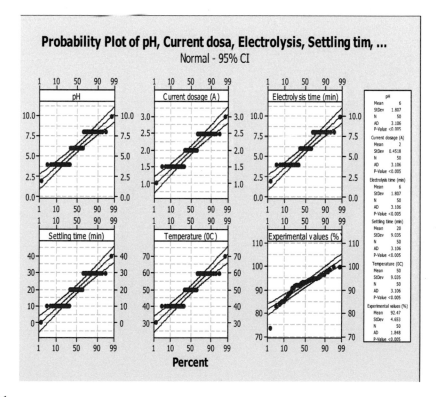

FIGURE 8.11

Probability plot of the parameters and the turbidity reduction.

Table 8.5 Pearson correlations for the parameters and the response variable (turbidity reduction).

		pH	Current dosage (A)	Electrolysis time (min)	Settling time (min)	Temperature (°C)	Experimental values (%)
pH	Pearson correlation	1	0.000	0.000	0.000	0.000	−0.254*
	Sig. (one-tailed)		0.500	0.500	0.500	0.500	0.038
	N	50	50	50	50	50	50
Current dosage (A)	Pearson correlation	0.000	1	0.000	0.000	0.000	0.268*
	Sig. (one-tailed)	0.500		0.500	0.500	0.500	0.030
	N	50	50	50	50	50	50
Electrolysis time (min)	Pearson Correlation	0.000	0.000	1	0.000	0.000	0.380**
	Sig. (one-tailed)	0.500	0.500		0.500	0.500	0.003
	N	50	50	50	50	50	50
Settling time (min)	Pearson correlation	0.000	0.000	0.000	1	0.000	0.431**
	Sig. (one-tailed)	0.500	0.500	0.500		0.500	0.001
	N	50	50	50	50	50	50
Temperature (°C)	Pearson correlation	0.000	0.000	0.000	0.000	1	0.103
	Sig. (one-tailed)	0.500	0.500	0.500	0.500		0.239
	N	50	50	50	50	50	50
Experimental values (%)	Pearson correlation	−0.254*	0.268*	0.380**	0.431**	0.103	1
	Sig. (one-tailed)	0.038	0.030	0.003	0.001	0.239	
	N	50	50	50	50	50	50

*$P \leq 0.05$.
**$P \leq 0.01$.

Electrode and electrical power consumption during the ECF process

Electrode consumption effects depend on the wastewater characteristics and operating conditions (Igwegbe, 2019; Ozyonar & Karagozoglu, 2011). According to Faraday's law (Eq. 8.5), the theoretical electrode consumption at the optimum conditions obtained from optimization using GA was 0.594088 gAl/m^3. It is clear that electrode consumption, in addition to electrochemical and chemical reactions, contributes significantly to the dissolution of aluminum electrodes to generate coagulants ($Al^{3+}_{(aq)}$), and will undergo further spontaneous reactions to produce corresponding hydroxides and/or polyhydroxides in the EC (Ozyonar & Karagozoglu, 2011).

One of the most significant parameters that affect the application of any method of wastewater treatment is cost (Safari et al., 2016). Energy consumption is the major cost in the EC process (Geraldino et al., 2015; Safari et al., 2016); hence this was calculated theoretically per m^3 of the effluent solution using Eq. (8.6), with an electrical power consumption of 1.51038×10^{-5} W h/m^3 being evaluated.

Conclusion

The results of turbidity reduction in municipal waste leachate via aluminum electrodes were modeled using the ANN tool. The network was trained for different numbers of iterations to obtain the best number of neurons for the hidden layer (Nbest). The optimum turbidity removal and the optimum parameters that influence the treatment process (initial pH, current density, electrolysis time, settling time, and temperature) were also obtained using the GA tool. The data were also statistically analyzed using Minitab software. The Nbest was observed as 10, having the lowest RMSE (0.0053), SSE (0.00279), and AAD (0.00106), and the highest R^2 value (0.9886). The R^2 values were close to 1 and the RMSE, SSE, and AAD values were low, indicating that the ANN can be used to model the process and the predicted and experimental responses are close and accurate. The optimal solutions for the input process parameters for pH, current dosage, electrolysis time, settling time, and temperature were 3.6004, 1.3502 A, 3.6004 minutes, 9.001 minutes, and 36.004°C, respectively, with 99.98% turbidity reduction. The GA optimization tool was efficient as the experimental value of 99.84 obtained from conducting experiments at the optimum conditions was close to 99.98%. The statistical analysis shows that the parameters have an influence on the response variable and are able to effectively and efficiently reveal the results of the experiments (P values less than .005). The theoretical electrode consumption and electrical power consumption at the optimum conditions were 0.594088 g/m^3 and 1.51038×10^{-5} W h/m^3.

Acknowledgment

The first author wishes to acknowledge her husband: Engr. George C. Igwegbe, and children: Divine Chinenye Igwegbe, Marvel Ifechukwu Igwegbe, Victory Chukwudubem Igwegbe, and Great Ekene Igwegbe for their spiritual and moral support.

References

Abbas, A. A., Jingsong, G., Ping, L. Z., Ya, P. Y., & Al-Rekabi, W. S. (2009). Review on landfill leachate treatments. *Journal of Applied Sciences Research*, *5*(5), 534−545. Available from http://www.insinet.net/jasr/2009/534-545.pdf.

Ahmadi, S., & Igwegbe, C. A. (2020). Removal of methylene blue on zinc oxide nanoparticles: Nonlinear and linear adsorption isotherms and kinetics study. *Sigma Journal of Engineering and Natural Sciences*, *38*(1), 289−303.

Ahmadi, S., & Mostafapour, F. K. (2017). Tea waste as a low cost adsorbent for the removal of COD from landfill leachate: Kinetic study. *Journal of Scientific and Engineering Research*, *4*(6), 103−108.

Amuda, O. S. (2006). Removal of COD and colour from sanitary landfill leachate by using coagulation— Fenton's process. *Journal of Applied Sciences and Environmental Management*, *10*(2), 49−53.

Arslan-Alaton, I., Kabdaşli, I., Vardar, B., & Tünay, O. (2009). Electrocoagulation of simulated reactive dye-bath effluent with aluminum and stainless steel electrodes. *Journal of Hazardous Materials*, *164*(2−3), 1586−1594. Available from https://doi.org/10.1016/j.jhazmat.2008.09.004.

Azari, A., Mahmoudian, M. H., Niari, M. H., Eş, I., Dehganifard, E., Kiani, A., Javid, A., Azari, H., Fakhri, Y., & Mousavi Khaneghah, A. (2019). Rapid and efficient ultrasonic assisted adsorption of diethyl phthalate onto FeIIFe2IIIO4@GO: ANN-GA and RSM-DF modeling, isotherm, kinetic and mechanism study. *Microchemical Journal*, *150*, 104144. Available from https://doi.org/10.1016/j.microc.2019.104144.

Aziz, S. Q., Aziz, H. A., Bashir, M. J. K., & Mojiri, A. (2014). *Municipal landfill leachate treatment techniques: An overview. Wastewater engineering: Types, characteristics and treatment technologies*. Penang: IJSR Publications.

Aziz, S. Q., Aziz, H. A., Yusoff, M. S., & Bashir, M. J. K. (2011). Landfill leachate treatment using powdered activated carbon augmented sequencing batch reactor (SBR) process: Optimization by response surface methodology. *Journal of Hazardous Materials*, *189*(1−2), 404−413. Available from https://doi.org/10.1016/j.jhazmat.2011.02.052.

Baig, S., Coulomb, I., Courant, P., & Liechti, P. (1999). Treatment of landfill leachates: Lapeyrouse and Satrod case studies. *Ozone: Science and Engineering*, *21*(1), 1−22. Available from https://doi.org/10.1080/01919519908547255.

Bashir, M. J. K., Aziz, H. A., Aziz, S. Q., & Abu Amr, S. S. (2012). An overview of electro-oxidation processes performance in stabilized landfill leachate treatment. *Desalination and Water Treatment*, *51* (10−12), 2170−2184.

Bazrafshan, E., & Ahmadi, S. (2017). Removal COD of landfill leachate using a coagulation and activated tea waste ($ZnCL_2$) adsorption. *International Journal of Innovative Science, Engineering & Technology*, *4*(4), 339−348.

Behin, J., & Farhadian, N. (2016). Response surface methodology and artificial neural network modeling of reactive red 33 decolorization by O_3/UV in a bubble column reactor. *Advances in Environmental Technology*, *2*(1), 33−44.

Betiku, E., & Ajala, S. O. (2014). Modeling and optimization of *Thevetia peruviana* (yellow oleander) oil biodiesel synthesis via *Musa paradisiacal* (plantain) peels as heterogeneous base catalyst: A case of artificial neural network vs. response surface methodology. *Industrial Crops and Products*, *53*, 314−322. Available from https://doi.org/10.1016/j.indcrop.2013.12.046.

Bhatti, M. S., Kapoor, D., Kalia, R. K., Reddy, A. S., & Thukral, A. K. (2011). RSM and ANN modeling for electrocoagulation of copper from simulated wastewater: Multi objective optimization using genetic algorithm approach. *Desalination*, *274*(1−3), 74−80. Available from https://doi.org/10.1016/j.desal.2011.j01.083.

Billah, M., Waheed, S., & Hanifa, A. (2016). *Stock market prediction using an improved training algorithm of neural network. 2016 Second international conference on electrical, computer & telecommunication engineering (ICECTE)*. IEEE.

Bui, H. M., Duong, H. T. G., & Nguyen, C. D. (2016). Applying an artificial neural network to predict coagulation capacity of reactive dyeing wastewater by chitosan. *Polish Journal of Environmental Studies*, *25*(2), 545−555. Available from https://doi.org/10.15244/pjoes/61114.

Chaouki, Z., Khalil, F., Ijjaali, M., Valdés, H., Rafqah, S., Sarakha, M., & Zaitan, H. (2017). Use of combination of coagulation and adsorption process for the landfill leachate treatment from Casablanca city. *Desalination and Water Treatment*, *83*, 262−271. Available from https://doi.org/10.5004/dwt.2017.20743.

Chen, Y. N., Liu, C. H., Nie, J. X., Luo, X. P., & Wang, D. S. (2013). Chemical precipitation and biosorption treating landfill leachate to remove ammonium-nitrogen. *Clean Technologies and Environmental Policy*, *15*(2), 395−399. Available from https://doi.org/10.1007/s10098-012-0511-4.

Cheng, W. P., & Chi, F. H. (2002). A study of coagulation mechanisms of polyferric sulfate reacting with humic acid using a fluorescence-quenching method. *Water Research*, *36*(18), 4583−4591. Available from https://doi.org/10.1016/S0043-1354(02)00189-6.

Ching, S. L., Yusoff, M. S., Aziz, H. A., & Umar, M. (2011). Influence of impregnation ratio on coffee ground activated carbon as landfill leachate adsorbent for removal of total iron and orthophosphate. *Desalination*, *279*(1−3), 225−234. Available from https://doi.org/10.1016/j.desal.2011.06.011.

Danial, R., Abdullah, L. C., & Sobri, S. (2017). *Potential of copper electrodes in electrocoagulation process for glyphosate herbicide removal*, . MATEC web of conferences (103). EDP Sciences. Available from https://doi.org/10.1051/matecconf/201710306019.

Dawood, A. S., & Li, Y. (2013). Modeling and optimization of new flocculant dosage and pH for flocculation: Removal of pollutants from wastewater. *Water (Switzerland)*, *5*(2), 342−355. Available from https://doi.org/10.3390/w5020342.

Devlin, T. R., Kowalski, M. S., Pagaduan, E., Zhang, X., Wei, V., & Oleszkiewicz, J. A. (2019). Electrocoagulation of wastewater using aluminum, iron, and magnesium electrodes. *Journal of Hazardous Materials*, *368*, 862−868. Available from https://doi.org/10.1016/j.jhazmat.2018.10.017.

Di Iaconi, C., Pagano, M., Ramadori, R., & Lopez, A. (2010). Nitrogen recovery from a stabilized municipal landfill leachate. *Bioresource Technology*, *101*(6), 1732−1736. Available from https://doi.org/10.1016/j.biortech.2009.10.013.

Elkacmi, R., Kamil, N., & Bennajah, M. (2017). Upgrading of Moroccan olive mill wastewater using electrocoagulation: Kinetic study and process performance evaluation. *Journal of Urban and Environmental Engineering*, *11*(1), 30−41. Available from https://doi.org/10.4090/juee.2017.v11n1.030041.

Gandhimathi, R., Durai, N. J., Nidheesh, P. V., Ramesh, S. T., & Kanmani, S. (2013). Use of combined coagulation-adsorption process as pretreatment of landfill leachate. *Iranian Journal of Environmental Health Sciences & Engineering*, *10*, 24.

Geraldino, H. C. L., Simionato, J. I., De Souza Freitas, T. K. F., Garcia, J. C., De Carvalho Júnior, O., & Correr, C. J. (2015). Eficiência e custo operacional de um sistema de eletrofloculação aplicado ao tratamento de efluente da indústria de laticínio. *Acta Scientiarum—Technology*, *37*(3), 401−408. Available from https://doi.org/10.4025/actascitechnol.v37i3.26452.

Ghafari, S., Aziz, H. A., Isa, M. H., & Zinatizadeh, A. A. (2009). Application of response surface methodology (RSM) to optimize coagulation-flocculation treatment of leachate using poly-aluminum chloride (PAC) and alum. *Journal of Hazardous Materials*, *163*(2−3), 650−656. Available from https://doi.org/10.1016/j.jhazmat.2008.07.090.

Ghalwa, N., Musabeh, A., & Farhat, N. B. (2017). Performance efficiency of electrocoagulation adsorption process of Oxyfluorfen herbicide from aqueous solutions using different anodes. *Journal of Environmental & Analytical Toxicology*, *7*(3), 12. Available from https://doi.org/10.4172/2161-0525.1000448.

Ghosh, A., Das, P., & Sinha, K. (2015). Modeling of biosorption of Cu(II) by alkali-modified spent tea leaves using response surface methodology (RSM) and artificial neural network (ANN). *Applied Water Science*, *5*(2), 191−199. Available from https://doi.org/10.1007/s13201-014-0180-z.

Gotvajn, A. Z., Tišler, T., & Zagorc-Končan, J. (2009). Comparison of different treatment strategies for industrial landfill leachate. *Journal of Hazardous Materials*, *162*(2−3), 1446−1456. Available from https://doi.org/10.1016/j.jhazmat.2008.06.037.

Igwegbe, C. A. (2019). Evaluation of bio- and electro- coagulants' activities on Fish pond wastewater and Solid waste leachate (Ph.D. dissertation). Submitted to the Department of Chemical Engineering. Awka, Nigeria: Nnamdi Azikiwe University.

Igwegbe, C. A., Mohmmadi, L., Ahmadi, S., Rahdar, A., Khadkhodaiy, D., Dehghani, R., & Rahdar, S. (2019). Modeling of adsorption of methylene blue dye on Ho-CaWO$_4$ nanoparticles using response surface methodology (RSM) and artificial neural network (ANN) techniques. *MethodsX*, *6*, 1779−1797. Available from https://doi.org/10.1016/j.mex.2019.07.016.

Igwegbe, C. A., Onukwuli, O. D., & Onyechi, P. C. (2019). Optimal route for turbidity removal from aquaculture wastewater by electrocoagulation-flocculation process. *Journal of Engineering and Applied Sciences*, *15*(1), 99−108.

Ilhan, F., Kabuk, H. A., Kurt, U., Avsar, Y., Sari, H., & Gonullu, M. T. (2014). Evaluation of treatment and recovery of leachate by bipolar membrane electrodialysis process. *Chemical Engineering and Processing: Process Intensification*, *75*, 67−74. Available from https://doi.org/10.1016/j.cep.2013.11.005.

Ilhan, F., Kurt, U., Apaydin, O., & Gonullu, M. T. (2008). Treatment of leachate by electrocoagulation using aluminum and iron electrodes. *Journal of Hazardous Materials*, *154*(1−3), 381−389. Available from https://doi.org/10.1016/j.jhazmat.2007.10.035.

Irki, S. (2018). Decolorizing methyl orange by Fe-electrocoagulation process—A mechanistic insight. *International Journal of Environmental Chemistry*, *21*(1), 18−28. Available from https://doi.org/10.11648/j.ijec.20180201.14.

Kalderis, D., Koutoulakis, D., Paraskeva, P., Diamadopoulos, E., Otal, E., Valle, J. O. d., & Fernández-Pereira, C. (2008). Adsorption of polluting substances on activated carbons prepared from rice husk and sugarcane bagasse. *Chemical Engineering Journal*, *144*(1), 42−50. Available from https://doi.org/10.1016/j.cej.2008.01.007.

Kamaruddin, M. A., Abdullah, M. M. A., Yusoff, M. S., Alrozi, R., & Neculai, O. (2017). Coagulation-flocculation process in landfill leachate treatment: Focus on coagulants and coagulants aid. *IOP Conference Series: Materials Science and Engineering*, *209*, 012083. Available from https://doi.org/10.1088/1757-899X/209/1/012083.

Kareem, S. S., & Pathak, Y. (2016). *Clinical applications of artificial neural networks in pharmacokinetic modeling. Artificial neural network for drug design, delivery and disposition* (pp. 393−405). Elsevier Inc. Available from https://doi.org/10.1016/B978-0-12-801559-9.00020-X.

Kashitarash, Z. E., Taghi, S. M., Kazem, N., Abbass, A., & Alireza, R. (2012). Application of iron nanoparticles in landfill leachate treatment-case study: Hamadan landfill leachate. *Journal of Environmental Health Science and Engineering*, *9*(1), 36.

Kobya, M., Can, O. T., & Bayramoglu, M. (2003). Treatment of textile wastewaters by electrocoagulation using iron and aluminum electrodes. *Journal of Hazardous Materials*, *100*(1−3), 163−178. Available from https://doi.org/10.1016/S03043894(03)00102-X.

Kobya, M., & Delipinar, S. (2008). Treatment of the baker's yeast wastewater by electrocoagulation. *Journal of Hazardous Materials*, *154*(1−3), 1133−1140. Available from https://doi.org/10.1016/j.jhazmat.2007.11.019.

Košutića, K., Dolara, D., & Strmeckya, T. (2014). Treatment of landfill leachate by membrane processes of nanofiltration and reverse osmosis. *Desalination and Water Treatment*, *55*(10), 1−10.

Kumar, S. S., & Bishnoi, N. R. (2017). Coagulation of landfill leachate by FeCl$_3$: Process optimization using Box−Behnken design (RSM). *Applied Water Science*, *7*, 1943−1953. Available from https://doi.org/10.1007/s13201-015-0372-1.

Lim, C. K., Seow, T. W., Neoh, C. H., Md Nor, M. H., Ibrahim, Z., Ware, I., & Mat Sarip, S. H. (2016). Treatment of landfill leachate using ASBR combined with zeolite adsorption technology. *3 Biotech*, *6*(2), 195. Available from https://doi.org/10.1007/s13205-016-0513-8.

Linde, K., & Jönsson, A. S. (1995). Nanofiltration of salt solutions and landfill leachate. *Desalination, 103*(3), 223–232. Available from https://doi.org/10.1016/0011-9164(95)00075-5.

Maleki, A., Daraei, H., Shahmoradi, B., Razee, S., & Ghobadi, N. (2014). Electrocoagulation efficiency and energy consumption probing by artificial intelligent approaches. *Desalination and Water Treatment, 52* (13–15), 2400–2411. Available from https://doi.org/10.1080/19443994.2013.797545.

Mouedhen, G., Feki, M., Wery, M. D. P., & Ayedi, H. F. (2008). Behavior of aluminum electrodes in electrocoagulation process. *Journal of Hazardous Materials, 150*(1), 124–135. Available from https://doi.org/10.1016/j.jhazmat.2007.04.090.

Moussa, D. T., El-Naas, M. H., Nasser, M., & Al-Marri, M. J. (2016). A comprehensive review of electrocoagulation for water treatment: Potentials and challenges. *Journal of Environmental Management, 186*(Part 1), 24–41.

Mucha, Z., & Kułakowski, P. (2016). Turbidity measurements as a tool of monitoring and control of the SBR effluent at the small wastewater treatment plant-preliminary study. *Archives of Environmental Protection, 42*(3), 33–36. Available from https://doi.org/10.1515/aep-2016-0030.

Murthy, Z. V. P., & Parmar, S. (2011). Removal of strontium by electrocoagulation using stainless steel and aluminum electrodes. *Desalination, 282*, 63–67. Available from https://doi.org/10.1016/j.desal.2011.08.058.

Naje, A. S., Chelliapan, S., Zakaria, Z., Ajeel, M. A., & Alaba, P. A. (2016). A review of electrocoagulation technology for the treatment of textile wastewater. *Reviews in Chemical Engineering, 33*(3), 263–292.

Nizam, M. M. K., Remy, R. M. A. Z. M., Ismail, A., & Norlia, B. (2016). Electrocoagulation process by using aluminium and Sstainless steel electrodes to treat total chromium, colour and turbidity. *Procedia Chemistry, 19*, 681–686. Available from https://doi.org/10.1016/j.proche.2016.03.070.

O'Dell, J. W. (1993). Method 180.1: Determination of turbidity by nephelometry. Environmental Monitoring Systems Laboratory Office of Research and Development, U.S. Environmental Protection Agency.

Ozyonar, F., & Karagozoglu, B. (2011). Operating cost analysis and treatment of domestic wastewater by electrocoagulation using aluminum electrodes. *Polish Journal of Environmental Studies, 20*(1), 173–179.

Pilkington, J. L., Preston, C., & Gomes, R. L. (2014). Comparison of response surface methodology (RSM) and artificial neural networks (ANN) towards efficient extraction of artemisinin from *Artemisia annua*. *Industrial Crops and Products*, 15–24. Available from https://doi.org/10.1016/j.indcrop.2014.03.016.

Prajapati, A. K., Chaudhari, P. K., Pal, D., Chandrakar, A., & Choudhary, R. (2016). Electrocoagulation treatment of rice grain based distillery effluent using copper electrode. *Journal of Water Process Engineering, 11*, 1–7. Available from https://doi.org/10.1016/j.jwpe.2016.03.008.

Raghab, S. M., Abd El Meguid, A. M., & Hegazi, H. A. (2013). Treatment of leachate from municipal solid waste landfill. *HBRC Journal, 9*, 187–192. Available from https://doi.org/10.1016/j.hbrcj.2013.05.007.

Renou, S., Givaudan, J. G., Poulain, S., Dirassouyan, F., & Moulin, P. (2008). Landfill leachate treatment: Review and opportunity. *Journal of Hazardous Materials, 150*(3), 468–493. Available from https://doi.org/10.1016/j.jhazmat.2007.09.077.

Safari, S., Azadi Aghdam, M., & Kariminia, H. R. (2016). Electrocoagulation for COD and diesel removal from oily wastewater. *International Journal of Environmental Science and Technology, 13*(1), 231–242. Available from https://doi.org/10.1007/s13762-015-0863-5.

Safwat, S. M., Hamed, A., & Rozaik, E. (2019). Electrocoagulation/electroflotation of real printing wastewater using copper electrodes: A comparative study with aluminum electrodes. *Separation Science and Technology (Philadelphia), 54*(1), 183–194. Available from https://doi.org/10.1080/01496395.2018.1494744.

Sanphoti, N., Towprayoon, S., Chaiprasert, P., & Nopharatana, A. (2006). The effects of leachate recirculation with supplemental water addition on methane production and waste decomposition in a simulated tropical landfill. *Journal of Environmental Management, 81*(1), 27–35. Available from https://doi.org/10.1016/j.jenvman.2005.10.015.

Sekman, E., Top, S., Varank, G., & Bilgili, M. S. (2011). Pilot-scale investigation of aeration rate effect on leachate characteristics in landfills. *Fresenius Environmental Bulletin, 20*(7A), 1841–1852.

SenthilKumar, P., Umaiyambika, N., & Gayathri, R. (2010). DYE removal from aqueous solution by electro-coagulation process using stainless steel electrodes. *Environmental Engineering and Management Journal*, *9*(8), 1031−1037. Available from https://doi.org/10.30638/eemj.2010.135.

Shabiimam, M. A., & Anil, K. D. (2012). Treatment of municipal landfill leachate by oxidants. *American Journal of Environmental Engineering*, *2*(2), 1−5. Available from https://doi.org/10.5923/j.ajee.20120202.01.

Sivakumar, D. (2013). Adsorption study on municipal solid waste leachate using *Moringa oleifera* seed. *International Journal of Environmental Science and Technology*, *10*(1), 113−124. Available from https://doi.org/10.1007/s13762-012-0089-8.

Sun, J., Li, X., Feng, J., & Tian, X. (2009). Oxone/Co^{2+} oxidation as an advanced oxidation process: Comparison with traditional Fenton oxidation for treatment of landfill leachate. *Water Research*, *43*(17), 4363−4369. Available from https://doi.org/10.1016/j.watres.2009.06.043.

Tamrat, M., Costa, C., & Márquez, M. C. (2012). Biological treatment of leachate from solid wastes: Kinetic study and simulation. *Biochemical Engineering Journal*, *66*, 46−51. Available from https://doi.org/10.1016/j.bej.2012.04.012.

Theepharaksapan, S., Chiemchaisri, C., Chiemchaisri, W., & Yamamoto, K. (2011). Removal of pollutants and reduction of bio-toxicity in a full scale chemical coagulation and reverse osmosis leachate treatment system. *Bioresource Technology*, *102*(9), 5381−5388. Available from https://doi.org/10.1016/j.biortech.2010.11.091.

Trujillo, D., Font, X., & Sánchez, A. (2006). Use of Fenton reaction for the treatment of leachate from composting of different wastes. *Journal of Hazardous Materials*, *138*(1), 201−204. Available from https://doi.org/10.1016/j.jhazmat.2006.05.053.

Tumuluru, J. S., & Heikkila, D. J. (2019). Biomass grinding process optimization using response surface methodology and a hybrid genetic algorithm. *Bioengineering*, *6*(1), 12. Available from https://doi.org/10.3390/bioengineering6010012.

Turro, E., Giannis, A., Cossu, R., Gidarakos, E., Mantzavinos, D., & Katsaounis, A. (2011). Electrochemical oxidation of stabilized landfill leachate on DSA electrodes. *Journal of Hazardous Materials*, *190*(1−3), 460−465. Available from https://doi.org/10.1016/j.jhazmat.2011.03.085.

Uygur, A., & Kargi, F. (2004). Biological nutrient removal from pre-treated landfill leachate in a sequencing batch reactor. *Journal of Environmental Management*, *71*(1), 9−14. Available from https://doi.org/10.1016/j.jenvman.2004.01.002.

Vasudevan, S., Lakshmi, J., & Packiyam, M. (2010). Electrocoagulation studies on removal of cadmium using magnesium electrode. *Journal of Applied Electrochemistry*, *40*(11), 2023−2032. Available from https://doi.org/10.1007/s10800-010-0182-y.

Vinitha, E. V., Mansoor Ahammed, M., & Gadekar, M. R. (2018). Chemical coagulation of greywater: Modelling using artificial neural networks. *Water Science and Technology*, *2017*(3), 869−877. Available from https://doi.org/10.2166/WST.2018.263.

Xu, Z. Y., Zeng, G. M., Yang, Z. H., Xiao, Y., Cao, M., Sun, H. S., Ji, L. L., & Chen, Y. (2010). Biological treatment of landfill leachate with the integration of partial nitrification, anaerobic ammonium oxidation and heterotrophic denitrification. *Bioresource Technology*, *101*(1), 79−86. Available from https://doi.org/10.1016/j.biortech.2009.07.082.

Yang, Z., & Zhou, S. (2008). The biological treatment of landfill leachate using a simultaneous aerobic and anaerobic (SAA) bio-reactor system. *Chemosphere*, *72*(11), 1751−1756. Available from https://doi.org/10.1016/j.chemosphere.2008.04.090.

Zangooei, H., Delnavaz, M., & Asadollahfardi, G. (2016). Prediction of coagulation and flocculation processes using ANN models and fuzzy regression. *Water Science and Technology*, *74*(6), 1296−1311. Available from https://doi.org/10.2166/wst.2016.315.

Zarei, A., Biglari, H., Mobini, M., Dargahi, A., Ebrahimzadeh, G., Narooie, M. R., Mehrizi, E. A., Yari, A. R., Mohammadi, M. J., Baneshi, M. M., Khosravi, R., & Poursadeghiyan, M. (2018). Disinfecting poultry slaughterhouse wastewater using copper electrodes in the electrocoagulation process. *Polish Journal of Environmental Studies, 27*(4), 1907−1912. Available from https://doi.org/10.15244/pjoes/78150.

Zhang, T., Ding, L., & Ren, H. (2009). Pretreatment of ammonium removal from landfill leachate by chemical precipitation. *Journal of Hazardous Materials, 166*(2−3), 911−915. Available from https://doi.org/10.1016/j.jhazmat.2008.11.101.

Ziyang, L., Youcai, Z., Tao, Y., Yu, S., Huili, C., Nanwen, Z., & Renhua, H. (2009). Natural attenuation and characterization of contaminants composition in landfill leachate under different disposing ages. *Science of the Total Environment, 407*(10), 3385−3391. Available from https://doi.org/10.1016/j.scitotenv.2009.01.028.

Zouboulis, A. I., Chai, X. L., & Katsoyiannis, I. A. (2004). The application of bioflocculant for the removal of humic acids from stabilized landfill leachates. *Journal of Environmental Management, 70*(1), 35−41. Available from https://doi.org/10.1016/j.jenvman.2003.10.003.

Application of deep learning and machine learning methods in water quality modeling and prediction: a review

Ugochukwu Ewuzie[1], Oladotun Paul Bolade[2] and Abisola Opeyemi Egbedina[3]

[1]*Department of Pure and Industrial Chemistry, Abia State University, Uturu, Nigeria* [2]*Department of Petroleum Chemistry, American University of Nigeria, Yola, Nigeria* [3]*Department of Chemistry, University of Ibadan, Ibadan, Nigeria*

Introduction

Water quality (WQ) has always been a critical issue due to the undeniable usefulness of water in every facet of life. Water for agriculture, industry, construction, consumption, or other domestic uses is required to be of a certain level of quality to guarantee its suitability for the intended use. This has instigated WQ assessment, which has become a well-known concept in environmental studies. The necessity for adequate WQ spans from the sustenance of soil structure and enhanced crop yields in agriculture, construction of sturdy and durable structures, conservation of water resources, to the preservation of human health and the environment. Originally, most water bodies may have already possessed the minimum quality required to meet these purposes, especially those that were not influenced by natural (geogenic) processes due to the existing lithostratigraphic characteristics of the area. An increase in human population density has resulted in a concomitant proliferation of human-led ecodamaging activities, industrialization, urbanization, exploration, and mining (Ukaogo et al., 2020), which has impacted negatively on aquatic systems and the environment generally. Moreover, the steady decline in WQ around the world has attracted justified concern, particularly in terms of domestic, industrial, and agricultural utilization (Abba et al., 2020). Worse still, the consumption of water, which was meant to be an "elixir of life," has turned into a "harbinger of death" (Ewuzie et al., 2020) owing to a myriad of natural and anthropogenic influences on water systems, making its quality questionable and in many cases unsatisfactory.

Monitoring WQ, especially with online sensors, has been conceded as reliable and cost-effective, replacing low-frequency monitoring that is characterized by grab sampling with its many shortcomings including the time lag in gathering data, the huge cost of analysis, and difficulty in accounting for scenarios that occur during sampling intervals (Castrillo & García, 2020), which may result in underestimation of risks. However, only well-known contaminants are monitored, often omitting emerging compounds of concern (Brack et al., 2017). When monitoring data are

Current Trends and Advances in Computer-Aided Intelligent Environmental Data Engineering.
DOI: https://doi.org/10.1016/B978-0-323-85597-6.00020-3

absent, modeled data may be used to gain a more comprehensive overview of the spatiotemporal variability of the stressors as well as the impacts on ecosystems (Brack et al., 2017). It is noteworthy that setting up monitoring points by water resource managers to observe changes in WQ cannot perform the eminent role of WQ modeling and prediction (Lu & Ma, 2020); rather, monitoring data can offer a predictive basis for a number of data-driven models. Essentially, WQ models remain a veritable tool that is extensively used to enhance the understanding of water systems and support decisions toward the management of water resources. Undoubtedly however, the use of traditional modeling approaches (deterministic, parametric, and statistical models) for WQ predictions served an indisputable role in pollution control and water resource management.

However, it has become clear that the complexity of environmental and hydrological processes of different water systems has rendered their quality modeling or even prediction by traditional methods ineffective, coupled with the fact that these models depend to a large degree on unspecified input dataset and arduous processes. Most of these models are adjudged to be time-consuming and susceptible to prediction errors due to the assumption that relationships between variables are a simple linear process (Ma et al., 2014). More so, the development of statistical models involves the use of long-term historical data, which, when unavailable, unfavorably affects the performance of the model due to difficulty in model parametrization. In addition, statistical models are limited in performing scenario analysis and dynamic modeling (Khan et al., 2020). Accurate and robust intelligent models for the prediction of WQ must be established to guide WQ experts and decision-makers in the protection, management, and preservation of water resources.

Interestingly, unlike the various traditional models used in WQ prediction, artificial intelligence (AI) technologies offer an influential ability to manage complex nonlinear relationships, and a precise interpretation of the general WQ processes. Therefore these technologies do not only possess the capacity to monitor the evolution of WQ, including analyzing and predicting WQ, but also revealing the processes involved in pollutant migration and transformation (Li et al., 2021). In other words, they are shifting the research focus from resolving current problems to identifying future risks, thereby optimizing the dynamics of WQ prediction, and safeguarding health and the environment. Machine learning (ML) is a field of AI that involves algorithms, which permit computer systems to deduce patterns from data (Hosseini et al., 2020). This is a process by which a machine practically learns from an input dataset and develops or improves a structure through the data for a particular purpose. In addition, deep learning (DL), a branch of ML, is a class of representation methods with multiple echelons of representation, which comprises numerous simple but nonlinear components, with each component converting the representation from a previous layer into another higher and more abstract layer of representation (Hosseini et al., 2020). That is to say, DL is ML but differs in its capability of using multilayer models that result in a higher-level representation of the dataset. In addition, without being instructed, DL has the capacity to extract considerable features, and therefore is more resistant to noisy data (Sahiner et al., 2019).

There has been a rapid advancement of DL and ML research in the field of hydrology, and numerous research papers, including reviews, have contributed immensely to the progress made on the predictive performance of different models. In addition, with the nascent fast Internet technologies for the transmission of big data, high capacity and fast computer systems, and improvement in learning algorithms, it is expected that more enhanced predictive performance models will soon emerge. Therefore there is a need for constant review of research works to keep abreast of these developments as they surface, and apply these for more robust management and conservation of water resources. Already, there are up-to-date reviews on the application of AI models for WQ modeling and prediction (Chen, Song, Liu, Yang, & Li, 2020c; Sit et al., 2020; Tiyasha, Tung, & Yaseen, 2020), which have somewhat replaced previous reviews that either focused on one model or the selection of water sources such as coastal or groundwater (Tiyasha et al., 2020). A recent study was extended however, to WQ prediction of various water bodies such as rivers, groundwater, reservoirs, stream, lakes, and ponds; notwithstanding, their focus was on artificial neural network (ANN) models (Chen et al., 2020c). However, due to the peculiarity of different water sources and prediction models, WQ prediction of different water bodies by different DL and ML models is worth considering, to gain a general understanding of the processes influencing the WQ of different water bodies and collate effective models for their prediction. Consequently, this chapter attempts to appraise DL and ML models that have been applied in WQ prediction, especially in recent times. Some of the water bodies whose WQ has been predicted include rivers, reservoirs, lakes, marshes, groundwater, and ponds/aquaculture, and the discussion on the application of DL and ML in WQ prediction is presented in this regard. The description of notations and abbreviations used in this work is given in Table 9.1.

Table 9.1 Meanings of notations and abbreviations.

ACF	Autocorrelation function	PACF	Partial autocorrelation function
ACO_R	Ant colony optimization for continuous domains	PCA	Principal component analysis
ARMA	Autoregressive moving average	PMI	Partial mutual information
A_T	Atmospheric temperature	P_O	Atmospheric pressure in the station
BOD	Biochemical oxygen demand	PO_4^{3-}	Phosphate
CART	Classification and regression tree	PSO	Particle swam optimization
CH	Carbonate hardness	Q	Water discharge
Chl-a	Chlorophyll-a	R	Coefficient of correlation
CNN	Convolutional neural network	R^2	Coefficient of determination
COD	Chemical oxygen demand	RBF	Radial basis function
C_ONN	Committee neural network	RBF-ANN	Radial basis function neural networks
CRF	Completely random tree forest	R-ELM	Radial basic activation function-extreme learning machine
CRT	Completely random tree	RF	Random forest
CTSI	Carlson trophic state index	RMSE	Root mean square error
DCF	Deep cascade forest	RMSPE	Root mean squared percentage error
DE	Differential evolutionary algorithm	RNN-DS	Recurrent neural network-Dempster/Shafer theory
DT	Decision tree	RWQ	River water quality
E	Coefficient of efficiency	SAL	Salinity
EC	Electrical conductivity	SAR	Sodium adsorption ratio
ELM	Extreme learning machine	SC	Specific conductance

(*Continued*)

Table 9.1 Meanings of notations and abbreviations. *Continued*

FDOM	Fluorescent dissolved organic matter	S-ELM	Sigmoid activation function-extreme learning machine
GP	Gaussian process	SRN	Elman neural network
GRU	Gated recurrent unit	SVM	Support vector machine
KNN	K-nearest neighbors	SVR	Support vector regression
LDA	Liner discriminant analysis	T_d	Dew point temperature
L_{int}	Light intensity	TH	Total hardness
LR	Logistic regression	TN	Total nitrogen
LSTM	Long short-term memory	TP	Total phosphorus
MAE	Mean absolute error	TURB	Turbidity
MAPE	Mean absolute percentage error	U	Relative humidity
MBUP	Multivariate Bayesian uncertainty processor	V	Horizontal visibility
MLP-ANN	Multilayer perceptron neural network	WA-ANFIS	Wavelet-adaptive neurofuzzy inference system
MODWT	Maximal overlap discrete wavelet transform	WA-ELM	Wavelet-extreme learning machine
MSE	Mean square error	WDT-ANFIS	Wavelet denoizing technique-adaptive neurofuzzy inference system
MT-BLSTM	Multitime scale bidirectional LSTM	WL	Water level
NB	Naive Bayes	WQ	Water quality
NMAE	Normalized mean absolute error	Ws	Wind speed
NRMSE	Normalized root mean square error	WT	Water temperature
NSE	Nash−Sutcliffe model efficiency coefficient	XGboost	Extreme gradient boosting
OP-ELM	Optimally pruned-extreme learning machine	δ	Delta percent
OS-ELM	Online sequential-extreme learning machine		

Deep learning and machine learning in WQ modeling and prediction

ML and DL architectures have been reportedly utilized in modeling and prediction of WQ parameters ranging from standalone (Bui et al., 2020; Rajaee et al., 2020) to hybrid architectures (Barzegar et al., 2020; Bui et al., 2020; Chou et al., 2018; Lu & Ma, 2020; Rajaee et al., 2020). A substantial increase in the application of DL and ML models in WQ prediction has occurred in recent times. However, many of the standalone models tend to generate unsatisfactory prediction results, due in part to the inability to identify or select appropriate input parameters or internal model parameters (Abba et al., 2020). Consequently hybrid models that can be obtained by appropriately utilizing a feature optimization or a data preprocessing method (Fijani et al., 2019) have been gaining attention. Nevertheless, DL together with ML standalone and hybrid models are still receiving attention in the field of hydrology as well as many other fields. Their use in modeling and prediction of WQ variables has been reported in the literature for decades, and recently, enormous progress has been made in fine-tuning different models for better prediction performances. Basically, the WQs of a number of water bodies, namely rivers (Azad et al., 2019; Liu et al., 2019; Lu & Ma, 2020; Sagan et al., 2020; Zhou, 2020; Zou et al., 2020), lakes (Barzegar, Aalami, & Adamowski, 2020; Chen et al., 2020a; Fijani, Barzegar, Deo, Tziritis, & Konstantinos, 2019; Hanson et al., 2020; Liang et al., 2020; Mohammed, Longva, & Razak, 2018), groundwater (Bui et al., 2020; Jalalkamali, 2015), marsh (Al-Mukhtar & Al-Yaseen, 2019), watersheds (Noori et al., 2020), reservoirs (Chen & Liu, 2014; Chou et al., 2018; Mamun et al., 2020), ponds/tanks for aquaculture (Li et al., 2021), ocean (Alizadeh & Kavianpour, 2015), and even wastewater (Chen et al., 2020a; Sharafati, Babak, Seyed, & Hosseinzadeh, 2020; Xu, Coco, & Neale, 2020; Liu, Zhang, & Zhang, 2020) have been successfully modeled and predicted utilizing ML and DL architectures. Furthermore, the application of these data-driven soft computing techniques has gone beyond the prediction of just individual water quality variables, and now, water quality index (WQI) for drinking and irrigation water can be predicted satisfactorily (Abba et al., 2020; Bui, Khosravi, Tiefenbacher, et al., 2020; El Bilali & Taleb, 2020; Isiyaka et al., 2019; Rezaie-Balf et al., 2020). Additionally, various DL and ML techniques have been effectively used for the prediction of other important aspects of water resources other than WQ; for instance, streamflow (Adnan et al., 2019, 2020; Danandeh Mehr, 2018; Kisi et al., 2019; Ni et al., 2020), groundwater level (Barzegar et al., 2017), sediment transport (Afan et al., 2016), river water level (Li et al., 2020), daily rainfall (Diez-Sierra & del Jesus, 2020; Ni et al., 2020), daily reference evapotranspiration (Wu et al., 2019), and groundwater flow and/or contaminant transport (Su et al., 2020; Yu et al., 2020).

Overview of learning methods

Just as training and learning are required to perform tactical work in real life, likewise, in both DL and ML, models used for prediction make use of certain underlying algorithms to deduce mathematical relationships from training data. Learning by a machine is said to have taken place when a machine that learns from experience about a certain class of tasks has its performance improved as a result. Kapitanova and coworker stated that ML is advantageous for tackling tasks that are very difficult to solve with preset programs written and designed by humans (Kapitanova & Son, 2012). However, they emphasized that the process of learning is not the task, rather the means of attaining the capability to execute the task. Four types of learning methods are presented, namely: supervised, unsupervised, reinforcement, and semisupervised learning.

Supervised learning

This form of learning is most common in DL and ML models (Lecun et al., 2015). It involves a model that is provided with a training dataset containing both input (observations) examples as well as their corresponding target (output) variables. Supervised learning is said to involve the observation of numerous examples of a random vector x and a related vector y, and then learning to predict *y* from *x*, typically by estimating $p(y|x)$ (Kapitanova & Son, 2012). The origin of supervised learning is having a picture of a target that is provided by a tutor or trainer that demonstrates to the ML system what to do (Kapitanova & Son, 2012). For instance, a supervised learning algorithm can study a river dataset and learn to classify the river WQ variables based on their measurements. Classification and regression are two groups of supervised learning according to the type of target variable; while the former learns and predicts using a classified target value, the latter uses a continuous numerical label (Bang et al., 2020).

Unsupervised learning

The model in unsupervised learning is provided with unclassified training data, being the inputs, then the model classifies the dataset into various classes by finding commonalities between them (Hosseini et al., 2020). It involves the observation of numerous samples of a random vector *x*, and trying to directly or indirectly learn the probability distribution $p(x)$, or some other interesting properties of the distribution (Kapitanova & Son, 2012). In other words, unsupervised learning functions exclusively on the input data without being tutored or guided, thereby learning to make sense of the data on its own. It equally implies that the target data are not contained in the learning data (Bang et al., 2020). In addition, instead of error-correction learning, unsupervised learning applies competitive learning (Sit et al., 2020). Supervised and unsupervised learnings are helpful in classifying some of the things done with ML algorithms but are not entirely formal or distinct concepts (Kapitanova & Son, 2012).

Reinforcement learning

In reinforcement learning, the algorithm attempts to find the optimum solution for a given input dataset utilizing a reward/penalty strategy and a trial-and-error method (Sit et al., 2020). Reinforcement learning algorithms have an interaction with the environment, thus there is the existence of a feedback loop between the learning system and its experiences (Kapitanova & Son, 2012). In this type of learning, the learner is not informed about the actions to be taken, rather it is expected to figure out the actions that will produce the desired result by experimenting with them. This could possibly be extremely relevant in a complex hydrological domain, where hydrogeochemical and anthropogenic processes pose difficulties for other forms of learning.

Semisupervised learning

This form of learning combines the properties of both supervised and unsupervised learning. In semisupervized learning, the training dataset principally contains a few classified (labeled) training data together with a large number of unclassified (unlabeled) data (Hosseini et al., 2020). The two major advantages of semisupervized learning that have been identified are being considerably more accurate than unsupervised learning with the inclusion of a small number of labeled data, and substantially less arduous compared to supervised learning (Hosseini et al., 2020). Semisupervised learning could likely be the most appropriate form of learning in most practical applications where unlabeled data are larger in number.

Machine learning architectures used in water quality modeling and prediction

The emergence of ML as a tool for WQ modeling and forecasting is borne out of the need to develop efficient and low-cost methods for processing large amounts of complex data (Najah Ahmed et al., 2019; Sahoo et al., 1969). Researchers have employed ML for different WQ parameters using various model architectures. A few of these are ANNs, decision tree (DT), and support vector machine (SVM) (Kim et al., 2014), which are briefly discussed next.

Artificial neural network

ANN is a data-mining approach that mimics the networks of the human brain and nervous system (Haghiabi et al., 2018; Khan & See, 2016). It has emerged as the most widely employed ML tool, finding application in fields of quality management of various water systems (Khan et al., 2020), ecology, medical, and biological fields (Gredell et al., 2019). In ANN, the input signal transmits through the network of neurons in a forward direction from one layer to the next. Each layer is connected to the adjacent layer by these neurons with weights assigned to each interlayer link. In a feedforward propagation process, the weights are multiplied by the input, and the resultant value moves forward to the next layer until it reaches the output layer (Khan & See, 2016). Recurrent or feedback propagation involves the flow of signals in both forward and backward directions for either a limited part or the entire network. Information about past inputs is fed back into and mixed with new inputs through recurrent connections.

ANN as a tool does not require prerequisite knowledge of the mathematical forms of the relationships between the inputs and corresponding outputs, and requires a liberal number of parameters to produce a satisfactory result. It is robust in noise, provides accurate predictions regardless of measurement error, fast data processing, and a higher tolerance for hardware support problems. It is also possible to apply unknown data to the already trained model while offering a great variety of models with different possibilities for solutions to problems (Farmaki et al., 2010). However, the major problem associated with the use of ANN is design issues, which are complex and can have an impact on its data-processing abilities. It can fail to generalize well when trained with limited data. Likewise, overfitting can occur due to the use of many weights (Farmaki et al., 2010). Despite these drawbacks, ANN has and is still gaining attention in research involving WQ prediction. ANN has been utilized to predict the nitrate concentration in shallow groundwater (Farmaki et al., 2010). Other authors have shown ANN to be a reliable prediction model when used to develop a comprehensive methodology for efficient WQ prediction and analysis for selected water parameters (Khan & See, 2016). ANN has been combined with genetic algorithms such as genetic programming (Joslyn, 2018) to accelerate the search for water optimization models. In fact, authors are of the opinion that a suitable combination of models gives better results than single models (Khan & See, 2016).

Neural networks models

In addition to the advantages highlighted previously, ANN offers a wide selection of neural networks that have been employed in different capacities. This section briefly discusses the common neural network architectures utilized in WQ modeling.

Multilayer perceptron neural network (MLP-ANN or MLP)

This is a feedforward ANN, and the most widely used of the neural networks (Sahoo et al., 1969). It consists of the basic structure of an ANN in which neurons are arranged in successive layers of the inner layer, hidden layers, and output layer (Barzegar, Fijani, et al., 2017). MLP-ANN overcomes the disadvantages of a single-layer neural network, which can only handle linear data (Solanki et al., 2015), as well as fitting challenges associated with ANN (Farmaki et al., 2010). It can adapt to changes according to the specific problem to be solved, yet still maintains its robustness. Some researchers compared the performance of MLP and SVM to predict the level of fluoride contamination in groundwater, and statistical evaluations showed that both models exhibited satisfactory potentials for WQ prediction (Barzegar et al., 2016). On the other hand, Najah Ahmed et al. conducted experiments to determine the ability of MLP and radial basis function (RBF-ANN) to predict several WQ parameters—pH, suspended solids, and ammoniacal nitrogen (Najah Ahmed et al., 2019). However, both models were inappropriate in predicting the WQ parameters due to their failure to acquire values lying outside the data used for calibration. A large number of neurons utilized also resulted in delayed convergence during the training of the network for MLP.

Radial basis function (RBF-ANN)

Similar to MLP, RBF-ANN is a feedforward neural network with architecture consisting of three layers interconnected to each other by a set of weights (Farmaki et al., 2010; Lu & Ma, 2020). The input layer is composed of input vectors, while the hidden layer composed of hidden neurons transforms the input data using a function that is usually Gaussian. These hidden neurons differentiate RBF-ANN from other types of neural networks (Lu et al., 2014). Each hidden neuron has a radial basis function and their number is based on the specific problems of the study (Huang & Yang, 2020). This neural network consists of a center position u, and a spread or width σ, which is the radial distance from the center. An advantage of RBF-ANN over MLP is its robustness and reliability in noisy data, faster network convergence and training, good generalizations with limited neurons, and a lower samples to variables ratio. A key component to the successful application of RBF-ANN is the selection of appropriate centers and spread, which limits its widespread application (Meng et al., 2018). A number of researches have been conducted using RBF-ANN, however, in a study, RBF-ANN was found to be less precise during the validation and testing stages (Najah Ahmed et al., 2019).

Self-organizing maps

Also known as Kohonen neural networks, self-organizing maps (SOMs) are feedforward neural networks with a single layer of neurons, fully connected to the inner layer arranged in rows and columns (Huang & Yang, 2020). SOMs map crucial points within the space characterized by weights onto a 2D layer. The closer the point to the pattern, the higher its likelihood of being picked. Previously defined learning rates are employed in calculating new weights and these are updated after each iteration (Farmaki et al., 2010). This ability to map input space while selecting the best matching units is SOM's greatest asset. However, a major demerit of SOM is that the performed mapping is discrete and mapping positions are limited by the size of the 2D Kohonen layer (Yotova et al., 2021). Alternative SOM architecture types include maps with no structure, with a linear structure, or 2D topologies. SOM was therefore used as a model to predict the quality of river basin water in Bulgaria (Yotova et al., 2021). The results obtained indicated that SOM is a suitable strategy for WQ monitoring.

Support vector machines

SVMs rely on statistical learning theory, otherwise known as Vapnik's theory, to provide methods for flexible estimation with limited data to achieve high levels of generalization and prediction accuracy (Barzegar, Asghari Moghaddam, et al., 2017). They are mostly used for pattern recognition and function fitting to maximize the distinction between the classes by visualizing data points plotted on a plane, which results in fewer errors (the difference between the model output and observed data) (Haghiabi et al., 2018; Najah Ahmed et al., 2019). Unlike ANN, SVM is characterized by a highly effective mechanism for avoiding overfitting that results in good determination, however it suffers from the absence of a probabilistic prediction capability that captures information about uncertainty, and from the number of support vectors that grows appreciably with the size of the training datasets. Haghiabi et al. (2018) investigated the performance of ANN and SVM in predicting the WQ component of the Tireh River in Iran. SVM was found to give the best performance, even though the results obtained with ANN show that its accuracy is acceptable for practical purposes. In addition, Joslyn (2018) employed SVM and genetic programming to explore the prediction accuracy of nine WQ factors: dissolved oxygen (DO), chlorophyll-a (Chl-a), temperature, nitrate, turbidity, electrical conductivity (EC), cyanobacteria, and fDOM. SVM gave a better result, and the temperature was found to have the highest prediction accuracy (98.4%) followed by DO (97.9%), while the lowest prediction accuracy was found for turbidity. However, SVM was found to be deficient in the time it took to run each prediction, which has also been reported in the literature (Barzegar, Asghari Moghaddam, et al., 2017).

Decision trees

DTs refer to ML architectures with a tree-like structure where each node represents an attribute, each link (branch) represents a decision, and each leaf represents an outcome. This structure makes it easy to use (Patel et al., 2012). DTs where the target variables can take a discrete set of values are called classification trees, and those where continuous values are the target variables are called regression trees. They possess the advantage of being simple to design and interpret with high accuracy and the ability to handle high-dimensional data. DTs exhibit some advantages over ANN. They can handle mixed data types and missing values. They are resistant to outliers and can handle irrelevant inputs. In addition, their lack of hidden layers enables better modeling performance (Bui, Khosravi, Tiefenbacher, et al., 2020). Azam and team used DT and compared it with logistic regression (LR) and linear discriminant function (LDM) to determine the quality of drinking water (Azam et al., 2017). Though LR performed better, DT was comparatively easy to draw and interpret. Some researchers used random forest, J48, LMT, and decision stump to separate water from different counties in Kenya into clean and unclean water, and by extension predict WQ using WQ predictors: pH, alkalinity, and electrical conductivity (Gakii & Jepkoech, 2019). J48 DT gave the highest accuracy (94%), while the decision stump had the lowest (83%) accuracy. Similarly, Chen and coworkers employed DT, RF, and deep cascade forest trained by datasets of pH, DO, chemical oxygen demand (COD), and NH_3-N for WQ prediction. All models were found to perform better than traditional models (Chen et al., 2020b).

However, DTs do not express themselves easily in some mathematical functions, cannot handle range inputs (i.e., predict within the range of labels seen before), and like ANN, there is also the possibility of overfitting (Patel et al., 2012). Some DT classifiers include the classification and regression tree (CART), which divides data into homogeneous subsets using binary recursive partition (Yang et al., 2013); ID3 which builds a tree based upon information obtained from the training process and subsequently uses these to classify the test data; and random forest (RF). RF comprises several DTs, which are each trained on a random subset of the data. The DTs are then aggregated to provide a single prediction (Ashwini et al., 2019; Nolan et al., 2015). Bui and fellow researchers employed 10 input variables: biological oxygen demand (BOD), COD, total solids, pH, phosphate, nitrates, EC, and turbidity to determine the efficiency of RF for predicting WQ (Bui, Khosravi, Karimi, et al., 2020). They concluded that the use of RF, which integrates DT and a classifier algorithm, improved prediction and eliminated certain shortcomings. In addition, RF also overcomes the problem of overfitting associated with DT and works better with a large range of data than a single DT does. They are very flexible and possess very high accuracy. However, they are complex, time-consuming, and less intuitive where a large collection of DTs is available.

Deep learning architectures used in water quality modeling and prediction

The DL technique consists of continuous transformations that map input vectors into output by training data. This implies that the model can learn by sampling from input and output datasets. DL techniques are capable of multiple nonlinear transformations owing to several layers of computational units at each layer. Basically, there are varied computational layers between the input and output. In classical ML methods, also called shallow learning, there are three key steps, which are data collection, feature selection, and regression/classification of interest variables. However, in DL, feature selection and regression of variables of interest succeed data collection as a single step.

Thus DL techniques do not require manual feature selection before model development, rather they are able to perform hierarchical feature learning. This accounts for the increasing popularity of DL when handling unstructured data such as images, text, audio, and video (Misra & Li, 2020).

This is an important difference between both approaches because, while in shallow learning it can be assumed that the optimal features can be chosen independent of the classification or interest variables, in DL, features cannot be selected independent of the interest variables. This implies that unlike classical ML where regression is carried out after features have been chosen based on prior data; this is done in parallel to the regression in DL. Merging both steps might appear a minor change, but it has been proven to have significant advantages; two of which include time saving and the ability to unravel and process complex features, which humans can overlook. In recent years, DL has become a good fit for data science problems in WQ modeling because WQ modeling data are increasing exponentially, and processing terabytes of information, particularly in real time, has necessitated more pragmatic approaches. Some important DL architectures are discussed below.

Convolutional neural network

Convolutional neural networks (CNNs) are mostly dedicated to solving image-processing challenges. CNNs are primarily made up of convolutional layers, which themselves are made up of filters. Image analysis is the most widely used application of CNNs. In CNNs, the transformation of input data into output is a convolutional operation. One key feature of CNNs is pattern analysis using extensive filtering/filters—that is, detecting patterns in images. These patterns may be shapes, textures, edges, and lots more. As the network goes deeper, it can detect more specific details. In regular neural networks, there are hidden layers embedded within the input and output layers, which connect neurons in each layer to neurons in the previous layers, creating a web of neurons, until output data are generated. However, in CNNs, neurons are not merely connected to previous neurons/neurons in the previous layer, rather, to closely related neurons within the same web, thereby creating a simplified system of connecting and processing spatial aspects of the dataset. CNNs are made of diverse networks, such as the convolution layer, pooling layer, rectified linear unit layer, and fully connected layer.

Convolutional layer—the convolutional layer creates a convolved feature map from a set of input data using a filter system. The output from a convolutional layer is a feature map, which serves as input into the next convolutional layer, which in turn learns more features.

Pooling layer—this layer finetunes the number of parameters the network needs to process by reducing the sample size of a feature map, creating a pooled feature map. Essentially, a pooling layer merges the features collected from one convolution layer before passing them to the next, thereby increasing computation efficiency.

Rectified linear unit layer—this layer ensures nonlinearity as data transit within the network.

Fully connected layer—this layer permits data classification.

To train a CNN, there are two approaches, namely: (1) working with labeled data and (2) working with unlabeled data, which is achieved with unsupervised learning tools such as autoencoders and generated adversarial networks (GANs). CNN has been applied as a tool for predicting WQ. One rapid area of development is the prediction of algal dynamics in water systems.

Spatiotemporal WQ data generated using a 3D model were used to investigate the ability of CNNs to predict cyanobacterial bloom in the short term (Pyo et al., 2020). Model output images of algal concentration for a section of the Nakdong River in South Korea were generated using the modified environmental fluid dynamics code (NEIR-EFDC). Input data consisted of algal biomass, as well as environmental, atmospheric, and WQ variables. Although model-generated synthetic data were used as input, and data volume decreased eventually, the performance of the CNN remained acceptable.

Emerging studies are increasingly exploring remote sensing as a source for high-quality input data (Choi et al., 2019; Ta & Wei, 2018). Choi et al. (2019) used a CNN model to predict the Chl-a concentration—which is responsible for algal bloom in some water systems. Log transformation and oversampling were used to account for extreme data imbalance and skewness. The dataset for WQ/physicochemical parameters collated over a 6-year period was selected as the input data, and trained. Furthermore, time-series data were generated to create additional features. The results show that using the synthetic minority oversampling technique and log transformation in the CNN model improved the performance of the model. A reverse CNN model approach (in which the pooling layer is removed) has also been proposed to predict changes in DO in aquatic systems (Ta & Wei, 2018). DO is critical to sustaining WQ, particularly for biological growth and aquatic life. The CNN approach presents a stable model that simplifies the overall computational complexity, which is a major drawback of most traditional models. In terms of prediction stability, reverse CNN performed better than the traditional model to which it was compared.

Recurrent neural network

RNNs are neural networks that model sequence data for predictions. Sequence data could be audio, text, or time series, among others. Traditional neural networks consist of input, hidden, and output layers, which operate via a feedforward mechanism (i.e., in one direction). RNNs, on the other hand, introduce a looping mechanism that can pass previous information forward—this is the hidden state, which represents information from all previous steps. This allows information to persist in RNNs, in contrast with traditional architectures. The feedback mechanism in RNNs can be from the hidden to the input layer or the output to the input layer, thereby allowing RNN to possess trainable memory for time-varying patterns (Bhattacharjee & Tollner, 2016). Unlike in convolutional neural networks where spatial data are filtered via a forward feed, a recurrent network feeds data back into itself. Hence they are better suited to sequential data, and are thereby able to predict patterns over time. Training RNN has three major steps: it does a forward pass and makes a prediction, compares the prediction to the ground truth and then generates an error value, and finally does a backpropagation using the error value to assign gradients to each node in the network.

Although RNNs are great for sequence predictions such as time series, they suffer from short-term memory (resulting from backpropagation). To overcome this, two specialized RNNs have been created, namely long short-term memory (LSTM) and gradient recurrent units (GRU). Although they both behave similarly to RNNs, they are capable of long-term dependencies using a mechanism called "gates." To train RNN models, an algorithm called backpropagation through time (BPTT) is used. The algorithm takes the gradient of the loss with respect to each parameter and then shifts parameters to minimize loss. This means that all the errors are flowing back through time to the beginning of the data sequence, and errors are backpropagated at each individual time step and finally across all time steps. Bhattacharjee and Tollner (2016) developed a WQ RNN model to identify important parameters in WQ prediction in windrow composting systems. They selected time-series data from 2001 to 2009 for WQ parameters such as total suspended solids, BOD, temperature, pond volume, and nitrate obtained in Georgia, United States, as input variables for the model. The study concluded that pond volume and air temperature are the most important input variables resulting in an understanding of WQ dynamics in the windrow composting system. Similarly, phytoplankton dynamics with seasonal variation in a river system were modeled and predicted using RNN (Jeong et al., 2001). Input data were sourced from atmospheric, hydrological, and limnological parameters compiled over 5 years, with Chl-a concentration serving as the output parameter. The mode accurately predicted Chl-a. The authors noted that not only was the model excellent for reductive purposes, but also in explaining the ecosystem dynamics. Subsequently, the authors compared the statistical regression model and RNN for understanding phytoplankton dynamics (Jeong et al., 2006). One important advantage of RNN based on the findings is that despite reducing the size of input parameters, the sensitivity analysis proved that the predictive effectiveness of the model for freshwater dynamics was not affected. The gated recurrent unit neural network model has been used to predict and monitor DO in freshwater aquaculture (Cao et al., 2020). Key input parameters with great significance on WQ were selected using principal component analysis (PCA), and object classification was carried out using K-means clustering (an unsupervised learning method). The model showed better performance in terms of accuracy over time when compared with other conventional PCA-based models.

Generative unsupervised models

Generative models are statistical models capable of generating new datasets based on the probability distribution, which is then estimated, thereby generating a distribution similar to the original one. They are nondiscriminative and capable of generating novel samples. Moreover, they are unsupervised models as they do not need labeled data, which implies that they can make do with existing data samples. The two most prominent generative models are variational autoencoders and generative adversarial networks (GANs). Other generative models include Gaussian mixture models, hidden Markov models, Boltzmann machines, and latent Dirichlet allocation (Harshvardhan et al., 2020).

Variational autoencoders: An autoencoder is made up of an encoder, a decoder, and a loss function. It has three layers—input, middle or bottleneck, and output layers. Inputs are encoded and stored in the middle layer through weights. Subsequently, an output similar to the input is generated. The loss is determined and backpropagated, leading to weight adjustments. The decoder receives input from the dataset and the output obtained is a representation of the sample at a stochastic lower dimension. This is then reconstructed into the original sample/dataset. Two losses are used, namely reconstruction loss and Kulback—Leiber divergence, which uses a Gaussian distribution to align the latent space and assumed distributions.

Generative adversarial networks: GANs have a unique advantage over variational encoders in the area of image datasets. They also train generative models but with better generated images.

GANs are made up of two complementary components—a generator and a discriminator. The generator creates fake data by integrating discriminator feedback, thereby making the discriminator classify its output as real. The discriminator takes real samples (from the ground truth) and fake samples (from the generator) for training, then discriminates/separates those which belong to the ground truth. Both are complementary because the generator keeps creating fake samples from the ground truth, while the discriminator keeps improving on its ability to separate the real and generated samples.

Generative models are nascent and have found very little application in WQ assessment and modeling yet. However, one area of marine research where this technique is finding breakthrough application is underwater image restoration and enhancement. Generative adversarial networks could provide significant insight into solving the challenge posed by turbidity and color distortion in underwater observation. Some researchers have described GAN models for underwater image restoration using the cycle-consistent adversarial network. Although the network they developed improved the contrast enhancement and color correction (quality) of images generated, the model could not replicate this performance under inhomogeneous illumination (Lu et al., 2019). Several other GAN-based DL models have been proposed for underwater image enhancement such as encoder–decoder models, block designs, dual-generator GANs, and multibranch designs (Anwar & Li, 2020).

Application of ML and DL models in WQ prediction of different water systems

Prediction of WQ is adjudged to be one of the reasons why models are being developed and used (Zheng et al., 2018), with the intention of achieving suitable management of water resources over a period of time. WQ models play crucial roles in the evaluation of WQ, in addition to revealing trends of WQ parameters. More importantly, the idea of WQ prediction is for the projection of the variation in WQ variables or index that could occur at a certain time in the near future (Chen et al., 2018). Therefore WQ modeling and prediction have immense practical benefits as they play a significant role in water resource management, pollution control, environmental monitoring, maintenance of human health, and serve as a prerequisite for timely control of future intelligence aquaculture (Fijani et al., 2019). For a thorough understanding of how the WQ of various water bodies have been modeled and forecast in recent times (for 2016–20) using ML and DL models, a step-by-step description is presented in Fig. 9.1.

Modeling and prediction of different water systems

The water systems that have been modeled in recent times include but are not limited to rivers, lakes, groundwater, marshes, and reservoirs. The provision of fresh water for domestic uses, agriculture, transportation, and industry illustrates the vital role these sources have played in society (Singh et al., 2019). However, the discharge of pollutants from point sources as well as indirect influences such as climate change, land management, and atmospheric precipitation could cause

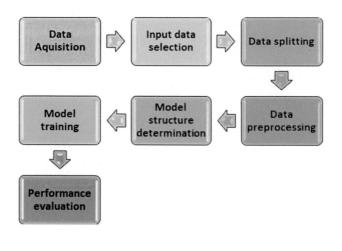

FIGURE 9.1

A proposed framework for modeling water quality of various water bodies.

changes in the quality of water bodies (Yotova et al., 2021). Therefore monitoring their quality, especially where they serve as the only water resource, is an integral part of water management. Their quality modeling and prediction are discussed in the following sections.

Data collection

Data collection for modeling WQ can be somewhat difficult, depending on the type of data. Depending on the nature of the source, the process involved in acquiring data can be costly—grab sampling, laboratory equipment, sensors, and meteorological stations. Although sensors are gaining widespread use for collecting data from rivers, lakes, streams, and oceans, traditional grab sampling is still in use, especially in developing countries. In addition, meteorological parameters such as rainfall, air temperature and pressure, and wind speed, which can also influence WQ, are also used. The literature indicates that researchers used dataset collected from water-monitoring stations (Ahmed, 2017; Chen et al., 2020b; Elkiran, Nourani, & Abba, 2019; Liu, Wang, Sangaiah, Xie, & Yin, 2019; Najah Ahmed et al., 2019), water authorities (Azad et al., 2019; Barzegar et al., 2016, 2018), or from open sources (Heddam & Kisi, 2017; Li et al., 2019; Lu & Ma, 2020; Zou et al., 2020) to model WQ. As illustrated in Table 9.2, modeling of river WQ could be performed with only water quality variables (WQVs) (Bui et al., 2020; Chen et al., 2020b; Fijani, Barzegar, Deo, Tziritis, & Konstantinos, 2019; Li et al., 2018; Lu & Ma, 2020), or a combination of WQVs and meteorological variables (MVs) (Li et al., 2018; Mamun, Kim, Alam, & An, 2020; Yu, Chen, Hassan, & Li, 2016; Zhou, 2020; Zou et al., 2020). In a rare case, Heddam and Kisi (2017) successfully utilized elements of a Gregorian calendar as a dataset in modeling river WQ without using WQVs. From the reviewed papers, some studies on lakes (Barzegar et al., 2020), groundwater (Kisi et al., 2019), rivers (Azad et al., 2019; Elkiran et al., 2019), and reservoirs (Mamun et al., 2020) did not explicitly give the number of their dataset (Table 9.2). This may not be appropriate, in that,

Table 9.2 Details of WQ modeling and prediction of various water systems by the reviewed papers.

Data collection	Input selection	Input/output	Data splitting	Data preprocessing	Model/structure determination	Model training	Model evaluation	Model order of performance	Source
Rivers									
Open-data source (WQV and MV): 2258 datasets	Domain knowledge	WT, Po, P, U, W, V, Td, R/ pH, DO, COD, NH$_3$-N	70% training and 30% testing	Data filling: linear imputation (LIN); normalization: standardization	Model: LSTM, MT-BLSTM; structure determination: no detail	Box–Behnken experimental design (BBD) for submodels	MAE	MT-BLSTM >BLSTM >LSTM > GRU > RNN	Zou et al. (2020)
Water authority (WQV): 336 datasets (1983–2011)	Pearson correlation/ sensitivity analysis	Ca^{2+}, Mg^{2+}, Na$^+$, SO$_4^{2-}$, and Cl$^-$/EC	Training: 1983–2003; validating: 2004–08; testing: 2009–11	Data filling: not mentioned; normalization: range scaling	Model: wavelet-ANFIS and wavelet-ANN; structure determination: trial and error	Levenberg–Marquardt training algorithm (TrainLM)	R^2, NRMSE, NSE, TS	WA-ANFIS > WA-ANN > ANFIS > ANN	Barzegar et al. (2016)
Water authority (WQV): dataset no. NA (2001–15)	Correlation (type not specified)	TDS, EC, pH, HCO$_3^-$, Cl$^-$, SO$_4^{2-}$, Mg^{2+}, Na$^+$, K$^+$, CO$_3^{2-}$, Ca^{2+}, CH, and TH/ TDS, EC, SAR, CH, and TH	70% training and 30% testing	Data filling: not mentioned; normalization: not mentioned	Model: ANFIS-PSO and ANFIS-ACO$_R$; structure determination: global method	Particle swarm optimization (PSO); ant colony optimization for continuous domain (ACO$_R$)	RMSE, R^2, MAPE, δ	ANFIS-PSO > ANFIS-ACO$_R$ > ANFIS	Azad et al. (2019)
Water station (WQV and MV): 5,789,520 datasets (2015–19)	PCA/Kendall tau coefficient/ PMI	DO, COD, pH, EC, TURB, WT, NH$_3$-N, WL, ORP, W, R, L/DO, NH$_3$-N, and COD	Training: 40% (2015–17); validation: 30% (2018) and testing: 30% (2018–19)	Data filling: transfer learning; normalization: not specified	Model: LSTM, TL-LSTM; structure determination: no detail	Transfer learning algorithm	RMSE and NSE	MBUP-TL-LSTM > TL-LSTM>LSTM	Zhou (2020)
Water stations (WQV): dataset no. NA 1999–2012	Pearson correlation	DO, BOD, COD, Q, pH, WT, NH$_3$/DO	75% training and 25% testing	Data filling: transfer learning; normalization: not specified	Model: BPNN, ANFIS, and SVM; structure determination: trial and error	BPNN, ANFIS: Lavenberg–Marquardt training algorithm; SVM: Gaussian kernel function	RMSE and R^2	ANFIS > BPNN > SVM	Elkiran et al. (2019)
Open-data source (WQV): 1448 datasets (2017–18)	Autocorrelation	Permanganate index, pH, TP, and DO/ permanganate index, pH, TP, and DO	70% training and 30% testing	Data filling: not specified; normalization: range scaling	Model: LSTM, GRU, and SRN; RNN-DS; structure determination: no detail	Backpropagation through time (BPTT) algorithm	RMSE, MAE, NSE, MAPE	RNN-DS >LSTM > GRU > SRN > SVR > BPNN	Li et al. (2019)
Water station (WQV): 731 datasets (2016–17)	Pearson correlation	DO, TURB, COD, EC, pH, WT, NH$_3$/DO, TURB, COD, EC, pH, NH$_3$	Training data: January 2016–December 2017; testing	Data filling: linear interpolation; normalization: range scaling	Model: SVR and LSTM; structure determination: no detail	LSTM: adaptive moment estimation (Adam) optimization algorithm; SVR:	MSE	LSTM > SVR	Liu et al. (2019)

Data source	Variable selection method	Input/output variables	Data split	Data preprocessing	Model and structure	Algorithm	Metrics	Model ranking	Reference
Water stations (WQV): 40 datasets (1998–2002)	Correlation (type not specified)/ sensitivity analysis	WT, EC, SAL, NO_3^-, TURB, PO_4^{3-}, CT, K, Na, Mg, Fe, and *Escherichia coli*/pH, SS, NH_3-N	Training data: 1998–2007; testing data: 2009–10 data January 2018–June 2018	Data filling: not mentioned; normalization: not mentioned	Model: MLP-ANN, RBF-ANN, WDT-ANFIS; structure determination: trial and error	Gaussian and RBF kernel function Levenberg–Marquardt algorithm	MSE, NSE, R	WDT-ANFIS > ANFIS > MLP > RBFNN	Najah Ahmed et al. (2019)
Open-data source (WQV): 1875 datasets (May 2009–July 2019)	Domain knowledge	WT, DO, pH, SC, TURB and FDOM/ WT, DO, pH, SC, TURB, and FDOM	90% training and 10% testing	Data filling: model based; normalization: range scaling; decomposition by CEEMDAN	Model: CEEMDAN-XGBoost and CEEMDAN-RF; structure determination: tree model	Gradient boosting algorithm	RMSPE, MAE, MAPE, RMSE	CEEMDAN-XGBoost > CEEMDAN-RF > XGBoost > RF	Lu and Ma (2020)
Water authority (WQV): 315 datasets (1984–2011)	Autocorrelation function (ACF) and partial ACF	EC/EC	90% training and 10% testing	Data filling: model based; normalization: range scaling; decomposition by MODWT	Model: WA-ELM, WA-ANFIS; structure determination: trial and error	Hybrid optimization method	RMSE, NSE, R^2	WA-ELM > WA-ANFIS	Barzegar et al. (2018)
Water station (WQV): 160 datasets (2010–12)	Correlation (type not specified)	BOD, BOD + COD/ DO	70% training, 15% validation, and 15% testing	Data filling: not mentioned; normalization: not mentioned	Model: FFNN, RBFNN; structure determination: no detail	Levenberg–Marquardt algorithm	NSE, R, MSE	RBFNN > FFNN	Ahmed (2017)
Open-data source (WQV): 260,602 datasets (2007–10)	Correlation (type not specified)	WT, SC, TURB, pH, Gregorian calendar, validation data/DO	70% training and 30% validation	Data filling: not mentioned; normalization: standardization	Model: S-ELM, R-ELM, OS-ELM, and OP-ELM; structure determination: analytically determined	Gaussian, sigmoid, hybrid activation functions	NSE, R, RMSE, MAE	OP-ELM > OS-ELM > S-ELM > R-ELM > MLPNN	Heddam and Kisi (2017)
Lakes Water stations (WQV): 33,612 datasets (2012–18)	Domain knowledge	COD, DO, NH_3-N, pH/ COD, DO, NH_3-N, pH	80% training and 20% validation	Data filling: deleted; normalization: standardization	Model: DT, NB, LR, LDA, CRT, KNN, SVM, RF, CRF, and DCF; structure determination: not mentioned	SVM: RBF kernel function; NB: Gaussian kernel function	Precision, recall, F1-score, weighted F1-score	DCF > RF > DT	Chen et al. (2020a, 2020b, 2020c)
Sensor measurement (WQV): dataset no. NA (2012–13)	Easily measured and accessible	pH, ORP, WT, EC/DO, Chl-a	70% training and 30% validation	Data filling: not mentioned; normalization: range scaling	Model: CNN, LSTM, CNN-LSTM; structure determination: trial and error	Adaptive gradient algorithm (AdaGrad)	WI, BIAS, NSE, NMAE, MAE, RMSE, R, NRMSE	CNN-LSTM > LSTMy > CNN > SVR > DT	Barzegar et al. (2020)

(Continued)

Table 9.2 Details of WQ modeling and prediction of various water systems by the reviewed papers. *Continued*

Data collection	Input selection	Input/output	Data splitting	Data preprocessing	Model/structure determination	Model training	Model evaluation	Model order of performance	Source
Environmental fluid dynamic code (EFDC): 4032 datasets (12 years)	Cross-correlation/ permutation importance (PI)	WT, Chl-a, TP, PO_4^{3-}, TN, NH_3-N/ Chl-a	Training: 9 years and testing: 3 years	Data filling: not mentioned; normalization: standardization	Model: LSTM; structure determination: not mentioned	Backpropagation through time (BPTT) algorithm	NSE, RMSE	LSTM	Liang et al. (2020)
Sensor measurement (WQV): 363 datasets (2012–13)	Correlation and partial ACF	DO, Chl-a/ DO, Chl-a	70% training, 15% validation, and 15% testing	Data filling: not mentioned; normalization: range scaling	Model: LSSVM, ELM, CEEMDAN-LSSVM, CEEMDAN-ELM, CEEMDAN-VMD-LSSVM, CEEMDAN-VMD-ELM; structure determination: randomization	LSSVM: RBF kernel function; ELM: radial basis activation function	NMAE, NRMSE, BIAS, R, MAE, RMSE, WI, LMI	VMD-CEEMDAN-ELM> VMD-CEEMDAN-LSSVM >CEEMDAN-ELM >CEEMDAN-LSSVM > ELM > LSSVM	Fijani, Barzegar, Deo, Tziritis, and Konstantinos (2019)
Water stations (WQV): 208 datasets (2012–15)	Sensitivity analysis	pH, WT, TURB, EC, color, alkalinity, coliform, *E. coli* coliform, *E. coli*	70% training and 30% validation	Data filling: not mentioned; normalization: range scaling and standardization	Model: ANN, SVM; structure determination: no detail	ANN backpropagation through time (BPTT) algorithm; SVM: Gaussian and RBF kernel function	MSE, RMSE	ANN > SVM	Mohammed et al. (2018)
Reservoir/aquaculture									
Sensor measurement (WQV and MV): 700 datasets (2012–13)	Not mentioned	WT, solar radiation, W, U, rainfall, DO/DO	Training: 500 data; testing: 200 data	Data filling: not mentioned; normalization: not mentioned	Model: RBFNN, IPSO-LSSVM, RBFNN-IPSO-LSSVM structure determination: no detail	Improved particle swarm optimization (IPSO) algorithm	MAE, RMSE, MSE, NSE	IPSO-LSSVM > LSSVM > BPNN	Yu et al. (2016)
Ministry of Environment (WQV and MV): dataset no. NA (2000–17)	Not mentioned	EC, TP, Chl-a, DO, WT, TN, BOD, COD, TP, rainfall/ transparency, Chl-a	K-fold cross-validation	Data filling: not mentioned; normalization: not mentioned	Model: ANN, SVM structure determination: no detail	ANN: no detail; SVM: RBF kernel	RMSE, SST, SSR, R^2, MAE	SVM > ANN	Mamun et al. (2020)
Water station (WQV): 1635 datasets (1995–2016)	Easily measured and accessible	DO, SS, COD, WT, NH_3-N/CTSI	K-fold cross-validation	Data filling: deleted normalization: range scale	Model: ANN, SVM, LSSVR; structure determination: no detail	SVM: RBF kernel LSSVR: metaheuristic firefly algorithm (MetaFA)	R, MAPE, RMSE, MAE, SI	MetaFA-LSSVM >ANN > SVM	Chou et al. (2018)

Data source	Feature selection	Water quality variables	Data division	Data preprocessing	Model	Algorithm	Metrics	Result	Reference
Measured in pond (WQV and MV): 2880 datasets	Not mentioned	pH, DO, WT, A_T, U, W_s, P_o/DO	Not mentioned	Data filling: interpolation; normalization: range scale	Model: SAE, SAE-LSTM; structure determination: no detail	SAE: BP algorithm, LSTM: TrainLM	MAE, MSE, MAPE, RMSE	SAE-LSTM > LSTM > SAE-BPNN > BPNN	Li et al. (2018)
Groundwater Laboratory measurement (WQV): 143 datasets (2004–08)	PCA	Na^+, K^+, Ca^{2+}, HCO_3^-/F^-	Cross-validation: 80% training and validation, 20% testing	Data filling: none; normalization: range scale	Model: ELM; structure determination: trial and error	Radial basis activation function	R^2, MAE, RMSE, NSE	ELM > SVM > MLP	Barzegar, Asghari Moghaddam, et al. (2017)
Laboratory measurement (WQV): 246 datasets (date NA)	Pearson correlation	HCO_3^-, SO_4^{2-}, pH, K^+, WT, Na^+, Mg^{2+}, Cl^-, F^-, EC, Ca^{2+}/NO_3^-, Sr	Cross-validation: 70% training, 30% testing	Data filling: none; normalization: range scale	Model: GP; structure determination: trial and error	Bayesian method	R^2, RMSE, PBIAS, NSE	GP > RF > M5P > RT	Bui et al. (2020)
Laboratory measurement (WQV): dataset No. NA (1998–2015)	Correlation/ sensitivity analysis	HCO_3^-, SO_4^{2-}, K^+, Na^+, Mg^{2+}, Cl^-, Ca^{2+}/EC, SAR, TH	60% training, 20% validation, and 20% testing	Data filling: none; normalization: not mentioned	Model: ANFIS-CGA, ANFIS-ACO$_R$, ANFIS-DE, ANFIS-PSO; structure determination: not mentioned	Evolutionary algorithms (CGA, ACO$_R$, PSO, and DE)	R^2, MAPE, RMSE, SI	ANFIS-CGA > ANFIS-ACO$_R$ > ANFIS-DE > ANFIS-PSO > ANFIS	Kisi et al. (2019)
Water company (WQV): 93 datasets (September–October 2013)	Pearson correlation	Na^+, SO_4^{2-}, Mg^{2+}, Ca^{2+}/EC	Cross-validation: 75% training, 25% testing	Data filling: none; normalization: range scale	Model: MLP, RBFNN, GRNN structure determination: trial and error	Levenberg–Marquardt algorithm	R^2, MARE, RMSE,	C$_o$NN > RBFNN > MLP > GRNN	Barzegar and Asghari Moghaddam (2016)
Laboratory measurement (WQV): 2400 datasets (1997–2013)	Coefficient of variation	HCO_3^-, pH, Na^+, Mg^{2+}, Cl^-, TH, TDS, EC, Ca^{2+}/SO_4^{2-}, SAR	50% training, 25% validation, and 25% testing	Data filling: none; normalization: not mentioned	Model: ANN-PSO, ANN-DE; structure determination: trial and error	Evolutionary algorithms (PSO and DE)	RMSE, MAE, R^2	ANN-DE > ANN-PSO	Kisi et al. (2017)
Marsh Laboratory measurement (WQV): 84 datasets (2009–18)	Pearson correlation/ sensitivity analysis	NO_3^-, Mg^{2+}, Cl^-, TH, SO_4^{2-}, Ca^{2+}/TDS, EC	75% training, 25% testing	Data filling: none; normalization: not mentioned	Model: ANN, ANFIS; structure determination: trial and error	Levenberg–Marquardt algorithm; BP algorithm	RMSE, NSE, R^2	ANFIS > ANN	Al-Mukhtar and Al-Yaseen (2019)

reproducing such work would likely be difficult because the performance of some models depends on the amount of data used for training.

Input data selection

Seeing that a vast number of variables are obtainable from monitoring WQ of different water bodies, it is expedient that the most significant indicator variables are selected for modeling and prediction. By selection, we mean the parameters that finally made the input dataset for the models. A case in point is that the initial selection of parameters usually includes: knowledge of the water source, knowledge from literature, theoretical knowledge of the parameter(s), parameters that can be measured with ease or at low cost, available data from water authorities and monitoring stations, and parameters for drinking or irrigation WQ purposes. Thereafter, several approaches will then be used to ascertain the relevance of the input parameter(s) that will determine their selection. The approaches that have been used when modeling WQ include sensitivity analysis (Al-Mukhtar & Al-Yaseen, 2019; Chen et al., 2020a, 2020b, 2020c; Kisi et al., 2019), statistical analysis (Al-Mukhtar & Al-Yaseen, 2019; Barzegar, Asghari Moghaddam, et al., 2017; Bui, Khosravi, Karimi, et al., 2020), and ad hoc (Chen et al., 2020c). Notably, the input layer needs to include all pertinent information on the target data for appropriate multistep-ahead prediction (Barzegar et al., 2018). The authors identified potential variables, which corresponded to distinct lag times using an autocorrelation function and partial autocorrelation function. These variables were then used as the input parameters for building multistep-ahead prediction models (Barzegar et al., 2018).

In another study, the Pearson correlation was applied to the initially chosen input variables, and those with weak correlation coefficients were ignored (Barzegar et al., 2016). Thereafter the effect of the selected input variables on the output of the model was ascertained using variance-based sensitivity analysis. This was based on the linearity of the input and output variables, and thus was calculated as the square of the correlation coefficient. This result indicated that Na^+, Ca^{2+}, Mg^{2+}, SO_4^{2-}, and Cl^- explained the output (EC) well, with Na^+ explaining 96.6% of the output variance (Barzegar et al., 2016). On the other hand, Zhou (2020) utilized the Kendall tau coefficient and Partial Mutual Information (PMI) methods to choose input variable combinations. They further observed that the selected time lags were identical, following the highest Kendall tau coefficient (≥ 0.6) and PMI (≥ 0.5). Again, instead of sensitivity analysis, principal component analysis (PCA) was used to investigate the WQV and MV that were vital in explaining the variability of the river (Zhou, 2020) and groundwater (Barzegar, Asghari Moghaddam, et al., 2017) WQ. Nevertheless, Table 9.2 clearly shows that some studies did not ascertain the impact of their input parameter on the output, rather utilizing the measured or collected dataset as input directly.

Data splitting

Data splitting is a vital stage in every modeling process, and all research dealing with modeling of WQ almost always describes data dividing. Usually, the dataset for training is used for model fitting, the dataset for validation is essential in adjusting the model's hyperparameters, whereas the dataset for testing is meant to ascertain the model's generalizability (Chen et al., 2020c). In WQ modeling, it is expedient that unseen data (different from the calibration data) are used in the validation of the model's performance to ensure that the model would exhibit similar performances with differing datasets (Rajaee et al., 2020). Also, the k-fold cross-validation method, which has the advantage of using all observations for both training and validation (Chen et al., 2020b), may be used to reduce bias that is connected with random samples of training and testing datasets (Chou et al., 2018). There is no strict pattern for data splitting, and sometimes researchers manually partition their data based on the year of sampling (Liu et al., 2019; Najah Ahmed et al., 2019), or based on data number (Yu et al., 2016). The time-series nature of data is retained when they are manually divided, thus it is the most useful method of data splitting (Rajaee et al., 2020). However, a more significant correlation usually exists between successive and close data points than separated data points, hence training or validating models by combining extreme (far apart) data points, even in time series, is worth considering. This ensures that the model is trained with an encompassing dataset that depicts the hydrological processes of the water body. From the reviewed papers (Table 9.2), the number of papers that divided their data into training and testing (two) outnumbers those that partitioned their data into training, validating, and testing (three). Generally, the percentage of training data for modeling WQ is greater than or equal to 70% (Table 9.2). In addition, some researchers instead reported their data splitting for training, validation, and testing (Barzegar et al., 2016; Zhou, 2020), as well as training and testing (Liu et al., 2019; Najah Ahmed et al., 2019), according to dates (Table 9.2). Nevertheless, other methods of data dividing are available in the literature (Chen et al., 2020c).

Data preprocessing

As indicated earlier, the method of data acquisition could be through manual WQ monitoring (e.g., grab sampling and analysis, use of portable multimeters and hand-held detectors, etc.) or automatic WQ monitoring (e.g., use of sensors or other automatic measuring devices). The majority of the data used in modeling WQ are time series dataset, meaning that they are collected at equally spaced, successive points in time. Although both manual and automatic WQ monitoring can yield time series data, the latter tend to entertain more missing data, which may arise due to routine maintenance, mechanical failures in sensor operation, network connectivity issues, changes to sensor settings, or inadvertent disruption of sensor operation by objects, for example, ship movement. For satisfactory performance of models, missing data from automatic WQ monitoring systems, which can never be retrieved because time is irreversible, can be estimated with a certain degree of accuracy (Zou et al., 2020). To alleviate the effects of missing values on prediction, transfer learning, and data imputation, algorithms have been used (Che, Purushotham, Cho, Sontag, & Liu, 2018; Lepot, Aubin, & Clemens, 2017; Yang, Cheng, & Chan, 2017). It has been stated that the former algorithm is indirect in estimating the missing values from the perspective of model and parameters transfer. In contrast, the latter algorithm is direct in filling the missing values from the spatiotemporal data viewpoint (Zou et al., 2020). Specifically, Liu and coworkers employed a single imputation (linear interpolation, LIN) algorithm, to model Yangtze River WQ in Yangzhou City, China, which yielded a better estimation effect for the missing dataset in stationary time series within a short time interval (Liu et al., 2019). The LIN function was structured according to formula 9.1.

$$y_{n} = y_{i,u} + \frac{\left(y_{i,u} - y_{i,v}\right)\left(t - T_{i,u}\right)}{T_{i,u} - T_{i,v}}$$

(9.1)

where y_n is the missing value at time t; $y_{i,u}$ and $y_{i,v}$ are monitoring data before and after the missing value at moments $T_{i,u}$ and $T_{i,v}$, respecitvely.

Similarly, Zou et al. (2020) not only used the LIN algorithm for missing data but also explored the use of autoregressive moving average (ARMA) for data augmentation. They posited that data augmentation could be beneficial in matching two different data (say WQ and meteorological variables) in the time dimension. Notwithstanding, some ML and DL models seem to have immunity to the hitches that missing data present. The ability of wavelet artificial neural network (WA-ANN) models to accurately estimate WQ parameters despite the downsides of missing data has been demonstrated (Barzegar et al., 2018), while DT-based models such as random forest (RF) and extreme gradient boosting (XGBoost) have been adjudged insensitive to missing values when used for WQ modeling (Lu & Ma, 2020). In addition, the maximum data-missing rate at which prediction models would begin to be impacted has been under investigation. DL ANN such as TL-LSTM was accurately utilized to forecast river WQ with an input data missing rate as high as 50% (Zhou, 2020), contrary to earlier reported models that it could only withstand missing data at rates lower than 30% (Yang et al., 2017). Overall, Table 9.2 depicts that some papers on WQ modeling and prediction did not specify the method used in taking care of missing data, which could either mean that their dataset was not acquired through automatic WQ monitoring systems or that they did not observe missing values. Moreover, data for groundwater studies were mostly laboratory-measured and are not likely to be termed missing, while some missing data were deleted (Chen et al., 2020b; Chou, Ho, & Hoang, 2018), which is not good practice.

Data normalization is another important preprocessing stage in the modeling of WQ. This is because, when data are normalized, the unit limit of the data is jettisoned and transformed into a totally dimensionless value. By so doing, various orders of magnitude or units can be compared and weighted (Li et al., 2019). Standardization and range scaling have been identified as the two categories of normalization often used in WQ modeling, with the latter mostly used by researchers. Standardization and range scaling formulas are presented in formulas (9.2) and (9.3), respectively.

$$X_{ni,k} = \frac{X_{i,k} - m_k}{Sd_k}$$

(9.2)

where $X_{ni,k}$ signifies the normalized data of variable k (input or output) for every sample, i, $X_{i,k}$ represents the original value of variable k, whereas mk and Sd_k represent the mean value and standard deviation of variance k, respectively.

$$X_n = a \times \frac{X - X_{min}}{X_{max} - X_{min}} + b$$

(9.3)

where X_n is the normalized value of the variable X; a and b are constants, whereas X_{min} and X_{max} are the minimum and maximum values of X of the original data, respectively.

Note that by using different values for the constants, different authors arrived at different scales for the WQ data. For instance, using $a = 1$ and $b = 0$, a scale range of [0, 1] is obtained

(Barzegar et al., 2018), while a range of [0.2, 0.8] was suggested to offer ANN the flexibility to measure beyond the training range. It is worthy noting that after completion of the model's training, the normalized model's outputs should be denormalized to their actual values by making X the subject in formula (9.3).

Furthermore, removing noise that is not only caused by external factors but also measuring and reading data, has been adjudged to be an essential preprocessing step toward having a satisfactory prediction, since uneliminated noise can distort model outcomes. Consequently, several authors have recommended wavelet denoizing techniques (WDTs) as a conventional denoizing method for multidimensional, temporal, or spatial signals having either stable or unstable noise (Ahmadianfar et al., 2020; Fijani et al., 2019; Najah Ahmed et al., 2019). Table 9.2 shows that some of the reviewed papers utilized either range scaling or standardization method for normalization (Barzegar, Asghari Moghaddam, Adamowski, & Ozga-Zielinski, 2018; Chen et al., 2020b; Fijani, Barzegar, Deo, Tziritis, & Konstantinos, 2019; Heddam & Kisi, 2017; Liang et al., 2020; Lu & Ma, 2020; Zou et al., 2020), whereas some did not specify the method of normalization used (Elkiran et al., 2019; Zhou, 2020), and yet others, especially those that studied groundwater sources, did not mention their preprocessing steps at all (Ahmed, 2017; Al-Mukhtar & Al-Yaseen, 2019; Azad et al., 2019; Barzegar & Asghari Moghaddam, 2016; Kisi et al., 2019; Najah Ahmed et al., 2019).

Model structure determination

Model structure determination and model training are essential steps in model development. Suffice it to say that each ML and DL model has a distinct structure. Notwithstanding, in the selection of an adequate structure for models like ANN, the vector of the inputs (x), the functional form of the model (f) that is controlled by the model architecture (e.g., radial basic function), the network geometry (i.e., type of transfer function, number of nodes, and hidden layers as well as how they are arranged), and the vector of network parameters (w) that comprises the bias and connection weights, should be defined. However, it is noted that the model structure determination step may be rather superfluous for other architectures with fixed structures (Maier et al., 2010). DT-based models such as the XGBoost model adopt an additive model, while when constructing each tree in a random forest (RF) model, it makes use of a random sample predictor prior to the segmentation of each node, which tends to reduce bias (Lu & Ma, 2020). In determining the structure in an SVR model, the adjustment of the penalty c and kernel function g parameters is key; thus the grid search method is usually employed to ascertain the optimal values (Granata et al., 2017). More importantly, the methods that have been used to determine the structure of ANN models in WQ prediction include ad hoc, stepwise trial and error, and global methods, with trial and error being the most frequently used (Chen et al., 2020c).

As depicted in Table 9.2, WQ modeling and prediction in the last 5 years have been mainly through the use of neural network techniques. RNNs, majorly LSTM, have either been employed in a standalone (Chou et al., 2018; Li et al., 2019; Liang et al., 2020; Liu et al., 2019) or hybrid form (Barzegar et al., 2020; Li et al., 2018; Zhou, 2020; Zou et al., 2020). However, most of the reviewed papers did not give details about the method utilized in determining the structure of these DL methods (Table 9.2). Notwithstanding, the structure of other ANN models (BPNN, MLP,

GRNN, ANFIS, and RBFNN) was determined using the trial-and-error method (Al-Mukhtar & Al-Yaseen, 2019; Barzegar et al., 2016; Barzegar & Asghari Moghaddam, 2016; Elkiran et al., 2019). For instance, Najah Ahmed et al. (2019) stated that through the trial-and-error method, $N = 1-20$ neurons were obtained through the randomization of the hidden layer's neurons, and they admitted that the best number of nodes usually offers the lowest error in the hidden layer. In similar research, Barzegar and coworkers posited that by varying the nodes in the hidden layer, efficient models can be established; thus through a trial-and-error method, they selected optimal hidden nodes of 10, 10, and 13, respectively, for predicting EC in Aji-Chay River, Iran, for 1, 2, and 3 months using extreme learning machine (ELM) models (Barzegar et al., 2018). In another research that used adaptive neurofuzzy inference system-particle swarm optimization (ANFIS-PSO) and adaptive neurofuzzy inference system-ant colony optimization for continuous domain (ANFIS-ACO_R) models, fuzzy c-means clustering (FCM) was used to first generate a fuzzy inference system (FIS), then, the selected FIS was optimized by global methods that have the capability to escape from local minima with high-speed convergence and the ability to solve complex natural issues (Azad et al., 2019).

Model training

Various learning (training) methods for ML and DL have been given above, of which the supervised learning approach was adjudged the most common. In WQ prediction, models are first trained; and for most classical standalone and hybrid ANN, Levenberg—Marquardt algorithm is the most common learning algorithm. However, in most DL models, neural networks are trained by backpropagation through time (BPTT) algorithm, transfer learning algorithm, and various evolutionary algorithms (EA) such as PSO, ACO_R, adaptive moment optimization algorithm (Adam), continuous genetic algorithm (CGA), and differential evolution (DE) (Azad et al., 2019; Kisi et al., 2017, 2019; Li et al., 2019; Liang et al., 2020; Liu et al., 2019; Najah Ahmed et al., 2019; Zhou, 2020). In training RNN, both real-time recurrent learning (RTRL) and BPTT can be used; however BPTT requires less computation compared with RTRL, and hence is effective in practical applications (Li et al., 2019). It is worth mentioning that various activation functions have been used together with different learning algorithms. Najah Ahmed et al. (2019) employed the Levenberg—Marquardt backpropagation algorithm and some activation functions [linear transfer function (purelin), trans-(Tansig), and log-(Logsig) sigmodal] to train all the hybrid networks applied in predicting pH, suspended solids (SS), and NH_3-N in Johor River, Malaysia. Another study utilized EA (PSO, ACO_R, DE, and CGA) to train various hybrid networks for the prediction of EC, SAR, and TH in groundwater (Kisi et al., 2019). In addition, the effect of activation functions on the prediction performance of an ELM model was tested by using optimally pruned ELM (with Gaussian, sigmoid, and linear activation functions), sigmoid ELM (with sigmoid activation function), and online sequential ELM, which is a modified version of the original radial ELM with radial basis activation function (Heddam & Kisi, 2017). It was observed that the learning performance of ELM was better with optimally pruned ELM. Overall, the various training algorithms that were used in the reviewed papers for the prediction of the identified water bodies are given in Table 9.2.

Performance evaluation measures

Performance evaluation is the final step in modeling and prediction of WQ, and various measures have been adopted to verify the performance of models. Various reviewed papers indicated that mean square error (MSE), synthesis index (SI), coefficient of determination (R^2), percentage of bias (PBIAS), Willmott's index (WI), root mean square error (RMSE), normalized mean absolute error (NMAE), mean absolute percentage error (MAPE), mean absolute relative error (MARE), coefficient of correlation (R), normalized root mean square error (NRMSE), Nash−Sutcliffe efficiency coefficient (NSE), delta (δ), precision, recall, F1-score, weighted F1-score, mean absolute error (MAE), RMSE, Legates and McCabe index (LMI), average absolute relative error (AARE), root mean square percentage error (RMSPE), sum of the square of residuals (SSR), total sum of squares (SST), and threshold statistics (TS) are the criteria used for performance appraisal (Table 9.2). Their definitions, as well as their formulas, can be found elsewhere (Azad, Karami, Farzin, Mousavi, & Kisi, 2019; Barzegar, Aalami, & Adamowski, 2020; Barzegar, Asghari Moghaddam, Adamowski, & Ozga-Zielinski, 2018; Chen et al., 2020b; Chou, Ho, & Hoang, 2018; Fijani, Barzegar, Deo, Tziritis, & Konstantinos, 2019; Kisi et al., 2019; Li et al., 2019; Liang et al., 2020; Mamun, Kim, Alam, & An, 2020; Rajaee, Khani, & Ravansalar, 2020). It is suggested that the measure of the model's performance should comprise at least one goodness-of-fit evaluator (e.g., R^2 or R) and at least an absolute error measure (e.g., MAPE, NRMSE, or RMSE) (Elkiran et al., 2019). However, NSE has been identified as having the ability to evaluate the prediction power of hydrological models with different sets of data because it is a relative criterion (Li et al., 2019). On the other hand, studies have maintained that only MAE, BIAS, or RMSE should not be used alone as performance since they are sensitive to outliers owing to their usage of average errors (Li et al., 2019; Rajaee et al., 2020). However, the WI metric is able to detect either sensitivity to outliers within the observations or insensitivity to the proportional or additive differences between prediction values and observation values (Barzegar et al., 2020). More so, it is vital to include evaluators such as AARE or TS that present a performance index not only in terms of prediction of a variable, but also depict the distribution of the prediction errors (Barzegar et al., 2016; Rajaee et al., 2020). Furthermore, of all the error measurement criteria, the Theil U statistics (Lu & Ma, 2020), WI metrics (Barzegar et al., 2020; Fijani et al., 2019), BIAS and PBIAS (Barzegar et al., 2020; Bui, Khosravi, Karimi, et al., 2020; Fijani et al., 2019), SI (Chou et al., 2018; Kisi et al., 2019), F1-score and weighted F1-score (Chen et al., 2020b), and LMI (Fijani et al., 2019) are seldomly used in the literature, whereas MAPE is explicit in categorizing errors into excellent (<10%), good (10%−20%), reasonable (21%−50%), and inaccurate (>50%) (Lu and Ma, 2020).

It has been observed from the reviewed papers that these error measurement criteria are not only used for comparing the performance of different models but also assist in model structure determination and model training. They are also important in selecting optimal epoch iterations, even though the epoch may have been chosen arbitrarily (Liu et al., 2019). For example, some authors used RMSE, MAE, and MAPE to determine the number of neurons in the hidden layer that are necessary to generate an optimum prediction performance without overfitting and consequently weakening the generalizability of the model (Li et al., 2019). Table 9.2 also elucidates the order of performance of different applied ML and DL models. Apparently, using these criteria, authors would be able to discern the prediction performance of various applied models in different scenarios, which is one of the intentions of this review, to guide future researchers on the possible best modeling techniques for different types of water bodies.

Challenges facing DL and ML predictions

Although DL is much stronger that classical ML in a lot of ways, new challenges have also arisen with this technique. Some of the drawbacks and limitations with DL and ML include:

1. DL is not suited for applications with a small sample or data size. Despite the suitability of DL for nonlinear classifications, it thrives on considerable data as input for training and validation. Such a dataset may be difficult to come by for WQ modeling and assessment. For instance, algal growth is subject to seasonal variability, hence this results in data skewness.
2. Difficulty in the interpretation of extracted features, particularly those arising from large datasets. Unlike shallow learning where features are easily selected and well understood, feature selection in DL is more complex based on the appropriateness for the regression step rather than interpretability.
3. Selection of input parameters while navigating extreme data skewness and imbalance could be arduous. For instance, DL applications for algal dynamics have been rarely reported owing to the difficulty in obtaining remote imagery data and the cost of satellite imagery. This has necessitated the use of synthetic datasets.
4. *Vanishing gradients*: When handling large neural networks, many parameters have to be optimized simultaneously, which could result in vanishing gradients. Additionally, when the error gradient propagates in the backward direction, gradient explosion results. This is a nonlinear behavior and requires advanced algorithms and computational power for optimization. An example is a grating algorithm, which allows RNNs to control the process of information accumulation. This reduces long-distance dependencies and prevents information overload.
5. *Overfitting*: This occurs when a model is excellent at predictions using training data but not with untrained validation data. In this case, the validation metric will be considerably worse than the training metric and the model is not capable of accurate generalization, because once a dataset different from the training data is inputted into the model, it deviates from the output. To minimize the challenge of overfitting, it is best to add more data to the training set. As the model becomes more diverse due to improved data input, its capacity for generalization increases, thereby minimizing overfitting. Additionally, it is possible to create augmented data using the training dataset. This process is known as data augmentation or modification and improves the predictive capability of the model by increasing the diversity of training data. Finally, reducing the complexity of the model can help overcome overfitting.
6. Setting up and training DL models could be slow and financially demanding, with requirements for considerable computing power.

Conclusions and future prospects

The management of water resources has become increasingly important in the face of industrialization and the dwindling supply of good-quality water. The emergence of AI has resulted in not only sophisticated but also efficient methods to deal with the complex data obtained from different water sources to evaluate and predict trends and variations in WQ. This chapter gave an overview of the various learning methods involved in DL and ML, as well as the process involved in the successful modeling and prediction of WQ. The different DL and ML models in use for WQ modeling and prediction are also discussed. Based on experimental research, all models are effective in predicting WQ to varying degrees. However, no particular model is entirely superior, as superiority is relative to the problem under study. One model can excel with a specific problem and not with an other. This, therefore, introduces the complexity of specificity to the use of ML in WQ determination as models can change severally depending on parameters and water body, making its use cumbersome. In comparison, however, these models could be confidently adopted as an efficient substitute for physical-based models.

Beyond their capacity to monitor and analyze WQ, these methods can solve environmental problems by identifying future associated risks. The way to go, therefore, is the development of an enhanced uniform and versatile predictive model that is efficient in different sources for a broad category of parameters. Future trends in the use of ML as a tool for WQ index can also focus on analyzing and predicting trends in variations of different organic and inorganic pollutants in various water bodies for more robust management of water resources.

References

Abba, S. I., Hadi, S. J., Sammen, S. S., Salih, S. Q., Abdulkadir, R. A., Pham, Q. B., & Yaseen, Z. M. (2020). Evolutionary computational intelligence algorithm coupled with self-tuning predictive model for water quality index determination. *Journal of Hydrology*, *587*, 124974. Available from https://doi.org/10.1016/j.jhydrol.2020.124974.

Adnan, R. M., Liang, Z., Heddam, S., Zounemat-Kermani, M., Kisi, O., & Li, B. (2020). Least square support vector machine and multivariate adaptive regression splines for streamflow prediction in mountainous basin using hydro-meteorological data as inputs. *Journal of Hydrology*, *586*, 124371. Available from https://doi.org/10.1016/j.jhydrol.2019.124371.

Adnan, R. M., Liang, Z., Trajkovic, S., Zounemat-Kermani, M., Li, B., & Kisi, O. (2019). Daily streamflow prediction using optimally pruned extreme learning machine. *Journal of Hydrology*, *577*, 123981. Available from https://doi.org/10.1016/j.jhydrol.2019.123981.

Afan, H. A., El-shafie, A., Mohtar, W. H. M. W., & Yaseen, Z. M. (2016). Past, present and prospect of an artificial intelligence (AI) based model for sediment transport prediction. *Journal of Hydrology*, *541*, 902–913. Available from https://doi.org/10.1016/j.jhydrol.2016.07.048.

Ahmadianfar, I., Jamei, M., & Chu, X. (2020). A novel hybrid wavelet-locally weighted linear regression (W-LWLR) model for electrical conductivity (EC) prediction in surface water. *Journal of Contaminant Hydrology*, *232*, 103641. Available from https://doi.org/10.1016/j.jconhyd.2020.103641.

Ahmed, A. A. M. (2017). Prediction of dissolved oxygen in Surma River by biochemical oxygen demand and chemical oxygen demand using the artificial neural networks (ANNs). *Journal of King Saud University—Engineering Sciences*, *29*(2), 151–158. Available from https://doi.org/10.1016/j.jksues.2014.05.001.

Alizadeh, M. J., & Kavianpour, M. R. (2015). Development of wavelet-ANN models to predict water quality parameters in Hilo Bay, Pacific Ocean. *Marine Pollution Bulletin*, *98*(1–2), 171–178. Available from https://doi.org/10.1016/j.marpolbul.2015.06.052.

Al-Mukhtar, M., & Al-Yaseen, F. (2019). Modeling water quality parameters using data-driven models, a case study Abu-Ziriq marsh in south of Iraq. *Hydrology, 6*(1), 24. Available from https://doi.org/10.3390/hydrology6010021.

Anwar, S., & Li, C. (2020). Diving deeper into underwater image enhancement: A survey. *Signal Processing: Image Communication, 89*, 115978. Available from https://doi.org/10.1016/j.image.2020.115978.

Ashwini, K., Vedha, J. J., & Priya, M. D. (2019). Intelligent model for predicting water quality. *International Journal of Advance Research, 5*(2), 70−75.

Azad, A., Karami, H., Farzin, S., Mousavi, S. F., & Kisi, O. (2019). Modeling river water quality parameters using modified adaptive neuro fuzzy inference system. *Water Science and Engineering, 12*(1), 45−54. Available from https://doi.org/10.1016/j.wse.2018.11.001.

Azam, M., Aslam, M., Khan, K., Mughal, A., & Inayat, A. (2017). Comparisons of decision tree methods using water data. *Communications in Statistics: Simulation and Computation, 46*(4), 2924−2934. Available from https://doi.org/10.1080/03610918.2015.1066807.

Bang, H. T., Yoon, S., & Jeon, H. (2020). Application of machine learning methods to predict a thermal conductivity model for compacted bentonite. *Annals of Nuclear Energy, 142*, 107395. Available from https://doi.org/10.1016/j.anucene.2020.107395.

Barzegar, R., & Asghari Moghaddam, A. (2016). Combining the advantages of neural networks using the concept of committee machine in the groundwater salinity prediction. *Modeling Earth Systems and Environment, 2*(1), 26. Available from https://doi.org/10.1007/s40808-015-0072-8.

Barzegar, R., Aalami, M. T., & Adamowski, J. (2020). Short-term water quality variable prediction using a hybrid CNN-LSTM deep learning model. *Stochastic Environmental Research and Risk Assessment, 34*(2), 415−433. Available from https://doi.org/10.1007/s00477-020-01776-2.

Barzegar, R., Adamowski, J., & Moghaddam, A. A. (2016). Application of wavelet-artificial intelligence hybrid models for water quality prediction: A case study in Aji-Chay River, Iran. *Stochastic Environmental Research and Risk Assessment, 30*(7), 1797−1819. Available from https://doi.org/10.1007/s00477-016-1213-y.

Barzegar, R., Asghari Moghaddam, A., Adamowski, J., & Fijani, E. (2017). Comparison of machine learning models for predicting fluoride contamination in groundwater. *Stochastic Environmental Research and Risk Assessment, 31*(10), 2705−2718. Available from https://doi.org/10.1007/s00477-016-1338-z.

Barzegar, R., Asghari Moghaddam, A., Adamowski, J., & Ozga-Zielinski, B. (2018). Multi-step water quality forecasting using a boosting ensemble multi-wavelet extreme learning machine model. *Stochastic Environmental Research and Risk Assessment, 32*(3), 799−813. Available from https://doi.org/10.1007/s00477-017-1394-z.

Barzegar, R., Fijani, E., Asghari Moghaddam, A., & Tziritis, E. (2017). Forecasting of groundwater level fluctuations using ensemble hybrid multi-wavelet neural network-based models. *Science of the Total Environment, 599−600*, 20−31. Available from https://doi.org/10.1016/j.scitotenv.2017.04.189.

Bhattacharjee, N. V., & Tollner, E. W. (2016). Improving management of windrow composting systems by modeling runoff water quality dynamics using recurrent neural network. *Ecological Modelling, 339*, 68−76. Available from https://doi.org/10.1016/j.ecolmodel.2016.08.011.

Brack, W., Dulio, V., Ågerstrand, M., Allan, I., Altenburger, R., Brinkmann, M., Bunke, D., Burgess, R. M., Cousins, I., Escher, B. I., Hernández, F. J., Hewitt, L. M., Hilscherová, K., Hollender, J., Hollert, H., Kase, R., Klauer, B., Lindim, C., Herráez, D. L., & Vrana, B. (2017). Towards the review of the European Union Water Framework management of chemical contamination in European surface water resources. *Science of the Total Environment, 576*, 720−737. Available from https://doi.org/10.1016/j.scitotenv.2016.10.104.

Bui, D. T., Khosravi, K., Karimi, M., Busico, G., Khozani, Z. S., Nguyen, H., Mastrocicco, M., Tedesco, D., Cuoco, E., & Kazakis, N. (2020). Enhancing nitrate and strontium concentration prediction in groundwater by using new data mining algorithm. *Science of the Total Environment, 715*, 136836. Available from https://doi.org/10.1016/j.scitotenv.2020.136836.

Bui, D. T., Khosravi, K., Tiefenbacher, J., Nguyen, H., & Kazakis, N. (2020). Improving prediction of water quality indices using novel hybrid machine-learning algorithms. *Science of the Total Environment, 721*, 136612. Available from https://doi.org/10.1016/j.scitotenv.2020.137612.

Cao, X., Liu, Y., Wang, J., Liu, C., & Duan, Q. (2020). Prediction of dissolved oxygen in pond culture water based on K-means clustering and gated recurrent unit neural network. *Aquacultural Engineering, 91*, 102122. Available from https://doi.org/10.1016/j.aquaeng.2020.102122.

Castrillo, M., & García, Á. L. (2020). Estimation of high frequency nutrient concentrations from water quality surrogates using machine learning methods. *Water Research, 172*, 115490. Available from https://doi.org/10.1016/j.watres.2020.115490.

Che, Z., Purushotham, S., Cho, K., Sontag, D., & Liu, Y. (2018). Recurrent neural networks for multivariate time series with missing values. *Scientific Reports, 8*(1), 6085. Available from https://doi.org/10.1038/s41598-018-24271-9.

Chen, H., Chen, A., Xu, L., Xie, H., Qiao, H., Lin, Q., & Cai, K. (2020a). A deep learning CNN architecture applied in smart near-infrared analysis of water pollution for agricultural irrigation resources. *Agricultural Water Management, 240*, 106303. Available from https://doi.org/10.1016/j.agwat.2020.106303.

Chen, K., Chen, H., Zhou, C., Huang, Y., Qi, X., Shen, R., Liu, F., Zuo, M., Zou, X., Wang, I, Zhang, Y., Chen, D., Chen, X., Deng, Y, & Ren, H. (2020b). Comparative analysis of surface water quality prediction performance and identification of key water parameters using different machine learning models based on big data. *Water Research, 171*, 115454. Available from https://doi.org/10.1016/j.watres.2019.115454.

Chen, S., Fang, G., Huang, X., & Zhang, Y. (2018). Water quality prediction model of a water diversion project based on the improved artificial bee colony-backpropagation neural network. *Water (Switzerland), 10*(6), 806. Available from https://doi.org/10.3390/w10060806.

Chen, W. B., & Liu, W. C. (2014). Artificial neural network modeling of dissolved oxygen in reservoir. *Environmental Monitoring and Assessment, 186*(2), 1203−1217. Available from https://doi.org/10.1007/s10661-013-3450-6.

Chen, Y., Song, L., Liu, Y., Yang, L., & Li, D. (2020c). A review of the artificial neural network models for water quality prediction. *Applied Sciences (Switzerland), 10*(17), 5776. Available from https://doi.org/10.3390/app10175776.

Choi, J. H., Kim, J., Won, J., & Min, O. (2019). *Modelling chlorophyll-a concentration using deep neural networks considering extreme data imbalance and skewness. International conference on advanced communication technology, ICACT* (Vol. 2019, pp. 631−634). Institute of Electrical and Electronics Engineers Inc. Available from https://doi.org/10.23919/ICACT.2019.8702027.

Chou, J. S., Ho, C. C., & Hoang, H. S. (2018). Determining quality of water in reservoir using machine learning. *Ecological Informatics, 44*, 57−75. Available from https://doi.org/10.1016/j.ecoinf.2018.01.005.

Danandeh Mehr, A. (2018). An improved gene expression programming model for streamflow forecasting in intermittent streams. *Journal of Hydrology, 563*, 669−678. Available from https://doi.org/10.1016/j.jhydrol.2018.06.049.

Diez-Sierra, J., & del Jesus, M. (2020). Long-term rainfall prediction using atmospheric synoptic patterns in semi-arid climates with statistical and machine learning methods. *Journal of Hydrology, 586*, 124789. Available from https://doi.org/10.1016/j.jhydrol.2020.124789.

El Bilali, A., & Taleb, A. (2020). Prediction of irrigation water quality parameters using machine learning models in a semi-arid environment. *Journal of the Saudi Society of Agricultural Sciences, 19*(7), 439−451. Available from https://doi.org/10.1016/j.jssas.2020.08.001.

Elkiran, G., Nourani, V., & Abba, S. I. (2019). Multi-step ahead modelling of river water quality parameters using ensemble artificial intelligence-based approach. *Journal of Hydrology*, *577*, 123962. Available from https://doi.org/10.1016/j.jhydrol.2019.123962.

Ewuzie, U., Nnorom, I. C., & Eze, S. O. (2020). Lithium in drinking water sources in rural and urban communities in Southeastern Nigeria. *Chemosphere*, *245*, 125593. Available from https://doi.org/10.1016/j.chemosphere.2019.125593.

Farmaki, E. G., Thomaidis, N. S., & Efstathiou, C. E. (2010). Artificial neural networks in water analysis: Theory and applications. *International Journal of Environmental Analytical Chemistry*, *90*(2), 85−105. Available from https://doi.org/10.1080/03067310903094511.

Fijani, E., Barzegar, R., Deo, R., Tziritis, E., & Konstantinos, S. (2019). Design and implementation of a hybrid model based on two-layer decomposition method coupled with extreme learning machines to support real-time environmental monitoring of water quality parameters. *Science of the Total Environment*, *648*, 839−853. Available from https://doi.org/10.1016/j.scitotenv.2018.08.221.

Gakii, C., & Jepkoech, J. (2019). A classification model for water quality analysis using decision tree. *Journal of Chemical Information and Modeling*, *7*(3), 1−8.

Granata, F., Papirio, S., Esposito, G., Gargano, R., & de Marinis, G. (2017). Machine learning algorithms for the forecasting of wastewater quality indicators. *Water (Switzerland)*, *9*(2), 105. Available from https://doi.org/10.3390/w9020105.

Gredell, D. A., Schroeder, A. R., Belk, K. E., Broeckling, C. D., Heuberger, A. L., Kim, S. Y., King, D. A., Shackelford, S. D., Sharp, J. L., Wheeler, T. L., Woerner, D. R., & Prenni, J. E. (2019). Comparison of machine learning algorithms for predictive modeling of beef attributes using rapid evaporative ionization mass spectrometry (REIMS) data. *Scientific Reports*, *9*(1), 5721. Available from https://doi.org/10.1038/s41598-019-40927-6.

Haghiabi, A. H., Nasrolahi, A. H., & Parsaie, A. (2018). Water quality prediction using machine learning methods. *Water Quality Research Journal of Canada*, *53*(1), 3−13. Available from https://doi.org/10.2166/wqrj.2018.025.

Hanson, P. C., Karpatne, A., Dugan, H. A., Stachelek, J., Ward, N. K., Zhang, Y., . . . Kumar, V. (2020). Predicting lake surface water phosphorus dynamics using process-guided machine learning. *Ecological Modelling*, *430*109136. Available from https://doi.org/10.1016/j.ecolmodel.2020.109136.

Harshvardhan, G., Kumar, G. M., Manjusha, P., & Swarup, R. S. (2020). A comprehensive survey and analysis of generative models in machine learning. *Computer Science Review*, *38*, 100285. Available from https://doi.org/10.1016/j.cosrev.2020.100285.

Heddam, S., & Kisi, O. (2017). Extreme learning machines: A new approach for modeling dissolved oxygen (DO) concentration with and without water quality variables as predictors. *Environmental Science and Pollution Research*, *24*(20), 16702−16724. Available from https://doi.org/10.1007/s11356-017-9283-z.

Hosseini, M. P., Lu, S., Kamaraj, K., Slowikowski, A., & Venkatesh, H. C. (2020). *Deep learning architectures. Studies in computational intelligence* (Vol. 866, pp. 1−24). Springer Verlag. Available from https://doi.org/10.1007/978-3-030-31756-0_1.

Huang, W., & Yang, Y. (2020). Water quality sensor model based on an optimization method of RBF neural network. *Computational Water, Energy, and Environmental Engineering*, *9*, 1−11. Available from https://doi.org/10.4236/cweee.2020.91001.

Isiyaka, H. A., Mustapha, A., Juahir, H., & Phil-Eze, P. (2019). Water quality modelling using artificial neural network and multivariate statistical techniques. *Modeling Earth Systems and Environment*, *5*(2), 583−593. Available from https://doi.org/10.1007/s40808-018-0551-9.

Jalalkamali, A. (2015). Using of hybrid fuzzy models to predict spatiotemporal groundwater quality parameters. *Earth Science Informatics*, *8*(4), 885−894. Available from https://doi.org/10.1007/s12145-015-0222-6.

Jeong, K. S., Joo, G. J., Kim, H. W., Ha, K., & Recknagel, F. (2001). Prediction and elucidation of phytoplankton dynamics in the Nakdong River (Korea) by means of a recurrent artificial neural network. *Ecological Modelling*, *146*(1−3), 115−129. Available from https://doi.org/10.1016/S0304-3800(01)00300-3.

Jeong, K. S., Kim, D. K., & Joo, G. J. (2006). River phytoplankton prediction model by artificial neural network: Model performance and selection of input variables to predict time-series phytoplankton proliferations in a regulated river system. *Ecological Informatics*, *1*(3), 235−245. Available from https://doi.org/10.1016/j.ecoinf.2006.04.001.

Joslyn, K. (2018). Water quality factor prediction using supervised machine learning. REU final reports research experiences for undergraduates on computational modeling serving the city.

Kapitanova, K., & Son, S. H. (2012). *Machine learning basics. Intelligent sensor networks: The integration of sensor networks, signal processing and machine learning* (pp. 3−29). CRC Press. Available from https://doi.org/10.1201/b14300.

Khan, U., Cook, F. J., Laugesen, R., Hasan, M. M., Plastow, K., Amirthanathan, G. E., Bari, M. A., & Tuteja, N. K. (2020). Development of catchment water quality models within a realtime status and forecast system for the Great Barrier Reef. *Environmental Modelling and Software*, *132*, 104790. Available from https://doi.org/10.1016/j.envsoft.2020.104790.

Khan, Y., & See, C. S. (2016). Predicting and analyzing water quality using machine learning: A comprehensive model. In *2016 IEEE long island systems, applications and technology conference, LISAT 2016*. Institute of Electrical and Electronics Engineers Inc. https://doi.org/10.1109/LISAT.2016.7494106

Kim, Y. H., Im, J., Ha, H. K., Choi, J. K., & Ha, S. (2014). Machine learning approaches to coastal water quality monitoring using GOCI satellite data. *GIScience and Remote Sensing*, *51*(2), 158−174. Available from https://doi.org/10.1080/15481603.2014.900983.

Kisi, O., Azad, A., Kashi, H., Saeedian, A., Hashemi, S. A. A., & Ghorbani, S. (2019). Modeling groundwater quality parameters using hybrid neuro-fuzzy methods. *Water Resources Management*, *33*(2), 847−861. Available from https://doi.org/10.1007/s11269-018-2147-6.

Kisi, O., Keshavarzi, A., Shiri, J., Zounemat-Kermani, M., & Omran, E. S. E. (2017). Groundwater quality modeling using neuro-particle swarm optimization and neuro-differential evolution techniques. *Hydrology Research*, *48*(6), 1508−1519. Available from https://doi.org/10.2166/nh.2017.206.

Lecun, Y., Bengio, Y., & Hinton, G. (2015). Deep learning. *Nature*, *521*(7553), 436−444. Available from https://doi.org/10.1038/nature14539.

Lepot, M., Aubin, J.-B., & Clemens, F. (2017). Interpolation in Time Series: An Introductive Overview of Existing Methods, Their Performance Criteria and Uncertainty Assessment. *Water*, *9*(10), 796. Available from https://doi.org/10.3390/w9100796.

Li, L., Jiang, P., Xu, H., Lin, G., Guo, D., & Wu, H. (2019). Water quality prediction based on recurrent neural network and improved evidence theory: A case study of Qiantang River, China. *Environmental Science and Pollution Research*, *26*(19), 19879−19896. Available from https://doi.org/10.1007/s11356-019-05116-y.

Li, L., Rong, S., Wang, R., & Yu, S. (2021). Recent advances in artificial intelligence and machine learning for nonlinear relationship analysis and process control in drinking water treatment: A review. *Chemical Engineering Journal*, *405*, 126673. Available from https://doi.org/10.1016/j.cej.2020.126673.

Li, Y., Shi, H., & Liu, H. (2020). A hybrid model for river water level forecasting: Cases of Xiangjiang River and Yuanjiang River, China. *Journal of Hydrology*, *587*, 124934. Available from https://doi.org/10.1016/j.jhydrol.2020.124934.

Li, Z., Peng, F., Niu, B., Li, G., Wu, J., & Miao, Z. (2018). Water quality prediction model combining sparse auto-encoder and LSTM network. *IFAC-PapersOnLine*, *51*(17), 831−836. Available from https://doi.org/10.1016/j.ifacol.2018.08.091.

Liang, Z., Zou, R., Chen, X., Ren, T., Su, H., & Liu, Y. (2020). Simulate the forecast capacity of a complicated water quality model using the long short-term memory approach. *Journal of Hydrology, 581*,
124432. Available from https://doi.org/10.1016/j.jhydrol.2019.124432.

Liu, P., Wang, J., Sangaiah, A. K., Xie, Y., & Yin, X. (2019). Analysis and prediction of water quality using
LSTM deep neural networks in IoT environment. *Sustainability (Switzerland), 11*(7), 2058. Available from
https://doi.org/10.3390/su1102058.

Liu, H., Zhang, Y., & Zhang, H. (2020). Prediction of effluent quality in papermaking wastewater treatment
processes using dynamic kernel-based extreme learning machine. *Process Biochemistry, 97*(April), 72−79.
https://doi.org/10.1016/j.procbio.2020.06.020

Lu, H., & Ma, X. (2020). Hybrid decision tree-based machine learning models for short-term water quality
prediction. *Chemosphere, 249*, 126169. Available from https://doi.org/10.1016/j.chemosphere.2020.126169.

Lu, J., Hu, H., & Bai, Y. (2014). Radial basis function neural network based on an improved exponential
decreasing inertia weight-particle swarm optimization algorithm for AQI prediction. *Abstract and Applied
Analysis, 2014*, 178313. Available from https://doi.org/10.1155/2014/178313.

Lu, J., Li, N., Zhang, S., Yu, Z., Zheng, H., & Zheng, B. (2019). Multi-scale adversarial network for underwater image restoration. *Optics and Laser Technology, 110*, 105−113. Available from https://doi.org/10.1016/
j.optlastec.2018.05.048.

Ma, Z., Song, X., Wan, R., Gao, L., & Jiang, D. (2014). Artificial neural network modeling of the water quality in intensive *Litopenaeus vannamei* shrimp tanks. *Aquaculture, 433*, 307−312. Available from https://
doi.org/10.1016/j.aquaculture.2014.06.029.

Maier, H. R., Jain, A., Dandy, G. C., & Sudheer, K. P. (2010). Methods used for the development of neural
networks for the prediction of water resource variables in river systems: Current status and future directions. *Environmental Modelling and Software, 25*(8), 891−909. Available from https://doi.org/10.1016/j.
envsoft.2010.02.003.

Mamun, M., Kim, J. J., Alam, M. A., & An, K. G. (2020). Prediction of algal chlorophyll-a and water clarity
in monsoon-region reservoir using machine learning approaches. *Water (Switzerland), 12*(1), 30. Available
from https://doi.org/10.3390/w12010030.

Meng, X., Rozycki, P., Qiao, J. F., & Wilamowski, B. M. (2018). Nonlinear system modeling using RBF networks for industrial application. *IEEE Transactions on Industrial Informatics, 14*(3), 931−940. Available
from https://doi.org/10.1109/TII.2017.2734686.

Misra, S., & Li, H. (2020). *Deep neural network architectures to approximate the fluid-filled pore size distributions of subsurface geological formations. Machine learning for subsurface characterization.* Elsevier.
Available from https://doi.org/10.1016/b978-0-12-817736-5.00007-7.

Mohammed, H., Longva, A., & Razak, S. (2018). Predictive analysis of microbial water quality using
machine-learning algorithms. *Environmental Research, Engineering and Management, 74*(1), 7−20.
Available from https://doi.org/10.5755/j01.erem.74.1.20083.

Najah Ahmed, A., Binti Othman, F., Abdulmohsin Afan, H., Khaleel Ibrahim, R., Ming Fai, C., Shabbir
Hossain, M., Ehteram, M., & Elshafie, A. (2019). Machine learning methods for better water quality prediction. *Journal of Hydrology, 578*, 124084. Available from https://doi.org/10.1016/j.jhydrol.2019.124084.

Ni, L., Wang, D., Singh, V. P., Wu, J., Wang, Y., Tao, Y., & Zhang, J. (2020). Streamflow and rainfall forecasting by two long short-term memory-based models. *Journal of Hydrology, 583*, 124296. Available from
https://doi.org/10.1016/j.jhydrol.2019.124296.

Nolan, B. T., Fienen, M. N., & Lorenz, D. L. (2015). A statistical learning framework for groundwater nitrate
models of the Central Valley, California, USA. *Journal of Hydrology, 531*, 902−911. Available from
https://doi.org/10.1016/j.jhydrol.2015.10.025.

Noori, N., Kalin, L., & Isik, S. (2020). Water quality prediction using SWAT-ANN coupled approach. *Journal
of Hydrology, 590*, 125220. Available from https://doi.org/10.1016/j.jhydrol.2020.125220.

Patel, B. N., Prajapati, S. G., & Lakhtaria, K. I. (2012). Efficient classification of data using decision tree. *Bonfring International Journal of Data Mining*, *2*(1), 06−12. Available from https://doi.org/10.9756/bijdm.1098.

Pyo, J. C., Park, L. J., Pachepsky, Y., Baek, S. S., Kim, K., & Cho, K. H. (2020). Using convolutional neural network for predicting cyanobacteria concentrations in river water. *Water Research*, *186*, 116349. Available from https://doi.org/10.1016/j.watres.2020.116349.

Rajaee, T., Khani, S., & Ravansalar, M. (2020). Artificial intelligence-based single and hybrid models for prediction of water quality in rivers: A review. *Chemometrics and Intelligent Laboratory Systems*, *200*, 103978. Available from https://doi.org/10.1016/j.chemolab.2020.103978.

Rezaie-Balf, M., Attar, N. F., Mohammadzadeh, A., Murti, M. A., Ahmed, A. N., Fai, C. M., Nabipour, N., Alaghmand, S., & El-Shafie, A. (2020). Physicochemical parameters data assimilation for efficient improvement of water quality index prediction: Comparative assessment of a noise suppression hybridization approach. *Journal of Cleaner Production*, *271*, 122576. Available from https://doi.org/10.1016/j.jclepro.2020.122576.

Sagan, V., Peterson, K. T., Maimaitijiang, M., Sidike, P., Sloan, J., Greeling, B. A., Maalouf, S., & Adams, C. (2020). Monitoring inland water quality using remote sensing: Potential and limitations of spectral indices, bio-optical simulations, machine learning, and cloud computing. *Earth-Science Reviews*, *205*, 103187. Available from https://doi.org/10.1016/j.earscirev.2020.103187.

Sahiner, B., Pezeshk, A., Hadjiiski, L. M., Wang, X., Drukker, K., Cha, K. H., Summers, R. M., & Giger, M. L. (2019). Deep learning in medical imaging and radiation therapy. *Medical Physics*, *46*(1), e1−e36. Available from https://doi.org/10.1002/mp.13264.

Sahoo, S., Russo, T., Elliott, J., & Foster, I. (1969). Water resources res. *Journal of the American Water Resources Association*, *2*. Available from https://doi.org/10.1111/j.1752-1688.1969.tb04897.x.

Sharafati, A., Babak, S., Seyed, H., & Hosseinzadeh, M. (2020). The potential of new ensemble machine learning models for effluent quality parameters prediction and related uncertainty. *Process Safety and Environmental Protection*, *140*, 68−78. Available from https://doi.org/10.1016/j.psep.2020.04.045.

Singh, K. R., Goswami, A. P., Kalamdhad, A. S., & Kumar, B. (2019). Assessment of surface water quality of Pagladia, Beki and Kolong rivers (Assam, India) using multivariate statistical techniques. *International Journal of River Basin Management*, *18*(4), 511−520. Available from https://doi.org/10.1080/15715124.2019.1566236.

Sit, M., Demiray Bekir, Z., Zhongrun, Z., Ewing Gregory, J., Sermet, Z., & Demir, I. (2020). A comprehensive review of deep learning applications in hydrology and water resources. *Water Science and Technology*, *82*(12), 2635−2670. Available from https://doi.org/10.2166/wst.2020.369.

Solanki, A., Agrawal, H., & Khare, K. (2015). Predictive analysis of water quality parameters using deep learning. *International Journal of Computer Applications*, *125*(9), 29−34. Available from https://doi.org/10.5120/ijca2015905874.

Su, Y. S., Ni, C. F., Li, W. C., Lee, I. H., & Lin, C. P. (2020). Applying deep learning algorithms to enhance simulations of large-scale groundwater flow in IoTs. *Applied Soft Computing Journal*, *92*, 106298. Available from https://doi.org/10.1016/j.asoc.2020.106298.

Ta, X., & Wei, Y. (2018). Research on a dissolved oxygen prediction method for recirculating aquaculture systems based on a convolution neural network. *Computers and Electronics in Agriculture*, *145*, 302−310. Available from https://doi.org/10.1016/j.compag.2017.12.037.

Tiyasha., Tung, T. M., & Yaseen, Z. M. (2020). A survey on river water quality modelling using artificial intelligence models: 2000−2020. *Journal of Hydrology*, *585*, 124670. Available from https://doi.org/10.1016/j.jhydrol.2020.124670.

Ukaogo, P. O., Ewuzie, U., & Onwuka, C. V. (2020). *Environmental pollution: Causes, effects, and the remedies* (pp. 419−429). Elsevier BV. Available from https://doi.org/10.1016/b978-0-12-819001-2.00021-8.

Wu, L., Peng, Y., Fan, J., & Wang, Y. (2019). Machine learning models for the estimation of monthly mean daily reference evapotranspiration based on crossstation and synthetic data. *Hydrology Research*, *50*(6), 1730−1750. Available from https://doi.org/10.2166/nh.2019.060.

Xu, T., Coco, G., & Neale, M. (2020). A predictive model of recreational water quality based on adaptive synthetic sampling algorithms and machine learning. *Water Research*, *177*, 115788. Available from https://doi.org/10.1016/j.watres.2020.115788.

Yang, J.-H., Cheng, C.-H., & Chan, C.-P. (2017). A time-series water level forecasting model based on imputation and variable selection method. *Computational Intelligence and Neuroscience*, *2017*, 8734214. Available from https://doi.org/10.1155/2017/8734214.

Yang, Y., Farid, S. S., & Thornhill, N. F. (2013). *Prediction of biopharmaceutical facility fit issues using decision tree analysis. Computer aided chemical engineering* (Vol. 32, pp. 61−66). Elsevier BV. Available from https://doi.org/10.1016/B978-0-444-63234-0.50011-7.

Yotova, G., Varbanov, M., Tcherkezova, E., & Tsakovski, S. (2021). Water quality assessment of a river catchment by the composite water quality index and self-organizing maps. *Ecological Indicators*, *120*, 106872. Available from https://doi.org/10.1016/j.ecolind.2020.106872.

Yu, H., Chen, Y., Hassan, S., & Li, D. (2016). Dissolved oxygen content prediction in crab culture using a hybrid intelligent method. *Scientific Reports*, *6*, 27292. Available from https://doi.org/10.1038/srep27292.

Yu, X., Cui, T., Sreekanth, J., Mangeon, S., Doble, R., Xin, P., Rassam, D., & Gilfedder, M. (2020). Deep learning emulators for groundwater contaminant transport modelling. *Journal of Hydrology*, *590*, 125351. Available from https://doi.org/10.1016/j.jhydrol.2020.125351.

Zheng, F., Tao, R., Maier, H. R., See, L., Savic, D., Zhang, T., Chen, Q., Assumpção, T. H., Yang, P., Heidari, B., Rieckermann, J., Minsker, B., Bi, W., Cai, X., Solomatine, D., & Popescu, I. (2018). Crowdsourcing methods for data collection in geophysics: State of the art, issues, and future directions. *Reviews of Geophysics*, *56*(4), 698−740. Available from https://doi.org/10.1029/2018RG000616.

Zhou, Y. (2020). Real-time probabilistic forecasting of river water quality under data missing situation: Deep learning plus post-processing techniques. *Journal of Hydrology*, *589*, 125164. Available from https://doi.org/10.1016/j.jhydrol.2020.125164.

Zou, Q., Xiong, Q., Li, Q., Yi, H., Yu, Y., & Wu, C. (2020). A water quality prediction method based on the multi-time scale bidirectional long short-term memory network. *Environmental Science and Pollution Research*, *27*(14), 16853−16864. Available from https://doi.org/10.1007/s11356-020-08087-7.

Intelligent systems in water pollution research: a review

Ali Sohani, Kiana Berenjkar, Mohammad Hassan Shahverdian, Hoseyn Sayyaadi and
Erfan Goodarzi

Lab of Optimization of Thermal Systems' Installations, Faculty of Mechanical Engineering-Energy Division, K. N. Toosi University of Technology, Tehran, Iran

Introduction

Water is one of the most essential needs of humanity (Sayed et al., 2020). Water is not only used for cleaning and temperature control, but also is necessary for all life on Earth (Elsayed et al., 2021). Due to water-scarcity issues, there has been a growing tendency to utilize desalination systems to enhance the quality of water form the oceans and other resources to the required standard for its use (Sohani, Hoscinzadeh, & Berenjkar, 2021; Sohani, Hoseinzadeh, Samiezadeh, & Verhaert, 2021). Therefore, many involved in both academia and industry are attempting to develop and improve the performance of different kinds of water desalination systems.

Owning to the complexity of solving problems related to water treatment and desalination systems, the application of artificial intelligence (AI), as a robust tool for modeling and predicting the performance of such technologies, has been increasing constantly (Bagheri et al., 2020; Charrouf et al., 2020; Yang et al., 2020b). AI includes several methods such as artificial neural networks (ANNs), regression methods, deep learning, statistical approaches, and machine learning (ML) (Sohani, Hoseinzadeh, & Berenjkar, 2021; Sohani, Hoseinzadeh, Samiezadeh, & Verhaert, 2021). There are various methods in ML that can be used in different areas related to water desalination systems, and there is concern that the most efficient algorithm for water quality monitoring is used (Al Aani et al., 2019; Rajesh et al., 2018; Zarei & Behyad, 2019). Considering these issues, this chapter aim to provide a framework to obtain information about the working principle of various water desalination technologies and reviews studies that have been carried out in this area.

In this chapter, initially, in the Water standards section, the quality level required for different uses is discussed. Then, in the Water desalination technologies section, different commercially developed water desalination technologies, through which water reaches the desirable quality, are introduced. After that, in the Review of the literature section, studies in the field of the application of AI methods for water desalination technologies are reviewed. Next, a case study for the application of AI in water desalination systems in a previous investigation by this research team is described in the Selected case study from the literature section, and finally, the chapter ends by presenting the Conclusions in the last section.

Current Trends and Advances in Computer-Aided Intelligent Environmental Data Engineering.
DOI: https://doi.org/10.1016/B978-0-323-85597-6.00011-2

Water standards

Water quality standards are fundamental to water quality control (Li & Jennings, 2017). They have been provided by authorized agencies such as the Bureau of Industry and Security (BIS), US Environmental Protection Agency (US EPA), European Union (EU), World Health Organization (WHO), and The Food and Agriculture Organization (FAO). The required water quality for different applications such as drinking, washing, and bathing, is different, and among the different applications, the water used for drinking must have the highest quality (Louckes et al., 1967).

The basis of water standards

As already mentioned, a variety of standards based on the application have been provided by different agencies. The defined quality for water in each standard should meet a number of requirements. Some criteria of the optimal water quality in a standard include (Wacławek et al., 2017):

1. Technologically accessible;
2. Economically justifiable;
3. Easily measurable;
4. Able to meet the critical requirements.

Examples of water standards based on different water applications are given in Tables 10.1 and 10.2. Table 10.1 lists the various drinking water quality parameters for the WHO, US EPA, and EU, as well as Iranian, Australian, and Canadian standards. In Table 10.2, various irrigation water quality parameters for the US EPA, and FAO, in addition to Iranian and Canadian standards are mentioned. Using these tables, different standards can be compared.

As observed in Tables 10.1 and 10.2, the standards for various applications cover different parameters, including mercury, sodium, nitrite, nitrate, benzene, dichloroethane, etc. In addition, it should be noted that various definitions in different standards are considered for different materials. Aesthetic objective (AO), which is defined as the level of a subtance leading to changes in the appearance, the guideline value, and the maximum acceptable concentration can be given as examples. Among the parameters, salt is one of the most important. Although in chemistry, salt is a

Table 10.1 Comparison of different standards for drinking water quality (values in milligrams per liter).

Material	Standard					
	Canadian	Australian	Iranian	WHO	EU	US EPA
Sodium	200	180	200	200	200	N.A.
Mercury	0.001	0.001	0.006	0.006	0.001	0.002
Lead	0.005	0.01	0.01	0.01	0.01	0.015
Nitrate	45	50	50	50	50	45
Benzene	0.005	0.001	0.010	0.010	0.001	0.005
1,2-Dichloroethane	0.005	0.003	0.030	0.030	0.003	0.005
Nitrite	3	3	3	3	0.5	3

Table 10.2 Comparison of different standards for irrigation water quality (values in milligrams per liter).

Material	Canadian	Standard		
		FAO	US EPA	Iranian
Aluminum	5	5	5	5
Arsenic	0.1	0.2	0.2	0.1
Beryllium	0.1	0.1	0.1	0.1
Cadmium	0.01	0.05	0.05	0.01
Copper	0.2 and 1.0 for sensitive and tolerant crops, respectively	0.5	0.5	0.2
Selenium	0.05	0.05	0.05	0.02
Iron	5	N.A.	N.A.	5

general name used to describe the combination of anions and cations, in the water quality control literature (including the rest of this chapter), it usually refers to the combination of sodium and chlorine, also known as sodium chloride. The amount of salt in the water should be controlled, as consuming more than the recommended amount can be harmful to the human body. This is discussed in more depth in the next subsection.

Harmful effects of salt

Sodium is an essential mineral in the human diet that is commonly found in the form of sodium chloride (salt). Sodium is essential for the human body's normal functioning and is found in all organisms and fluids of the body. In general, adequate salt intake through food and drinking water sources is not considered harmful. However, excessive salt intake causes kidney disease, directly affecting the kidneys so that when the sodium level in the body rises, the process of water balance by the kidneys is disrupted. As a result, kidney function declines. Kidney problems also cause less water to be expelled from the body, leading to high blood pressure, which can lead to severe problems such as stroke or heart failure, and premature aging. Therefore, reducing salt intake prevents excessive blood pressure. Moreover, because calcium excretion is increased in people who consume high sodium, a high salt intake can lead to kidney stones. Another disadvantage of excessive salt consumption is osteoporosis, especially in postmenopausal women.

Salt has no odor and dissolves in water. The taste threshold of sodium in water depends on the anion and temperature of the solution. For instance, at room temperature, the threshold values are about 20 mg/L for sodium carbonate, 190 mg/L for sodium nitrate, 220 mg/L for sodium sulfate, 420 mg/L for sodium bicarbonate, and 150 mg/L for sodium chloride (Joshua & Nazrul, 2015). However, the following people should be aware of the amount of sodium (salt) in drinking water when it is more than 20 mg/L:

1. People who control their salt levels due to high blood pressure;
2. People with cardiovascular disease;
3. People who have kidney problems;
4. People on a low-sodium diet.

Moreover, sodium metal has broad usage in different fields, including:

1. Manufacturing of tetraethyl lead;
2. A catalyst for synthetic rubber;
3. A coolant in nuclear reactors;
4. Roads lighting;
5. Heat transmission medium in solar electric generators;
6. Water treatment processes, including softening, disinfection, corrosion control, pH adjustment, and coagulation;
7. Road defrosting;
8. Paper, glass, soap, pharmaceutical, chemical, and food industries.

Uncontrolled sodium concentration in various industries causes deposits in equipment and then, their breakdown. Therefore, controlling and reducing the salt (sodium) concentration is a vital requirement not only for drinking but also is crucial in a variety of applications. Considering this point, several water desalination technologies have been developed. The most important ones are introduced in the next section.

Water desalination technologies

There are severe limitations to access to water of appropriate quality, despite more than two-thirds of our planet being covered by water as this is mostly seawater or water resources that have high levels of materials, such as salt. Therefore efforts have been made to boost the quality of seawater and other available resources through desalination systems. The main purpose of water desalination systems is to decrease the concentration of salt in water (e.g., seawater) and make it drinkable. There are different types of desalination methods, which can be categorized into two main groups:

1. Phase-changing desalination,
2. Non phase-changing desalination.

It is worth mentioning that choosing the best desalination technology for an application is dependent on different parameters, including the required water quality and costs.

Phase-changing desalination

The first category of desalination systems reduces the amount of salt in water by changing the liquid phase. This method is also called thermal desalination. There are different methods for phase-changing desalination. The best known processes are:

1. Multistage flash (MSF) distillation;
2. Multieffect distillation (MED) system;
3. Solar still desalination;
4. Humidification–dehumidification (HDH) desalination;
5. Vapor compression (VC) desalination.

In these processes that use thermal energy in desalination, the salt water gains heat to evaporate. Then, the vapor is collected and condensed to form water. Salt and other contaminants do not travel with the water in the vapor phase. Consequently, they remain in place, and can be used for other purposes (e.g., salt could be used for cooking). Some advantages of these desalination methods are:

1. The efficiency of these methods is not related to the quality of feed water.
2. If the distillation system is coupled with a power generation system (or other energy systems which have a high amount of heating energy as their outlet in desirable levels), the energy for evaporation will be provided at a low cost.
3. The maintenance and repair costs are lower in comparison with other types of desalination methods.

However, as already mentioned, providing the required energy for water evaporation is the main challenge of using phase-changing desalination systems.

For a better understanding, the working processes of each of these types of water desalination methods are explained in the remainder of this section.

Multistage flash (MSF) distillation

This system has been using in the water industry for more than a century. This kind of water desalination system requires a large amount of energy. Hence it is widely used in systems with waste energy or extra energy that is available. They also can be coupled with fossil fuel plants or solar plants.

There are two widely used types of MSF systems, namely:

1. Brine circulation;
2. Once through.

The first type of MSF system is the system with brine circulation, which is shown in Fig. 10.1.

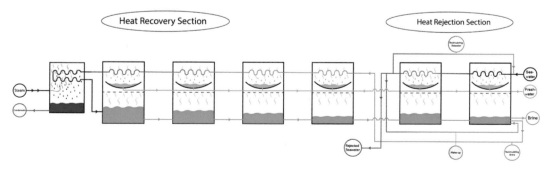

FIGURE 10.1

A multistage flash (MSF) distillation system with brine recirculation.

The MSF system with brine circulation contains three steps:

1. Brine heater;
2. Heat recovery section;
3. Heat rejection section.

In the brine heater, the saline water receives energy from an external source, for example, hot steam, which increases its temperature to a high level. The brine heater is the first unit on the left-hand side of Fig. 10.1. Then, the heated saline enters a number of units, which are similar to distillation columns. The schematic representation of one such unit is depicted in Fig. 10.2. According to Fig. 10.2, warm salt water enters the unit and passes through the flashing box, which leads to flashing of the saline water. This causes some of the water to evaporate. The evaporated water travels through the column, and becomes condensate through heat transfer that occurs at the top of the unit. At the top of the unit, the vapor passes on its energy to the saline water which is then goes to

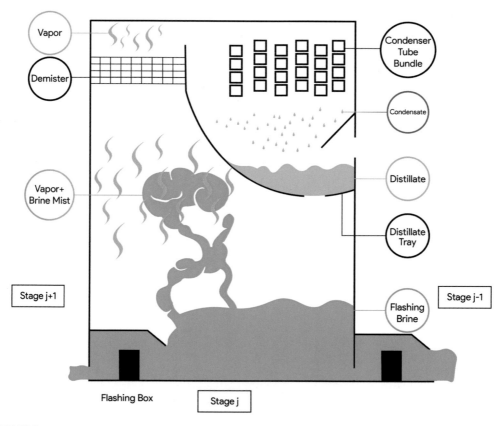

FIGURE 10.2

Schematic representation of the main unit of the heat recovery section in a multistage flash (MSF) distillation system with brine recirculation.

the brine heater. In this way, preheating of the saline water which is going to go to the brine heater also takes places. Therefore this part is known as the heat recovery section.

The condensate is collected in trays, as shown in Fig. 10.2.

In the units of the heat recovery section, the vapor passes through a demister, and the remaining salt is removed, therefore the output from these sections is almost pure. As mentioned earlier, the heat released from the vapor increases the feed water temperature in the tubes. Consequently the efficiency of desalination is enhanced. This process takes place in all stages, and the final output of the system is pumped out. This brine can be used for different purposes according to its quality.

Heat rejection is the third and final part of the brine recirculation-type MSF system. In this stage, the feed water enters the heat exchanger containing salt water. Using the pure water which is going to leave the system, temperature of that rises to the desired level. Using this part not only leads to saving energy, but also helps to reduce the temperature of the brine that will be dumped into the environment.

As already indicated, some of the brine is pumped out of the system, and can be used as a by-product or discharged in to the environment. However, the remaining part is returned to the system and recirculated, hence the term "recirculation" is used in its name. Before being pumped again into the heat recovery units, the brine which has been through desalination is mixed with fresh saline water which is preheated in the heat recovery section. The mixture then passes through the stages repeatedly until the defined ultimate goal is achieved (the required volume, the needed concentration of salt in the pure water, etc.).

In a commercial MSF system with brine recirculation, the density of saline water in all stages of the process is controlled at around $65,000-70,000$ ppm. The saline water temperature in the salt water heater output (maximum temperature of the cycle) is about $90°C-120°C$. In contrast, the water temperature in the final stage is significantly higher (about $6°C-10°C$) than seawater temperature. Furthermore, the saturation pressure in most evaporator stages is less than the vacuum pressure and varies from 1.5 to 50 bar. To prepare for the vacuum situation, noncondensable gases, including air, CO_2, etc., need to be vented to either the atmosphere or the next stages.

In most MSF systems using brine recirculation that are found in the market, the ratio of returned brine to the system is about $50\%-75\%$, which increases the system thermal efficacy and minimizes the amount of primary filtration and purification of the feed water. In addition, mixing brine with feedwater increases corrosion and sedimentation in the tubes. Thus there is a need to control this factor precisely to enable the optimum conditions of the system.

Another type of MSF water desalination technology is the once-through system. A schematic representation of an MSF system of a once-through type is shown in Fig. 10.3.

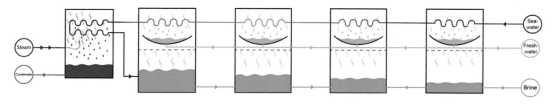

FIGURE 10.3

The schematic representation of a multistage flash (MSF) distillation system from a once-through type.

Table 10.3 Comparison of two types of multistage flash (MSF) distillation systems.

Advantages	MSF system with brine recirculation	MSF system from once-through type
Lower sediment and corrosion		×
Lower costs		×
More energy efficiency	×	
Higher levels of flexibility in the application (being more controllable)	×	

The main difference between these two types of MSF is the return of feedwater to the earlier stages. As the name suggests, feedwater (saline water) is used once in once-through systems, and it is released to the sea after passing the final step of flashing. Alternatively, there is a heat recovery section in brine recirculation systems, while a part of the brine is returned to the system.

Although adding more stages to the system improves efficiency, it leads to increased project costs. For that reason, once-through systems are utilized in some cases, depending on the project conditions.

There is a comparison between these two types of MSF systems presented in Table 10.3. Due to the mentioned differences between these two types of MSF system, the once-through systems are more suited to small plants.

MSF desalination systems enjoy a number of advantages, such as stable efficiency during years of operation. Nonetheless, one of the critical problems in MSF systems is the high energy usage that can be controlled by adjusting the following parameters:

1. Number of heating stages;
2. Increasing heat transfer during vapor condensation;
3. Reusing the waste energy of the brine and desalinated water;
4. Preventing the formation of sediment;
5. Venting noncondensable gases into the atmosphere;
6. Controlling corrosion in the system.

Several techniques have been developed to address some of the described problems, including controlling the maximum water temperature in the system, adding filtration to the feedwater, adding some components to the feedwater to avoid forming sediments, etc. Moreover, based on the reported data in the literature, in some commercially developed MSF systems, the processed water contained 50 ppm solid particles, which can be improved to 10 ppm using some solutions.

Although MSF systems play a vital role in seawater desalination, multieffect desalination (MED) systems have been enhanced in both efficiency and sediment decreasing level recently. Therefore, there is a growing tendency to using them. As discussed in the next subsection, these improvements have been achieved by replacing some parts of the system with new technologies.

Multieffect distillation (MED) system

Fig. 10.4 is a schematic representation of an MED system. As can be observed, an MED system is composed of a number of units. In each unit, saltwater is fed into the unit by spraying. Then, the

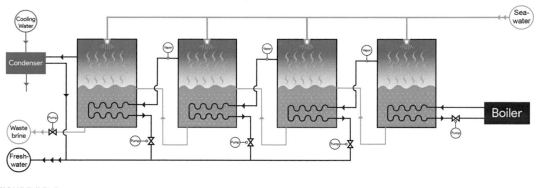

FIGURE 10.4

A schematic representation of the multieffect distillation (MED) system.

sprayed water gains heat from the vapor that passes through a pipe, and a some is evaporated, and so no longer contains salt. In the first unit, the vapor is provided by a boiler. Nonetheless, the evaporated water in unit 1 plays provides hot vapor for unit 2, which then condenses in that unit, and it leads to evaporation of a part of sprayed water to the unit 2. The condensed water in unit 2 is freshwater which is collected. In a similar way, the evaporated water in unit 2 goes through pipes to unit 3, and by losing energy and transferring to the liquid phase, it leads the evaporation of a part of the inlet water to unit 3. The condensed water is collected as in the previous unit. This process continues until the last unit. In the last unit, the produced vapor leaves the system, however it does not have heat transfer with saline water. Instead, it loses its energy through heat transfer to the atmosphere.

Based on the given explanations, an MED system reduces the salt in water by evaporating and condensation over several times. The outcome vapor from the first stage is known as desalinated water, and the quality of that can be enhanced by going through more stages. The number of required stages for this system is related to various parameters, including the temperature of the feedwater, boiler working pressure, atmospheric conditions, etc. By increasing the number of stages, the thermal efficiency of desalination increases. The cost, however, also increases. Like the MSF system, the optimum number of units can be determined by optimization.

It is worth adding that at each stage the pressure drops, so there is no need for extra heat to evaporate the brine. Due to stabilizing of the pressure in the final stages, the remaining steam is removed by a vacuum pump. A compressor provides the vacuum pressure. According to the compressor type, including thermal or electrical compressors, systems are called either MED-TVC or MED-MVC, respectively.

Solar still desalination

A solar still is a basin in which saltwater is kept, with some of the water being evaporated by absorbing heat from the sun. The evaporated water, then, is collected by condensing and it goes to a tank, which is located near the solar still (Sohani, Hoseinzadeh, & Berenjkar, 2021). Fig. 10.5 illustrates a solar still in a schematic way.

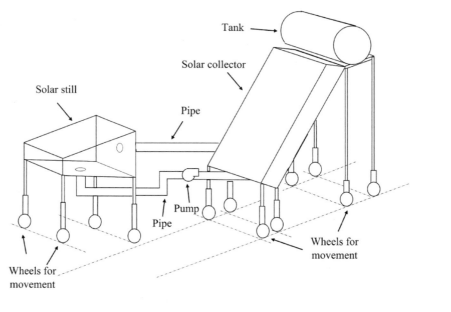

FIGURE 10.5

A solar still desalination system.

Reproduced with permission from: Sohani, A., Hoseinzadeh, S., & Berenjkar, K. (2021). Experimental analysis of innovative designs for solar still desalination technologies: An in-depth technical and economic assessment. Journal of Energy Storage, 33, *101862.*
https://doi.org/10.1016/j.est.2020.101862.

Solar still systems are much cheaper than other types of desalination technologies. However, their productivity is lower, including those methods that have been introduced already. They are the best fit for rural areas and areas that do not have access to an electricity or natural gas grid. The higher the energy prices, the more economically viable a solar still will be.

The temperature of water in the basin could be increased to higher levels, transforming the system from the passive into the active mode. The passive mode refers to a simple system, as already mentioned. On the other hand, the active system is a system in which the temperature of water in the basin increases by passing through a solar collector. Active solar systems have higher costs, but also enjoy higher yield and efficiency (Sohani, Hoseinzadeh, & Berenjkar, 2021).

Humidification–dehumidification (HDH) desalination

A schematic representation of an HDH desalination technology is shown in Fig. 10.6. In an HDH unit, the brine goes into a unit (the left-hand-side one), in which it absorbs heat from vapor coming from another side to the unit. It provides the possibility of preheating the saline water. Then, the saltwater leaves this unit, and receives more energy from a heater, which warms the saline. After that, the warm saltwater enters another unit (the right-hand-side one). After being sprayed, it flows on the packings. A gas is blown in to this unit, which makes some of the water on the packings evaporate (packings provide the possibility of greater contact between gas and water). The evaporated water goes to the next unit and loses its energy by heat transfer to the saltwater. This leads to

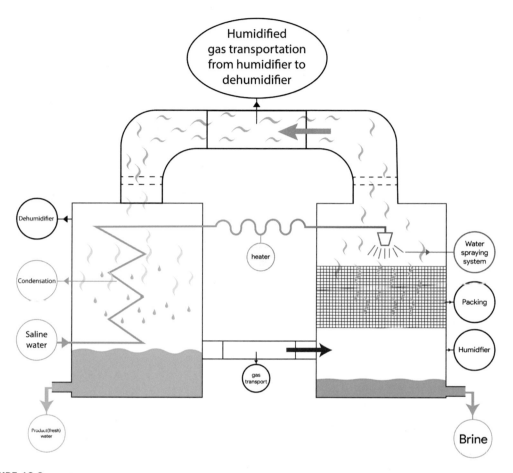

FIGURE 10.6

A schematic representation of a humidification–dehumidification (HDH) desalination technology.

the vapor changing to condensate. The condensate is collected on the left-hand side as freshwater, while nonevaporated saltwater forms brine on the bottom of the right-hand side.

The unit in which a part of salt water on packings is evaporated is called the humidification side. On the other hand, the unit in which the evaporated water (vapor) loses its energy and condensate is made is called the dehumidification side. Therefore, the whole process is called the HDH process.

HDH technology is reported as being suitable for small-scale applications. It does not have any expensive components, with a simple structure, which makes operating and maintenance easy. In addition, HDH systems are able to work properly in a wide range of water concentrations (Zubair et al., 2018). However, a relatively high amount of energy is required compared to other technologies, while solving the fouling of packings is another serious challenge.

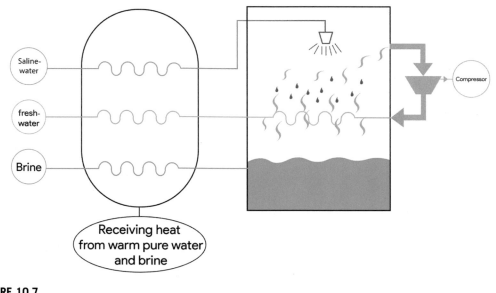

FIGURE 10.7

The vapor compression (VC) desalination system.

Vapor compression (VC) desalination

As per Fig. 10.7, in a VC desalination system, the brine enters the system and initially gives out heat from two hot streams, which are the pure water and brine flows. Then, it is sprayed into the main unit. In the main unit, some of the water gets vapor by spraying, and is conducted into a device that increases its pressure level. The device could be an ejector or a compressor. The temperature of vapor is also reduced by spraying. After passing through the compressor, the hot vapor loses its energy to the saltwater stream which has been sprayed. This leads to an increase in the amount of vapor generated in the system which goes into the compressor, and consequently, pure water production. The hot water that has lost its energy leaves the system in the form of a liquid. This liquid is water without salt, that is, freshwater. The water that has not evaporated is also collected in the form of brine at the bottom of the main unit. The brine stream passes its heat to the inlet saline water, and then it is either discharged or used for an other purpose.

Fast launching is one of the main positive aspects of VC desalination systems. Low complexity of maintenance is another advantage. However, they require a high amount of energy, which makes their operating costs significant (Warsinger et al., 2015).

Without phase-changing desalination

In the second category of desalination systems, reducing the concentration of salt in the water is done without changing the phase of water. The most important methods in this area are:

1. Reverse osmosis (RO);
2. Electrodialysis (ED).

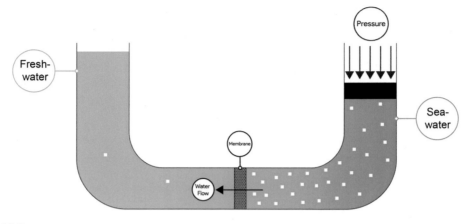

FIGURE 10.8

A schematic representation of a reverse osmosis (RO) water desalination system.

These methods reduce the salt in water by forcing the liquid to pass through a membrane. In the rest of this section, each of these systems and their functions are introduced.

Reverse osmosis (RO)

The working principle of this method is schematically shown in Fig. 10.8. In this figure, two storage columns, one containing pure water and the other with saltwater, are connected by a membrane that stops sodium and chloride ions from passing through.

If there is no external pressure, the water molecules in the pure water side tend to migrate to the saltwater side to make the concentration on both sides equal. Therefore the height of the saltwater column increases, whereas that of pure water goes down. The process continues until the hydraulic pressure (ρgh) in the saltwater side gets so high that it no longer allows the pure water molecules to enter the saltwater. This process is called osmosis, and the pressure at which the water molecule migration stops is known as the osmosis pressure. The osmosis pressure can be determined based on Vent Hoff's law, which is a function of the salt density (Lucy et al., 2013).

As the name indicates, in the RO process, by applying external pressure, the process takes place on the reverse side. In RO, the salt water is pushed through the semipermeable membrane, which allows water molecules to leave and prevents salt molecules from passing through. Therefore some of the salt water becomes pure.

This method was developed around 40 years ago, and is becoming increasingly popular with the discovery of new materials and decreased costs.

Some advantages of RO include:

1. It costs less in comparison with other types of desalination systems, and is economically friendly.
2. It is faster.
3. Development of the system has become more feasible.
4. The operation is at low temperature.
5. It needs smaller space for installation.

6. The initial cost for establishing the system is less than for other methods.
7. The system can be enhanced by using some other membranes which are able to remove nitrates or other contaminants from water.

However, the main issue with RO systems is providing electricity for building up the external pressure.

Electrodialysis (ED)

When salt is dissolved in water, it breaks into cations and anions, which have positive and negative charges, respectively. Therefore, if two surfaces, one with a negative, and the other with a positive charge, are attached to both sides of the saltwater container, the dissolved cations and anions will be absorbed, leading to a decrease in the concentration of both sodium and chloride, and consequently, salt.

An ED desalination system works based on the described principle, in which using a voltage, an electric field is generated. Fig. 10.9 shows a schematic representation of this system.

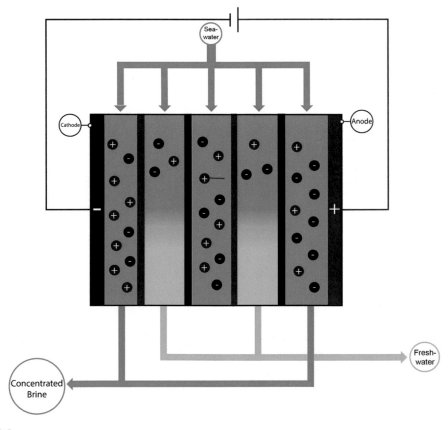

FIGURE 10.9

A schematic representation of a water desalination system using the electrodialysis (ED) method.

Table 10.4 Comparison of electrodialysis (ED) and reverse osmosis (RO), listing some advantages and disadvantages.

Type	Recovery capacity	Advantages	Disadvantages
RO	30%−60%	Lower energy and related costs; simple operation; fast start up; removal of other pollutants	Membrane replacement costs more; trained and qualified operators required; the possibility of mechanical failure at high pressures
ED	85%−94%	Maintenance is easier; operation pressure is lower; removal of other pollutants; membrane life is longer (around 7−10 years)	Periodic membrane cleaning required; possibility of leakage; not being able to remove bacteria; posttreatment is required for drinking water

Some membranes are also utilized in an ED system. They allow either anions or cations to pass through, while preventing some others from penetrating. In addition, some other membranes can be also used to filter other materials. To prevent material settlement on the surfaces of membranes, a reverse voltage can be used, which makes operating and maintenance easier.

Although the share of ED is smaller than RO, ED has some advantages in comparison with RO. One of the benefits of this kind of desalination is the ability to control the input and output easily (Mohtada & Toraj, 2008). A comparison of ED and RO, listing some advantages and disadvantages is provided in Table 10.4.

Review of the literature

AI and ML tools have become increasingly popular, and, considering this point, several studies have been carried out to simulate the performance of different types of desalination systems using AI and ML tools. In addition, another group of studies has considered a number of AI and ML tools, with the best model for prediction selected based on a number of error-related indicators. In some other investigations, one or more analyses, such as optimization, parametric study, sensitivity analysis, etc., have been done also. This section introduce recent research works in this field, which leads to obtaining a perspective from them and identifying any gaps in the research. Since a very good review work on the subject was provided by Al Aani et al. (2019) in 2019, here, the research works covered are in 2020 and 2021 are investigated, and for more information about the studies done before 2020, the mentioned review article should be referred to.

The performance of an RO unit that used wind energy was simulated by Cabrera et al. (2018). In that study, three ML approaches were employed. One was ANN, another was the support vector machine (SVM), while random forest (RF) was chosen as the third method. The prediction was done in two operating modes, while four parameters were selected as the output of modeling:

1. Inlet flow rate;
2. Flow rate of the water traveling through the membrane;

3. Conductivity of the water traveling through the membrane;
4. Pressure.

The performance prediction over a year was investigated, where SVM and RF were found to have a much better performance than ANN in the estimation of the studied indicators, offering around 5% more accurate results.

In the research work conducted by Kiran Naik et al. (2021), the performance of another renewable-based desalination system was investigated. In that study, the utilized renewable energy was solar energy. The system was designed in such a way that it could provide freshwater and regenerate desiccant at the same time. To analyze the system, a thermal model and *k*-nearest neighborhood, known as KNN, were utilized and validated using the data found in the literature. Then, by taking advantage of these, the optimal conditions of the system, to achieve the best conditions of two performance indicators, were found. One considered performance indicator was steam flux, while another was energy exchange. A number of working temperatures and pressures, as well as the received solar radiation, were taken into account as the input of modeling.

The performance of an innovative design for a solar still desalination system was simulated using different types of ANN in the investigation carried out by Sohani, Hoseinzadeh, Samiezadeh, and Verhaert (2021). The innovative design enjoyed side mirrors and tracking, which led to better performance compared to the conventional types. Prediction was done on a dynamic basis, which means it covered the operation during different months of the year. Basin temperature, as well as freshwater production, were selected as the output parameters. Three types of ANNs, namely, radial basis function (RBF), feedforward (FF), and backpropagation (BP) types were investigated. The results showed that RBF and FF had the foremost error-related criteria in the prediction of basin temperature and water production, respectively.

Faegh et al. (2021) simulated a heat pump which was coupled with an HDH desalination unit. Similar to the study of Sohani, Hoseinzadeh, Samiezadeh, and Verhaert (2021), three types of AI techniques were examined for modeling. They were RBF ANN, in addition to the multilayer perceptron (MLP) ANN and adaptive neurofuzzy inference systems (ANFIS). Models were developed for forecasting the ratio of gain output, as well as the heat transfer rate in the condenser and evaporator, using 180 series of data obtained from the experiments. The error analysis revealed that MLP ANN offered the best prediction accuracy for all three indicated performance criteria.

In another investigation, Kizhisseri et al. (2020) provided a prediction tool to estimate the capital cost of an RO plant. They used ANN, and trained, validated, and tested their found network by data obtained from 1806 large-scale RO plants. Six parameters were selected as the input for ANN, which were:

1. Daily freshwater production;
2. Type of feed water;
3. Year;
4. The location of the plant;
5. Type of unit;
6. Financing type.

The same type of desalination system, that is, RO technology, was also studied in the research work conducted by Choi et al. (2020). They developed models with the aim of accurate prediction of performance in a large-scale RO unit, in which there were complexities, including fouling issues. Among a variety of AI and ML tools, ANN and tree model (TM) were chosen, while the input data covered a number of effective parameters which could be measured easily, namely:

1. The working parameters, including time and input flow rate;
2. The water quality-related indicators, which were temperature of the input water and its total dissolved solids content.

There were also three output parameters, which were:

1. Input pressure;
2. Differential pressure;
3. Total dissolved solids of permeate.

The model development was done for long-term forecasting, and the error analysis showed that TM could be a better alternative than ANN. In fact, although they had relatively close error-related criteria, because it provided a mathematical function instead of a complex matrix structure, TM was preferred.

Modeling the performance of another type of membrane-based desalination technology, which worked based on vacuuming, was the subject of the studies carried out by Bagheri et al. (2020), Charrouf et al. (2020), and Yang et al. (2020a). For example, Yang et al. (2020a) took advantage of ANN and utilized 36 samples obtained from the experiment for model development. The temperature and flow rate of input water, as well as the length of the membrane, were considered as the input parameters, while the output parameters were energy consumption and flux of permeate. In that study, it was found that ANN could provide reliable performance within the whole investigated range of effective parameters.

Yeo et al. (2020) also utilized gradient boosting tree for prediction of membrane characteristics in an RO unit. The investigated membrane was a nanocomposite with low thickness. The modeling was done with the aim of determining two indicators, namely:

1. The passing rate of salt from the membrane;
2. Permeability of liquid.

The input parameters were:

1. The specifications of the membrane;
2. The imposed loading;
3. Particle size.

The developed ML approach was validated, and next, it was employed to discuss the possible opportunities to optimize the system.

The Internet of Things (IoT) is another AI- and ML-related tool that has been used to improve the performance of desalination units. As an example of such studies, Alshehri et al. (2021) utilized a new generation of the IoT to monitor, analyze, and optimize the performance of a number of desalination units with the aim of achieving the best possible conditions from the consumption of resources, such as solar energy and desalination resources. The data gathered by sensors and stored in a portal cloud space were employed, and an intelligence-based framework with decision-supporting ability was provided. The studies of Yaqub et al. (2019), Fu et al. (2020), and

Salam (2020) are other research works that have studied application of the IoT for water desalination installations.

In addition to the prediction of the performance criteria, such as those mentioned so far, AI and ML tools could be used for fault detection of desalination units. However, to the best of the authors' knowledge, the number of such research works is much lower. Taking part in such investigations, Achbi and Kechida (2020) employed integration of ANFIS and automata for accurate fault detection in a desalination plant. Their investigated system was an RO unit, while their approach was able to discover a variety of errors, including running and starting failures, valve and pump malfunctioning, and leakage issues. Moreover, Khirai et al. (2020) examined a decision tree and regression method to reveal a method for fault detection, in which the errors come from different issues, such as blocking, leakage, utility, devices, etc.

Selected case study from the literature

In this section, a case study is described and the details given to provide in-depth understanding of the process. The selected case study (Sohani, Hoseinzadeh, Samiezadeh, & Verhaert, 2021) is one of the last investigations by this research team on the topic.

The investigated system

The investigated system was a solar still desalination technology, which is illustrated in Fig. 10.5. In that system, the side mirrors and tracking technologies were utilized to receive the highest possible radiation from the sun. The system was originally proposed by Sohani, Hoseinzadeh, and Berenjkar (2021). Compared to a conventional solar still, in which there are no side mirrors or tracking technologies, the following enhancements were reported:

1. Daily freshwater production on a sample summer day: from 1.53 to 6.92 L;
2. Average efficiency on the sample summer day: from 28.11% to 54.29%;
3. Cost per liter (CPL): from 0.0289 to 0.0225 U$/L (despite the initial cost increase, the freshwater production goes up also, and the increase rate of the latter is more than that of the former).

The selected city

The data utilized for modeling using AI and ML tools were obtained through experiments over a year in Tehran, Iran. Iran is a country facing serious water shortages. Tehran, being the capital of Iran not only has a population of more than 10 million people (out of a total of population of 80 million), but also has much more severe drinking water supply issues than many other parts of Iran. Therefore, providing cheap methods like solar still desalination technologies could be very helpful for this city.

The utilized machine learning approaches

Showing high efficiency in several studies in the field, including those ones mentioned in the literature review section, ANN was chosen as the ML approach. Three different structures for ANN were considered, namely:

1. RBF;
2. FF;
3. BP.

Modeling was carried out for forecasting two main characteristics of the system, which were:

1. Water temperature in the basin;
2. Freshwater production.

ANN models were obtained using the developed codes using the MATLAB® software program. For each structure, several possibilities for the number of layers and neurons in each hidden layer, as well as transform and net functions, were examined, and by considering two error-related criteria, the best one for each structure was selected:

1. Mean absolute error (MAE);
2. Coefficient of determination (R^2).

Fig. 10.10 provides details of the stages done to develop ANN structures in a flowchart format. This figure was originally presented in one of the previous investigations of this research team, that is, Sohani et al. (2016).

The obtained results

As indicated, the best ANN was chosen for each output parameter by considering MAE and R^2 as the error-related criteria. The investigation showed that for the water temperature:

1. MAE: 4.47%, 3.56%, and 5.91% for RBF ANN, FF ANN, and BP ANN, respectively.
2. R^2: 0.956798, 0.963111, and 0.942567 for RBF ANN, FF ANN, and BP ANN, respectively.

Therefore, FF ANN was selected as the best prediction method for this case.
For freshwater production, the values were also:

1. MAE: 2.82%, 5.17%, and 5.25% for RBF ANN, FF ANN, and BP ANN, respectively.
2. R^2: 0.977057, 0.934889, and 0.934615 for RBF ANN, FF ANN, and BP ANN, respectively.

It was implied that RBF ANN was the best AI and ML tool for forecasting freshwater production.

Having determined the best data-driven model for each case, the accuracy of forecasting the monthly profiles of water temperature, as well as hourly and cumulative daily water production, was checked by plotting the error profiles. The monthly error profiles for the three indicated parameters are illustrated in Figs. 10.11−10.13, respectively.

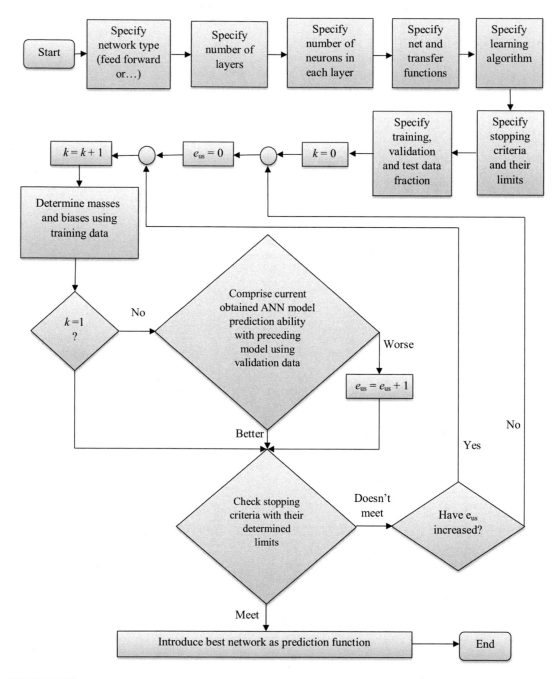

FIGURE 10.10

A flowchart reporting the stages carried out for developing an artificial neural network (ANN) model.

Reproduced with permission from: Sohani, A., Sayyaadi, H., Hasani Balyani, H., & Hoseinpoori, S. (2016). A novel approach using predictive models for performance analysis of desiccant enhanced evaporative cooling systems. Applied Thermal Engineering, 107, *227–252. https://doi.org/10.1016/j.applthermaleng.2016.06.121.*

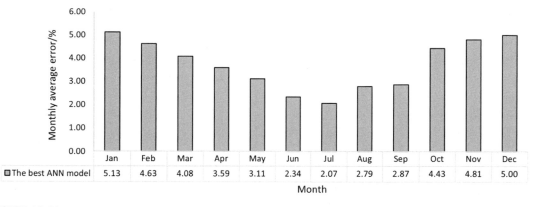

FIGURE 10.11

The monthly profiles of error in the estimation of water temperature.

Reproduced with permission from: Sohani, A., Hoseinzadeh, S., Samiezadeh, S., & Verhaert, I. (2021). Machine learning prediction approach for dynamic performance modeling of an enhanced solar still desalination system. Journal of Thermal Analysis and Calorimetry. https://doi.org/10.1007/s10973-021-10744-z.

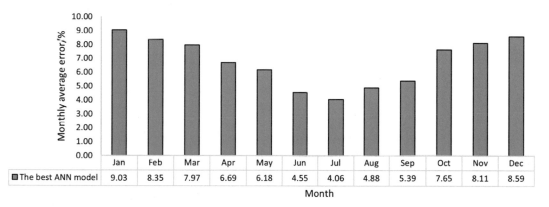

FIGURE 10.12

The monthly profiles of error in the estimation of water production in an hour.

Reproduced with permission from: Sohani, A., Hoseinzadeh, S., Samiezadeh, S., & Verhaert, I. (2021). Machine learning prediction approach for dynamic performance modeling of an enhanced solar still desalination system. Journal of Thermal Analysis and Calorimetry. https://doi.org/10.1007/s10973-021-10744-z.

The results demonstrated that the error levels in estimation of the three mentioned parameters were in the range of:

1. 2.07%–5.13% for water temperature;
2. 4.06%–9.03% for water production in an hour;
3. 2.41%–5.84% for water production in a day.

As a result, all the parameters could be precisely estimated by the foremost ANN structures.

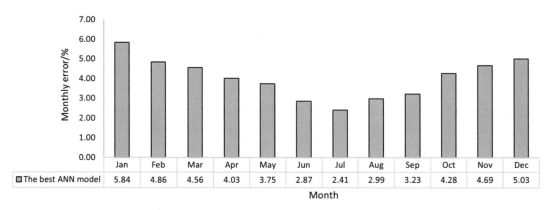

FIGURE 10.13

The monthly profiles of error in the estimation of water production in a day.

Reproduced with permission from: Sohani, A., Hoseinzadeh, S., Samiezadeh, S., & Verhaert, I. (2021). Machine learning prediction approach for dynamic performance modeling of an enhanced solar still desalination system. Journal of Thermal Analysis and Calorimetry. *https://doi.org/10.1007/s10973-021-10744-z.*

Conclusions

This chapter has presented a brief but extensive insight into water desalination technologies and recent investigations into them. After introducing the available standards, and various commercially developed technologies for desalination, the studies that have been recently carried out on the modeling of such systems using ML and AI tools were reviewed. The literature review highlighted that in addition to prediction, ML and AI have been employed for fault detection also. Moreover, ANN and tree-based modeling approaches were found to be the most popular AI and ML tools in the investigations for modeling. Additionally, it was found that there has been a strong tendency toward the application of new generations of AI- and ML-based methods, including the IoT.

References

Achbi, M. S., & Kechida, S. (2020). Methodology for monitoring and diagnosing faults of hybrid dynamic systems: A case study on a desalination plant. *Diagnostyka, 21*(1), 27−33.

Al Aani, S., Bonny, T., Hasan, S. W., & Hilal, N. (2019). Can machine language and artificial intelligence revolutionize process automation for water treatment and desalination? *Desalination, 458,* 84−96. Available from https://doi.org/10.1016/j.desal.2019.02.005.

Alshehri, M., Bhardwaj, A., Kumar, M., Mishra, S., & Gyani, J. (2021). Cloud and IoT based smart architecture for desalination water treatment. *Environmental Research, 195,* 110812. Available from https://doi.org/10.1016/j.envres.2021.110812.

Bagheri, A., Esfandiari, N., Honarvar, B., & Azdarpour, A. (2020). First principles vs artificial neural network modelling of a solar desalination system with experimental validation. *Mathematical and Computer Modelling of Dynamical Systems, 26*(5), 453−480.

Cabrera, P., Carta, J. A., González, J., & Melián, G. (2018). Wind-driven SWRO desalination prototype with and without batteries: A performance simulation using machine learning models. *Desalination Using Renewable Energy*, 435, 77−96. Available from https://doi.org/10.1016/j.desal.2017.11.044.

Charrouf, O., Betka, A., Abdeddaim, S., & Ghamri, A. (2020). Artificial neural network power manager for hybrid PV-wind desalination system. *Mathematics and Computers in Simulation*, 167, 443−460. Available from https://doi.org/10.1016/j.matcom.2019.09.005.

Choi, Y., Lee, Y., Shin, K., Park, Y., & Lee, S. (2020). Analysis of long-term performance of full-scale reverse osmosis desalination plant using artificial neural network and tree model. *Environmental Engineering Research*, 25(5), 763−770. Available from https://doi.org/10.4491/eer.2019.324.

Elsayed, M. L., Alharbi, S., & Chow, L. C. (2021). Utilization of waste heat from a commercial GT for freshwater production, cooling and additional power: Exergoeconomic analysis and optimization. *Desalination*, 513, 115127. Available from https://doi.org/10.1016/j.desal.2021.115127.

Faegh, M., Behnam, P., Shafii, M. B., & Khiadani, M. (2021). Development of artificial neural networks for performance prediction of a heat pump assisted humidification-dehumidification desalination system. *Desalination*, 508, 115052. Available from https://doi.org/10.1016/j.desal.2021.115052.

Fu, H., Manogaran, G., Wu, K., Cao, M., Jiang, S., & Yang, A. (2020). Intelligent decision-making of online shopping behavior based on internet of things. *International Journal of Information Management*, 50, 515−525. Available from https://doi.org/10.1016/j.ijinfomgt.2019.03.010.

Joshua, H., & Nazrul, I. (2015). Water pollution and its impact on the human health. *Journal of Environment and Human*, 2(1), 36−46. Available from https://doi.org/10.15764/EH.2015.01005.

Khirai, P., Shaikh, M., Kadole, A., Anehosur, U., & Gavali, A. (2020). Enhanced detection of faults in water desalination system using machine learning approaches. *Journal of Advances in Computational Intelligence Theory*, 2(2).

Kiran Naik, B., Chinthala, M., Patel, S., & Ramesh, P. (2021). Performance assessment of waste heat/solar driven membrane-based simultaneous desalination and liquid desiccant regeneration system using a thermal model and KNN machine learning tool. *Desalination*, 505, 114980. Available from https://doi.org/10.1016/j.desal.2021.114980.

Kizhisseri, M. I., Mohamed, M. M., & Hamouda, M. A. (2020). Prediction of capital cost of RO based desalination plants using machine learning approach. *E3S Web of Conferences*, 158(2), 06001. Available from https://doi.org/10.1051/e3sconf/202015806001.

Li, Z., & Jennings, A. (2017). Worldwide regulations of standard values of pesticides for human health risk control: A review. *International Journal of Environmental Research and Public Health*, 14(7), 826.

Louckes, D. P., Revelle, C. S., & Lynn, W. R. (1967). Linear programming models for water pollution control. *Management Science*, 14(4), B-166−B-181. Available from https://doi.org/10.1287/mnsc.14.4.B166.

Lucy, C., Ludovic, D., Jianhua, Z., Jun-de, L., Mikel, D., Juan, G., & Stephen, G. (2013). Advances in membrane distillation for water desalination and purification applications. *Water*, 5(1), 94−196. Available from https://doi.org/10.3390/w5010094.

Mohtada, S., & Toraj, M. (2008). Sea water desalination using electrodialysis. *Desalination*, 221(1−3), 440−447. Available from https://doi.org/10.1016/j.desal.2007.01.103.

Rajesh, M., Gaurav, M., Verma, O. P., & Shishir, S. (2018). Modelling and simulation of desalination process using artificial neural network: A review. *Desalination and Water Treatment*, 122, 351−364.

Salam, A. (2020). *Internet of things in water management and treatment. Internet of things* (pp. 273−298). Springer. Available from https://doi.org/10.1007/978-3-030-35291-2_9.

Sayed, E. T., Shehata, N., Abdelkareem, M. A., & Atieh, M. A. (2020). Recent progress in environmentally friendly bio-electrochemical devices for simultaneous water desalination and wastewater treatment. *Science of the Total Environment*, 748, 141046. Available from https://doi.org/10.1016/j.scitotenv.2020.141046.

Sohani, A., Hoseinzadeh, S., & Berenjkar, K. (2021). Experimental analysis of innovative designs for solar still desalination technologies: An in-depth technical and economic assessment. *Journal of Energy Storage*, *33*, 101862. Available from https://doi.org/10.1016/j.est.2020.101862.

Sohani, A., Hoseinzadeh, S., Samiezadeh, S., & Verhaert, I. (2021). Machine learning prediction approach for dynamic performance modeling of an enhanced solar still desalination system. *Journal of Thermal Analysis and Calorimetry*. Available from https://doi.org/10.1007/s10973-021-10744-z.

Sohani, A., Sayyaadi, H., Hasani Balyani, H., & Hoseinpoori, S. (2016). A novel approach using predictive models for performance analysis of desiccant enhanced evaporative cooling systems. *Applied Thermal Engineering*, *107*, 227–252. Available from https://doi.org/10.1016/j.applthermaleng.2016.06.121.

Wacławek, S., Lutze, H. V., Grübel, K., Padil, V. V., Černík, M., & Dionysiou, D. D. (2017). Chemistry of persulfates in water and wastewater treatment: A review. *Chemical Engineering Journal*, *330*, 44–62.

Warsinger, D. M., Mistry, K. H., Nayar, K. G., Chung, H. W., & Lienhard, J. H. (2015). Entropy generation of desalination powered by variable temperature waste heat. *Entropy*, *17*(11), 7530–7566. Available from https://doi.org/10.3390/e17117530.

Yang, C., Peng, X., Zhao, Y., Wang, X., Fu, J., Liu, K., Li, Y., & Li, P. (2020a). Prediction model to analyze the performance of VMD desalination process. *Computers & Chemical Engineering*, *132*, 106619. Available from https://doi.org/10.1016/j.compchemeng.2019.106619.

Yang, C., Peng, X., Zhao, Y., Wang, X., Fu, J., Liu, K., Li, Y., & Li, P. (2020b). Prediction model to analyze the performance of VMD desalination process. *Computers & Chemical Engineering*, *132*, 106619. Available from https://doi.org/10.1016/j.compchemeng.2019.106619.

Yaqub, U., Al-Nasser, A., & Sheltami, T. (2019). Implementation of a hybrid wind-solar desalination plant from an Internet of Things (IoT) perspective on a network simulation tool. *Applied Computing and Informatics*, *15*(1), 7–11. Available from https://doi.org/10.1016/j.aci.2018.03.001.

Yeo, C. S. H., Xie, Q., Wang, X., & Zhang, S. (2020). Understanding and optimization of thin film nanocomposite membranes for reverse osmosis with machine learning. *Journal of Membrane Science*, *606*, 118135. Available from https://doi.org/10.1016/j.memsci.2020.118135.

Zarei, T., & Behyad, R. (2019). Predicting the water production of a solar seawater greenhouse desalination unit using multi-layer perceptron model. *Solar Energy*, *177*, 595–603. Available from https://doi.org/10.1016/j.solener.2018.11.059.

Zubair, S. M., Antar, M. A., Elmutasim, S. M., & Lawal, D. U. (2018). Performance evaluation of humidification-dehumidification (HDH) desalination systems with and without heat recovery options: An experimental and theoretical investigation. *Desalination*, *436*, 161–175. Available from https://doi.org/10.1016/j.desal.2018.02.018.

A long short-term memory deep learning approach for river water temperature prediction

Salim Heddam[1], Sungwon Kim[2], Ali Danandeh Mehr[3], Mohammad Zounemat-Kermani[4], Ahmed Elbeltagi[5,6], Anurag Malik[7] and Ozgur Kisi[8,9]

[1]*Faculty of Science, Agronomy Department, Hydraulics Division, Laboratory of Research in Biodiversity Interaction Ecosystem and Biotechnology, University 20 Août 1955, Skikda, Algeria* [2]*Department of Railroad Construction and Safety Engineering, Dongyang University, Yeongju, Republic of Korea* [3]*Department of Civil Engineering, Antalya Bilim University, Antalya, Turkey* [4]*Department of Water Engineering, Shahid Bahonar University of Kerman, Kerman, Iran* [5]*College of Environmental and Resource Sciences, Zhejiang University, Hangzhou, China* [6]*Agricultural Engineering Department, Faculty of Agriculture, Mansoura University, Mansoura, Egypt* [7]*Punjab Agricultural University, Regional Research Station, Bathinda, India* [8]*Department of Civil Engineering, School of Technology, Ilia State University, Tbilisi, Georgia* [9]*Institute of Research and Development, Duy Tan University, Da Nang, Vietnam*

Introduction

Water temperature (T_w) is an important component of the freshwater system (Zaidel et al., 2020). Its importance is underlined by its variability and change in space and time, and by its control of several ecological processes, and it has a significant impact on the thermal habitat conditions in freshwater systems (Daniels & Danner, 2020), and a large number of physical and chemical processes are governed by T_w (Bogan et al., 2003). T_w is considered to be a key environmental variable that drives a large number of physical and chemical processes, and has a beneficial effect for aquatic species (King & Neilson, 2019). In addition, it has been reported that the biochemical quality of drinking water may be influenced positively or negatively by the amplitude of variation in T_w (Michel et al., 2020). River T_w depends on interactions of heat fluxes and the advective process occurring along the channel with river flow (Fabris et al., 2020). In general T_w has a strong diurnal cycle and is highly correlated to the air temperature (T_a). While T_w can be either higher or lower, it is more easily related to T_a, hence it needs to be considered as a whole that estimating T_w should be formulated based on T_a. Several approaches have been proposed for an accurate estimation of T_w, such as parametric and nonparametric (i.e., statistical) models, deterministic models (Caissie, 2006), and more recently machine learning models (Zhu & Piotrowski, 2020). Typical regression models rely on a linear regression formula between T_a and T_w (Seyedhashemi et al., 2020). Presently, the only machines learning models available for T_w estimation are through a direct link between T_w, T_a and river discharge (Q), which were used whether separately or combined together, and sometimes the periodicity (i.e., year, month, and day number) can be added to the T_a and Q as input variable for further improving the performances of machines learning models (Heddam et al., 2020).

Current Trends and Advances in Computer-Aided Intelligent Environmental Data Engineering.
DOI: https://doi.org/10.1016/B978-0-323-85597-6.00015-X

Benyahya et al. (2008) proposed two approaches for predicting mean weekly maximum river T_w: (1) the k-nearest neighbors' method (k-NN) and (2) the periodic autoregressive model with exogenous variables (PARX). The models were developed using data collected from Nivelle River, France, and two variables were selected as input variables, namely T_a and river Q. From the obtained results the k-NN model was more accurate compared to the PARX with low root mean square error (RMSE) and a high correlation between simulated and predicted T_w data. In a study conducted by Mohseni and Stefan (1999) using data measured on a weekly time scale at two rivers in the United States, namely, the Salt Fork of the Arkansas River and the Partridge River above Colby Lake, it was demonstrated that the T_w can be related to the T_a using a regression model, and the weekly equilibrium T_w/T_a relationship takes the form of an S-shaped function. Mohseni et al. (1998) developed a nonlinear regression model for predicting weekly stream T_w as a function of weekly T_a. The proposed model was based on logistic function having four parameters related to the maximum, minimum, and T_a temperature. By applying the proposed models for simulating T_w for more than 584 stations, they demonstrate that the T_w was highly fitted with a determination coefficient (R^2) superior to 0.90. Morrill et al. (2005) applied linear and nonlinear regression models for estimating river T_w to T_a using a large dataset from 43 stations located in 13 different countries including the United States and in Europe. The proposed models were validated using the R^2, Nash–Sutcliffe coefficient of efficiency (NSE) and the RMSE. They concluded that both linear and nonlinear regression equations can accurately fit T_w curves; however, the mathematical relation linking the T_a to T_w was more suitable to be a nonlinear relation rather than a linear relation. Pike et al. (2013) proposed a stochastic dynamics model called the RAFT and applied it for forecasting T_w at Sacramento River in California, United States, and demonstrated that the model achieved high performances in T_w prediction at 72 hours and also RAFT was able to simulate the river T_w fluctuation. In another study, Caldwell et al. (2013) used the generalized linear model (GLM) coupled with the k-NN for daily river T_w prediction. The proposed approach was applied using data collected from the Methow River near Winthrop, WA, United States. The river Q, precipitation, and maximal and minimal air temperatures (T_m, T_x) were used as input variables. Simulation results showed the high abilities of the GLM model for predicting daily T_w with NSE values reached 0.98, and also it was demonstrated that T_m and T_x were the most significant variables influencing the daily river T_w.

An in-depth analysis of the machine learning models proposed in earlier literature suggests that deep learning paradigms were rarely proposed for T_w prediction, which is one of the major motivations for the present study. For example, Wenxian et al. (2010) applied a hybrid model: the multilayer perceptron artificial neural network (MLPNN) and the particle swarm optimization (PSO) algorithm (PSO-MLPNN) for predicting monthly river T_w using data collected at the Yichang station in the middle reaches of the Yangtze River, China. The authors reported the high capacities of the new PSO-MLPNN model in predicting T_w, which significantly contributed to the increased overall prediction accuracies and to the decrease in prediction errors which were much lower than 3%. Hong and Bhamidimarri (2012) introduced a new model called the dynamic neurofuzzy local modeling system (DNFLMS) for modeling daily river T_w measured at the Huntly power station, Waikato River, south of New Zealand city, Auckland. The authors selected 13 variables for developing the model and the gamma test was used for feature extraction analysis and the best input combination selection. Compared to the MLPNN and the adaptive network-based fuzzy inference system (ANFIS), the best accuracies were achieved using the DNFLMS with an RMSE value of 0.240

compared to 0.258 and 0.363 obtained using the ANFIS and MLPNN models. Voza and Vuković (2018) used the MLPNN model for predicting the river T_w in the Morava River basin (Serbia) and reported moderate to good accuracies with an R^2 ranging from 0.648 to 0.839. Grbić et al. (2013) applied the Gaussian process regression (GPR) model for predicting daily river T_w at the Drava River, Croatia. The GPR model was calibrated and validated using T_a and the river Q, and the obtained results were compared to those obtained using the linear regression (LR), multiple linear regression (MLR), logistic regression (LG), stochastic (SR), and time-series (TR) models. The best accuracies were achieved using the GPR model with an NSE value of 0.984 compared to 0.866, 0.924, 0.876, 0.934, and 0.974 obtained using the LR, MLR, LG, TR, and SR models. In another study, Sahoo et al. (2009) examined the robustness of three models, namely, the MLPNN, the MLR, and the chaotic nonlinear dynamic algorithms (CNDA) models for modeling river T_w using solar radiation (SR) and T_a. High accuracies were achieved using the MLPNN model with a correlation coefficient reaching 0.98 and also it was highlighted that the inclusion of the SR contributed slightly to the improvement of the model performances. Several other machine learning models can be found in the literature, that is, the extremely randomized trees (Heddam et al., 2020); MLPNN with wavelet decomposition (Zhu et al., 2020); ANFIS model (Zhu, Heddam, Nyarko, Hadzima-Nyarko, Piccolroaz, Wu, 2019); and extreme learning machines (Zhu & Heddam, 2019; Zhu, Heddam, Wu, Dai, Jia, 2019).

Over the last few years, machine learning (Danandeh Mehr & Nourani, 2018; Hrnjica et al., 2019; Olyaie et al., 2017) and deep learning paradigms have received great attention from researchers worldwide, and the number of applications has greatly increased over the past few years. The long short-term memory (LSTM) deep learning model is one of the best and well-known deep learning models, with a large number of applications being found in the literature. The LSTM has been applied successfully for $PM_{2.5}$ concentration prediction (Chang et al., 2020; Zhang, Gao, Liu, & Zheng, 2020); solar radiation forecasting (Zang et al., 2020); predictions for COVID-19 (Shahid et al., 2020); prediction of the nutrient removal efficiency in a full-scale sewage treatment plant (Yaqub et al., 2020); and for forecasting short-term daily reference evapotranspiration (Yin et al., 2020). To the best of our knowledge no study has reported the application of the LSTM model for river water temperature estimation. Therefore the aims of the present study were:

1. To demonstrate how the LSTM deep learning model improves the prediction accuracies of the standalone machine learning using only the T_a as a predictor.
2. To examine to what degree the periodicity (i.e., year, month, and the day of the year corresponding to the number between 1 and 366) contributes to the improvement of the proposed machine learning models.

Materials and methods

Study area and data

In this study, we selected data from four stations. The selected stations were: (1) United States Geological Survey (USGS) 01104430 at Hobbs BK below Cambridge Res near Kendall Green, Middlesex County, MA, United States (latitude 42°23′53″, longitude 71°16′26″ NAD27), (2) USGS 14207200 at Tualatin River at Oswego Dam, near West Linn, Clackamas County, OR, United States (latitude 45°21′24″, longitude 122°41′02″ NAD27), (3) USGS 422302071083801 at, Fresh

Pond in Gate House at Cambridge, Middlesex County, MA, United States (latitude 42°23′02″, longitude 71°08′38″ NAD83), and (4) USGS 422622122004000 at, USGS 422622122004000 Mid-North-Lower-MDNL, Klamath County, OR, United States (latitude 42°26′21.5″, longitude 122°00′40.0″ NAD27). The data from these four selected stations were used to build machine learning models for predicting daily river T_w as a function of the daily T_a. The lengths of the dataset varied from one station to another ranging from 1746 to 9607 patterns. For each station, the dataset was randomly divided into two subgroups: one for the calibration period (70%) and the remaining part (30%) for validation. Statistical parameters of T_w and T_a are reported in Table 11.1.

Performance assessment of the models

The performances of the developed models were evaluated using four statistical indices, namely, RMSE, mean absolute error (MAE), correlation coefficient (R), and NSE, calculated as follows:

$$\text{RMSE} = \sqrt{\frac{1}{N}\sum_{i=1}^{N}\left[\left(Tw_{\text{obs},i}\right)-\left(Tw_{\text{est},i}\right)\right]^2}, 0 \leq \text{RMSE} < +\infty \tag{11.1}$$

$$\text{MAE} = \frac{1}{N}\sum_{i=1}^{N}|Tw_{\text{est},i}-Tw_{\text{obs},i}|0 \leq \text{MAE} < +\infty \tag{11.2}$$

$$R = \frac{\sum_{i=1}^{N}\left(Tw_{\text{obs},i}-\overline{Tw_{\text{obs}}}\right)\left(Tw_{\text{est},i}-\overline{Tw_{\text{est}}}\right)}{\sqrt{\sum_{i=1}^{N}\left(Tw_{\text{obs},i}-\overline{Tw_{\text{obs}}}\right)^2\sum_{i=1}^{N}(Tw_{\text{est},i}-\overline{Tw_{\text{est}}})^2}}, -1 \leq R \leq +1 \tag{11.3}$$

$$\text{NSE} = 1 - \left[\frac{\sum_{i=1}^{N}(Tw_{\text{obs},i}-Tw_{\text{est},i})^2}{\sum_{i=1}^{N}(Tw_{\text{obs},i}-\overline{Tw_{\text{obs}}})^2}\right], -\infty < \text{NSE} \leq +1 \tag{11.4}$$

In these, Tw_{obs} and Tw_{est} specify the observed and estimated daily river water temperature for ith observations, N shows the number of data points, and $\overline{Tw_{\text{obs}}}$ and $\overline{Tw_{\text{est}}}$ are the mean measured, and mean estimated T_w, respectively.

Methodology

Gaussian process regression

Rasmussen and Williams (2006) pioneered the idea of GPR based on two functions, that is, covariance and mean to solve the nonlinear regression and classification problems. In recent times, the GPR model has received extensive application in numerous engineering fields (Sihag et al., 2017; Sihag, Esmaeilbeiki, Singh, & Pandhiani, 2020; Sihag, Singh, Sepah Vand, & Mehdipour, 2020; Yaseen et al., 2021). In GPR, the covariance function is utilized to describe a prior probability distribution over function space. Overall, a group of random variables (RVs), any finite number of which have

Table 11.1 Summary statistics of water and air temperatures for the three stations.

Variables	Subset	Unit	X_{mean}	X_{max}	X_{min}	S_x	C_v	R
USGS 01104430								
T_w	Training	°C	12.420	26.700	0.200	7.536	0.607	1.000
	Validation	°C	12.379	26.900	0.700	7.680	0.620	1.000
	All data	°C	12.408	26.900	0.200	7.579	0.611	1.000
T_a	Training	°C	10.358	29.700	− 18.000	9.732	0.940	0.891
	Validation	°C	10.017	28.300	− 16.200	9.723	0.971	0.895
	All data	°C	10.256	29.700	− 18.000	9.730	0.949	0.892
USGS 14207200								
T_w	Training	°C	13.663	25.700	1.400	5.733	0.420	1.000
	Validation	°C	13.638	25.800	1.400	5.694	0.417	1.000
	All data	°C	13.656	25.800	1.400	5.721	0.419	1.000
T_a	Training	°C	11.772	29.000	− 7.200	6.014	0.511	0.920
	Validation	°C	11.764	27.300	− 5.200	5.906	0.502	0.917
	All data	°C	11.769	29.000	− 7.200	5.982	0.508	0.919
USGS 422302071083801								
T_w	Training	°C	13.046	28.300	0.500	8.484	0.650	1.000
	Validation	°C	12.886	28.200	0.200	8.552	0.664	1.000
	All data	°C	12.998	28.300	0.200	8.504	0.654	1.000
T_a	Training	°C	10.860	31.600	− 16.000	9.623	0.886	0.907
	Validation	°C	10.519	30.900	− 15.900	9.683	0.920	0.908
	All data	°C	10.758	31.600	− 16.000	9.641	0.896	0.907
USGS 422622122004000								
T_w	Training	°C	18.591	24.400	9.400	3.014	0.162	1.000
	Validation	°C	18.421	24.500	10.800	2.986	0.162	1.000
	All data	°C	18.540	24.500	9.400	3.006	0.162	1.000
T_a	Training	°C	16.777	25.800	2.600	4.350	0.259	0.839
	Validation	°C	16.531	26.000	2.200	4.505	0.272	0.850
	All data	°C	16.704	26.000	2.200	4.396	0.263	0.842

Note: C_v, Coefficient of variation; X_{max}, maximum; X_{mean}, mean; X_{min}, minimum; R, coefficient of correlation; S_x, standard deviation; T_a, air temperature; T_w, river water temperature.

a joint Gaussian distribution (JGD) is known as the Gaussian process (GP) (Schulz et al., 2018). In GP the mean and covariance functions are expressed as (Rasmussen & Williams, 2006):

$$f(y) \sim \mathrm{GP}\big(m\{y\}, k\{y, y'\}\big) \tag{11.5}$$

In which, f = distribution function (or signal), y = input variable, m = mean function of all the distribution functions estimated at y by setting $m(y) = 0$, and k is the covariance function at different inputs points, that is, between y and y'. Both mean and covariance are mathematically described by Eqs. (11.6) and (11.7):

$$m(y) = E(f\{y\})$$ (11.6)

$$k(y, y') = E[(f\{y\} - my)(f\{y'\} - my')]$$ (11.7)

In which, k = kernel of the GP (Jäkel et al., 2007). A variety of kernel functions including radial basis kernel function (RBF), polynomial, and Person VII universal kernel functions are available but the choice of a suitable one largely depends on the degree of flatness and expected patterns in the data. RBF is one of the popular functions to fulfill the earlier criteria and defined as (Schulz et al., 2018; Yaseen et al., 2021):

$$k(y, y') = \sigma_f^2 \exp\left(-\frac{y - y'^2}{2\lambda^2}\right)$$ (11.8)

Here, σ_f^2, and λ are the signal-variance and length-scale hyperparameters. Once the mean and kernel functions are elected then GP can be used to draw prior function values, along with posterior function values restricted upon the earlier observations. For more details about the theory and formulation of GPR refer to Rasmussen and Williams (2006) and Schulz et al. (2018).

Gene expression programming

In computer programming, gene expression programming (GEP) is an automatic problem-solving algorithm in which Darwin's principle of "survival of the fittest" is used to find and improve the best solution among various combinations of potential solutions, aka chromosomes. In the classic genetic programming (GP) developed by Koza (1994), each chromosome is represented by a tree structure with a root node, inner nodes, and terminal nodes (leaves), however, a GEP chromosome has a fixed-length string composed of a head h and tail t with different lengths and functionalities (Ferreira, 2001). The fundamentals of GP and GEP as well as their applications in water engineering have been reviewed by Danandeh Mehr et al. (2018). Therefore only a brief overview of GEP is given here in order to secure the integrity of the methodologies used in this study.

Like a classic GP algorithm, GEP begins with the creation of an initial population of chromosomes. The task is carried out via random selection of input variables and functions. Then, programs are evolved through the successive generation of new programs through reproduction, mutation, and crossover. The fitness of each program is determined by a specific objective function. Considering fitness values, the modeler can determine to iterate or terminate the evolution of new programs. Fig. 11.1 shows an example of a GEP model and its tree representation. To develop GEP-based models/solutions for a variety of regression or classification problems, software packages such as GeneXproTools, GEPPY, and gepR are available. GeneXproTools 5.0 (Ferriera, 2006) was used in this study.

Online sequential extreme learning machine

Extreme learning machines (ELMs) can be described as upgraded models of single hidden layer feedforward networks (SLFNs) (Huang et al., 2006). However, unlike the back

Chromosome1 : -2*2a22a2
Chromosome2 : *Ln 2+a222a
Linking function: +

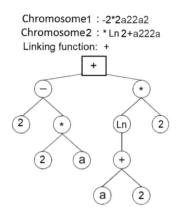

FIGURE 11.1

A gene expression programming model comprising two chromosomes and the addition linking function.

propagation (BP) algorithm in conventional feedforward artificial neural networks (ANNs), an ELM applies a random training methodology for the generation of hidden weights and biases for the tuning procedure of the network. Using this strategy, the output weights and biases are calculated in a single step by engaging the generalized Moore−Penrose pseudoinverse. As a result, the training speed of the ELM is much faster in comparison to the conventional BP algorithm in ordinary ANNs. The online sequential extreme learning machine (OSELM) was developed based on the ELM method using additive radial basis function (RFB) hidden nodes.

In the OSELM, N arbitrary independent samples $(x_i, t_i) \in R^n \times R^n$ are used for training an SLFN with L number of hidden nodes. Here, x_i is the training parameters and t_i stands for the target parameters. The target output can be determined by introducing a_i as the input weight vector and b_i as the biases of the ith hidden node, according to Eq. (11.9) (Scardapane et al., 2014; Zounemat-Kermani et al., 2020).

$$f_L(x_j) = \sum_{i=1}^{L} \beta_j G(a_i, b_i, x_i) = t_j, j = 1, 2, \ldots, N \tag{11.9}$$

where β_i denotes the output weight vector of the ith hidden node, and $G(a_i, b_i x_i)$ stands for the activation function, defined as follows:

$$G(a_i, b_i, x_i) = g(a_i.x_j + b_i), b_i \in R \tag{11.10}$$

The training process of the OSELM includes two main stages, including an initialization stage and an online sequential learning stage. In the initialization stage, a small training dataset is trained based on a fixed or varying chunk size on a chunk-by-chunk (one-by-one) block of data. Considering an SLFN with L hidden neurons, the data in an OSELM are introduced sequentially in the form of:

$$M = \left\{ (x_i, t_i), x_i \in R^n, t_i \in R^m, i = 1, \ldots, N \right\}, M_0 = \{x_i, t_i\}_{i=1}^{N_0} \not\subset M, \text{ and } N_0 \geq L \tag{11.11}$$

Stage I: In the initialization stage, some parts (a chunk) of the training data, which are denoted as M, are utilized to begin the learning procedure, and involve four steps:

1. First, the input weights and biases are randomly assigned for the range of $i = 1, \ldots, L$.
2. Subsequently, the initial hidden layer output matrix, H_0, is calculated:

$$H_0 = \begin{bmatrix} G(a_1, b_1, x_1) & \cdots & G(a_L, b_L, x_L) \\ \vdots & \cdots & \vdots \\ G(a_i, b_i, x_{N_0}) & \cdots & G(a_L, b_L, x_{N_0}) \end{bmatrix}_{N_0 \times L} \tag{11.12}$$

3. In the third step, the initial output weights β^0 are estimated using the formula:

$$\beta^0 = P_0 H_0^T T_0 \tag{11.13}$$

where

$$T_0 = \left[t_1, \ldots, t_{N_0}\right]^T_{N_0 \times m}, P_0 = \left(H_0^T H_0\right)^{-1}, \text{ and } K_0 = P_0^{-1} = H_0^T H_0 \tag{11.14}$$

4. In this step, the number of chunks in the network, k parameter, is set to zero ($k = 0$).

Stage II: In the second stage, known as the online sequential learning (OSL) stage, a new chunk of sample dataset, $(k+1)^{th}$, is considered.

$$M_{k+1} = \left\{(x_i + t_i)\right\}_{i = \left(\sum_{j=0}^{k} N_j\right)+1}^{\sum_{j=0}^{k+1} N_j} \tag{11.15}$$

where M_{k+1} indicates the quantity of sample data in the $(k+1)^{th}$ chunk. This stage involves three steps:

1. In the first step, the partial hidden layer output matrix H_{k+1} is determined:

$$H_{k+1} = \begin{bmatrix} G\left(a_1, b_1, x_{\left(\sum_{j=0}^{k} N_j\right)+1}\right) & \cdots & \left(a_L, b_L, x_{\left(\sum_{j=0}^{k} N_j\right)+1}\right) \\ \vdots & \cdots & \vdots \\ G\left(a_1, b_1, x_{\left(\sum_{j=0}^{k+1} N_j\right)}\right) & \cdots & G\left(a_L, b_L, x_{\left(\sum_{j=0}^{k+1} N_j\right)}\right) \end{bmatrix}_{N_{k+1} \times L} \tag{11.16}$$

2. In this step, the output weights (β^{K+1}) are calculated as follows:

$$\beta^{K+1} = \beta^K + K_{k+1}^{-1} H_{k+1}^T \left(T_{k+1} - H_{k+1}\beta^k\right) \tag{11.17}$$

where

$$T_{k+1} = \left[t_{\left(\sum_{j=0}^{k} N_j\right)+1}, \ldots, t_{\left(\sum_{j=0}^{k+1} N_j\right)}\right]^T_{N_{k+1} \times m}, K_{k+1} = K_k + H_{k+1}^T H_{k+1} \tag{11.18}$$

To avoid dealing with inverting matrices during the recursive process, such as K_{k+1}^{-1}, the least-squares solution defined as follows can be employed:

$$K_{k+1}^{-1} = K_k^{-1} - K_k^{-1} K_{k+1}^T \left(I + H_{k+1} K_k^{-1} H_{k+1}^T\right)^{-1} H_{k+1} K_k^{-1} \tag{11.19}$$

$$P_{k+1} = K_{k+1}^{-1} \tag{11.20}$$

$$P_{k+1} = P_k - P_k H_{k+1}^T \left(I + H_{k+1} P_k H_{k+1}^T\right)^{-1} H_{k+1} P_k \tag{11.21}$$

$$\beta^{K+1} = \beta^K + P_{k+1} H_{k+1}^T \left(T_{k+1} - H_{k+1} \beta^k\right) \tag{11.22}$$

In the final step, k is set as $k = k + 1$.

By returning to step 2 of the second stage (the OSL stage), this process will be repeatedly continued until the last chunk has arrived.

Support vector regression

The support vector machines (SVMs) were developed by Vapnik (2000) and mainly based on statistical and mathematical learning theory that use so-called structural risk minimization (Smola & Schölkopf, 2004; Vapnik, 2000). The SVM focused on regression problems are called support vector regression (SVR). From a mathematical point of view, a nonlinear approximation function linking a set of independent variables (the input: x_i) to one dependent variable (the output: Y_i) is achieved by projection in a high-dimensional feature space, and a linear function is constructed instead of a nonlinear problem (Balasundaram & Prasad, 2020). The linear function linking x_i to y_i can be formulated as follows:

$$y = f(x, w) = \sum_{i=1}^{m} w_i \varphi_i(x) + \lambda = w^T \phi(X) + \lambda \tag{11.23}$$

where y is the calculated value of the dependent variable or the output of the model, $w = [w_1, \ldots, w_n]$ is the weight vector, λ is the bias term, φ is the nonlinear mapping function, and ϕ is the nonlinear kernel function, generally the sigmoid, the radial basis function, or the polynomial kernel function (Lee et al., 2020; Xue et al., 2020). The radial basis function is the most commonly and widely used kernel function for the SVR model. During the model-building process, the goal will be to identify the best set of w_i and the correct nonlinear function (Kavaklioglu, 2011; Ko & Lee, 2013).

Long short-term memory

LSTM represents an artificial recurrent neural network (ARNN) used in the deep learning field, as reported by Zhang, Gao, Liu, and Zheng (2020). The RNN considers a form of ANN where a recurrent structure is created by links between hidden nodes. The original ARNN structure, namely, a vanilla ARNN, contains recurrent neural network chains, where each ARNN module comprises a hyperbolic tangent activation function layer sole structure (Choi, Cho, Kim, 2020; Choi, Lee, Kong, 2020). As the building unit of the RNN layer, which is commonly called the LSTM network, the LSTM unit is used. LSTM helps RNN to remember its input for a long time. The LSTM network solves the issue of RNN generating a gradient explosion when long time-series prediction is processed because the memory unit is connected to the LSTM network neurons to detect the effective data capacity used, which is superlative for the processing and forecasting significant events in long-term periods and time-series delays. When a message reaches the LSTM network, it can be decided if, according to the rules, it is helpful. The data only conforming to the algorithm rules will be left, while the incompatible information will be neglected through the forgetting gate.

Eq. (11.1) and Fig. 11.1 indicate that the current state h_{t-1} and input X_t are affected by the secret state h_t, which is modified within the RNN (Colah's Blog, 2015). The sequence data can be processed efficiently by the RNN structure, since the past information can influence the future as follows:

$$h_t = f_w(h_{t-1}, x_t)$$ (11.24)

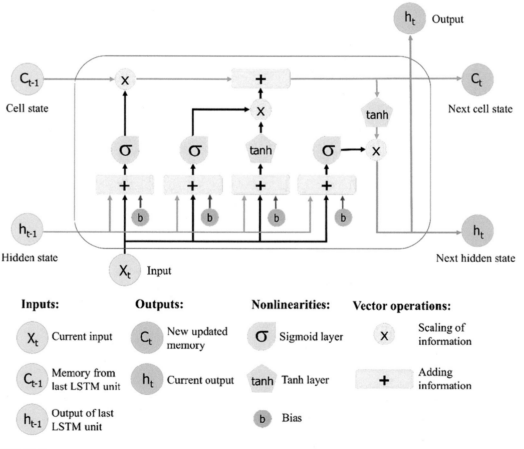

FIGURE 11.2

Structure of the long short-term memory neural network.

A standard LSTM layout has one cell and three gates divided into an input, a forget, and an output, respectively. Over nonregular time intervals, the cell recalls values and the three gates control the datasets into and out of the cell. Each gate has a specific function as follows: (1) the forget gate estimates the size of past data needs to be derelict and to evaluate the output value between 0 and 1, it receives h_{t-1} of the unseen state and input data x_t by applying the activation function of sigmoid, (2) the input gate estimates the volume of information required to recall. This gate also uses the same function of the forget gate with h_{t-1} and input x_t, and also implements the matrix operation of Hadamard product beside the hyperbolic tangent to input variables, (3) the output gate considers an interior gate that determines the output summation to the existing state. The active tan h function is utilized to identify the information of cell state that has been modified in advance, and the ht value represents the existing outcome and works as h_{t-1} in the following sequence functions, and (4) this arrangement minimizes information loss and facilitates the data distribution to all series. The LSTM structural feature allows the problem of long-term dependence to be solved and has been applied tthe o process the sequential data (Choi, Cho, Kim, 2020; Choi, Lee, Kong, 2020; Huang et al., 2020; Zhang, Zhang, Zhao, & Lian, 2020) (Fig. 11.2).

Multiple linear regression

The MLR models can be formulated as follows:

$$Y = \beta_0 + \beta_1 x_1 + \beta_2 x_2 + \beta_i x_i \tag{11.25}$$

β_i are the parameters of the MLR model, Y is the dependent variable (T_w), and x_i were the independent variables.

Results and discussion
USGS 01104430 station

Computed precision of applied models during training and validation stages is displayed in Table 11.2 for the USGS 01104430 station. Bold numbers show the values of superior precision during training and validation stages. It can be seen from Table 11.2 that the SVR1 model ($R = 0.982$, NSE $= 0.964$, RMSE $= 1.451°C$, and MAE $= 1.079°C$ for validation stage) was the optimized model during training and validation stages. However, the MLR2 model showed the worst achievement during training and validation stages. Also, a simple comparison between model scenarios 1 (i.e., using the air temperature and temporal indicators) and 2 (i.e., using only the air temperature) provided that covering the temporal indicators (i.e., year, months, and day number) to the air temperature (T_a) improved the computed precision of applied models during training and validation stages. The scatter diagrams between the measured and calculated water temperature (T_w) values utilizing model scenario 1 (i.e., OSELM1, LSTM1, GEP1, SVR1, GPR1, and MLR1) for USGS 01104430 station are illustrated in Fig. 11.3A−F covering the individual matching line ($y = x$), simple linear equation, and R^2 value, respectively. It can be considered from the scatter diagrams that the calculated values corresponding to the SVR1 model followed

Table 11.2 Performances of different models at the USGS 01104430 station.

Models	Training				Validation			
	R	NSE	RMSE	MAE	*R*	NSE	RMSE	MAE
OSELM1	**0.984**	**0.969**	1.331	1.045	**0.979**	**0.958**	1.563	1.208
OSELM2	0.911	0.830	3.108	2.387	0.917	0.841	3.054	2.342
LSTM1	**0.986**	**0.972**	1.261	0.933	0.956	0.914	2.246	1.734
LSTM2	**0.982**	**0.964**	1.434	1.089	0.956	0.911	2.282	1.821
GEP1	0.936	0.872	2.695	2.118	0.937	0.874	2.722	2.123
GEP2	0.909	0.823	3.170	2.488	0.914	0.833	3.124	2.445
SVR1	**0.989**	**0.979**	1.100	0.732	**0.982**	**0.964**	1.451	1.079
SVR2	0.911	0.828	3.129	2.368	0.917	0.839	3.068	2.310
GPR1	**0.987**	**0.974**	1.214	0.942	**0.982**	**0.963**	1.476	1.136
GPR2	0.911	0.830	3.110	2.391	0.917	0.841	3.053	2.344
MLR1	0.896	0.803	3.352	2.697	0.898	0.807	3.362	2.704
MLR2	0.891	0.794	3.421	2.760	0.895	0.801	3.412	2.745

the measured ones faithfully during the validation stage. Fig. 11.7A illustrates the box diagrams for the spatial dispersion of calculated water temperature values based on model scenario 1 (i.e., OSELM1, LSTM1, GEP1, SVR1, GPR1, and MLR1) during the validation stage. The brief statistics (e.g., first quartile, median, and third quartile) of spatial dispersion based on the OSELM1, LSTM1, SVR1, and GPR1 models traced the measured water temperature values similarly, while the GEP1 and MLR1 models could not trail the measured water temperature values accurately during validation stage. The interquartile ranges (e.g., first and third quartiles) of the OSELM1, LSTM1, SVR1, and GPR1 models were broader than those of GEP1 and MLR1 models, while the complete ranges (e.g., maximum and minimum) of the OSELM1, LSTM1, SVR1, and GPR1 models were narrower than those of the MLR1 model. The violin diagram, which displays the probability dispersion of measured and calculated water temperature values, is organized as a box plot with adjustment of the kernel density plot (Hintze & Nelson, 1998). Considering Fig. 11.8A, the violin diagram illustrated that the OSELM1, SVR1, and GPR1 models performed the minimum, 25th percentile, medium, and 75th percentile ranges of measured water temperature closely compared to the other models (i.e., LSTM1, GEP1, and MLR1) during the validation stage at USGS 01104430 station.

A polar figure suggested by Taylor (2001) was applied to obtain visual assistance of model achievement based on three statistics (i.e., correlation coefficient, normalized standard deviation, and RMSE) (Heo et al., 2014; Taylor, 2001; Zounemat-Kermani et al., 2019). Fig. 11.9A shows the Taylor diagram between the measured and calculated water temperature (T_w) values based on model scenario 1 (i.e., OSELM1, LSTM1, GEP1, SVR1, GPR1, and MLR1) at USGS 01104430 station. The Taylor diagram demonstrates that the SVR1 model supplied smaller RMSE values than the other models. Although the values of normalized standard deviation and correlation coefficient computed by the SVR1 model did not match the measured ones perfectly, the node equivalent to the SVR1 model was closer to the measured one compared to the other models.

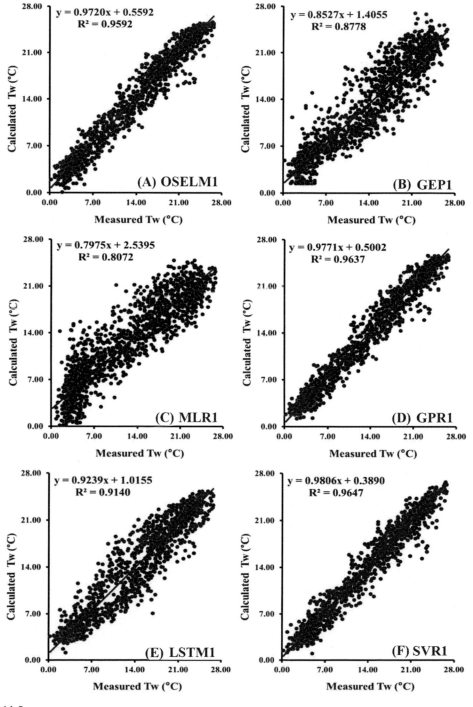

FIGURE 11.3

Scatter diagrams of measured versus calculated river water temperature (T_w) at the USGS 01104430 station (validation stage).

Nevertheless, the MLR1 was the poorest model which is highlighted by the optical aid of Taylor diagram.

USGS 14207200 station

The computed precision of the applied models during training and validation stages is illustrated in Table 11.3 for USGS 14207200 station. Bold numbers present the values of outstanding precision during training and validation stages. It can be judged from Table 11.3 that the LSTM1 model ($R = 0.992$, NSE = 0.985, RMSE = 0.708°C, and MAE = 0.547°C) was the optimized model during the training stage, whereas the GPR1 model ($R = 0.981$, NSE = 0.962, RMSE = 1.105°C, and MAE = 0.859°C) was the optimal model during the validation stage, with the lowest (i.e., RMSE and MAE) and highest (i.e., R and NSE) statistical values. However, the MLR2 model provided the worst performance during the training and validation stages. Also, a plain comparison between model scenarios 1 and 2 demonstrated that including the temporal indicators with the air temperature enhanced the computed precision of applied models during the training and validation stages at USGS 14207200 station. The scatter diagrams between the measured and calculated water temperature values using the model scenario 1 at USGS 14207200 station are clarified in Fig. 11.4A−F, including the individual matching line ($y = x$), simple linear equation, and R^2 value, respectively. It can be imagined from the scatter diagrams that the calculated values using the GPR1 model correspond perfectly to the measured ones undoubtedly during validation stage. Fig. 11.7B reveals the box diagrams for the spatial dispersion of calculated water temperature values based on model scenario 1 at USGS 14207200 station during the validation stage. The evident statistics (e.g., first quartile, median, and third quartile) of spatial dispersion based on the OSELM1, LSTM1, GEP1, SVR1, and GPR1 models followed the measured water temperature values equivalently, whereas the MLR1 model could

Table 11.3 Performances of different models at the USGS 14207200 station.

Models	Training				Validation			
	R	**NSE**	**RMSE**	**MAE**	**R**	**NSE**	**RMSE**	**MAE**
OSELM1	**0.978**	**0.956**	1.203	0.951	**0.975**	**0.950**	1.273	1.014
OSELM2	0.931	0.867	2.092	1.644	0.928	0.861	2.126	1.650
LSTM1	**0.992**	**0.985**	0.708	0.547	**0.972**	**0.945**	1.338	1.032
LSTM2	**0.987**	**0.974**	0.930	0.720	0.967	0.935	1.450	1.118
GEP1	0.966	0.933	1.481	1.175	0.964	0.929	1.512	1.195
GEP2	0.930	0.866	2.100	1.653	0.927	0.860	2.129	1.655
SVR1	**0.985**	**0.971**	0.980	0.705	**0.980**	**0.961**	1.131	0.856
SVR2	0.931	0.865	2.106	1.632	0.928	0.859	2.138	1.646
GPR1	**0.986**	**0.972**	0.961	0.746	**0.981**	**0.962**	1.105	0.859
GPR2	0.931	0.867	2.092	1.643	0.928	0.861	2.125	1.649
MLR1	0.924	0.854	2.192	1.758	0.920	0.847	2.230	1.770
MLR2	0.920	0.846	2.250	1.808	0.917	0.840	2.276	1.806

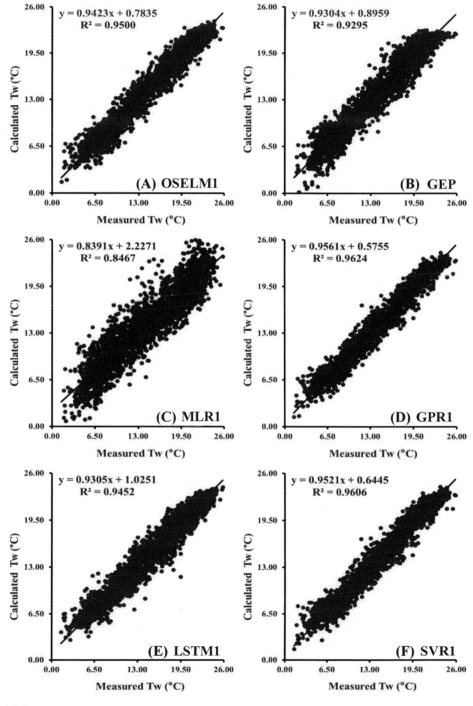

FIGURE 11.4

Scatter diagrams of measured versus calculated river water temperature (T_w) at the USGS 14207200 station (validation stage).

not track the measured water temperature values clearly during the validation stage. The interquartile ranges (e.g., first and third quartiles) of the OSELM1, LSTM1, GEP1, SVR1, and GPR1 models were wider than those of the MLR1 models, whereas the full ranges (e.g., maximum and minimum) of the OSELM1, LSTM1, SVR1, and GPR1 models were more restricted than those of the MLR1 model absolutely. With regard to the violin diagram in Fig. 11.8B, the addressed figure described that the OSELM1, SVR1, and GPR1 models accomplished the minimum, 25th percentile, medium, and 75th percentile ranges of measured water temperature more accurately compared to the other models (i.e., LSTM1, GEP1, and MLR1) during the validation stage.

Fig. 11.9B illustrates the Taylor diagram between the measured and calculated water temperature values based on the model scenario 1 at USGS 14207200 station. This figure indicates that the GPR1 model yielded smaller RMSE values than the other models. Although the values of normalized standard deviation and correlation coefficient computed by the GPR1 model did not match the measured ones completely, the point corresponding to the GPR1 model was closer to the measured one compared to the other models. However, the point for the MLR1 model was the poorest performance with the visual aid of a Taylor diagram.

USGS 422302071083801 station

Estimated accuracies of the developed models during the training and validation stages are given in Table 11.4 for the USGS 422302071083801 station. Bold numbers show the values of remarkable accuracy during the training and validation stages. It can be considered from Table 11.4 that the SVR1 model ($R = 0.994$, NSE $= 0.988$, RMSE $= 0.926°$C, and MAE $= 0.602°$C) was the optimized model during the training stage, while the GPR1 model ($R = 0.992$, NSE $= 0.985$, RMSE $= 1.057°$C, and MAE $= 0.794°$C) was the optimal model during the validation stage.

Table 11.4 Performances of different models at the USGS 422302071083801 station.

Models	Training				Validation			
	R	NSE	RMSE	MAE	*R*	NSE	RMSE	MAE
OSELM1	0.992	0.984	1.072	0.832	0.991	0.982	1.136	0.854
OSELM2	0.916	0.839	3.409	2.571	0.922	0.850	3.315	2.525
LSTM1	0.988	0.976	1.326	0.968	0.976	0.953	1.854	1.394
LSTM2	0.986	0.970	1.467	1.088	0.975	0.950	1.905	1.407
GEP1	0.940	0.883	2.898	2.275	0.940	0.883	2.928	2.305
GEP2	0.921	0.847	3.313	2.543	0.923	0.852	3.293	2.520
SVR1	0.994	0.988	0.926	0.602	0.992	0.984	1.068	0.762
SVR2	0.921	0.844	3.352	2.436	0.923	0.848	3.336	2.432
GPR1	0.993	0.986	1.004	0.763	0.992	0.985	1.057	0.794
GPR2	0.921	0.849	3.295	2.490	0.924	0.854	3.272	2.464
MLR1	0.920	0.847	3.317	2.609	0.919	0.845	3.364	2.656
MLR2	0.907	0.822	3.575	2.835	0.908	0.824	3.582	2.847

However, the MLR2 model gave the worst results during the training and validation stages. In addition, a clear comparison between model scenarios 1 and 2 displayed that involving the temporal indicators to the air temperature boosted the estimated accuracy of the developed models during the training and validation stages at USGS 422302071083801 station. The scatter diagrams of the measured and calculated water temperature values employing model scenario 1 for USGS 422302071083801 station are shown in Fig. 11.5A−F including the individual matching line ($y = x$), simple linear equation, and R^2 value, respectively. It can be assumed from the scatter diagrams that the estimated values corresponding to the GPR1 model tracked the measured ones clearly during the validation stage. Fig. 11.7C shows the box diagrams for the spatial distribution of calculated water temperature values based on model scenario 1 at USGS 422302071083801 station. The apparent statistics (e.g., first quartile, median, and third quartile) of spatial distribution based on the OSELM1, LSTM1, SVR1, and GPR1 models accompanied the measured water temperature values fairly accurately, while the GEP1 and MLR1 models could not calculate the measured water temperature values accurately during validation stage at USGS 422302071083801 station. The interquartile ranges (e.g., first and third quartiles) of the OSELM1, LSTM1, SVR1, and GPR1 models were much larger than those of the GEP1 and MLR1 models, while the entire ranges (e.g., maximum and minimum) of the OSELM1, LSTM1, SVR1, and GPR1 models were more limited than those of the MLR1 model. In accordance with the violin diagram in Fig. 11.8C, this figure illustrated that the OSELM1, SVR1, and GPR1 models achieved the minimum, 25th percentile, medium, and 75th percentile ranges of measured water temperature values clearly compared to the other models (i.e., LSTM1, GEP1, and MLR1) during the validation stage at USGS 422302071083801 station.

Fig. 11.9C represents the Taylor diagram between the measured and calculated water temperature values based on model scenario 1 at USGS 422302071083801 station. The underlying figure showed that the GPR1 model provided smaller RMSE values than the other models. Although the values of normalized standard deviation and correlation coefficient estimated by the GPR1 model could not match the measured ones entirely, the mark corresponding to the GPR1 model was closer to the measured one compared to the other models. However, the mark for the MLR1 model was the weakest attainment with the visual assistance of the Taylor diagram.

USGS 422622122004000 station

The estimated accuracy of the developed models during the training and validation stages is proposed in Table 11.5 for USGS 422622122004000 station. Bold numbers show the values of excellent accuracy during the training and validation stages. It can be seen from Table 11.5 that the GPR1 model ($R = 0.952$, NSE $= 0.906$, RMSE $= 0.914°C$, and MAE $= 0.660°C$ for validation stage) was the optimized model during the training and validation stages. Unfortunately, the MLR2 (training stage) and MLR1 (validation stage) models achieved the worst results. Also, an uncomplicated comparison between model scenarios 1 and 2 showed that using only the air temperature encouraged the estimated accuracy of developed models during the training and validation stages except for the MLR model at USGS 422622122004000 station. The scatter diagrams between the measured and calculated water temperature values for model scenario 1 for USGS 422622122004000 station are proposed in Fig. 11.5A−F enclosing the individual matching line

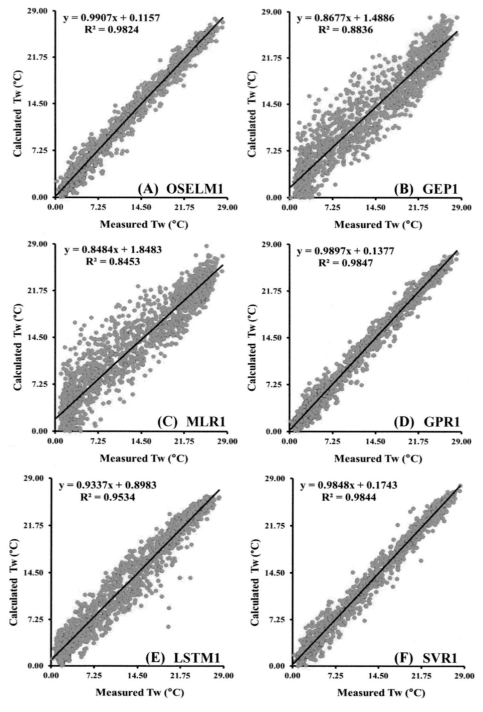

FIGURE 11.5

Scatter diagrams of measured versus calculated river water temperature (T_w) at the USGS 422302071083801 station (validation stage).

Table 11.5 Performances of different models at the USGS 422622122004000 station.

Models	Training				Validation			
	R	NSE	RMSE	MAE	R	NSE	RMSE	MAE
OSELM1	0.944	0.891	0.995	0.774	0.923	0.852	1.146	0.880
OSELM2	0.843	0.701	1.647	1.278	0.855	0.720	1.577	1.217
LSTM1	0.973	0.946	0.701	0.511	0.887	0.787	1.375	1.081
LSTM2	0.972	0.945	0.707	0.527	0.871	0.753	1.483	1.171
GEP1	0.881	0.775	1.427	1.118	0.883	0.779	1.402	1.106
GEP2	0.843	0.710	1.622	1.276	0.858	0.735	1.535	1.206
SVR1	0.973	0.945	0.704	0.453	0.949	0.899	0.949	0.689
SVR2	0.844	0.712	1.617	1.258	0.859	0.736	1.531	1.194
GPR1	0.991	0.983	0.398	0.298	0.952	0.906	0.914	0.660
GPR2	0.842	0.709	1.626	1.285	0.856	0.733	1.542	1.216
MLR1	0.841	0.707	1.631	1.293	0.849	0.720	1.578	1.249
MLR2	0.839	0.704	1.638	1.294	0.850	0.722	1.574	1.240

($y = x$), simple linear equation, and R^2 value, respectively. It can be understood from the scatter diagrams that the estimated values corresponding to the GPR1 model correspond to the measured ones definitely during the validation stage. Fig. 11.7D shows the box diagrams for the spatial distribution of calculated water temperature values based on the model scenario 1 at USGS 422622122004000 station. The obvious statistics (e.g., first quartile, median, and third quartile) of spatial distribution based on the OSELM1, LSTM1, SVR1, and GPR1 models guided the measured water temperature correctly, whereas the GEP1 and MLR1 models could not simulate the measured water temperature confidently during the validation stage at USGS 422622122004000 station. The interquartile ranges (e.g., first and third quartiles) of the OSELM1, LSTM1, SVR1, and GPR1 models were more extensive than those of the GEP1 and MLR1 models, whereas the total ranges (e.g., maximum and minimum) of the LSTM1, SVR1, GPR1, and MLR1 models provided a similar pattern. Concerning the violin diagram in Fig. 11.8D, this figure shows that the OSELM1, SVR1, and GPR1 models carried out the minimum, 25th percentile, medium, and 75th percentile ranges of measured water temperature values well compared to the other models (i.e., LSTM1, GEP1, and MLR1) during the validation stage at USGS 422622122004000 station.

Fig. 11.9D depicts the Taylor diagram between the measured and calculated water temperature values based on model scenario 1 at USGS 422622122004000 station. The figure shows that the GPR1 model supported smaller RMSE values than the other models. Although the values of normalized standard deviation and correlation coefficient estimated by the GPR1 model could not match the measured ones completely accurately, the circle corresponding to the GPR1 model was next to the measured one compared to the other models. However, the circle for the MLR1 model had the longest distance from the measured one with the visual support of the Taylor diagram (Figs. 11.6–11.9).

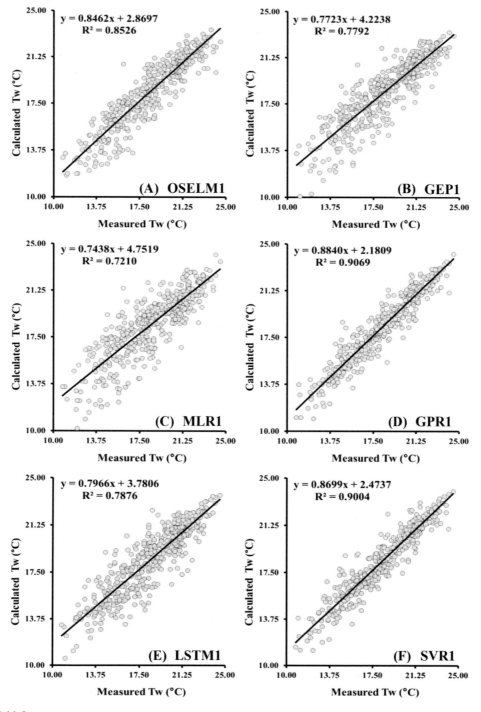

FIGURE 11.6

Scatter diagrams of measured versus calculated river water temperature (T_w) at the USGS 422622122004000 station (validation stage).

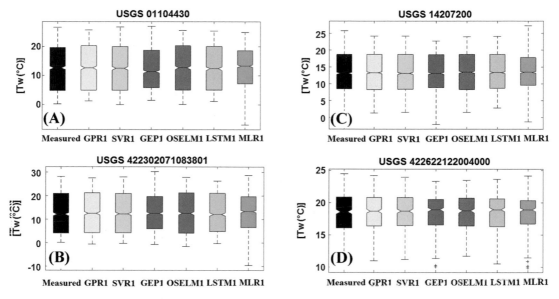

FIGURE 11.7

Box diagrams of measured versus calculated river water temperature (T_w: °C) for the four stations (validation stage).

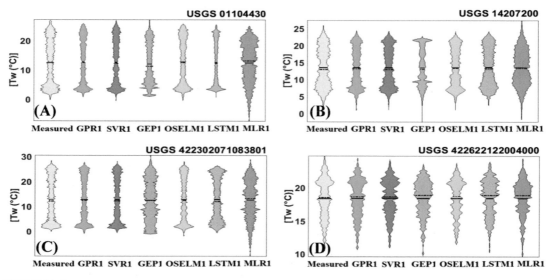

FIGURE 11.8

Violin diagrams showing the distributions of measured versus calculated river water temperature (T_w: °C) for the four stations (validation stage).

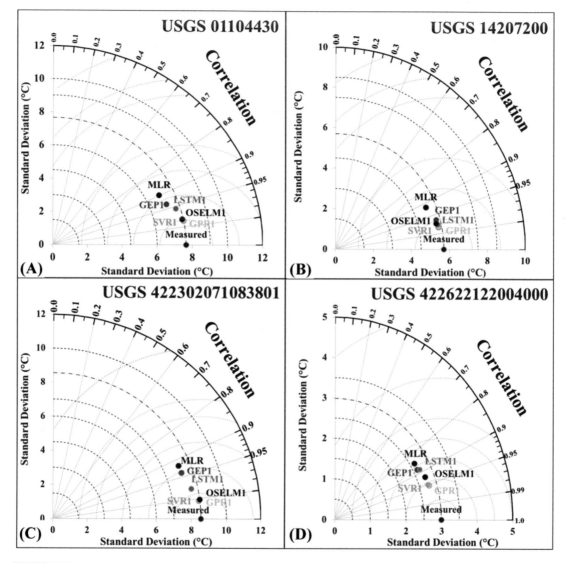

FIGURE 11.9

Taylor diagrams of measured versus calculated river water temperature (T_w: °C) for the four stations (validation stage).

Discussion

The discussed research indicates that the different machine learning (i.e., OSELM, GEP, SVR, GPR, and MLR) and deep learning (i.e., LSTM) models simulated the natural behaviors (e.g., non-linear and nonstationary time series) of water temperature in four stations in the United States. The computed accuracy of the developed models based on model scenario 1 provided better performance compared to the other models based on model scenario 2. However, only the MLR2 model was superior to the MLR1 model slightly during the validation stage at USGS 422622122004000 station. Considering the corresponding optimized models (i.e., OSELM1, LSTM1, GEP1, SVR1, GPR1, and MLR1 for USGS 01104430, USGS 14207200, and USGS 422302071083801 stations; OSELM1, LSTM1, GEP1, SVR1, GPR1, and MLR2 for USGS 422622122004000 station) in the four stations, the best models were selected as the SVR1 (USGS 01104430 station) and GPR1 models (USGS 14207200, USGS 422302071083801, and USGS 422622122004000 stations) during the validation stage, respectively.

Based on the RMSE values of SVR1 and GPR1 models for the corresponding stations, the SVR1 model enhanced the performance accuracy of the OSELM1, LSTM1, GEP1, GPR1, and MLR1 models by 7.17%, 35.40%, 46.69%, 1.69%, and 56.84% at USGS 01104430 station. In addition, the GPR1 model improved the achievement precision of the OSELM1, LSTM1, GEP1, SVR1, and MLR1 models by 13.20%, 17.41%, 26.92%, 2.30%, and 50.45% at USGS 14207200 station, and 6.95%, 42.99%, 63.90%, 1.03%, and 68.58% at USGS 422302071083801 station, respectively. Finally, the GPR1 model increased the results accuracy of the OSELM1, LSTM1, GEP1, SVR1, and MLR2 models by 20.24%, 33.53%, 34.81%, 3.69%, and 41.93% at USGS 422622122004000 station.

Earlier articles and reports have illustrated that the quality and quantity of employed data can affect the performance of machine learning and deep learning models critically (Kim & Kim, 2008; Londhe & Charhate, 2010; Zheng et al., 2018). If the different models (e.g., SVR1 and GPR1 models) demonstrate the best performance accuracy based on the specific data, the supplementary statistical methods (e.g., null hypothesis) and data addition are recommended to validate which model is better than the others definitely (Salas et al., 2002).

Regarding earlier literature for water temperature calculation using machine learning and deep learning models, Read et al. (2019) developed the process-guided deep learning (PGDP) model to predict lake water temperature. The PGDP model predicted lake water temperature accurately in the Midwestern United States. Zhu, Heddam, Wu, Dai, and Jia (2019) used the different machine learning models (i.e., ELM, MLPNN, and MLR) to calculate the river water temperature. The ELM model proved to be the best model to calculate river water temperature. Zhu, Nyarko, Hadzima-Nyarko, Heddam, and Wu (2019) employed the FFNN, GPR, and DT models to calculate the river water temperature in Croatia, Switzerland, and the United States.

The three machine learning models accomplished the calculation of river water temperature effectively. Therefore this research was a novel approach to calculate water temperature using different machine learning and deep learning models in the United States. To reinforce the calculated accuracy of this research, the combination processes using different machine learning, deep learning, evolutionary algorithm, and data-preprocessing technique can be recommended to improve the accuracy of the calculated river water temperature.

Conclusions and future recommendations

This study investigated the efficiency of the LSTM deep learning method in predicting river water temperature. Daily data obtained from four stations operated by USGS were used as case studies and air temperature-based two scenarios (scenario 1: air temperature and periodicity, and scenario 2: air temperature) were implemented and the predictions of the LSTM were compared with those of the OSELM, GEP, SVR, GPR, and MLR models. All the machine learning methods provided better accuracy in scenario 1 compared to scenario 2, and they were better than the MLR in predicting river water temperature. However, using only air temperature (scenario 2), among the machine learning methods, the LSTM performed better than the other methods. Compared to OSELM2, GEP2, SVR2, GPR2, and MLR2, applying a deep learning method (LSTM2) improved the prediction efficiency with respect to RMSE by 25.28%, 26.95%, 25.62%, 25.25%, and 33.12% for station USGS 01104430, by 31.80%, 31.89%, 32.18%, 31.76%, and 36.29% for station USGS 14207200, by 42.53%, 42.15%, 42.90%, 41.78%, and 46.82% for station USGS 422302071083801, and by 5.96%, 3.39%, 3.14%, 3.83%, and 5.78% for station USGS 422622122004000, respectively. Including periodicity considerably improved the machine learning methods in prediction of river water temperature; decreases in RMSE of LSTM, OSELM, GEP, SVR, and GPR were about 2%−8%, 27%−66%, 9%−29%, 38%−68%, and 41%−68%, respectively. The main limitation of the presented study is the use of a limited number of independent variables (e.g., air temperature). For future research, more input variables which are effective on river water temperature should be used to increase the models' efficiency. The LSTM may be compared with other deep learning and machine learning methods (e.g., fuzzy- or neurofuzzy-based methods with new metaheuristic algorithms) using river water temperature data at different time intervals (e.g., hourly, monthly).

References

Balasundaram, S., & Prasad, S. C. (2020). On pairing Huber support vector regression. *Applied Soft Computing*, *97*(Part B), 106708. Available from https://doi.org/10.1016/j.asoc.2020.106708.

Benyahya, L., St-Hilaire, A., Ouarda, T. B. M. J., Bobée, B., & Dumas, J. (2008). Comparison of non-parametric and parametric water temperature models on the Nivelle River, France. *Hydrological Sciences Journal*, *53*(3), 640−655. Available from https://doi.org/10.1623/hysj.53.3.640.

Bogan, T., Mohseni, O., & Stefan, H. G. (2003). Stream temperature-equilibrium temperature relationship. *Water Resources Research*, *39*(9). Available from https://doi.org/10.1029/2003WR002034.

Caissie, D. (2006). The thermal regime of rivers—A review. *Freshwater Biology*, *51*, 1389−1406. Available from https://doi.org/10.1111/j.1365-2427.2006.01597.x.

Caldwell, R. J., Gangopadhyay, S., Bountry, J., Lai, Y., & Elsner, M. M. (2013). Statistical modeling of daily and subdaily stream temperatures: Application to the Methow River Basin, Washington. *Water Resources Research*, *49*(7), 4346−4361. Available from https://doi.org/10.1002/wrcr.20353.

Chang, Y. S., Chiao, H. T., Abimannan, S., Huang, Y. P., Tsai, Y. T., & Lin, K. M. (2020). An LSTM-based aggregated model for air pollution forecasting. *Atmospheric Pollution Research*, *11*(8), 1451−1463. Available from https://doi.org/10.1016/j.apr.2020.05.015.

Colah's Blog. (2015). Understanding LSTM networks.

Choi, E., Cho, S., & Kim, D. K. (2020). Power demand forecasting using long short-term memory (LSTM) deep-learning model for monitoring energy sustainability. *Sustainability*, *12*(3), 1109. Available from https://doi.org/10.3390/su12031109.

Choi, Y., Lee, J., & Kong, J. (2020). Performance degradation model for concrete deck of bridge using pseudo-LSTM. *Sustainability*, *12*(9), 3848. Available from https://doi.org/10.3390/su12093848.

Danandeh Mehr, A., & Nourani, V. (2018). Season algorithm-multigene genetic programming: A new approach for rainfall-runoff modelling. *Water Resources Management*, *32*(8), 2665−2679. Available from https://doi.org/10.1007/s11269-018-1951-3.

Danandeh Mehr, A., Nourani, V., Kahya, E., Hrnjica, B., Sattar, A. M. A., & Yaseen, Z. M. (2018). Genetic programming in water resources engineering: A state-of-the-art review. *Journal of Hydrology*, *566*, 643−667. Available from https://doi.org/10.1016/j.jhydrol.2018.09.043.

Daniels, M. E., & Danner, E. M. (2020). The drivers of river temperatures below a large dam. *Water Resources Research*, *56*(5). Available from https://doi.org/10.1029/2019WR026751, e2019WR026751.

Fabris, L., Rolick, R. L., Kurylyk, B. L., & Carey, S. K. (2020). Characterization of contrasting flow and thermal regimes in two adjacent subarctic alpine headwaters in Northwest Canada. *Hydrological Processes*, *34* (15), 3252−3270. Available from https://doi.org/10.1002/hyp.13786.

Ferreira, C. (2001). Gene expression programming: A new adaptive algorithm for solving problems. *Complex Systems*, *13*(2). Available from https://doi.org/10.1007/978-1-4471-0123-9_54.

Grbić, R., Kurtagić, D., & Slišković, D. (2013). Stream water temperature prediction based on Gaussian process regression. *Expert Systems with Applications*, *40*(18), 7407−7414. Available from https://doi.org/10.1016/j.eswa.2013.06.077.

Heddam, S., Ptak, M., & Zhu, S. (2020). Modelling of daily lake surface water temperature from air temperature: Extremely randomized trees (ERT) vs Air2Water, MARS, M5Tree, RF and MLPNN. *Journal of Hydrology*, *588*, 125130. Available from https://doi.org/10.1016/j.jhydrol.2020.125130.

Heo, K. Y., IIa, K. J., Yun, K. S., Lee, S. S., Kim, H. J., & Wang, B. (2014). Methods for uncertainty assessment of climate models and model predictions over East Asia. *International Journal of Climatology*, *34*(2), 377−390. Available from https://doi.org/10.1002/joc.3692.

Hintze, J. I., & Nelson, R. D. (1998). Violin plots: A box plot-density trace synergism. *The American Statistician*, *52*(2), 181−184.

Hong, Y. S. T., & Bhamidimarri, R. (2012). Dynamic neuro-fuzzy local modeling system with a nonlinear feature extraction for the online adaptive warning system of river temperature affected by waste cooling water discharge. *Stochastic Environmental Research and Risk Assessment*, *26*(7), 947−960. Available from https://doi.org/10.1007/s00477-011-0543-z.

Hrnjica, B., Mehr, A. D., Behrem, Š., & Ağıralioğlu, N. (2019). Genetic programming for turbidity prediction: Hourly and monthly scenarios. *Pamukkale Üniversitesi Mühendislik Bilimleri Dergisi*, *25*(8), 992−997. Available from https://doi.org/10.5505/pajes.2019.59458.

Huang, G. B., Zhu, Q. Y., & Siew, C. K. (2006). Extreme learning machine: Theory and applications. *Neurocomputing*, *70*(1−3), 489−501. Available from https://doi.org/10.1016/j.neucom.2005.12.126.

Huang, L., Cai, T., Zhu, Y., Zhu, Y., & Wang, W. (2020). LSTM-based forecasting for urban construction waste generation. *Sustainability*, *12*(20), 8555. Available from https://doi.org/10.3390/su12208555.

Jäkel, F., Schölkopf, B., & Wichmann, F. A. (2007). A tutorial on kernel methods for categorization. *Journal of Mathematical Psychology*, *51*(6), 343−358.

Kavaklioglu, K. (2011). Modeling and prediction of Turkey's electricity consumption using support vector regression. *Applied Energy*, *88*(1), 368−375. Available from https://doi.org/10.1016/j.apenergy.2010.07.021.

Kim, S., & Kim, H. S. (2008). Uncertainty reduction of the flood stage forecasting using neural networks model. *JAWRA Journal of the American Water Resources Association*, *44*(1), 148−165.

King, T. V., & Neilson, B. T. (2019). Quantifying reach-average effects of hyporheic exchange on Arctic river temperatures in an area of continuous permafrost. *Water Resources Research*, *55*(3), 1951−1971. Available from https://doi.org/10.1029/2018WR023463.

Ko, C. N., & Lee, C. M. (2013). Short-term load forecasting using SVR (support vector regression)-based radial basis function neural network with dual extended Kalman filter. *Energy*, *49*, 413−422. Available from https://doi.org/10.1016/j.energy.2012.11.015.

Koza, J. R. (1994). *Genetic programming II* (Vol. 17). Cambridge: MIT Press.

Lee, S., Lee, S., & Moon, M. (2020). Hybrid change point detection for time series via support vector regression and CUSUM method. *Applied Soft Computing*, *89*, 106101. Available from https://doi.org/10.1016/j.asoc.2020.106101.

Londhe, S., & Charhate, S. (2010). Comparison of data-driven modelling techniques for river flow forecasting. *Hydrological Sciences Journal*, *55*(7), 1163−1174.

Michel, A., Brauchli, T., Lehning, M., Schaefli, B., & Huwald, H. (2020). Stream temperature and discharge evolution in Switzerland over the last 50 years: Annual and seasonal behaviour. *Hydrology and Earth System Sciences*, *24*(1), 115−142. Available from https://doi.org/10.5194/hess-24-115-2020.

Mohseni, O., & Stefan, H. G. (1999). Stream temperature/air temperature relationship: A physical interpretation. *Journal of Hydrology*, *218*(3), 128−141. Available from https://doi.org/10.1016/S0022-1694(99)00034-7.

Mohseni, O., Stefan, H. G., & Erickson, T. R. (1998). A nonlinear regression model for weekly stream temperatures. *Water Resources Research*, *34*(10), 2685−2692. Available from https://doi.org/10.1029/98WR01877.

Morrill, J. C., Bales, R. C., & Conklin, M. H. (2005). Estimating stream temperature from air temperature: Implications for future water quality. *Journal of Environmental Engineering*, *131*(1), 139−146. Available from https://doi.org/10.1061/(ASCE)0733-9372(2005)131:1(139).

Olyaie, E., Abyaneh, H. Z., & Mehr, A. D. (2017). A comparative analysis among computational intelligence techniques for dissolved oxygen prediction in Delaware River. *Geoscience Frontiers*, *8*(3), 517−527. Available from https://doi.org/10.1016/j.gsf.2016.04.007.

Pike, A., Danner, E., Boughton, D., Melton, F., Nemani, R., Rajagopalan, B., & Lindley, S. (2013). Forecasting river temperatures in real time using a stochastic dynamics approach. *Water Resources Research*, *49*(9), 5168−5182. Available from https://doi.org/10.1002/wrcr.20389.

Rasmussen, C. E., & Williams, C. K. I. (2006). *Gaussian processes for machine learning*. Cambridge: MIT Press.

Read, J. S., Jia, X., Willard, J., Appling, A. P., Zwart, J. A., Oliver, S. K., Karpatne, A., Hansen, G. J., Hanson, P. C., Watkins, W., & Steinbach, M. (2019). Process-guided deep learning predictions of lake water temperature. *Water Resources Research*, *55*(11), 9173−9190.

Sahoo, G. B., Schladow, S. G., & Reuter, J. E. (2009). Forecasting stream water temperature using regression analysis, artificial neural network, and chaotic non-linear dynamic models. *Journal of Hydrology*, *378*(3−4), 325−342. Available from https://doi.org/10.1016/j.jhydrol.2009.09.037.

Salas, J. D., Smith, R. A., Tabios, G. Q., & Heo, J. H. (2002). Statistical computer techniques in water resources and environmental engineering. Course notes, Department of Civil Engineering, Colorado State University, Fort Collins, Colorado.

Scardapane, S., Comminiello, D., Scarpiniti, M., & Uncini, A. (2014). Online sequential extreme learning machine with kernels. *IEEE Transactions on Neural Networks and Learning Systems*, *26*(9), 2214−2220.

Schulz, E., Speekenbrink, M., & Krause, A. (2018). A tutorial on Gaussian process regression: Modelling, exploring, and exploiting functions. *Journal of Mathematical Psychology*, *85*, 1−16. Available from https://doi.org/10.1016/j.jmp.2018.03.001.

Seyedhashemi, H., Moatar, F., Vidal, J. P., Diamond, J. S., Beaufort, A., Chandesris, A., & Valette, L. (2020). Thermal signatures identify the influence of dams and ponds on stream temperature at the regional scale. *Science of the Total Environment*, *766*, 142667. Available from https://doi.org/10.1016/j.scitotenv.2020.142667.

Shahid, F., Zameer, A., & Muneeb, M. (2020). Predictions for COVID-19 with deep learning models of LSTM, GRU and Bi-LSTM. *Chaos, Solitons & Fractals*, *140*, 110212. Available from https://doi.org/10.1016/j.chaos.2020.110212.

Sihag, P., Esmaeilbeiki, F., Singh, B., & Pandhiani, S. M. (2020). Model-based soil temperature estimation using climatic parameters: The case of Azerbaijan Province, Iran. *Geology, Ecology, and Landscapes*, *4*(3), 203−215. Available from https://doi.org/10.1080/24749508.2019.1610841.

Sihag, P., Singh, B., Sepah Vand, A., & Mehdipour, V. (2020). Modeling the infiltration process with soft computing techniques. *ISH Journal of Hydraulic Engineering*, *26*(2), 138−152. Available from https://doi.org/10.1080/09715010.2018.1464408.

Sihag, P., Tiwari, N. K., & Ranjan, S. (2017). Modelling of infiltration of sandy soil using gaussian process regression. *Modeling Earth Systems and Environment*, *3*(3), 1091−1100. Available from https://doi.org/10.1007/s40808-017-0357-1.

Smola, A. J., & Schölkopf, B. (2004). A tutorial on support vector regression. *Statistics and Computing.*, *14*, 199−222. Available from https://doi.org/10.1023/b:stco.0000035301.49549.88.

Taylor, K. E. (2001). Summarizing multiple aspects of model performance in a single diagram. *Journal of Geophysical Research: Atmospheres*, *106*(D7), 7183−7192.

Vapnik, V. N. (2000). *The nature of statistical learning theory*. New York: Springer. Available from https://doi.org/10.1007/978-1-4757-3264-1.

Voza, D., & Vuković, M. (2018). The assessment and prediction of temporal variations in surface water quality—A case study. *Environmental monitoring and assessment*, *190*(7), 434. Available from https://doi.org/10.1007/s10661-018-6814-0.

Wenxian, G., Hongxiang, W., Jianxin, X., & Wensheng, D. (2010). *PSO-BP neural network model for predicting water temperature in the middle of the Yangtze River, 2010 International* conference *on* intelligent computation technology *and* automation (Vol. 2, pp. 951−954). IEEE. Available from https://doi.org/10.1109/ICICTA.2010.501.

Xue, Z., Zhang, Y., Cheng, C., & Ma, G. (2020). Remaining useful life prediction of lithium-ion batteries with adaptive unscented Kalman filter and optimized support vector regression. *Neurocomputing*, *376*, 95−102. Available from https://doi.org/10.1016/j.neucom.2019.09.074.

Yaqub, M., Asif, H., Kim, S., & Lee, W. (2020). Modeling of a full-scale sewage treatment plant to predict the nutrient removal efficiency using a long short-term memory (LSTM) neural network. *Journal of Water Process Engineering*, *37*, 101388. Available from https://doi.org/10.1016/j.jwpe.2020.101388.

Yaseen, Z. M., Sihag, P., Yusuf, B., & Al-Janabi, A. M. S. (2021). Modelling infiltration rates in permeable stormwater channels using soft computing techniques. *Irrigation and Drainage*, *70*, 117−130. Available from https://doi.org/10.1002/ird.2530.

Yin, J., Deng, Z., Ines, A. V., Wu, J., & Rasu, E. (2020). Forecast of short-term daily reference evapotranspiration under limited meteorological variables using a hybrid bi-directional long short-term memory model (Bi-LSTM). *Agricultural Water Management*, *242*, 106386. Available from https://doi.org/10.1016/j.agwat.2020.106386.

Zaidel, P. A., Roy, A. H., Houle, K. M., Lambert, B., Letcher, B. H., Nislow, K. H., & Smith, C. (2020). Impacts of small dams on stream temperature. *Ecological Indicators*, *120*, 106878. Available from https://doi.org/10.1016/j.ecolind.2020.106878.

Zang, H., Liu, L., Sun, L., Cheng, L., Wei, Z., & Sun, G. (2020). Short-term global horizontal irradiance forecasting based on a hybrid CNN-LSTM model with spatiotemporal correlations. *Renewable Energy*, *160*, 26−41. Available from https://doi.org/10.1016/j.renene.2020.05.150.

Zhang, B., Zhang, H., Zhao, G., & Lian, J. (2020). Constructing a PM2.5 concentration prediction model by combining auto-encoder with Bi-LSTM neural networks. *Environmental Modelling & Software*, *124*, 104600. Available from https://doi.org/10.1016/j.envsoft.2019.104600.

Zhang, Q., Gao, T., Liu, X., & Zheng, Y. (2020). Public environment emotion prediction model using LSTM network. *Sustainability (Switzerland)*, *12*(4), 1665. Available from https://doi.org/10.3390/su12041665.

Zheng, F., Maier, H. R., Wu, W., Dandy, G. C., Gupta, H. V., & Zhang, T. (2018). On lack of robustness in hydrological model development due to absence of guidelines for selecting calibration and evaluation data: Demonstration for data-driven models. *Water Resources Research*, *54*(2), 1013−1030.

Zhu, S., & Piotrowski, A. P. (2020). River/Stream water temperature forecasting using artificial intelligence models: A systematic review. *Acta Geophysica*, 1−10. Available from https://doi.org/10.1007/s11600-020-00480-7.

Zhu, S., & Heddam, S. (2019). Modelling of maximum daily water temperature for streams: Optimally pruned extreme learning machine (OPELM) vs radial basis function neural networks (RBFNN). *Environmental Processes*, *6*(3), 789−804. Available from https://doi.org/10.1007/s40710-019-00385-8.

Zhu, S., Heddam, S., Nyarko, E. K., Hadzima-Nyarko, M., Piccolroaz, S., & Wu, S. (2019). Modeling daily water temperature for rivers: Comparison between adaptive neuro-fuzzy inference systems and artificial neural networks models. *Environmental Science and Pollution Research*, *26*(1), 402−420. Available from https://doi.org/10.1007/s11356-018-3650-2.

Zhu, S., Heddam, S., Wu, S., Dai, J., & Jia, B. (2019). Extreme learning machine based prediction of daily water temperature for rivers. *Environmental Earth Science*, *78*, 202. Available from https://doi.org/10.1007/s12665-019-8202-7.

Zhu, S., Nyarko, E. K., Hadzima-Nyarko, M., Heddam, S., & Wu, S. (2019). Assessing the performance of a suite of machine learning models for daily river water temperature prediction. *PeerJ*, *7*, e7065.

Zhu, S., Ptak, M., Yaseen, Z. M., Dai, J., & Sivakumar, B. (2020). Forecasting surface water temperature in lakes: A comparison of approaches. *Journal of Hydrology*, *585*, 124809. Available from https://doi.org/10.1016/j.jhydrol.2020.124809.

Zounemat-Kermani, M., Alizamir, M., Fadaee, M., Sankaran Namboothiri, A., & Shiri, J. (2020). Online sequential extreme learning machine in river water quality (turbidity) prediction: A comparative study on different data mining approaches. *Water and Environment Journal*, *35*, 335−348. Available from https://doi.org/10.1111/wej.12630.

Zounemat-Kermani, M., Seo, Y., Kim, S., Ghorbani, M. A., Samadianfard, S., Naghshara, S., Kim, N. W., & Singh, V. P. (2019). Can decomposition approaches always enhance soft computing models? Predicting the dissolved oxygen concentration in the St. Johns River, Florida. *Applied Sciences*, *9*(12), 2534.

Data-centric and intelligent systems in land pollution research

Machine learning and artifical intelligence application in land pollution research

Mohammad Hossein Moradi[1], Ali Sohani[2], Mitra Zabihigivi[1], Uwe Wagner[1], Thomas Koch[1] and Hoseyn Sayyaadi[2]

[1]Institute of Internal Combustion Engines, Karlsruhe Institute of Technology, Karlsruhe, Germany [2]Lab of Optimization of Thermal Systems' Installations, Faculty of Mechanical Engineering-Energy Division, K.N. Toosi University of Technology, Tehran, Iran

Introduction

Human life has changed significantly in a relatively short time. Issues such as urbanization, population growth, and increasing standards of living have led to much higher production and consequently consumption levels (Jin et al., 2018). These have also been accompanied by increased concerns about land pollution from contamination caused by trash, debris, and toxic chemicals such as pollutant emissions and pesticides (Huang et al., 2019).

Land pollution not only damages natural beauty but also is a very dangerous factor for the health of plants, animals, and humans. In addition, as another negative side effect it causes the release of greenhouse gas emissions, especially methane. Considering such a direct and strong relationship with the health and future of humanity, a number of studies have been carried out in monitoring, assessment, and mitigation of land pollution, and it has become a very hot topic, which has a very fast pace of growth, with data-centric (DC) and artificial intelligence (AI) methods being employed. Using DC and AI has been increasingly popular because the systems to be investigated are becoming increasingly complex, which makes data analysis so challenging. DC and AI could provide the opportunity for accurate prediction of performance criteria, without extensive knowledge about the modeled system and governing equations (Moradi et al., 2017). This can facilitate designers, scientists, and politicians to come together to develop better plans for pollution management. This chapter provides an in-depth but brief summary of the studies which have used DC and AI to study land pollution.

Therefore this chapter is divided into four parts. In the first section, Introduction, using AI and DC in flow modeling, landfill leachate is discussed. After that, in the Application of deep learning and machine learning methods in flow modeling of landfill leachate section, employing machine learning methods in soil quality assessment and remediation of soil quality are explained. Next, the Application of deep learning and machine learning methods in soil quality assessment and remediation section describes the nexus between nonbiodegradable waste and DC systems. Finally, in the Establishing a nexus between nonbiodegradable waste and data-centric systems section, first, the analysis of solid waste management techniques by deep learning and machine learning methods is investigated, and then, an artificial neural network (ANN) is developed by the research team for a very important case study in the automotive industry, which is

Current Trends and Advances in Computer-Aided Intelligent Environmental Data Engineering.
DOI: https://doi.org/10.1016/B978-0-323-85597-6.00008-2

modeling production amount of end-of-life vehicles (ELVs). It should be noted that to provide a better understanding for researchers who are in early stages of their careers or who do not have a broad background on these modeling tools, in each section, initially general information about the concepts is presented, and then the investigation of the case studies is carried out. Moreover, descriptions of the working principles of AI and DC methods are considered to be beyond the scope of this chapter, and readers are referred to the references cited in the text.

Application of deep learning and machine learning methods in flow modeling of landfill leachate

Main concepts

Garbage is gathered in a landfill, and in the rainy season, raindrops mix with some of the toxic elements in the landfill, forming the leachate. As is schematically depicted in Fig. 12.1, the leachate leaks to the soil and leads to soil and groundwater pollution.

To prevent damage to the soil and groundwater, usually the landfill is isolated by some layers and a leachate collection system also may be used. The leachate goes through pipes and is transferred to a treatment process. Treatment is either done in the site, or a pretreatment is performed and the rest is carried out in a central sewage treatment unit located elsewhere.

Fig. 12.2 shows the processes carried out in a leachate treatment plant.

1. Initially, leachate enters a pH-controlling unit, and the pH is adjusted if necessary.
2. Then, it enters a flash mixer. Here, the suspended solids are coagulated.
3. Next, the lower weight solids are removed in a clariflocculator.
4. After that, it passes through a lamella separator and sand filter, in which any remaining solid parts are gathered.

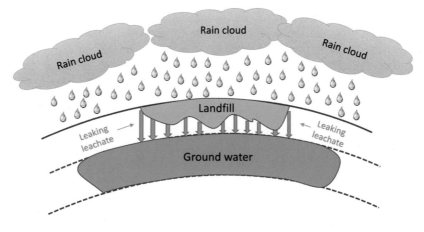

FIGURE 12.1

A schematic figure describing the process of leachate formation.

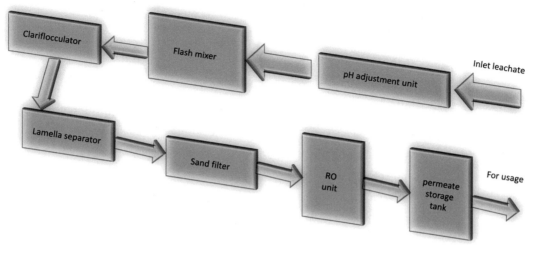

FIGURE 12.2

The processes carried out in a leachate treatment plant.

5. The liquid which has no solid parts at this time, goes to a reverse osmosis (RO) unit for further purification.
6. After leaving the RO unit, the liquid is fed into a permeate storage tank and the permeate can be employed for different purposes, including watering plants.

Selected recent studies

Different DC and AI methods have been utilized over recent years in this field. For instance, Abunama et al. (2019) employed a multilayer perceptron type of artificial neural network (known as MLP-ANN) for modeling. The authors selected leachate production rate as the output, while rainfall rate, garbage in the landfill, and emanated gases were the inputs. The prediction ability of MLP-ANN in comparison to support vector machine (SVM) was evaluated using relative error as the criterion. The comparisons made showed the significant superiority of MLP-ANN compared with SVM. Among the MLP-ANN models, the one with two hidden layers also had a better performance than the network which had one hidden layer.

In another study, Azadi et al. (2016) chose chemical oxygen demand load (COD load) as the output parameter of the modeling by their developed AI models. The landfill in the lab-scale was studied, and two DC and AI methods were examined. One was ANN, and the other was a method known as MP5 principal component analysis, abbreviated as PCA-MP5. The gathered experimental data by the authors was used to develop models. Like the investigation of Abunama et al. (2019), rainfall level was considered as an input, while four other were also taken into account. These were:

1. Days passed since deposition of waste;
2. Thickness of top cover;

3. Thickness of compacted clay liner's top cover;
4. Thickness of compacted clay liner's bottom cover.

According to the results, with a value of 4%, ANN has almost three times better absolute average error of PCA-MP5, that is, 12%, and as in the study by Abunama et al. (2019), ANN was found to be the best DC and AI tool for prediction.

Another example is the paper by Guo et al. (2015), in which the wastewater treatment plant of a food waste disposal landfill was considered, and a robust tool for predicting the total nitrogen was found. In that study, similar to the investigation by Abunama et al. (2019), ANN and SVM were selected as the employed DC and AI techniques, and their ability to predict were compared. Evaluation was done based on three parameters, which were:

1. Coefficient of determination (R^2);
2. Relative efficiency criteria;
3. Nash−Sutcliff efficiency.

The final results demonstrated that like the two previously conducted studies, ANN was able to predict the output more accurately than the other methods. In addition, the sensitivity of the output to the considered effective input parameters was evaluated by a combination of a pattern search method and an approach called Latin-hypercube one-factor-at-a-time. The results of the sensitivity analysis are shown in Fig. 12.3, where two methods introduced different levels of the importance

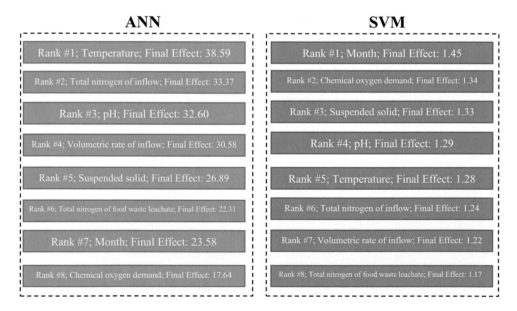

FIGURE 12.3

The predicted impact level of effective input parameters on the value of output, that is, total nitrogen in the study by Guo et al. (2015).

for the effective parameters. Among them, knowing that ANN is more accurate, its reported sensitivity that would be more reliable.

Application of deep learning and machine learning methods in soil quality assessment and remediation

Main concepts

In general, soil is a combination of mineral, water, and air, and different combinations of these three materials will lead to various conditions for soil, three examples of which are depicted in Fig. 12.4. As observed, for instance, in a good soil for plant growth, the contributions of the mentioned parts are around 50%, 25%, and 25%, respectively (Bünemann et al., 2018).

The quality of soil is a key factor in agriculture, building and road construction, and many other processes important to human life. Soil should have the "desirable" quality to meet the expected requirements. The quality of soil affects water resources, climate change, food industry, wildlife, etc. There are different parameters which have impacts on soil quality. They can be categorized in to three main aspects, which are:

1. Physical properties: Including temperature, moisture level, bulk density, texture, water retention, etc.
2. Chemical properties: pH, electricity conductivity, soil organic carbon, and the amount of nitrogen are considered as the most important chemical properties of soil.
3. Biological properties: These are the characteristics which describe the activity of microorganisms in the soil. Microbial biomass carbon is one of the well-known biological properties of soil.

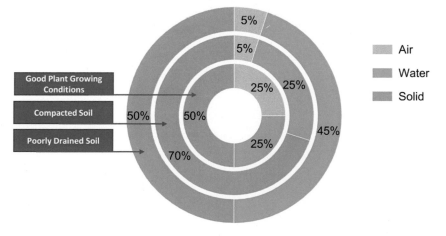

FIGURE 12.4

Three examples of possible combinations for soil.

As schematically shown in Fig. 12.5, in each application, a "healthy" soil is the one whose properties are in an acceptable range from the three described aspects. Moreover, based on the contribution of sand, slit, and clay, different names are given to different types of soil, as observed in Fig. 12.6.

Soil can be polluted in a number of ways, including:

- Leaking leachate (as has been discussed already), oil, or any other substances that are harmful to the soil;
- High utilization of fertilizers or pesticides;
- Destruction of the plants and trees in the region;
- Changing weather conditions.

When soil is polluted, the contamination should be removed. Soil remediation refers to such a process. There are five common ways to clean soil, which are:

1. *Excavation*: This is the fastest way to remove contaminated soil. In this method, the part of soil which is polluted is removed by means of various types of excavator. The removed part of the soil is then transferred for further treatment.
2. *Soil vapor extraction (SVE)*: As illustrated in Fig. 12.7, in SVE, initially a digging process is performed to create a number of wells. Then, in some of these wells, vapor is injected. The injected vapor leads contaminants to move to the other wells, where through a suction process,

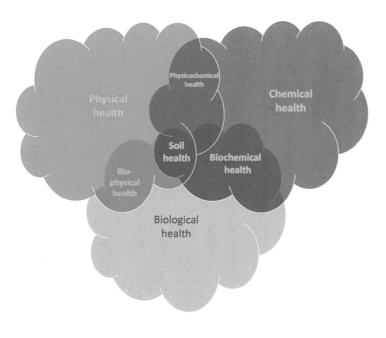

FIGURE 12.5

The definition of soil health in addition to introducing a number of important physical, chemical, and biological properties of soil.

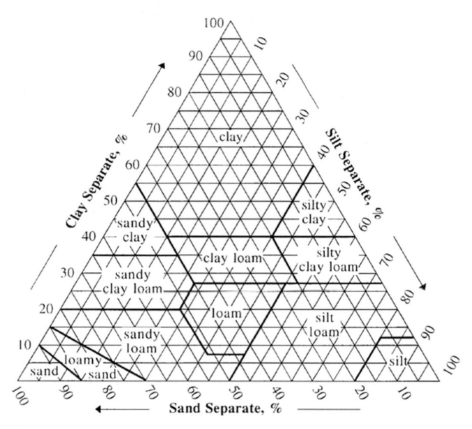

FIGURE 12.6

Different types of soil based on the contributions of clay, silt, and sand; this figure is known as the triangular diagram of soil texture classes by the United States Department of Agriculture (USDA).

From United States Department of Agriculture (USDA). (2020). Soil Texture Calculator. https://www.nrcs.usda.gov/wps/portal/nrcs/ detail/soils/survey/?cid = nrcs142p2_054167.

the mixture of vapor and contaminants is transferred to the ground level. After that, the vapor is separated and used again, while the contaminants are sent for further treatment. SVE is the most common and cheapest method of soil remediation.

3. *Electrical resistance heating (ERH)*: When ERH is applied, a number of conductor electrical resistances, such as that in Fig. 12.8, are installed in the polluted soil. Then, using electrical energy, an electrical current flows, and electrical resistances dissipate heat to the soil. By increasing the temperature of the soil, contaminants are gradually transferred to the ground level. They are then vacuumed and sent to treatment units.

4. *Chemical oxidation*: Chemical oxidation works based on the fact that some pollutants can react with oxidizers like H_2O_2. Therefore, as is schematically shown in Fig. 12.9, the oxidizer is injected into the ground, and then the product of the reaction is gathered from some of the wells.

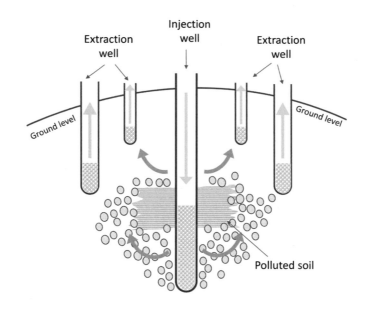

FIGURE 12.7

Soil vapor extraction process for soil remediation.

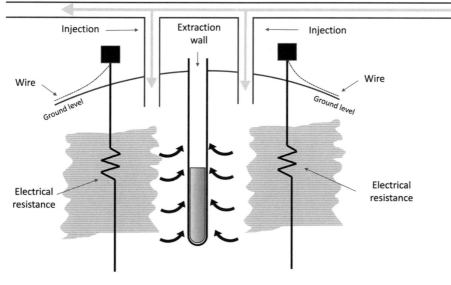

FIGURE 12.8

Electrical resistance heating process for soil remediation.

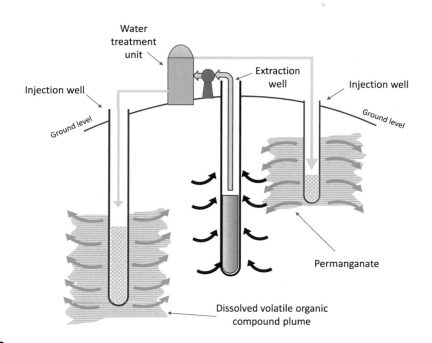

FIGURE 12.9

Chemical oxidation process for soil remediation.

5. *Bioremediation*: There are some bacteria which consume some contaminants and, when they enter polluted soil, are able to remove these pollutants. In this way, the probable biological consequences should be considered.

Selected recent studies

As with, studies on leachate, assessment of soil quality has been carried out using different techniques, among which AI has been one of the most frequently used. For example, Liu et al. (2016) employed SVM to classify the soil quality in urban areas. The authors used Taiyuan, China as their case study. The Chinese soil standard, mentioned in Table 12.1, was used to calculate the soil quality index for the training data. The results showed that the best found SVM model was able to predict the soil quality with an accuracy level of 98.3%.

In another investigation, Bayat et al. (2021) used ANN to predict the thermal conductivity of soil. They developed their model in such a way that the prediction became possible based on topographical attributes. A region in the United States, namely, the Southern Great Plains, was studied in this case. In that study, in addition to ANN, SVM and multiple linear regression (MLR) methods were also applied, and their prediction ability was compared with that of ANN. Their sample distributions are depicted in Fig. 12.10.

The authors examined 12 conditions, in each of which a specific combination of inputs was the input for modeling. The combinations are introduced in Table 12.2. Each series of inputs was called

Table 12.1 The soil quality indicators based on the Chinese standard.

Type of material	Category			Unit
Metals	Group I	Group II	Group III	N.A.
Copper	From 0 to 35	From 35 to 100	From 100 to 400	mg/kg
Zinc	From 0 to 100	From 100 to 300	From 300 to 500	mg/kg
Nickel	From 0 to 40	From 40 to 100	From 100 to 200	mg/kg
Chromium	From 0 to 90	From 90 to 350	From 350 to 400	mg/kg
Lead	From 0 to 35	From 35 to 80	From 80 to 500	mg/kg
Cadmium	From 0.000 to 0.200	From 0.200 to 0.800	From 0.800 to 1.000	mg/kg
Mercury	From 0.000 to 0.150	From 0.150 to 1.000	From 1.000 to 1.500	mg/kg
Arsenic	From 0 to 15	From 15 to 25	From 25 to 40	mg/kg
Fertilizers	Class A	Class B	Class C	N.A.
Whole nitrogen	From 0.15 to infinity	From 0.075 to 0.150	From 0.000 to 0.075	%
Usable nitrogen	From 120 to infinity	From 60 to 120	From 0 to 60	mg/kg
Usable phosphorus	From 20 to infinity	From 5 to 20	From 0 to 5	mg/kg
Usable potassium	From 150 to infinity	From 50 to 150	From 0 to 50	mg/kg
Amount of organic matter	From 3 to infinity	From 1 to 3	From 0 to 1	%

Data from Liu, Y., Wang, H., Zhang, H., & Liber, K. (2016). A comprehensive support vector machine-based classification model for soil quality assessment. Soil and Tillage Research, 155, 19–26. https://doi.org/10.1016/j.still.2015.07.006.

PTF, which is the acronym for PedoTransfer Function. The combination was composed of all or a number of the following parameters:

The silt to sand ratio;
Bulk density;
Water content in the soil;
General landscape information;
General weather during soil sampling;
East–west slope;
North–south slope.

Like almost all of the investigated studies in this section, ANN had the best performance among the examined AI techniques. TPF$_7$, with the specifications indicated in Table 12.3, was found to be the foremost ANN for prediction.

Moreover, some attempts have been made using AI and DC methods to help with soil remediation. Jia et al. (2021) published a review study on investigations which combined visible and infrared reflectance spectroscopy (VIRS) with AI methods for soil pollution mapping process. The authors studied the related research works based on a variety of criteria. For example, Table 12.4 is one of the tables presented by them, in which the conducted investigations are compared together based on the percentage of training and validation sets, number of observations, and the employed methods.

The use of hydrogel nanocomposites was investigated by Hou et al. (2018) for both detection and removing the soil pollution. In that study, a future scheme for employing AI to help the process was also drawn. Additionally, Boente et al. (2019) took advantage of geostatistical, statistics, and AI to detect and diminish soil pollution. The study was carried out for a region around a mercury

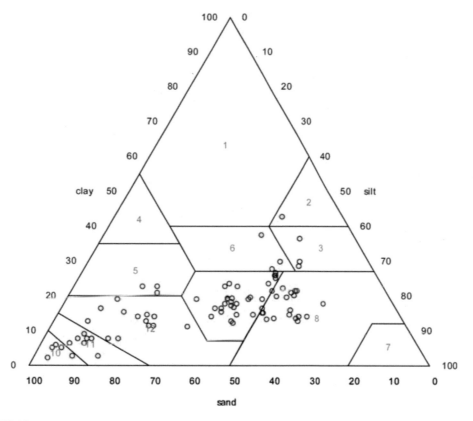

FIGURE 12.10

Distribution of soil samples employed for model development in the study of Bayat et al. (2021).

From Bayat, H., Ebrahimzadeh, G., & Mohanty, B. P. (2021). Investigating the capability of estimating soil thermal conductivity using topographical attributes for the Southern Great Plains, USA. Soil and Tillage Research, 206, 104811. https://doi.org/10.1016/j.still.2020.104811.

mine in Spain which was out of operation at the time of the study from the 1970s, but the pollution had already contaminated the soil.

Establishing a nexus between nonbiodegradable waste and data-centric systems

Main concepts

In general, the word nexus refers to the connection between two things (Safari et al., 2020). Considering this point, the nexus between nonbiodegradable waste and DC systems means the connections that DC and AI techniques have to the issues related to nonbiodegradable waste.

Table 12.2 Different combinations considered for the input parameters in Bayat et al. (2021).

PedoTransfer function number	Silt to sand ratio (Si/S)	Bulk density (BD)	Water content in the soil (WCS)	General landscape information (GLI)	General weather during soil sampling (GWS)	East–west slope (EWS)	North–south slope (NSS)
				Inputs			
1	✓	✗	✗	✗	✗	✗	✗
2	✓	✓	✗	✗	✗	✗	✗
3	✓	✗	✓	✗	✗	✗	✗
4	✓	✓	✓	✗	✗	✗	✗
5	✓	✓	✓	✓	✗	✗	✗
6	✓	✓	✓	✗	✓	✗	✗
7	✓	✓	✓	✗	✗	✓	✓
8	✓	✓	✓	✓	✗	✓	✓
9	✓	✓	✓	✓	✓	✓	✓
10	✓	✓	✓	✓	✓	✗	✗
11	✓	✓	✓	✓	✓	✓	✓
12	✗	✗	✓	✓	✓	✓	✓

From Bayat, H., Ebrahimzadeh, G., & Mohanty, B. P. (2021). Investigating the capability of estimating soil thermal conductivity using topographical attributes for the Southern Great Plains, USA. Soil and Tillage Research, 206. https://doi.org/10.1016/j.still.2020.104811.

Table 12.3 Specifications of artificial neural network (ANN) models developed in the study of Bayat et al. (2021).

Parameter	Description	PedoTransfer function number											
		1	2	3	4	5	6	7	8	9	10	11	12
Number of ANN	Radial basis function	31	30	34	13	7	16	14	14	13	6	7	15
	Multilayer perceptron	19	20	26	37	43	34	36	36	37	44	43	35
Hidden neurons	Bounds	From 3 to 19	From 3 to 19	From 3 to 19	From 3 to 19	From 3 to 19	From 3 to 19	From 3 to 19	From 3 to 19	From 3 to 19	From 3 to 19	From 3 to 19	From 3 to 19
	Mean	12	12	12	9	8	9	10	10	10	8	9	9
Transfer function for the output layer	Tanh	6	1	5	11	4	14	6	8	9	10	11	10
	Logistic	3	6	7	8	12	3	7	6	7	10	8	3
	Exponential	4	3	7	3	8	0	1	5	5	5	8	9
	Identity	32	36	29	19	18	26	24	22	24	17	17	19
	Sine	5	4	2	9	8	7	12	9	5	8	6	9
	Gaussian	31	30	24	13	7	16	14	14	14	6	7	15
Transfer function for the hidden layer	Identity	0	0	2	10	7	5	6	4	8	14	7	15
	Exponential	1	6	4	7	6	9	8	11	8	8	12	4
	Sine	0	0	3	5	8	8	7	6	6	8	10	2
	Logistic	11	7	10	6	11	4	6	9	8	5	7	10
	Tanh	7	7	7	9	11	8	9	6	6	9	7	4

From Bayat, H., Ebrahimzadeh, G., & Mohanty, B. P. (2021). Investigating the capability of estimating soil thermal conductivity using topographical attributes for the Southern Great Plains, USA. Soil and Tillage Research, 206, 104811. https://doi.org/10.1016/j.still.2020.104811.

Table 12.4 Classification of the studies carried out in the field of combining VIRS and AI for soil pollution mapping (Jia et al., 2021).

No.	Reference	Fraction of data employed for training and validation	Number of datasets	Corresponding statistical methods
1	Stazi et al. (2014)	75%, 25%	135	PLSR, SVM
2	Okparanma et al. (2014)	78%, 22%	137	PLSR
3	Shi et al. (2014)	66%, 34%	95	PLSR
4	Chakraborty et al. (2015)	75%, 25%	108	PLSR, RF, PSR
5	Peng et al. (2016)	75%, 25%	300	Cubist
6	Chakraborty et al. (2017)	70%, 30%	190	RF, PSR, ENet
7	Tayebi et al. (2017)	80%, 20%	120	PLSR, PCR
8	Zhao et al. (2018)	67%, 33%	225	MLR, BNPP, GA-BPNN

AI, Artificial intelligence; BNP, brain natriuretic peptide; ENet, elastic net regression; GA-BPNN, genetic algorithm back propagation neural network ; MLR, multiple linear regression; PCR, principal component regression; PLSR, partial least squares regression; PSR, penalized spline regression; RF, random forest; SVM, support vector machine; VIRS, visible and infrared reflectance spectroscopy.
Data from Jia, X., O'Connor, D., Shi, Z., & Hou, D. (2021). VIRS based detection in combination with machine learning for mapping soil pollution. Environmental Pollution, 268, 115845. https://doi.org/10.1016/j.envpol.2020.115845.

Treatment of nonbiodegradable waste is a challenging problem for landfill treatment and soil pollution management.

The unwanted materials, known as garbage, are classified into two main groups:

1. *Biodegradable waste*: These materials can be decomposed into simple compounds of soil (manure) by using natural agents and are called biodegradable waste. There are a variety of natural agents, including oxygen, microorganisms, macroorganism, water, acid rain, sun radiation, etc. In other words, biodegradable waste is recycled naturally. Examples of biodegradable waste include, paper fruits, and vegetables. Most biodegradable waste materials are organic.

2. *Nonbiodegradable waste*: Metals, glasses, fiber glasses, kitchenware, plastics, and arcopal plates are examples of nonbiodegradable waste. In contrast to biodegradable, nonbiodegradable waste waste cannot be decomposed into manure, even after hundreds or thousands of years. Therefore nonbiodegradable waste cannot be recycled naturally. Some types, such as metals, plastics, and glasses, can be recycled using developed processes. However, some other kinds, like acropal plates cannot, and they should be treated by one of the other processes could be done on the landfill treatment and mentioned in this chapter.

Selected recent studies

The study carried out by Sudha et al. (2016) is an examples of recent research works in this field. In that investigation, the authors employed a deep learning algorithm to develop a system which works based on processing the waste material image. A network was built and trained, and then employed for clustering.

In another work, Dubey et al. (2020) used the Internet of Things (IoT) and *k*-nearest neighbors algorithm for segregation of waste in both stages: household and society levels. The working principle of the algorithm developed by the authors is depicted in Fig. 12.11. Moreover, the process flowchart of the algorithm for the household and society levels is introduced in Figs. 12.12 and 12.13, respectively.

In addition, in the research work of Gupta et al. (2019) different systems have been introduced. One of these, which is illustrated in Fig. 12.14, is a smart system for gathering, transferring, and disposal of garbage. The system works based on a number of sensors, the IoT, and AI. It considers many aspects, including the volume of garbage in a trash bin, the predicted increasing rate of volume, and the estimated time and that the trash bin will be full. To minimize the cost and effort of the cleaning team, the smart waste management system also has a connection to traffic and geographical information system (GIS) data.

As observed, the detection and discovery of methods for better management have been the topic of one group of the studies in the field. In those studies, the IoT has been the most dominant means, while other techniques such as AI and DC methods have been employed also. In another group, AI and DC have been used to find a correlation for describing the performance. The found correlation has the potential of usage for different applications, including optimization.

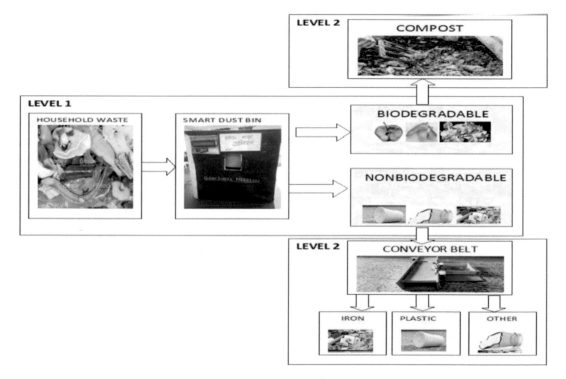

FIGURE 12.11

A schematic description of the developed algorithm of Dubey et al. (2020) for waste management.

From Dubey, S., Singh, P., Yadav, P., & Singh, K. K. (2020). Household waste management system using IoT and machine learning.
Procedia Computer Science, 167, *1950–1959. https://doi.org/10.1016/j.procs.2020.03.222.*

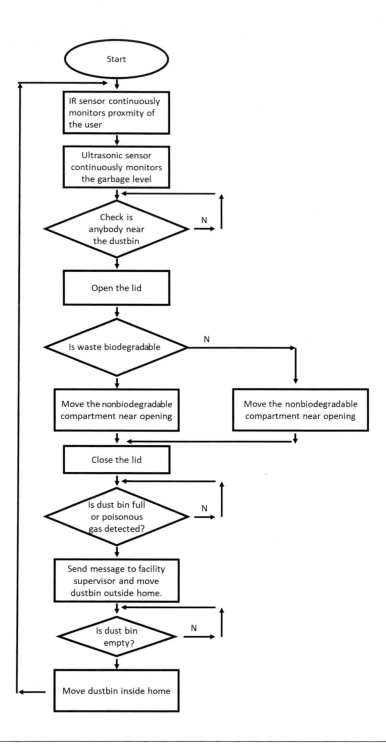

FIGURE 12.12

The process flowchart for the developed algorithm of Dubey et al. (2020) for waste management; stage 1, that is, household level.

From Dubey, S., Singh, P., Yadav, P., & Singh, K. K. (2020). Household waste management system using IoT and machine learning. Procedia Computer Science, 167, 1950—1959. https://doi.org/10.1016/j.procs.2020.03.222.

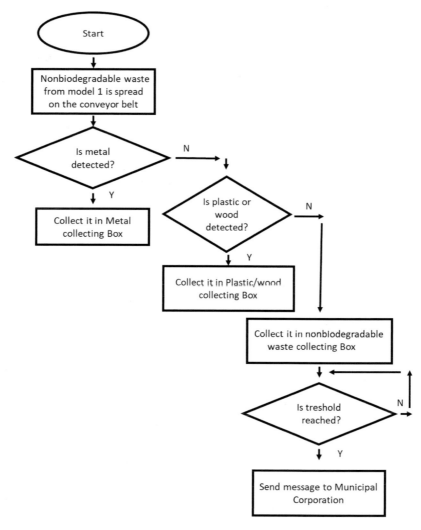

FIGURE 12.13

The process flowchart for the developed algorithm of Dubey et al. (2020) for waste management; (b) stage 2, that is, society level.

From Dubey, S., Singh, P., Yadav, P., & Singh, K. K. (2020). Household waste management system using IoT and machine learning. Procedia Computer Science, 167, 1950–1959. https://doi.org/10.1016/j.procs.2020.03.222.

Mukherjee et al. (2019) conducted a study to discover the optimum conditions in the tire waste treatment process. The authors took advantage of response surface methodology (RSM) and Box—Behnken design for this purpose. Three operating parameters were considered and analyzed. These were activation temperature, the fraction of potassium hydroxide to waste, and time of activation. These had the range of 400°C—600°C, 0.5—1.5, and 1—3 hours, respectively. The highest error level of

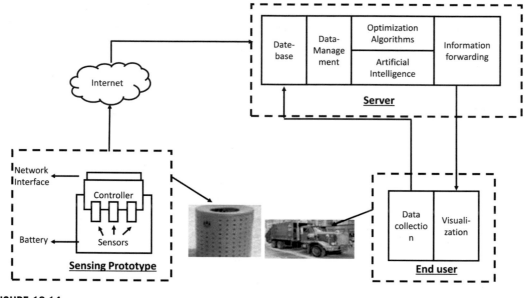

FIGURE 12.14

The schematic representation of the intelligent system discussed in Gupta et al. (2019) for smart waste management. As mentioned in Gupta et al. (2019), the figure is drawn based on the information in Gutierrez et al. (2015).

From Gupta, P. K., Shree, V., Hiremath, L., & Rajendran, S. (2019). The use of modern technology in smart waste management and recycling: Artificial intelligence and machine learning. In Studies in computational intelligence (Vol. 823, pp. 173–188). Springer Verlag. https://doi.org/10.1007/978-3-030-12500-4_11.

1.5% and coefficient of determination (R^2) of 0.975 were observed, which confirmed the good agreement of the provided regression. Furthermore, the values of 400°C, 1.5, and 165 minutes were found to be the optimal values for the three mentioned performance decision variables, respectively.

Case studies of evaluations and analysis of solid waste management techniques by deep learning and machine learning methods

The complexity of solid waste management techniques

All the solid materials produced by different human activities and that are useless or unwanted are called "solid waste." Based on different criteria, solid waste can be divided into several classifications. For example, three classifications are the following:

1. Organic or inorganic;
2. Disposable and undisputable;
3. The production source: residential, industrial, medical, agricultural, and so on.

Solid waste management refers to the process of collection, transportation, and final treatment of solid waste. As shown in Fig. 12.15, in the solid waste management process, initially, solid waste is gathered by waste containers, dust bins, trash cans, etc. Next, they are transferred from the production location to the disposal units during the transportation process, and then, the final treatment takes place. Based on what the solid waste is, a number of conditions take place. Some of the most important are the following:

- *Incineration*: In the incineration process, solid waste is burned, and thermal energy, ash, and flue gases are obtained. This process is suitable for organic materials, and can be used to generate heat or power. However, it is also accompanied by air pollution.
- *Composting*: Biodegradable materials can be converted into fertilizers, and are used again in agriculture. Sometimes, the process is facilitated using worms, which is called vermiculture.
- *Reuse*: Some parts, especially metals can be reused. They are heated through a smelting process.
- *Disposal*: The part of the solid waste which cannot be used anymore is disposed of in a landfill, sanitary landfill, open dump, etc.
- *Pyrolysis*: In the pyrolysis process, the substance is at high temperature, very low pressure, and with the absence of oxygen. Temperature ranges between 300°C–900°C, and the product is usually a fuel or other chemical substance.
- *Bioremediation*: As the name suggests, in this method, the environmental conditions are simulated in such a way that the activity of microorganisms increases significantly, leading to degradation of the waste.

As a key factor which plays a vital role in solid management, prediction of the amount of waste produced in a large scale is of great importance. Considering this point, a solution for accurate prediction of ELVs is provided using ANN by the research team in the rest of this section. This will open the road for policy-makers to perform solid waste management better.

Waste   **Waste collection**   **To plant**

FIGURE 12.15

A schematic diagram showing the processes that take place in solid waste management.

The analyzed case study

The volume of ELVs is an important factor in waste management (Idiano et al., 2020). To create a suitable waste management system for the vehicle, and organize the infrastructure for their reuse, prediction of the ELV value is a crucial factor (Rosa & Terzi, 2018; Zhou et al., 2019). There have been several studies that have attempted to find a suitable prediction model for ELVs, including Andersen et al. (2005), Hao et al. (2018), and Idiano et al. (2020).

In one of these studies, Idiano et al. (2020) developed a linear prediction methodology for estimation of the generated and recycled ELVs. In that study, gross domestic product (GDP) and population were considered as influencing variables. Data from European countries for the years 2006−16 were used to develop the model. The R^2 values for the generated models are listed in Table 12.5. As observed in this table, the achieved R^2 values in that study were all under 0.8.

Despite many efforts, there is still a long way to go, because determination of all the effective factors is a very complex challenge. In this sense, here, the use of ANN in waste management of vehicles is investigated.

In the present work, with the aim of improvement of the accuracy of modeling, ANN is used. GDP per capita and population of European countries for the years 2008−17 are assumed to be the effective factors, which indicates that a more up-to-date database is used. Moreover, the generated ELVs per capita and recycled ELVs are considered as the output parameters. All the data are extracted from Eurostat (2020). Figs. 12.16 and 12.17 introduce a schematic representation of the network for different models. The uncertainty values for the developed models are also listed in Table 12.6.

The results show that the application of neural networks could provide significant advantages compared to the linear models which have been proposed in the literature (Idiano et al., 2020). Although further improvements can be still achieved, the results of the evaluation of the model provided here by the research team have confirmed that with economic factors such as GDP and population, there is great potential for predicting the generated and recycled ELVs in a more precise way.

Table 12.5 Uncertainty of different models.

No.	Output	The considered effective factor	R^2
1	Generated ELVs (thousand tons)	GDP	0.7137
2	Generated ELVs per capita (kg/capita)	GDP per capita	0.7145
3	Recycled ELVs (thousand tons)	GDP	0.7354
4	Recycled ELVs per capita (kg/capita)	GDP per capita	0.7393
5	Generated ELVs (thousand tons)	Population	0.7508
6	Recycled ELVs (thousand tons)	Population	0.7662

ELVs, *End-of-life vehicles*; GDP, *gross domestic product.*
Data from Idiano, D., Massimo, G., & Paolo, R. (2020). Recycling of end-of-life vehicles: Assessing trends and performances in Europe. Technological Forecasting and Social Change, 152, *119887. https://doi.org/10.1016/j.techfore.2019.119887.*

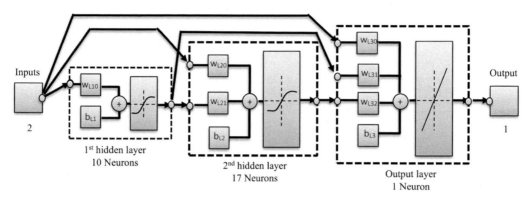

FIGURE 12.16

Schematic representation of the feedforward neural networks used in this study for recycled ELVs. *ELVs*, End-of-life vehicles.

Modified from Moradi, M. H., Sohani, A., Zabihigivi, M., & Wirbser, H. (2017). A comprehensive approach to find the performance map of a heat pump using experiment and soft computing methods. Energy Conversion and Management, 153, *224–242. https://doi.org/10.1016/j.enconman.2017.09.070.*

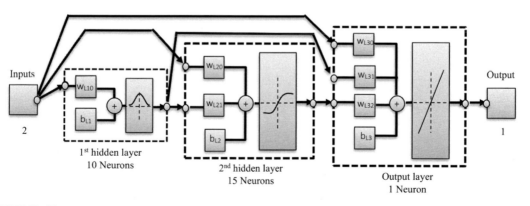

FIGURE 12.17

Schematic representation of the feedforward neural networks used in this study for generated ELVs. *ELVs*, End-of-life vehicles.

Modified from Sohani, A., Zabihigivi, M., Moradi, M. H., Sayyaadi, H., & Hasani Balyani, H. (2017). A comprehensive performance investigation of cellulose evaporative cooling pad systems using predictive approaches. Applied Thermal Engineering, 110, *1589–1608. https://doi.org/10.1016/j.applthermaleng.2016.08.216.*

Table 12.6 Uncertainty of different models.

Model	R^2	NRMSE	NMAE
Generated ELVs per capita (ton/capita)	0.986	0.029	0.013
Recycled ELVs per capita (ton/capita)	0.985	0.024	0.01

ELVs; *End-of-life vehicles;* NMAE, *normalized mean absoloute error;* NRMSE, *normalized root mean square error.*

Conclusions

According to the investigation carried out in this chapter, DC and AI techniques have been extensively utilized in studies with in the subject of monitoring, evaluation, and removing land pollution. In different investigations, various input and output parameters have been considered based on the studied issue. A variety of the available DC and AI methods, like SVM, MLR, RSM, ANN, etc. have been utilized. However, ANN has been used much more often than others in the research works, and has provided higher accuracy compared to other approaches, as has been proven in a number of studies. Considering this point, future works could be carried out for optimization of the ANN structure to have more accurate and faster calculations. Moreover, the IoT and GIS could be utilized in combination with ANN to provide more flexible prediction tools. Taking the impact of uncertainty and various policy-making scenarios into account are also other subjects that could be suggested for future investigations.

References

Abunama, T., Othman, F., Ansari, M., & El-Shafie, A. (2019). Leachate generation rate modeling using artificial intelligence algorithms aided by input optimization method for an MSW landfill. *Environmental Science and Pollution Research*, 26(4), 3368−3381. Available from https://doi.org/10.1007/s11356-018-3749-5.

Andersen, F. M., Larsen, H. V., & Skovgaard, M. (2005). Projection of end-of-life vehicles. Development of a projection model and estimates of ELVs for 2005−2030. European Topic Centre on Resource and Waste Management. ETC/RWM working paper No. 2008/2. http://www.risoe.dk/rispubl/art/2008_28.pdf.

Azadi, S., Amiri, H., & Rakhshandehroo, G. R. (2016). Evaluating the ability of artificial neural network and PCA-M5P models in predicting leachate COD load in landfills. *Waste Management*, *55*, 220−230. Available from https://doi.org/10.1016/j.wasman.2016.05.025.

Bayat, H., Ebrahimzadeh, G., & Mohanty, B. P. (2021). Investigating the capability of estimating soil thermal conductivity using topographical attributes for the Southern Great Plains, USA. *Soil and Tillage Research*, *206*, 104811. Available from https://doi.org/10.1016/j.still.2020.104811.

Boente, C., Albuquerque, M. T. D., Gerassis, S., Rodríguez-Valdés, E., & Gallego, J. R. (2019). A coupled multivariate statistics, geostatistical and machine-learning approach to address soil pollution in a prototypical Hg-mining site in a natural reserve. *Chemosphere*, *218*, 767−777. Available from https://doi.org/10.1016/j.chemosphere.2018.11.172.

Bünemann, E. K., Bongiorno, G., Bai, Z., Creamer, R. E., De Deyn, G., Goede, R., Fleskens, L., Geissen, V., Kuyper, T. W., Mäder, P., Pulleman, M., Sukkel, W., van Groenigen, J. W., & Brussaard, L. (2018). Soil quality—A critical review. *Soil Biology and Biochemistry*, *120*, 105−125. Available from https://doi.org/10.1016/j.soilbio.2018.01.030.

Chakraborty, S., et al. (2015). Development of a hybrid proximal sensing method for rapid identification of petroleum contaminated soils. *Science of the Total Environment*, *514*, 399−408. Available from https://doi.org/10.1016/j.scitotenv.2015.01.087.

Chakraborty, S., et al. (2017). Rapid assessment of regional soil arsenic pollution risk via diffuse reflectance spectroscopy. *Geoderma*, *289*, 72−81. Available from https://doi.org/10.1016/j.geoderma.2016.11.024.

Dubey, S., Singh, P., Yadav, P., & Singh, K. K. (2020). Household waste management system using IoT and machine learning. *Procedia Computer Science*, *167*, 1950−1959. Available from https://doi.org/10.1016/j.procs.2020.03.222.

Eurostat. (2020). https://ec.europa.eu/eurostat/home.

Guo, H., Jeong, K., Lim, J., Jo, J., Kim, Y. M., Park, J.-P., Kim, J. H., & Cho, K. H. (2015). Prediction of effluent concentration in a wastewater treatment plant using machine learning models. *Journal of Environmental Sciences*, *32*, 90−101. Available from https://doi.org/10.1016/j.jes.2015.01.007.

Gupta, P. K., Shree, V., Hiremath, L., & Rajendran, S. (2019). *The use of modern technology in smart waste management and recycling: Artificial intelligence and machine learning. Studies in computational intelligence* (Vol. 823, pp. 173−188). Springer Verlag. Available from https://doi.org/10.1007/978-3-030-12500-4_11.

Gutierrez, J.M., Jensen, M., Henius, M., Riaz, T. (2015). Smart waste collection system based on location intelligence. Procedia Computer Science. Available from https://doi.org/10.1016/j.procs.2015.09.170.

Hao, H., Zhang, Q., Wang, Z., & Zhang, J. (2018). Forecasting the number of end-of-life vehicles using a hybrid model based on grey model and artificial neural network. *Journal of Cleaner Production*, *202*, 684−696. Available from https://doi.org/10.1016/j.jclepro.2018.08.176.

Hou, X., Mu, L., Chen, F., & Hu, X. (2018). Emerging investigator series: Design of hydrogel nanocomposites for the detection and removal of pollutants: From nanosheets, network structures, and biocompatibility to machine-learning-assisted design. *Environmental Science: Nano*, *5*(10), 2216−2240. Available from https://doi.org/10.1039/c8en00552d.

Huang, Y., Wang, L., Wang, W., Li, T., He, Z., & Yang, X. (2019). Current status of agricultural soil pollution by heavy metals in China: A meta-analysis. *Science of the Total Environment*, *651*, 3034−3042. Available from https://doi.org/10.1016/j.scitotenv.2018.10.185.

Idiano, D., Massimo, G., & Paolo, R. (2020). Recycling of end-of-life vehicles: Assessing trends and performances in Europe. *Technological Forecasting and Social Change*, *152*, 119887. Available from https://doi.org/10.1016/j.techfore.2019.119887.

Jia, X., O'Connor, D., Shi, Z., & Hou, D. (2021). VIRS based detection in combination with machine learning for mapping soil pollution. *Environmental Pollution*, *268*, 115845. Available from https://doi.org/10.1016/j.envpol.2020.115845.

Jin, S., Bluemling, B., & Mol, A. P. J. (2018). Mitigating land pollution through pesticide packages—The case of a collection scheme in rural China. *Science of the Total Environment*, *622−623*, 502−509. Available from https://doi.org/10.1016/j.scitotenv.2017.11.330.

Liu, Y., Wang, H., Zhang, H., & Liber, K. (2016). A comprehensive support vector machine-based classification model for soil quality assessment. *Soil and Tillage Research*, *155*, 19−26. Available from https://doi.org/10.1016/j.still.2015.07.006.

Moradi, M. H., Sohani, A., Zabihigivi, M., & Wirbser, H. (2017). A comprehensive approach to find the performance map of a heat pump using experiment and soft computing methods. *Energy Conversion and Management*, *153*, 224−242. Available from https://doi.org/10.1016/j.enconman.2017.09.070.

Mukherjee, T., Rahaman, M., Ghosh, A., & Bose, S. (2019). Optimization of adsorbent derived from non-biodegradable waste employing response surface methodology toward the removal of dye solutions.

International Journal of Environmental Science and Technology, *16*(12), 8671−8678. Available from https://doi.org/10.1007/s13762-018-02184-4.

Okparanma, R. N., Coulon, F., Mayr, T., & Mouazen, A. M. (2014). Mapping polycyclic aromatic hydrocarbon and total toxicity equivalent soil concentrations by visible and near-infrared spectroscopy. *Environmental Pollution*, *192*, 162−170. Available from https://doi.org/10.1016/j.envpol.2014.05.022.

Peng, Y., et al. (2016). Digital mapping of toxic metals in Qatari soils using remote sensing and ancillary data. *Remote Sensing*, *8*(12), 1003.

Rosa, P., & Terzi, S. (2018). Improving end of life vehicle's management practices: An economic assessment through system dynamics. *Journal of Cleaner Production*, *184*, 520−536. Available from https://doi.org/10.1016/j.jclepro.2018.02.264.

Safari, M., Sohani, A., & Sayyaadi, H. (2020). A higher performance optimum design for a tri-generation system by taking the advantage of water-energy nexus. *Journal of Cleaner Production*, *284*, 124704. Available from https://doi.org/10.1016/j.jclepro.2020.124704.

Shi, T., Liu, H., Wang, J., Chen, Y., Fei, T., & Wu, G. (2014). Monitoring arsenic contamination in agricultural soils with reflectance spectroscopy of rice plants. *Environmental Science & Technology*, *48*(11), 6264−6272.

Stazi, S. R., et al. (2014). Hyperspectral visible−near infrared determination of arsenic concentration in soil. *Communications in Soil Science and Plant Analysis*, *45*(22), 2911−2920.

Sudha, S., Vidhyalakshmi, M., Pavithra, K., Sangeetha, K., & Swaathi, V. (2016). *An automatic classification method for environment: Friendly waste segregation using deep learning. 2016 IEEE international conference on technological innovations in ICT for agriculture and rural development, TIAR 2016* (pp. 65−70). Institute of Electrical and Electronics Engineers Inc. Available from https://doi.org/10.1109/TIAR.2016.7801215.

Tayebi, M., Naderi, M., Mohammadi, J., & Tayebi, M. H. (2017). Comparing different statistical models for assessing Fe-contaminated soils based on VNIR/SWIR spectral data. *Environmental Earth Sciences*, *76*(21), 734.

Zhao, L., et al. (2018). Estimation methods for soil mercury content using hyperspectral remote sensing. *Sustainability*, *10*(7), 2474.

Zhou, F., Lim, M. K., He, Y., Lin, Y., & Chen, S. (2019). End-of-life vehicle (ELV) recycling management: Improving performance using an ISM approach. *Journal of Cleaner Production*, *228*, 231−243. Available from https://doi.org/10.1016/j.jclepro.2019.04.182.

Application of artificial intelligence in the mapping and measurement of soil pollution

13

Chukwunonso O. Aniagor, Marcel I. Ejimofor, Stephen N. Oba and Matthew C. Menkiti

Department of Chemical Engineering, Nnamdi Azikiwe University, Awka, Nigeria

Introduction

The term "soil pollution" is often confused with "soil contamination," meanwhile, both terms have been clearly distinguished by the Intergovernmental Technical Panel on Soils, under the Global Soil Partnership. Soil contamination occurs when the concentrations of soil pollutants are higher than normal, but with no significant harmful environmental effects (Rodríguez-Eugenio et al., 2018). Conversely, for soil pollution, the high pollutant concentration sustains detrimental environmental effects. Rapid urbanization and population growth have resulted in the generation of huge volumes of waste, with the soil serving as their main sink. Thus, in most cases, soil pollutants (such as heavy metals and petroleum hydrocarbons) exist as a direct consequence of a number of anthropogenic activities (Hashem, Aniagor, Hussein, et al., 2021; Hashem, Aniagor, Nasr, et al., 2021), with some additional evidence for the toxicity (especially at high concentration) of naturally occurring soil minerals. It is erroneously believed that once these pollutants are placed into the soil, their negative human health and environmental impacts are neutralized. However, this is not usually the case as the danger associated with their persistent physicochemical evolution, as well as their assessment and perception difficulty in soil, persist.

Soil pollution is considered among the top 10 issues with far-reaching consequences on soil functionality in Europe, North Africa, Asia, and North America (FAO, 2015). This is because the soil nutrient balance and pH may be significantly altered by the presence of some of these pollutants (FAO, 2015). Based on an earlier soil pollution estimate by the International Soil Reference and Information Centre and the United Nations Environment Programme, about 22 million hectares are polluted globally (Centrum, 1990). Consequently, due to socioeconomic differences, all the soil pollutant mapping and measurement attempts have been conducted principally in developed countries. The available records show that about 35% of Chinese soil (Li et al., 2015), 3 million plots of the European Economic Area, 1300 American sites (Mench et al., 2018), and 80,000 Australian sites (Reijnders, 2009) are polluted. However, the aforementioned data are believed to be grossly underestimated in several quarters considering the complexity associated with soil pollution mapping and measurements. This issue of poor mapping and measurement underscores the paucity of data on soil pollution and its attendant consequences, hence the need for an effective soil pollution mapping and measurement approach.

Current Trends and Advances in Computer-Aided Intelligent Environmental Data Engineering.
DOI: https://doi.org/10.1016/B978-0-323-85597-6.00003-3

Previously, soil pollution surveys were achieved via laborious approaches, involving the collection of polluted soil samples from the field and subsequent chemical analyses of these samples in the laboratory. Despite their seemingly wide acceptability among environmental soil scientists, the aforementioned approach is both time-and cost-intensive, while the results are usually nonencompassing and incomprehensive (Abdallah et al., 2020). Currently, there is an increased research focus on the understanding and assessment of the soil pollution issue. This is due to the increasing perception of the implications of soil pollution and the urgent need for their mitigation, coupled with increasing technological advancements. Advanced technologies and artificial intelligence (AI) systems are revolutionizing the execution of soil pollution mapping and measurement. Composed of a computer program and design, AI has the capacity of imitating human features in terms of analytical evaluation, training, logic, and environmental cognitiveness (Voda & Radu, 2019; Zheng et al., 2017). Several AI-based models [such as artificial neural network (ANN) genetic algorithm, and fuzzy logic] have successfully depicted various environment-related issues.

AI-based models have demonstrated high efficiency in the evaluation of multivariate and nonlinear data, hence their increased adoption for addressing diverse problems in environmental engineering (Abdallah et al., 2020; Yetilmezsoy et al., 2011). For instance, the applications of ANN, multilayer perceptron (MLP), and adaptive neurofuzzy inference system (ANFIS) models for soil pollutant and particulate matter concentration have been reported (Gholami et al., 2011; Shu et al., 2006). The concentration level of some atmospheric gaseous pollutants such as carbon (II) oxide and ozone, have been effectively predicted using MLP (Agirre-Basurko et al., 2006). Also, the optimization of wastewater treatment processes (Cakmakci, 2007; George et al., 2021; Igwegbe et al., 2019) and methane yield prediction within a biodigester set-up (Niska & Serkkola, 2018) have been achieved with ANFIS. In soil pollution studies, AI is currently employed for soil pollutant mapping, measurement, reduction, management, etc. A preliminary literature survey showed that the major reviews on AI application in environmental science and engineering centers around the optimization of wastewater treatment, with some in specific solid waste-related applications. To the best of our knowledge and judging from the extensive literature survey conducted, there exists no comprehensive report on the application of AI-based systems in soil pollution mapping and measurement. Therefore there is a need to harness reported research findings toward providing a thorough discussion and assessment of the current AI applicational status in this field.

This work offers a detailed discussion of the various AI-based models with successful application in soil pollution mapping and measurement. In-depth exposition of the theoretical background of the respective AI models and their potential applications for mapping and measurement of soil pollution are also provided. This chapter further aims to elucidate the different merits, demerits, and operational efficiency of the different AI-based models applied in this research area.

Methodology

Systematic review protocol

Systematic literature reviewing (SLR) has wide application in several engineering fields, such as civil and environmental engineering, as it is key for holistic identification, assessment, and interpretation of works and findings in a given research sphere. Following the laid-down protocols of design, implementation, and discussion, SLR is adopted for the elimination of review blueprint-related bias to ensure a credible and comprehensive outcome (Staples & Niazi, 2008). In this study, the SLR deals with the identification and assessment of works relating to AI application in the mapping and measurement of soil pollution, adopting specific research questions. The adopted research questions are stated thus (1) Which AI models/algorithms are applied in soil pollution mapping and measurement? (2) How does the prediction performance of a given AI model contrast with others? (3) What are the comparative merits and demerits of the investigated AI models?

Search and selection criteria

To achieve this, journal articles were retrieved from notable digital libraries/repositories such as Google Scholar, PubMed, ScienceDirect, Web of Science, and Public Library of Science. In the present study, an attempt was made at reviewing all articles ever published in this field, since the AI application in soil pollution studies remains a recent development, with no much study as at yet. Upon the preliminary search, about 1964 works, with out-of-scope AI-related articles (such as those about wastewater treatment optimization and other statistical modeling papers) being in the majority. However, the adoption of certain inclusion terms, such as "deep learning," "machine learning," "artificial intelligence," "soil pollution mapping," and "soil pollution measurement," produced 98 articles. Further screening based on the significance of the paper title, abstract, and keywords, as well as the exclusion of duplicate studies, reduced the number of articles to 32 publications. Furthermore, the information presented in the final 32 publications was methodically evaluated and documented for further analyses and discussion.

Quality check and data extraction

For qualitative filtering of the selected studies of relevance, certain quality evaluation indices were adopted. These included: (1) credibility check to ascertain the presence of a well-designed experiment with a sufficient dataset, (2) ensuring that the scope of the respective studies and its field of application were well demarcated, (3) ensuring the clarity of the objective(s) of the respective studies and adequacy of the adopted methodology, and (4) ensuring their data computational and discussion accuracy, with a rich contribution(s) to existing scientific knowledge.

The use of some statistical and error function models as performance indicators for the evaluation and comparison of literature data was employed in this investigation. Meanwhile, the mathematical expressions of the different models are presented in Table 13.1. The R^2 (coefficient of determination), which explicates the extent of dependent variable discrepancies that is anticipated from the independent variable is the most commonly adopted model quality determination criterion. The closer R^2 and r (correlation coefficient) are to unity, the better the respective model fit (Aniagor & Menkiti, 2018). The root mean square error (RMSE) value is determined as the residuals of standard deviation. The smaller the RMSE and standard error values, the better the respective model's accuracy (Hashem, Aniagor, Taha, et al., 2021). Residual prediction deviation (RPD)

Table 13.1 The goodness-of-fit parameters.

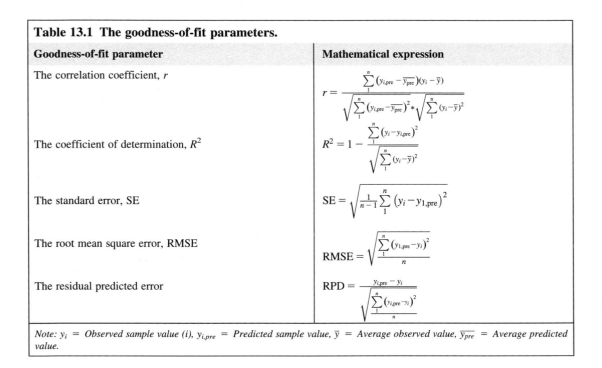

Goodness-of-fit parameter	Mathematical expression
The correlation coefficient, r	$r = \dfrac{\sum\limits_{1}^{n}\left(y_{i,pre} - \overline{y_{pre}}\right)(y_i - \overline{y})}{\sqrt{\sum\limits_{1}^{n}\left(y_{i,pre} - \overline{y_{pre}}\right)^2} * \sqrt{\sum\limits_{1}^{n}(y_i - \overline{y})^2}}$
The coefficient of determination, R^2	$R^2 = 1 - \dfrac{\sum\limits_{1}^{n}(y_i - y_{i,pre})^2}{\sqrt{\sum\limits_{1}^{n}(y_i - \overline{y})^2}}$
The standard error, SE	$SE = \sqrt{\dfrac{1}{n-1}\sum\limits_{1}^{n}\left(y_i - y_{1,pre}\right)^2}$
The root mean square error, RMSE	$RMSE = \sqrt{\dfrac{\sum\limits_{1}^{n}\left(y_{1,pre} - y_i\right)^2}{n}}$
The residual predicted error	$RPD = \dfrac{y_{i,pre} - y_i}{\sqrt{\dfrac{\sum\limits_{1}^{n}\left(y_{i,pre} - y_i\right)^2}{n}}}$

Note: y_i = Observed sample value (i), $y_{i,pre}$ = Predicted sample value, $\overline{y}$ = Average observed value, $\overline{y_{pre}}$ = Average predicted value.

is a goodness-of-fit parameter that obtained a quotient of the standard deviation and the RMSE, with values greater than 1.8 considered good (Jia et al., 2021).

Theoretical backgrounds to the different AI models
Artificial intelligence models applied in the field

During the literature survey, different AI models were applied in the mapping and measurement of soil pollution. Meanwhile, the ANN model of different algorithms [such as radial basis function (RBF), MLP, backpropagation, feedforward, and autoregressive and recurrent ANN] were the most commonly adopted AI models in this research field. The predicator and underlying mechanism relating to the key AI models will be elucidated in the subsequent subsections. Meanwhile, the advantages and limitations of the applied AI models are summarized in Table 13.2.

Artificial neural network

The nonlinear behavior of the multivariable originating from polluted soil makes their data modeling significantly tasking, hence the application of ANN models (Abdallah et al., 2020). Due to their

Table 13.2 Advantages and limitations of the most frequently used AI models.

AI model	Advantages	Disadvantages	Reference
ANN	Absence of fault bias. Able to simulate complicated data correlations in a multicomponent network. Minimal calibration data are required	Limited handling of analytical and computational issues that require high precision. Demands data pretreatment. Fixed datasets are not precisely analyzed. Poor correlation between factors involved	Shadrin et al. (2020)
SVM	Class distinctions and grouping errors are, respectively, maximized and minimized. Not prone to data overfitting. Efficiently reduces error approximation and model proportion concurrently. Low generalizing error and computing costs. Good prediction and appropriate running time.	Highly sensitive to the specific kernel and tuning variables	Akinpelu et al. (2020)
ANFIS	Possesses exceptional control over dataset vagueness, hence a smaller number of parameters are required. The system is readily managed. Its inherent design enables better working resolution for similar case studies. Its architectural makeup allows visualization of the intermediate result, hence the risk contribution to each tree is readily discerned	Effective parametric tuning requires a proficient training mechanism. There is a direct relationship between parametric convolution and the cost of computation. The larger the dataset, the greater the training and computing cost	Bazoobandi et al. (2019)
RF	Can tackle both grouping and regression problems, with appreciable accuracy. Ability to manipulate large data and can effectively approximate missing data. Efficient at error balancing, with a strong capacity to detect outliers. They can be readily tuned and can adapt to scattered computing. Not prone to data overfitting	The trainer has little control over the models' performance during training. It has a poor regression capacity, hence can overfit noisy datasets	Jia et al. (2021)
GBM	The algorithms are quite easy to read and interpret. Data handling is very easy and seamless. The modeling approach is very flexible and data overfitting is very unlikely	The approach is a function of outliers. Data scale-up and streamlining is usually difficult. Model training requires expertise	Hu et al. (2020)
BN	Incomplete data are accurately predicted. The issue of data overfitting is not prevalent. Depicts accurate data even with a limited dataset. Readily compatible with other decision-analytic tools for efficient data handling	They possess limited capacity for handling continuous data. The typical input dataset are usually discretized, which may cause certain difficulties	Boente et al. (2020)
Fuzzy system	The system is robust, with the capacity to handle nonprecise and indeterminate input data. The system can be readily reprogrammed in the case of malfunctioning. It has a flexible, simple, and valid design	The logic is not accurate sometimes. Its AI perception design varies from that of the neural network system. Often difficult to synchronize precise fuzzy rules	Lourenço et al. (2010)

ANFIS, *Adaptive neurofuzzy inference system;* ANN, *artificial neural network;* BN, *Bayesian network;* GBM, *gradient boosted machine;* RF, *random forest;* SVM, *support vector machine.*

unique design, ANNs can efficiently model undetermined and fragmented datasets from nonlinear processes, as well as analyze complex tasks, with high intuitive demands. ANN is a typical three-layered (an input layer, hidden layers, and an output layer) model of many node-to-node interlinkages between the different layers (Abdallah et al., 2020). Various ANN classifications exist and are further elucidated herein.

The multilayer perceptron neural network

This is considered to be one of the commonest feedforward ANN, whose structural design strongly influenced their modeling capacity. The number of input and output layer neurons is informed by independent and dependent parameters, respectively (Ghaedi & Vafaei, 2017). Meanwhile, the number of hidden layer neurons is arbitrarily determined since there is no set approach for the optimal neuron determination (Bahrami et al., 2017; Moosavi & Soltani, 2013). Meanwhile, the existence of an insufficient number of hidden neurons results in data underfitting due to the networks' inferior learning of the data laws, while unusually high parametric quantities originating from excess neurons lead to data overfitting (Zonouz et al., 2016).

The backpropagation neural network

This is one of the most widely applied AI models in the field of pollution control studies. The processing of its input variable and the output data generation are achieved via the hidden layers and nonlinear transformations, respectively (Abdallah et al., 2020). This model sustains a layer-to-layer interaction between neurons in the hidden layer, whose input and output variables' correlation is expressed as Eq. (13.1).

$$y_j = f\left(\sum_{i=1}^{n} w_{ij}x_i + b\right) \tag{13.1}$$

where y_j is the hidden neuron jth output, x_i input layer ith output, w_{ij} is the combined weight of elements i and j, while $f(x)$ and "n" are the transfer function and input variable number, respectively. Its gradient search operational mechanism is achieved upon the continual updating of the networks' weight and threshold, while minimizing the error variance between the actual and expected networks' outputs (Fan et al., 2018; Wang et al., 2018). The information processing involved in a single neuron an a two hidden layered multilayer perceptron neural network (MLPNN) is shown in Fig. 13.1 and Fig. 13.2, respectively. Further details on the MLPNN in particular and the general ANN operational principles are reported elsewhere (Ghaedi & Vafaei, 2017; Kalogirou, 2003; Khataee & Kasiri, 2010).

The radial basis function neural network

The radial basis function neural network (RBFNN) is a supervised learning feedforward ANN as is the MLPNN, however, the former is considered superior due to its online learning capacity and unique ability to model systems with high input noise, though with some additional data (Buyukyildiz et al., 2014; Buyukyildiz & Kumcu, 2017; Zhu et al., 2017). The RBFNN also

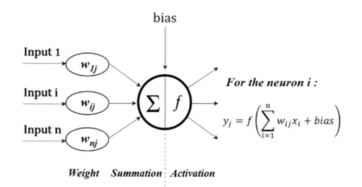

bias

Input 1 w_{1j}

Input i w_{ij}

Input n w_{nj}

Σ f

For the neuron i :

$$y_j = f\left(\sum_{i=1}^{n} w_{ij}x_i + bias\right)$$

Weight   Summation   Activation

FIGURE 13.1

The information processing involved in a single neuron layout.

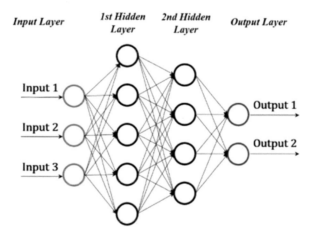

Input Layer   1st Hidden   2nd Hidden   Output Layer
Layer   Layer

Input 1

Input 2

Input 3

Output 1

Output 2

FIGURE 13.2

The information processing involved in a two hidden layered MLPNN. *MLPNN,* Multilayer perceptron neural network.

From Ye, Z., Yang, J., Zhong, N., Tu, X., Jia, J., & Wang, J. (2020). Tackling environmental challenges in pollution controls using artificial intelligence: A review. Science of the Total Environment, 699, *134279. https://doi.org/10.1016/j.scitotenv.2019.134279*

linearly combines three-layered RBFs, namely, input, Gaussian RBF, and linear output layer, and is distinguished from MLPNN based on their inherent computational design (Singh et al., 2013; Tatar et al., 2016). These RBFs consequently provide the model's activation function (Nandagopal et al., 2017; Turan et al., 2011). Fig. 13.3 presents the RBFNN single output structure, its hidden layers of the *m*th neutron are expressed as Eq. (13.2).

$$y_j = f\left(\sum_{i=1}^{n} w_k \theta_k [x(t)]\right) \tag{13.2}$$

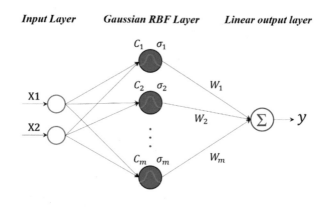

FIGURE 13.3

The RBFNN single output structure. *RBFNN,* Radial basis function neural network.

From Ye, Z., Yang, J., Zhong, N., Tu, X., Jia, J., & Wang, J. (2020). Tackling environmental challenges in pollution controls using artificial intelligence: A review. Science of the Total Environment, 699, *134279. https://doi.org/10.1016/j.scitotenv.2019.134279*

where "x" and "y" are the networks' input and output data, respectively. W_k is the kth hidden and output neuron weight connection, and $\Theta_k(x)$ is the kth hidden output data.

Support vector machines

As one of the many supervised data analysis AI algorithms, SVM was originally intended for non-parametric data classification due to their capacity to minimize and maximize grouping error and class partitioning, respectively (Chen et al., 2015; Dixon & Candade, 2008). Their subsequent evolution to regression problem-solving stems from the realization of their superior performance over other traditional regression approaches. The achievement of good generalized classification and regression results by SVM is due to its convergence principle which gives it a data analytical edge (Chen et al., 2015; Dixon & Candade, 2008). A dedicated regression version of SVM with extensive application in environmental control studies via the introduction of a discriminatory loss function is known as support vector regression (SVR). Its operational design is captured by Eq. (13.3).

$$f(x) = \left(\sum_{i=1}^{M} w_i \phi(x_i) + b \right) \tag{13.3}$$

where $x =$ SVR input data, $f(x)$ is the SVR output data, M is the number of data points, and $\phi(x_i)$ is high-dimensional featured space. The "w_i" and "b" are obtained upon minimization of the regularized risk.

Adaptive neurofuzzy inference system

ANFIS is one of the classical neurofuzzy systems that can efficiently tackle complex problems in many research areas. It has applications in data prediction, standardization, and mining, as well as

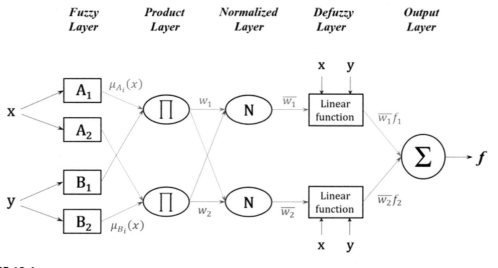

FIGURE 13.4

A typical ANFIS structural configuration. *ANFIS*, Adaptive neurofuzzy inference system.

From Ye, Z., Yang, J., Zhong, N., Tu, X., Jia, J., & Wang, J. (2020). Tackling environmental challenges in pollution controls using artificial intelligence: A review. Science of the Total Environment, *699, 134279. https://doi.org/10.1016/j.scitotenv.2019.134279*

noise suppression (Hong, Panahi, et al., 2018; Hong, Tsangaratos, et al., 2018; Wan et al., 2011). It is a feedforward neural network system that incorporates fuzzy logic for nonlinear behavioral interpretation in complex systems (Mingzhi et al., 2009). The ANFIS structural configuration shown in Fig. 13.4 presents a fuzzy rule network connection between the precursor and terminator. Meanwhile, the effectiveness of ANFIS is due to its combined advantage derived from the hybrid integration of the neural network learning capability and fuzzy logic (Ali et al., 2019; Huang & Chen, 2015).

Random forest

Random forest (RF) is a decision tree-based algorithm applied in a nonlinear and nonparametric procedure (Guio Blanco et al., 2018). It is principally distinguished from a decision tree as its modeling decision is made from multiple trees instead of a single tree which is obtainable in the decision tree model (Guio Blanco et al., 2018). Due to its intuitive algorithmic design, RF uses hierarchical and binary splits for handling regression and data groupings (Ellis et al., 2014). However, the data overfitting and high error variance associated with the aforementioned analytical approach have been highlighted, hence the integration of bagging (bootstrapping aggregation) (Jia et al., 2020). Furthermore, the RF combines many trees, whose respective dataset is repetitively segregated into progressively correlative output variable subgroups, predicated on improved residual sum of squares (Hu et al., 2020). Meanwhile, all the input variables are evaluated for

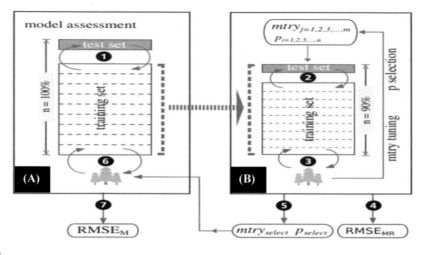

FIGURE 13.5

A schematic representation of random forest (A) model selection and (B) validation procedure.

From Guio Blanco, C. M., Brito Gomez, V. M., Crespo, P., & Ließ, M. (2018). Spatial prediction of soil water retention in a Páramo landscape: Methodological insight into machine learning using random forest. Geoderma, 316, 100–114. https://doi.org/10.1016/j. geoderma.2017.12.002

determining those that provide a principal dataset subdivision. A schematic representation of the RF model selection and validation procedure is presented in Fig. 13.5.

Gradient boosted machine

Friedman (2002) developed the GBM algorithm aimed at generating a useful and efficient model for estimating the different heavy metal bioaccumulation factors in an agricultural ecosystem. This algorithm is probabilistic and nonlinear gradient boosting that is fundamentally based on regression trees (Friedman, 2001). The GBM model aims at executing advanced modeling on predictable data via specific loss function minimization (Martin et al., 2009). The independent variables' contribution to the model effectiveness can be numerically evaluated from the individual performance of all independent variables in an exclusive tree.

Bayesian machine learning

Bayesian networks are stochastic graphical models that portray a variable set with subjective reliance via directed noncyclic graphs, whose convergence depicts a univariate correlation (Benavoli et al., 2017). The establishment of Bayesian networks based on machine-learnt data could ultimately and independently link, classify, and evaluate the variables of a given dataset.

Hybrid models

The combination of different AI models or an AI model with metaheuristic algorithms for performing a specific task gives rise to hybrid models. Such combinations have the advantages of eliminating the shortcomings associated with adopting a sole/single model separately (Ye et al., 2020). The hybrid models are targeted at integrating different problem-solving algorithms toward accomplishing distinct tasks with superior accuracy.

Application domain of the different AI models
AI models in soil pollution mapping

Soil pollution mapping is a worthwhile issue as it provides useful information on the soil pollutant distribution and pollutant point-source concentration within a given environment. However, the execution of a successful pollutant mapping operation is hampered due to the laborious, costly, and time-consuming processes involved in the manual collection of polluted soil samples from the field and subsequent chemical analyses of these samples in the laboratory. The aforementioned constraints have a significant influence on the robustness and quality of the generated soil contamination mapping data, hence the application of machine learning for rapid, seemingly inexpensive, and accurate mapping.

Table 13.3 summarizes the different studies conducted on AI application in soil pollution mapping, the type of model used, the mapped pollutant, and the key research findings. The reported

Table 13.3 Comparative studies of different AI model applications in soil pollution mapping.

AI models	Mapped pollutant	Key findings	Reference
Fuzzy classification	Cu, Pb, Zn	The correlation coefficients between measured and predicted values are relatively high for predictions based on spatial correlation in the vertical plane. The correlations between the spatial predictions in the horizontal plane and the original measurements are lower	Franssen et al. (1997)
Fuzzy classification	Cr, Hg, As, Pb, and Cd	Four classes that accurately represented the different risk areas of soil heavy metal pollution were obtained	Jia et al. (2020)
Fuzzy decision trees	Different suspected soil pollutants	The soil pollution risk of the sample groups was successfully demarcated as low, medium, and high	López et al. (2008)
Spatial analysis and fuzzy classification	Pb, Zn, Ni, and Cu	The map showed the levels of pollution risk within the study area. The coefficients of variation (CVs) for Cu (65.22%), Zn (55.33%), and Ni (50.32%) were higher than that for Pb, thus they have variations among the soil samples	Lourenço et al. (2010)

(Continued)

Table 13.3 Comparative studies of different AI model applications in soil pollution mapping. *Continued*

AI models	Mapped pollutant	Key findings	Reference
ANN-SOM	Polycyclic aromatic hydrocarbons, heavy metal, total petroleum hydrocarbon	The SOM was used as a powerful visualization tool to identify trends in the dataset. Areas with high concentrations of pollutants were easily identified from the c-planes which revealed vital information for interpretation of the results	Olawoyin et al. (2013)
ANN-AGA	As, Cd, Cr, Cu, Hg, Ni, Pb, and Zn	The city was found to be seriously polluted by heavy metals. Then, the possible heavy metal sources were identified through a correlation matrix	Zhou et al. (2015)
DL-ANN and RF	Generalized digital soil mapping	Modeling with DL-ANN produced the most accurate predictions, which on average were 4%–7% more accurate than modeling with random forests	Behrens et al. (2018)
PCA and ANN	Petrol and diesel	ANN application gave a validation quality of over 95%, an indication of the accuracy of the validation set mapping. A polluted soil mapping efficiency of about 100% was achieved in the study	Bieganowski et al. (2018)
ANN	Cu, Co, Ni, and Cr	The soil pollutant classification structure was efficiently supervised by ANN	Dai et al. (2020)
FFNN	Cs 137 and Sr 90	The NNRK was successfully used in modeling complex nonlinear pollutant distribution. The MSE-NNRK model was better than FFNN based on the independent data validation test	Kanevsky et al. (1996)
DTM	Zn	Although the DT modeling approach did not map with better accuracies than those reported in the literature, the approach was a quicker, simpler, and more realistic combination of geoenvironmental variables. The developed tree model explained 88% of the variance in zinc concentration. The quantitative zinc map (at 1:50,000 scale) was estimated at an overall accuracy of 78%	Kheir et al. (2010)
PLSR, SVM, BPNN, and ELM	Zn and Pb	The FD-ELM depicted the closest spatial patterns similarity with other maps obtained by value interpolation measurement. The combination of reflectance spectroscopy and the ELM algorithm provided a rapid, inexpensive, and accurate tool for mapping heavy metal spatial distribution in the selected dumpsite soils	Khosravi et al. (2018)

Note: AGA, *Adaptive genetic algorithm;* AI, *artificial intelligence;* ANN, *artificial neural network;* BPNN, *backpropagation neural network;* DL, *deep learning;* DTM, *decision tree model;* ELM, *extreme learning machine;* FD, *first derivative;* FFNN, *feedforward neural network;* PCA, *principal component analysis;* PLSR, *partial least squares regression;* RF, *random forest;* SOM, *self-organizing map;* SVM, *support vector machine.*

studies were limited, with the majority of studies undertaken in developed countries. This observation highlights the place and effect of countries, socioeconomic stability on the success and thoroughness of their soil pollution management approaches. Table 13.3 also presents heavy metals as the most often mapped soil pollutant. This may be due to their extreme toxicity to the biotic community and the high rate at which they are generated and consequently discharged into the environment by several process industries. The fuzzy classification and ANN algorithm are the most commonly applied AI models for soil pollution mapping judging from Table 13.3. Their extensive application in the field could be linked to the different convincing advantages of both models which are detailed in Table 13.2.

AI models in soil pollutant measurement

The hazards associated with soil pollution warrant a categorical determination of the level and extent of pollutants in a given site. Obtaining detailed knowledge on this subject will inform the selection of a suitable and effective remediation approach. A summary of the various AI algorithms applied for the measurement of soil pollution, as well as the main research objective and key findings from the reviewed articles, are presented in Table 13.4.

Table 13.4 Comparative studies on the applications of different AI models in soil pollution measurement.

AI model	Study objective	Key findings	Reference
Bayesian networks	The SPI was calculated to assess the degree of contamination and the pollution indicators were subjected to Bayesian network analysis	The scale factor altered the elemental contribution to SPIs. The restrictive regional SSL made it difficult to identify local anomalies	Boente et al. (2020)
RF	Combining the fuzzy k-means with the random forest (RF) method for classifying potential risk areas	The RF models performed well in predicting the concentrations of Cr, Pb, Hg, and As elements in soils, with RPIQ values of 1.85, 2.12, 2.09, and 1.68, respectively. Meanwhile, the prediction of Cd was poor	Jia et al. (2020)
Hybrid	Combination of SVM, MLP, RF, and ERF for predicting soil arsenic risk levels	The accuracy of ERF in test area 1 reached 0.87, performing better than RF (0.81), MLP (0.78), and SVM (0.77). The F1-score of ERF for discerning high-risk points in test area 1 was as high as 0.8	Jia et al. (2021)
Hybrid	Comparison of GA-SVR-Gaussian, GA-SVR-poly, and Ms-SVR	GA-SVR-Gaussian performed better than Ms-SVR and GA-SVR-poly with MAE and MAPD values of 63.89% and 36.32%, respectively. The order of model performance based on MAPD is GA-SVR-Gaussian > Ms-SVR > GA-SVR-poly	Akinpelu et al. (2020)

(Continued)

Table 13.4 Comparative studies on the applications of different AI models in soil pollution measurement. *Continued*

AI model	Study objective	Key findings	Reference
Hybrid	Comparative modeling of soil heavy metal pollution using ANN and MLR	Based on model performance criteria, the ANN depicted RMSE value ranging from 0.04 μg/kg (Cd) to 0.1 μg/kg (Cr) and its model efficiency (EF) ranged from 0.79 (Cr) to 0.94 (Cd, Zn). The ANN models performed better than the MLR model	Anagu et al. (2009)
Hybrid	Comparative study on the prediction of soil heavy metal content using SVM and GRNN	The SVM gave a faster and more accurate prediction than the GRNN, with superior R and RMSE values	Aryafar et al. (2012)
Hybrid	Comparative study on the Pb and Cd estimation from different soil samples using MLR, ANN, and ANFIS	The ANN model [RMSE = 1.04 (Cd) and 0.23 (Pb)] was better than the ANFIS model [RMSE = 2.56 (Cd) and 1.27 (Pb)]. The order of model performance was ANN > ANFIS > MLR model	Bazoobandi et al. (2019)
Hybrid	XGBoost was introduced to abstract the correlated input parameters for the Pb prediction and validated against PCA, RFE, and GA models	Findings show the XGBoost model dependence on sample size. XGBoost modeling accuracy decreased under an external feature selector. The XGBoost model exhibited a promising modeling algorithm due to its high accuracy and speed	Bhagat et al. (2021)
Hybrid	Evaluation of the combined effects of MIR-DRIFTS and different ANNs for soil Pb content prediction	Using two neurons in each hidden layer, the MLP 897-2-1 network produced the best prediction (RPD = 2.1, RMSE = 0.009 mg/kg) of all the tested ANN models. Notably, MLP 897-4-1 showed the worst generalization capacity among the MLP models with an RPD of 1.85	Chakraborty et al. (2015)
BPNN	Using reflectance spectra data, the Cd concentration of the different soil samples was estimated using PLSR and BPNN	Compared to PLSR modeling, BPNN achieved a more accurate estimation with the lowest RMSE in the range of 0.4068−0.4700	Chen et al. (2015)
ANN	Prediction of soil salinity based on measured reflectance spectra using PLSR and ANN methods	The results indicated that both methods have soil salinity mapping and estimation potentials. Although there exist strong similarities in the results from both methods, PLSR provided better prediction, thus the relationship between soil salinity and soil reflectance can be approximated by a linear function	Farifteh et al. (2007)
BPNN	Estimation of selected volatile organic compounds concentration in contaminated soils using a combination of PCA and BPNN	BPNN with a partially connected hidden layer provided a more satisfactory result. The adoption of normalized fractional conductance changes as the preprocessing algorithm gave the best results with the neural networks	Getino et al. (1999)
Hybrid	To predict the soil Ni and Fe concentration using SVM and BPNN	SVM performed better than BPNN in terms of its relatively high correlation coefficient (which is higher than that of BPNN) and the associated running time (which is lower than that of BPNN)	Gholami et al. (2011)

Table 13.4 Comparative studies on the applications of different AI models in soil pollution measurement. *Continued*

AI model	Study objective	Key findings	Reference
Hybrid	Comparative study on the prediction of soil heavy metal content by RF, GBM, and GLM	In terms of R^2 values, the RF model showed the best prediction ability, followed by GBM and GLM. The model was efficient in predicting the HM contents in crops as a function of the HM contents in soil, at significantly reduced cost, labor, and time requirements	Hu et al. (2020)
Hybrid	To apply machine learning calibration (PLSR, ANN, and RF) models for interpreting spectral data and predict soil contamination levels	The model predicted the soil pollution level with reasonable accuracy	Jia et al. (2020)
ANN	To predict heavy metals concentration in polluted soil using stepwise MLR and ANN	High accuracy prediction was achieved for six of the nine targeted elements, with significant R^2 values. A similar prediction result was achieved by both models	Kemper and Sommer (2002)
Hybrid	To calibrate spectra features using PLSR, SVM, BPNN, and ELM and further apply the models for soil heavy metal concentration prediction	Based on R^2, RMSE, R, and RPD values, FD-ELM provided the best heavy metal prediction accuracy. The combination of reflectance spectroscopy with the ELM algorithm served as a rapid, inexpensive, and accurate tool for indirect evaluation of soil Pb and Zn concentrations	Khosravi et al. (2018)
Hybrid	ANNs and SVMs were evaluated and compared for SPI prediction of heavy metals	Findings showed that the ANNs result was comparable to those of SVMs, but the SVMs had a better error generalization with earlier stopping than that of ANNs. The study preferred the application of SVMs	Sakizadeh et al. (2017)
Hybrid	To compare the effectiveness of two neural networks (GRNN and MLP), as well as two combined techniques (GRNNRK and MLPRK) for the real measurements of chromium surface contamination	MLPRK and GRNNRK show better predictive accuracy than kriging, MLP, and GRNN. The hybrid models provide more accurate predictions than single/sole models. The most significant improvement in RMSE (15.5% compared to kriging) was observed in the MLPRK model	Tarasov et al. (2018)

ANFIS, *Adaptive neurofuzzy inference system*; AI, *artificial intelligence*; ANN, *artificial neural network*; BPNN, *backpropagation neural network*; ELM, *extreme learning machine*; ERF, *extreme random forest*; GA, *genetic algorithm*; GBM, *gradient boosted machine*; GLM, *generalized linear model*; GRNN, *generalized regression neural network*; GRNNRK, *generalized regression neural network residual kriging*; MAE, *mean absolute error*; MAPD, *mean absolute percentage deviation*; MIR-DRIFTS, *mid-infrared-diffuse reflectance infrared Fourier transform spectroscopy*; MLP, *multilayer perceptron*; MLPRK, *multilayer perceptron residual kriging*; MLR, *multilinear regression*; PCA, *principal component analysis*; PLSR, *partial least squares regression*; RFE, *recursive feature elimination*; RMSE, *root mean square error*; RPD, *residual prediction deviation*; SPI, *soil pollution index*; SVM, *support vector machine*; SVR, *support vector regression*; XGBoost, *extreme gradient boosting*; RPIQ, *ratio of performance to interquartile distance*.

The extensive application of hybrid AI models as opposed to a sole model has been succinctly elucidated in Table 13.4. According to Ye et al. (2020), hybrid AI models have the advantages of eliminating the shortcomings associated with a single model application, as well as integrating the different problem-solving algorithms toward accomplishing distinct tasks with superior accuracy. Different types of neural network systems are among the predominant components of the different hybrid AI models presented in Table 13.4. Similarly, several studies (Anagu et al., 2009; Bazoobandi et al., 2019; Chakraborty et al., 2015; Chen et al., 2015; Getino et al., 1999) have reported the superior soil pollution prediction performance of neural network systems over their AI counterparts. This may be due to the superior architectural and structural design of the neural network models. For instance, their self-learning capacities permit their processing of huge data to yield exceptional results. Their processing units comprising of interconnected neuron nodes of input and output units like those in humans aptly execute large input data information processing. Despite their prediction performance, the neural network huge running time was reported as a major limitation to its applicability (Gholami et al., 2011). Meanwhile, there are exceptional cases where the neural networks were outperformed. Aryafar et al. (2012) and Gholami et al. (2011) reported that the SVM gave a faster and more accurate prediction than the generalized regression neural network and backpropagation neural network, with superior R and RMSE values. In their study, Sakizadeh et al. (2017) observed that the ANN results were comparable to those of SVMs, but the SVMs had a better error generalization with earlier stopping than that of ANNs. Hence the SVM algorithm was preferred to ANN. Consequently, Kemper and Sommer (2002) recorded a similar prediction result with both models. The results presented in Table 13.4 conclusively illustrate that artificial intelligence models could be efficiently adopted and applied in the measurement of soil pollution.

Conclusions

The application of AI models in soil pollution mapping and measurement has been methodically reviewed based on the findings and insights drawn from the 32 literature sources collated in the research field. The key findings from all the research articles, as well as the advantages and limitations of the different AI models, have been elucidated in this chapter. The comprehensive literature review informed of the successful adoption of both sole and hybrid AI models for the mapping and measurement of soil pollution. The general findings also portrayed heavy metal as the most commonly mapped and measured soil pollutant. The study also observed that the cost and time constraints associated with the implementation of traditional soil pollution mapping and measurement techniques were effectively addressed with the application of AI systems.

Considering the existence of scant literature in this research field, one can safely opine that AI-based soil pollution mapping and measurement is still developing, hence enumerating their probable applicational limitations is key to the subsequent design of robust AI-based soil pollution mapping and measurement systems/techniques. The identified applicational limitations include:

1. *Data inadequacy*: The insufficiency of input data remains one of the major impediments to widespread acceptance and application of AI systems since their algorithms require some relatively elaborate datasets for model training and normalization. Meanwhile, the

socioeconomic differences and variations in technological advancement between countries have significantly widened this gap. Developing countries have very poor data repositories, as they largely rely on traditional sampling approaches due to their increasing deficiency in applying modern data-capturing techniques.

2. *Lack of passion*: There has been a rapid evolution of the IoT and numerous other AI-based systems, even in developing countries, but there has not been as much attendant and corresponding effort aimed at deploying such developments in soil pollution studies. Although there are some exceptions to this assertion, the overall AI-based research progress in the field of soil pollution studies is not very significant judging by the existent scant literature.

3. *Research continuity*: The issue of research continuity still subsists as most AI black box (which is key to the sustained application and development of the AI techniques) is either hidden or absent from published articles.

References

Abdallah, M., Abu Talib, M., Feroz, S., Nasir, Q., Abdalla, H., & Mahfood, B. (2020). Artificial intelligence applications in solid waste management: A systematic research review. *Waste Management*, *109*, 231−246. Available from https://doi.org/10.1016/j.wasman.2020.04.057.

Agirre-Basurko, E., Ibarra-Berastegi, G., & Madariaga, I. (2006). Regression and multilayer perceptron-based models to forecast hourly O_3 and NO_2 levels in the Bilbao area. *Environmental Modelling and Software*, *21*(4), 430−446. Available from https://doi.org/10.1016/j.envsoft.2004.07.008.

Akinpelu, A. A., Ali, M. E., Owolabi, T. O., Johan, M. R., Saidur, R., Olatunji, S. O., & Chowdbury, Z. (2020). A support vector regression model for the prediction of total polyaromatic hydrocarbons in soil: An artificial intelligent system for mapping environmental pollution. *Neural Computing and Applications*, *32*(18), 14899−14908.

Ali, H., Khan, E., & Ilahi, I. (2019). Environmental chemistry and ecotoxicology of hazardous heavy metals: Environmental persistence, toxicity, and bioaccumulation. *Journal of Chemistry*, *2019*, 6730305. Available from https://doi.org/10.1155/2019/6730305.

Anagu, I., Ingwersen, J., Utermann, J., & Streck, T. (2009). Estimation of heavy metal sorption in German soils using artificial neural networks. *Geoderma*, *152*(1−2), 104−112. Available from https://doi.org/10.1016/j.geoderma.2009.06.004.

Aniagor, C. O., & Menkiti, M. C. (2018). Kinetics and mechanistic description of adsorptive uptake of crystal violet dye by lignified elephant grass complexed isolate. *Journal of Environmental Chemical Engineering*, *6*(2), 2105−2118. Available from https://doi.org/10.1016/j.jece.2018.01.070.

Aryafar, A., Gholami, R., Rooki, R., & Doulati Ardejani, F. (2012). Heavy metal pollution assessment using support vector machine in the Shur River, Sarcheshmeh copper mine, Iran. *Environmental Earth Sciences*, *67*(4), 1191−1199. Available from https://doi.org/10.1007/s12665--012--1565--7.

Bahrami, S., Niaei, A., Illán-Gómez, M. J., Tarjomannejad, A., Mousavi, S. M., & Albaladejo-Fuentes, V. (2017). Catalytic reduction of NO by CO over CeO_2-MOx (0.25) (M = Mn, Fe and Cu) mixed oxides— modeling and optimization of catalyst preparation by hybrid ANN-GA. *Journal of Environmental Chemical Engineering*, *5*(5), 4937−4947. Available from https://doi.org/10.1016/j.jece.2017.09.023.

Bazoobandi, A., Emamgholizadeh, S., & Ghorbani, H. (2019). Estimating the amount of cadmium and lead in the polluted soil using artificial intelligence models. *European Journal of Environmental and Civil Engineering*. Available from https://doi.org/10.1080/19648189.2019.1686429.

Behrens, T., Schmidt, K., MacMillan, R. A., & Rossel, R. A. V. (2018). Multi-scale digital soil mapping with deep learning. *Scientific reports*, *8*(1), 1–9.

Benavoli, A., Corani, G., Demšar, J., & Zaffalon, M. (2017). Time for a change: A tutorial for comparing multiple classifiers through Bayesian analysis. *Journal of Machine Learning Research*, *18*, 1–36. Available from http://jmlr.csail.mit.edu/papers/volume18/16-305/16-305.pdf.

Bhagat, S. K., Tiyasha, T., Awadh, S. M., Tung, T. M., Jawad, A. H., & Yaseen, Z. M. (2021). Prediction of sediment heavy metal at the Australian Bays using newly developed hybrid artificial intelligence models. *Environmental Pollution*, *268*, 115663.

Bieganowski, A., Józefaciuk, G., Bandura, L., Guz, Ł., Łagód, G., & Franus, W. (2018). Evaluation of hydrocarbon soil pollution using E-nose. *Sensors*, *18*(8), 2463.

Boente, C., Gerassis, S., Albuquerque, M., Taboada, J., & Gallego, J. (2020). Local versus regional soil screening levels to identify potentially polluted areas. *Mathematical Geosciences*, *52*(3), 381–396.

Buyukyildiz, M., & Kumcu, S. Y. (2017). An estimation of the suspended sediment load using adaptive network based fuzzy inference system, support vector machine and artificial neural network models. *Water Resources Management*, *31*(4), 1343–1359. Available from https://doi.org/10.1007/s11269-017-1581-1.

Buyukyildiz, M., Tezel, G., & Yilmaz, V. (2014). Estimation of the change in lake water level by artificial intelligence methods. *Water Resources Management*, *28*(13), 4747–4763. Available from https://doi.org/10.1007/s11269-014-0773-1.

Cakmakci, M. (2007). Adaptive neuro-fuzzy modelling of anaerobic digestion of primary sedimentation sludge. *Bioprocess and Biosystems Engineering*, *30*(5), 349–357. Available from https://doi.org/10.1007/s00449-007-0131-2.

Centrum, S. (1990). World map on status of human-induced soil degradation.

Chakraborty, S., Weindorf, D. C., Paul, S., Ghosh, B., Li, B., Ali, M. N., Ghosh, R. K., Ray, D. P., & Majumdar, K. (2015). Diffuse reflectance spectroscopy for monitoring lead in landfill agricultural soils of India. *Geoderma Regional*, *5*, 77–85. Available from https://doi.org/10.1016/j.geodrs.2015.04.004.

Chen, T., Chang, Q., Clevers, J. G. P. W., & Kooistra, L. (2015). Rapid identification of soil cadmium pollution risk at regional scale based on visible and near-infrared spectroscopy. *Environmental Pollution*, *206*, 217–226. Available from https://doi.org/10.1016/j.envpol.2015.07.009.

Dai, H., Huang, D., & Mao, H. (2020). Evaluation model of soil heavy metal pollution index based on machine learning and particle image recognition. *Microprocessors and Microsystems*, 103411. Available from https://doi.org/10.1016/j.micpro.103411.

Dixon, B., & Candade, N. (2008). Multispectral landuse classification using neural networks and support vector machines: One or the other, or both? *International Journal of Remote Sensing*, *29*(4), 1185–1206. Available from https://doi.org/10.1080/01431160701294661.

Ellis, K., Kerr, J., Godbole, S., Lanckriet, G., Wing, D., & Marshall, S. (2014). A random forest classifier for the prediction of energy expenditure and type of physical activity from wrist and hip accelerometers. *Physiological Measurement*, *35*(11), 2191–2203. Available from https://doi.org/10.1088/0967-3334/35/11/2191.

Fan, M., Hu, J., Cao, R., Ruan, W., & Wei, X. (2018). A review on experimental design for pollutants removal in water treatment with the aid of artificial intelligence. *Chemosphere*, *200*, 330–343. Available from https://doi.org/10.1016/j.chemosphere.2018.02.111.

FAO. (2015). *Status of the world's soil resources (SWSR)—main report*. Food and Agriculture Organization of the United Nations.

Farifteh, J., Van der Meer, F., Atzberger, C., & Carranza, E. (2007). Quantitative analysis of salt-affected soil reflectance spectra: A comparison of two adaptive methods (PLSR and ANN). *Remote Sensing of Environment*, *110*(1), 59–78.

Franssen, H. H., Van Eijnsbergen, A., & Stein, A. (1997). Use of spatial prediction techniques and fuzzy classification for mapping soil pollutants. *Geoderma*, *77*(2–4), 243–262.

Friedman, J. H. (2001). Greedy function approximation: A gradient boosting machine. *Annals of Statistics*, *29* (5), 1189−1232. Available from https://doi.org/10.1214/aos/1013203451.

Friedman, J. H. (2002). Stochastic gradient boosting. *Computational Statistics & Data Analysis*, *38*(4), 367−378. Available from https://doi.org/10.1016/s0167-9473(01)00065-2.

George, A. A., Adaobi, I. C., & Ighalo, J. O. (2021). ANN modelling of the adsorption of herbicides and pesticides based on sorbate-sorbent interphase. *Chemistry Africa*, *4*, 443−449. Available from https://doi.org/10.1007/s42250-020-00220-w.

Getino, J., Arés, L., Robla, J. I., Horrillo, M. C., Sayago, I., Fernández, M. J., Rodrigo, J., & Gutiérrez, J. (1999). Environmental applications of gas sensor arrays: Combustion atmospheres and contaminated soils. *Sensors and Actuators B: Chemical*, *59*(2), 249−254. Available from https://doi.org/10.1016/S0925-4005 (99)00229-4.

Ghaedi, A. M., & Vafaei, A. (2017). Applications of artificial neural networks for adsorption removal of dyes from aqueous solution: A review. *Advances in Colloid and Interface Science*, *245*, 20−39. Available from https://doi.org/10.1016/j.cis.2017.04.015.

Gholami, R., Kamkar-Rouhani, A., Doulati Ardejani, F., & Maleki, Sh (2011). Prediction of toxic metals concentration using artificial intelligence techniques. *Applied Water Science*, *1*, 125−134. Available from https://doi.org/10.1007/s13201-011-0016-z.

Guio Blanco, C. M., Brito Gomez, V. M., Crespo, P., & Ließ, M. (2018). Spatial prediction of soil water retention in a Páramo landscape: Methodological insight into machine learning using random forest. *Geoderma*, *316*, 100−114. Available from https://doi.org/10.1016/J.geoderma.2017.12.002.

Hashem, A., Aniagor, C. O., Nasr, M. F., & Abou-Okeil, A. (2021). Efficacy of treated sodium alginate and activated carbon fibre for Pb(II) adsorption. *International Journal of Biological Macromolecules*, *176*, 201−216. Available from https://doi.org/10.1016/j.ijbiomac.2021.02.067.

Hashem, A., Aniagor, C., Hussein, D., & Farag, S. (2021). Application of novel butane-1, 4-dioic acid-functionalized cellulosic biosorbent for aqueous cobalt ion sequestration. *Cellulose*, *28*, 3599−3615.

Hashem, A., Aniagor, C., Taha, G., & Fikry, M. (2021). Utilization of low-cost sugarcane waste for the adsorption of aqueous Pb(II): Kinetics and isotherm studies. *Current Research in Green and Sustainable Chemistry*, *4*, 100056. Available from https://doi.org/10.1016/j.crgsc.2021.100056.

Hong, H., Panahi, M., Shirzadi, A., Ma, T., Liu, J., Zhu, A. X., Chen, W., Kougias, I., & Kazakis, N. (2018). Flood susceptibility assessment in Hengfeng area coupling adaptive neuro-fuzzy inference system with genetic algorithm and differential evolution. *Science of the Total Environment*, *621*, 1124−1141. Available from https://doi.org/10.1016/j.scitotenv.2017.10.114.

Hong, H., Tsangaratos, P., Ilia, I., Liu, J., Zhu, A. X., & Chen, W. (2018). Application of fuzzy weight of evidence and data mining techniques in construction of flood susceptibility map of Poyang County, China. *Science of the Total Environment*, *625*, 575−588. Available from https://doi.org/10.1016/j.scitotenv.2017. 12.256.

Hu, B., Xue, J., Zhou, Y., Shao, S., Fu, Z., Li, Y., Chen, S., Qi, L., & Shi, Z. (2020). Modelling bioaccumulation of heavy metals in soil-crop ecosystems and identifying its controlling factors using machine learning. *Environmental Pollution*, *262*, 114308. Available from https://doi.org/10.1016/j.envpol.2020. 114308.

Huang, Y. W., & Chen, M. Q. (2015). Artificial neural network modeling of thin layer drying behavior of municipal sewage sludge. *Measurement: Journal of the International Measurement Confederation*, *73*, 640−648. Available from https://doi.org/10.1016/j.measurement.2015.06.014.

Igwegbe, C. A., Mohmmadi, L., Ahmadi, S., Rahdar, A., Khadkhodaiy, D., Dehghani, R., & Rahdar, S. (2019). Modeling of adsorption of Methylene Blue dye on Ho-CaWO$_4$ nanoparticles using response surface methodology (RSM) and artificial neural network (ANN) techniques. *MethodsX*, *6*, 1779−1797. Available from https://doi.org/10.1016/j.mex.2019.07.016.

Jia, X., Cao, Y., O'Connor, D., Zhu, J., Tsang, D. C. W., Zou, B., & Hou, D. (2021). Mapping soil pollution by using drone image recognition and machine learning at an arsenic-contaminated agricultural field. *Environmental Pollution*, *270*, 116281. Available from https://doi.org/10.1016/j.envpol.2020.116281.

Jia, X., Fu, T., Hu, B., Shi, Z., Zhou, L., & Zhu, Y. (2020). Identification of the potential risk areas for soil heavy metal pollution based on the source-sink theory. *Journal of Hazardous Materials*, *393*, 122424. Available from https://doi.org/10.1016/j.jhazmat.2020.122424.

Kalogirou, S. A. (2003). Artificial intelligence for the modeling and control of combustion processes: A review. *Progress in Energy and Combustion Science*, *29*(6), 515−566. Available from https://doi.org/10.1016/S0360-1285(03)00058-3.

Kanevsky, M., Arutyunyan, R., Bolshov, L., Demyanov, V., & Maignan, M. (1996). Artificial neural networks and spatial estimation of Chernobyl fallout. *Geoinformatics*, *7*(1−2), 5−11.

Kemper, T., & Sommer, S. (2002). Estimate of heavy metal contamination in soils after a mining accident using reflectance spectroscopy. *Environmental Science and Technology*, *36*(12), 2742−2747. Available from https://doi.org/10.1021/es015747j.

Khataee, A. R., & Kasiri, M. B. (2010). Artificial neural networks modeling of contaminated water treatment processes by homogeneous and heterogeneous nanocatalysis. *Journal of Molecular Catalysis A: Chemical*, *331*(1−2), 86−100. Available from https://doi.org/10.1016/j.molcata.2010.07.016.

Kheir, R. B., Greve, M. H., Abdallah, C., & Dalgaard, T. (2010). Spatial soil zinc content distribution from terrain parameters: A GIS-based decision-tree model in Lebanon. *Environmental Pollution*, *158*(2), 520−528.

Khosravi, V., Ardejani, F. D., Yousefi, S., & Aryafar, A. (2018). Monitoring soil lead and zinc contents via combination of spectroscopy with extreme learning machine and other data mining methods. *Geoderma*, *318*, 29−41.

Li, X. N., Jiao, W. T., Xiao, R. B., Chen, W. P., & Chang, A. C. (2015). Soil pollution and site remediation policies in China: A review. *Environmental Reviews*, *23*(3), 263−274. Available from https://doi.org/10.1139/er-2014-0073.

López, E. M., García, M., Schuhmacher, M., & Domingo, J. L. (2008). A fuzzy expert system for soil characterization. *Environment international*, *34*(7), 950−958.

Lourenço, R. W., Landim, P. M. B., Rosa, A. H., Roveda, J. A. F., Martins, A. C. G., & Fraceto, L. F. (2010). Mapping soil pollution by spatial analysis and fuzzy classification. *Environmental Earth Sciences*, *60*(3), 495−504.

Martin, M. P., Lo Seen, D., Boulonne, L., Jolivet, C., Nair, K. M., Bourgeon, G., & Arrouays, D. (2009). Optimizing pedotransfer functions for estimating soil bulk density using boosted regression trees. *Soil Science Society of America Journal*, *73*(2), 485−493. Available from https://doi.org/10.2136/sssaj2007.0241.

Mench, M. J., Dellise, M., Bes, C. M., Marchand, L., Kolbas, A., Coustumer, P. L., & Oustrière, N. (2018). Phytomanagement and remediation of cu-contaminated soils by high yielding crops at a former wood preservation site: Sunflower biomass and ionome. *Frontiers in Ecology and Evolution*, *6*, 123. Available from https://doi.org/10.3389/fevo.2018.00123.

Mingzhi, H., Jinquan, W., Yongwen, M., Yan, W., Weijiang, L., & Xiaofei, S. (2009). Control rules of aeration in a submerged biofilm wastewater treatment process using fuzzy neural networks. *Expert Systems with Applications*, *36*(7), 10428−10437. Available from https://doi.org/10.1016/j.eswa.2009.01.035.

Moosavi, M., & Soltani, N. (2013). Prediction of hydrocarbon densities using an artificial neural network-group contribution method up to high temperatures and pressures. *Thermochimica Acta*, *556*, 89−96. Available from https://doi.org/10.1016/j.tca.2013.01.038.

Nandagopal, M. S. G., Abraham, E., & Selvaraju, N. (2017). Advanced neural network prediction and system identification of liquid-liquid flow patterns in circular microchannels with varying angle of confluence. *Chemical Engineering Journal*, *309*, 850−865. Available from https://doi.org/10.1016/j.cej.2016.10.106.

Niska, H., & Serkkola, A. (2018). Data analytics approach to create waste generation profiles for waste management and collection. *Waste Management*, *77*, 477−485. Available from https://doi.org/10.1016/j.wasman.2018.04.033.

Olawoyin, R., Nieto, A., Grayson, R. L., Hardisty, F., & Oyewole, S. (2013). Application of artificial neural network (ANN)−self-organizing map (SOM) for the categorization of water, soil and sediment quality in petrochemical regions. *Expert Systems with Applications*, *40*(9), 3634−3648.

Reijnders, L. (2009). Are soil pollution risks established by governments the same as actual risks? *Applied and Environmental Soil Science*, *2009*, 237038. Available from https://doi.org/10.1155/2009/237038.

Rodríguez-Eugenio, N., McLaughlin, M., & Pennock, D. (2018). *Soil pollution: A hidden reality*. FAO.

Sakizadeh, M., Mirzaei, R., & Ghorbani, H. (2017). Support vector machine and artificial neural network to model soil pollution: A case study in Semnan Province, Iran. *Neural Computing and Applications*, *28*(11), 3229−3238. Available from https://doi.org/10.1007/s00521-016-2231-x.

Shadrin, D., Pukalchik, M., Kovaleva, E., & Fedorov, M. (2020). Artificial intelligence models to predict acute phytotoxicity in petroleum contaminated soils. *Ecotoxicology and environmental safety*, *194*, 110410.

Shu, H. Y., Lu, H. C., Fan, H. J., Chang, M. C., & Chen, J. C. (2006). Prediction for energy content of Taiwan municipal solid waste using multilayer perceptron neural networks. *Journal of the Air and Waste Management Association*, *56*(6), 852−858. Available from https://doi.org/10.1080/10473289.2006.10464497.

Singh, K. P., Gupta, S., Ojha, P., & Rai, P. (2013). Predicting adsorptive removal of chlorophenol from aqueous solution using artificial intelligence based modeling approaches. *Environmental Science and Pollution Research*, *20*(4), 2271−2287. Available from https://doi.org/10.1007/s11356-012-1102-y.

Staples, M., & Niazi, M. (2008). Systematic review of organizational motivations for adopting CMM-based SPI. *Information and Software Technology*, *50*(7−8), 605−620. Available from https://doi.org/10.1016/j.infsof.2007.07.003.

Tarasov, D., Buevich, A., Sergeev, A., & Shichkin, A. (2018). High variation topsoil pollution forecasting in the Russian Subarctic: Using artificial neural networks combined with residual kriging. *Applied Geochemistry*, *88*, 188−197.

Tatar, A., Naseri, S., Bahadori, M., Hezave, A. Z., Kashiwao, T., Bahadori, A., & Darvish, H. (2016). Prediction of carbon dioxide solubility in ionic liquids using MLP and radial basis function (RBF) neural networks. *Journal of the Taiwan Institute of Chemical Engineers*, *60*, 151−164. Available from https://doi.org/10.1016/j.jtice.2015.11.002.

Turan, N. G., Mesci, B., & Ozgonenel, O. (2011). The use of artificial neural networks (ANN) for modeling of adsorption of Cu(II) from industrial leachate by pumice. *Chemical Engineering Journal*, *171*(3), 1091−1097. Available from https://doi.org/10.1016/j.cej.2011.05.005.

Voda, A. I., & Radu, L. D. (2019). *How can artificial intelligence respond to smart cities challenges? Smart cities: Issues and challenges mapping political, social and economic risks and threats* (pp. 199−216). Elsevier. Available from https://doi.org/10.1016/B978-0-12-816639-0.00012-0.

Wan, J., Huang, M., Ma, Y., Guo, W., Wang, Y., Zhang, H., Li, W., & Sun, X. (2011). Prediction of effluent quality of a paper mill wastewater treatment using an adaptive network-based fuzzy inference system. *Applied Soft Computing Journal*, *11*(3), 3238−3246. Available from https://doi.org/10.1016/j.asoc.2010.12.026.

Wang, C., Ye, Z., Yu, Y., & Gong, W. (2018). Estimation of bus emission models for different fuel types of buses under real conditions. *Science of the Total Environment*, *640−641*, 965−972. Available from https://doi.org/10.1016/j.scitotenv.2018.05.289.

Ye, Z., Yang, J., Zhong, N., Tu, X., Jia, J., & Wang, J. (2020). Tackling environmental challenges in pollution controls using artificial intelligence: A review. *Science of the Total Environment*, *699*, 134279. Available from https://doi.org/10.1016/j.scitotenv.2019.134279.

Yetilmezsoy, K., Ozkaya, B., & Cakmakci, M. (2011). Artificial intelligence-based prediction models for environmental engineering. *Neural Network World*, *21*(3), 193–218. Available from https://doi.org/10.14311/NNW.2011.21.012.

Zheng, N. N., Liu, Z. Y., Ren, P. J., Ma, Y. Q., Chen, S. T., Yu, S. Y., Xue, J. R., Chen, B. D., & Wang, F. Y. (2017). Hybrid-augmented intelligence: Collaboration and cognition. *Frontiers of Information Technology and Electronic Engineering*, *18*(2), 153–179. Available from https://doi.org/10.1631/FITEE.1700053.

Zhou, P., Zhao, Y., Zhao, Z., & Chai, T. (2015). Source mapping and determining of soil contamination by heavy metals using statistical analysis, artificial neural network, and adaptive genetic algorithm. *Journal of Environmental Chemical Engineering*, *3*(4), 2569–2579.

Zhu, S., Han, H., Guo, M., & Qiao, J. (2017). A data-derived soft-sensor method for monitoring effluent total phosphorus. *Chinese Journal of Chemical Engineering*, *25*(12), 1791–1797. Available from https://doi.org/10.1016/j.cjche.2017.06.008.

Zonouz, P. R., Niaei, A., & Tarjomannejad, A. (2016). Modeling and optimization of toluene oxidation over perovskite-type nanocatalysts using a hybrid artificial neural network-genetic algorithm method. *Journal of the Taiwan Institute of Chemical Engineers*, *65*, 276–285. Available from https://doi.org/10.1016/j.jtice.2016.05.020.

Further reading

Chen, K. Y. (2011). Combining linear and nonlinear model in forecasting tourism demand. *Expert Systems with Applications*, *38*(8), 10368–10376. Available from https://doi.org/10.1016/j.eswa.2011.02.049.

Jaramillo, F., Orchard, M., Muñoz, C., Antileo, C., Sáez, D., & Espinoza, P. (2018). On-line estimation of the aerobic phase length for partial nitrification processes in SBR based on features extraction and SVM classification. *Chemical Engineering Journal*, *331*, 114–123. Available from https://doi.org/10.1016/j.cej.2017.07.185.

Artificial intelligence in the reduction and management of land pollution

Marcel I. Ejimofor, Chukwunonso O. Aniagor, Stephen N. Oba, Matthew C. Menkiti and Victor I. Ugonabo

Department of Chemical Engineering, Nnamdi Azikiwe University, Awka, Nigeria

Introduction

Globally, pollution of the environment is a great concern (Aniagor & Menkiti, 2018; Bai, 2007; Hashem, Aniagor, Nasr, et al., 2021a, 2021b). All foreign deposits on land, water, and air spaces have an effect that may take years to remedy or may never be contained without a deficit to environment (Aniagor & Menkiti, 2018; Bai, 2007; Hashem, Aniagor, Nasr, et al., 2021a, 2021b). Land pollution is severe and constantly increasing and so its management requires stringent measures. Land pollution is another term for soil contamination resulting from anthropogenic sources (Kowalska et al., 2018; Tetteh, 2015). Land contamination with factory chemicals or sewage, other wastewaters and industrial wastes, garbage, agricultural pesticides, and fertilizers, impacts from mining, systematic destruction of soil through overintensive agriculture, and the impact of erosion can be classified under land pollution (Tetteh, 2015). Another general overview of land pollution is the deterioration of the Earth's land surfaces, at and below ground level, due to the accumulation of solid and liquid waste materials that contaminate groundwater and soil (Popp et al., 2014). Hence, in summary, land pollution means any kind of long-term land damage, destruction, degradation, or loss as a result of the introduction of a foreign substance onto the land. Fig. 14.1 shows different sites of land pollution from different sources.

All causes of land pollution can be categorized into major areas such as deforestation, urbanization, and industrialization (Tanrivermis, 2003). While deforestation can be directly managed or regulated, urbanization and industrialization cannot be directly controlled; however, management of their impacts if done adequately can help cushion their overall effects. For the safety of the environment, systematic control of land pollution is urgent. Conventionally, many control measures are in use. Currently, the emphasis is on methods such as recycling of wastes, use of organic or reduction in the use of pesticides and herbicides, proper management of wastes dumps and land fills, source reduction and minimization, process modification, and reforestation, among others (Arshad et al., 2020).

Despite the usefulness of these methods, there remains the need for further systematic upgrading of land pollution management and control techniques, hence the recent adoption of machine learning or artificial intelligence (AI) (Li et al., 2021; Ye et al., 2018). This is an enhanced method of solving difficult and complex issues (Mellit & Kalogirou, 2008), which works by combining large amounts of data with fast, iterative processing and intelligent algorithms, allowing the software to learn automatically from

FIGURE 14.1

Sites of land pollution from different sources.

patterns or features in the data (Yaghini et al., 2013; Yao et al., 2019). AI by definition refers to the simulation of human intelligence in machines that are programmed to think like humans and mimic their actions (Barredo Arrieta et al., 2020). The term may also be applied to any machine that exhibits traits associated with a human mind such as learning and problem solving (Syam & Sharma, 2018), while robotics is the field of studies that uses the knowledge of science, engineering, and technology in designing and fabrication of robots, that can be a substitute for (or replicate) human actions (Yang et al., 2018).

This chapter is a review of the use of AI and robotics for the control of land pollution. The chapter is considered under the following subsections (1) the use of AI and robotics in system modification for effective on-the-spot minimization of wastes in process industries; (2) AI in the disposal and smart recycling of wastes; (3) impact of drones and neural network in reforestation; and (4) the use of machine learning in sustainable green agriculture.

The use of artificial intelligence and robotics in system modification for effective on-the-spot minimization of wastes in process industries

Manufacturing system adjustment and process modification targeted at the reduction of unrecyclable waste will aid the minimization of available waste materials that enter the environment (Briassoulis et al., 2019). These will in turn reduce the extent of the pressure on land as the final recipient of these wastes and also reduce land pollution (Menkiti & Ejimofor, 2016). System modification can be achieved with the use of applications that can improve the process performance and efficiency via mechanisms such as intelligent monitoring, optimization, and control and enhanced human—machine collaboration (Klumpp, 2018; Zhu et al., 2020). AI and robotics augment and amplify human potentials, increase productivity, and are moving from simple reasoning toward human-like cognitive abilities (Barile et al., 2019; Zheng et al., 2017). Through machine learning, robotics, drones, and the Internet of Things (IoT) (AI and robotics-related applications), society can achieve better process understanding, monitoring, modification, adjustment, and reduction of process wastes. In this area of thought, strong AI using the correct software/programming can optimize production processes through sets of algorithms to better performances, which will not only reduce cost but also reduce significantly the amount of by-products of conversion processes and enhance immediate reduction of disposable waste products (Wirtz, 2019). This will drastically reduce the extent of waste being deposited on the available land and in turn reduce land pollution. Dematerialization as a result of deep learning, which leads to conversion of some traditional physical products to software, has achieved such targeted waste reduction in music recording industries, where CDs and DVDs are now being replaced by streaming services. The introduction of machine learning and the IoT in the oil production industries has help check and minimize oil spillage, which has greatly contributed to land pollution (Aalsalem et al., 2018). Since the 19th century, production robots have been replacing employees because of the advancements in technology. They work more precisely than humans, for example, the "Robo Gas Inspector," 23 an inspection robot equipped with remote gas-sensing technology, can inspect technical facilities even in difficult-to-reach areas without putting humans at risk, for example, to detect leaks in above ground and underground gas pipelines (Soldan & Kroll, 2014).

The introduction of the so-called "smart factory" allows automated and machine-controlled production. The core target of Industry 4.0 was aimed at modification of the existing production facilities to the use of intelligent machines (smart factories) (Frank et al., 2019; Lasi et al., 2014; Schumacher et al., 2016). This production set up will be able to run with few or no humans, with the ability to calculate the optimal utilization capacity of the production facility (Lasi et al., 2014). It is targeted at achieving greater production accuracy with minimal process waste (which may be subjected to smart classification and recycling or safe disposal if not recyclable). This can be achieved via deep learning, robotics, and integration of a world-covering and fast-moving data-based network (IoT) (Schumacher et al., 2016). This on-the-spot minimization of waste through AI will help in the reduction of land pollution.

Artificial intelligence in the disposal and smart recycling of wastes
Artificial intelligence and robotics in waste classification

For a workable system of control, an efficient waste classification system precedes other important considerations before the correct decision of management or general policy. For fast and efficient waste classification, an AI-influenced system and the use of robotics can be of great help, such systems are discussed in the subsequent subsections.

Convolutional neural network model system of waste classification

A convolutional neural network (CNN) is a neural network that has one or more convolutional layers and these are used mainly for image processing, classification, segmentation, and also for other autocorrelated data (Yamashita et al., 2018; Zhang et al., 2017). It is a momentous class of deep learning with tremendous progress in image recognition (Park et al., 2017). In general, they are applied to evaluate visual imagery and often work beside the image classification (Park et al., 2017; Yamashita et al., 2018; Zhang et al., 2017). They can be identified at the core of everything from online photo tagging to self-driving cars (Chen et al., 2016; Dibaei et al., 2019). They are working hard behind the scenes in everything from health care to security. The agenda for this field is to enable machines to view the world as humans do, perceive it similarly, and even use this knowledge for a multitude of tasks such as image and video recognition, image analysis and classification, media recreation, recommendation systems, and natural language processing. The advancements in computer vision with deep learning have been constructed and perfected over time, primarily over one particular algorithm. The working principles of CNNs enable the acceptance of input via the input layer (Dibaei et al., 2019). The CNN explicitly assumes the input is an image, assigns learnable weights, and biases to various aspects of the image and is able to differentiate one from the other and reflect classifications onto its architecture (Fig. 14.2).

In waste classification, various systems of classification and segregation can be developed using image processing and CNN (Bobulski & Kubanek, 2019). A system of classifying and segregating polyethylene wastes was successfully developed and performed using several experiments to detect terephthalate, polyethene, high-density polyethylene, polypropylene, and polystyrene (Gené-Mola et al., 2019). The computer system was based on images obtained by an RGB digital camera and software for computer-based image preprocessing and convolution neural network with deep learning for object recognition (Agarwal et al., 2020). Also, capsule neural network (Capsule-Net) is very useful for the detection of waste types and classification into plastic and nonplastic materials (Sreelakshmi et al., 2019). The complete integration of CNN and Capsule-Net could resolve the

FIGURE 14.2

Typical CNN classification sequence (*CNN*, convolutional neural network).

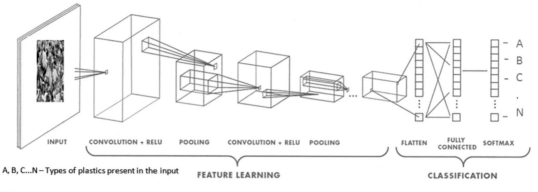

FIGURE 14.3

Convolutional neural network system of plastic classification.

issue of plastic detection and holistic classification, while separation could be achieved using an air stream to direct the waste to a specific container, assuming that the waste is transported separately on the conveyor belt. A schematic representation of the CNN system of plastic classification is presented in Fig. 14.3.

Support vector machine

Support vector machines (SVMs) are supervised learning models with associated learning models that analyze data for grouping and analysis (Cristianini & Schölkopf, 2002). They are a new type of learning machine for two-group classification problems. SVMs were first introduced in the late 1970s and early 1980s by Vladimir Vapnik and became famous as a classifier method based on the principle of structural risk minimization. They use a technique called the kernel trick to transform data and then, based on these transformations, find an optimal boundary between the possible outputs. The outstanding limitation of SVMs is that in their most simple form, they do not support multiclass classification (Tomas & Virginijus, 2017; Winters-Hilt et al., 2006). However, they are excellent in recognition and binary classification. Hence, for multiclass classification, a hybrid system of SVM and CNN could be used. In waste classification, SVM has been used for the classification of wastes into biodegradable and nonbiodegradable wastes, with 89.51% accuracy (Hanbal et al., 2020).

Artificial intelligence-robotics pickup system

A robot is a machine that can be controlled by a computer and is able on its own to automatically carry out functions irrespective of the degree of complexity of the task. Usually, it can yield to an external control device or the control may be embedded within. Robots can mimic a lifelike appearance or automated movements, and may convey a sense of intelligence of their own (Larson, 2010). An AI-robotics intelligence pickup robot was designed to help in a waste pickup program.

FIGURE 14.4

Garbage pickup system.

From Bai, J., Lian, S., Liu, Z., Wang, K., & Liu, D. (2018). Deep learning based robot for automatically picking up garbage on the grass. IEEE Transactions on Consumer Electronics, 64(3), 382–389. https://doi.org/10.1109/TCE.2018.2859629

The first intelligent waste pickup robot was designed by ZenRobotics (Ayub & ABM, 2020). It uses multiple in-built sensors for accurate analysis, upon which the robot can make independent decisions to pick up the objects from the waste stream or not. The robotic waste pickup machine consists of four units: locomotion, detection, pick up, and control system. It has the following components: metal detector, ultrasonic sensor, control and power unit, and actuators. This autonomous robot can perform tasks such as obstacle avoidance and metal detection. The locomotion unit was designed for movement, the pickup unit depends on the control unit, while the ultrasonic sensor is responsible for changing the path of the robot when there is an obstacle. This pickup system can handle metal wastes with high efficiency. A similar design was proposed for garbage pickup (Aniagor & Menkiti, 2018; Bai, 2007; Hashem, Aniagor, Nasr, et al., 2021a, 2021b). A pictorial representation of the garbage pickup system is shown in Fig. 14.4.

Artificial intelligence and robotics in waste recycling

Waste recycling as a measure of limiting land pollution is about the idea that all recyclable wastes should be kept from littering the environment by converting them useful products. Waste, such as plastics, nonbiodegradable materials, and litter, can accumulate on fertile land, polluting and altering the chemical and biological properties of soil. Recycling in clear terms is the conversion of waste into reusable material through a series of steps that takes a used material and processes, remanufactures it, and sells it as a new product (Yang et al., 2018). In addition to the economic impacts, it reduces the need for landfilling and incineration, and prevents pollution caused by the manufacturing of products from virgin materials. In addition, it saves energy, and decreases emissions of greenhouse gases that contribute to global climate change, conserves natural resources such as timber, water, and minerals, and helps sustain the environment for future generations. Recycling can keep wastes away from the environment and save the land from pollution. Both degradable and nonbiodegradable products can be recycled: the nonbiodegradables are sent back to the production line, while the biodegradables are sent to the composting pot for organic farming. Generally, two major parts of recycling include waste sorting and the conversion process (Demirbas, 2011). AI and robotics can also find relevance in the recycling process.

Robotic recycle sorting system

Robotic recycle sorting uses AI and robotics to sort recyclable wastes such as plastics, aluminum, and metals. The recycle sorting system is not only fast and efficient, but also reduces the cost of labor and the health risks associated with such work (Chin et al., 2019).

Working principle of the robotic sorting system

A robotic sorting system is comprised of a set of programmed robots and a waste conveyor system. The robots are equipped with cameras and computer systems that are highly trained to recognize specific objects, identify different colors, textures, shapes, and sizes of target materials, and have sensored fingers able to detect and snag recyclable items out of other waste materials and place them in their respective bins (Saxena et al., 2008). Though their usage is still developing, they work fast, with better efficiency than humans. A robotic sorting system called "optical sorting robotics" is currently under use by Recology in San Francisco Bay. The ZenRobotics heavy picker can pickup to 6000 pieces of waste in an hour. The fast picker can pickup to 4000 pieces of material per hour.

Advantages and disadvantages of a recycling robotic sorting system

An AI-powered robot can replace human workers effectively. Those workers can then be moved to other places that need attention, thus speeding up the process. It is faster at sorting off line and has the ability to self-update using available stored data. The benefits of AI are rapidly increasing and soon, robots may be able to make all the necessary adjustments on their own. Also, the recycle sorter's ability to store and process data will add to a database that can enhance waste recycling in future and is another a good advantage. In addition, its operation is quicker, more precise, and provides better sorting quality. In contrast to its numerous merits, the initial start-up cost remains a major challenge.

Artificial intelligence-robotic quality assessment system

AI and robotics also find relevant uses in product processing quality control. An automated quality assessment system uses machine learning and a smart intelligence algorithm for proper coordination and function execution. An AI-robotic quality assessment system uses high-powered sensors coupled with pickers (Silwal et al., 2017). This system can work both for the process feedstock and at the end of the product line. After sorting, waste conversion processes target making new products from the recyclable wastes. Before the conversion process, the robots scan the feed material to identify what each piece is and its location/size relative to each other piece on the belt, and then make a pick based on the programming installed and past experiences. This will aid the robots in picking off any odd material on the line. In addition, at the product end, robots can picking out any odd products different from the target products. The application of AI-robotic systems in quality control has been demonstrated in the single-stream sector of C & D Company, where the system was referred to as a quality control agent whose "eyes" never stop searching for impurities (Bai et al., 2018). Some of the benefits of this system include: it is a more focused system than manual handling, in the case of a threat of exposure to hazardous materials, it removes the risk from humans. By having a machine that can recognize multiple materials that do not belong on the line and removing them, commodity purity is increased (Aniagor & Menkiti, 2018; Bai, 2007; Hashem, Aniagor, Hussein, & Farag, 2021a; Hashem, Aniagor, Nasr, & Abou-Okeil, 2021b). According to *Waste Advantage* magazine of October 2017 report, the machines never take a break, their sensors do not get tired, and they do not take sick days. Whether it is an 8-hour shift or a 24-hour shift, the software does not stop working, resulting in higher quality product and less downtime for the process plant.

Reforestation for land pollution management: impact of drones and neural network

In the management and control of land pollution, reforestation is vital. Without trees, the land is exposed to pollution (Savard, 2010). Reforestation involves replanting an area with trees. This process helps to bind the soil, preventing soil erosion and flooding, which can be activated when there are no trees to prevent the top layer of soil from being carried away. In addition, trees help cushion the effect of acid rain by absorbing the toxins it contains, which would otherwise increase land pollution (Tasneem et al., 2013). However, effective global reforestation may be slow if not impossible using the method of planting trees by hand. In this respect, the use of AI and robotics can play the utmost role and make reforestation easy, faster, and efficient. Effective applications of AI and robotics in reforestation include site assessment and data/information curation, information/data analysis using a deep learning algorithm, site and planting pattern selection based on an analysis report, efficient and fast seed-firing planting method using drones, and postplanting monitoring and assessment. These important aspects are discussed below.

Site assessment, data/information curation, and site planting pattern for reforestation: Area and location assessment is the first step involved in the use of AI and robotics for reforestation. The drones fly over the target area to gather information about the topography and soil conditions (planting site condition) and make an accurate 3D map (Ajayi et al., 2018). This is used to assess the area conditions and suitability for tree planting. The area surveys obtained supply images (Figs. 14.5 and 14.6) that are combined and analyzed using deep learning algorithms.

Based on the drone's report analysis, informed decisions such as available space for planting, selection of trees, and planting pattern, among others, are made (Liu et al., 2017). In addition, the fast and efficient seed-planting drones, equipped with guidance and control software and fitted with pressurized canisters of seed pods with germinated seeds proceed to fire biodegradable pods and nutrients into designated spots, as shown in Fig. 14.7.

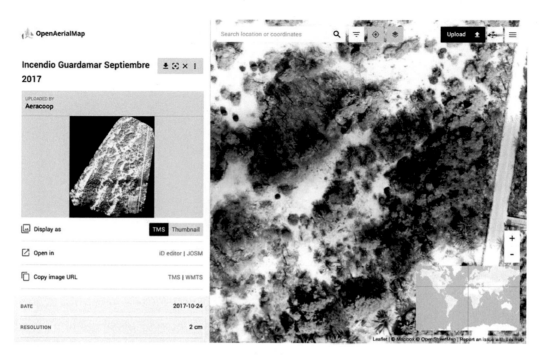

FIGURE 14.5

Degraded site image captured using drones.

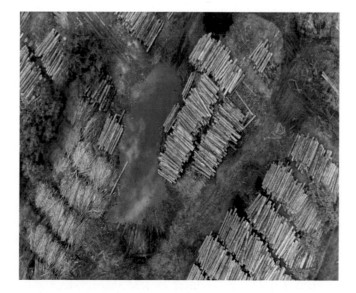

FIGURE 14.6

Degraded site image captured using drones.

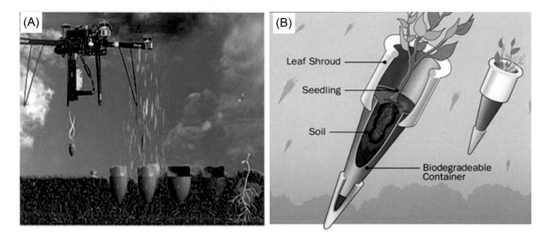

FIGURE 14.7

(A) Seed-firing drones and (B) pressurized canisters of seed pods.

From https://dronecoria.org

The reality of the use of AI and robotics in reforestation has been demonstrated by BioCarbon Engineering in conjunction with The Worldview International Foundation via the BioCarbon reforestation scheme. Hence successful reforestation will prevent the effects of acid rain and erosion, which are among the major courses of land degradation and pollution.

Land pollution management via sustainable green agriculture: use of machine learning and robotics

Among the major factors that contribute to land pollution through agriculture is the overuse of chemical pesticides, fertilizers, and herbicides. Hence, limiting the use of an excess of chemical pesticides, fertilizers, and herbicides will reduce land pollution. To this effect, the use of AI and robotics can help reduce the excess use of herbicides, chemical fertilizers, and pesticides, and also enhance productivity. To limit the use of chemical herbicides, autonomous robotic weed control systems have been proposed and are currently in use. The robotic weed control system combines the deep learning algorithm and robotics in providing an interactive technology for guidance, detection and identification, precision in-row weed control, and mapping. Among the functions, detection and identification of weeds under the wide range of conditions common to agricultural fields remain the greatest challenge (Sabanci & Aydin, 2017). However, few complete robotic weed control systems have demonstrated the potential of weed detection and identification and more research has been directed toward this challenge. Some of the methods for weed detection and identification include morphological characteristic measurement of leaf shape, which differentiates the weeds from the crops by determining the variation leaf sizes. Varying effectiveness ($\leq 75\%$) was recorded using this method (Tanha et al., 2020). Another method involves the use of digital imaging which

Table 14.1 Summary of the existing AI-robotic applications in weeding operations.

Application	Crop	Algorithms for weed detection	Weed removal methods
Precision weed management	Pepper plants, artificial plants	Machine vision, AI	A smart sprayer
Autonomous weeding robot	Sugar beat	Machine vision algorithm	High-power lasers for intrarow weeding
Robot for weed control	Sugar beets	Machine vision	Rotatory hoe/mechanical removal
Weeding robot	Rice	–	Motion of robot prevents weed growth
Weed prevention robot	Rice		Motion of robot
Weed detection	Sugar cane	Color-based and texture-based algorithms; greenness identification; fuzzy real-time classifier	Robotic arms for mechanical removal
Robotic weed control	Cotton	Machine vision algorithm based on mathematical morphology	Chemical spraying

AI, Artificial intelligence.

involved a self-organizing neural network; this method enables a weed identification accuracy above 75% (Tanha et al., 2020). Table 14.1 shows the existing technologies based on AI-robotics systems either as alternatives to herbicides or for a reduction in the number of chemical herbicides needed for effective weed removal.

Also, the use of fertilizers and pesticides, whether chemical or natural, can be effectively optimized using AI and robotics. AI and robotics can be used for soil assessment and the detection of chemical levels in the soil, which can be used to determine the nature of fertilizer and optimum levels of fertilizers required for maximum productivity (Golicz et al., 2019). In addition, the Blue River Technology See and spray model built around machine learning and robotics for weed and pest control uses computer vision to precisely find pests and spray pesticides only where needed. This technology has reduced the use of excess pesticide which can cause soil contamination and pollution, and limited the use of such chemicals to only when highly necessary.

Conclusion

The uses of AI and robotics have become very important in daily global activities. Their usage has cut across all areas of life; in medicine and diagnostics, industries, agriculture, and other sectors. This chapter has demonstrated that AI and robotics can be very useful also in the control and reduction of land pollution. Measures such as on-the-spot waste minimization during the production via process optimization, smart disposal and recycling, reforestation and sustainable green agriculture can be easily enhanced using AI and robotics. Hence, AI and robotics, if effectively channeled can help the global fight in the reduction and control of land pollution.

References

Aalsalem, M. Y., Khan, W. Z., Gharibi, W., Khan, M. K., & Arshad, Q. (2018). Wireless sensor networks in oil and gas industry: Recent advances, taxonomy, requirements, and open challenges. *Journal of Network and Computer Applications*, *113*, 87−97. Available from https://doi.org/10.1016/j.jnca.2018.04.004.

Agarwal, S., Gudi, R., & Saxena, P. (2020). One-shot learning based classification for segregation of plastic waste. ArXiv. https://arxiv.org.

Ajayi, O. G., Palmer, M., & Salubi, A. A. (2018). Modelling farmland topography for suitable site selection of dam construction using unmanned aerial vehicle (UAV) photogrammetry. *Remote Sensing Applications: Society and Environment*, *11*, 220−230. Available from https://doi.org/10.1016/j.rsase.2018.07.007.

Aniagor, C. O., & Menkiti, M. C. (2018). Kinetics and mechanistic description of adsorptive uptake of crystal violet dye by lignified elephant grass complexed isolate. *Journal of Environmental Chemical Engineering*, *6*(2), 2105−2118. Available from https://doi.org/10.1016/j.jece.2018.01.070.

Arshad, Z., Robaina, M., Shahbaz, M., & Veloso, A. B. (2020). The effects of deforestation and urbanization on sustainable growth in Asian countries. *Environmental Science and Pollution Research*, *27*(9), 10065−10086. Available from https://doi.org/10.1007/s11356-019-07507-7.

Ayub, A. A. A., & ABM, A. (2020). Artificial intelligence and machine learning in waste management and recycling. *Engineering International*, *8*(1), 43−52. Available from https://doi.org/10.18034/ei.v8i1.498.

Bai, X. (2007). Integrating global environmental concerns into urban management: The scale and readiness arguments. *Journal of Industrial Ecology*, *11*(2), 15−29. Available from https://doi.org/10.1162/jie.2007.1202.

Barile, S., Piciocchi, P., Bassano, C., Spohrer, J., & Pietronudo, M. C. (2019). *Re-defining the role of artificial intelligence (AI) in wiser service systems*, . Advances in intelligent systems and computing (787, pp. 159−170). Springer Verlag. Available from https://doi.org/10.1007/978-3-319-94229-2_16.

Barredo Arrieta, A., Díaz-Rodríguez, N., Del Ser, J., Bennetot, A., Tabik, S., Barbado, A., Garcia, S., Gil-Lopez, S., Molina, D., Benjamins, R., Chatila, R., & Herrera, F. (2020). Explainable explainable artificial intelligence (XAI): concepts, taxonomies, opportunities and challenges toward responsible AI. *Information Fusion*, *58*, 82−115. Available from https://doi.org/10.1016/j.inffus.2019.12.012.

Bobulski, J., & Kubanek, M. (2019). *Waste classification system using image processing and convolutional neural networks*, . Lecture notes in computer science *(including subseries* Lecture notes in artificial intelligence *and* Lecture notes in bioinformatics*)* (11507, pp. 350−361). Springer Verlag. Available from https://doi.org/10.1007/978-3-030-20518-8_30.

Briassoulis, D., Pikasi, A., & Hiskakis, M. (2019). End-of-waste life: inventory of alternative end-of-use recirculation routes of bio-based plastics in the European Union context. *Critical Reviews in Environmental Science and Technology*, *49*(20), 1835−1892. Available from https://doi.org/10.1080/10643389.2019.1591867.

Chen, Y., Yang, X., Zhong, B., Pan, S., Chen, D., & Zhang, H. (2016). CNNTracker: online discriminative object tracking via deep convolutional neural network. *Applied Soft Computing Journal*, *38*, 1088−1098. Available from https://doi.org/10.1016/j.asoc.2015.06.048.

Chin, L., Lipton, J., Yuen, M. C., Kramer-Bottiglio, R., & Rus, D. (2019). *Automated recycling separation enabled by soft robotic material classification*. RoboSoft 2019−2019 IEEE international conference on soft robotics (pp. 102−107). Institute of Electrical and Electronics Engineers Inc. Available from https://doi.org/10.1109/ROBOSOFT.2019.8722747.

Cristianini, N., & Schölkopf, B. (2002). Support vector machines and kernel methods: the new generation of learning machines. *AI Magazine*, *23*(3), 31–41.

Demirbas, A. (2011). Waste management, waste resource facilities and waste conversion processes. *Energy Conversion and Management*, *52*(2), 1280–1287. Available from https://doi.org/10.1016/j.enconman.2010.09.025.

Dibaei, M., Zheng, X., Jiang, K., Maric, S., Abbas, R., Liu, S., Zhang, Y., Deng, Y., Wen, S., Zhang, J., Xiang, Y., & Yu, S. (2019). An overview of attacks and defences on intelligent connected vehicles. ArXiv. https://arxiv.org

Frank, A. G., Dalenogare, L. S., & Ayala, N. F. (2019). Industry 4.0 technologies: Implementation patterns in manufacturing companies. *International Journal of Production Economics*, *210*, 15–26. Available from https://doi.org/10.1016/j.ijpe.2019.01.004.

Gené-Mola, J., Vilaplana, V., Rosell-Polo, J. R., Morros, J. R., Ruiz-Hidalgo, J., & Gregorio, E. (2019). Multimodal deep learning for Fuji apple detection using RGB-D cameras and their radiometric capabilities. *Computers and Electronics in Agriculture*, *162*, 689–698. Available from https://doi.org/10.1016/j.compag.2019.05.016.

Golicz, K., Hallett, S. H., Sakrabani, R., & Pan, G. (2019). The potential for using smartphones as portable soil nutrient analyzers on suburban farms in central East China. *Scientific Reports*, *9*(1), 16424. Available from https://doi.org/10.1038/s41598-019-52702-8.

Hanbal, I. F., Ingosan, J. S., Oyam, N. A. A., & Hu, Y. (2020). Classifying wastes using random forests, Gaussian Naïve Bayes, support vector machine and multilayer perceptron. *IOP Conference Series: Materials Science and Engineering*, *803*(1), 012017. Available from https://doi.org/10.1088/1757-899X/803/1/012017.

Hashem, A., Aniagor, C. O., Hussein, D. M., & Farag, S. (2021a). Application of novel butane-1, 4-dioic acid-functionalized cellulosic biosorbent for aqueous cobalt ion sequestration. *Cellulose*, *28*, 3599–3615. Available from https://doi.org/10.1007/s10570-021-03726-9.

Hashem, A., Aniagor, C. O., Nasr, M. F., & Abou-Okeil, A. (2021b). Efficacy of treated sodium alginate and activated carbon fibre for Pb(II) adsorption. *International Journal of Biological Macromolecules*, *176*, 201–216. Available from https://doi.org/10.1016/j.ijbiomac.2021.02.067.

Klumpp, M. (2018). Automation and artificial intelligence in business logistics systems: Human reactions and collaboration requirements. *International Journal of Logistics Research and Applications*, *21*(3), 224–242. Available from https://doi.org/10.1080/13675567.2017.1384451.

Kowalska, J. B., Mazurek, R., Gąsiorek, M., & Zaleski, T. (2018). Pollution indices as useful tools for the comprehensive evaluation of the degree of soil contamination—a review. *Environmental Geochemistry and Health*, *40*(6), 2395–2420. Available from https://doi.org/10.1007/s10653-018-0106-z.

Larson, D.A. (2010). Artificial intelligence: Robots, avatars, and the demise of the human mediator. Faculty Scholarship. Paper 351. https://open.mitchellhamline.edu/facsch/351

Lasi, H., Fettke, P., Kemper, H. G., Feld, T., & Hoffmann, M. (2014). Industry 4.0. *Business and Information Systems Engineering*, *6*(4), 239–242. Available from https://doi.org/10.1007/s12599-014-0334-4.

Li, L., Rong, S., Wang, R., & Yu, S. (2021). Recent advances in artificial intelligence and machine learning for nonlinear relationship analysis and process control in drinking water treatment: A review. *Chemical Engineering Journal*, *405*, 126673. Available from https://doi.org/10.1016/j.cej.2020.126673.

Liu, W., Wang, Z., Liu, X., Zeng, N., Liu, Y., & Alsaadi, F. E. (2017). A survey of deep neural network architectures and their applications. *Neurocomputing*, *234*, 11–26. Available from https://doi.org/10.1016/j.neucom.2016.12.038.

Mellit, A., & Kalogirou, S. A. (2008). Artificial intelligence techniques for photovoltaic applications: A review. *Progress in Energy and Combustion Science*, *34*(5), 574–632. Available from https://doi.org/10.1016/j.pecs.2008.01.001.

Park, W. B., Chung, J., Jung, J., Sohn, K., Singh, S. P., Pyo, M., Shin, N., & Sohn, K. S. (2017). Classification of crystal structure using a convolutional neural network. *IUCrJ*, *4*, 486−494. Available from https://doi.org/10.1107/S205225251700714X.

Popp, J., Lakner, Z., Harangi-Rakos, M., & Fari, M. (2014). The effect of bioenergy expansion: Food, energy, and environment. *Renewable and Sustainable Energy Reviews*, *32*, 559−578. Available from https://doi.org/10.1016/j.rser.2014.01.056.

Sabanci, K., & Aydin, C. (2017). Smart robotic weed control system for sugar beet. *Journal of Agricultural Science and Technology*, *19*(1), 73−83. Available from http://jast.modares.ac.ir/article_15928_c74-c5a1ad5cdd87aa22fcf2e5fb04641.pdf.

Savard, M. M. (2010). Tree-ring stable isotopes and historical perspectives on pollution—an overview. *Environmental Pollution*, *158*(6), 2007−2013. Available from https://doi.org/10.1016/j.envpol.2009.11.031.

Saxena, A., Driemeyer, J., & Ng, A. Y. (2008). Robotic grasping of novel objects using vision. *International Journal of Robotics Research*, *27*(2), 157−173. Available from https://doi.org/10.1177/0278364907087172.

Schumacher, A., Erol, S., & Sihn, W. (2016). *A maturity model for assessing industry 4.0 readiness and maturity of manufacturing enterprises*. *Procedia CIRP* (52, pp. 161−166). Available from https://doi.org/10.1016/j.procir.2016.07.040.

Silwal, A., Davidson, J. R., Karkee, M., Mo, C., Zhang, Q., & Lewis, K. (2017). Design, integration, and field evaluation of a robotic apple harvester. *Journal of Field Robotics*, *34*(6), 1140−1159. Available from https://doi.org/10.1002/rob.21715.

Soldan, S., & Kroll, A. (2014). Übersicht zu Sensordatenfusionsansätzen in der Thermografie. *Technisches Messen*, *81*(10), 474−484. Available from https://doi.org/10.1515/teme-2014-1044.

Sreelakshmi, K., Akarsh, S., Vinayakumar, R., & Soman, K.P. (2019). Capsule neural networks and visualization for segregation of plastic and non-plastic wastes. In 2019 Fifth international conference on advanced computing and communication systems, ICACCS 2019 (pp. 631−636). Institute of Electrical and Electronics Engineers Inc. https://doi.org/10.1109/ICACCS.2019.8728405

Syam, N., & Sharma, A. (2018). Waiting for a sales renaissance in the fourth industrial revolution: machine learning and artificial intelligence in sales research and practice. *Industrial Marketing Management*, *69*, 135−146. Available from https://doi.org/10.1016/j.indmarman.2017.12.019.

Tanha, T., Dhara, S., Nivedita, P., Hiteshri, Y., & Manan, S. (2020). Implementation of artificial intelligence in agriculture for optimisation of irrigation and application of pesticides and herbicides. *Artificial Intelligence in Agriculture*, *4*, 58−73. Available from https://doi.org/10.1016/j.aiia.2020.04.002.

Tanrivermis, H. (2003). Agricultural land use change and sustainable use of land resources in the Mediterranean region of Turkey. *Journal of Arid Environments*, *54*(3), 553−564. Available from https://doi.org/10.1006/jare.2002.1078.

Tasneem, A., P., P., T., K., & S.A., A. (2013). Acid rain: past, present, and future. *International Journal of Environmental Engineering*, *229*, 054703. Available from https://doi.org/10.1504/IJEE.2013.054703.

Tetteh, R. N. (2015). Chemical soil degradation as a result of contamination: a review. *Journal of Soil Science and Environmental Management*, *6*(11), 301−308. Available from https://doi.org/10.5897/JSSEM15.0499.

Tomas, P., & Virginijus, M. (2017). Comparison of Naive Bayes, random forest, decision tree, support vector machines, and logistic regression classifiers for text reviews classification. *Baltic Journal of Modern Computing*, *5*(2), 221−232. Available from https://doi.org/10.22364/bjmc.2017.5.2.05.

Winters-Hilt, S., Yelundur, A., McChesney, C., & Landry, M. (2006). Support vector machine implementations for classification & clustering. *BMC Bioinformatics*, *7*(2), S4. Available from https://doi.org/10.1186/1471-2105-7-S2-S4.

Wirtz, J. (2019). Organizational ambidexterity: cost-effective service excellence, service robots, and artificial intelligence. *Organizational Dynamics*, *49*(3), 1−9.

Yaghini, M., Khoshraftar, M. M., & Fallahi, M. (2013). A hybrid algorithm for artificial neural network training. *Engineering Applications of Artificial Intelligence*, 26(1), 293–301. Available from https://doi.org/10.1016/j.engappai.2012.01.023.

Yamashita, R., Nishio, M., Do, R. K. G., & Togashi, K. (2018). Convolutional neural networks: An overview and application in radiology. *Insights into Imaging*, 9(4), 611–629. Available from https://doi.org/10.1007/s13244-018-0639-9.

Yang, G. Z., Bellingham, J., Dupont, P. E., Fischer, P., Floridi, L., Full, R., Jacobstein, N., Kumar, V., McNutt, M., Merrifield, R., Nelson, B. J., Scassellati, B., Taddeo, M., Taylor, R., Veloso, M., Wang, Z. L., & Wood, R. (2018). The grand challenges of science robotics. *Science Robotics*, 3(14), eaar7650. Available from https://doi.org/10.1126/scirobotics.aar7650.

Yao, K., Unni, R., & Zheng, Y. (2019). Intelligent nanophotonics: Merging photonics and artificial intelligence at the nanoscale. *Nanophotonics*, 8(3), 339–366. Available from https://doi.org/10.1515/nanoph-2018-0183.

Ye, H., Liang, L., Li, G. Y., Kim, J., Lu, L., & Wu, M. (2018). Machine learning for vehicular networks: Recent advances and application examples. *IEEE Vehicular Technology Magazine*, 13(2), 94–101. Available from https://doi.org/10.1109/MVT.2018.2811185.

Zhang, Q., Zhou, D., & Zeng, X. (2017). HeartID: A multiresolution convolutional neural network for ECG-based biometric human identification in smart health applications. *IEEE Access*, 5, 11805–11816. Available from https://doi.org/10.1109/ACCESS.2017.2707460.

Zheng, Nn, Liu, Zy, Ren, Pj, Ma, Yq, Chen, St, Yu, Sy, Xue, Jr, Chen, Bd, & Wang, Fy (2017). Hybrid-augmented intelligence: Collaboration and cognition. *Frontiers of Information Technology and Electronic Engineering*, 18(2), 153–179. Available from https://doi.org/10.1631/FITEE.1700053.

Zhu, M., He, T., & Lee, C. (2020). Technologies toward next generation human machine interfaces: From machine learning enhanced tactile sensing to neuromorphic sensory systems. *Applied Physics Reviews*, 7(3), 031305. Available from https://doi.org/10.1063/5.0016485.

Further reading

Bai, J., Lian, S., Liu, Z., Wang, K., & Liu, D. (2018). Deep learning based robot for automatically picking up garbage on the grass. *IEEE Transactions on Consumer Electronics*, 64(3), 382–389. Available from https://doi.org/10.1109/TCE.2018.2859629.

Menkiti, M. C, & Ejimofor, M. I (2016). Experimental and artificial neural network application the optimization of paint effluent (PE) coagulation using novel Achatinoidea shell extract (ASE). *Journal of Water Process Engineering*, 10, 172–187. Available from https://doi.org/10.1016/j.jwpe.2015.09.010.

Data-centric and intelligent systems in noise pollution research and other environmental engineering issues

Advanced soft computing techniques in modeling noise pollution health impacts

Manoj Yadav, Bhaven Tandel and M. Mansoor Ahammed

Civil Engineering Department, S.V. National Institute of Technology, India

Introduction

Humanity currently faces countless challenges as a result of industrialization and urbanization in the modern era. Some common examples include the pollution of water, land, and air, global warming, and climate change. The magnitudes of these problems have become large enough that they can no longer be ignored. Noise pollution is one such problem that has grown in the age of modernization (Guarnaccia, 2010). The primary impact of noise pollution on humans is mostly psychological, and includes annoyance, stress, lack of concentration, interference to verbal communication, and social-behavioral issues such as bad temper (Chuang et al., 2014; Passchier-Vermeer & Passchier, 2000). Auditory health impacts can include be hearing impairment and loss of hearing. Nonauditory impacts on health include headache, hypertension, high blood pressure, and cardiovascular diseases (Anitha et al., 2017; Baridalyne et al., 2014).

In many cases of noise-induced health-impact modeling or work efficiency, prediction modeling requires analysis, ranking, and optimization, based on available or collected data that are uncertain or ambiguous, or frequently incomplete (Rahmani et al., 2011). Moreover, this kind of prediction modeling integrates judgment based on engineering mathematics and opinion given by experts in the area (Bakker et al., 2012). The ambiguity, as well as uncertainty in the available data, can be overcome by employing various optimization techniques available such as sensitivity analysis, multicriteria decision-making, artificial neural network, fuzzy optimization, swarm optimization, structural equation modeling (SEM), and adaptive control (Flintsch & Chen, 2004). Also, soft computing techniques propose an attractive substitute because these evolving computational systems combine numerous problem-solving methods that give the corresponding reasoning and methods to solve real-world problems that involve imprecision, uncertainty, subjectivity, and partial truth.

Two arithmetical methods, SEM and exploratory factor analysis (EFA), have come into focus in recent years due to their ability in identifying and assessing the relations in hypothetical models (Wen et al., 2018). Precisely, EFA is beneficial in the case of studies based on direct interview responses; it helps to recognize the relationships among variables acquired from questionnaire items without past knowledge factors and the patterns of the acquired variables (Finch & West, 1997). Second, the SEM approach is advantageous in studying complicated relationships between acquired

Current Trends and Advances in Computer-Aided Intelligent Environmental Data Engineering.
DOI: https://doi.org/10.1016/B978-0-323-85597-6.00014-8

337

variables as well as simultaneously calculating all coefficients in the system model (Bo et al., 2015).

The neuro-fuzzy computing method is becoming a choice of researchers for use in prediction modeling studies. It gives the interpretation and identification strength of fuzzy logic systems and the capability of learning by neural networks in a single system (Ghosh et al., 2014). Over the last decade, various neuro-fuzzy systems have been developed. Among them, the adaptive neuro-fuzzy inference system (ANFIS) gives an organized and directed approach to constructing the prediction model. It provides the design parameters that are best suited in the lowest possible time (Sharad et al., 2018).

The objective of this chapter is to introduce an integrated approach to study assistive and predictive modeling for noise pollution-induced health implications. The approach integrates two soft computing techniques called EFA and SEM followed by an ANFIS. Often, while studying noise-induced health effects, the number of parameters considered will be high. In such cases, traditional mathematical modeling does not provide precise outcomes (Ramalingeswara Rao & Seshagiri Rao, 1992). Here the EFA and SEM approaches will be helpful as EFA summarizes and reduces the data parameters and SEM gives correlations between parameters as well as explaining the most significant parameters to the desired output. ANFIS is then used to build a prediction model based on the most significant parameters as inputs for predicting the desired output.

Effect of noise pollution on human health

The perception of sound in humans plays a very significant role in day-to-day life and is directly related to satisfaction with life (World Health Organization. Regional Office for Europe, 2011). According to the International Programme on Chemical Safety (Okokon et al., 2018), "an adverse effect of noise is defined as a change in the morphology and physiology of an organism that results in impairment of functional capacity, or impairment of capacity to compensate for additional stress, or increases the susceptibility of an organism to the harmful effects of other environmental influences." As explained in this definition, effects can be short-lived or have long-term effects on the physical, psychological, or functional ability of humans or a particular organ (Bruce et al., 2012). The World Health Organization (WHO) has established seven classes of harmful health effects of noise pollution on humans (World Health Organization. Regional Office for Europe, 2011).

Hearing impairment

When the threshold of hearing increases, it is typically called hearing impairment. Hearing impairment can be quantified by audiometric testing. One can suffer from hearing handicap due to noise, which is a stage of hearing impairment, where the person is unable to hear adequately in background noise (Mathias et al., 2014). On a global level, impairment by noise pollution is the most common occupational hazard. In developing countries like India, noise impairment not only exists in occupations but also through environmental noise (Pandya, 2003). "Over 120 million people are suffering by hearing impairment all over the world"; it was concluded in the world health assembly 1995 (Smith et al., 2003). Men and women are at equal risk of hearing impairment due to noise (Karin et al., 2014).

Interference with speech communication

Due to noise, spoken communication is more often interrupted, leading to functional as well as behavioral problems. This problem is most commonly observed in hearing-impaired children and older people (World Health Organization. Regional Office for Europe, 2011). Noise in commercial or industrial areas leads to interference in speech communication and can cause various problems such as not understanding precisely what a is being communicated (Omar et al., 2018).

Sleep disturbances

Uninterrupted sleep is one of the essential aspects for human well-being and proper functionality (Maria et al., 2016). On the other hand, sleep disturbance is the most commonly reported impact of noise (Mary et al., 2019). Due to outdoor noise, one can suffer from difficulty in falling asleep as well as frequent awakenings.

Cardiovascular and physiological

Laboratory as well as epidemiological studies have shown that those in noisy areas and people living near noisy streets, airports, railway stations, or industries have some temporary or permanent physiological impacts (Jurica et al., 2018). Noise is an environmental stressor (Passchier-Vermeer & Passchier, 2000). Short-term high noise exposure can activate hormonal imbalance and cause an increase in blood pressure and heartbeat rate (Marta et al., 2015). Long-term noise exposure can cause severe implications to humans such as heart diseases and hypertension (Thomas et al., 2018). Also, noise can cause reflux reactions, especially when it is unwanted or sudden. The extent and interval of cardiovascular and physiological effects are dependent on personal characteristics, lifestyle, and environmental conditions (Konstantina et al., 2017).

Disturbances to mental health

Noise pollution is not a direct cause of mental illness, but it is identified as an accelerator of mental illness (Belojevic et al., 2003). Ill effects of noise pollution on mental health include emotional stress, nervous complaints, nausea, headaches, instability, argumentativeness, sexual impotence, mood changes, increase in social conflicts, as well as general psychiatric disorders such as neurosis, psychosis, and hysteria (Beutel et al., 2016).

The effects of noise on performance

It has been discovered in many types of research as well as laboratory studies that occupational noise decreases cognitive task performance (Håkan et al., 2014). Especially among children in school, it noise has been identified as causing a lack of concentration, which leads to lowering the understanding of tasks given to children (Charlotte et al., 2013). If a person is working in a noisy area, the chances of making errors are high, depending upon the noise levels and type of task (Tao et al., 2017). Reading, solving problems, memory, and attention can by affected by surrounding noise, which ultimately results in lowered performance.

Negative social behavior and annoyance reactions

Annoyance is globally felt as a noise-induced adverse effect. Annoyance can be defined as displeasure felt by individuals or groups by any agent (Al-Mutairi et al., 2011). Several studies have reported that noise-induced annoyance is a significant discomforting phenomenon in daily life. It can lead to anger, disappointment, dissatisfaction, depression, anxiety, withdrawal, and exhaustion (Beutel et al., 2016). Noise pollution also affects social behavior. For example, in loud noise, people may behave angrily with other people or may become less helpful and aggravated (World Health Organization. Regional Office for Europe, 2011).

Noise pollution health-impact modeling

The health impacts of noise pollution can vary from person to person or area to area. Noise pollution health impacts modeling and drawing specific conclusions is subjective. As the data collection in noise pollution health-impact prediction is uncertain, inconsistent, and complicated in nature, advanced soft computing tools/techniques are a necessity in such scenarios. Here, the authors have discussed three such methods with an approach for assistive and then predictive modeling for noise pollution health impacts. The first is EFA, the second is SEM, and the third is prediction modeling by the adaptive neuro-fuzzy inference system.

Exploratory factor analysis

EFA is a mathematical tool used to detect the underlying function of a relatively large number of variables. It is a factor evaluation method where the primary purpose is to define the theoretical relationship between different studied variables. EFA is used when the researcher wants to reduce a large number of variables into a few meaningful ones. Therefore, it is basically a data reduction technique that is used to create a better explanation of a process (Thompson, 2004). EFA is a bivariate statistical method for modeling the covariance structure of the variables found across the following three parameter groups: factor loadings related to latent, residual variance referred to as unique variance, and the correlations.

The purpose of EFA is to clarify a comparatively smaller number of factors for the interaction between several observed variables. Therefore EFA is known as one of the strategies for data reduction. In the study of noise pollution health impacts modeling, a high number of variables must be considered to draw precise conclusions. The variables may be personal/socioeconomic variables such as the age of the person, and their education, awareness, and economic status; other variables can be related to noise pollution in areas, that is, noise source, noise levels, noise indices, noise exposure time, and noise dose received by the person. Apart from variables explaining personal and noise pollution characteristics, primary noise pollution impacts such as headache, stress, sleep disturbance, annoyance, and interference in spoken communication also have to be considered in the study. Hence, it is clear that a large number of observed variables may be involved in noise pollution studies. Here EFA is very useful, as the goal of EFA is to identify the groups of items that, when considered together, explain as much of the observed covariance as possible. Each of these groups made of observed variables is called a factor or latent factor. These latent factors can be considered as groups depending upon their correlated observed variables, as shown in Fig. 15.1. As can be seen in Fig. 15.1, observed variables 1, 2, and 3 can be represented by latent factor 1. Later these latent factors can be used for various hypotheses testing in SEM. It helps to discover a meaningful pattern by identifying the items where responses seem to clump together or vary in a predictable way (Rajalahti & Kvalheim, 2011). Hence, EFA in noise pollution health-impact studies can be successfully used for data summarization and data reduction.

Structural equation modeling

SEM is an efficient, multivariate approach used commonly for the testing and evaluation of multivariate causal links in science research. SEMs vary as they measure the direct and indirect effects on previously presumed causal interactions from other modeling techniques. SEM has evolved over more than three decades and is an almost 100-year-old statistical process. The very first phase of SEMs established the idea of causal modeling by way of path analysis (Surajit, 2015). SEM was later morphed into the social sciences also to include factor analysis. SEM has increased its

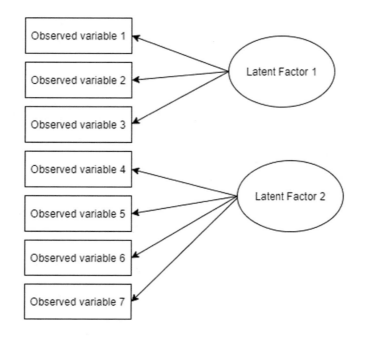

FIGURE 15.1

Representation of exploratory factor analysis.

potential through the second generation. The third generation of SEM began in 2000 with the creaton of Judea Pearl's "structural causal model," accompanied by the incorporation of Bayesian modeling.

SEM has the ability to analyze the dependence relationships series simultaneously. It is particularly useful in evaluating hypotheses that involve many equations involving relationships of dependency. In other words, if we assume the picture creates satisfaction, so material generates commitment, and happiness is a contingent and independent variable. Though in a corresponding dependency relationship, a hypothesized dependent variable becomes an independent variable. None of the traditional methods permit analysis of the 0th calculation properties and to assess in one methodology the theoretical relations. These kinds of questions are answered by SEM (Abbas et al., 2017).

SEM is a blend of different statistical techniques: path analysis as well as confirmatory factor analysis. Confirmatory factor analysis, which evolved in psychometrics, has the goal of estimating latent psychological characteristics, such as behavior and satisfaction direction analysis (Rajendran & Manoranjan, 2019). On one of the other sides, it began with biometrics and sought to identify the causal relationship between variables by constructing a route map. In noise pollution health impacts assistive modeling, these features of SEM are advantageous. After the completion of satisfactory results of EFA, one can opt for SEM through the following steps. The six stages are as follows and are also represented in Fig. 15.2.

Stage 1: Defining individual constructs

Defining individual constructs is the first step in SEM analysis in which latent factors are defined with their measured variables, as shown in Fig. 15.1. EFA achieves this first step as it defines unobserved or latent factors with their indicator measured variables. A good theory of measurement is important if valuable results of SEM are to be obtained. Hypotheses testing of structural relations between structures is no more accurate or true than a measuring model is when describing how these structures are built. Researchers often need to select a certain number of stated scales, each with minor variance. However, the researcher faces the absence of a developed scale in some contexts and must create a new scale or dramatically change an existing scale into a new sense. In each scenario, it sets the basis for the whole remainder of the SEM study to be chosen by researchers to calculate each house. Early in the testing process, the researcher must spend a great deal of time and resources to ensure accurate results can be attained with respect to the measurement accuracy.

Stage 2: Developing and specifying the measurement model

In this step, each latent construct to be included in the model is identified, and the measured indicator variables (items) are assigned to latent constructs. Preparing and explaining the measurement model is very important as here the hypothesis is made according to the desired output; this is

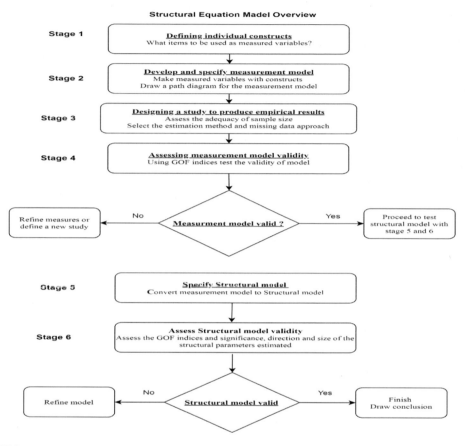

FIGURE 15.2

Steps in structural equation modeling.

explained in Fig. 15.3. As shown in Fig. 15.3, the constructs of latent factors 1, 2, and 3 are linked together by arrows representing their direct and indirect effects on each other. Here latent factor 3 is the desired output. The e1, e2, ... are error terms associated with the respective observed variables.

Stage 3: Designing a study to produce empirical results

In this third step, the prepared measurement model will be run in suitable software to obtain imperial results in the form of standardized and unstandardized regression weights and path coefficients. This can be done in the AMOS software suit. The researcher must concentrate on problems concerning study architecture and estimation by defining the fundamental model in terms of measured and constructs indicators/variables. In the research designs areas, the following are deliberated (1)

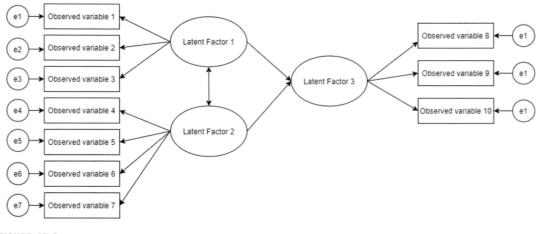

FIGURE 15.3

Hypothetical measured model.

the data type to be analyzed, either correlations or covariance; (2) the remedies as well as impact for missing data; and (3) the sample impact size.

Stage 4: Assessing measurement model validity

This is the most crucial step in the SEM method. Here one can assess the validity of the constructed measurement model. This can be achieved by comparing goodness-of-fit (GoF) indices calculated in AMOS software. GOF indicates replication of the covariance matrix observed among indicating objects by the defined model (such that the covariance matrix similarity, observed and estimated). Since the development of the first GOF measure, researchers have sought to enhance, develop, and introduce new measures which reflect different aspects of the data representation model's ability. Researchers are also willing to take a variety of alternate GOF steps. Every GOF is distinct, but it is grouped into three main forms: parsimony fit measures, incremental measures, and absolute. By comparing these indices, one can decide whether the model is final for drawing conclusions.

Stage 5: Specifying the structural model

In this stage, the finalization of the measurement model to the structural model is achieved. If the GoF indices satisfy all of its values, the model can be directly considered the structural equation model and can go for Step 6. If the model is not satisfying GoF indices, modes have to be revised as it is not statistically valid. For revision of the model, a series of changes can be carried out in measured variables as addition or deletion; this can be achieved by regression weight values in an invalid model.

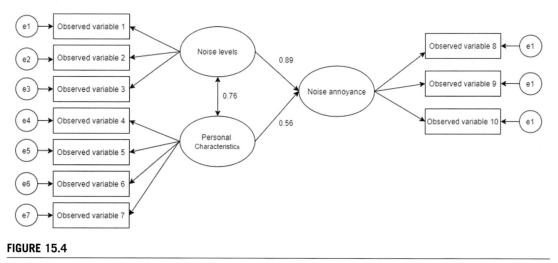

FIGURE 15.4

Final structural equation model.

Stage 6: Assessing the structural model validity

In this final stage of the SEM model, model validity will be again checked by GoF indices, and accordingly, the structural model is finalized for path coefficient analysis or for conclusions to be drawn. Three numerical values as shown in Fig. 15.4 are path coefficients, that is, regression weight or correlation coefficients between latent factors. Consider latent factor "noise annoyance" a the desired output having indicator observed variables 8, 9, and 10 and inputs are latent factors "noise levels" and "personal characteristics" with its respective indicator observed variables, as shown in Fig. 15.4. The path coefficient between noise levels and noise annoyance is 0.89, which can be interpreted as noise levels highly or positively affect noise annoyance. Latent factor personal characteristics show a path coefficient of 0.56 toward noise annoyance, which can be interpreted as personal characteristics that moderately affect noise annoyance. Similarly, conclusions can be made for other path coefficients.

By using this EFA and SEM method, one can discover the observed and unobserved relationships between collected or observed variables data and come to a significant conclusion for noise pollution health impacts modeling.

Adaptive neuro-fuzzy inference system

Neuro-fuzzy computation is the intelligent synthesis of neural merits and fuzzy methods. This introduces the popular benefits of artificial neural networks, such as robustness, massive parallelism, and learning inside data-rich settings, into the framework (Zadeh, 1994). The use of fluid logic is able to model imprecise and qualitative know-how and communicate confusion. The neuro-fuzzy solution also offers the required applications-specific benefit in addition to these generic advantages (Abdulshahed et al., 2015).

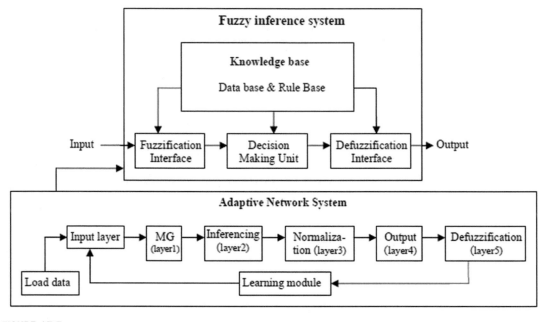

FIGURE 15.5

Conceptional diagram of adaptive neuro-fuzzy inference system.

From Tooy, D., & Murase, H. (2007). Neuro-fuzzy approach in determining human interest for decision making. The International Journal of Applied Management and Technology, 5, 186–204.

Some neuro-fuzzy systems are best known by their short names, for instance, FLEXNFIS, SANFIS, DENFIS, ANFIS, etc. An ANFIS has been introduced as a fuzzy inference method in adaptive neural networks. ANFIS either utilizes output/input datasets to create a fading inference system whose membership functions are tuned utilizing a learning algorithm, or an expert may determine a fading inference system. Fig. 15.5 displays ANFIS's logical diagram based on the discussed approach. It contains two main elements: the adaptive neural network and fuzzy inference system. There are five logical blocks in a floating inference method. A fuzzifier transforms individual input numbers into fuzzy sets. In essence, this dynamic unit translates crisp inputs into linguistic meaning compatibility. The database (or dictionary) includes fuzzy sets' component functions. In modeling, linguistic words are widely employed, for example, "the noise level is low" or "the person is young," and the membership functions provide versatility for fuzzy set. A rule foundation requires a set of linguistic declarations of the formula if X is A then Y is B, where A and B are labels (like "high" or "low") of fuzzy sets on the variables X and Y, respectively. These fuzzy labels are identified by the required database member function. An inference engine executes the inference operations of the rules to evaluate the performance by a fuzzy reasoning approach. Defuzzifier transforms the inference engine fuzzy outputs into the real number domain of the nonfuzzy output. A corresponding adaptive neural network is designed to integrate the ability to learn from datasets in input and output in fuzzy inference systems. A multilayer feedforward network is an adaptive network composed of directional as well as node links that bind nodes. Fig. 15.5

reveals that Layer 1 is a layer of input and Layer 2 defines each input fuzzy member function. Layer 3 is an inference layer, and in Layer 4, normalization is performed. The output is given in Layer 5 and the defuzzification layer is Layer 6. Adaptive and fixed nodes form the layers. Every adaptive node has a number of parameters that perform a basic function on input signals (node function). Either backpropagation or the hybrid-learning algorithm can be the learning module. The learning rule shows how the adaptive node parameters need to be adjusted to minimize the specified calculation of error. The parameter changes contribute to a change in the type of membership functionality relevant to the fuzzy inference method.

The ANFIS is a data-driven adaptive network and fuzzy logic-based inference system modeling methods generally used for solving function approximation issues. Data-driven methods involved in the construction of ANFIS are commonly based on the clustering of sets of numerical data available of the unidentified patterns/variables to be predicted or approximated (Mrinal, 2008). Since the development of ANFIS, it is mostly used for solving problems such as rule-based control of processes, tasks of classifications, recognization of unidentified patterns, and similar issues. The results and conclusions given by ANFIS are widely accepted. ANFIS works as a preparation of fuzzy rule-based input and output datasets based on Takagi, Sugeno, and Kang inference methods. ANFIS prefers a multiple-input—single-output (MISO) system rather than multiple input—multiple output (MIMO) systems, and it is recommended that five to six input variables are used for good results (Al-Hmouz et al., 2012). In noise pollution health impacts prediction, modeling ANFIS has been widely used by many researchers successfully (Zaheeruddin & Garima, 2006).

As mentioned previously, using the EFA and SEM approach, one can identify the most affecting observed variables with the greatest effect for the desired output. For example, from Fig. 15.4, it is clear that the most influencing latent factor for noise annoyance is noise levels. Now noise levels latent factor is made up with its indicator observed variables 1, 2, and 3. By taking these observed variables 1, 2, and 3 as input and indicator observed variables 8, 9, or 10 as output for noise annoyance, an ANFIS prediction model can be built. After knowing the desired input and output, data pairs have to be made in a Microsoft Excel worksheet as the final column is the desired output. The ANFIS toolbox of MATLAB® software is represented in Fig. 15.5. The input and output data pairs have to be divided for training, testing, and checking/validation purposes as 70—15—15% or 60—20—20%, respectively, according to the number of samples. By incorporating inputs and desired output data pairs in the ANFIS toolbox of MATLAB software, a successful prediction model can be constructed with the lowest possible error margin.

SEM and ANFIS case studies

Some of the important studies in noise pollution health modeling using SEM and ANFIS computing methods are briefly described here.

The relation between road and rail traffic noise and life satisfaction, in general, was explored by Jan & Vojtěch (2013). Although the negative association between traffic noise and residential satisfaction is relatively strong, the impact of traffic noise on life satisfaction is much less well known. According to previous research, a paradigm incorporates objective noise, noise annoyance, noise sensitivity, and life and residential satisfaction. As the association between life satisfaction and residential satisfaction is not obvious from the top down or bottom up, authors define models which integrate these theoretical ideas. SEM and survey data among inhabitants of high road traffic noise regions (n1 = 354) and rail traffic noise (n2 = 228) have been used in the test for analytical models. Traffic noise influences residential satisfaction but does not impact the overall life satisfaction directly or indirectly in a substantial way. Noise annoyance because of noise caused by road and rail traffic noise impacts residential fulfillment rather than overall life satisfaction dramatically. These findings for road and rail traffic noise are quite similar, whether the model suggests that the effect between residential satisfaction as well as life satisfaction is bottom up or top down.

The impact of road traffic noise on elevated and ischemic heart disease and also hypertension was studied by Fyhri and Klæboe (2008). One concern with some experiments is the inability to define the direction of causal relationships. This also occurs as cross-sectional knowledge and multivariate methods of regression are used. The study was aimed at examining the link between health and road traffic noise. The connection between noise sensitivity and noise issues, and heart-related issues and hypertension, was more specifically explored. A total of 1842 respondents in Oslo, Norway, were asked about their experience and subjective health issues with the local climate. Two surveys were used to carry out the interviews. Individual air pollution measures (NO_2) and noise measures (Lden) were calculated. The data were evaluated utilizing structural equation models. Chest pain and hypertension were only associated with noise sensitivity. No associations were observed between health conditions and noise exposure. The findings indicate that the noise—health relations in such experiments are partly incorrect. The human health can be adversely affected by its existing poor health and a exposure to high noise. It promotes the advantage of considering and integrating more qualitative factors into a noise—health model.

The relation between landscapes and soundscapes within different space functions has been examined (Chan et al., 2015) and the effect of functional features of locations on soundscape perceptions in urban environments was studied also. Landscape and soundscape perceptions were analyzed at 25 locations in Seoul through surveys. The urban contexts were categorized into four major purposes, events, and visual features of areas: industrial, residential, business, and leisure. A model of structural equations in the soundscape of the city has been designed based on seven factors: sound (traffic, human, and natural), pleasantness and operation, visual quality, and environmental harmony. The model correlates correctly to the survey results. The findings state that dominant conditions influencing soundscapes varied according to the location's key functions. Sounds from human actions played a major role in the measurement of soundscapes in industrial fields. Traffic noise was a primary sound source for business and residential functional areas that influenced the sound quality. Human sound from leisure activities is also a significant element in creating a significant soundscape in urban areas. The research results indicate that the role of a location should be taken on board as a significant framework for sounder architecture and an analytical understanding of the holistic interactions between soundscape influences in urban contexts.

Maarten et al. (2008) attempted to create a model scientifically for describing noise discomfort ability based on the principle that psychological tension is evaluated empirically. This model was evaluated using the model of structures based on data from inhabitants of Amsterdam Schiphol Airport in the Netherlands. This model gives an outstanding model match, revealing that the most significant factors to describe noise annoyance are fears about negative health consequences of air and noise pollution, responsive disorders and their regulation, and perceived coping ability. In addition, the model showed that two reciprocal connations occur between (1) noise annoyances and perceived disturbance and (2) coping capacity, perceived control along with noise annoyance. Finally, two unexpected findings emerged from this model. First, factors, such as noise exposure and the fear associated with the noise source, did not describe external variances in the model's endogenous versions, and, thus, the model was removed. The second was the comparatively limited scale of the average noise sensitivity effect on noise annoyance.

Zaheeruddin and Garima (2006) prepared a neuro-fuzzy model to predict a decrease in work proficiency as a function of noise level, type of task, and exposure time. Their work demonstrates that the efficiency of work is to a large degree based on the sound level and form of work with the same exposure period. This has also been confirmed where very high noise levels impact basic tasks, whereas complex tasks are greatly impaired at a much lower noise level.

Golmohammadi et al. (2011) suggested a workplace noise emission calculation approach based on fuzzy sets. This method of assessment took the noise level function, the number of staff exposed, noise reverberation time, and exposure duration into consideration. The proposed approach allows an unconsidered evaluation of cases to determine the probability of noise exposure. It was found the results of fuzzy logic evaluation are more useful and versatile for analysis as compared to traditional evaluations. Fuzzy logic gives the potential to acquire a noise exposure risk model based on noise parameters, occupational dimension, and human experience.

Conclusion

The primary focus of this chapter has been to lay the foundation for researchers to conduct a valid research study using an EFA-SEM and ANFIS approach, as it is a meaningful and fast approach for assistive and predictive modeling of noise pollution health impacts. First, EFA can be used for understanding data patterns, data summarization, and data reduction in the form of latent factors derived by it. Later, using these latent factors, one can use the structural equation model method to discover unobserved casual relationships among observed and unobserved variables for drawing precise conclusions as well as finding most affecting measured/observed variable associated with desired outcome/output. Once the most parameters with the greatest effect have been discovered, using these variables, one can opt for ANFIS predictive modeling for predicting a desired output in the future or on another location with the same characteristics. Noise is now considered a primary pollutant mostly because of its adverse effect on human psychological health that may directly reduce productivity. Hence, more research is needed into this to identify and reduce noise pollution impacts.

References

Abbas, M., Dalia, S., Edmundas, Z., Fausto, C., Mehrbakhsh, N., Ahmad, J., & Habib, Z. (2017). Application of structural equation modeling (SEM) to solve environmental sustainability problems: A comprehensive review and meta-analysis. *Sustainability*, 1814. Available from https://doi.org/10.3390/su9101814.

Abdulshahed, A. M., Longstaff, A. P., Fletcher, S., & Myers, A. (2015). Thermal error modelling of machine tools based on ANFIS with fuzzy c-means clustering using a thermal imaging camera. *Applied Mathematical Modelling*, 39(7), 1837–1852. Available from https://doi.org/10.1016/j.apm.2014.10.016.

Al-Hmouz, A., Shen, J., Al-Hmouz, R., & Yan, J. (2012). Modeling and simulation of an adaptive neuro-fuzzy inference system (ANFIS) for mobile learning. *IEEE Transactions on Learning Technologies*, *5*(3), 226–237. Available from https://doi.org/10.1109/TLT.2011.36.

Al-Mutairi, N. Z., Al-Attar, M. A., & Al-Rukaibi, F. S. (2011). Traffic-generated noise pollution: Exposure of road users and populations in Metropolitan Kuwait. *Environmental Monitoring and Assessment*, *183*(1–4), 65–75. Available from https://doi.org/10.1007/s10661-011-1906-0.

Anitha, P., Regina, H., Kathrin, W., Ute, K., Josef, C., Wolfgang, B., Annette, P., & Alexandra, S. (2017). Long-term associations of modeled and self-reported measures of exposure to air pollution and noise at residence on prevalent hypertension and blood pressure. *Science of the Total Environment*, 337–346. Available from https://doi.org/10.1016/j.scitotenv.2017.03.156.

Bakker, R. H., Pedersen, E., van den Berg, G. P., Stewart, R. E., Lok, W., & Bouma, J. (2012). Impact of wind turbine sound on annoyance, self-reported sleep disturbance and psychological distress. *Science of the Total Environment*, *425*, 42–51. Available from https://doi.org/10.1016/j.scitotenv.2012.03.005.

Baridalyne, N., SanjeevKumar, G., & Limalemla, J. (2014). Community noise pollution in urban India: Need for public health action. *Indian Journal of Community Medicine*, 8. Available from https://doi.org/10.4103/0970-0218.126342.

Belojevic, G., Jakovljevic, B., & Slepcevic, V. (2003). Noise and mental performance: Personality attributes and noise sensitivity. *Noise and Health*, *6*(21), 77–89. Available from http://www.noiseandhealth.org.

Beutel, M. E., Jünger, C., Klein, E. M., Wild, P., Lackner, K., Blettner, M., Binder, H., Michal, M., Wiltink, J., Brähler, E., & Münzel, T. (2016). Noise annoyance is associated with depression and anxiety in the general population—The contribution of aircraft noise. *PLoS One*, e0155357. Available from https://doi.org/10.1371/journal.pone.0155357.

Bo, X., Martin, S., & Bo, X. (2015). A critical review of structural equation modeling applications in construction research. *Automation in Construction*, 59–70. Available from https://doi.org/10.1016/j.autcon.2014.09.006.

Bruce, K. D., Eric, E., Dobie, R. A., Peter, R., James, C., Richard, K., & Warner, H. T. (2012). Occupational noise-induced hearing loss. *Journal of Occupational and Environmental Medicine*, 106–108. Available from https://doi.org/10.1097/JOM.0b013e318242677d.

Chan, L. S., Young, H. J., & Yong, J. J. (2015). Effects of acoustic characteristics of combined construction noise on annoyance. *Building and Environment*, 657–667. Available from https://doi.org/10.1016/j.buildenv.2015.05.037.

Charlotte, C., Jenny, H., & Stansfeld, S. A. (2013). Longitudinal effects of aircraft noise exposure on children's health and cognition: A six-year follow-up of the UK RANCH cohort. *Journal of Environmental Psychology*, 1–9. Available from https://doi.org/10.1016/j.jenvp.2013.03.002.

Chuang, L., Elaine, F., Tiesler, C. M. T., Matthias, B., Wolfgang, B., Carl-Peter, B., Sibylle, K., Andrea, von B., Barbara, H., & Joachim, H. (2014). The associations between traffic-related air pollution and noise with blood pressure in children: Results from the GINIplus and LISAplus studies. *International Journal of Hygiene and Environmental Health*, 499–505. Available from https://doi.org/10.1016/j.ijheh.2013.09.008.

Finch, J. F., & West, S. G. (1997). The investigation of personality structure: Statistical models. *Journal of Research in Personality*, *31*(4), 439–485. Available from https://doi.org/10.1006/jrpe.1997.2194.

Flintsch, G. W., & Chen, C. (2004). Soft computing applications in infrastructure management. *Journal of Infrastructure Systems*, *10*(4), 157–166. Available from https://doi.org/10.1061/(ASCE)1076-0342(2004)10:4(157).

Fyhri, A., & Klæboe, R. (2008). Road traffic noise, sensitivity, annoyance and self-reported health—A structural equation model exercise. *Environment International*, *35*(2009), 91–97. Available from https://doi.org/10.1016/j.envint.2008.08.006.

Ghosh, S., Biswas, S., Sarkar, D., & Sarkar, P. P. (2014). A novel neuro-fuzzy classification technique for data mining. *Egyptian Informatics Journal*, *15*(3), 129–147. Available from https://doi.org/10.1016/j.eij.2014.08.001.

Golmohammadi, R., Eshaghi, M., & Khoram, M. R. (2011). Fuzzy logic method for assessment of noise exposure risk in an industrial workplace. *International Journal of Occupational Hygiene*, *3*(2), 49−55.

Guarnaccia, C. (2010). Analysis of traffic noise in a road intersection configuration. *WSEAS Transactions on Systems*, *9*(8), 865−874. Available from http://www.wseas.us/e-library/transactions/systems/2010/88-138.pdf.

Håkan, H., Magnus, E., Rachel, E., Stephen, W., Claes, M., & Björn, L. (2014). Cognitive skills and the effect of noise on perceived effort in employees with aided hearing impairment and normal hearing. *Noise and Health*, *79*. Available from https://doi.org/10.4103/1463-1741.132085.

Jan, U., & Vojtěch, M. (2013). Linking traffic noise, noise annoyance and life satisfaction: A case study. *International Journal of Environmental Research and Public Health*, 1895−1915. Available from https://doi.org/10.3390/ijerph10051895.

Jurica, I., Tino, B., & Petar, A. (2018). Effects of interior aircraft noise on pilot performance. *Applied Acoustics*, 8−13. Available from https://doi.org/10.1016/j.apacoust.2018.04.006.

Karin, S., Marit, A. G., Geir, A., Bente, O., & Hjertager, K. N. (2014). Road traffic noise, sleep and mental health. *Environmental Research*, 17−24. Available from https://doi.org/10.1016/j.envres.2014.02.010.

Konstantina, D., Konstantinos, K., Ifigeneia, P., Maria-Iosifina, K., Haralabidis, A. S., Panayota, S., Evangelia, S., Danny, H., Wim, S., Hansell, A. L., & Klea, K. (2017). Is aircraft noise exposure associated with cardiovascular disease and hypertension? Results from a cohort study in Athens, Greece. *Occupational and Environmental Medicine*, 830−837. Available from https://doi.org/10.1136/oemed-2016-104180.

Maarten, K., Molin, E. J. E., & van Wee, B. (2008). Testing a theory of aircraft noise annoyance: A structural equation analysis. *The Journal of the Acoustical Society of America*, 4250−4260. Available from https://doi.org/10.1121/1.2916589.

Maria, F., Eze, I. C., Danielle, V., Mark, B., Christian, C., Seraina, C., Harris, H., Emmanuel, S., Christian, S., Miriam, W., Jean-Marc, W., Martin, R., & Nicole, P.-H. (2016). Long-term transportation noise annoyance is associated with subsequent lower levels of physical activity. *Environment International*, 341−349. Available from https://doi.org/10.1016/j.envint.2016.03.011.

Marta, N.-K., Anna, P.-D., Mirosław, B., Mariusz, S., & Ryszard, P. (2015). Effects of noise and mental task performance upon changes in cerebral blood flow parameters. *Noise and Health*, 422. Available from https://doi.org/10.4103/1463-1741.169709.

Mary, P. K., Alves, C. M. R., & Trombetta, Z. P. H. (2019). Exposure to road traffic noise: Annoyance, perception and associated factors among Brazil's adult population. *Science of The Total Environment*, 978−986. Available from https://doi.org/10.1016/j.scitotenv.2018.09.041.

Mathias, B., Wolfgang, B., Adrian, D., Mark, B., Charlotte, C., Sabine, J., & Stephen, S. (2014). Auditory and non-auditory effects of noise on health. *The Lancet*, 1325−1332. Available from https://doi.org/10.1016/s0140-6736(13)61613-x.

Mrinal, B. (2008). *Adaptive network based fuzzy inference system (ANFIS) as a tool for system identification with special emphasis on training data minimization*.

Okokon, E. O., Yli-Tuomi, T., Turunen, A. W., Tiittanen, P., Juutilainen, J., & Lanki, T. (2018). Traffic noise, noise annoyance and psychotropic medication use. *Environment International*, 287−294. Available from https://doi.org/10.1016/j.envint.2018.06.034.

Omar, H., Manfred, B., Tommaso, G., Andreas, S., Maria, B., Norbert, P., Thomas, R., Karl, L., Mette, S., Prochaska, J. H., Wild, P. S., & Thomas, M. (2018). Annoyance to different noise sources is associated with atrial fibrillation in the Gutenberg Health Study. *International Journal of Cardiology*, 79−84. Available from https://doi.org/10.1016/j.ijcard.2018.03.126.

Pandya, G. H. (2003). Assessment of traffic noise and its impact on the community. *International Journal of Environmental Studies*, *60*(6), 595−602. Available from https://doi.org/10.1080/0020723032000093973.

Passchier-Vermeer, W., & Passchier, W. F. (2000). Noise exposure and public health. *Environmental Health Perspectives*, *108*(1), 123−131. Available from https://doi.org/10.1289/ehp.00108s1123.

Rahmani, S., Mousavi, S. M., & Kamali, M. J. (2011). Modeling of road-traffic noise with the use of genetic algorithm. *Applied Soft Computing Journal*, *11*(1), 1008−1013. Available from https://doi.org/10.1016/j.asoc.2010.01.022.

Rajalahti, T., & Kvalheim, O. M. (2011). Multivariate data analysis in pharmaceutics: A tutorial review. *Advanced Characterization Techniques*, *417*(1), 280−290. Available from https://doi.org/10.1016/j.ijpharm.2011.02.019.

Rajendran, B. G., & Manoranjan, P. (2019). Modelling perceived pedestrian level of service of sidewalks: A structural equation approach. *Transport*, 339−350. Available from https://doi.org/10.3846/transport.2019.9819.

Ramalingeswara Rao, P., & Seshagiri Rao, M. G. (1992). Community reaction to road traffic noise. *Applied Acoustics*, 51−64. Available from https://doi.org/10.1016/0003-682x(92)90010-p.

Sharad, T., Richa, B., & Gagandeep, K. (2018). Performance evaluation of two ANFIS Models for predicting water quality index of River Satluj (India). *Advances in Civil Engineering*, 1−10. Available from https://doi.org/10.1155/2018/8971079.

Smith, D. G., Baranski, J. V., Thompson, M. M., & Abel, S. M. (2003). The effects of background noise on cognitive performance during a 70 hour simulation of conditions aboard the International Space Station. *Noise and Health*, *6*(21), 3−16.

Surajit, B. (2015). A short review on structural equation modeling: Applications and future research directions. *Journal of Supply Chain Management Systems*. Available from https://doi.org/10.21863/jscms/2015.4.3.014.

Tao, L., Chin-Chiuan, L., Kuo-Chen, H., & Yi-Chang, C. (2017). Effects of noise type, noise intensity, and illumination intensity on reading performance. *Applied Acoustics*, 70−74. Available from https://doi.org/10.1016/j.apacoust.2017.01.019.

Thomas, M., Schmidt, F. P., Sebastian, S., Johannes, H., Andreas, D., & Mette, S. (2018). Environmental noise and the cardiovascular system. *Journal of the American College of Cardiology*, 688−697. Available from https://doi.org/10.1016/j.jacc.2017.12.015.

Thompson, B. (2004). *Exploratory and confirmatory factor analysis: Understanding concepts and applications. Exploratory and confirmatory factor analysis: Understanding concepts and applications* (p. 195) American Psychological Association. Available from https://doi.org/10.1037/10694-000.

Tooy, D., & Murase, H. (2007). Neuro-fuzzy approach in determining human interest for decision making. *The International Journal of Applied Management and Technology, 5*, 186–204.

Wen, L., Tingshen, Z., Wei, Z., & Jingjing, T. (2018). Safety risk factors of metro tunnel construction in China: An integrated study with EFA and SEM. *Safety Science*, 98−113. Available from https://doi.org/10.1016/j.ssci.2018.01.009.

World Health Organization. Regional Office for Europe. (2011). Burden of disease from environmental noise: Quantification of healthy life years lost in Europe. World Health Organization. Regional Office for Europe. https://apps.who.int/iris/handle/10665/326424.

Zadeh, L. A. (1994). Soft computing and fuzzy logic. *IEEE Software*, *11*(6), 48−56. Available from https://doi.org/10.1109/52.329401.

Zaheeruddin., & Garima. (2006). A neuro-fuzzy approach for prediction of human work efficiency in noisy environment. *Applied Soft Computing Journal*, *6*(3), 283−294. Available from https://doi.org/10.1016/j.asoc.2005.02.001.

Intelligent and knowledge-based waste management: smart decision-support system

Emmanuel Emeka Okoro[1] and Samuel Eshorame Sanni[2]

[1]Department of Petroleum and Gas Engineering, University of Port Harcourt, Port Harcourt, Nigeria [2]Department of Chemical Engineering, Covenant University, Ota, Nigeria

Introduction

The exploration for and production of crude oil and natural gas generate significant waste compared to many other industries. Hydrocarbon exploration and production (E&P) activities in the subsurface represent an ever-growing disposal and handling problem globally (Janajreh et al., 2020). These activities range from drilling, production, and refining operations. Johnson and Affam (2019) further classified the waste generated from hydrocarbon exploration, production, and processing as bottom tank sludge, drilling fluids, petroleum effluent treatment plant sludge, drill-cuttings, petroleum wastewater, etc. The three streams of the oil and gas industry generate both solid and liquid wastes with different toxicity levels, and this has put the sector under inspection by environmental organizations and government regulators on issues bordering around oil field chemicals pollution and waste disposal. Improper handling and disposal of these wastes can impose severe and long-lasting effects on the environment and people in the locality (Okoro, Okolie, Sanni, & Omeje, 2020; Okoro, Okolie, Sanni, Joel, et al., 2020). Direct health impacts from mismanagement of these wastes have been established in the literature, and there is a need to correctly classify these wastes for proper management. Pollard et al. (1992) highlighted the need for cost-effective and informative techniques that can address the waste mixtures at source; and thus improve source efforts in selecting and assessing possible remedial technologies.

The exploration phase in oil and gas production generates a significant volume of drilling fluid systems and subsurface formation (drill-cuttings), and these wastes are often contaminated with the drilling fluid system used as the transportation medium from the wellbore subsurface. Drilling wastes are classified as the second largest volume of wastes, after water, generated by the oil and gas industry (Onwukwe & Nwakaudu, 2012). The physical and chemical properties of the drilling wastes, such as the nature of the additives used for the drilling fluid system formulation and the type of formation being drilled, influence the hazardous waste characteristics and the potential environmental impact. Imarhiagbe and Obayagbona (2019), in their study, stated that an average offshore well generates approximately 1100 million tons of drill-cuttings, while 3900 billion barrels of drill-cuttings are produced in a typical 4054-m onshore drilling operation. The volume of waste generated for a particular oil and gas well is a function of the depth and diameter. Thus, the deeper the wellbore, the more drill-cuttings that will be generated. Many waste management approaches have been adopted for handling drilling waste by contractors depending on the location of the well and the regional regulations. Ideally, industry operators prefer a waste management technique that integrates solid and fluid control for cost-effective waste management (Fisher et al., 2020).

Waste generated during the production and processing (refining) of hydrocarbons is of different forms, and has a larger volume than other operations. Wastes generally generated during production are mostly made up of fluids and particles that settle and accumulate in effluents, pits, storage, and other equipment within the production line. These solids consist of sludge and sediments, and are subject to the position of the sludge accumulation in the production line; there also may be different mixtures and other substances that may precipitate out of the solution (Ferrar et al., 2013). These solids often require regular removal from pits and tanks; thus they are treated as a separate waste stream. Oil and gas exploration can generate a number of additional waste streams that are less than the volume of water periodically produced. Backwash and other wastewaters can be treated in the same pits and tanks as the water produced, but used filters and sorbents should be considered as separate waste streams for disposal (Estrada & Bhamidimarri, 2016). In general, there is no national dataset on the amount of waste generated by each E&P company. Although some countries collect waste data to an appropriate extent, the methods and parameters for collecting these data are not uniform across these countries. In addition, some states exempt some categories of waste from their regulations, so these data may not be available (Ahammad et al., 2017). This makes it difficult to compare and collect data on a larger scale.

An estimation of exploration and production wastes has been attempted by the American Petroleum Institute (API). The API used 1995 data from their survey to calculate the relationship between production (i.e., the volume of crude oil produced with a period) and produced waste. These ratios were later used in 2000 to measure the amount of waste based on different production ratios. Since then, existing drilling inventory has been aging, and new wellbores have been drilled (Chen et al., 2013). The depths of new wellbores used for deepwater and ultra-deepwater field development are of significant distances; thus they will generate more significant quantities of waste if the process is not optimized for proper waste management. However, these calculations using API-established relationships still provide a reasonable comparison of the relative amount of waste, but these estimates only provide a partial measure of the waste generated. This study evaluates the gaps in expert systems in oil and gas waste management and disposal (Walid & Abdulqader, 2005). Expert systems are poised to take over the no-less essential tasks of the ill-structured and less-deterministic parts of the planning, design, and management processes with respect to oil and gas waste management. This study shows the technical limitations and also reveals a variety of oil and gas waste measurement, collection, and identification technologies that can be integrated through the application of the Internet of Things.

Trends in exploration and production wastes in the oil and gas industry

Produced water and used drilling fluid systems account for over 95% of the total volume of waste generated by the oil and gas industry during hydrocarbon exploration and production. There are other forms of waste, which include but are not limited to sludge, effluents, wax, and other wastes that can be comanaged in the existing waste management processes. This section provides information on the waste classification (exploration and production/refining), with enormous variability in the volume, composition, and waste management.

Exploration waste in the oil and gas industry

Before the extensive application of hydraulic technology in hydrocarbon exploration, the wastes generated during drilling operations were predominately formation cuttings and spent drilling fluid for each hole section. However, hydraulic technology has introduced additional volumes of waste, such as a large volume of water and chemicals that are used to create fractures that facilitate the migration of hydrocarbons to the wellbore for collection (Walid & Abdulqader, 2005). The generation of waste from drilling mud and formation cuttings can be investigated at different stages of the drilling process. The enormous volume of cuttings is generated during the first few thousand meters of drilling because the wellbore diameter is largest at this stage. Ahammad et al. (2017) classified solids generated during drilling according to their sizes into coarse ($>2000\,\mu$m), intermediate ($250-2000\,\mu$m), medium ($74-250\,\mu$m), fine ($44-74\,\mu$m), ultra-fine ($2-44\,\mu$m), and colloidal ($<2\,\mu$m); and also highlighted that the early removal of these solids will help avoid accumulation and clogging of the system and separation devices.

The most economical method to solve the problem of waste management without affecting the drilling process is to optimize the disposal of solids from the source, and thus limit the amount of waste generated, with on-site cleaning and disposal of treated waste. The processing and disposal of waste that is not harmful to the environment are relatively inexpensive and straightforward. Environmentally toxic wastes, such as produced fluids, contaminated formation cuttings, and diesel- or petroleum-based mud systems create severe problems for the environment and people in the locality (Shahryar, 2017). For the offshore drilling waste-handling process, United States Environmental Protection Agency (USEPA) data from 15 Gulf of Mexico operators showed that more than 90% of cuttings associated with water-based drilling fluids are discharged. At the same time, those that do not meet the regulation toxicity limits are transported back to shore. In some cases, some of these drilling fluid systems are recycled for reuse, but very small portions are injected into the formation, and the cost for injection is between \$18/bbl and \$45/bbl. The cost of disposal for most companies ranged from \$7/bbl to over \$140/bbl, depending on whether the cost of transportation, cutting box rental, and cleanup charges are included.

Oil-based mud (OBM) systems are mostly recycled and reused because of their nature, and the cost of transporting these oil-based muds to the shore for recycling ranged from \$35/bbl to \$50/bbl; while the cost of disposal onshore was between \$4/bbl and \$30/bbl, depending on the distance. The cost of disposing of OBM through injection technology is between \$400/bbl and \$500/bbl. Fig. 16.1 shows a sample of drilling waste management for an offshore company (Islam et al., 2012). A synthetic-based mud (SBM) system is an example of OBM mud, but the oil continuous phase for the SBM system is not a petroleum product; thus it is more environmental friendly when compared to OBM. Onshore operations have a more comprehensive range of management options than offshore operations (Cevat et al., 2020). For onshore operations, there are many other control options available as there is space around the field. The most common method for disposing of cuttings associated with aqueous mud systems is on-site burial. Other methods include waste pit

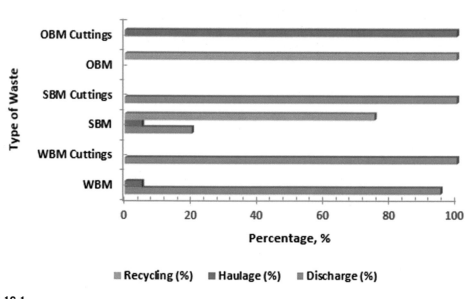

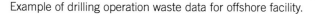

FIGURE 16.1

Example of drilling operation waste data for offshore facility.

construction, as well as thermal and biological processes. Formation cuttings can be treated and used for other useful purposes.

Four waste volume estimation methods for drilling cuttings and associated mud have been identified from the literature, which include but are not limited to the volume of waste haulage data, volume by mud usage mass balance, volume in the pit, and volume from mud deliveries. The disposal cost of formation cuttings associated with a water-based mud (WBM) system ranged from $5/bbl to $13/bbl. However, some operators have dedicated injection wells where they inject both cuttings from WBM and OBM systems (Onwuka et al., 2018). The annual costs for operating and maintaining some of these injection facilities are between $4 and 9 million per annual, and the percentage is now gradually increasing. The cost of treating and disposing of cuttings from WBM and OBM systems differ. Cuttings associated with synthetic or enhanced mineral OBMs can be disposed of through reinjection after cuttings have been treated to an acceptable level (concentration of oil must be below 6.9 g/100 g wet solid).

Drilling fluids perform several functions when drilling a well. However, in most cases, the base fluid will not have the proper physical and chemical properties to achieve these goals. Therefore other components called additives are added to provide various unique functional properties. Traces of these additives can contaminate both drilling fluids and cuttings, making the composition of the cuttings toxic and harmful (Pam, 2015). Heavy metals can enter drilling fluids through two routes, either they are natural metals present in the subsurface formations or as part of the mud system additives, which can enter the drilling fluid system and change the fluid characteristics. The environmental impact of these cuttings is determined by the degree and nature of contamination of

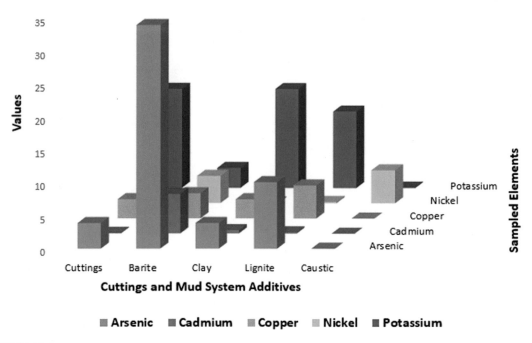

FIGURE 16.2

Sampled elemental composition of mud system constituents.

drilling fluids and heavy metals (Fig. 16.2). Many materials and wastes associated with drilling can have a negative impact on the environment (Olah & Molnar, 2003). The possible effects depend mainly on the material, its concentration after release, and the biotic community it is exposed to.

Production and refining waste in the oil and gas industry

The fluids produced from a hydrocarbon well are mostly a mixture of crude oil, natural gas, and associated water. This mixture is immediately directed to one or more oil and gas separators that use baffles or other means to partition the different phases based on density (Altaş & Büyükgüngör, 2008). The waste generated in the most significant volume during the separation process is produced water that flows from the well (Fig. 16.3). Other wastes usually generated during hydrocarbon production are particles that have accumulated in effluents, pits, tanks, and other equipment along the production line. These solids are commonly referred to as sludge, sediments, or tank bottom. It is clear that there are also numerous organic compounds that may be present in produced water. The most commonly detected organic compounds are commonly associated with hydrocarbons (e.g., benzene and toluene), but these compounds do not always originate from the formation (Cheremisinoff, 2003).

Environmental impacts associated with crude oil and natural gas production primarily result from long-term changes to the habitat in oil and gas fields, as well as from production activities (including maintenance or replacement of oil and gas components), waste management and disposal

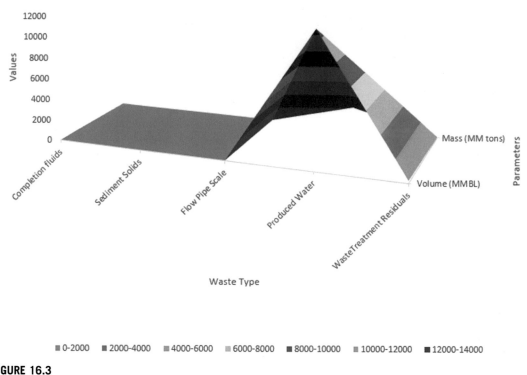

FIGURE 16.3

Estimated waste type generation.

(such as sediments and produced water), and people in the locality (Johnson & Affam, 2019). The routine operations for the production of crude oil and natural gas could lead to the emission of some compounds that constitute a risk to the environment and public health. Exposure can occur when these wastes are improperly handled and released into the environment, and contamination can result from accidental spills. Sand separated from the produced water must be properly disposed of, as it is often contaminated with oil, heavy metals, or other natural components (Chavan & Mukherji, 2008). Production operation can also cause large amounts of scale and sludge to build up in pipes and storage tanks, and these wastes can be disposed of to remote locations. Produced water can be a significant waste stream in crude oil and natural gas production.

The refinery unavoidably generates an enormous quantity of tank bottom oily sludge as well as oil-contaminated soil waste, which constitutes a significant challenge for hazardous waste management as well as environmental management. Crude oil tank sludge, residual from upgrading, catalysts from hydro-refining, off-spec products, sulfur complex sludge, desalting sludge, and spent caustic are examples of waste generated from refining processes (Coelho et al., 2006). The literature has shown that the waste management practices adopted by most hydrocarbon refining industries are changing significantly as the processes are being modified or undergoing significant restructuring due to new technology; thus no one unique solution can serve all the different classifications. Refineries produce industrial process wastes that are inherent to the activities they carry out in the handling and processing of crude petroleum and petroleum products, and these waste streams are often managed together. The actual substances present in refinery wastes will depend upon the combination of the individual process technology used and the specific crude oils being processed (El-Naas et al., 2010).

Refinery size and production output contribute to the volume of waste generated in the facility, and managing wastes produced by these refineries is a massive task because these wastes tend to be collected together and are mostly in sludge, solid, or liquid form (Walid & Abdulqader, 2005). Data concerning volumes of wastes from refinery and production operations are not routinely collected in most countries and facilities; thus making it necessary to develop methods for estimating these volumes by direct or indirect methods. It is more convenient to divide wastes into categories and also propose their management in relation to the sequence of operations that occurs in the process cycle of a refinery. Operation units in the refinery have different needs; for example, desalting, distillation, catalytic, thermal cracking, and treatment processes require a significant volume of water to produce products such as feedstocks, diesel, liquefied petroleum gas, gasoline, and asphalt (Otadi et al., 2010).

Refined wastes are generally generated from the process of refining crude oil, fuels, lubricants, and petrochemicals. This is the primary source of sewage or sewage water pollution. Wastewater consists mainly of grease, oil, and many other toxic organic compounds (Okiel et al., 2011). Crude oil refining requires a great deal of water; therefore a large amount of wastewater is generated. The demand for water depends on the size, raw feed, and complexity of the process, and the resulting wastewater can contain various volumes of hydrocarbons. Singh and Shikha (2008) highlighted that the volume of petroleum refinery effluents generated during processing is 0.4−1.6 times the amount of crude oil that is being processed. Assuming a yield of 84 million barrels per day of crude oil, a total of 33.6 million barrels per day of effluent are reported to be generated from this case study. Refineries are complex systems with many operations and processes that depend on the type of oil and the desired products. Not all refineries are the same due to the different techniques and types of oil processed. Refineries use a huge amount of water compared to other industries, depending on the size, crude oil, products, and complexity of operations (Wong & Hung, 2009).

Oil and gas waste management

Onwuka et al. (2018) defined waste management as a means of controlling, collection, storage, transportation, processing, and disposal of wastes generated during drilling in a safe and acceptable environment that is in context with the existing regulatory requirements. Over the past decade, there has been increasing international concern for proper waste management in order to minimize their potential to cause harm to the environment and people in the locality. Efficient and effective waste management is an important part of a company's environmental management system. In addition, effective waste management practices will be a source of information not only for waste reduction programs, but also for contamination liability and treatment technology (Onwukwe & Nwakaudu, 2012). Waste management involves incorporating a hierarchy of waste management practices into the development of waste management plans. Determining and quantifying waste flows and assessing the impact on the environment can provide a basis for identifying specific operations for improvements in practice.

Different waste management methods depend on local environmental regulations, disposal costs, technical feasibility, and the amount of waste generated. The method should be carefully evaluated before being used on the waste management process (Solomon et al., 2018). Fig. 16.4 shows a field estimate of waste from two hole sections during the drilling operation. The large diameter (12.25 in.) was drilled from the surface to 3000 ft. into the subsurface, while the second hole section (9.625 inch) was drilled from 3000 to 10,000 ft.; that is, a 7000 ft. interval. The amount of waste generated from these hole sections (12.25 and 9.625 in.) was 534.3 and 748 bbl, respectively. The lower diameter hole section generated more waste because of the long hole section interval (depth). To effectively study the waste management approach, the assessment process should include a comprehensive economic and environmental analysis (Wang & McTernan, 2002). Disposal of drilling waste is no longer a matter of environmental friendliness for the operator but can be used proactively to reduce well construction costs.

Hydrocarbon is currently obtained primarily by drilling a wellbore after conducting structural geology studies of the reservoir, analyzing the sedimentary basin, and characterizing the reservoir (i.e., the porosity and permeability of the geological structures where the deposit is located). Some practices that are seen as routine in one facility can be regarded as innovative or alternative in another; thus every waste management practice that exists can be considered vital in one specific condition or another (Bakke et al., 2013). This is because different climatological or geological settings may demand other management procedures, either for technical convenience in designing and running a facility or because environmental settings in a particular region may be unique. The oil and gas industry process includes exploration, production, treatment, transportation, refining, etc.

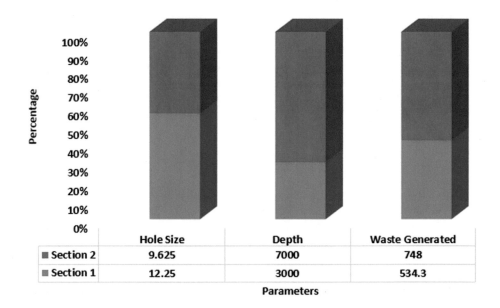

	Hole Size	Depth	Waste Generated
■ Section 2	9.625	7000	748
■ Section 1	12.25	3000	534.3

Parameters

■ Section 1 ■ Section 2

FIGURE 16.4

Waste volume estimation for two hole sections.

Waste streams are typically managed on-site or off-site through a combination of storage, handling, and disposal methods. Waste treatment procedures and equipment should be developed and documented. Refinery activities and processes can generate large amounts of wastewater, including oil, water, and sludge (Nandy et al., 1999). The discharge of this wastewater not only pollutes the environment but also reduces oil and water production. Different wastewater treatment methods are used in the industry, but the effectiveness, compatibility, and cost vary among them. The assessment of the most efficient technology depends on various considerations such as the quality of influent, treatment cost, the environmental footprint, and energy consumption (Ahammad et al., 2017). There are four categories of wastewater generated in the refining process: process water, surface water runoff, cooling water, and sanitary wastewater.

Waste minimization should first be integrated into the waste management system of each enterprise to identify ways to prevent waste generation and, if possible, to reduce waste generation. Treatment may be required to minimize the potential waste effects and internal risks (e.g., toxicity, corrosion, etc.) of the waste (Okoro, Okolie, Sanni, & Omeje, 2020). An excellent integrated approach to waste management is to learn general methods of waste management in a facility. An iterative process of collecting, analyzing, applying, and measuring the results for each waste stream should be carried out to determine which method of waste management is the most technically feasible and inexpensive compared to other methods. Improved and optimized waste management technology in the oil and gas industry could potentially result in a significant reduction in the quantity and cost of handling generated waste and a reduction in the flow or contaminant load of waste.

Conventional waste management approach in the oil and gas industry

This industry is generally divided into three main components: upstream, middle, and downstream. Upstream operations include the exploration, development, and production of hydrocarbons. As the name suggests, the middle segment (midstream) contains processes and facilities that lie between the upstream and downstream sectors. Refining and trading activities, processing, storage, and transportation of hydrocarbons are classified under downstream activities (Ambituuni et al., 2014). The major challenge throughout these three streams is that their waste streams can become contaminated by oily or hazardous fluids, and naturally occurring radioactivity that requires careful handling, treatment, and disposal (Johnson & Affam, 2019). However, the industry-based research and development institutions, and governmental and nongovernmental environmental agencies have proposed some international best practices that should be adopted during E&P operations with regards to adequately dealing with any form of inconvenience that may arise. But, there is a need to systematically identify the challenges facing the oil and gas industry in achieving sustainable management of all waste from onshore or offshore facilities.

Waste handling hierarchy

There are several waste management options available for hazardous waste. It is highly desirable to reduce the amount of waste at the source or to recycle the materials for other production purposes (Wan Ahmad et al., 2016). Reduction and recycling are desirable options, but they are not considered the ultimate solutions to the problem of hazardous waste management. Particular hazardous wastes must always be treated, stored, or disposed of depending on what state and federal regulations allow and how costly those options are for the facility in question. Cost and environmental factors are the key drivers of oilfield waste management (Sadiq et al., 2003). The industry has based its research on waste management approaches that reduce waste generation from source and disposal techniques that offer significant environmental safety. Fig. 16.5 shows the three-tiered waste management hierarchy often adopted in managing waste in the most environment-friendly scenario. The first is waste minimization from source; it involves process modifications, adoption of new technologies, and product substitution to generate less waste (reduce approach). The second tier is the reuse or recycling of waste approach. This approach involves the conversion of wastes into usable materials and/or extraction of energy or materials from wastes. The result of this is a significant cost saving and highly reduced waste management concerns. Some wastes that cannot be handled and managed by these first two tiers are then managed through disposal (third tier). Disposal also involves the most significant potential liability and, as such, is the least preferred waste management option (Ahmadun et al., 2009).

Storage, handling, distribution, and transportation are integrated processes in all areas of oil and gas industry operations. Significant quantities of crude oil and/or natural gas are stored, handled, and transported through terminals. Emissions to air, sewage, and solid waste can arise at storage, transportation, sales, and marketing terminals (Al-Futaisi et al., 2007). These emissions originate from different activities and processes of the waste management cycle, that is, from collection to recovery, thermal and biological processes, and disposal. A high percentage of the Sustainable Development Goals for the 2030 Sustainable Development Agenda currently signed by the 193 United Nations Member States are linked to effective handling and management of waste, and the lack of an integrated smart system and planned frameworks has significantly impacted the progress on sustainable waste management in the oil and gas industry. However, the magnitude differs from region to region.

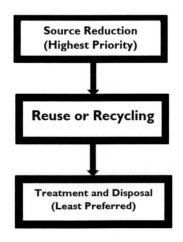

FIGURE 16.5

Three tiers of waste handling.

There are recorded cases in the literature where the treated waste exceeds the maximum contaminant levels and the presence of incomplete removal of organic compounds using conventional methods (Hill et al., 2019). Depending on timing and location, even relatively minor pollution can cause significant harm to individual organisms or entire populations. Waste management plans play a significant role in attaining sustainable waste management in line with international best practice and waste legislation. Incorporating a hierarchy of waste management practices into the development of waste management plans is an integral part of waste management (Maarten, 2012). The waste hierarchy generally prioritizes what represents the best overall environmental vision in waste legislation and policy.

Waste treatment techniques in the oil and gas industry

The increased global activity in the oil and gas industry to meet future energy needs on a global scale has contributed significantly to the huge generation of waste; thus, making zero to minimal discharge of harmful waste almost impossible (Bojes & Pope, 2007). Treatment is used to reduce the volume and/or toxicity of waste and place it in a convenient place for final disposal. Treatment and disposal options are highly dependent on the characteristics of the waste and legal requirements. Best treatment practice criteria are designed to be flexible and allow practices to be matched and adapted to the needs of the specific field operations and environment (Cholakov, 2009). Treatment techniques typically used in relation to oil and gas industry waste streams can involve physical, chemical, thermal, or biological processes, or a combination of two or more of these.

Physical treatment techniques have been developed to improve the waste management and physical characteristics of E&P wastes, reduce the area through which contaminants can be transported or lost, and limit the solubility or detoxification of hazardous components in waste (Barik et al., 2012). Physical waste treatment techniques remove substances using natural forces such as gravity, electrical attraction, and van der Waal forces, as well as physical barriers. In general, the mechanisms of physical treatments do not lead to changes in the chemical structure of the waste. In some cases, the physical state of the waste changes, as in vaporization, and often dispersed substances are caused to agglomerate as observed during the filtration process (Kesari et al., 2011). Physical waste treatment techniques include but are not limited to sedimentation, flotation, and adsorption, as well as barriers such as sieves, depth filters, and membranes.

The chemical treatment technique forces contaminants that are dissolved or inherent in the waste to separate more quickly through the application of specific substances. Chemical methods include ion exchange, reduction, precipitation, and neutralization. The chemical treatment technique involves an ion exchange reaction, in which charges of atoms or groups of atoms are exchanged between two substances so that they can bond together (Buyukkamaci & Kucukselek, 2007). Chemical precipitation is another technique that uses a chemical reaction to form separable solids in solution, either by converting a substance to an insoluble form or by modifying the properties of a solution to reduce the solubility of the contaminant (Pollard et al., 1992). The efficiency of this process can be increased through the use of coagulants and flocculants.

Biological treatment of particular organic wastes, such as those from the oil and gas industry, is also used. This technique uses natural processes to help with the decomposition of organic substances. Microbes can be added to metabolize both waste and nutrients. In some cases, genetically modified bacteria are used (Chojnacka & Noworyta, 2004). Microbes can also be used to stabilize hazardous waste at contaminated sites, using a process called bioremediation. Advances in biological processes have resulted in systems that permit faster degradation rates and treatment of higher levels of contamination by raising treatment temperature and improving oxygen transfer rates (Cain et al., 2008). The oxygen stimulates the growth of bacteria and microorganisms, which feed off any organic contaminants in the water and convert them into inorganic substances.

The most common thermal technique is high-temperature incineration, which despite being somewhat controversial, is increasingly becoming the preferred option for some specific wastes. In fact, it is very suitable for certain types of wastes, such as aqueous solvent mixtures, drilling mud, rock waste, and some resins. The thermal technique as a method of waste treatment must be monitored and verified, by continuously monitoring the operating parameters with a physicochemical profile in all combustion and discharge zones and by measuring the concentration of pollutants in the combustion gases relative to the gases emission limit values (Andersson et al., 1998). New thermal processes have utilized technologies such as plasma arc combustion and gasification to improve destruction efficiencies and produce an inert, vitrified ash product.

For combined techniques, chemical, biological, or physical treatments are often carried out in separate steps, depending on the composition and the operation that generated the waste. It is ideal to combine these process steps with the appropriate waste treatment technology for an efficient and cost-effective solution for waste treatment in the oil and gas industry (Hansel et al., 1996). Chemical treatment is often combined with physical treatment techniques for optimal results, for example, using coagulants with physical flocculation methods to accelerate the formation of hard clumps that must be removed by dehydration methods. Physical and chemical techniques are fundamental within the waste treatment systems and prior to any biological and advanced treatment technologies (Hill et al., 2019). Continuing innovation is seen as the key to providing more cost-effective and environmentally acceptable solutions to both long-standing and, as yet, unresolved problems with E&P generated wastes (Cecal et al., 2012). Physicochemical techniques have an important role in today's E&P operation wastes treatment scenario and will continue to have an increased application due to their established practice and continued improvisation.

Environmental impact of oil and gas generated wastes

The global revitalization of the oil and gas industry to meet future energy needs is often associated with increased environmental pollution, and waste reduction is seen as a more environment-friendly approach to a clean society (Thomas et al., 1990). Optimized and efficient waste disposal is an essential part of the hydrocarbon exploration and production industry because some of the wastes are potentially harmful due to their composition. This helps to minimize risks to people and the environment; thus improving the use of resources and reducing cost. The USEPA has specific guidelines common between the E&P industries that present new technologies, including pretreatment and advanced treatment, to achieve the necessary limitations of wastes (Radelyuk et al., 2019). Enforcement of legislation has allowed developed and developing countries to eliminate risks to the environment and public health. Effective legislation, as well as the ensuing use of new technologies and smart systems in waste management systems, is the only effective way to prevent potential damage to the environment and people in the locality.

The environmental impact of oil and gas operations and associated waste generation can affect species, populations, communities, or ecosystems by changing various ecological parameters such as biodiversity, productivity, and biomass (Rahmat et al., 2017). Regulatory bodies generally offer advice on the appropriate assessment of potential impacts on environmental parameters. Routine oil and gas activities can have detrimental environmental and public health effects during each of the main phases of upstream, midstream, and downstream. It is critical that all of the potential impacts of routine operations are accounted for when designing generated waste management strategies, whether local or regional, for offshore or onshore oil and gas activities (Bakke et al., 2013). The industry places great emphasis on establishing effective management systems and ensuring that environment-related issues are key components of corporate culture. The oil and gas industry, through research and development, has worked for a long time to meet waste management challenges to provide environmental protection, however it also recognizes that even more can be accomplished.

The impact of generated waste on the environment is dependent on the process stage, quantity, complexity of the operation/ project, composition, surrounding environment sensitivity (offshore/ onshore), mitigation, and control techniques. In assessing potential impacts, it is crucial to consider the geographical scale over which they might occur (Clark et al., 2016). The fundamental examination of the environmental impact of waste generated in E&P operations should start with identification and understanding of the sources and nature of the emissions to be able to efficiently identify their relative contribution to the environment (Demopoulos et al., 2014). The toxicity and make-up of wastes generated during exploration and production and their possible environmental significant constituents have been described in the literature. Examples of the constituents in varying amounts are heavy metals, inorganic salts, solids, hydrocarbons, production chemicals, polyaromatic hydrocarbons (PAHs), benzene, and sometimes, depending on the operation, naturally occurring radioactive materials (NORM) (Pires et al., 2011). The extent of the constituents' impact can only be judged through an environmental impact assessment.

The most widespread and dangerous consequence of oil and gas industry activities is pollution (Ugochukwu & Ertel, 2012). Pollution is associated with virtually all activities throughout all stages of oil and gas production, from exploratory activities to refining. Wastewater, gas emissions, solid waste, and aerosols are generated during drilling, production, refining (responsible for the most pollution), etc. (Uwe, 2006). Most potential environmental impacts related to oil and gas industry activities are already well documented. Taking into account environmental variables in production processes has been a serious and important challenge for the oil industry. The desire for sustainable development today goes beyond ethical and moral obligations; it has become a social requirement (Olalekan & Gordon, 2011). This commitment alone is a limiting factor in the survival of companies, as society at large can be affected by the negative image associated with polluting companies.

There are potential impacts when these toxic concentrations of constituents contaminate the environment if there is any exposure pathway present. Environmental contamination may arise from leakage or accidental spill age of chemicals and other toxic substances from the generated waste, causing possible harmful impact to both flora and fauna (Bhatia, 2002). Environmental contamination by hydrocarbons, particularly PAHs, is a particular concern because these compounds can persist for decades, posing a significant risk of prolonged toxicological effects (Chilaka & Nwaneke, 2016). The price of this pollution weighs most heavily on rural, low-income, and minority communities in the form of increased exposure to toxic chemicals and related health risks such as cancer, neurological disease, and many other serious health complications.

Heavy metals can be found in waste generated during the exploration and production operations in two ways: (1) many metals that occur naturally in the subsurface formations and (2) metals contained in additives. The heavy metals found in most oil and gas wastes are associated with various environmental problems, depending on the metal and its concentration (Gupta, 2006). In very low concentrations, certain metals are essential for healthy cellular activity. Since most concentrations in some wastes are relatively low, environmental impacts are pronounced only after chronic exposure (Giwa et al., 2017). Excessive concentrations of metals suppress normal biochemical processes in cells. This inhibition can damage the liver, kidneys, and reproductive and nervous systems. These effects can also include mutations or tumors (Pathak et al., 2012).

Challenges of conventional waste management systems

Most oil and gas facilities for waste management lack a holistic approach covering the whole chain of operations. These waste management processes are not synchronized, thus giving rise to sustainability challenges in the waste management system (Parvathamma, 2014). Another issue of concern is the lack of a systematic regulatory framework regarding monitoring NORM (Okoro, Okolie, Sanni, Joel, et al., 2020). Unfortunately, currently, there are no specifically designed safety standards, guidelines, and regulations for the oil and gas industry that provide reliable protection for workers engaged in oil and gas industry processes involving radiological exposure. Also, the lack of understanding of other factors that affect the different phases of waste management and the relationships that are required to ensure the operation of the overall waste management system is efficient directly affects the E&P waste management process (Fell et al., 2010). Other factors that affect oil and gas waste management systems are:

1. Waste reduction and management are not sufficient from a long-term sustainability perspective.
2. Lack of comprehensive information on the quantity of waste generated from oil and gas operations.
3. Underutilized intelligent control technology and decision support system.
4. There is a knowledge-based waste management gap.
5. Seasonal characterization, quantification, and management practice for E&P waste.
6. Inadequate intelligent decision-making/support process for waste management and disposal.
7. Lack of integrated waste management for E&P operations.
8. The potential application of the Internet of Things is not utilized in the waste management process.
9. Lack of a smart protocol and communication techniques (networking and integration).
10. Nonutilization of an integrated waste management information system.

Management information systems are important aspects of the waste handling and treatment process. The smart system provides the idea of managing, monitoring, and handling waste management in any facility, as well as collecting data and managing records that are captured in the waste generation points in real time using channels of remote sensors (Rafique, 2018). This idea allows the operator of a remote system to view, monitor, and control a system even for a large volume of different types of waste and offers an improved level of optimization and safety. A clear understanding and regulation of the multiscale interconnection mechanism for the waste management process are vital in achieving a multiscale integrated conceptual framework for intelligent waste management systems (Ge et al., 2020). The growing awareness of the problem associated with efficient E&P waste management has prompted initiatives to solve the problem, leading to the proposal of a smart integrated decision-making and handling system to support good waste management practice.

Expert system for the oil and gas waste management system

The role of smart technologies can be very important and useful in solving the waste management problems that the oil and gas industry is facing today and laying the foundation for a sustainable future. A smart approach is the ability to incorporate the knowledge necessary to solve the major problems of modern society. The main challenge is to manage and reduce the impact of the waste generated and to guarantee balanced, sustainable development (Sandro et al., 2019). Close cooperation between all relevant engineering professions is essential for interdisciplinary collaboration and can address the complex technical challenges associated with waste management in the oil and gas industry. Intensive research efforts should be directed toward balanced use of resources, efficient energy conversion technologies, the integration of the Internet of Things, efficient approaches to creating a closed environmental framework, and efficient integration of processes, as well as other important issues for the waste management structure.

Expert systems are poised to take over the no less vital tasks of the ill-structured and less-deterministic parts of the planning, design, and management processes with respect to oil and gas waste management (Phil et al., 2020). Sustainable development reconciles economic progress and waste management without jeopardizing the planet's natural balance. The challenge is to meet the current energy needs of humanity without compromising its future development, future generations, and the means and resources necessary to meet current and future needs (Ion & Gheorghe, 2014). It is imperative to control and minimize the cost of waste management within the limits established by law. To achieve this goal, every waste treatment and disposal facility needs smart technology and tools, as well as modern equipment for the collection, processing, and application of specific procedures (Serna-Loaiza et al., 2019).

Research and development activities in the oil and gas industry should also focus on how best to conserve or even improve these various types of waste from an economic and environmental point of view through the documentation of quantitative information, such as the location and properties of the waste, possible treatment technologies, and potential target products, and frameworks to support decision-making (Chang & Wang, 1996). The integration of disparate knowledge is often prevented by insufficiently structured experience, and this gap can be addressed using an expert system approach. Expert systems provide new opportunities for harnessing the scarce and often scattered pieces of valuable knowledge, and experience in waste management (Basri & Stentiford, 1995). Attempts to use this new information and computing technology in other areas of engineering show that the experience of waste management in various forms has enormous potential to be encoded successfully in expert systems.

Sensor application in a waste management expert system

An expert system is "a knowledge-based system whose performance must be complimented with human experts." Expert systems consist of a knowledge base, an inference engine, and an input/output mechanism (Thomas et al., 1990). Fig. 16.6 shows a sensor-based expert system for the identification and classification of waste generated in E&P streams operations, and it is data-driven. The sensor in the proposed expert system does not have a set solution algorithm, only a goal and some known conditions. The execution of the program is based on data received by the sensor. The data are used to select a rule or heuristic that can be followed with reasonable safety and adapt to changing waste streams. At the same time, the traditional method will likely have to undergo extensive structural review if the decision pattern changes, but the proposed expert system sensor only requires that the characteristics of the new method be entered into the knowledge base (Meyers et al., 2006). When the data match the new attributes in the knowledge base, the expert system selects the heuristics that lead to the target state. Expert systems can deal effectively with uncertainty, which is present in varying degrees in forecasts of waste generation, treatment, and disposal (Ahuja & Bahukhandi, 2012). Expert systems can easily grow and adapt to new information on waste generation and technologies as it becomes available. The new data sensor would be incorporated into the knowledge base as the system generates the report.

Improving waste management efficiency is the critical factor of a sensor approach on expert system. The sensors are designed to detect three categories of possible pollutants, including acidic gas, heavy metals, and NORM (Katz, 2012). With the sensors, inherent properties, they will be able to detect the presence of any of these pollutants as they come in contact with the waste stream, and with their response, the process is either terminated if there is no particular pollutant for the sensor or it moves to the next stage if pollutants are present. The data from the sensor are used to determine the level of the pollutant in the waste stream by comparing it with the established model for the facility. If the detected limit is higher than the allowable standard limits set by the regulatory authority, the system recommends the particular treatment required before disposal/storage, otherwise, the system returns to the initial starting point. This approach is oriented on the movement from one point to another during handling of the waste stream. The goal of the process is to find a minimal-cost cyclic tour through a set of points such that every point is visited once (Chiodo & Ijomah, 2014).

The proposed sensor for identification and classification of E&P wastes is a multicriteria decision framework that has the capability to weigh different criteria and calculate them so as to provide a comparative decision in the waste management process (Ardjmand & Daneshfar, 2020). The proposed framework will be used to identify the best option and determine the ranking of options by simultaneous incorporation of all decision-making criteria from the sensor data. The expert system includes several decision options and allows analysis of the sensitivity of the criteria and subcriteria. This method is based on a pairwise comparison, which simplifies evaluation and calculation, indicating the degree of compatibility and inconsistency of the solution (Abdel-Shafy & Mansour, 2018). Several studies have been conducted in recent years to select the best waste management model. Still, it should be noted that each of the economic, technical, or environmental

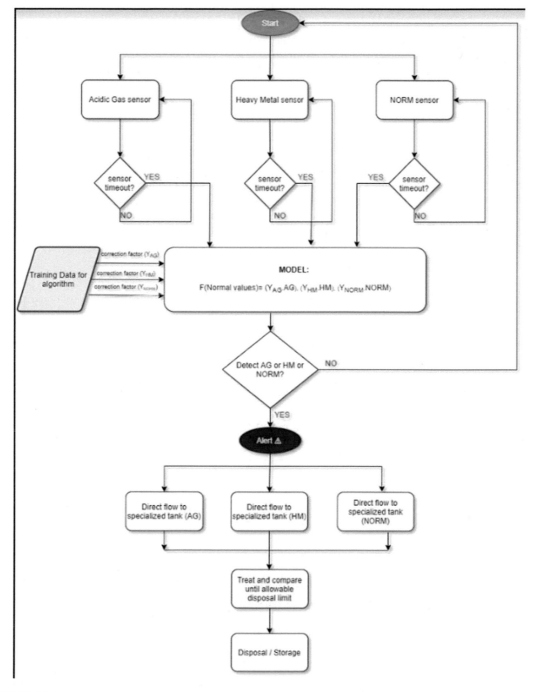

FIGURE 16.6

Sensor-driven expert system for waste management.

parameters alone does not lead to choosing the best waste management model. A waste management system must simultaneously consider environmental, technical, economic, and other criteria (Huang et al., 2018). During waste management, technological, environmental, and system performance are the most important criteria in the process.

The lack of an expert system in waste management planning, especially at the decision-making level, makes some rational decision guides unattractive. By developing an expert system, savings can be made over the repetitive use of consultants to identify and evaluate waste management alternatives. Additionally, the objective nature of the expert system results can help the planning process to better meet the needs of the entire industry operations (Basri, 2000). The proposed sensor expert system is an efficient system with choices of proper management of the oil and gas industry waste depending upon the scenario; thus creating a useful assessment and identification process. The choice of waste treatment and identification methods is complicated by changing technology, uncertain waste generation rates, and waste stream composition, as well as environmental and regulatory pressures. Expert systems approaches are useful in developing waste management plans that are cost-effective and capable of meeting a variety of qualitative and quantitative system objectives (Thomas et al., 1990).

Algorithm of the proposed sensor approach

Sometimes, the constraints of complex task execution might be changed online. The sensor might detect these changes, and the control-based approach should reorganize the task execution. The main idea behind this is that a complex task is separated into a set of subtasks. The sequence of these subtasks is represented as a stack. The general idea of the proposed method is to manipulate the current challenges in waste management facilities in order to satisfy the desired constraints on the sequence (Bonello et al., 2017). The main idea of the approach is straightforward: calculate the possible challenges and then apply an algorithm to solve the inherent problems. The goal of the approach is to minimize the cycle time while considering both kinematics and dynamics. Fig. 16.7 shows an algorithm flowchart of the proposed expert system. The solution process was split into three stages: the input, model, and output, where the model is the stage where the decision is made, and the optimization problem is solved with the algorithm.

Oil and gas wastes are managed in such ways that have been found to be most convenient or less costly. Most approaches often recommended for waste management looks at ways to minimize the generation of waste and with a disposal technique that offers better environmental protection. Wastes that are cancerous and/or toxic to humans and the ecosystems are often regulated by government agencies (Kadafa, 2018). In the absence of government regulations, guidelines issued by relevant international or regional organizations are generally used. The input section is the primitive tasks, while the output relates to the sequence of the process. The input section considers the model parameter setup, which considers the topology, hyperparameter tuning, initialization of the weight, and the loading of the training data. The training, validation, and configuration of the AI model take place at the model section. The output section shows the results of the training and detection test results from the waste management process. The real-time data from the sensors are used for the configuration of a specific facility model (De Almeida & Borsato, 2019).

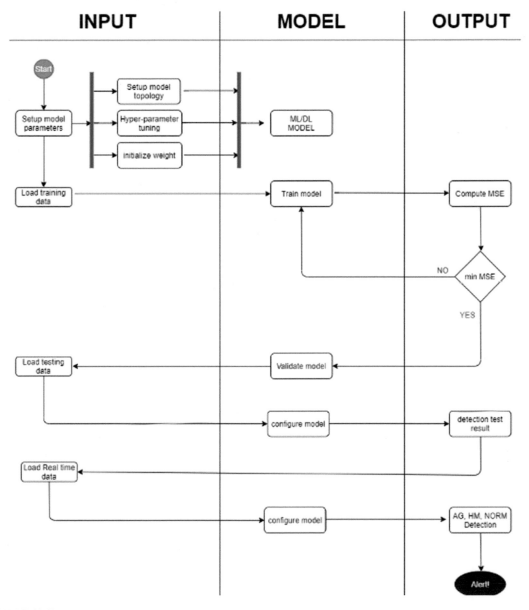

FIGURE 16.7

Algorithm flowchart of the proposed waste management expert system.

Gaps in a waste management expert system

The global search for sustainability will depend on the resource management system, which mediates on the one hand the relationship between society and the economy and, on the other hand, the continuity of the functional processes of the ecosystem. Waste generation and management issues are known to have an increasing impact on human health, socioeconomics, aesthetics, and quality of life in many communities, states, and countries around the world (Naushad et al., 2009). Many scientific fields are already using an expert system approach to solve a variety of problems in their field of study. The uncertainty in the oil and gas waste generation rates, the composition of waste streams, and sociopolitical pressures have made it difficult to select the most appropriate waste treatment and disposal methods; expert systems approaches have proven useful for the development of management plans (Chau, 2006). Economical waste disposal through expert systems will also help protect the environment by contributing to proper waste planning and management (Kaplan et al., 2005).

A critical factor in successfully implementing waste management is the need for specialized knowledge in the form of a human expert or a written program, such as an expert system. Operational problems can be more easily identified if the waste management facility is incorporated with an expert system; thus expert systems are not only designed in order to provide specialized knowledge (Ahuja & Bahukhandi, 2012). Expert systems have evolved from simple decision support systems to sophisticated tools suitable for many common problems. They were originally created as computer programs that required a lot of code to be written from scratch. Later, the development cycle was shortened considerably using special development tools, such as expert shell systems (Dyson & Chang, 2005). Expert systems have also been enriched with their integration into neural networks, fuzzy logic, and the genetic algorithm (Fleming et al., 2007). Expert system development is a collective effort because it requires the input of experts in the related field to define the knowledge framework and gather the necessary facts, information, and knowledge for the development of the knowledge-base.

The gaps and challenges in establishing effective and efficient expert systems in the oil and gas industry include:

1. Lack of understanding of both physical and chemical parameters in oil and gas waste streams, which in turn govern the behavior in the natural environment.
2. The E&P industry attachment to existing rules-of-thumb, thus, it is unwilling to integrate these smart systems into already-existing management systems.
3. The need for comprehensive data and human expertise that will be used to develop the knowledge-base of the system.
4. A nonuniform standardized analytical hierarchy process for designing the specific knowledge-base for each oil and gas industry operation and its associated waste streams.
5. Expert systems are effective in modeling heuristic concepts rather than analytical mathematical relations.
6. Expert system simulations must adopt a concurrent object-orientation approach.
7. No standardized rules exist on how to address data gaps and process completeness.
8. Expert systems are data-driven instead of methodology-driven; thus it is driven by the goal and certain known conditions.
9. The need to develop better tools to make expert systems cost-effective in the industry.
10. Changes in the waste composition can have a significant impact on waste management practices.

Effective utilization of expert systems in oil and gas industry waste management

AI, and expert systems, in particular, are an exciting and relatively new approach for effective waste handling and management. They provide unique opportunities for harnessing the scarce and often scattered pieces of valuable knowledge and experience in oil and gas waste streams management, which at present is in possession of the privileged few. Real-time data on the quantities, composition, and characterization of wastes are essential as they determine the appropriateness of different waste management and treatment options. An ideal waste management system must involve waste segregation at source to allow much more efficient value extraction, treatment, and disposal/utilization (Kumar et al., 2017). AI and its subfield of expert systems with the best record of successful applications are consequently the areas with the most immediate potential for the industry, and these are the highly-rated topics in modern waste management. The aim of interpretation, diagnosis, monitoring, and control is mostly to recognize known patterns, that is, to identify an object, composition, or an alarm condition. Here, a solution is selected from a set of given alternatives; in contrast, the resolution in design.

Based on current data, program execution in expert systems continues in a forward direction. The data are used to select a rule or heuristic that can be followed with reasonable safety. These systems can easily be adapted to changes in solution techniques (Bani et al., 2009). If the data fits the new characteristics in the knowledge base platform, the expert system will select those heuristics that lead toward the goal for the process. User interaction helps the planner to better understand the simulation process and, to a greater degree, communicate the simulation results to the decision maker (Pollard et al., 1992). Expert systems can effectively deal with the uncertainties that exist to some extent in the forecasts of waste generation, the composition of waste streams, new technologies in the field of recovery, and use of resources, energy, and other factors (Chang et al., 2011). Expert systems can easily be expanded and adapted to new information on waste generation and compositions as it becomes available. In advanced expert systems, findings that no longer lead to the achievement of the target state can be identified and avoided, making future process decisions more efficient (Imarhiagbe & Obayagbona, 2019).

A heuristic algorithm can take into account several factors, as a human expert thinks, without having to convert each aspect into standard units of comparison. Developing an expert system can include the knowledge of a group of experts, which offers a clear advantage over using the experts available for a particular project. The lack of full experience in oil and gas waste management planning, especially at the local decision-making level, makes some waste management decision aids attractive (den Boer et al., 2007). There is room for economies of scale in the development of an expert system versus the reuse of consultants to identify and evaluate alternatives for waste management. Additionally, the objective nature of the expert system results can help the planning process to better meet the needs of the entire industry operations (Banar et al., 2009). In addressing the range of issues described as challenges in handling, managing, and disposing of the oil and gas industry generated waste streams, expert systems would be most applicable to technical decisions since the industry has considerable leeway in recommending a preferred technology to meet the established regulations in waste management.

Economic considerations can be effectively addressed using expert systems that are linked to more appropriate financial analysis and optimization approaches that will align with the industry objectives (Bovea & Powell, 2006). Some aspects of the policy and regulations can be dealt with by an expert system (e.g., compliance with different levels of environmental legislation). However, it is best to deal with other policy issues while selecting or considering a list of possible alternatives during decision-making. Environmental considerations generally depend on the technology chosen and the location of the field or plant and can be evaluated more effectively by operators or resource economists in other ways (Beigl & Salhofer, 2004). Technical problems lend themselves well to the expert system environment due to the rapid development of waste-handling technologies. Data on past successes and failures can be archived in an expert systems database to aid in planning for new systems. The strength of expert systems lies in their ability to automatically react or "learn" from new information on the latest technologies. As new effective methods are developed, they will be preferred over less effective methods.

Failed methods should be avoided, as they are less likely to reach the target state or the objective of the waste management process. In this way, technology transfer can maximize the efficiency of new facilities by recognizing the strengths and weaknesses of previous projects. Expert systems can determine the conditions for the successful implementation of a new program based on previous experience with that technology (Page, 1990). Expert systems are well suited to making qualitative decisions. An expert system could provide a list of potential problems or environmental considerations to be dealt with prior to the implementation of any waste management alternative. Expert systems are suitable for storing knowledge of different types and origins, and for providing this information for troubleshooting purposes. The representation of heuristic knowledge, as well as the management of vague and incomplete knowledge, are well understood in expert systems engineering. Editing the expert knowledge base is usually easier.

Conclusion

The composition of waste streams is determined by several factors, which may include the specific environmental conditions that exist during formation (i.e., degree and extent of anoxia and local water composition), the degree of subsequent change (e.g., thermal maturity of hydrocarbons and degree of evaporation), and external disturbances (e.g., uplift and invasion of neighboring aquifers). All of these factors lead to a high degree of variability between and within the subsurface bedrock encountered during exploration and production activities in the oil and gas industry.

The relationships identified in the literature cannot be used to predict the exact concentration of toxic materials or components in a waste stream from a particular well. Too many sources of variability remain, resulting in a range of potential concentrations that span an order of magnitude or more. However, these relationships can provide probability distributions from which the probable concentrations in an area can be predicted, and thus, contribute to the development of the knowledge base for the expert system.

The use of expert systems can minimize the effects of toxic and hazardous E&P operation waste streams to the ambient environment, especially in the case of large-volume waste management in the field. The proposed sensor-equipped expert system has reasonably achieved the objective of harnessing scarce expertise in a critical domain, and exploiting the potential of the latest software technology and algorithms in order to create a user-friendly expert system for effective and efficient waste streams management.

To prevent expert systems from becoming obsolete, they need to be developed and kept up to date. This includes a mechanism for making knowledge changes and needs to change so as to incorporate new knowledge from new compositions or regulations. The existing knowledge base of the expert system can be improved by clarifying, expanding, and strengthening its knowledge base using new results in the literature or new experience in the field of knowledge, added functionality, and demonstration of the preliminary system design.

References

Abdel-Shafy, H. I., & Mansour, M. S. M. (2018). Solid waste issue: Sources, composition, disposal, recycling, and valorization. *Egyptian Journal of Petroleum*, *27*(4), 1275–1290. Available from https://doi.org/10.1016/j.ejpe.2018.07.003.

Ahammad, S. M. D., Nagalakshmi, N. V. R., Srigowri, R. S., Vasanth, G., & Uma, S. K. (2017). Drilling waste management and control the effects. *Journal of Advanced Chemical Engineering*, *7*(1).

Ahmadun, F.-R., Alireza, P., Chuah, A. I., Awang, B. D. R., Siavash, M. S., & Zainal, A. Z. (2009). Review of technologies for oil and gas produced water treatment. *Journal of Hazardous Materials*, 530–551. Available from https://doi.org/10.1016/j.jhazmat.2009.05.044.

Ahuja, N. J., & Bahukhandi, K. D. (2012). Expert systems for solid waste management: A review. *International Review on Computers and Software*, *7*(4), 1608–1613.

Al-Futaisi, A., Jamrah, A., Yaghi, B., & Taha, R. (2007). Assessment of alternative management techniques of tank bottom petroleum sludge in Oman. *Journal of Hazardous Materials*, *141*(3), 557–564. Available from https://doi.org/10.1016/j.jhazmat.2006.07.023.

Altaş, L., & Büyükgüngör, H. (2008). Sulfide removal in petroleum refinery wastewater by chemical precipitation. *Journal of Hazardous Materials*, *153*(1–2), 462–469. Available from https://doi.org/10.1016/j.jhazmat.2007.08.076.

Ambituuni, A., Amezaga, J., & Emeseh, E. (2014). Analysis of safety and environmental regulations for downstream petroleum industry operations in Nigeria: Problems and prospects. *Environmental Development*, *9*(1), 43–60. Available from https://doi.org/10.1016/j.envdev.2013.12.002.

Andersson, P., Rappe, C., Maaskant, O., Unsworth, J. F., & Marklund, S. (1998). Low temperature catalytic destruction of PCDD/F in flue gas from waste incineration. *Organohalogen Compounds*, *36*, 109–112.

Ardjmand, M., & Daneshfar, M. A. (2020). Selecting a suitable model for collecting, transferring, and recycling drilling wastes produced in the operational areas of the Iranian offshore oil company (IOOC) using analytical hierarchy process (AHP). *Journal of Environmental Management*, *259*, 109791.

Bakke, T., Klungsøyr, J., & Sanni, S. (2013). Environmental impacts of produced water and drilling waste discharges from the Norwegian offshore petroleum industry. *Marine Environmental Research*, *92*, 154–169. Available from https://doi.org/10.1016/j.marenvres.2013.09.012.

Banar, M., Cokaygil, Z., & Ozkan, A. (2009). Life cycle assessment of solid waste management options for Eskisehir, Turkey. *Waste Management*, *29*(1), 54–62. Available from https://doi.org/10.1016/j.wasman.2007.12.006.

Bani, M. S., Rashid, Z. A., Hamid, K. H. K., Harbawi, M. E., Alias, A. B., & Aris, M. J. (2009). The development of decision support system for waste management; a review. *World Academy of Science, Engineering and Technology*, *37*, 161–168. Available from http://www.waset.org/pwaset/v37/v37-33.pdf.

Barik, S. P., Park, K. H., Parhi, P. K., Park, J. T., & Nam, C. W. (2012). Extraction of metal values from waste spent petroleum catalyst using acidic solutions. *Separation and Purification Technology, 101,* 85−90. Available from https://doi.org/10.1016/j.seppur.2012.09.020.

Basri, H. B. (2000). An expert system for landfill leachate management. *Environmental Technology,* 157−166. Available from https://doi.org/10.1080/09593330.2000.9618896.

Basri, H. B., & Stentiford, E. I. (1995). Expert systems in solid waste management. *Waste Management & Research, 13*(1), 67−89.

Beigl, P., & Salhofer, S. (2004). Comparison of ecological effects and costs of communal waste management systems. *Resources, Conservation and Recycling, 41*(2), 83−102. Available from https://doi.org/10.1016/j.resconrec.2003.08.007.

Bhatia, S. C. (2002). *Handbook of industrial pollution and control* (Vol. 2). CBS Publishers.

den Boer, J., den Boer, E., & Jager, J. (2007). LCA-IWM: A decision support tool for sustainability assessment of waste management systems. *Waste Management, 27,* 1032−1045.

Bojes, H. K., & Pope, P. G. (2007). Characterization of EPA's 16 priority pollutant polycyclic aromatic hydrocarbons (PAHs) in tank bottom solids and associated contaminated soils at oil exploration and production sites in Texas. *Regulatory Toxicology and Pharmacology, 47*(3), 288−295. Available from https://doi.org/10.1016/j.yrtph.2006.11.007.

Bonello, D., Saliba, M. A., & Camilleri, K. P. (2017). An exploratory study on the automated sorting of commingled recyclable domestic waste. *Procedia Manufacturing, 11,* 686−694.

Bovea, M. D., & Powell, J. C. (2006). Alternative scenarios to meet the demands of sustainable waste management. *Journal of Environmental Management, 79*(2), 115−132. Available from https://doi.org/10.1016/j.jenvman.2005.06.005.

Buyukkamaci, N., & Kucukselek, E. (2007). Improvement of dewatering capacity of a petrochemical sludge. *Journal of Hazardous Materials, 144*(1−2), 323−327. Available from https://doi.org/10.1016/j.jhazmat.2006.10.034.

Cain, A., Vannela, R., & Woo, L. K. (2008). Cyanobacteria as a biosorbent for mercuric ion. *Bioresource Technology, 99*(14), 6578−6586. Available from https://doi.org/10.1016/j.biortech.2007.11.034.

Cecal, A., Humelnicu, D., Rudic, V., Cepoi, L., Ganju, D., & Cojocari, A. (2012). Uptake of uranyl ions from uranium ores and sludges by means of *Spirulina platensis, Porphyridium cruentum* and *Nostok linckia* alga. *Bioresource Technology, 118,* 19−23. Available from https://doi.org/10.1016/j.biortech.2012.05.053.

Cevat, Y., Ismail, A., & Omar, A. (2020). Potential for greenhouse gas reduction and energy recovery from MSW through d15ifferent waste management technologies. *Journal of Cleaner Production,* 121432. Available from https://doi.org/10.1016/j.jclepro.2020.121432.

Chang, N. B., & Wang, S. F. (1996). The development of an environmental decision support system for municipal solid waste management. *Computers, Environment and Urban Systems, 20*(3), 201−212. Available from https://doi.org/10.1016/S0198-9715(96)00015-4.

Chang, N. B., Pires, A., & Martinho, G. (2011). Empowering systems analysis for solid waste management: Challenges, trends, and perspectives. *Critical Reviews in Environmental Science and Technology, 41*(16), 1449−1530. Available from https://doi.org/10.1080/10643381003608326.

Chau, K. W. (2006). An expert system on site selection of sanitary landfill. *International Journal of Environment and Pollution, 28*(3−4), 402−411. Available from https://doi.org/10.1504/IJEP.2006.011219.

Chavan, A., & Mukherji, S. (2008). Treatment of hydrocarbon-rich wastewater using oil degrading bacteria and phototrophic microorganisms in rotating biological contactor: Effect of N:P ratio. *Journal of Hazardous Materials, 154*(1−3), 63−72. Available from https://doi.org/10.1016/j.jhazmat.2007.09.106.

Chen, C., Huang, X., Lei, C., Zhang, T. C., & Wu, W. (2013). Effect of organic matter strength on anammox for modified greenhouse turtle breeding wastewater treatment. *Bioresource Technology, 148,* 172−179. Available from https://doi.org/10.1016/j.biortech.2013.08.132.

Cheremisinoff, N. P. (2003). Handbook of solid waste management and waste minimization technologies. *Chemical Engineer*, *744*, 48. Available from http://www.tcetoday.com.

Chilaka, M. A., & Nwaneke, P. K. (2016). Integrating corporate social responsibility, health improvement, and community support in development programmes: A case for enhancing the application of health impact assessment in programme implementation in the Niger Delta region. *Local Environment*, *21*(3), 383–395. Available from https://doi.org/10.1080/13549839.2014.1000287.

Chiodo, J. D., & Ijomah, W. L. (2014). Use of active disassembly technology to improve re-manufacturing productivity: Automotive application. *International Journal of Computer Integrated Manufacturing*, *27*(4), 361–371.

Chojnacka, K., & Noworyta, A. (2004). Evaluation of Spirulina sp. growth in photoautotrophic, heterotrophic and mixotrophic cultures. *Enzyme and Microbial Technology*, *34*(5), 461–465. Available from https://doi.org/10.1016/j.enzmictec.2003.12.002.

Cholakov, G. (2009). Pollution Control Technologies. In Control of Pollution in the Petroleum Industry: Vol. III.

Clark, M. R., Althaus, F., Schlacher, T. A., Williams, A., Bowden, D. A., & Rowden, A. A. (2016). The impacts of deep-sea fisheries on benthic communities: A review. *ICES Journal of Marine Science*, *73*, i51–i69. Available from https://doi.org/10.1093/icesjms/fsv123.

Coelho, A., Castro, A. V., Dezotti, M., & Sant'Anna, G. L. (2006). Treatment of petroleum refinery sourwater by advanced oxidation processes. *Journal of Hazardous Materials*, *137*(1), 178–184. Available from https://doi.org/10.1016/j.jhazmat.2006.01.051.

De Almeida, S. T., & Borsato, M. (2019). Assessing the efficiency of End of Life technology in waste treatment—A bibliometric literature review. *Resources, Conservation and Recycling*, *140*, 189–208. Available from https://doi.org/10.1016/j.resconrec.2018.09.020.

Demopoulos, A. W. J., Bourque, J. R., & Frometa, J. (2014). Biodiversity and community composition of sediment macrofauna associated with deep-sea *Lophelia pertusa* habitats in the Gulf of Mexico. *Deep-Sea Research Part I: Oceanographic Research Papers*, *93*, 91–103. Available from https://doi.org/10.1016/j.dsr.2014.07.014.

Dyson, B., & Chang, N. B. (2005). Forecasting municipal solid waste generation in a fast-growing urban region with system dynamics modeling. *Waste Management*, *25*(7), 669–679. Available from https://doi.org/10.1016/j.wasman.2004.10.005.

El-Naas, M. H., Al-Zuhair, S., & Alhaija, M. A. (2010). Removal of phenol from petroleum refinery wastewater through adsorption on date-pit activated carbon. *Chemical Engineering Journal*, *162*(3), 997–1005. Available from https://doi.org/10.1016/j.cej.2010.07.007.

Estrada, J. M., & Bhamidimarri, R. (2016). A review of the issues and treatment options for wastewater from shale gas extraction by hydraulic fracturing. *Fuel*, *182*, 292–303. Available from https://doi.org/10.1016/j.fuel.2016.05.051.

Fell, D., Cox, J., & Wilson, D. C. (2010). Future waste growth, modelling and decoupling. *Waste Management and Research*, *28*(3), 281–286. Available from https://doi.org/10.1177/0734242X10361512.

Ferrar, K. J., Michanowicz, D. R., Christen, C. L., Mulcahy, N., Malone, S. L., & Sharma, R. K. (2013). Assessment of effluent contaminants from three facilities discharging marcellus shale wastewater to surface waters in Pennsylvania. *Environmental Science and Technology*, *47*(7), 3472–3481. Available from https://doi.org/10.1021/es301411q.

Fisher, O. J., Watson, N. J., Escrig, J. E., Witt, R., Porcu, L., Bacon, D., Rigley, M., & Gomes, R. L. (2020). Considerations, challenges and opportunities when developing data-driven models for process manufacturing systems. *Computers and Chemical Engineering*, *140*. Available from https://doi.org/10.1016/j.compchemeng.2020.106881.

Fleming, G., Merwe, M. V. D., & McFerren, G. (2007). Fuzzy expert systems and GIS for cholera health risk prediction in southern Africa. *Environmental Modelling and Software*, *22*(4), 442–448. Available from https://doi.org/10.1016/j.envsoft.2005.12.008.

Ge, H., Yagu, D., Li, Z., Yiyang, D., Yi, Q., & Xu, J. (2020). Architecture model proposal of innovative intelligent manufacturing in the chemical industry based on multi-scale integration and key technologies. *Computers & Chemical Engineering*, 106967. Available from https://doi.org/10.1016/j.compchemeng.2020.106967.

Giwa, S. O., Layeni, A. T., Nwaokocha, C. N., & Sulaiman, M. A. (2017). Greenhouse gas inventory: A case of gas flaring operations in Nigeria. *African Journal of Science, Technology, Innovation and Development*, *9*(3), 241−250. Available from https://doi.org/10.1080/20421338.2017.1312778.

Gupta, V. (2006). Break-through in oil-water separation. *Environment Science and Engineering*, 57−58.

Hansel, S., Castegnaro, M., Sportouch, M. H., Méo, M. D., Milhavet, J. C., Laget, M., & Duménil, G. (1996). Chemical degradation of wastes of antineoplastic agents: Cyclophosphamide, ifosfamide and melphalan. *International Archives of Occupational and Environmental Health*, *69*, 109−114. Available from https://doi.org/10.1007/s004200050124.

Hill, L. A., Czolowski, E. D., DiGiulio, D., & Shonkoff, S. B. C. (2019). Temporal and spatial trends of conventional and unconventional oil and gas waste management in Pennsylvania, 1991−2017. *Science of the Total Environment*, *674*, 623−636. Available from https://doi.org/10.1016/j.scitotenv.2019.03.475.

Huang, Z., Xu, Z., Quan, Y., Jia, H., Li, J., Li, Q., et al. (2018). A review of treatment methods for oil-based drill cuttings. IOP Conference Series: Earth and Environmental Science, 170.

Imarhiagbe, E. E., & Obayagbona, N. O. (2019). *Environmental Evaluation and Biodegradability of Drilling Waste: A case study of Drill Cuttings from Ologbo Oil Field wells at Edo State*. IntechOpen. Available from http://doi.org/10.5772/intechopen.88612.

Ion, I., & Gheorghe, F. F. (2014). The innovator role of technologies in waste management towards the sustainable development. *Procedia Economics and Finance*, *8*, 420−428.

Islam, A. B. M. S., Jameel, M., Jumaat, M. Z., Shirazi, S. M., & Salman, F. A. (2012). Review of offshore energy in Malaysia and floating Spar platform for sustainable exploration. *Renewable and Sustainable Energy Reviews*, *16*(8), 6268−6284. Available from https://doi.org/10.1016/j.rser.2012.07.012.

Janajreh, I., Alshehi, A., & Elagroudy, S. (2020). Anaerobic co-digestion of petroleum hydrocarbon waste and wastewater treatment sludge. *International Journal of Hydrogen Energy*, *45*, 11538−11549.

Johnson, O. A., & Affam, A. C. (2019). Petroleum sludge treatment and disposal: A review. *Environmental Engineering Research*, *24*(2), 191−201.

Kadafa, A. A. (2018). Environmental impacts of oil exploration and exploitation in the Niger Delta of Nigeria. *Global Journal of Science Frontier Research*, *12*(3).

Kaplan, Ö. P., Barlaz, M. A., & Ranjithan, S. R. (2005). A procedure for life-cycle-based solid waste management with consideration of uncertainty. *Journal of Industrial Ecology*, *8*, 155−172.

Katz, R. S. (2012). Environmental pollution: Corporate crime and cancer mortality. *Contemporary Justice Review*, *15*(1), 97−125. Available from https://doi.org/10.1080/10282580.2011.653523.

Kesari, K. K., Verma, H., & Behari, J. (2011). Physical methods in wastewater treatment. *International Journal of Environmental Technology and Management*, *14*, 43−66.

Kumar, S., Smith, S. R., Fowler, G., Velis, C., Kumar, S. J., Arya, S., Rena., Kumar, R., & Cheeseman, C. (2017). Challenges and opportunities associated with waste management in India. *Royal Society Open Science*, *4*(3). Available from https://doi.org/10.1098/rsos.160764.

Maarten, D. (2012). Extended producer responsibility for consumer waste: The gap between economic theory and implementation. *Waste Management & Research*, 36−42. Available from https://doi.org/10.1177/0734242X12453379.

Meyers, G. D., McLeod, G., & Anbarci, M. A. (2006). An international waste convention: Measures for achieving sustainable development. *Waste Management and Research*, *24*(6), 505−513. Available from https://doi.org/10.1177/0734242X06069474.

Nandy, T., Kaul, S. N., Husain, M. Z., & Gajghata, D. G. (1999). Waste water management in refinery- A case study. *Environmental Pollution Control Journal*, 5−15.

Naushad, K., Huan, F., & Eric, S. (2009). A purview of waste management evolution: Special emphasis on USA. *Waste Management*, 974−985. Available from https://doi.org/10.1016/j.wasman.2008.06.032.

Okiel, K., El-Sayed, M., & El-Kady, M. Y. (2011). Treatment of oil−water emulsions by adsorption onto activated carbon, bentonite and deposited carbon. *Egyptian Journal of Petroleum*, *20*(2), 9−15. Available from https://doi.org/10.1016/j.ejpe.2011.06.002.

Okoro, E. E., Okolie, A. G., Sanni, S. E., Joel, E. S., Agboola, O., & Omeje, M. (2020). Assessment of naturally occuring radiation in lithofacies of oil field in Niger Delta region and its possible health implications. *Journal of Environmental Management*, *264*, 110498.

Okoro, E. E., Okolie, A. G., Sanni, S. E., & Omeje, M. (2020). Toxicology of heavy metals to subsurface lithofacies and drillers during drilling of hydrocarbon wells. *Scientific Reports*, *10*, 6152.

Olah, G. A., & Molnar, A. (2003). *Hydrocarbon Chemistry* (Second Edition). Wiley-Interscience, John Wiley & Sons, Inc.

Olalekan, A., & Gordon, M. (2011). The Niger Delta wetlands: Threats to ecosystem services, their importance to dependent communities and possible management measures. *International Journal of Biodiversity Science, Ecosystem Services & Management*, 50−68. Available from https://doi.org/10.1080/21513732.2011.603138.

Onwuka, O. S., Igwe, O., Ifediegwu, S. I., & Uwon, C. S. (2018). An assessment of the effectiveness of drilling waste treatment process in X-gas field, Niger Delta, Nigeria. *Geology, Ecology, and Landscapes*, *2*(4), 288−302.

Onwukwe, S. I., & Nwakaudu, M. S. (2012). Drilling waste generation and management approach. *International Journal of Environment Science and Development*, *3*(2), 252−257.

Otadi, N., Hassani, A. H., Javid, A. H., & Khiabani, F. F. (2010). Oily compounds removal in wastewater treatment system of pars oil refinery to improve its efficiency in a lab scale pilot. *Journal of Water Chemistry and Technology*, 370−377. Available from https://doi.org/10.3103/s1063455x1006010x.

Page, B. (1990). An analysis of environmental expert system applications. *Environmental Software*, *5*(4), 177−197. Available from https://doi.org/10.1016/S0266-9838(05)80009-7.

Pam, B. (2015). Produced and flowback water recycling and reuse: Economics, limitations, and technology. *Oil and Gas Facilities*, 16−21. Available from https://doi.org/10.2118/0214-0016-OGF.

Parvathamma, G. I. (2014). An analytical study on problems and policies of solid waste management in India −Special reference to Bangalore City. *IOSR Journal of Environmental Science, Toxicology and Food Technology*, *8*(10), 6−15.

Pathak, C., Hiren, C., & Mandalia. (2012). Petroleum industries: Environmental pollution effects, management and treatment methods. *International Journal of Separation for Environmental Sciences*, *1*, 55−62.

Phil, S., Guillermo, G.-G., Jamie, S., & Shahin, R. (2020). A complete decision-support infrastructure for food waste valorisation. *Journal of Cleaner Production*, 119608. Available from https://doi.org/10.1016/j.jclepro.2019.119608.

Pires, A., Martinho, G., & Chang, N. B. (2011). Solid waste management in European countries: A review of systems analysis techniques. *Journal of Environmental Management*, *92*(4), 1033−1050. Available from https://doi.org/10.1016/j.jenvman.2010.11.024.

Pollard, S. J., Hrudey, S. E., Fuhr, B. J., Alex, R. F., Holloway, L. R., & Tosto, F. (1992). Hydrocarbon wastes at petroleum- and creosote-contaminated sites: Rapid characterization of component classes by thin-layer chromatography with flame ionization detection. *Environmental Science & Technology*, 2528−2534. Available from https://doi.org/10.1021/es00036a029.

Radelyuk, I., Tussupova, K., Zhapargazinova, K., Yelubay, M., & Persson, M. (2019). Pitfalls of wastewater treatment in oil refinery enterprises in Kazakhstan—A system approach. *Sustainability*, *11*, 1618.

Rafique, H. (2018). *Energy management in network systems*, . *Comprehensive energy systems* (Vols. 5−5, pp. 581−647). Elsevier Inc. Available from https://doi.org/10.1016/B978-0-12-809597-3.00531-9.

Rahmat, Z. G., Niri, M. V., Alavi, N., Goudarzi, G., Babaei, A. A., Baboli, Z., & Hosseinzadeh, M. (2017). Landfill site selection using GIS and AHP: A case study: Behbahan, Iran. *KSCE Journal of Civil Engineering*, *21*(1), 111−118. Available from https://doi.org/10.1007/s12205-016-0296-9.

Sadiq, R., Husain, T., Bose, N., & Veitch, B. (2003). Distribution of heavy metals in sediment pore water due to offshore discharges: An ecological risk assessment. *Environmental Modelling and Software*, *18*(5), 451−461. Available from https://doi.org/10.1016/S1364-8152(03)00010-0.

Sandro, N., Nedjib, D., Agis, P., & Rodrigues, J. J. P. C. (2019). Smart technologies for promotion of energy efficiency, utilization of sustainable resources and waste management. *Journal of Cleaner Production*, 565−591. Available from https://doi.org/10.1016/j.jclepro.2019.04.397.

Serna-Loaiza, S., García-Velásquez, C. A., & Cardona, C. C. (2019). Strategy for the selection of the minimum processing scale for the economic feasibility of biorefineries. *Biofuels, Bioproducts and Biorefining*, 107−119. Available from https://doi.org/10.1002/bbb.1941.

Shahryar, J. (2017). (pp. 269−345). Elsevier BV. https://doi.org/10.1016/b978-0-12-809243-9.00007-9.

Singh, S., & Shikha. (2018). Treatment and recycling of wastewater from oil refinery/petroleum industry. *Chapter 10: Advances in biological treatment of industrial waste water and their recycling for a sustainable future*, 303−332. Available from https://doi.org/10.1007/978-981-13-1468-1_10.

Solomon, O. O., Ogbonnaya, I., Ikenna, I. S., & Stella, U. C. (2018). An assessment of the effectiveness of drilling waste treatment process in X-gas field, Niger Delta, Nigeria. *Geology, Ecology, and Landscapes*, 288−302. Available from https://doi.org/10.1080/24749508.2018.1473751.

Thomas, B., Tamblyn, D., & Baetz, B. (1990). Expert systems in municipal solid waste management planning. *Journal of Urban Planning and Development*, *116*(3), 150−155. Available from https://doi.org/10.1061/(ASCE)0733-9488(1990)116:3(150).

Ugochukwu, C. N. C., & Ertel, J. (2012). Negative impacts of oil exploration on biodiversity management in the Niger Delta area of Nigeria. *Impact Assessment and Project Appraisal*, *26*(2), 139−147.

Uwe, K. (2006). *Environmental engineering* (Vol. 718). Irwin McGraw-hill.

Walid, E., & Abdulqader, A. (2005). Solid waste generation from oil and gas industries in United Arab Emirates. *Journal of Hazardous Materials*, 89−99. Available from https://doi.org/10.1016/j.jhazmat.2004.12.036.

Wan Ahmad, W. N. K., Rezaei, J., Tavasszy, L. A., & de Brito, M. P. (2016). Commitment to and preparedness for sustainable supply chain management in the oil and gas industry. *Journal of Environmental Management*, *180*, 202−213. Available from https://doi.org/10.1016/j.jenvman.2016.04.056.

Wang, T. A., & McTernan, W. F. (2002). The development and application of a multilevel decision analysis model for the remediation of contaminated groundwater under uncertainty. *Journal of Environmental Management*, *64*(3), 221−235. Available from https://doi.org/10.1006/jema.2001.0470.

Wong, J.M., & Hung, Y. (2009). Treatment of Oilfield and Refinery Wastes'. Waste Treatment in the Process. Fundamentals of Petroleum Refining.

Computer-aided modeling of solid waste conversion: case study of maize (*Zea mays*) residues air gasification

Adewale George Adeniyi[1], Joshua O. Ighalo[1,2] and Chinenye Adaobi Igwegbe[2]

[1]*Department of Chemical Engineering, Faculty of Engineering and Technology, University of Ilorin, Ilorin, Nigeria*
[2]*Department of Chemical Engineering, Nnamdi Azikiwe University, Awka, Nigeria*

Introduction

Maize (*Zea mays*) is a major cereal crop that is cultivated all around the world. Annual production worldwide averages about 520×10^9 kg (Ioannidou et al., 2009). Maize (*Z. mays*) is also one of the major agricultural products of tropical West Africa, and Nigeria in particular. The stalk and cob of the plant are currently incinerated by both commercial and local farmers. These are very rich cellulosic and lignocellulosic sources for energy recovery processes (Sun et al., 2016). Considering the need for energy and environmental sustainability (Ighalo & Adeniyi, 2020c), energy recovery from biomass is of paramount concern to researchers in energy and environmental engineering (Ighalo & Adeniyi, 2020a). Maize residues are good feedstock for thermochemical processes (Anukam et al., 2017; Kumar et al., 2008).

Several studies have attempted to evaluate several aspects of the gasification of different maize residues. The advantage of using maize residues as fuel for internal combustion engines after the first-stage gasification or anaerobic digestion process has been estimated (Allesina et al., 2015). The potential for electricity generation in Ghana via a gasification process based on the availability of maize residues has been evaluated (Otchere-Appiah & Hagan, 2014). The effect of potassium addendum in the feed in the supercritical water gasification (also known as supercritical steam reforming) of maize residues has been studied (D'Jesús et al., 2005). In an experimental study (Perkins et al., 2008), investigations into the use of a solar-thermal technology for the high-temperature gasification of corn stover were conducted. In another experimental study (Tavasoli et al., 2009), a research team utilized a fixed-bed microreactor to produce hydrogen via the gasification of corn and wheat dry distiller grains. The air—steam gasification of corn stover in a simulation study on ASPEN Plus has also been reported (Kumar et al., 2009).

Besides the dearth of studies involving a thermodynamic approach in simulation modeling, few efforts have been made to place comparisons between the different maize residues. ASPEN Plus can be used to simulate and study the process of biomass gasification in the domain of preheating effect (Doherty et al., 2009), the effect of the gasifying agent (Gu et al., 2019), nature and

Current Trends and Advances in Computer-Aided Intelligent Environmental Data Engineering.
DOI: https://doi.org/10.1016/B978-0-323-85597-6.00017-3

381

composition of the product (Khezri et al., 2016), preliminary study (Mustafa et al., 2015), comparative performance analysis (Ramzan et al., 2011), and process modeling (Abdelouahed et al., 2012).

To the best of the authors' knowledge, the thermodynamic modeling of maize residue gasification to compare the product quality and based on residue type has not been investigated. This is the knowledge gap that this novel study attempts to explore. In this study, ASPEN Plus v8.8 was used to develop a model for the gasification of maize (*Z. mays*) residues based on a thermodynamic approach. The study takes a comparative approach between stalks and cobs. The developed model was used to investigate the effect of process temperature, pressure, and air–fuel ratio (AFR) on the molar composition of the product stream.

Methodology

In this section, a detailed explanation of the modeling approach is presented. The component specifications, model specifications, process description, and simplifying assumptions are also given. For a thermodynamic simulation like this, the technique employed was minimization of the Gibbs-free energy. Further details about the technique are available elsewhere (Adeniyi & Ighalo, 2020a,b; Ighalo & Adeniyi, 2020b).

Component specifications

The components added to the simulation are solid carbon (C), carbon dioxide (CO_2), hydrogen (H_2), carbon monoxide (CO), oxygen (O_2), methane (CH_4), nitrogen (N_2), silicon oxide (SiO_2), and water (H_2O). SiO_2 was in the simulation to represent ash in the biomass (Adeniyi & Ighalo, 2020a, b; Ighalo & Adeniyi, 2020b). The ultimate and proximate analyses of maize (*Z. mays*) residues are required to successfully model it as a nonconventional material in an ASPEN Plus v8.8 simulation environment. The specific property methods for the computation of biomass enthalpy and density were HCOALGEN and DGOALIGT, respectively (Adeniyi & Ighalo, 2020c; Adeniyi, Ighalo, & Abdulsalam, 2019). The ultimate analyses and proximate analyses of maize (*Z. mays*) residues utilized in this study are presented in Table 17.1 (Ioannidou et al., 2009).

Model specifications

In this subsection, some basic specifications about the simulation are described. The global calculation method selected for the simulation was the Peng–Robinson with Boston–Mathias alpha-function equation of state. The alpha-function (a temperature-dependent parameter) is included in the Peng–Robinson fluid package to improve the prediction of pure component vapor pressure (especially at very high temperatures). It has been used in thermodynamic simulations on ASPEN Plus by other researchers (Adeniyi, Ighalo, & Abdulsalam, 2019; Adeniyi, Ighalo, & Amosa, 2019). The approach of a recent study (Atikah and Harun, 2019) was replicated in converting the nonconventional maize (*Z. mays*) residues to conventional simulation components. The RYIELD block was assigned initial mass yields similar to those reported in another study (Atikah & Harun, 2019). A CALCULATOR was then included to the simulation. This was to specify the yield of the

Table 17.1 Proximate and ultimate analyses of maize (*Zea mays*) residues.

	Maize stalk	Maize cob
Proximate analysis (wt.% wet basis)		
Moisture	6.44	7.57
Fixed carbon	8.19	27.10
Volatile matter	83.07	57.27
Ash	2.30	8.07
Ultimate/elemental analysis (wt.% moisture free)		
Carbon	43.80	43.77
Hydrogen	6.42	6.23
Sulfur	—	—
Oxygen	49.78	50.00
Nitrogen	—	—
Chemical analysis (wt.%)		
Cellulose	32.40	34.30
Hemicclluloses	40.80	40.53
Lignin	2.50	18.80
Extractives	NS	NS
NS, Not stated.		

conventional simulation components based on proximate and ultimate analyses data of the feed-stock. The Fortran formulas used in the current study are available elsewhere (Adeniyi & Ighalo, 2019a,b; Adeniyi, Otoikhian, & Ighalo, 2019). The ambient conditions for the simulation were set as 25°C and 1 atm.

Model description

In this subsection, a general description of the process simulation and the integration of the different blocks for the air gasification process is presented. The "BREAK" block was used to represent the initial stage of biomass pyrolysis when heating commences where the major constituents disintegrate and thermally crack into chemical species of lower molecular weight. The reactions of the gasification process were computed by the "RGIBBS" block. This block computes the phase and chemical equilibrium and predicts final product composition and conditions based on input composition, temperature, and pressure. This is carried out using the nonstoichiometric approach to the minimization of Gibbs-free energy calculation method. The SEP block was used to represent the separation of the solid gasification products (char and ash) from the volatile products. This is carried out by specifying the split ratio.

The maize cob and stalk were sent into the simulation using an input flow rate of 100 kg/h as basis. This was at ambient conditions (25°C and 1 atm). A summary of the blocks in the air gasification simulation and their descriptions is given elsewhere (Ighalo & Adeniyi, 2020a). The effects

Table 17.2 Description of model blocks and streams.

ASPEN Plus ID	Name	Description
MATERIAL	BIOMASS	The maize cob and stalk feedstock
RYIELD	BREAK	Models the initial biomass pyrolysis at heating
CALCULATOR	DECOMP	Specifies the yield of the conventional simulation components based on analysis data
MATERIAL	OUT1	The output stream from the RYIELD block
MATERIAL	AIR	The air stream needed for biomass gasification
RGIBBS	GASIFIER	Computes the conditions and product of the biomass gasification process (nonstoichiometric approach to the minimization of Gibbs-free energy calculation method)
MATERIAL	OUT	The output stream from the RGIBBS block
SSPLIT	SEP	For separating the solids from the vapor product
MATERIAL	SYN-GAS	The vapor product stream of synthesis gas and nitrogen
MATERIAL	BIO-CHAR	The solid product stream

of process temperature, pressure, and AFR on the molar composition of the product stream were investigated using this model. The gasification pressure and temperature were varied from the user panel on the RGIBBS block. Temperature was varied between 400°C and 1000°C, while pressure was varied between 1 and 5 atm. The AFR is the mass ratio of the inlet air to the biomass feedstock. This was varied by retaining the feedstock basis (100 kg/h) and varying the inlet flow rate of air at the user panel. The AFR is a measure of the equivalence ratio of the combustion fuels. The AFR was varied between 0.01 and 1 kg/kg. The choice of range for varying the parameters was based on information obtained from other studies (Adeniyi, Ighalo, Onifade, & Adeoye, 2019; Ighalo & Adeniyi, 2020a,b,c).

In the process of model development, several simplifying assumptions were considered and implemented (Atikah & Harun, 2019). The gasification simulation was a steady-state model and hence process time was not a variable. The gasifier is considered to operate isothermally, hence temperature zones and variations within the reactor do not exist and heat loss is negligible. It was also considered that the drop in process pressure due to losses from tortuosity is negligible. With respect to the reaction, it is assumed that oxides of sulfur and nitrogen are not formed in the reactor. All elements in the inlet stream to the reactor take part in the process (there are no inert species or catalyst). The gasification reactions take place at equilibrium. The ash content of the solid product is considered to be silicon oxide while the char is carbon. The particle size distribution of biomass was neither investigated as a factor nor specified for the feedstock. A description of all the simulation components is given in Table 17.2. The ID shows the type of block that it is, while the name is the user-given name in the simulation.

Results and discussion

Upon implementation of the methodology, the simulation was successfully run without any errors and warnings from computation. Though the simulation product stream contains nitrogen, the

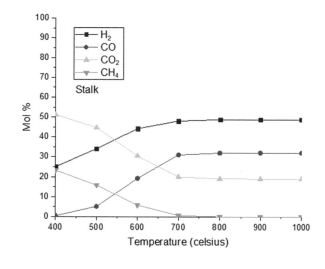

FIGURE 17.1

Effect of temperature on gas composition at 1 atm and AFR 1 kg/kg for stalk (nitrogen-free basis).

syngas discussed in the results is in a nitrogen-free basis. Based on this, CO, CO_2, CH_4, and H_2 make up the product stream. The parameter of interest is the percentage molar composition of the different chemical species in the product stream. The way the process factors affect this composition helps to show the selectivity of the species to various levels of these factors.

Effect on temperature on product selectivity

Figs. 17.1 and 17.2 show the effects of temperature on the synthesis gas composition at 1 atm and 1 kg/kg AFR for stalks and cobs, respectively. The trends for each chemical species with temperature are similar for both stalks and cobs though the values are different. When considered holistically, the difference in the values is slight. Looking at Table 17.1, it can be observed that the ultimate analysis reveals great similarity between both the cobs and the stalks. Considering that the RYIELD blocks do the conversion into conventional simulation components based on ultimate analysis information, then this similarity is expected. With increasing temperature, the H_2 and CO content increase, while the CO_2 and CH_4 content reduce. Equilibrium is attained at about 700°C, beyond which increasing temperature does not have a significant effect on the gas composition. It can be deduced that the optimum temperature for both maize and corn stalk air gasification is 700°C. From the plots, the H_2 content is 48.1% and 47.9% for stalk and cob, respectively.

Effect of pressure on product selectivity

Figs. 17.3 and 17.4 show the effects of pressure on the synthesis gas composition at 600°C and 1 kg/kg AFR for stalks and cobs, respectively. It can be observed that H_2 and CO decrease with

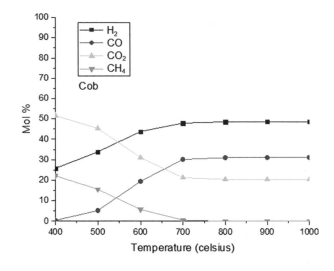

FIGURE 17.2

Effect of temperature on gas composition at 1 atm and AFR 1 kg/kg for cob (nitrogen-free basis).

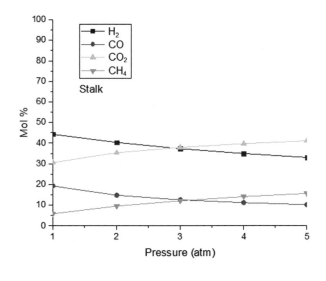

FIGURE 17.3

Effect of pressure on gas composition at 600°C and AFR 1 kg/kg for stalk (nitrogen-free basis).

increasing pressure and vice versa for the other two chemical species. The chemical equilibrium will always shift in favor of the heavier species at higher pressures (Adeniyi & Ighalo, 2019a,b; Adeniyi, Ighalo, & Otoikhian, 2019). At atmospheric conditions, the hydrogen content of the product stream is 44.2% and 43.8% for stalks and cobs, respectively. When the ease and lower

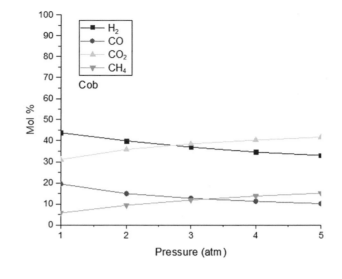

FIGURE 17.4

Effect of pressure on gas composition at 600°C and AFR 1 kg/kg for cob (nitrogen-free basis).

cost of designing systems to operate at atmospheric conditions are considered, it can be surmised that the optimum pressure for steam reforming of the maize residues is 1 atm. At 0.2 kg/kg, 1 atm, and 700°C for the gasification of maize stalks, the composition of the synthesis gas was 50% H_2, 35% CO, 12% CO_2, and 3% CH_4. The product stream was 95.5% gas and 5% char. At 0.2 kg/kg, 1 atm and 700°C for the gasification of maize cobs, the composition of the synthesis gas was 49% H_2, 36% CO, 12.5% CO_2, and 2.5% CH_4. The product stream was 96% gas and 4% char. It can be observed that while the stalks will give a product of marginally higher syngas quality, the cobs will give a marginally higher syngas yield.

Effect of air – fuel ratio on product selectivity

Figs. 17.5 and 17.6 shows the effects of AFR on the synthesis gas composition at 600°C and at 1 atm AFR for stalks and cobs, respectively. The AFR is a measure of the equivalence ratio and/ or the availability of oxygen in the gasification system (Ighalo & Adeniyi, 2020a,b,c). It can be observed that the oxygenate species (CO and CO_2) increase with higher AFR and vice versa for the others. However, this change is observed to be only marginal. The barest minimal AFR cannot ordinarily be considered as the optimum for the hydrogen content because the total flow rate of the product stream is higher at higher AFR as the overall amount of feed (sum of biomass and air) will invariably be greater. For both stalks and cobs, there was a 4% drop in hydrogen content when AFR rose from 0.01 to 1 kg/kg. In this case, it would be difficult to pinpoint an apparent optimal for AFR. However, valuable understanding has been gained from the AFR effect on the process. An AFR of 0.2 kg/kg will be considered to compare both residues of interest.

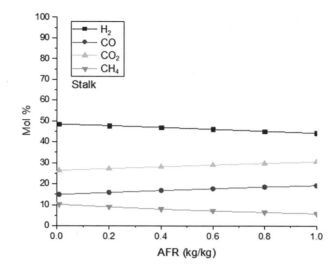

FIGURE 17.5

Effect of air—fuel ratio (AFR) on gas composition at 600°C and 1 atm for stalk (nitrogen-free basis).

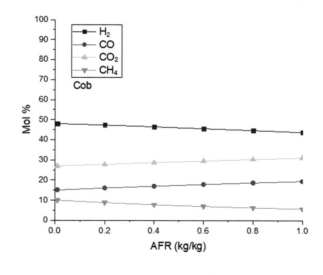

FIGURE 17.6

Effect of air—fuel ratio (AFR) on gas composition at 600°C and 1 atm for cob (nitrogen-free basis).

Conclusion

ASPEN Plus was successfully used to develop a model for the gasification of maize (*Z. mays*) residues based on a thermodynamic method (the nonstoichiometric approach to the minimization of Gibbs-free energy calculation method). The developed model was used to investigate the effect of process temperature, pressure, and AFR on the molar composition of the product stream. The optimum conditions were found to be 1 atm and 700°C. At 0.2 kg/kg, 1 atm, and 700°C for the gasification of maize stalks, the composition of the synthesis gas was 50% H_2, 35% CO, 12% CO_2, and 3% CH_4. The product stream was 95.5% gas and 5% char. At 0.2 kg/kg, 1 atm, and 700°C for the gasification of maize cobs, the composition of the synthesis gas was 49% H_2, 36% CO, 12.5% CO_2, and 2.5% CH_4. The product stream was 96% gas and 4% char. It was observed that while the stalks give a product of marginally higher syngas quality, the cobs give a marginally higher syngas yield. It can be surmised that both biomass samples are excellent feedstocks for the air gasification process. Instead of incineration or composting, biomass can be more efficiently utilized via this technique.

References

Abdelouahed, L., Authier, O., Mauviel, G., Corriou, J. P., Verdier, G., & Dufour, A. (2012). Detailed modeling of biomass gasification in dual fluidized bed reactors under ASPEN Plus. *Energy and Fuels*, *26*(6), 3840–3855. Available from https://doi.org/10.1021/ef300411k.

Adeniyi, A., & Ighalo, J. (2020a). Computer-aided modeling of thermochemical conversion processes for environmental waste management. In C. M. Hussain (Ed.), *Handbook of Environmental Materials Management* (pp. 1–16). Available from https://doi.org/10.1007/978-3-319-58538-3_185-1.

Adeniyi, A., & Ighalo, J. (2020b). Computer-aided modelling of the pyrolysis of rubber saw dust (Hevea Brasiliensis) using ASPEN Plus acta technica corviniensis. *Bulletin of Engineering*, *13*, 105–108.

Adeniyi, A. G., & Ighalo, J. O. (2019a). A review of steam reforming of glycerol. *Chemical Papers*, *73*(11), 2619–2635. Available from https://doi.org/10.1007/s11696-019-00840-8.

Adeniyi, A. G., & Ighalo, J. O. (2019b). Study of process factor effects and interactions in synthesis gas production via a simulated model for glycerol steam reforming. *Chemical Product and Process Modeling*. Available from https://doi.org/10.1515/cppm-2018-0034.

Adeniyi, A. G., & Ighalo, J. O. (2020c). ASPEN Plus predictive simulation of soft and hard wood pyrolysis for bio-energy recoviery. *International Journal of Environment and Waste Management*, 234. Available from https://doi.org/10.1504/ijewm.2020.10028695.

Adeniyi, A. G., Ighalo, J. O., & Abdulsalam, A. (2019). Modeling of integrated processes for the recovery of the energetic content of sugar cane bagasse. *Biofuels, Bioproducts and Biorefining*, *13*(4), 1057–1067. Available from https://doi.org/10.1002/bbb.1998.

Adeniyi, A. G., Ighalo, J. O., & Amosa, M. K. (2019). Modelling and simulation of banana (Musa spp.) waste pyrolysis for bio-oil production. *Biofuels*. Available from https://doi.org/10.1080/17597269.2018.1554949.

Adeniyi, A. G., Ighalo, J. O., & Otoikhian, K. S. (2019). Steam reforming of acetic acid: Response surface modelling and study of factor interactions. *Chemical Product and Process Modeling*. Available from https://doi.org/10.1515/cppm-2019-0066.

Adeniyi, A. G., Ighalo, J. O., Onifade, D. V., & Adeoye, S. A. (2019). Modeling the valorization of poultry litter via thermochemical processing. *Biofuels, Bioproducts and Biorefining*, 242–248. Available from https://doi.org/10.1002/bbb.2056.

Adeniyi, A. G., Otoikhian, K. S., & Ighalo, J. O. (2019). Steam reforming of biomass pyrolysis oil: A review. *International Journal of Chemical Reactor Engineering*, *17*(4). Available from https://doi.org/10.1515/ijcre-2018-0328.

Allesina, G., Pedrazzi, S., Guidetti, L., & Tartarini, P. (2015). Modeling of coupling gasification and anaerobic digestion processes for maize bioenergy conversion. *Biomass and Bioenergy*, *81*, 444−451. Available from https://doi.org/10.1016/j.biombioe.2015.07.010.

Anukam, A. I., Goso, B. P., Okoh, O. O., & Mamphweli, S. N. (2017). Studies on characterization of corn cob for application in a gasification process for energy production. *Journal of Chemistry*, 2017. Available from https://doi.org/10.1155/2017/6478389.

Atikah, M. S. N., & Harun, R. (2019). Simulation and optimization of Chlorella vulgaris gasification using ASPEN Plus. *Process Integration and Optimization for Sustainability*, *3*(3), 349−357. Available from https://doi.org/10.1007/s41660-019-0080-7.

D'Jesús, P., Artiel, C., Boukis, N., Kraushaar-Czarnetzki, B., & Dinjus, E. (2005). Influence of educt preparation on gasification of corn silage in supercritical water. *Industrial and Engineering Chemistry Research*, *44*(24), 9071−9077. Available from https://doi.org/10.1021/ie0508637.

Doherty, W., Reynolds, A., & Kennedy, D. (2009). The effect of air preheating in a biomass CFB gasifier using ASPEN Plus simulation. *Biomass and Bioenergy*, *33*(9), 1158−1167. Available from https://doi.org/10.1016/j.biombioe.2009.05.004.

Gu, H., Tang, Y., Yao, J., & Chen, F. (2019). Study on biomass gasification under various operating conditions. *Journal of the Energy Institute*, *92*(5), 1329−1336. Available from https://doi.org/10.1016/j.joei.2018.10.002.

Ighalo, J. O., & Adeniyi, A. G. (2020a). A perspective on environmental sustainability in the cement industry. *Waste Disposal & Sustainable Energy*, *2*(3), 161−164. Available from https://doi.org/10.1007/s42768-020-00043-y.

Ighalo, J. O., & Adeniyi, A. G. (2020b). Biomass to biochar conversion for agricultural and environmental applications in Nigeria: Challenges, peculiarities and prospects. *Materials International*, 111−116. Available from https://doi.org/10.33263/materials22.111116.

Ighalo, J. O., & Adeniyi, A. G. (2020c). Modelling of thermochemical energy recovery processes for switchgrass (Panicum virgatum). *Indian Chemical Engineer*. Available from https://doi.org/10.1080/00194506.2020.1711535.

Ioannidou, O., Zabaniotou, A., Antonakou, E. V., Papazisi, K. M., Lappas, A. A., & Athanassiou, C. (2009). Investigating the potential for energy, fuel, materials and chemicals production from corn residues (cobs and stalks) by non-catalytic and catalytic pyrolysis in two reactor configurations. *Renewable and Sustainable Energy Reviews*, *13*(4), 750−762. Available from https://doi.org/10.1016/j.rser.2008.01.004.

Khezri, R., Azlinaa, W., & Tana, H. (2016). An experimental investigation of syngas composition from small-scale biomass gasification. *International Journal of Biomass & Renewables*, *5*(1), 6−13.

Kumar, A., Noureddini, H., Demirel, Y., Jones, D. D., & Hanna, M. A. (2009). Simulation of corn stover and distillers grains gasification with ASPEN Plus. *Transactions of the ASABE*, *52*(6), 1989−1995. Available from http://asae.frymulti.com/azdez.asp?JID = 3&AID = 29195&CID = t2009&v = 52&i = 6&T = 2.

Kumar, A., Wang, L., Dzenis, Y. A., Jones, D. D., & Hanna, M. A. (2008). Thermogravimetric characterization of corn stover as gasification and pyrolysis feedstock. *Biomass and Bioenergy*, *32*(5), 460−467. Available from https://doi.org/10.1016/j.biombioe.2007.11.004.

Mustafa, N., Li, C. S., Doevendans, T., Chin, S. A., & Ghani, W. A. W. A. K. (2015). Fluidised bed gasification of Oil Palm Frond (OPF) and Napier Grass (NG): A preliminary study. *Chemical Engineering Transactions*, *45*, 1441−1446. Available from https://doi.org/10.3303/CET1545241.

Otchere-Appiah, G., & Hagan, E. (2014). Potential for electricity generation from maize residues in rural Ghana: A case study of Brong Ahafo region. *International Journal of Renewable Energy Technology Research*, *3*(5), 1−10.

Perkins, C., Woodruff, B., Andrews, L., Lichty, P., Lancaster, B., Weimer, C., & Bingham, A. W. (2008). Synthesis gas production by rapid solar thermal gasification of corn stover. 14th Biennial CSP

SolarPACES (Solar Power and Chemical Energy Systems) Symposium, 4-7 March 2008, Las Vegas, Nevada.

Ramzan, N., Ashraf, A., Naveed, S., & Malik, A. (2011). Simulation of hybrid biomass gasification using Aspen plus: A comparative performance analysis for food, municipal solid and poultry waste. *Biomass and Bioenergy*, *35*(9), 3962–3969. Available from https://doi.org/10.1016/j.biombioe.2011.06.005.

Sun, H., Shao, X., & Ma, Z. (2016). Effect of incorporation nanocrystalline corn straw cellulose and polyethylene glycol on properties of biodegradable films. *Journal of Food Science*, *81*(10), E2529–E2537. Available from https://doi.org/10.1111/1750-3841.13427.

Tavasoli, A., Ahangari, M. G., Soni, C., & Dalai, A. K. (2009). Production of hydrogen and syngas via gasification of the corn and wheat dry distiller grains (DDGS) in a fixed-bed micro reactor. *Fuel Processing Technology*, *90*(4), 472–482. Available from https://doi.org/10.1016/j.fuproc.2009.02.001.

Neural network model for biological waste management systems 18

Ravi Rajamanickam[1] and Divya Baskaran[2]

[1]*Department of Chemical Engineering, Annamalai University, Chidambaram, India* [2]*Department of Chemical Engineering, Sri Venkateswara College of Engineering, Sriperumbudur, Tamil Nadu, India*

Introduction

The hydrophobic chlorinated volatile organic compound (VOC) dichloromethane (DCM) is a health serious hazard through its acute and chronic effects. DCM is considered an efficient solvent and is used in a wide range of industrial applications such as paint removers, pharmaceutical processes, acetate film production, metal degreasing and cleaning, solvent formulation, as a gaseous propellant, and polycarbonate resin production (Deng et al., 2020; Watson et al., 2019). Due to its high vapor pressure (57.3 kPa at 25°C) and low boiling point (39.6°C at 760 mm Hg), DCM easily vaporizes in the environment. Henry's law constant of 3.25 L atm/mol also confirms that the DCM has high volatility in nature and pollutes the atmosphere via gaseous emission (Shirono et al., 2008). In addition, accumulation in the food chain and drinking water supply could result in toxicity to both humans and ecosystems (Ravi et al., 2010a, 2010b; Shestakova & Sillanpää, 2013). Moreover, exposure to highly concentrated DCM has potential adverse human health effects including central nervous system damage, liver and lung cancers, cardiac effects, and mammary gland tumors (Han et al., 2019). The global consumption of DCM has increased by 7.7% per year up to 2012, and it is expected to increase in the future due to its extensive application (Hossaini et al., 2017). The emissions of DCM from individual sites increased from 2.8 pounds to 1,016,106 pounds per year with a median of 5562 pounds and a mean of 3,414,787 pounds (Park et al., 2017). According to the World Health Organization, the maximum limited concentration of DCM in work areas as well as in ambient air should be 360 mg/m^3. As a consequence of these adverse effects on health and the environment, emission control of DCM-like VOCs has been strictly regulated in several countries. Thus such reasonable concerns have given rise to the search for treatment techniques for the removal of contaminated industrial waste gases. With the outstanding recognition of lower energy consumption, eco-friendliness, and less secondary pollution, biological removal techniques are being seen as effective treatment methods for contaminated gaseous organic compounds in low concentrations at higher flow rates than conventional treatments (Li et al., 2020). DCM can be freely degraded under aerobic and anaerobic conditions by various microbial communities using it as a sole carbon and energy source (Almomani et al., 2021). Aerobic biodegradation of DCM produces carbon dioxide (1 mole), hydrochloric acid (2 moles), organic intermediates, and soluble microbial products with a new microbial colony (Mattes et al., 2010). A biotrickling filter reactor (BTF) is a free liquid phase bioreactor that has proven to be superior in the removal of acid by-products and to control pH during the biodegradation of chlorinated VOCs compared with other bioreactors (Quan et al., 2018). Therefore in this chapter, a trial was carried out to develop the BTF for the treatment of poorly soluble DCM. The microbial metabolism of contaminated waste gases comprises a series of steps including adsorption, absorption, diffusion, and biodegradation in the filter bed (Cheng et al., 2016; Yang et al., 2018). The nature of the biodegradability, reactivity, and solubility of the pollutant in the biofilm could affect the removal rate of contaminants in BTF. In addition, the characterization of packing material, ecology of microorganism, nutrient and oxygen availability, pH, and temperature are involved in a successful biofiltration operation (Malakar et al., 2017). Mixed bacterial consortia are readily degraded to DCM, which is derived from activated sludge and polluted water and soil samples in contrast to the pure strain of bacteria (Justicia-Leon et al., 2012; Torgonskaya et al., 2019; Wright et al., 2017). Yu et al. (2014) evaluated the performance of a DCM biotrickling reactor using an isolated strain of *Pandoraea pnomenusa*, where more than 85% DCM removal was achieved at a concentration of $150-700$ mg/m^3. Several steady-state models have been proposed to describe the elimination of volatile pollutants under different gas and liquid loading rates, and some analytical solutions are available (Vergara-Fernández et al., 2018; Wantz et al., 2021). Almenglo et al. (2019) developed a dynamic model to describe an anoxic BTF for hydrogen sulfide removal. An artificial neural network model (ANN) has been shown to be an effective model for waste gas treatment systems such as BTFs, biofilters, and continuous stirred tank reactors. The complex biochemical process and molecular dynamic behavior has made an interest to model the bioreactor performance using a neural network (Reneet al., 2011). In the black box model, multilayer perceptions are interconnected by neurons to form a network called topology. López et al. (2017) and Boojari et al. (2019) developed the two-liquid phase BTF for the treatment of toluene under transient-state conditions and has been effectively modeled using neural network. However, few reports have been published for the different bioreactors for treating various VOCs. Therefore this study is aimed at predicting the performance of a BTF and modified rotating biological contactor (RBC) using ANN for efficient removal of synthetic DCM vapor.

Materials and methods

Experimental details related to the microorganism cultivation, culture media composition, preparation of packing media, experimental setup, and operation of BTF and modified RBC and analytical techniques for each data collection have been given in the authors' earlier reported works (Ravi et al., 2010a, 2010b).

Data-driven modeling approaches

The modeling methodology adopted in this study is shown schematically using a unidirectional block diagram in Fig. 18.1.

Artificial neural network-based predictive modeling

A multilayer perceptron (MLP) is a powerful data-driven modeling tool in ANNs (Heidari et al., 2019). An MLP normally consists of three layers, these being the input layer, a hidden layer, and

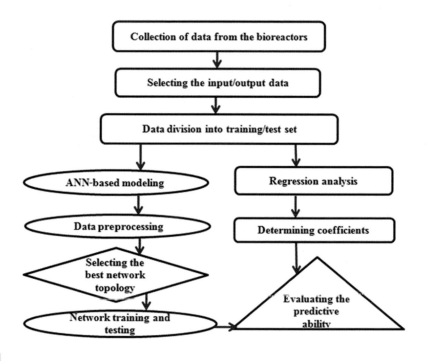

FIGURE 18.1

The methodology used for a modeling study.

an output layer (Fig. 18.2). This is a completely black box model that accepts inputs and produces the desired output for the processing dataset (Baskaran, Sinharoy, Pakshirajan, et al., 2020; Baskaran, Sinharoy, Paul, et al., 2020). Each layer consists of neurons that are interconnected by weights to the previous and following layers. An additional bias term is provided to introduce a threshold for the activation of neurons. The critical parameters of any biological gas treatment process with the greatest effects are inlet pollutant concentration and gas residence time or flow rate. These parameters are easily measurable and are common to any biological reactors, irrespective of the type of filter material and microbial culture used. Hence, these parameters were taken as inputs to the network, whereas removal efficiency (RE) values were used as the output. The datasets used for developing the ANN model for BTF and modified RBC were obtained from Ravi et al. (2010a, 2010b). The modeling methodology adopted in this study consists of the following sequence of steps (Fig. 18.2).

Choosing the activation function

$$f(x) = \frac{1}{1 + e^{-x}} \tag{18.1}$$

The activation function denoted by $f(x)$ defines the output of a neuron in terms of the induced local field x. The most commonly used activation function within the neurons is the logistic

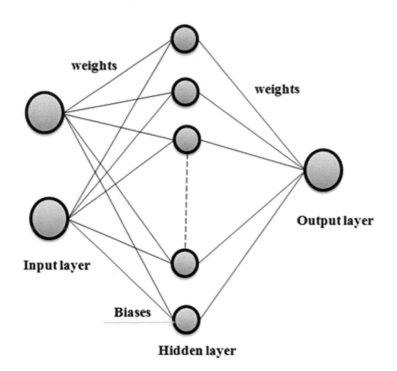

FIGURE 18.2

Schematic representation of a basic three-layered neural network structure consisting of two inputs and one output.

sigmoid function, which takes the form shown in Eq. (18.1). This transfer function produces output in the range of $0-1$ and introduces a certain amount of nonlinearity into the output.

$$E = \frac{1}{2}\sum (O_d - O_p)^2 \tag{18.2}$$

$$\Delta W(t) = \sum_{(s=1)}^{\epsilon} -\eta\frac{\partial E}{\partial W} + \mu\Delta W(t-1) \tag{18.3}$$

Choosing the appropriate training algorithm

The standard backpropagation (BP) algorithm was used to train the respective models (Boojari et al., 2019). A neural network is the most popular method of optimizing the connection weights during network training. This process involves adjusting the weights of the connections in the network so as to minimize the difference between the output vector predicted by the trained network and the desired (experimental) output vector. Hence, when a training vector sample is presented to the network, the global error function (E) is calculated according to Eq. (18.2), where, E is the global error function, O_d is the desired output, and O_p is the output predicted by the network. In

BP, the error of the output layer in the network propagates backward to the input layer through the hidden layer to obtain the final desired output. During the learning process, the connection weights are adjusted using a form of the generalized delta learning rule in order to minimize the error function, E, and obtain the desired output from a given set of inputs. The connection weights (W) are updated using the gradient descent algorithm as described by Rene et al. (2008), which is given in Eq. (18.3), where W is the connection weight between neurons i and j, η is the learning rate, μ is the momentum term, and e is the epoch size, which is the number of training samples presented to the network at any given time. This value was kept constant at 100 during the training process.

Data preprocessing and randomization

$$\hat{X} = \frac{X - X_{min}}{X_{max} - X_{min}} \tag{18.4}$$

The experimental data collected from the biological reactors (BTF and modified RBC) during the continuous operation were randomized to obtain spatial distribution of the data, which accounts for both steady-state and unsteady-state operations. The data were also normalized and scaled to the range of 0−1 using Eq. (18.4), so as to suit the transfer function in the hidden (sigmoid) and output (linear) layers, where $\hat{X}$ is the normalized value, and X_{min} and X_{max} are the minimum and maximum values of X, respectively.

Data division

The experimental observations from individual BTF and modified RBC were divided into training and testing sets. Seventy-five percent (N_{Tr}) of the data points were used for training the network and carrying out regression analysis, and the remaining 25% (N_{Te}) were used for testing the developed models. The testing data were kept aside during the training process and were used only for validation purposes. The performance parameter of RE of both bioreactors was predicted under different operating conditions.

Internal parameters of the network and performance evaluation

$$R = \frac{\sum (x - \bar{x})(y - \bar{y})}{\sqrt{\sum ((x - \bar{x})^2) \sum ((y - \bar{y})^2)}} \tag{18.5}$$

The effects of internal network parameters such as the number of neurons in the hidden layer (N_H), training count (T_c), learning rate (η), and momentum term (μ) on the predictive ability of the network were studied using the 2^k full factorial design. The coefficient of determination (R^2) between the experimental and predicted values was used as an error-estimating index to evaluate the accuracy of the models. R^2 is the square of the correlation coefficient described in Eq. (18.5).

The network configuration yielding the best value of R^2 in the testing dataset was chosen for predicting performance parameters in the test set, where and x and y are experimental and predicted values of the model, and $\bar{x}$ and $\bar{y}$ are the average value of the samples, respectively.

Sensitivity analysis

$$S_{ki,\text{avg}} = \sqrt{\frac{\sum_{p=1}^{p}\left(\left[s_{ki}^{(p)}\right]^2\right)}{p}} \tag{18.6}$$

$$S_{ki,\text{abs}} = \frac{\sqrt{\sum_{p=1}^{p}\left|s_{ki}^{(p)}\right|}}{p} \tag{18.7}$$

$$S_{ki,\text{max}} = \max_{p=1,\dots p}\left\{s_{ki}^{(p)}\right\} \tag{18.8}$$

In order to evaluate the significant effect of the input parameters on the developed models, a sensitivity analysis was carried out by estimating the absolute average sensitivity (AAS). The sensitivity is calculated by summing the changes in the output variables caused by moving the input variables by a small amount over the entire training set. The different sensitivity indices described by Rene et al. (2011) were used in this study for a specific training pattern, p. The mean square average sensitivity (AS) of $S_{ki,\text{avg}}$ is defined in Eq. (18.6). The absolute value AS matrix $S_{ki,\text{abs}}$ is defined in Eq. (18.7). The maximum sensitivity matrix $S_{ki,\text{max}}$ is defined in Eq. (18.8), where $s_{ki}^{(p)}$ is the sensitivity of a trained output O_k and P is the number of training patterns.

Statistical analysis

Statistical calculations and analyses were done using the software MINITAB (Version 12.2, PA, United States). Regression analysis was carried out using the Data Analysis Tool Pack in Microsoft Excel. ANN-based predictive modeling was carried out using the shareware version of the neural network and multivariable statistical modeling software, NNMODEL (Version 1.4; Neural Fusion, NY, United States). The experimental data were preprocessed using the "randomize rows" function in the software—NeuroSolutions for Excel (Version 4.3).

Results and discussions
Process modeling of biological reactors for DCM removal

In any scientific investigation, mathematical models are built to simulate the behavior of a physical system or to explain a hypothesis. Such models can then be used to predict the performance of the systems under various operating conditions (Tomlin & Axelrod, 2007). In order to achieve this, a model was proposed, and experiments were performed to gather relevant data for estimating model parameters and to evaluate the predictability of the model. The approach of pursuing mathematical modeling is basically achieved in two ways: it can be derived in a deductive manner using laws of nature called mechanistic modeling or it can be inferred from a set of data collected from experimental observations called black box modeling (Ismail et al., 2019). In general, the field of environmental engineering relies on a number of complex phenomenological processes, which make mathematical modeling intractable. In particular reference to this study, the extent of biodegradation of pollutants primarily depends on waste gas concentration and composition, moisture content, gas flow rate, microbial ecology and distribution, biofilm characteristics and thickness, nutrient and oxygen availability, temperature, and pH. A considerable amount of modeling work has been done with bioreactors explaining the micro- and macrokinetics of the degradation process (Deshusses et al., 1995; Rajamanickam & Baskaran, 2017). These knowledge-driven models explain the underlying phenomenon of the system with prior knowledge of sensitive parameters such as microbial growth rate, biofilm thickness, overall mass transfer coefficient, partition, distribution and diffusion coefficients, Henry's rate constant, porosity, O_2 consumption rate, and biomass yield coefficient. However, the accurate measurement of these variables in a bioreactor involves elaborate experimentation that is not only complex but also difficult (for instance, biofilm thickness, porosity within the bed, and biofilm—pollutant partition coefficients). Hence, under such circumstances, a mere assumption of the state variables helps a researcher to develop appropriate models describing the performance of the system. The most proficient way to overcome such practical limitations is to quantify or predict the performance of the system under consideration from the knowledge gained from experimental trials using techniques capable of indicating the nonlinearity of the process (Abiodun et al., 2018). These data-driven models, borrowed heavily from artificial intelligence techniques, are based on limited knowledge of the modeling process and can rely on the data describing the input and output functions. ANN is used to make an abstract and generalization of the process behavior, and plays a complementary role to knowledge-driven models. In this study, the experimental data from laboratory-scale biological reactors (BTF and modified RBC) treating DCM were used to formulate different models based on regression analysis and neural networks. The parameters that are readily available in any biodegradation process in the gas phase are inlet pollutant concentration and gas flow rate. These parameters can be used as inputs to predict the performance in any data-driven model. Two modeling approaches were tested to evaluate the performance of the biological reactors: the first is a simple regression analysis (nonlinear) and the second is the use of ANNs to predict the RE. There are few reports in the literature on the use of these types of models for predicting the performance of biological reactor systems of BTF and modified RBC (Khalil Arya & Ayati, 2013; López et al., 2014). This being the first of its kind to comprehensively report on the application of ANNs in biological reactors for DCM removal, substantial effort has been taken to analyze these ANN models and pertinent information has been given to understanding the effect of internal parameters that are more likely to affect the network topology.

Artificial neural modeling of the different biological reactors

The second part of the data-driven modeling study explores the possibility of using ANN as a predictive tool for performance evaluation in the biological reactor. The same approach used for developing the regression models was used for formulating ANN-based predictive models also by training three-fourths of the available data and testing the developed model with the rest of the experimental data. The effect of internal network parameters on the architecture of the network on the model fitting was evaluated by a statistical evaluation procedure, and the degree of model prediction was ascertained by the determination coefficient R^2 between the experimental and model predicted values. A sensitivity analysis was performed for the developed model to examine the influence of input parameters on the output of the network.

Effect of internal network parameters on the network architecture-modified RBC

The factorial design of experiments was used to choose the best network architecture, as it requires the minimum set of runs. The run order and the values of the internal parameter chosen (low and high levels) for the ANN models are given in Table 18.1. The other network factors were set to maximize the performance during training for the developed models in this study. The number of neurons in the input layer (N_I) and output layer (N_o) was equal to the number of input and output parameters chosen for the models, respectively. The R^2 of the test data (determination of coefficient between the experimental RE and ANN predicted value) was used as the response to obtain the best network with the least error in the training data. The main effect plots from Fig. 18.3 show the effects of each of the internal training parameters on the R^2 value of the training dataset. Increasing the number of neurons in the hidden layer had very little effect on the R^2 value, but an increase in the training count, learning rates, and momentum term values increased the R^2 value. Changes in input-hidden layer learning rates and momentum term showed a significant increase in the R^2 value. Maier and Dandy (1998) studied the effects of internal parameters such as epoch size, momentum, learning rate, transfer function, initial weight distribution, and a number of neurons on the performance of BP neural network with special reference to forecasting salinity in a river. Their study used randomized trial-and-error runs for choosing the values of the internal parameters, whereas in this work we used a much simpler and statistically significant 2^5 full factorial design by studying the effects at two levels, that is, low and high, for each of the factors. Statistical analysis in the form of ANOVA (analysis of variance) was performed to ascertain the influence of various parameters on the response variable, R^2. The main effects were by and large more significant than the interaction effects as described by their high F and low P values (14.76, .065). Deshmukh et al. (2012) reported a comparison of the radial basis function neural network and response surface methodology for predicting the performance

Table 18.1 Ranges of input and output parameters used for training and testing an ANN model developed to represent biodegradation of DCM in modified RBC.

Parameter	Training, N_{Tr}-180			Testing, N_{Te}-59		
	Min	Max	Mean	Min	Max	Mean
Input						
DCM initial concentration (g/m^3)	0.1809	1.4165	0.79872	0.1802	1.4129	0.7955
Flow rate (LPM)	5.3	12.86	9.08	5.3	12.86	9.08
Output						
DCM removal efficiency, %	28.26	76.56	52.41	26.3454	76.416	51.3807

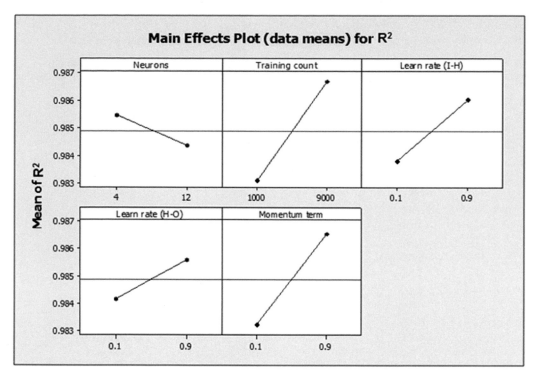

FIGURE 18.3

The main effects plot of network internal parameters on the R^2 value for DCM removal during training in RBC performance.

of biofilter treating toluene. The R^2 for each combination of the parameters is given in Table 18.2 for testing data. The high values of R^2 observed in this study indicate the ability of a trained network with two levels of internal parameters to satisfactorily explain the system behavior. Of the 33 trials of neural networks, the one which gave the maximum R^2 for test data was chosen as the best network architecture. The best network for the ANN model for DCM removal was obtained with the following conditions of the internal network parameters: $N_H = 4$, $T_c = 1000$, $\eta_{ih} = 0.90$, $\eta_{ho} = 0.1$, and $\mu = 0.9$. With these best network conditions, the ANN model was applied to the testing data, and predicted removal efficiencies were compared with the experimental values. Rene et al. (2006) developed two models using inlet benzene, toluene, and xylene treated in a BTF. During statistical analysis, the predictive capability of the model decreased when increasing the N_H and η_{ih} and the model predictability increasing with increasing T_c and μ from 1000 to 10,000 and 0.1 to 0.9.

Predictive capability of the model for modified RBC

Figs. 18.4 and 18.5 depict the experimental and ANN model predicted REs in the training and testing data, respectively. The predictive capacities of the models were also evaluated in terms of the

Table 18.2 Full 2^5 factorial design for estimating the best network architecture along with their determination coefficients for training and test data for DCM removal in RBC.

Run order	Neurons, N_H	Training count, T_c	Learning rate, h_{ih}	Learning rate, h_{ho}	Momentum term, m	Determination coefficient, R^2 (testing)
1	4	1000	0.1	0.1	0.1	0.97678
2	12	1000	0.1	0.1	0.1	0.97169
3	4	9000	0.1	0.1	0.1	0.98577
4	12	9000	0.1	0.1	0.1	0.98582
5	4	1000	0.9	0.1	0.1	0.98068
6	12	1000	0.9	0.1	0.1	0.97808
7	4	9000	0.9	0.1	0.1	0.98752
8	12	9000	0.9	0.1	0.1	0.98718
9	4	1000	0.1	0.9	0.1	0.98115
10	12	1000	0.1	0.9	0.1	0.97992
11	4	9000	0.1	0.9	0.1	0.98582
12	12	9000	0.1	0.9	0.1	0.98572
14	12	1000	0.9	0.9	0.1	0.98578
13	4	1000	0.9	0.9	0.1	0.98611
15	4	9000	0.9	0.9	0.1	0.98714
16	12	9000	0.9	0.9	0.1	0.98657
17	4	1000	0.1	0.1	0.9	0.98604
18	12	1000	0.1	0.1	0.9	0.98593
19	4	9000	0.1	0.1	0.9	0.98673
20	12	9000	0.1	0.1	0.9	0.98536
21	4	1000	0.9	0.1	0.9	0.98873
22	12	1000	0.9	0.1	0.9	0.98608
23	4	9000	0.9	0.1	0.9	0.98747
24	12	9000	0.9	0.1	0.9	0.98858
25	4	1000	0.1	0.9	0.9	0.98603
26	12	1000	0.1	0.9	0.9	0.9857
27	4	9000	0.1	0.9	0.9	0.98729
28	12	9000	0.1	0.9	0.9	0.98639
29	4	1000	0.9	0.9	0.9	0.98707
30	12	1000	0.9	0.9	0.9	0.98355
31	4	9000	0.9	0.9	0.9	0.98712
32	12	9000	0.9	0.9	0.9	0.98846
33	8	5000	0.5	0.5	0.5	0.95446

relative deviations $(RE_{exp} - RE_{pred})/RE_{exp}$ for the ANN model. The performance of the RBC for the DCM removal indicated by these deviations is shown in Figs. 18.6 and 18.7 for the training and testing data, respectively. With a few exceptions, the values of the variables showed a good agreement (within 20% error) with the experimental data shown in Fig. 18.8. Table 18.3 presents the

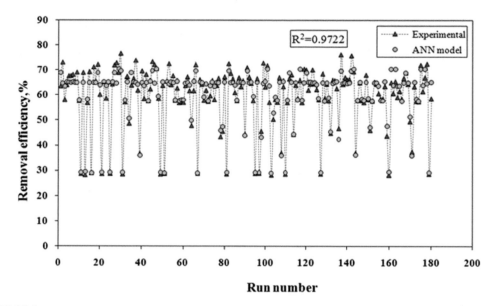

FIGURE 18.4

Comparison of experimental and predicted values of DCM removal efficiency in RBC during model training.

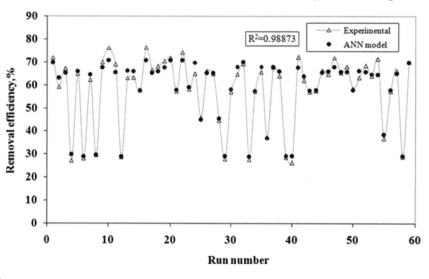

FIGURE 18.5

Comparison of experimental and predicted values of DCM removal efficiency in RBC during model testing.

weights of the neural network model used for predicting the REs. Elías et al. (2006) demonstrated a laboratory-scale biofilter packed with pig manure and sawdust. In this modeling, a 2-2-1 network topology was found and the predicted RE was well fitted with experimental efficiency which has a high R^2 value of 0.9200 which is lower than our R^2 value (0.9722) obtained in the present study.

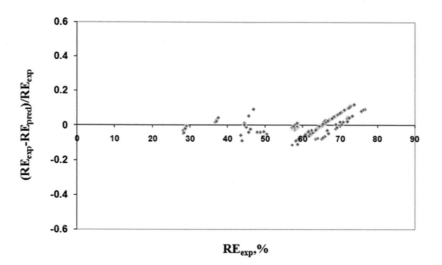

FIGURE 18.6

Relative deviations between predicted (RE_{pred}) and experimental (RE_{exp}) values of DCM removal efficiency in RBC from ANN models for data in the training set.

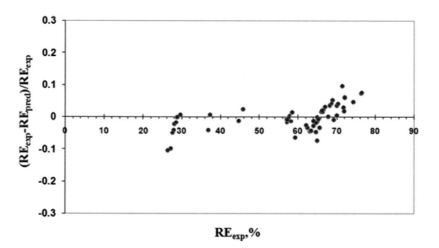

FIGURE 18.7

Relative deviations between predicted (RE_{pred}) and experimental (RE_{exp}) values of DCM removal efficiency in RBC from ANN model for data in the testing set.

Sensitivity analysis of inputs

The strength of the relationship between the output variable and the input variable is normally estimated by carrying out a sensitivity analysis, that is, a small change in the input variable could have

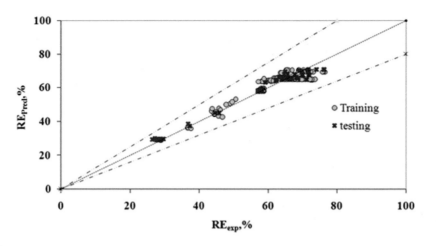

FIGURE 18.8

Comparison between experimental and predicted values of DCM removal efficiency in RBC.

Table 18.3 Weights ascertained after neural network training for the prediction of DCM removal efficiency in RBC.

Neurons	W_{ih}			Neurons	W_{ho}
	X_1	X_2	Bias		Y
1	6.1421	4.6916	−7.1395	1	−3.3312
2	−3.3529	−0.7775	4.0728	2	1.2345
3	−5.0692	−5.9417	2.7812	3	−3.8582
4	1.68212	−2.6723	−0.04306	4	1.2721
				Bias	−0.7918

W_{ih}, Weights between input and hidden layers; W_{ho}, weights between hidden and output layers.

a very large and significant impact on the output variable. This analysis was performed for the ANN model after determining the best network architecture. The sensitivity is calculated by summing the changes in the output variables caused by moving the input variables by a small amount over the entire training set. There are three variables accumulated during the calculation. The AAS variable is the average of the absolute values of the change in the output (Ravi et al., 2010b; Shestakova & Sillanpää, 2013). This value is then divided by the total amount of change for all input variables to normalize the values. The AS is calculated in the same way as the AAS variable except the absolute values are not taken. If the direction of the change in the output variable is always the same, then both these sensitivity values would be identical. The third variable calculated is the peak sensitivity (PS) and the row in the training data where it occurred. The result from this analysis is given in Table 18.4. These results indicate that inlet concentration plays a major role in predicting the RE; flow rate appears to have a lesser effect. Rene et al. (2009) identified the most influential input parameter of the developed model, and sensitivity analysis in the form of AAS and

Table 18.4 Sensitivity analysis of process input variables after network training (N_{Tr}-180) in modified RBC.

Order	Parameter	AAS	AS	PS	Peak row
1	DCM concentration	0.54305	−0.43657	0.01542	135
2	Flow rate	0.45695	−0.15846	0.001437	150

AS was determined. Here, the + or − sign shown in the AS values indicates the positive or negative effect of that variable on the RE of the system. The negative value of the AS shows that, apparently decreases the performance of the biofilter.

Removal of DCM in the biotrickling filter

In the effect of internal network parameters on the network architecture-modified RBC section, ANN models developed for the removal of DCM in modified RBC performed well in predicting the REs. Hence, ANN was attempted for the removal of DCM in BTF. Here X_1 and X_2 are the two input variables and also Y_1 is the response as DCM RE.

Effect of internal network parameters on the network architecture

The range of parameters chosen for the ANN modeling is shown in Table 18.5. The value of R^2 is significant for studying the effect of network parameters as well as for finding the best network architecture. The values of R^2 for the test data were used as the response to obtain the best network with the least error in the training data. The main effect plot is given in Fig. 18.9. The decreasing effect for N_H is shown clearly. The learning rate (η_{ih}) increases the R^2 value but, in general, this increasing effect is not significant. The learning rate (η_{ho}), momentum term (η), and training count increase as R^2 increases. Cabrera et al. (2007) developed the dynamic neural network observer in the biofilter for modeling toluene elimination capacity performances. About 350 data points were trained and tested to predict the elimination capacity, which is perfectly fitted with the experimental data points. The maximum R^2 value of 1 has been achieved by using Sigmoid Tensorflow as network parameters. The factorial design table with responses obtained for training and test data is shown in Table 18.6. The best network for the ANN model for DCM removal was obtained with the following conditions of the internal network parameters: $N_H = 4$, $T_c = 9000$, $\eta_{ih} = 0.1$, $\eta_{ho} = 0.1$, and $\mu = 0.9$. With this best network condition of the ANN model, the predicted values from the model were compared with the experimental values using the training data. Rene et al. (2011) modeled the styrene continuous-stirred tank bioreactor using BP with gradient descent neural network. The obtained network parameters are $T_c = 10,000-50,000$, $h = 0.75$, and $m = 0.9$ with topology of 2-5-1 to attain a high R^2 value of 0.9667. The value of the momentum term is higher than the present study, which is due to the type of reactor performance and the number of data points used for the neural modeling. The comparison plots are shown in Figs. 18.10 and 18.11 for training and testing response, respectively. The maximum obtained R^2 values of 0.9752 and 0.9844 were achieved for training and testing

Table 18.5 Range of input and output parameters used for training and testing of the ANN model developed to represent the biodegradation of DCM in BTF.

Parameter	Training, N_{Tr}-110			Testing, N_{Te}-36		
	Min	Max	Mean	Min	Max	Mean
Input						
DCM initial concentration (g/m^3)	0.351	1.19	0.7705	0.3595	1.1832	0.7713
Flow rate (LPM)	0.491	0.818	0.6545	0.491	0.818	0.6545
Output						
DCM removal efficiency (%)	25.2	74.63	49.915	25.02	73.45	49.235

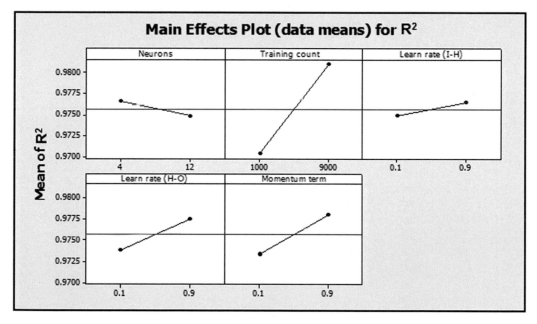

FIGURE 18.9

The main effects plot of network internal parameters on the R^2 value during the training of ANN models for the biodegradation of DCM in BTF.

response, respectively. The RE has been increased due to a significant increase in momentum value and learning rate in the bioreactor performance modeling (Ravi et al., 2010a).

Predictive capability and sensitivity of the ANN model

The experimental and ANN model-predicted REs in the test data are described in Figs. 18.10 and 18.11, respectively. The predictive capacity of the model was also evaluated in terms of the relative

Table 18.6 Full 2^5 factorial design for estimating the best network architecture along with their determination coefficients for training and test data for DCM removal in BTF.

Run order	Neurons, N_H	Training count, T_c	Learning rate, h_{ih}	Learning rate, h_{ho}	Momentum term, m	Determination coefficient, R^2 (testing)
1	4	1000	0.1	0.1	0.1	0.957561
2	12	1000	0.1	0.1	0.1	0.957149
3	4	9000	0.1	0.1	0.1	0.981563
4	12	9000	0.1	0.1	0.1	0.976301
5	4	1000	0.9	0.1	0.1	0.973343
6	12	1000	0.9	0.1	0.1	0.970059
7	4	9000	0.9	0.1	0.1	0.957522
8	12	9000	0.9	0.1	0.1	0.983183
9	4	1000	0.1	0.9	0.1	0.972381
10	12	1000	0.1	0.9	0.1	0.969803
11	4	9000	0.1	0.9	0.1	0.981791
12	12	9000	0.1	0.9	0.1	0.98204
14	12	1000	0.9	0.9	0.1	0.974541
13	4	1000	0.9	0.9	0.1	0.969838
15	4	9000	0.9	0.9	0.1	0.98419
16	12	9000	0.9	0.9	0.1	0.982626
17	4	1000	0.1	0.1	0.9	0.973188
18	12	1000	0.1	0.1	0.9	0.969246
19	4	9000	0.1	0.1	0.9	0.984395
20	12	9000	0.1	0.1	0.9	0.983671
21	4	1000	0.9	0.1	0.9	0.981512
22	12	1000	0.9	0.1	0.9	0.96712
23	4	9000	0.9	0.1	0.9	0.983927
24	12	9000	0.9	0.1	0.9	0.981871
25	4	1000	0.1	0.9	0.9	0.972381
26	12	1000	0.1	0.9	0.9	0.96903
27	4	9000	0.1	0.9	0.9	0.984032
28	12	9000	0.1	0.9	0.9	0.983842
29	4	1000	0.9	0.9	0.9	0.979957
30	12	1000	0.9	0.9	0.9	0.969933
31	4	9000	0.9	0.9	0.9	0.982756
32	12	9000	0.9	0.9	0.9	0.981283
33	8	5000	0.5	0.5	0.5	0.945212

deviations $(RE_{exp} - RE_{pred})/RE_{exp}$ for the ANN model. The performance of the BTF for DCM removal is indicated by deviations shown in Figs. 18.12 and 18.13. The model-predicted removal of DCM showed good agreement (within 20% error) with the experimental data (Fig. 18.14). The deviation is much less and can be negligible due to achieving a high value of R^2 in both the

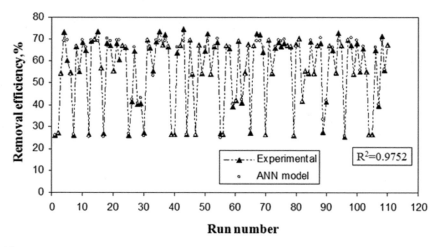

FIGURE 18.10

Comparison of experimental and predicted values of DCM removal efficiency in BTF during model training.

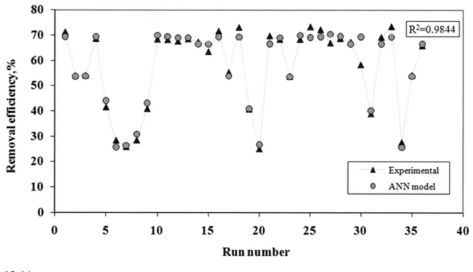

FIGURE 18.11

Comparison of experimental and predicted values of DCM removal in BTF during model testing.

training and testing sets. Table 18.7 presents the weights of the neural network model developed for predicting the removal efficiencies. The input and hidden layer weight matrix and biases of input and output layers are developed to discover the optimum neural network topology of 2-4-1 for predicting the reactor performance (Baskaran, Sinharoy, Pakshirajan, et al., 2020). The results from a sensitivity analysis are given in Table 18.8. These results indicate that the pollutant

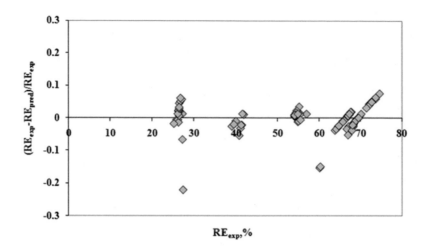

FIGURE 18.12

Relative deviations between predicted (RE_{pred}) and experimental (RE_{exp}) values of DCM removal in BTF by the ANN model for data in the training set.

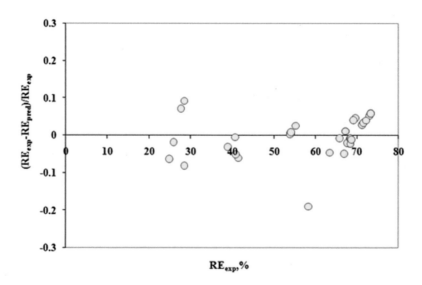

FIGURE 18.13

Relative deviations between predicted (RE_{pred}) and experimental (RE_{exp}) values of DCM removal in BTF by the ANN model for the test dataset.

concentration plays a major role in predicting the RE and the flow rate appears to have slightly less effect. Baskaran et al. (2019) reported the experimental studies and neural network modeling of the removal of trichloroethylene vapor in a biofilter. To predict the accuracy, the different statistical parameters were checked and an accuracy factor of 1.0039 was found which revealed that the inlet

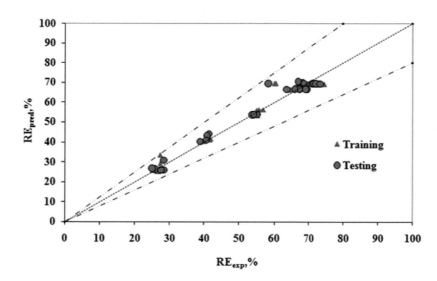

FIGURE 18.14

Comparison of experimental and predicted values of DCM removal efficiency in BTF during model training.

Table 18.7 Weights ascertained after neural network training in the biodegradation of DCM in biotrickling filter.

Neurons	W_{ih}			W_{ho}	
	X_1	X_2	Bias	Neurons	Y_1
1	0.22502	5.2512	−6.0529	1	−25.2312
2	−8.6998	−3.399	9.9312	2	−12.2345
3	−4.3444	1.3321	0.4751	3	−9.5124
4	1.1212	−2.2699	−0.409	4	−2.9512
				Bias	3.5213

Note: W_{ih}, *Weights between input and hidden layers;* W_{ho}, *weights between hidden and output layers.*

Table 18.8 Sensitivity analysis of process input variables after network training for DCM removal in biotrickling filter (N_{Tr}-23).

Order	Parameter	AAS	AS	PS	Peak row
1	DCM concentration	0.61293	−0.612	0.03374	64
2	Flow rate	0.38707	−0.35985	0.03642	54

pollutant concentration has great ability for predicting RE. In recent years the neural network has been used in the field of environmental biotechnology, particularly in bioreactors for modeling the treatment of waste gas streams. Chairez et al. (2009) applied a dynamic neural network observer to model laboratory-scale toluene biofilter. Similarly, more reports have been published to model the different types of bioreactor performance using the neural network model (Abdel daiem et al., 2021; Salehi & Sigit Lestari, 2021; Szulczyński et al., 2019). The retrieved data from the real-time bioreactor can be merged with the previously available original data, and the neural network can be trained in online mode effectively. Therefore the accurately predicted performance of a modified RBC and BTF can be used for real-time monitoring and control of waste gas treatment systems.

Conclusion

ANN-based models were successfully developed using easily measurable input parameters (inlet concentration and flow rate) and tested to predict the performance of bioreactor systems (RBC and BTF). After proper optimization of network parameters and through vigorous training and testing, the best network for BTF was obtained with the following conditions of the internal network parameters: $N_H = 4$, $T_c = 9000$, $\eta_{ih} = 0.1$, $\eta_{ho} = 0.1$, and $\mu = 0.9$ and for RBC the internal network parameters: $N_H = 4$, $T_c = 1000$, $\eta_{ih} = 0.1$, $\eta_{ho} = 0.1$, and $\mu = 0.9$. The results from sensitivity analysis showed that the most critical factor that antagonistically affects the RE in both the bioreactors was pollutant concentration and flow rate, which appears to have a slightly lesser effect. The results from this study reveal that the neural network model can predict the exact performance of both bioreactors for DCM treatment. Therefore the proposed model in environmental biotechnology proved that is a potential alternative model through training and testing in a safer way.

References

Abdel daiem, M. M., Hatata, A., El-Gohary, E. H., Abd-Elhamid, H. F., & Said, N. (2021). Application of an artificial neural network for the improvement of agricultural drainage water quality using a submerged bio-filter. *Environmental Science and Pollution Research*, 28(5), 5854–5866. Available from https://doi.org/10.1007/s11356-020-10964-0.

Abiodun, O. I., Jantan, A., Dada, K. V., Mohamed, N. A., Arshad, H., & Omolara, A. E. (2018). State-of-the-art in artificial neural network applications: A survey.

Almenglo, F., Ramírez, M., & Cantero, D. (2019). Application of response surface methodology for H2S removal from biogas by a pilot anoxic biotrickling filter. *ChemEngineering*, 3(3), 1–12. Available from https://doi.org/10.3390/chemengineering3030066.

Almomani, F., Rene, E. R., Veiga, M. C., Bhosale, R. R., & Kennes, C. (2021). Treatment of waste gas contaminated with dichloromethane using photocatalytic oxidation, biodegradation and their combinations. *Journal of Hazardous Materials*, 405. Available from https://doi.org/10.1016/j.jhazmat.2020.123735.

Baskaran, D., Rajamanickam, R., & Pakshirajan, K. (2019). Experimental studies and neural network modeling of the removal of trichloroethylene vapor in a biofilter. *Journal of Environmental Management*, 250. Available from https://doi.org/10.1016/j.jenvman.2019.109385.

Baskaran, D., Sinharoy, A., Pakshirajan, K., & Rajamanickam, R. (2020). Gas-phase trichloroethylene removal by Rhodococcus opacus using an airlift bioreactor and its modeling by artificial neural network. *Chemosphere*, 247, 125806. Available from https://doi.org/10.1016/j.chemosphere.2019.125806.

Baskaran, D., Sinharoy, A., Paul, T., Pakshirajan, K., & Rajamanickam, R. (2020). Performance evaluation and neural network modeling of trichloroethylene removal using a continuously operated two-phase partitioning bioreactor. *Environmental Technology and Innovation*, *17*. Available from https://doi.org/10.1016/j.eti.2019.100568.

Boojari, M. A., Zamir, S. M., Rene, E. R., & Shojaosadati, S. A. (2019). Performance assessment of gas-phase toluene removal in one- and two-liquid phase biotrickling filters using artificial neural networks. *Chemosphere*, *234*, 388−394. Available from https://doi.org/10.1016/j.chemosphere.2019.06.040.

Cabrera, A. I., Chairez, J. I., & Ramírez, M. G. (2007). Computational soft sensor for fungal biofiltration process. *IFAC Proceedings Volumes*, *40*(4), 399−404. Available from https://doi.org/10.3182/20070604-3-mx-2914.00068.

Chairez, I., García-Peña, I., & Cabrera, A. (2009). Dynamic numerical reconstruction of a fungal biofiltration system using differential neural network. *Journal of Process Control*, *19*(7), 1103−1110. Available from https://doi.org/10.1016/j.jprocont.2008.12.009.

Cheng, Y., He, H., Yang, C., Zeng, G., Li, X., Chen, H., & Yu, G. (2016). Challenges and solutions for biofiltration of hydrophobic volatile organic compounds. *Biotechnology Advances*, *34*(6), 1091−1102. Available from https://doi.org/10.1016/j.biotechadv.2016.06.007.

Deng, H., Pan, T., Zhang, Y., Wang, L., Wu, Q., Ma, J., Shan, W., & He, H. (2020). Adsorptive removal of toluene and dichloromethane from humid exhaust on MFI, BEA and FAU zeolites: An experimental and theoretical study. *Chemical Engineering Journal*, *394*. Available from https://doi.org/10.1016/j.cej.2020.124986.

Deshmukh, S. C., Senthilnath, J., Dixit, R. M., Malik, S. N., Pandey, R. A., Vaidya, A. N., Omkar, S. N., & Mudliar, S. N. (2012). Comparison of radial basis function neural network and response surface methodology for predicting performance of biofilter treating toluene. *Journal of Software Engineering and Applications*, 595−603. Available from https://doi.org/10.4236/jsea.2012.58068.

Deshusses, M. A., Hamer, G., & Dunn, I. J. (1995). Behavior of biofilters for waste air biotreatment. 1. Dynamic model development. *Environmental Science and Technology*, *29*(4), 1048−1058. Available from https://doi.org/10.1021/es00004a027.

Elías, A., Ibarra-Berastegi, G., Arias, R., & Barona, A. (2006). Neural networks as a tool for control and management of a biological reactor for treating hydrogen sulphide. *Bioprocess and Biosystems Engineering*, *29*(2), 129−136. Available from https://doi.org/10.1007/s00449-006-0062-3.

Han, M. F., Wang, C., Yang, N. Y., & Li, Y. F. (2019). Determination of design parameters and cost-effectiveness analysis for a two-liquid phase biofilter treating gaseous dichloromethane. *Biochemical Engineering Journal*, *143*, 81−90. Available from https://doi.org/10.1016/j.bej.2018.12.018.

Heidari, A. A., Faris, H., Aljarah, I., & Mirjalili, S. (2019). An efficient hybrid multilayer perceptron neural network with grasshopper optimization. *Soft Computing*, *23*(17), 7941−7958. Available from https://doi.org/10.1007/s00500-018-3424-2.

Hossaini, R., Chipperfield, M. P., Montzka, S. A., Leeson, A. A., Dhomse, S. S., & Pyle, J. A. (2017). The increasing threat to stratospheric ozone from dichloromethane. *Nature Communications*, *8*(1), 1−9.

Ismail, S., Elsamadony, M., Fujii, M., & Tawfik, A. (2019). Evaluation and optimization of anammox baffled reactor (AnBR) by artificial neural network modeling and economic analysis. *Bioresource Technology*, *271*, 500−506. Available from https://doi.org/10.1016/j.biortech.2018.09.004.

Justicia-Leon, S. D., Ritalahti, K. M., Mack, E. E., & Löffler, F. E. (2012). Dichloromethane fermentation by a Dehalobacter sp. in an enrichment culture derived from pristine river sediment. *Applied and Environmental Microbiology*, *78*(4), 1288−1291. Available from https://doi.org/10.1128/AEM.07325-11.

Khalil Arya, F., & Ayati, B. (2013). Application of artificial neural networks for predicting cod removal efficiencies of rotating disks and packed-cage rbcs in treating hydroquinone. *Iranian Journal of Science and Technology - Transactions of Civil Engineering*, *37*(2), 325−336. Available from http://www.shirazu.ac.ir/en/index.php?page_id = 1691.

Li, T., Li, H., & Li, C. (2020). A review and perspective of recent research in biological treatment applied in removal of chlorinated volatile organic compounds from waste air. *Chemosphere*, *250*. Available from https://doi.org/10.1016/j.chemosphere.2020.126338.

López, M. E., Boger, Z., Rene, E. R., Veiga, M. C., & Kennes, C. (2014). Transient-state studies and neural modeling of the removal of a gas-phase pollutant mixture in a biotrickling filter. *Journal of Hazardous Materials*, *269*, 45−55. Available from https://doi.org/10.1016/j.jhazmat.2013.11.023.

López, M. E., Rene, E. R., Boger, Z., Veiga, M. C., & Kennes, C. (2017). Modelling the removal of volatile pollutants under transient conditions in a two-stage bioreactor using artificial neural networks. *Journal of Hazardous Materials*, *324*, 100−109. Available from https://doi.org/10.1016/j.jhazmat.2016.03.018.

Maier, H. R., & Dandy, G. C. (1998). The effect of internal parameters and geometry on the performance of back-propagation neural networks: An empirical study. *Environmental Modelling and Software*, *13*(2), 193−209. Available from https://doi.org/10.1016/S1364-8152(98)00020-6.

Malakar, S., Saha, P. D., Baskaran, D., & Rajamanickam, R. (2017). Comparative study of biofiltration process for treatment of VOCs emission from petroleum refinery wastewater—A review. *Environmental Technology and Innovation*, *8*, 441−461. Available from https://doi.org/10.1016/j.eti.2017.09.007.

Mattes, T. E., Alexander, A. K., & Coleman, N. V. (2010). Aerobic biodegradation of the chloroethenes: Pathways, enzymes, ecology, and evolution. *FEMS Microbiology Reviews*, *34*(4), 445−475. Available from https://doi.org/10.1111/j.1574-6976.2010.00210.x.

Park, A. S., Ritz, B., Ling, C., Cockburn, M., & Heck, J. E. (2017). Exposure to ambient dichloromethane in pregnancy and infancy from industrial sources and childhood cancers in California. *International Journal of Hygiene and Environmental Health*, *220*(7), 1133−1140. Available from https://doi.org/10.1016/j.ijheh.2017.06.006.

Quan, Y., Wu, H., Guo, C., Han, Y., & Yin, C. (2018). Enhancement of TCE removal by a static magnetic field in a fungal biotrickling filter. *Bioresource Technology*, *259*, 365−372. Available from https://doi.org/10.1016/j.biortech.2018.03.031.

Rajamanickam, R., & Baskaran, D. (2017). Biodegradation of gaseous toluene with mixed microbial consortium in a biofilter: Steady state and transient operation. *Bioprocess and Biosystems Engineering*, *40*(12), 1801−1812. Available from https://doi.org/10.1007/s00449-017-1834-7.

Ravi, R., Philip, L., & Swaminathan, T. (2010a). An intelligent neural network model for evaluating performance of compost biofilter treating dichloromethane vapours. In *Proceedings of the Duke-UAM conference in biofiltration for air pollution control* (pp. 49−57).

Ravi, R., Philip, L., & Swaminathan, T. (2010b). Comparison of biological reactors (biofilter, biotrickling filter andmodified RBC) for treating dichloromethane vapors. *Journal of Chemical Technology and Biotechnology*, *85*(5), 634−639. Available from https://doi.org/10.1002/jctb.2344.

Rene, E. R., Estefanía López, M., Veiga, M. C., & Kennes, C. (2011). Neural network models for biological waste-gas treatment systems. *New Biotechnology*, *29*(1), 56−73. Available from https://doi.org/10.1016/j.nbt.2011.07.001.

Rene, E. R., Joo, K. S., & Park, H. S. (2008). Experimental results and neural prediction of sequencing batch reactor performance under different operational conditions. *Journal of Environmental Informatics*, *11*(2), 51−61. Available from https://doi.org/10.3808/jei.200800111.

Rene, E. R., Maliyekkal, S. M., Philip, L., & Swaminathan, T. (2006). Back-propagation neural network for performance prediction in trickling bed air biofilter. *International Journal of Environment and Pollution*, *28*(3−4), 382−401. Available from https://doi.org/10.1504/IJEP.2006.011218.

Rene, E. R., Veiga, M. C., & Kennes, C. (2009). Experimental and neural model analysis of styrene removal from polluted air in a biofilter. *Journal of Chemical Technology and Biotechnology*, *84*(7), 941−948. Available from https://doi.org/10.1002/jctb.2130.

Salehi, R., & Sigit Lestari, R. A. (2021). Predicting the performance of a desulfurizing bio-filter using an artificial neural network (ANN) model. *Environmental Engineering Research*, *26*(6). Available from https://doi.org/10.4491/eer.2020.462, 200462-0.

Shestakova, M., & Sillanpää, M. (2013). Removal of dichloromethane from ground and wastewater: A review. *Chemosphere*, *93*(7), 1258−1267. Available from https://doi.org/10.1016/j.chemosphere.2013.07.022.

Shirono, K., Morimatsu, T., & Takemura, F. (2008). Gas solubilities (CO2, O2, Ar, N2, H 2, and He) in liquid chlorinated methanes. *Journal of Chemical and Engineering Data*, *53*(8), 1867−1871. Available from https://doi.org/10.1021/je800200j.

Szulczyński, B., Rybarczyk, P., Gospodarek, M., & Gębicki, J. (2019). Biotrickling filtration of n-butanol vapors: Process monitoring using electronic nose and artificial neural network. *Monatshefte Für Chemie - Chemical Monthly*, *150*(9), 1667−1673. Available from https://doi.org/10.1007/s00706-019-02456-w.

Tomlin, C. J., & Axelrod, J. D. (2007). Biology by numbers: Mathematical modelling in developmental biology. *Nature Reviews Genetics*, *8*(5), 331−340. Available from https://doi.org/10.1038/nrg2098.

Torgonskaya, M. L., Zyakun, A. M., Trotsenko, Y. A., Laurinavichius, K. S., Kümmel, S., Vuilleumier, S., & Richnow, H. H. (2019). Individual stages of bacterial dichloromethane degradation mapped by carbon and chlorine stable isotope analysis. *Journal of Environmental Sciences (China)*, *78*, 147−160. Available from https://doi.org/10.1016/j.jes.2018.09.008.

Vergara-Fernández, A., Revah, S., Moreno-Casas, P., & Scott, F. (2018). Biofiltration of volatile organic compounds using fungi and its conceptual and mathematical modeling. *Biotechnology Advances*, *36*(4), 1079−1093. Available from https://doi.org/10.1016/j.biotechadv.2018.03.008.

Wantz, E., Kane, A., Lhuissier, M., Amrane, A., Audic, J.-L., & Couvert, A. (2021). A mathematical model for VOCs removal in a treatment process coupling absorption and biodegradation. *Chemical Engineering Journal*, 130106. Available from https://doi.org/10.1016/j.cej.2021.130106.

Watson, J., Lu, J., de Souza, R., Si, B., Zhang, Y., & Liu, Z. (2019). Effects of the extraction solvents in hydrothermal liquefaction processes: Biocrude oil quality and energy conversion efficiency. *Energy*, *167*, 189−197. Available from https://doi.org/10.1016/j.energy.2018.11.003.

Wright, J., Kirchner, V., Bernard, W., Ulrich, N., McLimans, C., Campa, M. F., Hazen, T., Macbeth, T., Marabello, D., McDermott, J., Mackelprang, R., Roth, K., & Lamendella, R. (2017). Bacterial community dynamics in dichloromethane-contaminated groundwater undergoing natural attenuation. *Frontiers in Microbiology*, 8. Available from https://doi.org/10.3389/fmicb.2017.02300.

Yang, C., Qian, H., Li, X., Cheng, Y., He, H., Zeng, G., & Xi, J. (2018). Simultaneous removal of multicomponent VOCs in biofilters. *Trends in Biotechnology*, *36*(7), 673−685. Available from https://doi.org/10.1016/j.tibtech.2018.02.004.

Yu, J., Cai, W., Cheng, Z., & Chen, J. (2014). Degradation of dichloromethane by an isolated strain Pandoraea pnomenusa and its performance in a biotrickling filter. *Journal of Environmental Sciences*, *26*(5), 1108−1117. Available from https://doi.org/10.1016/s1001-0742(13)60538-0.

The role of artificial neural networks in bioproduct development: a case of modeling and optimization studies

Abiola Ezekiel Taiwo[1], Anthony Ikechukwu Okoji[1], Andrew C. Eloka-Eboka[2] and Paul Musonge[3]

[1]*Department of Chemical Engineering, Landmark University, Omu-Aran, Nigeria* [2]*Centre of Excellence in Carbon-based Fuels, School of Chemical and Mineral Engineering, North-West University, Potchefstroom, South Africa* [3]*Faculty of Engineering, Mangosuthu University of Technology, Durban, South Africa*

Introduction

The rapidly growing population, and the associated environmental issues coupled with increasing global demand for energy, chemicals, and other value-added products have stimulated growing concern for the management and use of natural resources toward the improvement of human quality of life (Owusu & Asumadu-Sarkodie, 2016). Because of their availability and environmental efficiency, renewable and sustainable products have become the focus of the most recent research (Moustakas et al., 2020). Unlike traditional chemical synthesis, bioprocessing is the current manufacturing process trend globally. This is because biotechnology methods are more environmentally friendly than the latter, which adds pollutants and waste to the environment (Ezeonu et al., 2012; Saxena & Pandey, 2021).

Bioproducts are biologically synthesized and known by their chemical composition, structure, and functions in various industrial processes or production (Taiwo et al., 2020). Bioprocesses that make use of renewable resources have increased industrial product efficiency and optimization without causing depletion, reduced environmental degradation, and improved overall quality of life. Bioproducts not only reduce the reliance on synthetic chemicals in industries such as agriculture, pharmaceutics, nutrients, flavors, and energy but also help meet current demands as well as future generational social, economic, and other requirements (Taiwo, 2020).

Modeling and optimization of a value-added product in studies such as bioremediation, biofuel production, and biopharmacy (drug production and dosage) will contribute to a better understanding of process inputs for maximum yield and production rate for sustainable development (Betiku & Taiwo, 2015; Lefnaoui et al., 2020; Olawoyin, 2016; Sadollah et al., 2020). Bioprocess modeling and optimization studies are trending subjects in the discussion about bioprocess development and the need for an optimal operating condition for microorganisms to grow, multiply, and produce the targeted bioproduct. This includes specific concentrations of nutrients to the culture, removing any toxic metabolites, pH, and temperature control (Nicoletti et al., 2009). Many state and input variables characterize a bioprocess operation leading to bioproduct development. Generally, they are classified into physical control variables such as agitation rate, temperature, pressure, fermentation broth, biomass mass composition; chemical variables such as cultivation medium composition, selected gas concentrations (O_2, N_2, CO_2), pH;

Current Trends and Advances in Computer-Aided Intelligent Environmental Data Engineering.
DOI: https://doi.org/10.1016/B978-0-323-85597-6.00007-0

biochemical control variables such as cell mass composition, enzymes, proteins; and macrobiological variables including contamination, degeneration, aggregation, and mutation (Heinzle et al., 2007). The discussed bioprocess operation variables are transient and germane to the bioproduct development of any targeted product of high importance. Traditional modeling and bioprocess control are based on a set of differential equations that are equivalent to mass (and, more often, energy) balances (Subramanian et al., 2018). Finding a suitable mathematical set of equations as well as reliable parameters is a time-consuming task mainly because biological processes are inherently difficult to conduct (Bardini et al., 2017; Nicoletti et al., 2009). The traditional optimization method (one factor at a time) is not only labor-intensive but also lacks interactions between physicochemical parameters and fails to capture the full effects of process variables (Ashok & Kumar, 2017; Upendra et al., 2014). This method, which employs a one-by-one search with subsequent variable variance, has at least two distinct flaws: first, variable relationships are overlooked because other variables are inherently kept constant, and second, obtaining targeted optimal results in a minimal series of experiments is extremely difficult (Nor et al., 2017). When evaluating more than five variables at four levels, the full factorial design of an experiment becomes undesirable in terms of effort, resources, and operating costs (Muralidharan et al., 2019).

In recent years, research have shown that computational intelligence techniques may be used to model and regulate bioprocess operations with the goal of optimizing production variables, allowing for more flexible and alternate solutions to the shortcomings of conventional modeling approaches (Betiku & Ishola, 2020; Sewsynker-Sukai et al., 2017; Taiwo et al., 2018).

Artificial neural network (ANN) and genetic algorithm (GA) are two computational intelligence techniques used in fermentation research for searching the optimal results (media combination and process operating parameters) in bioprocess studies. Similarly, different modeling tools such as fuzzy logic, ant algorithm, and particle swarm optimization are being examined. ANNs are appropriate for developing bioprocess models that do not require prior knowledge of the kinetics of metabolic fluxes within the cell or the cultural environment (Gueguim Kana et al., 2012). ANNs can be applied in the prediction of various processes; they are useful for virtual experiments and could potentially enhance the optimization of value-added products and development (Sewsynker-Sukai et al., 2017). This chapter highlights the application of computational modeling in selected bioprocess operations and also discusses future developments and trends.

Bioproduct development

Biorenewable resources are typically organic materials of biological origin that can be processed, further developed, or converted to generate heat and power, chemicals, fiber liquids, and solid fuels using various biochemical, chemical, and thermochemical conversion technologies (Morgan et al., 2019). Thermochemical conversion could decompose biocomponents into a wide range of final products in a short period of time, with less constraints, suitable environmental conditions, and a lower cost of catalysts. Common thermochemical conversion technologies include pyrolysis, gasification, solvolysis, and direct combustion. Pyrolysis has been deployed for years in the production of solid fuels like charcoal, while gasification of biomasses produces synthetic natural gas and other feedstocks of chemical synthesis (Bhoi et al., 2021). Solvolysis makes use of solvents to enhance and speed up decomposition, in addition to the separation of various compounds and compositions of biomasses, while direct combustion is targeted at the primary delivery of heat and power being generated from different biomasses (Brown & Brown, 2013). Bioproducts can be developed from raw materials or feedstocks through various innovative processes which can be explored to yield valued and finished products. Thermochemical, chemical, and biochemical conversion processes have been deployed to convert biomasses to transportation fuels; there has been the development of biochar-bioenergy-pyrolysis platforms to produce carbon-neutral and carbon-negative forms of energy. Some of the processes are ranked, compared, and comprehensively evaluated for feasibility using various methodologies. Process modeling, life cycle analysis (benefit–cost analysis), sensitivity and uncertainty assessments (risk detection and quantification), technoeconomic analysis are a few examples. Numerical and computational techniques are sometimes used in addition to experimental investigations and validations to quantify, model, and optimize these technologies typical of response surface methodologies (RSMs), ANNs, and computational fluid dynamics (Seok et al., 2019). Some factors drive the economic impacts of technological development and environmental issues, and contribute to the development of bioproducts in general. Innovate techniques or new tools for bioprocessing activate improvements in bioproduct potential and production systems (Dearing, 2000). There are impacts on climate change, economic competitiveness, environmental quality, and sustainability as a result of innovative modeling techniques in bioprocess operation (Singh et al., 2003). Bioproducts of interest that have undergone development and attained commercialization into real industrial establishment include absorbents, activated carbons, adhesives, agricultural chemicals, alternative fibers, biofuels such as bioethanol, biodiesel, biogas, bioenergy products, bioplastics, composite/phase change materials, cleaning agents including soaps, detergents, surfactants; food and beverages, nutrients; fuel additives, fertilizers, dyes and pigments, bio-lubricants/greases, waxes, biooils, cosmetics, hair products, pharmaceutics and medicines, soil/water/air remediation, solvents, specialty chemicals, fatty acids, glycerols, carboxylic acids, paper, pulp and related products, and water and wastewater treatments and technologies (Singh et al., 2003). These products generally undergo identification, characterization, formulation, and scale-up in their developmental trajectory (Neubauer et al., 2013).

Product formulation

Product formulation is one of the transitional stages in any product development process and when the focus is on a bioproducts (materials, chemicals, and energy derived from renewable biological resources), then a bioprocess [any process that uses complete living cells or their components (e.g., bacteria, enzymes) to obtain desired products for commercial use] is the required approach (Forde, Rainey, Speight, Batchelor, & Pattenden, 2016; Neubauer et al., 2013). This entails any process(es) that would add value to wastes from renewables constituting an improvement in environmental sustainability, which are compatible with industrial processes with long-lasting effects and greater efficiency. Generally, bioproducts are products formulated from biomasses characterized by a variety of properties, compositions, and processes, in addition to several benefits and, to some extent, risks. As bioproducts relate to inputs derived from biological sources, including biomass, agriculture, and/or food processing, formulation strategies differ from product to product (Tan et al., 2016). There is no universally accepted formulation approach from feedstock generation to the production of end products, in addition to research, development, and commercialization processes. An example of such a formulation approach is presented from the process development in the production and recovery of choice bioproducts (bioethanol, acetoin, and vanillin) from lignocellulosic materials derivable from agroindustries, animal husbandry, food processing, municipal and forestry residues, marine products, and wastes (Taiwo et al., 2020). The potential of bioethanol was formulated from arrays of agricultural wastes of cassava peels, sugarcane bagasse, corn cobs, mango peels, sorghum straw, and rice rusks using earlier elucidated technologies inclusive of biological pathways of hydrolysis and fermentation in bioproduct formulation studies (Awoyale & Lokhat, 2019). The product formulation involved the decomposition of lignocellulose into carbohydrates, which were further processed to yield the value-added bioproducts efficiently and was achievable using various optimization and modeling approaches.

Product deformulation

Product deformulation or reverse engineering, on the other hand, can be a process of developing bioproducts using decoupling and identification of component materials making up the product (Bhatti, Syed, & John, 2018). The tools of process modeling, optimization, prediction, and validation akin to ANN are essential in the process, rather than the limitations and herculean burden of simple analysis, experimentation, and spectrometric scanning of various analyses. Deformulation of complex biomass-based matrices, analysis, and characterization can be made easier using the computational and numerical approach in combination with any necessary spectrometry depending on the targeted functionality of the inherent active materials (Banerjee & Mazumdar, 2012). Deformulation stages do not only allow simplification of the bioproduct to be X-rayed but also looking at the structural matrices on the foundation of the chemical and physical properties of the spectroscopic chromatograms produced, in which case their target exploitation is facilitated providing necessary information on the chemical composition of the bioproducts which can be better enhanced using ANNs for prediction and validation. For more complex and detailed characterization, this approach becomes even more indispensable in combination with chemometric data analysis. A great deal of product reverse engineering laboratories have recently begun to rely extensively on an artificial intelligence (AI) approach to unravel product mysteries in juxtaposition to the relevant order analysis, scanning, and characterization of functionalities in bioproducts (Gupta, 2020). Once the desired functional elements or compounds are obtained, the bioproduct is deformulated, redirected, and/or reproduced.

Selected optimization tools used in bioprocess development as computational intelligence

Artificial intelligence

ANNs offer one of the most versatile methods of modeling diverse nonlinear processes. When it comes to structure and function, ANN mimics the capability of the human brain. Neurons are the building blocks of the brain, and can store, retrieve, and link data (Bhowmik et al., 2000; Upendra et al., 2014). Based on previous learning and training, it can identify patterns. Biological neurons are made up of dendrites (which can pick up signals), cell bodies (which process information), axons (which transmit information), and synapses (which connect neurons; communicating with other neurons) (Mandlik et al., 2016). The nonlinear relationship between the input(s) and output(s) is created using a set of basic building blocks known as neurons or nodes. The nodes are interconnected and usually occur in multiple layers. Each internodal link or connection is weighted. At each node, the weighted inputs (from other nodes or the external inputs) are summed up with an external bias known as the threshold, and the sum is passed through a nonlinear function. A multilayered perceptron (MLP) is a multilayer feedforward neural network with one input layer, one or more hidden layers, and one output layer. It has been established that a three-layered perceptron with the backpropagation learning algorithm can model a wide range of nonlinear relationships to a reasonable degree of accuracy (Bhowmik et al., 2000).

The ANN is a mathematical model that is used to implement machine learning techniques that are algorithm-based and designed. The weights of neural inputs are calculated for ANN communication, which is based on mathematical operations such as multiplication and addition. Before activation, each node's input is multiplied by its weights and added together. A biological neuron's dendrites receive information, which is processed at the soma (cell body) and transmitted to the axon (output). Likewise, in ANN, the artificial neuron is the fundamental unit of information reception, where inputs are received, multiplied, summed, and processed before being routed to the output via a transfer function. An ANN model, similar to a biological neural network, can handle extremely complex real-world problems in a nonparallel and distributed manner. Fig. 19.1 shows an overview of biological and ANNs in diagram form, and Eq. (19.1) (Puri et al., 2016) can be used to understand the mathematical definition of an ANN:

$$A(t) = F\left[\sum_{i=1}^{n}(B_i(t)C_i(t) + d)\right] \tag{19.1}$$

where $B_i(t)$ represents the input signal at time t, $C_i(t)$ is the weight of neural input at time t, d is the bias, F is the transfer function, and $A(t)$ represents the output value at time t (Puri et al., 2016).

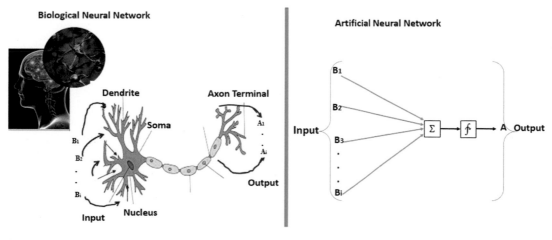

FIGURE 19.1

Overview of biological and ANNs in diagram form. *ANNs,* Artificial neural networks.

ANNs are categorized as either feedforward or recurrent networks based on their design and analysis pattern. According to Mandlik et al. (2016), there are five different types of neural networks:

1. *Multilayered perceptron/backpropagation networks*: MLP is the most widely used neural network model. The backpropagation algorithm is used to build these supervised networks. The error obtained in each run is backpropagated in the network, which greatly reduces the error.
2. *Kohonen neural networks*: Unsupervised networks in which the property under examination is not used during training are known as Kohonen neural networks. The Kohonen network is a two-dimensional network that translates points from a three-dimensional space to a two-dimensional plane.
3. *Counterpropagation (CPG) networks*: CPG networks are supervised networks that use Kohonen's training algorithm. Only the input layer is used to measure distance in CPG networks, while the weights of both the input and output layers are modified during the adaptation steps.
4. *Bayesian neural networks (BNNs)*: Neural networks that operate from a Bayesian paradigm and provide a clear structure for pattern classification and data analysis are known as BNNs.
5. *Recurrent neural networks (RNNs)*: These control the network's complex temporal activity and use internal memory to process inputs. Elman neural networks are RNNs in which the input is propagated in a normal feedforward manner before the learning rule is applied. During learning, this type of neural network always stores a memory of the previous values present in the hidden units.

ANN is a technique that uses adapted biological neural networks. As a learning technique, it is particularly capable of predicting system goals in exchange for exact input variables with biases and weights. The information signal reaching "adjusted weights" and "biases" will determine the number of ANN nodes. Furthermore, modified biases are values that are applied to weights at a later stage of the ANN model's preparation. The ANN training procedure aims to reduce the error caused by discrepancies in observed and expected results, as shown in Fig. 19.2. Because it is a training procedure, it attempts to adjust and improve

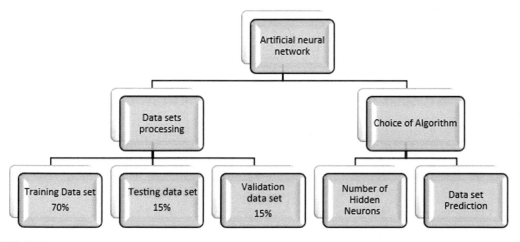

FIGURE 19.2

A diagrammatic training procedure for an ANN. *ANN*, Artificial neural network.

the biases and weights on a regular basis to suggest the best target. It should be noted that function estimation is one of the most important applications of ANN models (Abdel-Sattar et al., 2021).

Genetic algorithms

Genetic algorithms (GAs) are based on the artificial selection theory and imitate the basic evolutionary processes of mutation and selection. In such algorithms, a population of individuals (potential solutions) is subjected to a sequence of mutation and crossover transformations (Schmitt, 2001). These individuals compete for survival using a selection scheme that favors fitter individuals in the next generation's selection. After a certain number of generations, the software converges, and the best individual represents the optimum solution (Gueguim Kana et al., 2012). Its application in optimizing bioprocess processes is summarized as follows: each bioprocess experiment's conditions, such as medium composition and physical parameters, are coded in "chromosomes," with one "gene" representing each medium constituent at the defined concentration or physical parameter. A chromosome population is created to produce a generation whose performance is evaluated. Higher-performing chromosomes are chosen and replicated in proportion. Following replication, chromosome crossover and random gene mutations are carried out. In this way, a new generation of experiments is created (Gueguim Kana et al., 2012).

Evolutionary optimization algorithms for multiobjective optimization have now been applied because of their methodology by employing a population-based technique to create a new population of solutions from one solution in duplication and each iteration (Wang & Sobey, 2020).

Defining a baseline GA involves the following steps, according to Burugari et al. (2020). (1) Build a population of arbitrary individuals such that each individual represents a potential solution to the problem being faced. (2) Calculate increasing human fitness, that is, its capacity to solve a specific problem. This requires searching for the so-called fitness function. (3) Select individual members of the community to become parents. The fitness-proportionate selection is the basic selection method, where persons are chosen with a potential proportional to their relative fitness. This ensures the estimated number of times a person is selected in correspondence to their relative population results. Therefore individuals with high fitness have a greater chance of "reproducing," whereas those with poor fitness are likely to vanish. (4) Produce offspring and introduce them to the population by recombining novel material through crossover (Burugari et al., 2020). Fig. 19.3 depicts a diagrammatic representation of the GA.

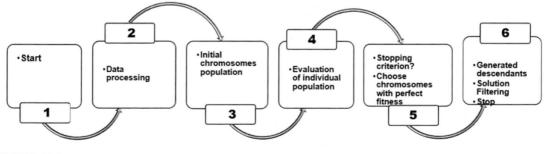

FIGURE 19.3

A diagrammatic representation of a genetic algorithm.

Fuzzy logic

A fuzzy inference system's basic concept is to integrate human intelligence into a collection of fuzzy IF—THEN rules, which entails four operations: a fuzzifier, a fuzzy rule base, a fuzzy inference engine, and a defuzzifier (Honda & Kobayashi, 2000). The general inference system can be seen in Fig. 19.4. Fuzzy logic findings vary from 0 to 1. In essence, fuzzy logic determines certain transitional values including absolute truth and absolute false between sharp evaluations. This is an indication that fuzzy sets can manage ideas that are usually encountered daily, such as very small, small, big, and very big. Fuzzy logic works with fuzzy sets which have membership degrees/notches in their components.

Essentially, a member element from a multiple set associated with different membership values may be an object (Burugari et al., 2020). For example, weekdays are usually assigned from Monday to Friday, and weekends include Saturday and Sunday. Alternatively, it could be assumed that, on Friday, individuals begin to feel the optimistic impact of the approaching weekend. Therefore it may be thought that while Friday is classed within the "weekdays" set with a membership value of 0.95, it belongs to the "weekend" set with a value of 0.05 (Kayacan & Khanesar, 2015). Several studies have been conducted to investigate the application of fuzzy reasoning. Details have been reported elsewhere (Borges et al., 2020; Horiuchi, 2002; Kayacan & Khanesar, 2015).

Application of optimization tools in bioprocessing operations

Modeling and optimization are two of the most crucial phases in a biological process for increasing process efficiency (Betiku & Taiwo, 2015). Bioprocess design and optimization from a modeling

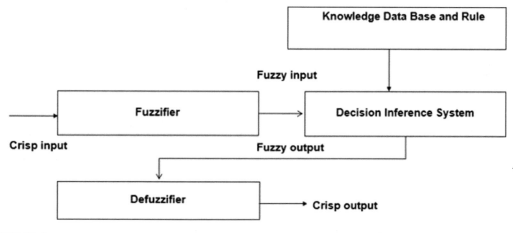

FIGURE 19.4

A diagrammatic representation of a fuzzy logic system.

standpoint have been shown to be a capable method for this purpose, in conjunction with additional tools such as bioprocess monitoring, to promote methodical design and optimization studies to swiftly enhance the productivity of the feedstock process for the development of biofuels. Process optimization of biomass-based processes to boost the yield and productivity of the biofuels required is crucial to the lucrative economic outlook of bioprocesses (Burugari et al., 2020). The ability of ANN to extract meaningful information from complex data is astounding. The formulation and optimization of media are critical to the success of bioprocess development because they directly affect the time and cost of bioproducts (Rangel et al., 2020). The ability of ANN methodology to be used in biotechnology and pharmaceutical sciences ranges from data interpretation to drug production and dosage optimization, as well as the optimization of polluted processes, wastewater treatment, and conception by biopharmaceuticals or clinical pharmacy (Bourquin et al., 1997; Ghaffari et al., 2006).

Bioremediation

Bioremediation is the use of biological processes to minimize contamination in the air, water, and land. It also entails removing microbes from the atmosphere and exposing them to a contaminant of interest to minimize the toxicity (Azubuike et al., 2016). It is referred to as an optimization method because it entails correctly matching decaying microbes to environments, comprehending and monitoring the movement of the contaminant so that it comes into contact with microbes, and characterizing the abiotic conditions that influence each of these factors (Ezeonu et al., 2012). Bioremediation aims to reduce the potential toxicity of environmental contamination by reducing, transforming, and immobilizing undesirable compounds using biosystems such as microbes and higher organisms such as plants and animals. One of the most promising methods for extracting heavy metals from wastewater or soil is bioremediation. Depending on the heavy metal, sample composition, and bacteria used, a variety of factors may affect the process. As a result, one of the most important steps in achieving the best results during bioremediation is the optimization process. To improve the bioremediation process, optimization tools such as RSM and ANNs can be used (El-Naggar & Rabei, 2020).

The conventional one-variable-at-a-time optimization technique, which has been used for decades, is not only time-consuming and labor-intensive, but also fails to display the total interactions and effects of each parameter measured during the study, potentially resulting in inaccurate results (Talib et al., 2019). Because of the large number of influencing parameters in the composting process and the time-consuming nature of the process, it is experimentally impossible to determine the optimum conditions for maximum removal of hydrocarbons from polluted soil (Cipullo et al., 2019). Long-term studies with multiple soil sampling are often needed to accurately track the bioremediation process and support risk evaluation and degradation assessment, which are labor-intensive, time-consuming, and expensive (Varjani, Agarwal, Gnansounou, & Gurunathan, 2018). As a consequence, the use of computational intelligence, such as ANN, which is trained on empirical evidence, may be useful in predicting possible degradation and toxicity reduction during remediation (Adesina et al., 2021). ANNs are useful instruments for predicting toxicant levels in the microenvironment, such as polycyclic aromatic hydrocarbons resulting from anthropogenic activities.

Biofuel production

As a result of the depletion of fossil fuels and the negative environmental effects of their burning, one area of research gaining significant traction is biofuels (Taiwo et al., 2018). Renewable energy growth, such as bioethanol, biodiesel, and biogas, is receiving a great deal of attention, with laboratory- and pilot-scale production being pursued (Betiku & Ishola, 2020; Betiku & Taiwo, 2015; Oloko-Oba et al., 2018; Pabon-Pereira et al., 2019). Computational modeling has the potential to be a cost-effective tool that enhances both productivity and economics for biofuel processes (Petrides, 2000). Advances in artificial intelligence (AI) and its subclasses are making it possible to predict several items including process yields, substrate medium components, and optimal process conditions, among others. It has been employed in many bioprocesses such as pretreatment of lignocellulosic biomass and various biofuel production processes (Burugari et al., 2020; Nicoletti et al., 2009). Further implementation of this computer-based tool may potentially mitigate the need for preliminary experiments and, in some cases, laboratory-scale experiments. In biofuel production, there are more parameters to be considered, including temperature, pH, agitation, substrate concentration, inoculum concentration, and oxygen levels (Moodley & Kana, 2015). All these parameters play a crucial role in how the process proceeds and are also determinants of the final output yield. For this reason, these parameters must be modeled and optimized in their respective stages to ensure maximum productivity. To fully realize the potential of biofuel production, these processes must undergo thorough modeling and optimization to enhance process economics and scalability. Modeling and optimization of biogas production using organic wastes and codigestion of industrial potato waste with aquatic weed have been done using ANNs and GAs. In addition, the authors have demonstrated that GA is a useful tool for optimizing the biogas production process (Gueguim Kana et al., 2012; Oloko-Oba et al., 2018).

Biopharmacy

Biopharmaceutical research into drug production, drug stability of modified-release solid dosage forms, and delivery has grown considerably since its emergence, with the properties of active substances and preparations being examined in living organisms, and modeling of accompanying processes of interaction being needed to be explored for optimization of production (Upendra et al., 2014). The physical, chemical, and pharmacological properties of the bioproducts, as well as the complex relationships of pharmacodynamic and toxicological responses of the organism, need to be determined (Seiler, 2002). Computer intelligence has given a significant boost to the fields of drug design and delivery, with applications ranging from understanding chemical structure and molecule characteristics to analyzing medication's pharmacological and toxicological aspects and developing efficient and novel drug-delivery systems (Puri et al., 2016). ANNs can predict the chemical properties of a variety of compounds, making them a valuable tool for drug preformulation research. The ability of ANNs to model and recognize nonlinear patterns expands their possible applications in a broad variety of pharmaceutical research studies (Damiati, 2020). Drug modeling, pharmacokinetic and pharmacophore perception modeling, chemical library design, data interpretation, and, most notably, in vitro/in vivo correlations are among these applications (Mandlik et al., 2016).

Future developments or trends

Research is trending on the benefits and future opportunities of existing AI technologies in clinical practice for physicians, healthcare facilities, medical education, and bioethics. AI is expected to improve quality of life by conducting early diagnoses, reducing complications, improving care and/or offering less invasive alternatives, and reducing hospitalization time. AI in clinical practice is a key area of research that is rapidly evolving alongside other modern fields, such as precision medicine, genomics, and teleconsultation. The literature demonstrates AI's promising solutions to complex issues in a variety of applications in areas with massive amounts of data but very low levels of theory, and it has played a variety of different roles in scientific research. Recent research has focused on knowledge-based thinking for disease classification and learning, as well as the discovery of new biomedical knowledge for disease treatment. AI techniques are becoming more prevalent in biomedical engineering and computer science. AI techniques can be used to solve complex problems in biomedical engineering and informatics. A significant portion of the cost in biotechnological production is accounted for by downstream operations. The search for cost-effective separation techniques to reduce production costs is still ongoing using different artificial intelligence approaches.

Conclusion

To remain ahead of the competition in the industrial production market, there is currently a search to improve the productivity and economics of bioprocess operations. Studies have shown that there is a rapid increase in the use of computational modeling in almost every industry, with the scaling up of the rate(s) of production. Because complex biological systems make empirical approaches difficult, modeling and simulations are effective tools for bringing such processes, which are often more cost-effective, closer to technical implementation. Traditional mathematical modeling is difficult to employ and simulate due to the complexity of the process(es). ANN has been used as an optimization tool in many science and engineering fields due to its simplicity in simulation. The accuracy of ANN prediction depends on the level of mimic network trainings, and process performance modeling. Analyzing complex, nonlinear, and dynamic data with multiple inputs applies to ANN. ANNs have been greatly enhanced by the fact that the models understand the nonlinear and complex relationship between inputs and outputs, and do not limit the input or output space. These make ANNs valid as a tool to study biological processes. Several disciplines, including chemistry, medicine, molecular biology, and chemical engineering, have successfully used ANNs. ANNs have been used in biotechnology for a variety of applications, including variable prediction, optimization and modeling, and process control. This chapter has demonstrated the application of computational intelligence and the various roles it can play in bioprocesses.

References

Abdel-Sattar, M., Aboukarima, A. M., & Alnahdi, B. M. (2021). Application of artificial neural network and support vector regression in predicting mass of ber fruits (Ziziphus mauritiana Lamk.) based on fruit axial dimensions. *PLoS One*, *16*(1). Available from https://doi.org/10.1371/journal.pone.0245228.

Adesina, O. A., Taiwo, A. E., Akindele, O., & Igbafe, A. (2021). Process parametric studies for decolouration of dye from local 'tie and dye' industrial effluent using Moringa oleifera seed. *South African Journal of Chemical Engineering*, *37*, 23−30. Available from https://doi.org/10.1016/j.sajce.2021.03.005.

Ashok, A., & Kumar, D. S. (2017). Different methodologies for sustainability of optimization techniques used in submerged and solid state fermentation. *3 Biotech*, *7*(5). Available from https://doi.org/10.1007/s13205-017-0934-z.

Awoyale, A. A., & Lokhat, D. (2019). Harnessing the potential of bio-ethanol production from lignocellulosic biomass in Nigeria − A review. *Biofuels, Bioproducts and Biorefining*, *13*(1), 192−207. Available from https://doi.org/10.1002/bbb.1943.

Azubuike, C. C., Chikere, C. B., & Okpokwasili, G. C. (2016). Bioremediation techniques−classification based on site of application: Principles, advantages, limitations and prospects. *World Journal of Microbiology and Biotechnology*, *32*, 1−18.

Banerjee, S., & Mazumdar, S. (2012). Electrospray ionization mass spectrometry: A technique to access the information beyond the molecular weight of the analyte. *International Journal of Analytical Chemistry*, *2012*, 1−40. Available from https://doi.org/10.1155/2012/282574.

Bardini, R., Politano, G., Benso, A., & Di Carlo, S. (2017). Multi-level and hybrid modeling approaches for systems biology. *Computational and Structural Biotechnology Journal*, *15*, 396−402. Available from https://doi.org/10.1016/j.csbj.2017.07.005.

Betiku, E., & Ishola, N. B. (2020). Optimization of sorrel oil biodiesel production by base heterogeneous catalyst from kola nut pod husk: Neural intelligence-genetic algorithm vs neuro-fuzzy-genetic algorithm. *Environmental Progress and Sustainable Energy*, *39*(4). Available from https://doi.org/10.1002/ep.13393.

Betiku, E., & Taiwo, A. E. (2015). Modeling and optimization of bioethanol production from breadfruit starch hydrolyzate vis-à-vis response surface methodology and artificial neural network. *Renewable Energy*, *74*, 87−94. Available from https://doi.org/10.1016/j.renene.2014.07.054.

Bhatti, A., Syed, N. A., & John, P. (2018). Reverse engineering and its applications. In D. Barh, & V. Azevedo (Eds.), *Omics technologies and bio-engineering: Towards improving quality of life* (Vol. 1, pp. 95−110). Elsevier Inc. Available from https://doi.org/10.1016/B978-0-12-804659-3.00005-1.

Bhoi, R., Saharan, V. K., & George, S. (2021). *Sustainability of the catalytic process for biomass conversion: Recent trends and future prospects* (pp. 237−272). Springer Science and Business Media LLC. Available from https://doi.org/10.1007/978-3-030-65017-9_9.

Bhowmik, U. Kr, Saha, G., Barua, A., & Sinha, S. (2000). On-line detection of contamination in a bioprocess using artificial neural networks. *Chemical Engineering & Technology*, *23*(6), 543−549. Available from https://doi.org/10.1002/1521-4125. (200006)23:6 < 543::aid-ceat543 > 3.0.co;2-0.

Borges, A. S., Montano, I. D. C., Sousa Junior, R., & Suarez, C. A. G. (2020). Automatic solids feeder using fuzzy control: A tool for fed batch bioprocesses. *Journal of Process Control*, *93*, 28−42. Available from https://doi.org/10.1016/j.jprocont.2020.07.006.

Bourquin, J., Schmidli, H., Van Hoogevest, P., & Leuenberger, H. (1997). Basic concepts of Artificial Neural Networks (ANN) modeling in the application to pharmaceutical development. *Pharmaceutical Development and Technology*, *2*(2), 95−109. Available from https://doi.org/10.3109/10837459709022615.

Brown, R. C., & Brown, T. R. (2013). *Biorenewable resources: engineering new products from agriculture*. John Wiley & Sons. Available from https://onlinelibrary.wiley.com/doi/book/10.1002/9781118524985.

Burugari, V. K., Selvaraj, P., Praneel, V., Kondaveeti, H. K., & Pravin Kumar, M. (2020). The application of computational modeling for the optimization of bio fuel production processes. *International Journal of Advanced Trends in Computer Science and Engineering*, *9*(5), 7883−7893. Available from https://doi.org/10.30534/ijatcse/2020/140952020.

Cipullo, S., Snapir, B., Prpich, G., Campo, P., & Coulon, F. (2019). Prediction of bioavailability and toxicity of complex chemical mixtures through machine learning models. *Chemosphere*, *215*, 388−395. Available from https://doi.org/10.1016/j.chemosphere.2018.10.056.

Damiati, S. A. (2020). Digital pharmaceutical sciences. *AAPS PharmSciTech*, *21*(6). Available from https://doi.org/10.1208/s12249-020-01747-4.

Dearing, A. (2000). Sustainable innovation: Drivers and barriers. *Innovation and the Environment*, 103−125, World Business Council for Sustainable Development 4 chemin de Conches 1231 Geneva.

El-Naggar, N. E. A., & Rabei, N. H. (2020). Bioprocessing optimization for efficient simultaneous removal of methylene blue and nickel by Gracilaria seaweed biomass. *Scientific Reports*, *10*(1). Available from https://doi.org/10.1038/s41598-020-74389-y.

Ezeonu, C. S., Tagbo, R., Anike, E. N., Oje, O. A., & Onwurah, I. N. E. (2012). Biotechnological tools for environmental sustainability: Prospects and challenges for environments in Nigeria—A standard review. *Biotechnology Research International*, 1−26. Available from https://doi.org/10.1155/2012/450802.

Forde, G. M., Rainey, T. J., Speight, R., Batchelor, W., & Pattenden, L. K. (2016). Matching the biomass to the bioproduct: Summary of up- and downstream bioprocesses. In R. Luque, & C. Xu (Eds.), *Biomaterials* (pp. 1−44). Berlin, Boston: De Gruyter. Available from https://doi.org/10.1515/9783110342420-002.

Ghaffari, A., Abdollahi, H., Khoshayand, M. R., Bozchalooi, I. S., Dadgar, A., & Rafiee-Tehrani, M. (2006). Performance comparison of neural network training algorithms in modeling of bimodal drug delivery. *International Journal of Pharmaceutics*, *327*(1−2), 126−138. Available from https://doi.org/10.1016/j.ijpharm.2006.07.056.

Gueguim Kana, E. B., Oloke, J. K., Lateef, A., & Adesiyan, M. O. (2012). Modeling and optimization of biogas production on saw dust and other co-substrates using Artificial Neural network and Genetic Algorithm. *Renewable Energy*, *46*, 276−281. Available from https://doi.org/10.1016/j.renene.2012.03.027.

Gupta, P. (2020). Reverse engineering of human brain for the field of artificial intelligence. *International Journal of Engineering Research & Technology (IJERT)*, *9*, 252−257.

Heinzle, E., Biwer, A. P., & Cooney, C. L. (2007). *Development of sustainable bioprocesses: Modeling and assessment* (pp. 1−294). John Wiley and Sons. Available from https://doi.org/10.1002/9780470058916.

Honda, H., & Kobayashi, T. (2000). Fuzzy control of bioprocess. *Journal of Bioscience and Bioengineering*, *89*(5), 401−408. Available from https://doi.org/10.1016/S1389-1723(00)89087-8.

Horiuchi, J. I. (2002). Fuzzy modeling and control of biological processes. *Journal of Bioscience and Bioengineering*, *94*(6), 574−578. Available from https://doi.org/10.1016/S1389-1723(02)80197-9.

Kayacan, E., & Khanesar, M. A. (2015). *Fuzzy neural networks for real time control applications: Concepts, modeling and algorithms for fast learning* (pp. 1−242). Elsevier Inc. Available from https://doi.org/10.1016/C2014-0-02444-6.

Lefnaoui, S., Rebouh, S., Bouhedda, M., & Yahoum, M. M. (2020). Artificial neural network for modeling formulation and drug permeation of topical patches containing diclofenac sodium. *Drug Delivery and Translational Research*, *10*(1), 168−184. Available from https://doi.org/10.1007/s13346-019-00671-w.

Mandlik, V., Bejugam, P. R., & Singh, S. (2016). *Application of artificial neural networks in modern drug discovery. Artificial neural network for drug design, delivery and disposition* (pp. 123−139). Elsevier Inc. Available from https://doi.org/10.1016/B978-0-12-801559-9.00006-5.

Moodley, P., & Kana, E. B. G. (2015). Optimization of xylose and glucose production from sugarcane leaves (Saccharum officinarum) using hybrid pretreatment techniques and assessment for hydrogen generation at semi-pilot scale. *International Journal of Hydrogen Energy*, *40*(10), 3859−3867. Available from https://doi.org/10.1016/j.ijhydene.2015.01.087.

Morgan, T. J., Youkhana, A., Turn, S. Q., Ogoshi, R., & Garcia-Pérez, M. (2019). Review of biomass resources and conversion technologies for alternative jet fuel production in Hawai'i and tropical regions. *Energy and Fuels*, *33*(4), 2699−2762. Available from https://doi.org/10.1021/acs.energyfuels.8b03001.

Moustakas, K., Loizidou, M., Rehan, M., & Nizami, A. S. (2020). A review of recent developments in renewable and sustainable energy systems: Key challenges and future perspective. *Renewable and Sustainable Energy Reviews*, *119*. Available from https://doi.org/10.1016/j.rser.2019.109418.

Muralidharan, K., Romero, M., & Wuthrich, K. (2019). *Factorial designs, model selection, and (incorrect) inference in randomized experiments*. National Bureau of Economic Research.

Neubauer, P., Cruz, N., Glauche, F., Junne, S., Knepper, A., & Raven, M. (2013). Consistent development of bioprocesses from microliter cultures to the industrial scale. *Engineering in Life Sciences*, *13*(3), 224–238. Available from https://doi.org/10.1002/elsc.201200021.

Nicoletti, M. C., Jain, L. C., & Giordano, R. C. (2009). Computational intelligence techniques as tools for bioprocess modeling, optimization, supervision and control. *Studies in Computational Intelligence*, *218*, 1–23. Available from https://doi.org/10.1007/978-3-642-01888-6_1.

Nor, N. M., Mohamed, M. S., Loh, T. C., Foo, H. L., Rahim, R. A., Tan, J. S., & Mohamad, R. (2017). Comparative analyses on medium optimization using one-factor-at-a-time, response surface methodology, and artificial neural network for lysine–methionine biosynthesis by *Pediococcus pentosaceus* RF-1. *Biotechnology and Biotechnological Equipment*, *31*(5), 935–947. Available from https://doi.org/10.1080/13102818.2017.1335177.

Olawoyin, R. (2016). Application of backpropagation artificial neural network prediction model for the PAH bioremediation of polluted soil. *Chemosphere*, *161*, 145–150. Available from https://doi.org/10.1016/j.chemosphere.2016.07.003.

Oloko-Oba, M. I., Taiwo, A. E., Ajala, S. O., Solomon, B. O., & Betiku, E. (2018). Performance evaluation of three different-shaped bio-digesters for biogas production and optimization by artificial neural network integrated with genetic algorithm. *Sustainable Energy Technologies and Assessments*, *26*, 116–124. Available from https://doi.org/10.1016/j.seta.2017.10.006.

Owusu, P. A., & Asumadu-Sarkodie, S. (2016). A review of renewable energy sources, sustainability issues and climate change mitigation. *Cogent Engineering*, *3*(1), 1167990. Available from https://doi.org/10.1080/23311916.2016.1167990.

Pabon-Pereira, C., Slingerland, M., Hogervorst, S., van Lier, J., & Rabbinge, R. (2019). A sustainability assessment of bioethanol (EtOH) production: The case of cassava in Colombia. *Sustainability (Switzerland)*, *11*(14). Available from https://doi.org/10.3390/su11143968.

Petrides, D. (2000). Bioprocess design and economics. *Bioseparations Science and Engineering*, 1–83.

Puri, M., Solanki, A., Padawer, T., Tipparaju, S. M., Moreno, W. A., & Pathak, Y. (2016). *Introduction to artificial neural network (ann) as a predictive tool for drug design, discovery, delivery, and disposition: basic concepts and modeling*. Basic concepts and modeling. *Artificial neural network for drug design, delivery and disposition* (pp. 3–13). Elsevier Inc. Available from https://doi.org/10.1016/B978-0-12-801559-9.00001-6.

Rangel, A. E. T., Gómez Ramírez, J. M., & González Barrios, A. F. (2020). From industrial by-products to value-added compounds: The design of efficient microbial cell factories by coupling systems metabolic engineering and bioprocesses. *Biofuels, Bioproducts and Biorefining*, *14*(6), 1228–1238. Available from https://doi.org/10.1002/bbb.2127.

Sadollah, A., Nasir, M., & Geem, Z. W. (2020). Sustainability and optimization: From conceptual fundamentals to applications. *Sustainability (Switzerland)*, *12*(5). Available from https://doi.org/10.3390/su12052027.

Saxena, S., & Pandey, A. K. (2021). *Emerging and eco-friendly approaches for waste management* (pp. 61–81). Springer Science and Business Media LLC. Available from https://doi.org/10.1007/978-981-33-4347-4_3.

Schmitt, L. M. (2001). Theory of genetic algorithms. *Theoretical Computer Science*, *259*(1–2), 1–61. Available from https://doi.org/10.1016/S0304-3975(00)00406-0.

Seiler, J. P. (2002). Pharmacodynamic activity of drugs and ecotoxicology - Can the two be connected? *Toxicology Letters*, *131*(1–2), 105–115. Available from https://doi.org/10.1016/S0378-4274(02)00045-0.

Seok, W., Kim, G. H., Seo, J., & Rhee, S. H. (2019). Application of the design of experiments and computational fluid dynamics to bow design improvement. *Journal of Marine Science and Engineering*, *7*(7). Available from https://doi.org/10.3390/jmse7070226.

Sewsynker-Sukai, Y., Faloye, F., & Kana, E. B. G. (2017). Artificial neural networks: An efficient tool for modelling and optimization of biofuel production (a mini review). *Biotechnology and Biotechnological Equipment*, *31*(2), 221–235. Available from https://doi.org/10.1080/13102818.2016.1269616.

Singh, S. P., Ekanem, E., Wakefield, T., & Comer, S. (2003). Emerging importance of bio-based products and bio-energy in the United States economy: Information dissemination and training of students. *International Food and Agribusiness Management Review*, *5*(3). Available from http://www.ifama.org/members/articles/v5i3/singh.pdf.

Subramanian, A. S. R., Gundersen, T., & Adams, T. A. (2018). Modeling and simulation of energy systems: A review. *Processes*, *6*(12). Available from https://doi.org/10.3390/pr6120238.

Taiwo, A. E. (2020). Application of bioprocess-supercritical fluid extraction techniques in the production and recovery of some selected bioproducts. PhD Thesis (Chemical Engineering). http://hdl.handle.net/20.500.11838/3072

Taiwo, A. E., Madzimbamuto, T. F., & Ojumu, T. V. (2020). *Development of an integrated process for the production and recovery of some selected bioproducts from lignocellulosic materials. Green Energy and Technology* (pp. 439–467). Springer Science and Business Media Deutschland GmbH. Available from https://doi.org/10.1007/978-3-030-38032-8_21.

Taiwo, A. E., Madzimbamuto, T. N., & Ojumu, T. V. (2018). Optimization of corn steep liquor dosage and other fermentation parameters for ethanol production by saccharomyces cerevisiae type 1 and anchor instant yeast. *Energies*, *11*(7). Available from https://doi.org/10.3390/en11071740.

Talib, N. S. R., Halmi, M. I. E., Ghani, S. S. A., Zaidan, U. H., & Shukor, M. Y. A. (2019). Artificial neural networks (anns) and response surface methodology (RSM) approach for modelling the optimization of chromium (VI) reduction by newly isolated Acinetobacter radioresistens strain NS-MIE from agricultural soil. *BioMed Research International*, 2019. Available from https://doi.org/10.1155/2019/5785387.

Tan, H. T., Corbin, K. R., & Fincher, G. B. (2016). Emerging technologies for the production of renewable liquid transport fuels from biomass sources enriched in plant cell walls. *Frontiers in Plant Science*, *7*(2016). Available from https://doi.org/10.3389/fpls.2016.01854.

Upendra, R., Khandelwal, P., Amiri, Z. R., Banu, R., Barade, V. K., Gayathri, V., & Yamini, D. (2014). Artificial Neural Network: A novel method for optimization of bioproducts and bioprocesses: A critical review. *Journal of Membrane Science and Research*, *1*, 21–34.

Varjani, S. J., Agarwal, A. K., Gnansounou, E., & Gurunathan, B. (Eds.), (2018). *Bioremediation: applications for environmental protection and management*. Singapore: Springer. Available from https://link.springer.com/book/10.1007%2F978-981-10-7485-1.

Wang, Z. Z., & Sobey, A. (2020). A comparative review between Genetic Algorithm use in composite optimisation and the state-of-the-art in evolutionary computation. *Composite Structures*, 233. Available from https://doi.org/10.1016/j.compstruct.2019.111739.

Modeling of grains sun drying: from theoretical methods to intelligent systems

Joshua O. Ighalo[1,2], Adewale George Adeniyi[2] and Chinenye Adaobi Igwegbe[1]

[1]*Department of Chemical Engineering, Nnamdi Azikiwe University, Awka, Nigeria* [2]*Department of Chemical Engineering, Faculty of Engineering and Technology, University of Ilorin, Ilorin, Nigeria*

Introduction

Drying is a food-processing technique that has been in use since the beginning of human civilization. It remains a very popular practice in current times. Crop drying is also popular in Africa as most agricultural practices on this continent are carried out on small and medium-sized scales, and is usually located in rural/remote areas (Adeniyi et al., 2020). These areas usually lack electricity and infrastructure to utilize more modern drying equipment and techniques, hence solar drying remains prominent (Ekechukwu & Norton, 1999). The basic aim of drying is a reduction of the moisture content to a level where preservation without deterioration is assured within a given time frame (Ekechukwu & Norton, 1999; Fortes & Okos, 1981). Other areas of importance of drying include maintenance of product quality, early harvest, and year-round availability of certain agricultural products (Hall, 1970). Generally, drying is one of the most energy-intensive processes in the industry (Peishi & Pei, 1989). Sun drying is considered cheap because the source of energy is free and renewable (Toğrul & Pehlivan, 2003). Although considered cheap, if the solar drying operation takes too long, the time, energy, and labor costs will rise, thereby adversely affecting productivity (Aregbesola et al., 2015; Plumb et al., 1985).

Utilizing the sun for drying may be classified into three types: direct (open), indirect, and mixed modes (Bala & Woods, 1994). Numerous processes in food processing involve heat and mass transfer and these include open drying, frying, microwave heating, and roasting (Datta, 2007; Farkas et al., 1996). Open sun drying is a heat and mass transfer phenomenon that involves the direct heating of the crops through exposure to solar radiation (Adeniyi et al., 2020). The heat propagates to the interior of the crop (causing a temperature increase) and is also utilized in evaporating the moisture from the surface (Anwar & Tiwari, 2001). Heat transfer patterns are also affected by moisture movement (Adeniyi & Ighalo, 2018; De Vries, 1958). It has been shown that depending on the airflow rate, drying air temperature, and initial grain temperature, 12%−15% of the actual heat used in drying is transferred to the grain as sensible heat (Boyce, 1965). Both simple and complex dryers have been developed for solar drying of agricultural products (for all drying modes), and Ekechukwu and Norton (1999) in their review comprehensively presented a plethora of these types of equipment.

Current Trends and Advances in Computer-Aided Intelligent Environmental Data Engineering.
DOI: https://doi.org/10.1016/B978-0-323-85597-6.00016-1

Grains are small hard dry seeds with or without an attached hull. The term can be applied to both cereals and legumes. Grains and granular products are a class of agricultural products that require drying in their production step (Mhimid et al., 2000). The theoretical representation of drying data, consisting of the moisture content of the material and its temperature responses, is fundamentally a heat and mass transfer problem under transient conditions. The result is a system of nonlinear partial differential equations, which represent the heat and mass balances in the solid and air phases of the systems undergoing drying (Kaya et al., 2006; Kiranoudis et al., 1995). Key characteristics of drying models are movement, structural and thermodynamic assumptions, and methods of material property measurement, model solution, and model evaluation (Simal et al., 1994). Accuracy levels differ for different models as these expressions cannot always fully represent all the interdependencies of certain process factors. For example, the thermal properties of grains have been established as a function of moisture content (Kazarian & Hall, 1965) and will vary as the moisture content varies, and similarly with other properties such as size (Adeniyi et al., 2019). Hence, fully accurate mathematical modeling of drying is considered very difficult due to the constantly changing moisture content (Sander et al., 2003).

Numerous theoretical and experimental studies (Bruce & Giner, 1993; Jayas et al., 1991) have been carried out to elucidate the different aspects of drying (direct and indirect) of grains to different levels of accuracy. Among the grains, studies have been conducted for rice (Bala & Woods, 1994), barley (Boyce, 1965, 1966), corn (Fortes & Okos, 1981; Peishi & Pei, 1989; Thompson et al., 1968), wheat (Fortes et al., 1981; Jia et al., 2000), and sorghum (Sharma & Thompson, 1973; Suarez et al., 1980). Generalized models have also been developed for agricultural products (Laws & Parry, 1983; Parry, 1983; Parti, 1993; Peishi & Pei, 1989; Sun & Woods, 1997; Sun et al., 1995; Sutherland et al., 1971) while considering the substrate as an isotropic sphere (Haghighi & Segerlind, 1991) and as porous media (De Vries, 1958; Maroulis et al., 1995; Nasrallah & Perre, 1988). The heat and mass drying coefficients for grain drying have also been investigated (Miketinac et al., 1992; Sharma & Thompson, 1973).

Intelligent systems are computer-based systems that are trained based on input data and can predict system behavior after training (Adeniyi et al., 2020; Adeniyi et al., 2021). Intelligent data-driven systems have become more popularly utilized for the modeling of grain drying. Artificial neural networks (ANNs) are inspired by the behavior and functionality of the neurons in the brain (Ighalo, Igwegbe, & Adeniyi, 2020; Ighalo, Adeniyi, & Marques, 2020). They have been extensively applied for the modeling of various aspects of the grain-drying process, as reviewed by Aghbashlo et al. (2015). In another recent review (Sun et al., 2019), the limitations to the use of intelligent systems for the modeling of drying processes were explained (Farkas et al., 2000). In general, there is a transition from theoretical methods to intelligent systems in the modeling of processes. These systems can predict very complex and nonlinear engineering problems (Ighalo, Igwegbe, & Adeniyi, 2020; Ighalo, Adeniyi, & Marques, 2020), and hence their inherent suitability for the drying process.

In this chapter, progression in the research in to the modeling of drying of grains is discussed, taking a historical perspective. Reports such as these help to create an archive of the research progress and catalogs some of the key advances made. These help to direct and guide contemporary researchers to potential gray areas to explore, and highlight the transition from a theoretical approach to intelligent systems in mathematical modeling.

An account of early theoretical modeling efforts

As part of his PhD work at the University of Newcastle, Boyce (1965) looked at the changes in moisture and temperature as a function of time and position during the drying of barley. His study presented a system of equations for predicting the changes and also considered methods of determining the relevant physical properties using a step-by-step solution. His study was able to show that a layer-by-layer calculation can be done for the specific scenario. He suggested that noncomputer methods can be investigated for determining moisture and temperature in deep beds. In a continuation of his 1965 work, Boyce (1966) considered properly the transfer of heat and moisture in deep beds in 1966. He observed that the existing theories at that time were inadequate when high humidity was involved. He also emphasized the need for researchers at that time to develop more satisfying theoretical expressions for mass transfer in grain drying. Fortes et al. (1981) looked at heat and mass transfer during the drying and rewetting of wheat grains. The study was based on a nonequilibrium thermodynamic approach. The model was validated with experiments and found to be reasonably accurate for the intended purpose. However, they observed that its suitability did not hold for early harvested wheat because it was physiologically immature above 0.4 db (28.5% wet basis). Fortes and Okos (1981) conducted a similar study in the same year, albeit for corn kernels.

Haghighi and Segerlind (1991) utilized a finite element approach in modeling heat and mass transport in soybean kernels. The substrate was considered to be an isentropic sphere. The proposed technique by Haghighi and Segerlind had the potential of explaining the complicated coupled phenomena of transient heat and mass transfer in a sphere. One of the strong points of the technique was that the moisture gradients, as well as the temperature gradients, can be developed very easily and in a form directly usable for any further analysis. The authors suggested that the technique could be further explored in the domain of other geometries such as cuboids (slabs) and cylinders. Bruce and Giner (1993) considered heat and mass transfer modeling during the drying of grains in a counterflow bed. The drying equations was solved using three different solution methods. The first was Euler's method, the second were the improved Euler plus fourth-order Runge–Kutta method, while the third method was by finite difference. The models were validated and shown to be accurate. How crossover air affected grain temperatures was studied using these models.

In a very important early review paper (Parti, 1993), Parti summarized the different lumped parameter models, distributed parameter models, and thin-layer drying equations used for grain drying modelling. The study attempted to clarify the limitations of the different models, their basic assumptions, and the best scenarios in which they could be safely utilized. He observed that the popular assumptions in model development are temperature equilibrium and surface moisture content equilibrium. The lumped parameter model is applicable when the Biot number is greater than 10 and 1.5 for mass and heat transfer, respectively. Temperature and surface moisture equilibrium exists when the Biot number is above 4000 and 1000, respectively.

In 1994, Bala and Woods (1994) performed a numerical simulation of indirect natural convection during the solar drying of rough rice. From their investigations, it was observed that the thermal buoyancy effect is primarily controlled by the collector height, with the chimney having little effect. A pressure drop was also observed to occur primarily across the grain bed, as would be expected, with some contribution to airflow resistance from the chimney. The performance of the system was, therefore, sensitive to grain depth. It was proposed that chimneys in the system should be reconsidered as they do not contribute to airflow. Frequent mixing of the grains was also proposed to avoid overdrying. Kiranoudis et al. (1995) harnessed an experimental dataset of multiple responses (moisture content and temperature) in modeling the heat and mass transfer in grain drying. They utilized an iterative approach, as described in Fig. 20.1. The significance and correlation of model parameters were evaluated by determining their joint confidence regions. Sensitivity analysis of the model parameters concerning the output helped to portray which transfer mechanism prevailed in the region where the tendencies were observed. This was then either suitably transformed so that lumped dependencies of model parameters were taken into consideration or completely changed into another form that might describe transport phenomena more efficiently. This iterative model modification was continued until any tendency in the residuals was removed.

Sun et al. (1995) conducted a mathematical modeling study and dynamic simulation of the drying of grains at near ambient conditions. This study utilized the process software known as gPROMS (general-purpose process modeling software) in implementing the model. There were

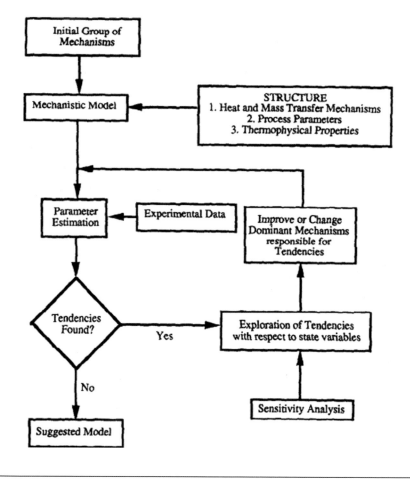

FIGURE 20.1

Model-building iterative procedure.

three novel features in the nonequilibrium mechanistic model proposed by Sun et al. First, they included a condensation term in a mathematically rigorous way. Second, the software implementation of the models was efficient and fast (this was still considered to be a major advantage in the early years of modeling although it is now commonplace). Finally, the heuristic control strategies were easily implemented and tested. Sun and Woods (1997) studied heat and mass transport during the drying of barley grains in a deep bed. The system of nonlinear partial differential equations was solved using the finite difference method.

Jia et al. (2000) conducted a mathematical simulation of heat and mass transport and how they vary within the kernels of grains during the drying process. The authors used a finite element method to solve the generated nonlinear partial differential equations involved in the analysis. The simulated results were fairly accurate, with an average error of 5% when validated with experimental findings. Mhimid et al. (2000) used both conductive and convective boundary conditions in the heat and mass transfer modeling of grains. The study was essentially numerical modeling of a combination of conductive and convective drying. The analysis was based on a cylindrical bed. The authors considered two mathematical models of heat and mass transfer through a granular medium: a two-temperature model (No Local Temperature Equilibrium Model) and a one-temperature model (Local Temperature Equilibrium Model). The models were validated with experiments, and sensitivity analysis was summarily conducted.

In 2001, Anwar and Tiwari (2001) evaluated the convective heat transfer coefficient of green chilies, green peas, Kabuli *chana*, onions, potatoes, and cauliflower a in open sun-drying conditions. From their investigations, they observed that the value of the convective heat transfer coefficient varied from crop to crop due to differences in porosity, moisture content, and the shape and size of the crops. For Kabuli *chana* the experimental errors in terms of per cent uncertainty were found to be in the range of 6%−16% for open sun-drying and 35% for natural cooling. The higher values in the case of natural cooling were due to the removal of small amounts of moisture. Other mathematical early models that may be of interest to readers for the heat and mass transfer during the drying of grains (using a variety of approaches) were proposed by Thompson et al. (1968), Sutherland et al. (1971), Laws and Parry (1983), Nasrallah and Perre (1988), Peishi and Pei (1989), Miketinac et al. (1992), and Maroulis et al. (1995).

Intelligent systems in the modeling of grain sun drying

Investigations have begun to employ intelligent systems for the modeling of grain drying. In an early study, Farkas attempted the modeling of grain drying using ANN (Datta, 2007; Farkas et al., 1996). The study observed that the model was quite sensitive to the nature of the training data, hence randomized training pairs were recommended. In his subsequent discussion, Farkas (2013) explained that the selection of training and validation data has a strong influence on the performance and accuracy of the model. Liu et al. (2007) studied the decrease in grain moisture content during the drying process and modeled it using the neural network modeling tool incorporated with a genetic algorithm. The genetic algorithm was used to select the optimum neural network topology for the training, validation, and testing of the dataset. The results of their study findings were positive and significant. They were significant because this was one of the earliest papers in the domain of research and paved the way for more intricate investigations involving other aspects of drying beyond moisture content prediction.

Momenzadeh et al. (2011) modeled corn drying based on a dataset from microwave-assisted corn drying in a fluidized bed. Using a neural network model with 170 neurons, excellent results were achieved, albeit with the hyperbolic tangent sigmoid transfer function. The accuracy of the ANN models is usually determined by error and statistical indices like root mean square error, coefficient of determination, mean squared error, mean bias error, mean absolute error, average absolute relative error, and standard error. Tohidi et al. (2012) modeled the deep bed drying of rough rice using neural networks. This study compared multilayered perceptron, generalized feedforward, and modular neural network for the modeling. The generalized feedforward architecture was the most suitable, with a hyperbolic tangent sigmoid transfer function.

Golpour et al. (2015) modeled the diminishing moisture content of paddy rice using ANN. They achieved optimal results with 5-7-1 ANN topology and with the Logsig and Tansig transfer function. Unlike the conventional approach of predicting moisture content, Beigi, Torki-Harchegani, and Mahmoodi-Eshkaftaki (2017) and Beigi, Torki-Harchegani, and Tohidi (2017) used a neural network model to predict the energy performance of the grain-drying process. The study was able to determine the energy-efficient drying conditions using the modeling approach. In another study in the same year, Beigi, Torki-Harchegani, and Tohidi (2017) also investigated the prediction of rice kinetics. This time the approach was to consider a direct comparison between mathematical models and a neural network model. They achieved optimal results with 4-18-18-1 ANN topology with a hyperbolic tangent sigmoid transfer function.

Dai et al. (2018) used intelligent systems for the drying process, albeit for the control. They developed an intelligent control system that could regulate the drying conditions of wheat based on a hybrid support vector machine algorithm and genetic algorithm. This was incorporated with a PID controller and tested with the achievement of positive results. Thant et al. (2018) investigated moisture content prediction of paddy rice using neural networks based on data from fluidized bed drying. Optimal results were obtained using 12 neurons and the Logsig and Tansig transfer function. Alam et al. (2018) employed an independent multilayered perceptron neural network for the modeling of rice drying. Under optimized modeling conditions and parameters, the model was able to accurately predict the moisture content of the rice grains with time. The data used were based on a BAU-STR dryer.

Conclusion

Grains are small hard dry seeds (cereals or legumes) with or without an attached hull, that form an important part of the human diet. Grains are dried to maintain product quality and to permit year-round availability. In this chapter, the progress in research in to the heat transfer and mass transfer modeling of the drying of grains was discussed, taking a historical perspective. The models developed for heat and mass transfer during the drying of grains were lumped parameter models, distributed parameter models, and thin-layer drying equations. The popular assumptions in model development are temperature equilibrium and surface moisture content equilibrium. The system of nonlinear partial differential equations is usually solved numerically using a variety of solution methods sometimes implemented on in silico platforms. Intelligent data-driven systems have become more popularly utilized for the modeling of grain drying. It was observed that most studies use it for moisture content prediction, but it has also been applied for energy efficiency optimization and in-process control.

References

Adeniyi, A. G., Ighalo, J., Adeyanju, C., & Ogunniyi, S. (2020). Fabrication of solar dehydrators: Effect of sunlight/heat on food drying: A mini review. In *Proceedings of the 19th Annual International Materials Congress for the Materials Society of Nigeria (MSN)*.

Adeniyi, G., & Ighalo, J. (2018). Heat transfer modelling of the open sun drying of ogbono (Irvingia gabonensis) seeds. In *Proceedings of the 29th Colloquium and Congress of the Nigerian Association of Mathematical Physics*.

Adeniyi, A., Ighalo, J., & Ajala, E. (2019). Mathematical modelling of heat transfer during Ogbono (Irvingia Spp.) seeds open-sun drying. *Annals of the Faculty Engineering Hunedoara-International Journal of Engineering*, *17*, 187−196.

Adeniyi, A. G., Igwegbe, C. A., & Ighalo, J. O. (2021). ANN modelling of the adsorption of herbicides and pesticides based on sorbate-sorbent interphase. *Chemistry Africa*. Available from https://doi.org/10.100 // s42250-020-00220-w.

Aghbashlo, M., Hosseinpour, S., & Mujumdar, A. S. (2015) Application of artificial neural networks (ANNs) in drying technology: A comprehensive review. *Drying Technology*, *33*(12), 1397−1462. Available from https://doi.org/10 1080/07373937.2015.1036288.

Alam, M. A., Saha, C. K., Alam, M. M., Ashraf, M. A., Bala, B. K., & Harvey, J. (2018). Neural network modeling of drying of rice in BAU-STR dryer. *Heat and Mass Transfer/Waerme- Und Stoffuebertragung*, *54*(11), 3297−3305. Available from https://doi.org/10.1007/s00231-018-2368-5.

Anwar, S. I., & Tiwari, G. N. (2001). Evaluation of convective heat transfer coefficient in crop drying under open sun drying conditions. *Energy Conversion and Management*, *42*(5), 627−637. Available from https://doi.org/10.1016/S0196-8904(00)00065-0.

Aregbesola, O. A., Ogunsina, B. S., Sofolahan, A. E., & Chime, N. N. (2015). Mathematical modeling of thin layer drying characteristics of dika (Irvingia gabonensis) nuts and kernels. *Nigerian Food Journal*, 83−89. Available from https://doi.org/10.1016/j.nifoj.2015.04.012.

Bala, B. K., & Woods, J. L. (1994). Simulation of the indirect natural convection solar drying of rough rice. *Solar Energy*, *53*(3), 259−266. Available from https://doi.org/10.1016/0038-092X(94)90632-7.

Beigi, M., Torki-Harchegani, M., & Mahmoodi-Eshkaftaki, M. (2017). Predviđanje kinetike sušenja pirinča: Komparativno proučavanje matematičkog modelovanja i veštačke neuronske mreže. *Chemical Industry and Chemical Engineering Quarterly*, *23*(2), 251−258. Available from https://doi.org/10.2298/CICEQ160524039B.

Beigi, M., Torki-Harchegani, M., & Tohidi, M. (2017). Experimental and ANN modeling investigations of energy traits for rough rice drying. *Energy*, *141*, 2196−2205. Available from https://doi.org/10.1016/j.energy.2017.12.004.

Boyce, D. S. (1965). Grain moisture and temperature changes with position and time during through drying. *Journal of Agricultural Engineering Research*, *10*(4), 333−341. Available from https://doi.org/10.1016/0021-8634(65)90080-6.

Boyce, D. S. (1966). Heat and moisture transfer in ventilated grain. *Journal of Agricultural Engineering Research*, *11*(4), 255−265. Available from https://doi.org/10.1016/S0021-8634(66)80033-1.

Bruce, D. M., & Giner, S. A. (1993). Mathematical modelling of grain drying in counter-flow beds: Investigation of crossover of air and grain temperatures. *Journal of Agricultural Engineering Research*, *55*(2), 143−161. Available from https://doi.org/10.1006/jaer.1993.1039.

Dai, A., Zhou, X., Liu, X., Liu, J., & Zhang, C. (2018). Intelligent control of a grain drying system using a GA-SVM-IMPC controller. *Drying Technology*, *36*(12), 1413−1435. Available from https://doi.org/10.1080/07373937.2017.1407938.

Datta, A. K. (2007). Porous media approaches to studying simultaneous heat and mass transfer in food processes. I: Problem formulations. *Journal of Food Engineering*, *80*(1), 80−95. Available from https://doi.org/10.1016/j.jfoodeng.2006.05.013.

De Vries, D. A. (1958). Simultaneous transfer of heat and moisture in porous media. *Eos, Transactions American Geophysical Union*, *39*(5), 909−916. Available from https://doi.org/10.1029/TR039i005p00909.

Ekechukwu, O. V., & Norton, B. (1999). Review of solar-energy drying systems II: An overview of solar drying technology. *Energy Conversion and Management*, *40*(6), 615−655. Available from https://doi.org/10.1016/S0196-8904(98)00093-4.

Farkas, B. E., Singh, R. P., & Rumsey, T. R. (1996). Modeling heat and mass transfer in immersion frying. I, model development. *Journal of Food Engineering*, *29*(2), 211−226. Available from https://doi.org/10.1016/0260-8774(95)00072-0.

Farkas, I. (2013). Use of artificial intelligence for the modelling of drying processes. *Drying Technology*, *31*(7), 848−855. Available from https://doi.org/10.1080/07373937.2013.769002.

Farkas, I., Reményi, P., & Biró, A. (2000). Modelling aspects of grain drying with a neural network. *Computers and Electronics in Agriculture*, 99−113. Available from https://doi.org/10.1016/s0168-1699(00)00138-1.

Fortes, M., & Okos, M. (1981). Nonequilibrium thermodynamics approach to heat and mass transfer in corn kernels. *Transactions of the ASAE*, *24*, 761−0769.

Fortes, M., Okos, M. R., & Barrett, J. R. (1981). Heat and mass transfer analysis of intra-kernel wheat drying and rewetting. *Journal of Agricultural Engineering Research*, *26*(2), 109−125. Available from https://doi.org/10.1016/0021-8634(81)90063-9.

Golpour, I., Amiri Chayjan, R., Amiri Parian, J., & Khazaei, J. (2015). Prediction of paddy moisture content during thin layer drying using machine vision and artificial neural networks. *Journal of Agricultural Science and Technology*, *17*(2), 287−298. Available from http://jast.modares.ac.ir/pdf_11982_cb1ef2c08-b8388e1c8e2af97bebe1bf7.html.

Haghighi, K., & Segerlind, L. (1991). Modeling simultaneous heat and mass transfer in an isotropic sphere: A finite element approach. *Transactions of the ASAE*, *31*, 629−637.

Hall, C. (1970). Drying farm crops. In Lyall Book Depot.

Ighalo, J. O., Igwegbe, C. A., Adeniyi, A. G., & Abdulkareem, S. A. (2020). Artificial neural network modeling of the water absorption behavior of plantain peel and bamboo fibers reinforced polystyrene composites. *Journal of Macromolecular Science, Part B: Physics*. Available from https://doi.org/10.1080/00222348.2020.1866282.

Ighalo, J., Adeniyi, A. G., & Marques, G. (2020). Application of artificial neural networks in predicting biomass higher heating value: An early appraisal. *Energy Sources, Part A: Recovery, Utilization, and Environmental Effects*, 1−8. Available from https://doi.org/10.1080/15567036.2020.1809567.

Jayas, D. S., Cenkowski, S., Pabis, S., & Muir, W. E. (1991). Review of thin-layer drying and wetting equations. *Drying Technology*, *9*(3), 551−588. Available from https://doi.org/10.1080/07373939108916697.

Jia, C. C., Sun, D. W., & Cao, C. W. (2000). Mathematical simulation of temperature and moisture fields within a grain kernel during drying. *Drying Technology*, *18*(6), 1305−1325. Available from https://doi.org/10.1080/07373930008917778.

Kaya, A., Aydin, O., & Dincer, I. (2006). Numerical modeling of heat and mass transfer during forced convection drying of rectangular moist objects. *International Journal of Heat and Mass Transfer*, *49*(17−18), 3094−3103. Available from https://doi.org/10.1016/j.ijheatmasstransfer.2006.01.043.

Kazarian, E., & Hall, C. (1965). Thermal properties of grain. *Transactions of the ASAE*, *8*(1), 33−37.

Kiranoudis, C. T., Maroulis, Z. B., & Marinos-Kouris, D. (1995). Heat and mass transfer model building in drying with multiresponse data. *International Journal of Heat and Mass Transfer*, *38*(3), 463−480. Available from https://doi.org/10.1016/0017-9310(94)00166-S.

Laws, N., & Parry, J. L. (1983). Mathematical modelling of heat and mass transfer in agricultural grain drying. *Proceedings of The Royal Society of London, Series A: Mathematical and Physical Sciences*, *385*(1788), 169−187.

Liu, X., Chen, X., Wu, W., & Peng, G. (2007). A neural network for predicting moisture content of grain drying process using genetic algorithm. *Food Control*, *18*(8), 928−933. Available from https://doi.org/10.1016/j.foodcont.2006.05.010.

Maroulis, Z. B., Kiranoudis, C. T., & Marinos-Kouris, D. (1995). Heat and mass transfer modeling in air drying of foods. *Journal of Food Engineering*, *26*(1), 113−130. Available from https://doi.org/10.1016/0260-8774(94)00040-G.

Mhimid, A., Ben Nasrallah, S., & Fohr, J. P. (2000). Heat and mass transfer during drying of granular products - simulation with convective and conductive boundary conditions. *International Journal of Heat and Mass Transfer*, *43*(15), 2779−2791. Available from https://doi.org/10.1016/S0017-9310(99)00286-0.

Miketinac, M. J., Sokhansanj, S., & Tutek, Z. (1992). Determination of heat and mass transfer coefficients in thin layer drying of grain. *Transactions of the ASAE*, *35*(6), 1853−1858.

Momenzadeh, L., Zomorodian, A., & Mowla, D. (2011). Experimental and theoretical investigation of shelled corn drying in a microwave-assisted fluidized bed dryer using Artificial Neural Network. *Food and Bioproducts Processing*, *89*(1), 15−21. Available from https://doi.org/10.1016/j.fbp.2010.03.007.

Nasrallah, S. B., & Perre, P. (1988). Detailed study of a model of heat and mass transfer during convective drying of porous media. *International Journal of Heat and Mass Transfer*, *31*(5), 957−967. Available from https://doi.org/10.1016/0017-9310(88)90084-1.

Parry, J. (1983). Mathematical modelling and computer simulation of heat and mass transfer in agricultural grain drying, PhD Thesis, Department of Mathematics, Cranfield Institute of Technology, United Kingdom.

Parti, M. (1993). Selection of mathematical models for drying grain in thin-layers. *Journal of Agricultural Engineering Research*, *54*(4), 339−352. Available from https://doi.org/10.1006/jaer.1993.1026.

Peishi, C., & Pei, D. C. T. (1989). A mathematical model of drying processes. *International Journal of Heat and Mass Transfer*, *32*(2), 297−310. Available from https://doi.org/10.1016/0017-9310(89)90177-4.

Plumb, O. A., Spolek, G. A., & Olmstead, B. A. (1985). Heat and mass transfer in wood during drying. *International Journal of Heat and Mass Transfer*, *28*(9), 1669−1678. Available from https://doi.org/10.1016/0017-9310(85)90141-3.

Sander, A., Skansi, D., & Bolf, N. (2003). Heat and mass transfer models in convection drying of clay slabs. *Ceramics International*, *29*(6), 641−653. Available from https://doi.org/10.1016/S0272-8842(02)00212-2.

Sharma, D., & Thompson, T. (1973). Specific heat and thermal conductivity of sorghum. *Transactions of the ASAE*, *16*, 114−0117.

Simal, S., Rossello, C., Berna, A., & Mulet, A. (1994). Heat and mass transfer model for potato drying. *Chemical Engineering Science*, *49*(22), 3739−3744. Available from https://doi.org/10.1016/0009-2509(94)00199-5.

Suarez, C., Viollaz, P., & Chirife, J. (1980). Diffusional analysis of air drying of grain sorghum. *International Journal of Food Science & Technology*, *15*(5), 523−531. Available from https://doi.org/10.1111/j.1365-2621.1980.tb00971.x.

Sun, D. W., & Woods, J. L. (1997). Simulation of the heat and moisture transfer process during drying in deep grain beds. *Drying Technology*, *15*(10), 2479−2492. Available from https://doi.org/10.1080/07373939708917371.

Sun, Q., Zhang, M., & Mujumdar, A. S. (2019). Recent developments of artificial intelligence in drying of fresh food: A review. *Critical Reviews in Food Science and Nutrition, 59*(14), 2258−2275. Available from https://doi.org/10.1080/10408398.2018.1446900.

Sun, Y., Pantelides, C. C., & Chalabi, Z. S. (1995). Mathematical modelling and simulation of near-ambient grain drying. *Computers and Electronics in Agriculture, 13*(3), 243−271. Available from https://doi.org/10.1016/0168-1699(95)00018-Y.

Sutherland, J. W., Banks, P. J., & Griffiths, H. J. (1971). Equilibrium heat and moisture transfer in air flow through grain. *Journal of Agricultural Engineering Research, 16*(4), 368−386. Available from https://doi.org/10.1016/S0021-8634(71)80036-7.

Thant, P., Robi, P., & Mahanta, P. (2018). ANN modelling for prediction of moisture content and drying characteristics of paddy in fluidized bed. *International Journal of Engineering and Applied Sciences, 5,* 245−257.

Thompson, T., Peart, R., & Foster, G. (1968). Mathematical simulation of corn drying-a new model. *Transactions of the ASAE, 11*(4), 582−586.

Toğrul, I. T., & Pehlivan, D. (2003). Modelling of drying kinetics of single apricot. *Journal of Food Engineering, 58*(1), 23−32. Available from https://doi.org/10.1016/S0260-8774(02)00329-1.

Tohidi, M., Sadeghi, M., Mousavi, S. R., & Mireei, S. A. (2012). Artificial neural network modeling of process and product indices in deep bed drying of rough rice. *Turkish Journal of Agriculture and Forestry, 36*(6), 738−748. Available from https://doi.org/10.3906/tar-1106-44.

Index

Note: Page numbers followed by "*f*" and "*t*" refer to figures and tables, respectively.

A

Absolute average sensitivity (AAS), 398
Activation function, 395–396
Adam. *See* Adaptive moment optimization algorithm (Adam)
Adaptive moment optimization algorithm (Adam), 208
Adaptive network–based fuzzy inference system (ANFIS), 38, 244–245
Adaptive neurofuzzy inference system (ANFIS), 298, 304–305, 338, 345–347
  case studies, 347–349
Adaptive neurofuzzy inference system-ant colony optimization for continuous domain (ANFIS-ACOR) model, 207–208
Adaptive neurofuzzy inference system-particle swarm optimization (ANFIS-PSO), 207–208
Adaptive neurofuzzy inference systems (ANFIS), 234
Additives, 356–357
Air gasification simulation, 383–384
Air pollution, 11, 105–106
Air quality. *See also* Water quality (WQ)
  AI methods for air quality monitoring, 38–42
  assessment, 25–26
  control, 41
  modeling, 39
    data and AQI, 13–14
    data integration and data preprocessing, 15–17
    data profiling, 12–14
    datasets, 12–13
    learning from data, 14–19
    machine learning and deep learning algorithms, 17–18
    validation metrics, 18–19
  monitoring systems, 41–42
  review of few previous and more recent studies on air quality modeling, 42–47
  sensors, 41
  standards, 40
Air quality index (AQI), 13–14, 37
  visualization of, 97–98
Air temperature (T_a), 243
Air–fuel ratio (AFR), 382
  effect on product selectivity, 387
    gas composition at 600°C, 388*f*
Alpha-function, 382–383
Ambient $PM_{2.5}$ air pollution, 83
Ambient sensors, 85–86
American Petroleum Institute (API), 354
Ammonia (NH_3), 83
Ammonical nitrogen (NH_3-N), 161–162

Anaerobic digestion process, 381
Anaerobic/anoxic/oxic processes (A/A/O processes), 148–149
Analysis of variance (ANOVA), 400–401
Annoyance reactions, 340
Anthropogenic activities, 25–26
Anthropogenic sources, 328–329
Application domain of AI, 307–309
Artificial intelligence (AI), 1, 25–26, 131–149, 186, 219, 273, 298, 319–320, 420–423
  AI-based technologies, 26–28
    AI methods for air quality monitoring, 38–42
    data mining with, 31
    machine learning and AI models, 32–38
    for pollution control, 26–49
  AI-influenced system, 321
  application domain of, 307–309
  artificial intelligence-robotic quality assessment system, 325–326
  artificial intelligence-robotics pickup system, 323–324
    garbage pickup system, 324*f*
  comparative studies of, 307*t*, 309*t*
  convolutional neural network model system of waste classification, 322–323
  data extraction, 299–300
  hybrid models, 307
  land pollution management by sustainable green agriculture, 328–329
  methods for water quality modeling and contaminant hydrology, 132–145
  models in
    field, 300
    soil pollutant measurement, 309–312
  quality check, 299–300
  reforestation for land pollution management, 326–328
  robotic recycle sorting system, 325
    advantages and disadvantages of, 325
    working principle of, 325
  and robotics in waste recycling, 324–325
  search and selection criteria, 299
  sites of land pollution from different sources, 320*f*
  support vector machine, 323
  in system modification for effective on-the-spot minimization of wastes, 320–321
    in disposal and smart recycling of wastes, 321
  systematic review protocol, 298–299
Artificial neural network (ANN), 1, 17–18, 27–28, 32–33, 59, 130–131, 135–136, 163, 186, 191–192, 219,

248–249, 273–275, 300–304, 393–394, 418, 420–421, 434
backpropagation neural network, 302
based predictive modeling, 394–395
of biological reactors, 399–401
    effect of internal network parameters, 400–401
MLPNN, 302
modeling, 166–169
    results, 170–173
predictive capability and sensitivity of, 407–412
RBFNN, 302–304
sensitivity analysis of inputs, 404–406
Artificial neuron fuzzy inference system (ANFIS), 142–143
    for suspended sediment load modeling of water quality, 143–144
Artificial recurrent neural network (ARNN), 251–252
Asbestos, 111–112
ASPEN Plus, 381
ASPEN Plus v8.8, 382
ATMO Index, 14
Atmosphere, 59–60
    structure, 60–62
Attention-based Air Quality Predictor (AAQP), 17–18
Attribute noise, 15
Autoencoders, 195–197
Automated quality assessment system, 325–326
Automobile environment detection system, 46–47
Autoregression moving average model (ARMA model), 37–38, 43–45, 206
AutoRegressive Integrated Moving Average (ARIMA), 18–19
Average absolute relative error (AARE), 209
Average sensitivity (AS), 398

B

Backpropagation (BP), 163
    algorithm, 248–249, 396–397
    networks, 422
    neural network, 302
Backpropagation through time algorithm (BPTT algorithm), 196–197, 208
Batch electrocoagulation experiments, 164–165
Bayesian machine learning, 306
Bayesian neural networks (BNNs), 422
Behavioral sensors, 85–86
Bidirectional Gated Recurrent Unit (BGRU), 17
Bidirectional Long Short-Term Memory network (BLSTM network), 19
Biochemical conversion processes, 418–419
Biochemical oxygen demand (BOD), 161–162
Biodegradable wastes, 286, 323
Biofuel production, 426
Biological neurons, 420–421
Biological oxygen demand (BOD), 194

Biological treatment, 363–364
Biomass
    feedstock, 383–384
    gasification, 381–382
    pyrolysis, 383
Biomass fuel (BMF), 107
Biopharmacy, 426
Bioprocessing, 417
    application of optimization tools in bioprocessing operations, 424–425
Bioproducts, 417
    application of optimization tools in bioprocessing operations, 424–425
    biofuel production, 426
    biopharmacy, 426
    bioremediation, 425
    development, 418–419
    future developments or trends, 427
    fuzzy logic, 424
    genetic algorithms, 423
    product deformulation, 420
    product formulation, 419–420
    selected optimization tools used in bioprocess development as computational intelligence, 420–423
Bioremediation, 281, 291, 363–364, 425
Biorenewable resources, 418–419
Biosphere, 60
Biotechnology, 417
Biotrickling filter (BTF), 406–407
    removal of DCM in, 406–407
Biotrickling reactor, 393–394
    choosing activation function, 395–396
    choosing appropriate training algorithm, 396–397
    data division, 397
    data preprocessing and randomization, 397
    data-driven modeling approaches, 394
    internal parameters of network and performance evaluation, 397–398
    materials and methods, 394
    sensitivity analysis, 398
    statistical analysis, 398
Black box modeling, 398–399
Box–Behnken design, 289–290
BREAK block, 383
Bureau of Industry and Security (BIS), 220

C

C++, 130–131
Canada Air Quality Health Index (AQHI), 14
Cancer, 108
Carbon (C), 382
Carbon dioxide (CO_2), 59, 65–66, 382
Carbon monoxide (CO), 59, 65–66, 83, 382
Cardiovascular dysfunctions, 107–108

Case-based reasoning (CBR), 28–30, 35–36
Cataract, IAQ and, 109
Chance Weighted Support Vector Regression (chWSVR), 17
Chaotic nonlinear dynamic algorithms (CNDA), 244–245
ChARM Health, 85
Chemical component forecast data, 13
Chemical conversion processes, 418–419
Chemical hazards, 105
Chemical herbicides, 328–329
Chemical oxidation, 279–280
Chemical oxygen demand (COD), 161–162, 193–194, 275–276
Chemical precipitation, 363
Chemical treatment technique, 363
ChiMerge, 16
Chronic obstructive pulmonary disease (COPD), 106
Chronic pulmonary disease, 108
Class noise, 15
Classification and regression tree (CART), 194
Classification approach, 15–16
Clustering approach, 15–16
Coactive neurofuzzy inference system (CANFIS), 38
Coefficient of correlation (R), 209
Coefficient of determination (R^2), 69, 209, 237
Combined visible and infrared reflectance spectroscopy (VIRS), 282
Combining Human Assessment and Reasoning Aids for Decision-making in Environmental Emergencies (CHARADE), 31
Common Air Quality Index (CAQI), 14
Complementary Ensemble Empirical Mode Decomposition (CEEMD), 18
Composting, 291
Computational intelligence techniques, 418
    selected optimization tools used in bioprocess development as computational intelligence, 420–423
Computational modeling, 426
Computer engineering, 2
Computer-aided intelligent environmental data engineering
    book structure and relevant audience, 2–3
    future, 4
    intelligent systems in environmental engineering research, 3
Constraint satisfaction, 28–30
Contaminant hydrology, AI methods and ML methods for, 132–145
Continuous genetic algorithm (CGA), 208
Control policies for IAQ, 113–114
Control system, 323–324
Conventional feedforward ANNs, 248–249
Conventional one-variable-at-a-time optimization technique, 425
Conversion processes, 320–321
Convolutional layer, 195

Convolutional neural network (CNN), 195–196, 322. *See also* Artificial neural network (ANN)
    model system of waste classification, 322–323, 322*f*, 323*f*
Convolutional Neural Network-LSTM (CNN-LSTM), 19
Convolutional-based Bidirectional Gated Recurrent Unit (CBGRU), 17
Correlation coefficient, 246
Counterpropagation networks (CPG networks), 422
Crop drying, 433
Cryosphere, 60
Cyber-physical systems, 1

D

Daily Air Quality Index (DAQI), 14
Data acquisition, 41
    and integration from environmental monitoring devices, 97
    and integration from wearable devices, 94–96
Data collection, 199–204
Data division, 397
Data extraction, 299–300
Data gathering, 25–26
Data integration, 15–17
Data interpretation method, 30–31
Data mining
    with AI, 31
    method, 30–31
Data normalization, 206
Data preprocessing, 15–17, 205–207
    and randomization, 397
Data profiling, 12–14
Data science, 11
Data splitting, 204–205
Data-centric intelligent systems
    AI methods and ML methods for water quality modeling and contaminant hydrology, 132–145
    AI-based technologies and data-centric systems for pollution control, 26–49
    air quality standards, 40
    artificial intelligence, 131–149
    future opportunities, 47–48
    machine learning and AI models, 32–38
    problems associated with numerical modeling in hydraulic transport and water quality prediction, 131
    recent advances in water quality modeling, 146–149
    review of few previous and more recent studies on air quality modeling, 42–47
Data-centric method (DC method), 273
Data-centric systems (DCS), 25–26
    data interpretation and mining methods, 30–31
    establishing nexus between nonbiodegradable waste and, 283–290
    fundamental principles of data mining with AI, 31
    for pollution control, 26–49
        decision support systems, 28–30

Data-centric systems (DCS) (*Continued*)
  design principles, 28
Data-driven method, 16
Data-driven modeling approaches, 394
Data/information curation, 326
Datasets, 12–13
Decision support system (DSS), 28–30, 132–133
Decision support techniques, 30–31
Decision tree (DT), 33–34, 142–145, 193–194
Decision Tree Regression (DTR), 17
Deep belief network (DBN), 37–38
Deep learning (DL), 17–18, 186, 219
  application in
    flow modeling of landfill leachate, 274–277
    soil quality assessment and remediation, 277–283
    WQ prediction of different water systems, 198
  architectures used in WQ modeling and prediction, 194–195
  case studies of evaluations and analysis of solid waste management techniques, 290–293
  challenges facing DL and ML predictions, 210
  in WQ modeling and prediction, 188–189
Deep Neural Network (DNN), 18
Deforestation, 319
Delta (δ), 209
Detection unit, 323–324
DGOALIGT, 382
Dichloromethane (DCM), 393–394
  process modeling of biological reactors for, 398–399
  removal of DCM in biotrickling filter, 406–407
Differential evolution (DE), 208
Direct combustion, 418–419
Discretization, 16
Disposal, 291
  artificial intelligence in, 321
Distributed Chemical Emergencies Manager (DCHEM), 31
Doctor31 app, 85
Doxtar platform, 84–85
Doxy.me, 85
Drilling wastes, 353–354
Drying, 433
Dynamic neurofuzzy local modeling system (DNFLMS), 244–245

E

Earth system, 60
Echo state network (ESN), 43–45
Eco-Management and Audit Scheme (EMAS), 25–26
ElasticNet, 19
Electrical energy consumption (EEC), 170
Electrical power consumption during ECF process, 177
Electrical resistance heating (ERH), 279
Electrocoagulation (EC), 162
Electrocoagulation-flocculation process (ECF process), 163

genetic algorithm optimization of, 169
Electrode
  calculation of, 170
  during ECF process, 177
Electrode consumption (ELC), 170
  calculation of, 170
Electrodialysis (ED), 230, 232–233
End-of-life vehicles (ELVs), 273–274
Enhanced IAQ
  and prevention strategies, 109–112
  technologies and control policies for, 112–114
Environment Protection Agency (EPA), 111
Environmental Data Management Flow process, 97
Environmental decision support systems (EDSS), 25–26
Environmental engineering, 2
  intelligent systems in environmental engineering research, 3
Environmental informatics, 25–26
Environmental monitoring devices, data acquisition and integration from, 97
Environmental Protection Agency (EPA), 40
Environmental quality analysis (EQA), 31
Environmental science, 25–26
Error-related criteria, 71–72
ESTABLISH project, 84
  architecture, 90–91
  data acquisition and integration
    from environmental monitoring devices, 97
    from wearable devices, 94–96
  decision support system, 90–91
  deployment, data acquisition, and integration, 91
  platform presentation, 98–99
  preliminary testing of sensors, 91–94
  related work, 84–85
  user guide
    for patients, 99–100
    for therapists, 100–101
  user requirements, 85–89
  visualization of air quality index, 97–98
Eulerian–Lagrangian methods, 130–131
European Union (EU), 220
Eutrophication process, 131–132
Evolutionary algorithms (EA), 208
Excavation, 278
Expert system (ES), 27
Exploration and production (E&P), 353
  wastes in oil and gas industry, 354–359
Exploratory factor analysis (EFA), 337–338, 340–341
eXtreme Gradient Boosting (XGboost), 18, 206–207
Extreme learning machines (ELMs), 43–45, 207–208, 248–249

F

F1-score, 209
Feature selection, 16

Feedforward artificial neural network (FFANN), 31
Feedforward backpropagation (FB), 43—45
Feedforward backpropagation-neural network (FFBP-NN), 46—47
Finite difference (FD), 130—131
Finite element, 130—131
Fitness function, 423
Fixed-bed microreactor, 381
Flow modeling of landfill leachate, 274—277
Food and Agriculture Organization (FAO), 220
Formaldehyde emission, 111
Fourth-generation models, 131—132
Fractional bias (FB), 43—45
Frames, 30
France Air Quality Index, 14
Fully connected layer, 195
Fuzzy c-means clustering (FCM), 207—208
Fuzzy inference system (FIS), 130—131, 136—137, 207—208
Fuzzy logic (FL), 27, 136—137, 144—145, 424

G

Gama test for SSL of water quality, 143—144
Garbage, 286
Garmin activity tracker, 91
Gasification, 418—419
  process, 381
  products, 383
Gasifier, 384
Gated Recurrent Unit (GRU), 17
Gaussian process regression (GPR), 244—248
Gene expression programming (GEP), 248
General-purpose process modeling software (gPROMS), 436—437
Generalized linear model (GLM), 244
Generalized models, 434
Generalized Regression Neural Network (GRNN), 18
Generated adversarial networks (GANs), 195—198
Generative unsupervised models, 197—198
Genetic algorithm (GA), 1, 35, 130—131, 135, 163—164, 418, 423
  optimization
    of ECF process, 169
    results, 173—175
Geographical information system (GIS), 287
Gibbs—free energy, 382
  calculation method, 383
Global warming, 25—26
Goodness-of-fit (GoF), 344
Gradient boosted machine (GBM), 306
Gradient Boosting Decision Tree (GBDT), 18
Gradient boosting regression (GBR), 17, 141—142
Gradient recurrent units (GRU), 196—197
Grains, 434
Granular products, 434

Gravity Recovery and Climate Experiment (GRACE), 141—142
Grey Correlation Analysis (GCA), 18
Gross domestic product (GDP), 292

H

Harmful effects of salt, 221—222
Hazard identification (Haz-in), 39
HCOALGEN, 382
Hearing impairment, 338—339
Heat recovery ventilator (HRV), 112
Heat transfer patterns, 433
Heating, ventilation, and air-conditioning (HVAC), 46
Heavy metals, 161—162, 366
High-efficiency particulate air filters (HEPA filters), 111—112
Human health
  noise pollution on, 338—340
    annoyance reactions, 340
    cardiovascular and physiological, 339
    disturbances to mental health, 339
    effects of noise on performance, 339—340
    hearing impairment, 338—339
    interference with speech communication, 339
    negative social behavior, 340
    sleep disturbances, 339
Human intelligence, 319—320
Human life, 273
Humidification—dehumidification (HDH) desalination, 222, 228—229
Hybrid models, 307
Hybrid system of SVM, 323
Hydraulic transport, numerical modeling in, 131
Hydrocarbons, 353, 360
Hydrogel nanocomposites, 282—283
Hydrogen (H_2), 382
Hydrosphere, 60

I

ID3, 16
Imbalanced learning, 16
Incineration, 291
Individual constructs, 342
Indoor air pollution (IAP), 105. *See also* Land pollution
  enhanced IAQ and prevention strategies, 109—112
  extensive review, 114
  indoor air quality and public health, 107—109
  primary pollution sources for IAQ, 116t
  research areas and open questions, 118f
  technologies and control policies for enhanced IAQ, 112—114
Indoor air quality (IAQ), 105
  enhanced IAQ and prevention strategies, 109—112
  primary pollution sources for, 116t
  and public health, 107—109

Indoor air quality (IAQ) (*Continued*)
  technologies and control policies for enhanced IAQ, 112–114
    control policies for IAQ, 113–114
    management technologies, 112–113
Indoor pesticides, 111
Industrialization, 11, 319
Industry 4.0, 321
Infant mortality, IAQ and, 108–109
Integrated long-short-term memory network, 137–140
Intelligent Environmental Quality System (INTELLEnvQ System), 31
Intelligent systems
  in air pollution research, 59
  analyzing error for smaller ranges of input parameters, 74–79
  atmosphere, 59–60
    structure, 60–62
  carbon monoxide and carbon dioxide, 65–66
  different contaminants in air, 62
  in environmental engineering research, 3
  error-related criteria, 71–72
  input and output parameters, 71
  investigated city, 70–71
  machine learning method, 70
  in modeling of grains sun drying, 437–438
  new studied case, 69–70
  particle matters, 64–65
  reviewof literature, 66–69, 233–236
  selected case study from literature, 236–239
    investigated system, 236
    obtained results, 237–239
    selected city, 236
    utilized machine learning approaches, 237
  specifications and validation of developed models, 72–73
  sulfur dioxide, 66
  tropospheric ozone, 62
  uncertainty of different models, 73
  water desalination technologies, 222–233
  in water pollution research, 219
  water standards, 220–222
Intelligent systems, 434
Internal parameters of network and performance evaluation, 397–398
International Standard Organization, 25–26
Internet of Things (IoT), 26–27, 235–236, 287, 320–321
Intervention decision-making, 40
Inverse Distance Weighting technique (IDW technique), 19

K

k-fold cross-validation method, 204–205
'*k*-nearest neighbors' method (k-NN), 244, 287
Kendall tau coefficient, 204
Knowledge engineering, 31

Knowledge-based system (KBS), 1, 130–134
Knowledge-driven models, 398–399
Kohonen neural networks, 422
Kyoto Summit, 25–26

L

Land pollution, 273, 319. *See also* Indoor air pollution (IAP)
  DL and ML methods
    establishing nexus between nonbiodegradable waste and DC systems, 283–290
    evaluations and analysis of solid waste management techniques by, 290–293
    in flow modeling of landfill leachate, 274–277
    in soil quality assessment and remediation, 277–283
    management by sustainable green agriculture, 328–329
      summary of existing AI-robotic applications in weeding operations, 329*t*
Latent factor, 340–341
Latin-hypercube one-factor-at-a-time approach, 276–277
Layer-recurrent neural network (LNN), 43–45
Leachate generation, 161–162
Leaky integrator echo state network (LI-ESN), 43–45
Learning methods, 189
  reinforcement, 190
  semisupervised, 190–191
  supervised, 189–190
  unsupervised, 190
Least square support vector machine (LSSVM), 35
Legates and McCabe Index (LMI), 209
Levenberge–Marquardt method (LM method), 163
Libelium air quality IoT kit, 42
Libelium Plug, 93
Light Gradient Boosting Machine (LightGBM), 18
Linear discriminant function (LDM), 193–194
Linear interpolation (LIN), 205–206
Linear regression (LR), 244–245
Lithosphere, 60
Loading rate, 393–394
Locomotion unit, 323–324
Logistic regression (LR), 193–194, 244–245
Logsig and Tansig transfer function, 438
Long short-term memory (LSTM), 17, 67, 137–138, 196–197, 245, 251–253
Long-term disease management, 84
Low birth weight, IAQ and, 108–109

M

Machine learning (ML), 11, 31–32, 67, 186, 219, 264–265
  and AI models, 32–38
    adaptive network-based inference fuzzy system, 38
    AI methods for air quality monitoring, 38–42
    ANN, 32–33
    CANFIS, 38
    deep belief network, 37–38

DT, 33–34
  genetic algorithm, 35
  LSSVM and SVM, 35
  multilayer perceptron neural network, 38
  RBFNN, 38
  RFM, 37
algorithms, 17–18
application in
  flow modeling of landfill leachate, 274–277
  WQ prediction of different water systems, 198
approaches, 67, 237
architectures used in WQ modeling and prediction, 191
case studies of evaluations and analysis of solid waste
    management techniques, 290–293
challenges facing DL and ML predictions, 210
employed machine learning method, 70
methods for water quality modeling and contaminant
    hydrology, 132–145
ML-based method, 16
in soil quality assessment and remediation, 277–283
used for land pollution management, 328–329
in WQ modeling and prediction, 188–189
Maize (*Zea mays*), 381
  residues air gasification, 381
    methodology, 382–384
    results, 384–387
Mass transfer, 433
MATLAB software program, 72, 130–131
Mean absolute error (MAE), 18–19, 43–45, 69, 209, 237,
    246
Mean absolute percentage error (MAPE), 18–19, 209
Mean absolute relative error (MARE), 209
Mean square error (MSE), 163, 209
Measurement model, 342–343
  validity, 344
Mechanistic modeling, 398–399
Mediterranean Expert (MEDEX), 30–31
Mental health, 339
Mesosphere, 62
Meteorological data, 13
Meteorological variables (MV), 199–204
Methane (CH_4), 59, 382
Microbes, 363–364
Minimum Description Length Principle (MDLP), 16
Minimum efficiency reposting value (MERV), 112
Minimum redundancy maximum relevance (MRMR), 43–45
Missing At Random (MAR), 16
Missing Completely At Random (MCAR), 16
Missing Not At Random (MNAR), 16
Missing value treatment, 16
Model(ing), 417–418
  of grain-drying process, 434
  model-based method, 16
MP5 principal component analysis (PCA-MP5), 275–276

Multieffect distillation (MED) system, 222, 226–227
Multilayer perceptron (MLP), 18, 163, 234, 298, 394–395,
    420–422
Multilayer perceptron neural network (MLPNN), 38,
    144–145, 192, 244–245, 302
Multiple complementary problem-solving techniques
    (MCPTs), 28–30
Multiple input–multiple output system (MIMO system), 347
Multiple kernel learning model with support vector classifier
    (MKSVC), 18
Multiple linear regression (MLR), 43–45, 244–245, 253, 281
Multiple objective decision support system, 30
Multiple-input–single-output system (MISO system), 347
Multistage flash (MSF) distillation, 222–226
Municipal solid waste leachate treatment
  artificial neural network modeling, 166–169
  basic EC cell, 162*f*
  batch electrocoagulation experiments, 164–165
  calculation of electrode and electrical consumption, 170
  electrode and electrical power consumption during ECF
    process, 177
  genetic algorithm optimization of ECF process, 169
  leachate characteristics, 164*t*
  results
    ANN modeling results, 170–173
    genetic algorithm optimization results, 173–175
    statistical analysis results, 175–176
  statistical analysis of data, 169

N

Nanovalent batch reactor (nZVI batch reactor), 146–148
Nash–Sutcliffe coefficient of efficiency (NSE), 209, 244
National Ambient Air Quality Standard (NAAQS), 40
National Environmental Policy Act (NEPA), 25–26
Naturally occurring radioactive materials (NORM), 365
Network architecture-modified RBC, 400–401
Neural Fitting app, 167
Neural networks, 17
  MLP-ANN, 192
  models, 192–193
  RBF-ANN, 192
  SOM, 193
  technology, 27–28
Neuro-fuzzy computing method, 338
Neurons, 420–421
Neuropsychiatric complications, 108
Nitrogen (N_2), 382
Nitrogen dioxide (NO_2), 59, 62–64
Nitrogen oxides (NOx), 83
Noise pollution, 337
  assessing measurement model validity, 344
  assessing structural model validity, 345–347
  empirical results, 343–344
  health-impact modeling, 340–342

Noise pollution (*Continued*)
EFA, 340–341
SEM, 341–342
on human health, 338–340
annoyance reactions, 340
cardiovascular and physiological, 339
disturbances to mental health, 339
effects of noise on performance, 339–340
hearing impairment, 338–339
interference with speech communication, 339
negative social behavior, 340
sleep disturbances, 339
individual constructs, 342
measurement model, 342–343
SEM and ANFIS case studies, 347–349
specifying structural model, 344
Noise reduction, 15
Noise-induced health-impact modeling, 337
Nonbiodegradable waste, 286
and data-centric systems, 283–290
Nonbiodegradable wastes, 323
Nonlinear autoregressive exogenous type (NARX), 67
Nonlinearity, 195
Nonmethane volatile organic compounds (NMVOCs), 83
Normalization, 16
Normalized Difference Vegetation Index (NDVI), 13
Normalized mean absolute error (NMAE), 76, 209
Normalized root mean square error (NRMSE), 43–45, 209
Novelty approach, 15–16

O

Office of Air Quality Planning and Standards (OAQPS), 40
Oil and gas industry
E&P wastes in, 354–359
exploration waste in, 355–357
production and refining waste in, 357–359
waste management approach in, 361–364
waste handling hierarchy, 361–363
waste treatment techniques in, 363–364
Oil and gas waste management system, 359–361
challenges of, 366–367
effective utilization of expert systems in, 373–374
environmental impact of waste, 364–366
expert system for, 367–370
algorithm of proposed sensor approach, 370
sensor application in, 368–370
Oil-based mud systems (OBM systems), 355–356
One-temperature model, 437
Online DO monitoring, 148–149
Online sequential extreme learning machine (OSELM), 208, 248–251
Open sun drying, 433
Optical particle counter (OPC), 91
Optical sorting robotics, 325

Optimally pruned-ELM, 208
Optimization, 417–418
application of optimization tools in bioprocessing operations, 424–425
selected optimization tools used in bioprocess development as computational intelligence, 420–423
Outdoor air pollution, 83
Outlier detection, 15
Oxygen (O_2), 382
Ozone (O_3), 25–26, 59

P

Partial Mutual Information (PMI), 204
Particle swarm optimization algorithm (PSO algorithm), 244–245
Particle Swarm Optimization and Gravitational Search Algorithm (PSOGSA), 18
Particulate Matter (PM), 46, 59, 64–65, 83, 107
PCA-MP5. *See* MP5 principal component analysis (PCA-MP5)
Peak sensitivity (PS), 404–406
Pearson's correlation coefficient (PCC), 18–19, 43–45
PedoTransfer Function (PTF), 281–282
Percentage of bias (PBIAS), 209
Performance assessment of models, 246
Periodic autoregressive model with exogenous variables (PARX), 244
Phase-changing desalination, 222–230
HDH desalination, 228–229
MED, 226–227
MSF, 223–226
solar still desalination, 227–228
VC desalination, 230
Physiological sensors, 85–86
Pickup unit, 323–324
Point of interest (POI), 13, 37
Polish State Environmental Monitoring System (PSEMS), 42–43
Pollutant concentration, 297
Pollutants, 107, 129–130
Polluted air, 11
Pollution control, AI-based technologies and data-centric systems for, 26–49
Polyaromatic hydrocarbons (PAHs), 365
Pooling layer, 195
Precision, 209
Preliminary testing of sensors, 91–94
Pressure effect on product selectivity, 385–387
Principal component analysis (PCA), 43–45, 196–197, 204
Process-guided deep learning (PGDP), 265
Product deformulation, 420
Product formulation, 419–420
Product selectivity
air–fuel ratio effect on, 387

pressure effect on, 385—387
temperature effect on, 385
Product stream, 385—387
Public health, IAQ and, 107—109
    cancer, 108
    cardiovascular dysfunctions, 107—108
    cataract, 109
    chronic pulmonary disease, 108
    low birth weight and infant mortality, 108—109
    neuropsychiatric complications, 108
    respiratory illness, 107
    SBS, 109
Pyrolysis, 291, 418—419

Q

Quality check, 299—300
Quality control agent, 325—326
Quality of air, 59
Quantum computing, 48

R

Radial basis function (RBF), 248—249, 300
Radial basis function ANN (RBF-ANN), 192
Radial basis function neural network (RBFNN), 38, 144—145,
    302—304
Random forest (RF), 18, 206—207, 233—234, 305—306
Random forest model (RFM), 37
Range scaling, 206
Real-time recurrent learning (RTRL), 208
Recall, 209
Rectified linear unit layer, 195
Recurrent neural network (RNN), 17, 196—197, 422
Recycling process, 324—325
Refining waste in oil and gas industry, 357—359
Reforestation for land pollution management, 326—328
    degraded site picture captured using drones, 327f, 328f
Regression
    methods, 219
    trees, 66—67
Regression analysis coefficient (R^2), 163
Rehabilitation programs, 84—85
Reinforcement learning, 189—190
Remote sensors, 41—42
    Libelium air quality IoT kit, 42
    urban clouds spatial mapping air quality sensor, 41
Removal efficiency (RE), 394—395
Residual prediction deviation (RPD), 299—300
Respiratory illness, 107
Response surface methodologies (RSMs), 289—290, 418—419
Reuse, 291
Reverse osmosis (RO), 230—232
RGIBBS block, 383
Risk assessment, 39
Risk evaluation, 39—40

River water temperature prediction
    box diagrams of measured *vs.* calculated river water
        temperature, 263f
    computation, 265
    machine learning, 264—265
    materials and methods, 245—246
        performance assessment of models, 246
        study area and data, 245—246
    methodology
        GEP, 248
        GPR, 246—248
        LSTM, 251—253
        MLR, 253
        OSELM, 248—251
        SVMs, 251
    results
        USGS 01104430 station, 253—256
        USGS 14207200 station, 256—258
        USGS 422302071083801 station, 258—259
        USGS 422622122004000 station, 259—263
Robo Gas Inspector, 320—321
Robot, 323—324
Robotic(s)
    recycle sorting system, 325
        advantages and disadvantages of, 325
        working principle of, 325
    in system modification for effective on-the-spot
        minimization of wastes, 320—321
    used for land pollution management, 328—329
    in waste classification, 321
    in waste recycling, 324—325
    weed control system, 328—329
Root mean square error (RMSE), 18—19, 43—45, 72,
    168—169, 209, 244, 299—300
Root mean square percentage error (RMSPE), 209
Rotating biological contactor (RBC), 393—394
    network architecture-modified RBC, 400—401
    predictive capability of model for modified RBC, 401—403
Ruled induction, 144—145
RYIELD block, 382—383

S

Salt, harmful effects of, 221—222
Satellite-retrieved data, 13
Search and selection criteria, 299
Self-organizing maps (SOM), 193
Semisupervised learning, 189—191
Sense SCP, 93
Sensitivity analysis, 398
Sensors
    different type of equipment, 93—94
    preliminary testing of, 91—94
    same type of equipment, 94
SEP block, 383

Sequencing batch biofilm reactor (SBBR), 148–149
Sick building syndrome (SBS), 109
Sigmoid-ELM, 208
Silicon oxide (SiO$_2$), 382
Single hidden layer feed-forward networks (SLFNs), 248–249
Site assessment, 326
Site planting pattern, 326
Sleep disturbances, 339
Smart Cities Pro (SCP), 91
Smart factory, 321
Smart recycling of wastes, artificial intelligence in, 321
Sodium, 221
Soft computing techniques, 337
Soil pollutant measurement, 309–312
Soil pollution, 297
    AI in mapping, 307–309
Soil quality assessment, DL and ML methods application in, 277–283
Soil remediation, DL and ML methods application in, 277–283
Soil vapor extraction (SVE), 278–279
Solar radiation (SR), 244–245
Solar still desalination, 222, 227–228
Solid waste conversion, computer-aided modeling of methodology, 382–384
    component specifications, 382
    model description, 383–384
    model specifications, 382–383
    results, 384–387
        effect of air–fuel ratio on product selectivity, 387
        effect on temperature on product selectivity, 385
        effect of pressure on product selectivity, 385–387
Solid waste management techniques, 273–274
    case studies of evaluations and analysis by DL and ML methods, 290–293
        analyzed case study, 292–293
        complexity of solid waste management techniques, 290–291
Solvolysis, 418–419
Spatial data, 13
Spatiotemporal artificial neural network (STANN), 37–38
Spatiotemporal deep learning (STDL), 37–38
Speech communication, 339
SST. *See* Total sum of squares (SST)
Stacked autoencoder (SAE), 37–38
Standardization, 206
Statistical analysis, 398
    of data, 169
    results, 175–176
Statistical approach, 219
Status (online application), 85
Steady-state model, 384
Stepwise regression method (SRM), 66–67
Stochastic model (SR model), 244–245
Stratosphere, 60–62

Structural equation modeling (SEM), 337, 341–342
    case studies, 347–349
Structural model
    assessing validity, 345–347
    specifying, 344
Sulfur dioxide (SO$_2$), 59, 66
Sulfuric oxides (SOx), 83
Sum of the square of residuals (SSR), 209
Sun drying, 433
    account of early theoretical modeling efforts, 435–437
    intelligent systems in modeling of grains sun drying, 437–438
Supercomputers, 25–26
Supercritical steam reforming. *See* Supercritical water gasification
Supercritical water gasification, 381
Supervised learning, 189–190
Supplementary leaky integrator echo state network (SLI-ESN), 43–45
Support vector machines (SVM), 1, 18, 35, 142–143, 193, 233–234, 251, 275, 304, 323
Support vector regression (SVR), 18, 37–38, 251, 304
Suspended sediment load (SSL), 143–144
    Gama test and ANFIS for SSL of water quality, 143–144
Suspended solids (SS), 208
Sustainable green agriculture, land pollution management by, 328–329
Symmetric mean absolute percentage error (SMAPE), 43–45
Syngas, 385–387
Synthesis index (SI), 209
Synthetic Minority Oversampling TEchnique (SMOTE), 16
Synthetic-based mud system (SBM system), 355–356
Systematic literature reviewing (SLR), 298–299
Systematic review protocol, 298–299

T
Temperature effect on product selectivity, 385, 385*f*
Temporal data, 13
Thermochemical conversion processes, 418–419
Thermodynamic approach, 381–382
Thermosphere, 62
Threshold, 420–421
Threshold statistics (TS), 209
Time-series (TR model), 244–245
Tobacco smoke, 108
Total sum of squares (SST), 209
Total volatile carbon (TVoC), 46, 105–106
Transfer learning algorithm, 208
Tree model (TM), 234–235
Trial-and-error method, 167
Tropical Rainfall Measuring Mission, 141–142
Troposphere, 60
Tropospheric ozone (O$_3$), 62, 83
Turbidity, 162–163
2D coastal modeling, 131–132

Two-temperature model, 437

U

Ultraviolet Index (UV Index), 13
Underground parking garages (UPGs), 46
United States Environmental Protection Agency (USEPA),
     97−98, 220, 355
     AQI, 14
United States Geological Survey (USGS), 245−246
Unsupervised learning, 189−190
uRADMonitor, 93
Urban Clouds spatial mapping air quality sensor, 41
Urbanization, 11, 129−130, 319
User guide
     for patients, 99−100
     for therapists, 100−101

V

Validation metrics, 18−19
Vapor (H_2O), 59
Vapor compression (VC) desalination, 222, 230
Visual Basic, 130−131
Visualization of air quality index, 97−98
Volatile organic compounds (VOCs), 62, 105, 393−394
VSee, 85

W

Waste classification
     AI and robotics in, 321
     CNN model system of, 322−323
Waste conversion processes, 325−326
Waste management
     approaches, 353−354
     gaps in waste management expert system, 371−372
     in oil and gas industry, 361−364
          waste handling hierarchy, 361−363
          waste treatment techniques in, 363−364
Waste recycling, 324−325
     AI and robotics in, 324−325
Wastewater disposal systems, 129−130
Wastewater treat plants (WWTPs), 148−149
Water (H_2O), 219, 382
     desalination technologies, 222−233
          phase-changing desalination, 222−230
          without phase-changing desalination, 230−233
     pollution, 129−130
     protection schemes/systems, 129−130
     standards, 220−222
          basis, 220−221
          harmful effects of salt, 221−222
     turbidity, 162−163
     water-scarcity, 219
Water quality (WQ), 185. *See also* Air quality
     ANN, 191−192
     challenges facing DL and ML predictions, 210

CNN, 195−196
     data collection, 199−204
     data preprocessing, 205−207
     data splitting, 204−205
     DL
          and ML in WQ modeling and prediction, 188−189
          architectures used in WQ modeling and prediction,
               194−195
     DT, 193−194
     engineering, 131−132
     generative unsupervised models, 197−198
     input data selection, 204
     learning methods, 189
     ML
          and DL models application in WQ prediction of different
               water systems, 198
          architectures used in water quality modeling and
               prediction, 191
     model(ing)
          AI methods and ML methods for, 132−145
          and prediction of different water systems, 198−199
          recent advances in, 146−149
          structure determination, 207−208
          training, 208
     monitoring, 185−186
     neural networks models, 192−193
     numerical modeling in water quality prediction, 131
     performance evaluation measures, 209−210
     RNN, 196−197
     simulation, 130−131
     support vector machines, 193
Water quality index (WQI), 188−189
Water quality variables (WQV), 199−204
Water temperature (T_w), 243
Water-based mud system (WBM system), 356
Wavelet artificial neural networks model (WAANN model),
     206
Wavelet denoizing techniques (WDT), 207
Wearable device, 91
     data acquisition and integration from, 94−96
Weather forecast data, 13
Weighted F1-score, 209
Willmott's Index (WI), 209
Without phase-changing desalination, 230−233. *See also*
     Phase-changing desalination
     electrodialysis, 232−233
     reverse osmosis, 231−232
World Health Organization (WHO), 11, 59, 106, 220, 338
Worldview International Foundation, 328

X

XGboost. *See* eXtreme Gradient Boosting (XGboost)

Z

Zea mays. See Maize (*Zea mays*)

Printed in the United States
by Baker & Taylor Publisher Services